THE IRISH ANNALS

From Some Reviews:

'This is a book to be reckoned with. It is an exhilarating read for its entirely fresh approach to the evidence; for the way it debunks and revises so much of the pre-existing scholarship on the Irish annals; for the penetrating light it shines on the shortcomings of the methodologies of Irish manuscript scholarship over the past 200 years and not least for the courteous but devastating way in which it exposes the perils of past failures to re-examine at first hand the primary manuscript evidence, a practice which we all know must form the raw material of worthwhile scholarly research.'

Dr Bernadette Cunningham, *Irish Archives*

'This is a truly wonderful production. I am simply stunned by the breadth and depth of learning contained within its covers and by the scope and quality of the enormous body of careful, sustained, lucid and minutely detailed argumentation in this magnificent volume. Dr Mc Carthy with this book has filled an enormous (and indeed astonishing, and even shameful) gap in Irish scholarly literature.'

Dr Nollaig Ó Muraíle, Department of Irish, NUI, Galway

'*The Irish Annals* [...] presents a survey of the sources for these medieval Christian chronicles from the fifth century to the late sixteenth century. Mc Carthy introduces the annals as chronicles that "represent a window onto the collective memory of the past preserved by one of its most privileged groups, its literate class". He carries out a critical review of the sources and modern analyses to arrive at a new account of the origins and evolution of the annals. There is much detail in this volume and it will lend to a better understanding of these early chronicles.'

Archaeology Ireland

'In this study and in his previous articles Mc Carthy has used his talents to improve our understanding of the chronological framework of the Irish annals, achieving far more than historians have managed before.'

Nicholas Evans, *The Medieval Review*

'Mc Carthy's book is a milestone in Irish Annalistic research, and will provide the foundation for further research in coming decades.'

Immo Warntjes, *Historische Zeitschrift*

Don dream scoláirí foighdeach, faid-bhreathnaitheach,
fiosúil a scríobh síos scéal na hÉireann

To all of those patient, far-seeing, knowledgeable scholars
who wrote down Ireland's story

The Irish Annals

Their Genesis, Evolution and History

Daniel P. Mc Carthy

FOUR COURTS PRESS

Typeset in 10.5 pt on 13 pt Ehrhardt by
Carrigboy Typesetting Services for
FOUR COURTS PRESS LTD
7 Malpas Street, Dublin 8, Ireland
e-mail: info@fourcourtspress.ie
and in North America for
FOUR COURTS PRESS
c/o ISBS, 920 NE 58th Avenue, Suite 300, Portland, OR 97213.

First published 2008
Reprinted 2010

A catalogue record for this title is available
from the British Library.

ISBN 978–1–84682–048–9

Printed in England by
Antony Rowe Ltd., Chippenham, Wilts.

Contents

Illustrations

Abbreviations

AA	*Anno Abrahami*
AB	*Annals of Boyle*; see Freeman 1924–7.
AC	*Annals of Clonmacnoise*, an earlier siglum for MB; see Murphy 1896, 1993.
AI	*Annals of Inisfallen*; see Mac Airt 1951.
AM	*Anno Mundi*
AR	*Annals of Roscrea*; see Gleeson & Mac Airt 1959.
AT	*Annals of Tigernach*; see Stokes 1895–7, 1993.
AU	*Annals of Ulster*; see Hennessy 1887, Mac Carthy 1893–1901, Mac Airt & Mac Niocaill 1983 and Ó Muraíle 1998.
BL	British Library
BOT	*Bedae opera de temporibus*; see Jones 1943.
c.	*circa*
cit(s).	citation(s)
cm.	centimetre
CCSL	*Corpus Christianorum, Series Latina*
CELT	*Corpus of Electronic Texts*; see www.ucc.ie/celt/
CG	*Cogadh Gaedhel re Gallaibh*; see Todd 1867.
CM	*Chronica maiora* by Bede, i.e. DTR cap. 66; see Jones 1977.
CMCS	*Cambridge/Cambrian Medieval Celtic Studies*
CT	*Annals of Connacht*; see Freeman 1944.
CS	*Chronicum Scotorum*; see Hennessy 1866, 1964.
CSEL	*Corpus Scriptorum Ecclesiasticorum Latinorum*
DIAS	Dublin Institute for Advanced Studies, Dublin 2.
DT	*De temporibus* by Bede 703; see Jones 1980.
DTR	*De temporum ratione* by Bede 725; see Jones 1977.
EH	*Ecclesiastical History* by Eusebius *c.*316; see Schwartz & Mommsen.
f./ff.	folio(s) or following
fl.	*floruit*, flourished
FA	*Fragmentary Annals*; see Radner 1978 and O'Donovan 1860.
FF	*Foras feasa ar Eirinn*; see Comyn & Dinneen 1902–15.
FM	*Annals of the Four Masters*; see O'Donovan 1848–51, 1966.
GCS	*Die Griechischen Christlichen Schriftsteller der Ehrsten Jahrhunderte*
H,H¹,H²	Sigla for the hands in TCD 1282; see Mac Airt & Mac Niocaill, *AU*, p. viii.
HE	*Historia ecclesiastica* by Bede 731; see Colgrave & Mynors 1991.
IIC	*Irish inaugural chronicle*, E. MacNeill's hypothesis
ITS	*Irish Texts Society*
IER	*Irish Ecclesiastical Record*

IWC   *Irish world chronicle*, E. MacNeill's hypothesis
JRSAI   *Journal of the Royal Society of Antiquaries of Ireland*
LC   *Annals of Loch Cé*; see Hennessy 1871, 1939.
LG   *Lebor Gabála*; see Macalister 1938–56.
LP   *Liber Pontificalis*; see Mommsen 1898.
m.   *mac* (son of)
MA   *Miscellaneous Irish Annals*; see Ó hInnse 1947.
MB   *Mageoghagan's Book*; see AC and Murphy 1896, 1993.
MGH   *Monumenta Germaniae Historica* (Munich)
MIA   *The Medieval Irish Annals*; see Mac Niocaill 1975.
MM   *Lectures on the Manuscript Materials of Ancient Irish History*; see
         O'Curry 1861.
MS/S   manuscript/s
n./nn.   note(s), i.e. footnotes
NHI   *A new history of Ireland* 1–9, Dublin 1987–2005.
NLI   National Library of Ireland
NUI   National University of Ireland
ODCC   *The Oxford Dictionary of the Christian Church*; see Cross & Livingstone
         1983.
p.   *post*
p./pp.   page(s)
PL   *Patrologia Latina*; see Migne 1844–64.
PRIA   *Proceedings of the Royal Irish Academy*
r.   reigned, ruled
RC   *Revue Celtique*
repr.   reprinted
RIA   Royal Irish Academy
SR   Micheál Ó Cléirigh's *Seanchas Riogh Eireann*; see Walsh 1918.
s.a.   *sub annum*
s.v.   *sub verbum*
TCD   Trinity College, Dublin
VC   *Vita Columbae*; see Anderson & Anderson 1961, and Sharpe 1995.
vs   versus
ZCP   *Zeitschrift für celtische Philologie*

Preface

My interest in the Irish Annals arose directly from an early curiosity concerning Easter and its peripatetic date. As a child, the mystery of the table of dates for the celebration of the moveable feast of Easter in the front of my prayer book provided welcome relief from the more demanding spiritual exercises. Later, a juvenile encyclopaedia provided my first specification, 'The first Sunday after the first full moon after 21 March', readily comprehensible but afterwards discovered to be an oversimplification. Subsequently I learned that the early Irish Church, like its Insular neighbours, had celebrated Easter according to a Paschal tradition not known elsewhere in Christendom, and naturally I wondered how it differed, and why and when Irish Christians had conformed to the Roman Church. Then in about 1972 I happened on Daniel O'Connell's lucid account of the subject in his 'Easter cycles in the early Irish Church', where I learned that indeed the early Insular churches had followed a unique eighty-four year Easter cycle, whereas the Roman Church followed a nineteen-year cycle. It was here in O'Connell's introduction that I first encountered the name of Bartholomew Mac Carthy and 'his erudite Introduction to the Annals of Ulster'. Thus was I directed towards stall seventy-nine in that treasure trove of scholarship's nuggets known as the Research Floor of the Berkeley Library at Trinity College, Dublin. There I beheld a whole shelf of volumes bearing the word 'Annals' on their spines, and conspicuous amongst these were the handsome four-volume edition of the *Annals of Ulster* (AU) by Hennessy and Mac Carthy. Opening the first volume I was intrigued to find each year marked with a kalend, which was often followed by ferial and lunar epactal data, though perplexity ensued when examination showed that the lunar data followed a nineteen-year cycle, rather than the Insular eighty-four year cycle. Thus my relationship with the Irish Annals commenced with a question mark.

Down the subsequent years I returned occasionally to browse AU and discovered that astronomical observations were sprinkled through the text, and footnotes showed that entries recording eclipses corresponded closely with the predictions of Newtonian mechanics. This disposed me to trust the entries in general, though it was disconcerting that some of these eclipse entries showed up in other published editions of annals under different AD years. Then in 1985 my head of department, Professor John Byrne, invited me to assist in the preparation of an exhibition of material illustrating the history of computation, and so I approached Dr Dáibhí Ó Cróinín of University College Galway for examples of early Insular Easter material for display, and he responded generously. Subsequently, in 1987, Dáibhí sent me a copy of the eighty-four year Insular Easter table that he had then only recently discovered in a manuscript at Padua, and he requested assistance to try to establish how the table had been constructed. This was the crucial document that sealed my relationship with the Irish Annals, for it was immediately apparent that in it each year commenced with a kalend followed by a ferial datum, just as I had observed in AU.

Sometime later, in 1993, having resolved the construction of the eighty-four year table, I returned to the Annals and was in the fortunate position of being able to examine the primary manuscript for the *Annals of Ulster*, which resides in the College Library as TCD 1282. As a result of this examination, my first paper dealing with the Irish Annals was published in 1994. At that time I unquestioningly accepted and reflected the view of scholarship that AU best represented the archetype of the Irish Annals, and that other annals which lacked early lunar data, such as the *Annals of Tigernach* (AT) and the *Chronicum Scotorum* (CS), must have somehow abandoned it. On this basis in 1995 I gave a paper regarding AU's papal succession to the Irish Conference of Medievalists at Maynooth College, and it was here that Dr Catherine Swift, then of University College, Dublin, literally placed in my hand a second crucial document. This was Gearóid Mac Niocaill's remarkable monograph, *The Medieval Irish Annals*, where in a mere forty-nine pages he not only provided a cogent survey of the principal annalistic texts, but also offered guidelines on how they should be analyzed and collated.

Having read Mac Niocaill's work and having good access to the advantages of computer technology, I began in 1996 to collate the entries from AT, CS, and AU, and it quickly emerged that my belief in the archetypal status of AU was ill-founded. It also became apparent that it was possible to recover a single, authoritative chronology for the Annals and to synchronize this with the Julian calendar, and I began making this available on the Internet. At the same time I was reading through the twentieth-century literature on the Annals, and here I found views expressed, some of which, particularly those concerning the textual history and precedence of the Annals, could not be reconciled with the results of my collation. The Irish Annals are a most substantial and valuable body of historical records, not only preserving literary elements of the culture of both Christianity and Ireland from the fifth century, but also reflecting how Irish scholarship adapted to Christianity, and providing a chronological framework for all of Irish medieval history. But the primacy that has been mistakenly attributed to AU, and the difficulty of their conflicting chronologies has hindered access to them by scholars. One consequence of this has been that no substantial review of the corpus of material has been written, so that Mac Niocaill's brief monograph remains to the present day by far the best published account of it. These then were the circumstances that prompted me to write this book. In the introduction to his monograph Mac Niocaill modestly invited his readers to try to remedy his own 'abundant avowals of ignorance and uncertainty', and this book is therefore my response to that invitation.

It is commonplace in a preface to review the organization and content of a book, but a glance at the table of contents will provide the reader with an effective overview of the content and arrangement of this book. Perhaps however something needs to be said concerning the book's title. Since the arrival of Christianity in the fifth century Ireland's scholars have compiled a wide variety of chronicles. It is the case that the most substantial of these systematically represent each successive year over most of their range, and it is this characteristic that qualifies them as annalistic chronicles, or annals for short. The Irish received this form of chronicle with Christianity and maintained it down to the seventeenth century. Their compilations of annals constitute the climax achievement of Irish chroniclers, and it is the purpose of this book to examine and document the processes of their initiation, development and role, that is their genesis, evolution and history. This is a considerable task and consequently the parallel development of Irish non-annalistic chronicles, most notably *Lebor Gabála*, while of great cultural interest, has received only summary treatment.

There remains the agreeable task of acknowledging the many kindnesses shown to me in relation to my interest in chronicles down the years, and the contributions made to this work. I would like to acknowledge and to thank the following: Trinity College Dublin for the award of a Berkeley Fellowship for 2002–3 which provided me with the space, time and resources necessary for researching and writing this book, and enabled me to examine most of the primary Annalistic manuscripts; Professor Fergus Kelly for making me welcome as a visiting scholar at DIAS for 2003–4, and Dr David Abrahamson for supporting my request for sabbatical leave that made that visit possible and for his constant support for my research; Professor John Byrne for his humane approach to engineering, and his all-embracing attitude to scholarship; Professor Dáibhí Ó Cróinín of the Department of History, National University of Ireland, Galway, for his sustained encouragement and patient and informative responses to a very long series of my questions; Dr Bernard Meehan, Felicity O'Mahony and Stuart Ó Seinóir of the Manuscripts Room, Trinity College, for sharing their expertise with respect to many manuscripts and texts; Charles Benson and his staff at the Early Printed Books at Trinity College for their assistance with many early published chronicles; †Anne Walsh and Mary Higgins of the Research Floor, Berkeley Library, Trinity College, for their encouraging and efficient responses to many bibliographic enquiries; Carol Conlin of the Armagh Public Library; the Library staff at the Duke Humfrey's Room, Bodleian Library, Oxford University, the Manuscript Room at the British Library, the Reading Room at the Royal Irish Academy, the Archives Department, National University of Ireland, Dublin, and the Library of the School of Celtic Studies, Dublin Institute for Advanced Studies; Fr Ignatius Fennessy of the Franciscan Library, Killiney; Anthony Caines and Ray Jordan of the Trinity College Conservation Laboratory for their advice on the codicology of TCD 1282; the support staff at the Department of Computer Science, Trinity College, who enthusiastically and efficiently resolved numerous problems relating to computing, communications and printing; Dr Bart Jaski who voluntarily read the entire manuscript and identified numerous corrections and submitted many constructive suggestions; the TCD Association and Trust whose two generous grants covered reproduction rights and photography and the expert compilation of the index by Helen Litton; Steven Collins who skillfully ensured that all of the manuscript images in the plates are legible; Michael Adams and Martin Fanning at Four Courts Press for their sustained encouragement, patience and always helpful counsel.

I would also like to thank a wide circle of scholars and friends who have kindly offered advice and encouragement, and graciously shared their knowledge on many details of chronicles and their history, viz., Sumiki Awaya, Mike Baillie, Bruce Barker-Benfield, Liam Breatnach, Pádraig Breatnach, Aidan Breen, Francis John Byrne, Ian Elliott, Peter Berrisford-Ellis, Anne Connon, David Dumville, Colmán Etchingham, Menso Folkerts, Adriano Gaspani, Anthony Harvey, Leofranc Holford-Strevens, David Howlett, Colin Ireland, Fergus Kelly, Brian Lacey, † Proinsias Mac Cana, Dónall Mac Giolla Easpaig, Damien Mc Manus, † Jennifer Moreton, Aoibheann Nic Dhonnchadha, Tomás Ó Concheanainn, Donnchadh Ó Corráin, Donnchadh Ó hAodha, Marius Ó hEarcáin, Pádraig Ó Macháin, Roibeard Ó Maolalaigh, Nollaig Ó Muraíle, Pádraig Ó Riain, Michelle O Riordain, Richard Sharpe, Katharine Simms, Peter J. Smith, Wesley Stevens, Robert Strevick, Peter Verbist, Faith Wallis, and Immo Warntjes. Finally I wish to express my unbounded gratitude to my wife Brídín for her constant support and encouragement, and to our family, Pádraig, Áine and Eoghan for their sustained forbearance and interest.

CHAPTER ONE

Chronicles and Annals – origins, compilation, taxonomy and nomenclature

Origins

The accumulated written chronicles of any culture represent a window onto the collective memory of the past preserved by one of its most privileged groups, its literate class. A knowledge of how this literate class compiled these chronicles, their sources, circumstances, and motives, is a prerequisite for an informed understanding of their account of the past. In the case of European cultures scholarship holds that Greece was the origin of the written chronicle tradition, and Christianity acted as the catalyst to spread this tradition to neighbouring parts of Europe. Because early Christianity preached a millenariast creed in a Greek milieu, this creed was linked directly to time measurement and it was natural therefore that Christianity should adopt the Greek chronicle form. Two early examples of such chronicles are the Χρονογραφίαι, or *Chronography*, by Julius Africanus †*c*.240, and the chronicle of Hippolytus, bishop of Rome †236. The most sophisticated and successful example of the early Christian chronicles was the Χρονικοὶ κανόνεσ, or *Chronological Canons*, of Eusebius of Caesarea †*c*.340, which work was translated into Latin and extended to AD 378 by S. Jerome †420, and this circulated widely throughout the Latin-literate world. Jerome's translation provided an inspiration and important source for many subsequent Western chronicles, including those of Orosius †*p*.417, Prosper †463 and Isidore †636. Another Latin chronicle which drew on both Eusebius' and Jerome's chronicles was compiled by Rufinus of Aquileia †410, a contemporary and one time friend of Jerome. As we shall see Rufinus' chronicle played a seminal role in the formation of the Irish chronicles, and it is the purpose of this book to examine this formation and their subsequent development up until the seventeenth century.[1]

1 For these chroniclers, their dates and works, and millenarianism see the *ODCC s.v.* The critical editions of these chronicles are: Julius Africanus' fragments in Routh, *Reliquae Sacrae*; Helm, *Hippolytus – die Chronik*; Schoene, *Eusebi Chronicorum* i, 1–296 (*Liber prior* or *Chronography*), id., ii, 11–199 (*Canones*); Helm, *Hieronimus – die Chronik*; Zangmeister, *Orosii historiarum*; Mommsen, 'Prosperi chronicon'; Mommsen, 'Isidori chronica'. For the Greek chronicle tradition see Mosshammer, *The Chronicle*, 15–17, 105–10, and also Muhlberger, *Fifth-century chroniclers*, 10–22. For Rufinus' chronicle and its transmission to Ireland see Mc Carthy, 'Status', 131–42, 148–50, and Mc Carthy, 'Emergence of AD', 46–9.

Terminology

It will assist the forthcoming discussion if the necessary terminology is first defined. These definitions will be presented here informally with the principal definition of each term identified in italics. The essentials of a *chronicle* are a sequence of textual entries embedded within a chronological apparatus which distributes these entries across time in a measured fashion. These *entries* comprise written accounts of earlier events, and if there is reason to believe that the entry was composed contemporaneously with the event it may be termed a *record*. On the other hand, if there is evidence that an entry represents a later addition to the chronicle, it may also be termed an *interpolation*. When an interpolation refers not to the chronicle events as such, but to the affairs of the scribes who were compiling the chronicle it will be termed an *interjection*. Examples of interjections are colophons, source identifications, and allusions to the scribes and their work. Given the frequently anonymous character of chronicles these interjections sometimes provide invaluable clues to the compilation of a chronicle. Regarding the entries, while these could register any *events* from the full gamut of human affairs, in practice a rather limited variety is observed, typically consisting of obituaries of secular and religious leaders, conflicts of all kinds, particularly if they involve violence, transfers of power in both the secular and religious spheres, civil disasters, and terrestrial, meteorological and astronomical extremes and rarities. These categories correspond in fact fairly closely with the headline material found in present day quality newspapers. The *purview* of a chronicle identifies the geographical and cultural focus of the events registered by its entries; Christian chronicles usually show an *ecclesiastical* emphasis in their purview, but also normally include some *secular*, i.e. non-ecclesiastical entries. The *provenance* of a chronicle refers specifically to its geographical purview. Regarding *language*, Western chronicles of late antiquity and early medieval times were in Latin, however, as written forms of *vernaculars* became established increasingly these tended to be used, since they often better reflected the purview of the chronicle.

Regarding the *chronological apparatus*, while it could in principle employ any unit of time, because human affairs are so closely linked to the annual cycle of the seasons in practice chronicles nearly always utilize a calendrical approximation to the solar year as their basic *unit of time*. This is not to suggest that chronicles must necessarily register entries and chronological apparatus for every year, for some gather entries by a larger unit of time, often employing the successive reigns of kings of an important dynasty; for example the chronicles of Isidore and Bede both use this arrangement.[2] However, some chronicles

2 Mc Carthy, 'Status', 124 n. 70 (discussion of the chronological apparatus of both Isidore and

whose chronological apparatus does register virtually each successive year are designated as *annals* in recognition of their annual character, and the usage of this word requires careful consideration. For the word 'annals', derives from the Latin 'annalis' meaning annual, and the plural of this word was used nominatively to identify the collection of records entitled *Annales Maximi* which were extended annually by the pontifex maximus in Rome during the Republican period. Thus originally 'annales' specified a compilation with a strictly annual character. However, later 'annales' was also used with a much more generalized sense to entitle the compilations of Roman history by Quintus Ennius †169 BC and Cornelius Tacitus †120 AD. Since neither of these provided a chronological apparatus, much less an annual account, it is clear that this word has been used ambiguously since the second century BC. Moreover, even the specific sense of 'annales' was not employed systematically in Latin, for some relentlessly annalistic compilations are never referred to as 'annales', but always as 'chronica'; Jerome's chronicle is an instance. But in this book I intend to use 'annals' only in its specific sense to identify those compilations whose chronological apparatus registers nearly every year; the qualification 'nearly' is required here since the annual character quite often breaks down near the start and end. However, even when restricted to its specific sense to identify strictly annual compilations the word 'annals' suffers from a serious disadvantage. Because the plural form is used to designate a singular collection there is no simple way to distinguish between one annalistic compilation and a plurality of such compilations. Of course, when the word is applied as a title to a named extant compilation, no such uncertainty can arise, but in the case of lost compilations this ambiguity is a problem. For this reason I will use the inclusive term 'chronicle' to identify non-extant annalistic compilations such as the 'Iona chronicle' and the 'Clonmacnoise chronicle'.

An early example of Roman annals from Christian times are the consular annals of late antiquity, which systematically registered every consular year using a chronological apparatus consisting simply of the names of the two consuls for each year. Since the consuls took office on 1 January, the implicit year of these consular annals ran from 1 January to 31 December, just as in our present Gregorian calendar year.[3] This chronological apparatus is unusual in that it is entirely literate, but more commonly an apparatus consists of a combination of literate and numerate elements, sometimes called *criteria*. For example, 'Anno Domini' followed by the year number, or a regent's name followed by the length of his reign. It is the resultant *series* of these data that provide the quantified temporal framework on which the chronicle entries are distributed. In some

Bede).   3 Muhlberger, *Fifth-century chroniclers*, 23–46 (consular annals).

chronicles with more than one such series a dependence exists between them, and in these cases it is convenient to distinguish them as the *independent series*, and *dependent series*. For example, Isidore's chronicle presents both regnal and *Anno Mundi* (AM) series, and since the AM is simply the accumulation of the regnal years, the AM is the dependent series. Published editions and discussions of chronicles often treat the chronological apparatus very briefly or not at all, and while this may be understandable it is a serious omission. For, while in textual terms the chronological apparatus is normally a small percentage of the whole text, its dispersal throughout that text together with the strong inter-relationships between the elements of its constituent series usually make it by far the most complex component of the chronicle. Consequently, the chronological apparatus is often the most conservative component of a chronicle and as such offers valuable insight into its history and compilation.

When we must deal with either two chronicles, or a single chronicle whose chronological apparatus comprises two or more series, the question of the *synchronism* of the chronological series is important. For example, consider a chronicle whose independent series identifies each year by the textual 'an.', standing for 'annus', and whose dependent series counts these years serially in Roman numerals. If this chronicle presented the apparatus, 'an. xxxxvi; an. xxxxvii; an. xxxxviii', then the series 'an.; an.; an.' harmonizes with the series 'xxxxvi; xxxxvii; xxxxviii', and we say that the two series are *synchronized*. If, on the other hand, the apparatus continued as, 'an. xxxxvi; an. xxxxvii; an. xxxxviii; an. l', then we see that the number 'xxxxviiii' has been omitted and say that the two series exhibit an *asynchronism* at 'an. l', and thenceforward they are *asynchronous*.[4] Another important aspect of a chronological apparatus is the *range* of years that it registers, and it is helpful to be able express this concisely. For the Christian era the *Anno Domini* (AD) will be employed to identify inclusively the initial and final years of the range. For example, AD 431–1014 identifies an inclusive range of AD 431 to AD 1014, a total of 1014–431+1=584 years; when the context makes clear that the era is Christian then the 'AD' may be omitted. In the pre-Christian era *Anno Mundi* years which count from the Creation of the world will normally be used, though sometimes it is more satisfactory to use the names of the Biblical *epochs*, such as Creation (or Adam), Flood, or Incarnation. It is important to note that the Septuagint and Vulgate traditions place these epochs at different AM; viz., in an Insular context typically Septuagint Flood=AM 2242 and Incarnation=AM 5200, whereas Vulgate Flood=AM 1656 and Incarnation=AM 3952. Thus the range Creation–Flood may equal Septuagint AM 1–2242, but Vulgate AM 1–1656.

---

4 Both chronological apparatus and example are based on the *Annales Cambriae*, see Morris, *Nennius*, 44, 85.

Because MSS often lose folios from their start and end, we frequently find that chronicles are *acephalous* and/or *truncated*. In such cases the stated range will include any vestigial apparatus and entries preserved at the start and end. When intermedial folios are lost, *lacunae* result and the chronicle is *lacunose*, and when precision is required its range must be given as a list of sub-ranges, e.g. AD 488–766, 974–1003, 1018–1178.

Compilation

It is in the nature of the human life span that any one chronicler can only personally record about fifty years of events. Thus any chronicle that extends for substantially more than fifty years must be the result of some *accumulative mechanism*. There are two well attested such mechanisms by which longer chronicles are compiled. The first is where a powerful institution such as a monastery or a secular dynasty has sufficient resources to maintain a professional historiographer to care for their existing chronicle, and to extend it on an annual basis. This *institutional compilation* is known from the sixth century BC from both China and Greece right up to the present day, where most national governments and many large institutions accumulate some kind of annual summary of their affairs. Such chronicles are naturally annalistic in character and are often entitled as 'Annals'. These being the work of a series of functionaries tend to be anonymous and they are usually identified by the name of their institution. For example, the *Annales Fuldenses* register the affairs of the Benedictine abbey of Fulda in Germany from the seventh up to the early tenth century.[5] These chronicles generally strongly reflect the character of the institution in their purview, language, entries, and chronological apparatus over long periods of time, all of which help to identify the institutional origin of the chronicle. The second mechanism by which chronicles are accumulated is that of *individual compilation* when a highly motivated editor gathers source material, often including the major current chronicle sharing his own purview, and compiles these materials into a new chronicle, to which he often adds an extension, or *end chronicle*, bringing the chronicle up to his own time. In the course of this compilation entries from the earlier sources may be re-written, updated orthographically, interpolated, translated, or omitted altogether. Where the entries from an earlier source are systematically abbreviated the resulting summary is often termed an *abridgement*. Regarding the chronological apparatus, on account of its aforementioned complexity such editors sometimes simply transcribe all or part of the chronological apparatus of their most extensive source. However, should an editor impose his own chronological

5 Pertz, 'Annales Fuldenses'.

apparatus on his compilation it is a hallmark of the resulting chronicle that its chronological apparatus exhibits a noticeably uniform character over the entire compilation. The chronicle resulting from this process of individual compilation represents a new *recension* of its sources. A third, smaller scale accumulative mechanism is that of *interpolation* whereby additions are inscribed marginally or interlinearly by chronicle users. In general it is entries that refer to famous persons and events that attract these additions, and these are often incorporated into a later recension when the interpolated chronicle is subsequently used as an exemplar by a copyist. Of course these three compilation mechanisms are not mutually exclusive and examples of an individual compiler employing as source an earlier interpolated institutional compilation, or an institution interpolating excerpts from an earlier individual compilation are commonplace, so that substantial chronicles usually exhibit multiple layers of compilation. Against these accumulative mechanisms the processes of omission by individual compilers and folio loss cause *attrition* of both chronicle entries and apparatus. Thus the investigation of old chronicles is the literary analogue of an archaeo-logical excavation on an old habitation site, for both present a multiplicity of layers that require separation and identification.

The chronicles of Eusebius, Jerome, Orosius, Prosper, Isidore, and Bede, to name a few, are all examples of individual compilations; indeed the very fact that these chronicles are each identified by an individual's name signifies this. Regarding their chronological apparatus, Jerome copied Eusebius' multiple series of regnal years, but Orosius, Prosper, Isidore and Bede each derived their own significantly simplified apparatus. Regarding their entries, of course in each case only that part of their compilation that derives from the earlier chronicle can be said to be a recension of it. For example, Jerome's chronicle may be described as a recension of Eusebius only up to AD 325, and the years 326–78 represent Jerome's own end chronicle. Examples of medieval European institutional compilations are the aforementioned annals of Fulda, the annals of Ghent, and the annals of S. Bertin.[6]

Irish medieval chronicles

Where then do Irish chronicles stand in respect of the foregoing definitions? I commence by considering the general characteristics of all the substantial medieval Irish chronicles. The following are all substantial with respect either to their range or to the quantity of their entries: *Cogadh Gaedhel re Gallaibh* (CG), *Lebor Gabála* (LG), *Foras Feasa ar Eirinn* (FF), *Chronicum Scotorum*

---

6 Burgess, 'Dates and editions' (date of Eusebius), 471; Reuter, *Annals of Fulda*; Johnstone, *Annals of Ghent*; Nelson, *Annals of S.-Bertin*.

(CS), and the annals of *Tigernach* (AT), *Ulster* (AU), *Inisfallen* (AI), *Loch Cé* (LC), *Connacht* (CT), the *Four Masters* (FM), the *Fragmentary Annals* (FA), and Conell Mageoghagan (MB).[7] The collective range of these chronicles is Adam–AD 1616, and both the scale of this and their multiplicity represent a remarkable achievement by Ireland's literate class, particularly given the relatively small population and geographical extent of the island. The first three of these chronicles are non-annalistic, each using a regnal series as the chronological apparatus for its narrative. All the remainder are substantially annalistic, as indeed is indicated by the appearance of 'Annals' in nearly every published title, and this too is remarkable in that no other European literate class compiled the annalistic genre with such vigour as the Irish. Thus an important characteristic of the major Irish chronicles is that they are predominantly annalistic and consequently this book will concentrate its attention on this key group and its affiliates, referring to them collectively as the 'Irish Annals', or 'Annals'. Regarding their purview, before the arrival of Christianity in Ireland in the early fifth century these Annals reflect in some degree the Mediterranean Christian purview of Eusebius' chronicle. But after the arrival of Christianity their purview shifts to reflect first eastern and then northern Irish and also Scots affairs. Then in the mid-eighth century the Scots component suddenly diminishes and thereafter the purview becomes and remains broadly Irish, with a noticeable emphasis first on Clonmacnoise and then on Connacht from the thirteenth century. Colmán Etchingham has made a careful thematic study of the Annals over the ninth and tenth centuries and shown that ecclesiastical affairs, and obits in particular, completely dominate their purview. However, in the second half of the tenth century he has identified a significant increase in the inclusion of secular events.[8] Although no corresponding study exists for later centuries a sampling of entries shows that this secular trend continues. Up until the fifth century in most cases their language is Latin, but thereafter place and personal names are generally registered in Irish, and this is followed by an inexorable shift to the vernacular in the subsequent centuries, so that by the tenth century about fifty percent of the text preserving most of the oldest orthography, AU, is in Irish, as David Dumville has documented.[9] It is remarkable, however, that even though their purview becomes increasingly secular from the mid-tenth century onwards absolutely no reference, citation,

---

7 Todd, *Cogadh Gaedhel*; Macalister, *LG*; Comyn & Dineen, *Foras Feasa*; for other texts see Abbreviations. By comparison with these works the *Leabhar Oiris* is not substantial, cf. Best, 'Leabhar Oiris', 74–112.   8 Etchingham, 'Cas des annales', 42–50, 55–6 diags. 1–4, cf. 52, 'Une evolution importante dans les annals du Xe siècle manifest par le nombre d'avis de décès plus réduit que dans celles du IXe siècle ... On note un accroissement important des notices se rapportant aux événements politiques séculiers dans les annals du Xe siècle.' See also Etchingham, 'Viking raids', 18–19, 28–9.   9 Dumville, 'Latin and Irish', 336–7, cf. Ó Máille, *Language of AU*, 17–18 (Irish dates).

or even gloss referencing the Annals is found in any legal text of whatever age.[10] It seems unlikely, therefore, that the Annals ever played any significant role in the administration of law in Ireland.

The predominant chronological apparatus of these Annals is one of their most distinctive features and it consists simply of the letters 'K' or 'Kł', standing for 'Kalendae Ianuarii', i.e. 1 January, thereby providing a precise temporal boundary between the entries for successive years. Commonly this is accompanied by another series, namely the ferial or weekday of 1 January, expressed as a Roman numeral between 'i' and 'uii', where 'Kł.i.' represents Sunday, and 'Kł.uii.' Saturday. Because, among chronicles, this apparatus is found only in the Irish Annals it was at one time assumed to be an Irish invention, however research has shown that this feature was transmitted by Rufinus' chronicle, and it derived most likely from the Paschal table of Anatolius †c.282, bishop of Laodicea, which employs the same apparatus.[11] This correspondence seems to have been in part responsible for the mistaken hypothesis that the Irish Annals developed from marginal entries on Easter tables.[12] In the eleventh century lunar epactal and AD series derived from the Paschal table of Dionysius Exiguus were introduced and the AD series remained part of the chronological apparatus thereafter.[13] Where necessary to identify the components of an apparatus I shall list these series in their customary order joined by '+', e.g. 'kalend+ferial'. The epochs used in Irish chronology are the aforementioned Biblical epochs, and the arrivals of Palladius, Patrick and the Normans at AD 431, 432 and 1169 respectively, yielding the terms pre/post-Palladian, pre/post-Patrician and pre/post-Norman.

Regarding the compilation mechanisms observed in Irish chronicles, their annalistic emphasis and ecclesiastical/dynastic purview point strongly to institutional compilation, and this conclusion is borne out by systematic investigation. For example, Alfred Smyth has shown that most of the entries over c.550–740 were compiled in the monastery of Iona, and John Bannerman introduced the term 'Iona chronicle' for this. Similarly investigation of the purview of entries from the eighth to the twelfth centuries has prompted many scholars to infer that a chronicle was maintained at the monastery of

---

10 I am grateful to Professor Fergus Kelly of DIAS for this information, pers. corresp. 21 January 2003. Compare also Binchy, 'Lawyers', 50–1 where he contrasted the stagnation of the Irish legal genre with the flourishing of the annalistic genre over 1000–1700.   11 Morris, 'Chronicle of Eusebius', 81 'The Irish, however, devised an ingenious but troublesome dating system of their own.' Mc Carthy, 'Chronology', 212–15, 245–50 (ferial sequences); idem, 'Lunar and Paschal tables', 289 (fig. 1), 308 (Anatolius' Paschal table and its apparatus); idem, 'Status', 148–51 (Rufinus' chronicle and its transmission of Anatolius' apparatus); Mc Carthy & Breen, *De ratione paschali*, 45–53 (critical edition of Anatolius), 60–1 (MS reproduction).   12 Ó Cróinín, 'Early Irish annals', 74–86 (Easter table hypothesis and literature).   13 Mc Carthy, 'AU apparatus 82–1019', 273–81 (epacts & AD); cf. infra figure 51, p. 345 and figure 53, p. 348 (ferials & epacts).

Clonmacnoise, and this is supported by Mícheál O Cléirigh's identification in 1636 of 'leabhar cluana mic nóis' as the first of his list of sources for the compilation of the Four Masters. Likewise an interjection in AU attributes an entry institutionally as 'secundum Librum Monachorum'.[14] The monastery is not the only institution concerned with annals however, for from the thirteenth century onwards interjections, purview and other evidence point to compilation by hereditary learned families attached to secular dynasties. The best manuscript evidence that we have for institutional compilation is that of AI, with forty hands accumulating the entries for 1093–1326.[15] On the other hand, the interjections of names such as 'Africanus', 'Eusebius', 'Marcellinus', 'Isidore', 'Bede', 'Cuana', 'Tigernach', 'Dubdáleithe' also shows that our Annals incorporate excerpts from individual compilations. However, none of our Annals can be considered the compilation of a single monastery or dynasty, rather they all incorporate to different degrees a number of separate institutional compilations. It is a principal objective of this book to try to identify the layers of these compilation processes, and so to derive a coherent text history for the Irish Annals.

Taxonomy of Irish Annals

I commence by examining the characteristics of all but one of the substantial Irish annals listed above, viz. CS, AT, AU, AI, LC, CT, FM, MB. If we examine the chronological apparatus of these we find that all except FM and MB systematically employ the kalend, 'Kl' or 'K', as their primary chronological series. The two FM and MB, on the other hand, employ a regnal-canon comprising an extended sequence of kings and their regnal years. Thus FM and MB may be accurately designated as belonging to the *regnal-canon tradition*, while the remainder belong to the *kalend tradition*. Regarding the kalend tradition we find that AT and CS share an emphatic Clonmacnoise purview over *c*.750–1150, a unique ferial series over 336–644, a simple kalend series over 645–1018, and cognate ferial, epactal and AD series over 1019–1150. Thus AT and CS are best placed together in a *Clonmacnoise group*. Of the remaining four AU and AI share common ferial and nineteen-year Dionysiac epactal series over 433–1014, and since I have associated these epacts with the 'Liber Cuanach' acknowledged in AU interjections, AU and AI are best placed in a *Cuana group*. Finally the pair LC and CT share an emphatically Connacht purview and common chronological apparatus so that they are best placed together in a *Connacht group*.

14 Smyth, 'Earliest Irish annals', 31–43 (Iona compilation); Bannerman, 'Scottish entries', 169 (Iona chronicle), cf. Moisl, 'Bernician dynasty', 106–7. O'Donovan, *FM* i, p. lxiv ('l. cluana mic nóis'). Mac Airt & Mac Niocaill, AU 511.4 (Librum Monachorum). 15 Best & Mac Neill, *AI facsimile*, 5–25 (the hands of AI).

If we expand our review to include lesser Irish annals two more emerge which fit readily into the above taxonomy. Namely the annals of Roscrea (AR) and of Boyle (AB) both qualify for the kalend tradition, and AR's post-Patrician ferial series and Clonmacnoise purview place it firmly in the Clonmacnoise group. On the other hand, AB's kalend series arranged in regular nineteen-year cycles and other characteristics to be discussed below place it in the Cuana group. When including these two lesser sources it will be as well to explain why I have chosen above to omit FA from both this taxonomy and ensuing discussion. This chronicle is found in a single MS, Bruxelles Bibl. Royale 5301–20 pp. 1–70, and in the valuable introduction to her edition Joan Radner set forth that its five fragments extend over c.573–914 and she gave the following account of their chronological apparatus:[16]

> The dating information in the FA text is minimal and untrustworthy. There are four A.D. dates in the entire text, three of them wrong ... There are no indications of ferials or epacts in FA, and although 'Kl.' appears, it is used irregularly. The number of kalends noted within a section is never equal to the number of years represented in the entries ... Generally 'Kl.' is a fossil in FA ...

Thus while it is clear that FA partially transmit the chronological apparatus of an annalistic source of the kalend tradition this is severely fragmented and corrupted, and to include such a distorted source as this in our analysis would simply further complicate an already demanding discussion with very little return. Accordingly I have elected to omit FA.

The foregoing brief, informal evaluation has divided the most important Irish annals into four groups based on their chronological apparatus and purview, and this taxonomy provides an effective basis on which to discuss their inter-relationships. Before proceeding with that it will be helpful to discuss more fully the common characteristics of each group of our corpus.

Clonmacnoise group

The three texts AT, CS, AR have been characterised as 'Clonmacnoise' texts by Thomas O'Rahilly, Kathleen Hughes, Kathryn Grabowski and David Dumville, and Gearóid Mac Niocaill, assigning this name on the basis of their relative emphasis on the affairs of that monastery and its hinterland.[17] Textually a collation over every common range shows that all three share many regular features, for example: common entries are closely related semantically and

---

16 Radner, *Fragmentary annals*, x (fragment ranges and cit.).   17 O'Rahilly, *Early Irish history*, 258; Hughes, *Introduction to the sources*, 45–7; Grabowski & Dumville, *Chronicles*, 42; Mac Niocaill, *MIA*, 22–4; Dumville, 'Millennium', 109.

textually; the sequence of the entries within each year and their overall chronology is virtually identical; the surviving kalend+ferial chronological apparatus in AT/CS/AR is textually cognate.[18] Taken together the three are witness to an annalistic institutional compilation maintained at Clonmacnoise, which commenced at Adam and continued with either a bare kalend or a kalend+ferial to *c.*1019, and continued from thence with ferials, annalistic epacts and intermittent AD until its termination at *c.*1227. I shall refer to this now lost institutional compilation as the 'Clonmacnoise chronicle'.

Cuana group

This group consists of AU, AI and AB, and it is named from the interjections found in AU over 467–628 referring to a now lost 'Liber Cuanach' written by 'Cuana'. This Cuana has been identified as Cuán Ua Lothcháin †1024, and his compilation with the range Adam – *c.*1019 was completed between 1022 and 1024. This individual compilation was a most significant development in Irish chronicling for it successfully introduced into the Annals both the lunar epacts and AD synchronized to those criteria in the Dionysiac Paschal table.[19] Hence membership of the Cuana group is principally determined by evidence of nineteen-year lunar epacts occurring before 1019. The interjections in AU referring to 'Cuana' arise from AU's compiler having collated his primary source against 'Liber Cuanach' over the interval AD 471–632 wherein the Clonmacnoise chronicle and AU diverge chronologically. Thus, even though AU has lost all of its pre-Christian section, over AD 81–1019 it is the best surviving witness that we have to the chronology and chronological apparatus of the now lost 'liber Cuanach'.[20] The reasons for including AI in this group are that collation of AI's chronological apparatus with AU over AD 433–1000 show that they share a cognate chronological apparatus including nineteen-year lunar epacts, and, as well, collation of AI's S. Brigit entries with AU shows that they share distinctive textual and chronological characteristics.[21] The reasons for including AB in this group are: its post-Creation kalends are arranged in groups of nineteen; these kalends are expressed as 'Kł.eñ', similarly to those of pre-Palladian AU; a number of its entries correspond textually and/or chronologically with pre-Palladian entries in AU that can be associated with 'Liber Cuanach'; the close correlation in the incidence of AB and AU entries over the interval

---

18 Mc Carthy, 'S. Brigit', 258, 261, (examples of textual identity); idem, 'Synchronization', *s.a.* 336–358, 488–644 (AT/CS) and 571–642 (AT/CS/AR) for cognate apparatus and corresponding entry sequences.   19 Mc Carthy, 'AU apparatus 82–1019', 261–9 (the introduction of epacts and AD), 273–81 (identity of Cuana and the chronology of his compilation).   20 Mc Carthy, 'Chronology', 232–6 (AU chronological divergence).   21 Mc Carthy, 'S. Brigit', 258–63, 281; Mc Carthy, 'AU apparatus 82–1019', 274–6 (AI's apparatus).

81–387.[22] Furthermore AB shows that originally Liber Cuanach commenced at Adam. Of course these three texts only represent a group as far as *c.*1019, after which they each possess their own distinct end chronicles, AU presenting in turn entries with Armagh, Derry, Connacht and Fermanagh purviews, AI presenting a Munster purview, and AB presenting first a purview of the Cistercian monastery of Boyle to 1228, when a transition to the nearby Premonstratensian monastery of the Holy Trinity occurs, and this purview is maintained until the termination of the text at 1257.

Connacht group

Of this group LC ranges over 1014–1577 with two substantial lacunae, and CT over 1224–1544 with three small lacunae. Both of these texts provide extensive coverage of the affairs of Connacht, and indeed Mac Niocaill placed the common source of both texts with a specific Connacht family writing: 'The two chief sets of annals for the later middle ages, *Conn* and *L1–L3* [i.e. CT and LC], both derive from a text compiled by a member of the Ó Maoilchonaire family, probably in the mid fifteenth century.'[23] From *c.*1231 to 1482 the Uí Maoil Chonaire of north Roscommon provided the hereditary *ollamh* or professor of history to the dynasty of the Uí Chonchobhair who then controlled a large part of the province of Connacht. Thus the two members of this group incorporate a secular institutional compilation that will be referred to as the 'Connacht chronicle'.

Regnal-canon group

The defining characteristic of this group is that their primary chronological series consists of a canon of the 'kings of Ireland' that extends from the time of the supposed Fir Bolg inhabitation of Ireland up to the death of Máel Sechnaill mac Domhnaill in 1022. Each kingship has been assigned a reign expressed in an integral number of years, and for FM a dependent series of AM or AD based upon these reigns has been provided for every year from AM 2242 onwards. At first this apparatus is intermittent but for AM 3266–5200 it is systematically written for every year and thereafter for AD 1–1616 likewise, so

---

22 Mc Carthy, 'AU apparatus 82–1019', 274 n. 45 shows that the following AB entries correspond textually and/or chronologically with critical entries found in the pre-Palladian section of AU: a) AB §1–7 the apparatus 'Kł.eñ', with nearly every nineteenth year citing a ferial datum as, e.g., §3 'Kł.eñ.uii.f'. b) Kalends arranged in groups of nineteen in AB §1–17. c) Verbatim entry AB §92 noting 'Hic est annus primus noni magni paschalis ... indictionis annus', cf. AU §95. d) Verbatim entry AB §93 for the Incarnation 'secundum Dionisium', cf. AU §96. See Mc Carthy, 'Synchronization', *s.a.* 81–387 for collation of the corresponding AU and AB entries.   23 Mac Niocaill, *MIA*, 32.

that FM is annalistic for the range AM 3266–AD 1616. In the case of MB its AD apparatus is independent of its regnal series and it becomes annalistic only from the middle of the seventh century. Even thereafter the AD series is frequently disrupted by lacunae, so that this compilation is chronologically the least coherent of our corpus. In MB this regnal-canon commences with the Fir Bolg Slane who 'was the first king that ever absolutely ruled Ireland', and similarly in FM at AM 3267 'Slainghe mac Deala do beith i ríghe Erionn' is the first king registered and his reign marks FM's transition to annals.[24] Thereafter this succession of kings of Ireland is continued in both texts down to Máel Sechnaill's death in 1022, and in both cases their regnal-canon corresponds closely with the regnal series found in recensions *a* and *m* of *Lebor Gabála*.[25] In both FM and MB their pre-Christian period is dominated by material derived from *Lebor Gabála*. In the case of FM its regnal-canon corresponds chronologically and orthographically with the *Seanchas Riogh Eireann* compiled by Mícheál Ó Cléirigh in 1630.[26] For further details of these relationships see chapter 10, p. 293 ff. Hitherto MB has always been classified as a 'Clonmacnoise' compilation on account of the semantic correspondence of many of its entries with those of the Clonmacnoise group from the fifth to the twelfth century.[27] However, the regnal-canon here used to determine its affinity with FM represents a far more fundamental and pervasive feature of its compilation than just the semantic correspondence of some of its entries with those of the Clonmacnoise group.

Annalistic nomenclature and referencing

The vernacular system of nomenclature for chronicles employed the word 'liber' or 'leabhar' qualified by the name of either its place of compilation or compiler, as for example 'Liber Cuanach' and 'leabhar cluana mic nóis'. However, when the names of the aforementioned annals are examined it transpires that with the exceptions only of 'Chronicum Scotorum' and the 'Annales Roscreenses' the customary titles of the remainder have no vernacular or MS basis whatsoever. Rather the customary titles used for AT, AU, AI, AB, LC, CT and MB all derive from titles used or suggested by James Ussher and James Ware. Ussher introduced the word 'annales' into the nomenclature in 1609 with his title 'Annales Ultonienses', and Ware followed suite, employing it systematically in his titles for annalistic compilations in his book catalogues over

---

24 Murphy, *AC*, 16 (cit.); O'Donovan, *FM* i, 14 (cit.), 4, 8, 12 (where earlier leaders are termed *toisigh* or *airig*). 25 Scowcroft, '*LG* I', 118–19 (LG 'king lists'); Macalister, *LG* v, 137–51 ('Roll of the Kings' terms these recensions 'R'' and 'Min'). 26 Walsh, *Genealogiae*, 3–35. 27 Mac Niocaill, *MIA*, 22; Sanderlin, *Conall Mageoghagan*, 3–4; Grabowski & Dumville, *Chronicles*, 7–8 (MB 'Clonmacnoise').

1625–48.[28] Some of these titles have been justifiably challenged by subsequent scholars, notably the 'Annals of Tigernach', as will appear from the discussion in chapter 6, p. 191 ff. However, in this book I need to be able to refer unambiguously to all of these works, and the best title for this purpose is normally the familiar title used for the most accessible published edition of the text. For this reason I adopt those published edition titles with the three following exceptions.

The first and most important of these is Conell Mageoghagan's compilation of 1627. At least by 1648 James Ware when citing extracts had referred to this in Latin and English as 'Annal. Clonmacnoisensibus' and the 'Annals of Clonmacnois' respectively.[29] Now as discussed already, while this chronicle has preserved in translation many entries originating in the Clonmacnoise chronicle, it has also completely supplanted the kalend apparatus with a regnal-canon apparatus. As such it is a very poor representative of the Clonmacnoise chronicle. It was therefore most unfortunate that Denis Murphy, author of the only published edition, chose to follow Ware and commence the lengthy title for his edition with the words, 'The Annals of Clonmacnoise', for that has become the accepted short title for the text.[30] Thus for over one hundred years now the important institutional qualifier 'Clonmacnoise' has been uniquely attached to this chronicle which preserves nothing of the chronological apparatus of the Clonmacnoise chronicle. This has been acknowledged as a source of confusion even among scholars who considered it a member of the Clonmacnoise group; for example, in 1984 Grabowski issued the warning, 'the reader should take care not to confuse AClon with the hypothetical exemplar of the Clonmacnoise-group texts'.[31] Consequently, in order to avoid this confusion in my own discussion, and because Mageoghagan referred repeatedly to his principal source as the 'old book' I will refer to this text using the vernacular style 'Mageoghagan's Book' and the siglum 'MB'. Since Mageoghagan was indeed responsible for its compilation and his name already appears in Murphy's full title, this title is unambiguous, accurate and readily understood.

The second exception, FM, presents an interesting case study in Annalistic nomenclature. It appears that when writing in Irish Mícheál Ó Cléirigh himself used no specific title for the work, for in his preface he referred to it repeatedly simply either as 'an leabhar', or 'an céid leabhar' or 'an dara leabhar' when he

28 Ussher, 'Corbes', 423, 432–3 (Annales Ultonienses). O'Sullivan, 'Finding List', 71–2, 86–7, 89–90, 94, 96 (Ware's 'Annales'). The word 'annalad' was used occasionally in Irish in its generalised sense of 'chronicle', e.g. Gilla Cóemáin's poem *Annálad anall uile* q.v. Best et al., *Book of Leinster* iii, 496–503. 29 Sanderlin, *Conell Mageoghagan*, 36 (Ware's extracts in BL MS 4787 f. 247 and MS 4791 f. 26; both MSS are included in his 1648 catalogue). 30 Murphy, *AC*, title page. In his preface, Murphy expressed a reservation about this title, p. v, 'These Annals have, in later times at least, usually gone by the name of the "Annals of Clonmacnoise". In the book itself there is nothing to show why it should be called by this name.' 31 Grabowski & Dumville, *Chronicles*, 7 (cit.).

wished to distinguish the first or second volume of the work. Similarly the two approbations written in Irish referred to it simply as, 'an leabhair si', or, 'an leabhar airis & annaladh'. However, three of the four approbations written in Latin stated explicitly that the work was entitled, 'Annales Regni Hiberniae', from which it would appear that in Latin Ó Cléirigh had imposed this title.[32] Subsequently, when the Franciscan copy reached Louvain it was used to index both their copy of Mac Fhirbhisigh's *Fragmentary Annals* and Brendan O'Conor's AR, and the indexer Thomas O'Sheerin always referred to it as 'Annales Dungallenses', naming it by its place of compilation. However, in 1645 John Colgan, having acknowledged this name, proposed the title 'Annales Quatuor Magistrorum' as a compliment to the principal compilers whom he designated as 'peritissimi Magistri'.[33] Subsequently, Colgan's title or its English translation were widely adopted, crucially including the Revd O'Conor who was the first to publish an edition of the text. But not subsequently by John O'Donovan who in 1854 published the first complete edition, which he entitled, 'ᵹnnᴀᴌᴀ Rıoᵹhᴀchᵗᴀ Єıreᴀnn. Annals of the Kingdom of Ireland, by the Four Masters, from the earliest period to the year 1616.' O'Donovan offered no discussion concerning these titles, but the first two are plainly Irish and English word-for-word renderings of Ó Cléirigh's 'Annales Regni Hiberniae'. Remarkably, in his own dedication O'Donovan described himself as, 'the Editor of the Annals of the Four Masters'.[34] Since then both Colgan's and O'Donovan's titles have been in use, with a general preference evident for Colgan's, but naturally O'Donovan's must be used if his published edition is to be referenced.[35] In these circumstances Colgan's title, in use since 1645, being the most familiar and acknowledged by O'Donovan's longer title seems preferable, and consequently I choose it and the siglum 'FM'.

The third exception is AB where, because Robin Flower expressed certainty that the annals in Cotton MS Titus A xxv were the annals of 'the Premonstratensian monastery of the Holy Trinity on Holy Trinity Island in Loch Cé', and this conflicted with the title 'Annales Buellensis' used by both

---

32 O'Donovan, *FM* i, pp. lxiii–lxvi (Ó Cléirigh's references); lxviii–ix (the Irish approbations); lxx (the Latin, viz., 'in opere quod intitulatur *Annales Regni Hiberniae*', 'Opus cui titulus *Annales Regni Hiberniae*', 'Opere quod intitulatur *Annales Regni Hiberniae*'); the fourth Latin approbation referred simply to 'hoc opere'.   33 The indices to FA and AR accompany their texts in Bruxelles Bibl. Royale 5301–20, pp. 71–88, 163–234, and these are in the hand of O'Sheerin, see chapter 2 n. 27. They are arranged alphabetically and their chronology column is headed on each page, 'iuxta Annal. Dungallenses'. Colgan, *Acta Sanctorum* i, preface p. [7], 'Sed cùm Annales hi ... à loco *Annales Dungallenses* appellare; nam in Conuentu nostro Dungallensi inchoati & consummati sunt, sed posteà ob alias rationes, potiùs ab ipsis compilatoribus, qui in facultate antiquaria erant quatuor peritissimi Magistri, duximus *Annales Quatuor Magistrorum* appelládos.'   34 O'Donovan, *FM* i, p. vi (cit.).   35 For examples of FM: O'Conor, *Bibliotheca* i, 178; Mac Niocaill, *MIA*, 18; Ó Muraíle, *Mac Fhirbhisigh*, 409 (all references to FM under 'Annals of the Four Masters', with a cross reference from '*Annála Ríoghachta Éireann*'); CELT s.v. 'Four Masters'.

Ussher and the Revd O'Conor, Martin Freeman proposed the title 'The Cottonian Annals'.[36] But examination of the text shows that it represents a Cistercian purview from 1096, a Boyle purview from its foundation as a Cistercian monastery in 1161 up to 1228, and a Holy Trinity purview only from 1229 until the text terminates in 1257.[37] Moreover, as will be shown, there are good reasons to believe that this end chronicle was compiled by monks from Boyle. Therefore Ussher's title 'Annals of Boyle' accurately represents the purview of these annals over 1161–1228, and it identifies an important location and ecclesiastical affiliation in respect of the final stages in their compilation. Where institutional or geographical terms are used in chronicle titles it is surely desirable that they identify the most substantial and important affiliation of the compilation? Flower's title only identifies the purview of the twenty-nine year end chronicle, whereas Freeman's title, 'Cottonian Annals', only indicates where the primary manuscript came to rest after it was removed far from its own context. In these circumstances I have no hesitation in adopting Ussher's title and its siglum 'AB'.

Next, I turn to the problem of concisely and accurately referencing chronicles since this will be required repeatedly in the following discussions. All references to chronicles will use their siglum followed by appropriate AM, AD, paragraph '§', or page data. Where a published edition provides a systematic marginal AM, AD, or paragraph reference system, this will be cited. The sigla, editions, and data used are as follows: AR post-Patrician – Gleeson & Mac Airt's paragraphs; AU post-Palladian – Mac Airt & Mac Niocaill's paragraphs; AU post-Palladian – Hennessy & Mac Carthy's AD; AI pre-Patrician – Mac Airt's paragraphs; AI post-Patrician – Mac Airt's AD; AB – Freeman's paragraphs; LC – Hennessy's AD; CT – Freeman's AD; FM – O'Donovan's AM and AD. Bede's chronicles in DT and DTR will be cited from Jones' editions in CCSL; that in DT cap. 16–22 will be cited by chapter and line number so it extends over DT 16.1–22.80, while that in DTR cap. 66 will simply use the paragraph numbers so it extends over DTR §1–593. These mechanisms work well unless the entries for the year in question extend over many pages. In these cases an *entry number* preceded by a period '.' will be used to provide an index of location. Although not all of the above cited editions provide entry numbers they have been added for most of the CELT electronic editions of these texts.

In the case of the published editions of AT and CS no satisfactory published AM/AD/§ apparatus exists, so for the Christian era I will cite the AD from my Internet synchronization of AT and CS. However, for the pre-Christian era of

---

36 Freeman, *AB* 44(1927), 337–40 (title); cf. Miller, 'World-chronicle', 79, eschewing 'Annals of Tigernach', identified AT *passim* as 'the Rawl. B 502' fragment or text. 37 Freeman, AB §283 'fundatum est Cistertium', §347 'Abbatia Buellensis hoc anno fundata est', §§390, 392, 393, 395, 397, 398, 401 (Holy Trinity purview).

AT and CS, and also for MB which all completely lack any coherent reference system, I will reference them by their published page followed by a *quarter letter*, i.e. the letters a–d used to identify the four quarters of their textual page, where a=first quarter, ... , d= fourth quarter. As well as providing a more precise reference this quarter letter will distinguish page references and ensure they cannot be confused with AD/AM references. The editions used will be: AT pre-Christian – Stokes, Llanerch page numbers; CS pre AD 336 – Hennessy's page numbers; MB – Murphy's page numbers. For the pre-Patrician era of AR which has not yet been published the same system will be used employing the pagination of its MS, Bruxelles Bibl. Royale 5301–20 pp. 1–24. For example:

AT 21d = AI §191 = AB §87 = DT 21.12 = DTR §200 = Alexander reg.
AT 225 = AU §74 = AI §279 = AB §126 = DT 22.25 = DTR §359 = [AD 225] Origines claruit.
AT 336 = CS 336 = AU §163 = AI §313 = [AD 336] Patricius natus.
AT 497 = CS 497 = MB 77a = AU 496 =AI 497 = [AD 497] Cormac pausauit.
AU 1376.1 = CT 1376.2 = MB 305a = [AD 1376] Tadhg h-Ua Ruairc d'eg.

Finally regarding orthography, I have followed where possible the orthography of *A New history of Ireland* and M.A. O'Brien's *Corpus genealogiarum Hiberniae*, giving the former priority in the case of conflict. However, because in the Annalistic corpus generally the family or tribal affiliation is indicated by 'Ua' I have used the year 1600 as the changeover boundary from 'Ua' to 'Ó', so that if the individual flourished before 1600 then 'Ua' will be used, but after that 'Ó' will be used.[38]

---

38 Ó Cróinin, *New history* i, p. v & Moody et al., *New history* viii, 4–5 (orthography). In AI 'O' predominates from *c.*1216, cf. Mac Airt, *AI*, li with the first instance at AI 1176.7.

CHAPTER TWO

Witnesses to the Annals – the primary manuscripts

Since, with the exception of a few brief prefaces and the interjections, no contemporary account of the Annalists or their Annals has come down to us, the principal witnesses to their work are their manuscripts. Consequently, to obtain an understanding of the Annals it is essential to examine carefully the evidence provided by these manuscripts. However, when one sets about this a number of serious impediments quickly emerge. First, the manuscripts themselves, some in fragile condition, are only accessible to those who can present a convincing case to the custodian library. Second, they are written predominantly in Middle Irish employing a formidable array of scribal abbreviations, so that reading and understanding the text are major obstacles for many scholars. Third, most of the texts have no AD apparatus, so that knowing where any particular entry is located in time is a difficulty for many scholars. None of these problems is unique to the Irish Annals, and all of them could and ideally would be solved by the publication of printed critical editions with parallel translations. However, a number of factors specific to Ireland's circumstances have combined to prevent the production of the requisite critical editions. First, with the English invasions of Ulster and Connacht following the battle of Kinsale in 1601, the remainder of the social structure and economy which had created and supported Gaelic scholarship, was, in the space of a couple of decades, effectively destroyed. Within these decades many of the principal literary monuments of Gaelic scholarship passed into the possession of Anglo-Irishmen who, in many instances, were illiterate in Irish. Henceforth the funding, and increasingly the personnel, for Gaelic scholarship were to be derived from alien cultures; Fearghal Ó Gadhra's funding of the compilation of FM over 1632–6 was the last such compilation sponsored and executed by individuals whose first language was Irish. All subsequent editions have been organized and executed in an English-speaking context. Second, relative to its size and population a remarkably large collection of texts has survived from the scholarship of medieval Ireland, of which the Annals are just a part. Third, neither the scale nor the circumstances of the Irish economy over the last four hundred years has been favourably disposed to the business of funding scholars with the time and resources necessary for the production of critical editions of these works. As a result, production of even published editions of the Irish Annals has been slow and spasmodic, most of them the result of the determination and enthusiasm of an individual, usually working alone with very limited financial and physical resources. Some idea of how this has evolved may be obtained by reviewing the availability of published editions at fifty-year intervals, as is shown in Figure 1.

AD	Published editions
1800	None available.
1850	Editions with parallel Latin translation of parts of AT, AI, AB, FM, AU published by the Revd Charles O'Conor working alone over 1814–26.
1900	Editions with parallel English translations of: FM and FA by John O'Donovan in 1848–51, 1860; CS, LC and part of CT, and part of AU by William Hennessy in 1866, 1871, 1887; the remainder of AU by Bartholomew Mac Carthy in 1893, 1895; AT with English translations of Irish passages by Whitley Stokes over 1895–97; MB by Denis Murphy in 1896. All these editors worked alone.
1950	Editions with English translations of Irish passages of AB and CT by Martin Freeman in 1924, 1944, and of MA by Séamus Ó hInnse in 1947; both these editors worked alone. A full facsimile edition of AI by R.I. Best and Eoin Mac Neill in 1933.
2000	Editions with parallel English translation of: AI by Seán Mac Airt in 1951; FA by Joan Radner in 1978; part of AU by Seán Mac Airt and Gearóid Mac Niocaill in 1983. Edition of part of AR with no translation by Dermot Gleeson and Seán Mac Airt in 1958.

Figure 1. The publication of editions of the Irish Annals over 1800–2000.

It is apparent that the peak of publishing activity was over the years 1851–1900, while the subsequent one hundred years has seen just the publication of two smaller works, two facsimiles, and five re-editions. While the re-editions of AT, CT, AI, FA, and AU all represented substantial improvements on the earlier editions, none can be described as a critical edition since none comprehensively surveys and incorporates into its published text the witness of all the available manuscripts. Moreover, up to c.AD 1000, while they share many entries registering the same events, there is repeated chronological disagreement between the marginal AD apparatus supplied by the various editors. Thus the present situation with respect to the Annals is that we have just printed editions, partial in the case of AR, mostly with English translations but with widely divergent editorial AD chronologies. Consequently, access to the witnesses via the published editions is relatively difficult and unsatisfactory, and there have been repeated complaints about this from scholars down the whole twentieth century.[1] Unfortunately these complaints have usually been directed against the editors, rather than the acute shortage of resources that in my view has been the principal cause of the deficiencies in the published editions. The effect has been dispiriting for editors and publishers alike, with the consequence that some recent projects have not come to fruition. For example, Mac Airt prepared an index for his re-edition of AU for AD 81–1056, and Mac Niocaill gave notice of its impending publication.[2] But, perhaps as a consequence of Dumville's trenchant criticisms of both the Mac Airt-Mac Niocaill edition of AU and of DIAS who published it, the index has not been published. Further, Mac Niocaill also prepared a re-edition of CS, ironically warmly anticipated by Dumville in the same review, and this likewise has not been published.[3] The present outlook for the production of critical editions appears substantially less promising than it did twenty-five years ago.

On the other hand various technological developments over the last fifty years have materially improved matters. The first of these has been the wide-spread production of black-and-white microfilms of many MSS, now widely available in universities and national libraries. These microfilms, while not easy to view and difficult to print satisfactorily, have significantly improved access to these MSS. The second development has been the on-line provision by the CELT project at the National University of Ireland, Cork of electronic versions of the principal published editions of the Annals. The speed, ease and precision with which these CELT editions may be searched and collated represents an invaluable contribution to Annalistic studies. Third, computerized information technology has facilitated the construction of a synchronized chronology for the principal Annals, available online since 1998, and which now extends over AD 1–1590. The fourth development has been the recent availability of high-resolution digitized images of the folios of primary manuscripts on the Internet. Oxford University has led this development with reproductions of their important manuscript witnesses for AT, AU and AI, followed more recently by the Dublin Institute for Advanced Studies' ISOS project which to date has made available numerous important texts including primary manuscripts for CT and FM. These splendid digitized reproductions, with their potential for comfortable, detailed examination, enlargement, enhancement and copying, when combined with the electronic CELT editions of the texts, have greatly improved access to the primary witnesses for the Annals.[4]

1 Complaints: Mac Carthy, *AU* iv, pp. xii–iv; Stokes, 'Notes', *passim*; Mac Neill, 'Authorship', 45; Binchy, 'Lawyers', 57; Hughes, *Early Christian Ireland*, 99–100; Sanderlin, 'Manuscripts', 111; Grabowski & Dumville, *Chronicle*, 5–6; Dumville, 'Editing', *passim*. 2 Mac Airt & Mac Niocaill, *AU*, vii–viii (index notice). 3 Dumville, 'Editing', *passim* (criticism), 69, 86 (Mac Niocaill's CS, now available on the CELT website). 4 CELT at www.ucc.ie/celt/ where at 15 June 2007 most of AT/CS/AU/AI/AB/LC/CT/FM/FA/MA were available. Mc Carthy, 'Synchronization' at www.irish-annals.cs.tcd.ie. Oxford, Bodleian at www.image.ox.ac.uk/ and ISOS at www.isos.dias.ie.

To give the reader a clear impression of these witnesses for our corpus I provide below for each an account of its primary MS(S), illustrated with a reproduction. Also since observation of the distribution and character of scribal hands and marginalia often helps to identify compilation stages, brief accounts of these are included. Finally brief details of the published editions will be given. These accounts will be presented in the order of the groups of chapter 1. In general for all Irish manuscripts at Oxford University we are in the fortunate position of having Brian Ó Cuív's splendid catalogue completed shortly before his much regretted death in 1999; in this he provides a very detailed physical and content description of each MS, and an account of its known history. Appendix 1 provides a list of the shelf-marks of known Annalistic MSS.

Clonmacnoise group

This group comprises AT/CS/AR and I will describe them in that order.

Annals of Tigernach

The two Bodleian manuscripts Rawl. B. 502 and B. 488, with ranges $c.770$ BC–AD 140 and $c.318$ BC–AD 1178 respectively, provide the primary witnesses to AT.[5] All the important Irish annals MSS at Oxford are in the Bodleian library and carry a Rawlinson shelfmark; all were originally Ware manuscripts, and passed to his son Robert, thence to the earl of Clarendon, thence to the duke of Chandos, and thence to Richard Rawlinson in 1747. Rawl. B. 502 ff. 1–12 consists of twelve vellum leaves averaging $c.27 \times 20.5$ cm., bound as a single gathering and dated to the late eleventh or early twelfth century.[6] The annals, which are both acephalous and truncated, in Irish miniscule in two columns were written according to Best and Oskamp by two scribes on ff. 1–4 and ff. 5–12 respectively. The occasional paragraph breaks are used to identify significant chronological epochs and these are further emphasized by the use of enlarged, decorated capitals, see plates 1–2. The date of this MS makes it a contemporary witness to the Clonmacnoise chronicle and a number of scribal details identified by Ó Cuív provide good reasons to believe that it was written in the Clonmacnoise scriptorium.[7]

---

5 Since there has been no conclusive work done on the pre-Christian chronology of the Irish annals I use my own kalend counts of Rawl. B. 502 as an approximate BC index, and hence prefix all such citations with *circa*.   6 Ó Cuív, *Catalogue*, xxiii–viii (Rawlinson's acquisition of Ware's MSS), 163–5, 181–2 (Rawl. B. 502), 141–51 (Rawl. B. 488).   7 Ó Cuív, *Catalogue*, 165 (Two scribes, Clonmacnoise).

There are repeated marginal and interlinear AM annotations, some by the first scribe, often enclosed in coloured cartouches, showing that a process of synchronizing these annals with Bede's DTR cap. 66 was in progress at the time of writing. This is also shown by interlinear citations from DTR cap. 66, some explicitly attributed to Bede; for example on f. 11[ra], '.i. in Roma singulariter, ut Beda ait' glossing 'Marcus in Italia euangelium scripsit'. Ff. 9–12 have been glossed in a hand identified by Best as the 'interpolator H' of the Clonmacnoise MS *Lebor na hUidre*.[8] The earliest identifiable reference to this manuscript is by Ware in his catalogue of 1648, and from his description of it as 'Annales ab Urbe condita ad imperium usque Antonini Pii' it is clear that nothing has been lost since his time. Since Ware wrote of it 'Huius Libri ignoratur Author' it appears certain that he did not realize that the text of ff. 6[vb]–12[vb] was cognate with Rawl. B. 488 ff. 1[r]–4[ra], which he also owned and had entitled 'Annales Tigernaci'.[9]

Rawl. B. 488 ff. 1–26 is a vellum MS of the later fourteenth century with leaves of size *c.*30.5×22.5 cm., written in two columns in a neat, regular Irish minuscule by a single scribe, apart from three brief interventions in ff. 7–10. The first scribe has not been identified but Best observed that he had written part of the Yellow Book of Lecan compiled in the Mac Fhir Bhisigh school in Sligo over *c.*1350–70, and also the LG passages in RIA MSS 537–9.[10] Clearly this was a skilled scribe involved in important compilations so there are good reasons to conclude that he made an accurate copy of his exemplar; see chapter 11, p. 304 ff. where it is argued that this scribe was a member of the Uí Duibhgeannáin. Hoewever, collation of the cognate text of ff. 1–4ra with that of Rawl. B. 502 ff. 6–12 reveals numerous omissions and orthographic errors in the Latin. These Latin errors continue in ff. 4rb–6 and are prominently registered in Stokes' *apparatus criticus* and they imply that the compiler of the archetype of the exemplar did not accurately reproduce his Clonmacnoise chronicle source.[11] This unfamiliarity with Latin, and the omission of important Clonmacnoise ecclesiastical series suggest that the compiler of the archetype worked in a secular context, cf. plate 3 and also chapter 9, p. 249 ff. The MS now comprises four distinct fragments, all acephalous and truncated as follows: ff. 1ra–6vb for *c.*318 BC–AD 358; ff. 7ra–14rb for AD 488–766; ff. 15ra–15vb for AD 974–1003; ff. 16ra–26vb for AD 1018–1178. In 1975 Oskamp examined the binding and asserted that these surviving fragments relate to the original

---

8 Stokes, *AT*, 7, 11, 13, 36, 37, 41 (Bede citations); Ó Cuív, *Catalogue*, 165 ('interpolator H'). 9 O'Sullivan, 'Finding list', 87 (citations from Ware's entries for Rawl. B. 488 & 502). 10 Ó Cuív, *Catalogue*, 144–5 (scribes); Best, 'Yellow Book', 190–2 (contributions to Yellow Book and LG); Oskamp, 'Yellow Book', 108 Plates I–VII (facsimile reproductions). 11 Stokes, *AT*, 50–77 (Latin orthographical errors); Mc Carthy, 'Chronology', 221 (Rawl. B. 488 vs B. 502); Byrne, 'Ut Beda boat', 52–3 (collations of Rawl. B. 502 vs 488).

gatherings, and estimated that a further 41–3 folios had been lost. O Cuív however considered that Oskamp's estimate 'must be regarded as speculative', and my own estimate is rather *c*.30 lost folios. But whichever estimate is accepted it is clear that we have the lacunose remains of a very substantial chronicle written essentially by a single accomplished scribe, which originally commenced before 318 BC and extended beyond AD 1178.[12]

The textual annotations have been well summarized by Ó Cuív but it is important to add that collation of the inscription on the bottom margin of f. 4^r with TCD 1293 ff. 95–101 shows that it was written by Brian Mac Diarmada, cf. LC below. This inscription cites both the year 1584, at which time Mac Diarmada was compiling LC, and also the Uí Ruairc whom he references in twenty-one entries over 1581–90. Furthermore, it will be helpful to describe the chronological annotations more fully here than does Ó Cuív:[13]

1. AM years derived from Bede's DTR cap. 66 in Roman numerals, usually in cartouches, some coloured, have been entered by the first scribe for the leading imperial reigns, cf. plate 5 a–b). For ff. 1rb–5va these are usually incorporated in the text, and thereafter they are marginal to f. 12vb, where they cease, and since these cartouches and their AM data appear marginally in Rawl. B. 502, cf. plates 1–2, there is every reason to conclude these have been inherited from that MS.

2. Marginal AD system-A on ff. 17^v–18^r, running for 1046–63, the last eighteen years of the second great Dionysiac cycle, written in Roman numerals, e.g. the last is 'M.lx.íii'. Examination of the ink and the hand leads to the conclusion that at least on f. 18^r these were written by the first scribe as he wrote the text. For example at f. 18rb he wrote 'M.lvíiíi' *before* he wrote the enlarged 'G' of 'Gallbrat' of AT 1058.6, since the 'G' transgresses the minims. Evidently therefore these AD marginalia were a feature of the exemplar.

3. Marginal AD system-B on ff. 15ra–17^r, 18^v–26^v, running for 978–1045, 1064–1178, written in a mixture of Irish words and Roman numerals, e.g. 'ocht mbl– .lxx.ix.c..a.in.t.', read as 'ocht mbliadna sechtmogat naí cét áis in tigerna', which is the Uí Duibhgeannáin style of AD found in the Connacht group MSS, cf. plates 10–11 and also chapter 11, p. 258.[14] The least significant digit of these annotations has been systematically emended from f. 15^v to 16^r up to AD 1024, and since this system ceases for 1046–63 it is clear that system-B postdates system-A. Indeed examination of both the ink and hand suggests that these may be the work of the hand that annotated on the upper margin of f. 5^r 'Glés nach maith ⁊ amen don dub', which hand Ó Cuív described as 'possibly sixteenth century'.[15]

12 Oskamp, 'Yellow book', 103 (binding), 111–13 (folio loss); Ó Cuív, *Catalogue*, 143 (cit.). 13 Ó Cuív, *Catalogue*, 143–4, 149–50 (textual annotations), 149 (inscription on f. 4^r).   14 Ó Cuív, *Catalogue*, 144 (cits.).   15 Ó Cuív, *Catalogue*, 149 (cits.).

4. Marginal AD system-C on ff. 6^v–26^v, found intermittently over 372–1178 written by Ware in Arabic numerals, which clearly postdates system-B.

The earliest reference to this MS is a simple 'Tigernacus' by Ware in one of his lists of books lent over 1630–6. Ware also foliated the manuscript, and from discrepancies between this and the modern foliation cited here it is clear that one leaf has since been lost.[16] However, the start of the present manuscript does effectively correspond with Ware's description in his 1648 catalogue, 'meus MS. caret principio, & incipit à morte Alexandri Magni', and the text of ff. 1–6 is continuous so it appears that the leaf was lost from a later lacuna.[17] As mentioned the MS is truncated during 1178 and it is remarkable therefore that Roderick O'Flaherty, having first stated that 'Tigernachus Cluanensis' had equated AM 3952 with the second year of the decennovenal cycle, continued thus:[18]

> In vetustis penes me annalibus pergameno olim mandatus, annus 1180 characteribus designatur his: Kalenda Januariae Martis die, Luna Prima: bissextilis annus: tertius annus Decennovenalis cycli:

These four chronological criteria for 1180 parallel those in Rawl. B. 488 at 1178, and this and the conspicuous way in which O'Flaherty identified his vellum source as 'annalibus pergameno olim mandatus' suggests that he had then in his possession the continuing folios of Rawl. B. 488. I will give in chapter 6, p. 172 ff. my reasons for concluding that the Clonmacnoise chronicle and hence Rawl. B. 488 formerly extended to $c.$1227.

The first printed edition of AT was published in 1825 by the Revd Charles O'Conor †1828 who edited Rawl. B. 488 ff. 1–19 for $c.$318 BC–AD 1088, filling lacunae from AU and FM and giving a parallel Latin translation. This was the first of his five editions of Irish annals, and represented a pioneer undertaking by O'Conor and his patron, the marquis of Buckingham. Unfortunately O'Conor's textual skills were not equal to the task and the inaccuracy of both his text and translations have been repeatedly remarked.[19] Next, over 1895–7 Whitley Stokes incrementally published the full text of Rawl. B. 502 for $c.$770 BC–AD 140, and Rawl. B. 488 for AD 141–1178, with interspersed English translations of the Irish passages. Stokes' edition was reproduced in a two-volume facsimile in 1993, and in 1997 Diarmuid Ó Murchadha published a valuable series of indices to this.[20]

---

16 Ó Cuív, *Catalogue*, 142 (foliation and lost leaf). 17 O'Sullivan, 'Finding list', 71–2 ('Tigernacus'), 87 (cit.); Stokes, *AT*, 23 where the first substantial entry on f. 1^r describes the division of Alexander's empire following his death. 18 O'Flaherty, *Ogygia*, 7 (cit.); Stokes, *AT*, 446 (criteria for 1178). 19 O'Conor, *Rerum Hib.* ii, 1–314 (edition); Reeves, *Columba*, 312 (O'Conor's inaccuracy); Ó Muraíle, *Celebrated antiquary*, 315–16 (O'Conor's life). 20 Stokes, *AT*, (edition); Murchadha, *Index*.

Chronicum Scotorum

The fact that of the fourteen known MSS of this text ten paper copies were written in the nineteenth century attests to the enduring popularity of the annalistic genre among Gaelic scholars. Thanks to the work of Nollaig Ó Muraíle we know that these ten together with the two eighteenth-century MSS and a solitary vellum MS all derive from that MS written in *c.*1640 by Dubhaltach Mac Fhirbhisigh †1671, now TCD 1292 ff. 162ʳ–216ᵛ. These fourteen MSS thus constitute a single family, and Ó Muraíle has extensively documented the scribes (mostly Ó Longáin), dates, and places of writing of all thirteen paper MSS. However, the origins of the only vellum copy are obscure as Ó Muraíle has also documented. A colophon in the hand of the scribe states that it was written in 1611 by Michéal Peadair Ó Longáin *fl. c.*1750, but Ó Muraíle pointed out that a great number of difficulties exist in relation to both this date and scribe, as well as the text being incomplete and interpolated with passages from AT. Thus on substantial grounds he has concluded that 'the work is an early nineteenth-century forgery'.[21] His collation of readings shows that this vellum copy incorporates textual emendations made by Roderick O'Flaherty to Dubhaltach's MS, and in support of this I may point out that the series of intermittent embedded AD data running for 373–806 likewise show close dependence upon O'Flaherty's marginal AD data, but include occasional copying errors. They are expressed in characteristic late medieval Irish style, for example 'se.chet.iiii.xxit.u' = $6 \times 100 + 4 \times 20 + 5 = 685$ mis-copied from O'Flaherty's marginal '695'.

Thus TCD 1292 is unquestionably the primary witness to CS, and the principal accounts of it are by William Hennessy and Nollaig Ó Muraíle.[22] The MS comprises fifty-five paper leaves measuring *c.*19×28.5 cm, with ff. 162ʳ–214ʳ commencing with an abridged account of the Irish origin legend extending from the Flood to the Milesian invasion, followed by annals for AD 336–1135 with a lacuna for 723–803. These were written by Dubhaltach Mac Fhirbhisigh alone in *c.*1640, but the last two leaves covering 1141–50 he wrote jointly with an unidentified scribe who also assisted him in writing his Book of Genealogies.[23] The incipit on f. 162ʳ reading, 'Incipit cronicũ Scotorum .i. tinsgantar croinic na Scot andso', followed by a preface addressed to the reader is unique in the Irish Annals, and the incipit provides the title of the text. In chapter 11, p. 307 ff. it will be shown that Dubhaltach himself compiled both this title and preface and nine subsequent interjections, and on this account alone this MS must be

---

21 Ó Muraíle, *Celebrated antiquary*, 100–1 (date), 308–9 (scribes & MSS), 309 (cit.). Idem, *Background*, 326–7 (early copies), 329–30 (Uí Longáin copies), 330–7 (vellum MS problems). 22 Hennessy, *CS*, ix, xxv–xli (MS description); Ó Muraíle, *Celebrated antiquary*, 97–104 (MS date & description), 308–9 (secondary MSS). 23 Ó Muraíle, *Celebrated antiquary*, 98 (second hand).

accorded priority. At the year 1135 Mac Fhirbhisigh's kalend on f. 214ʳ is conspicuously large, and he left half column b and the entire verso blank, so it appears his first compilation ended here. On the other hand at the end of the continuation for 1141–50 on ff. 215–16 the catch-word 'Muredach' is written alone in the bottom right-hand corner of f. 216ᵛ, so this continuation appears to have been truncated. Mac Fhirbhisigh wrote Irish minuscule in a clear bold hand in two columns with frequent paragraphing made by enlarged initials offset into the left-hand margin, and there is extensive use made of scribal abbreviations, cf. plate 4. The chronological apparatus for AD 336–644 consists of kalend+ferial, and because it straddles AT's lacuna over 359–487, it provides the crucial witness to the chronology of early Christian Ireland.[24] The MS has extensive, untidy marginalia by Roderick O'Flaherty, mostly just providing AD data, but some making reference to 'Cod. Cluan[ensis]' and 'Tigernacus', and to the work of Ussher and Ware. O'Flaherty's references to 'Cod. Cluan apud Goghaganum' on f. 167ʳ and to 'Tigernacus' show that he had adopted Ware's annalistic nomenclature for MB and AT, while his folio references to 'Tigernacus' show that he was using the copy of AT bound in TCD 1292 ff. 113ʳ–53ʳ. On the other hand O'Flaherty's extensive annotations to the Armagh MS of MB suggest that this was his 'Cod. Cluan'.

The only printed edition of the text is that published by Hennessy in 1866 based upon TCD 1292, which was reprinted in 1964, and my collation of the ferial data of the MS with Hennessy's edition showed that he transcribed these data very accurately. However, his own marginal AD data were obtained by simply counting the kalends and are without any chronological value, as indeed his own introduction indicates, but collation against AT and other annals has provided a reliable chronology for the work.[25] In 2002 an electronic version of Gearóid Mac Niocaill's edition from the same MS was made available at the CELT website.

Annals of Roscrea

Bruxelles Bibl. Royale 5301–20 pp. 97–162 is a seventeenth-century Franciscan MS, and the only witness to AR. The published descriptions by Bindon, Van den Gheyn, and Gleeson and Mac Airt are all brief and contain a considerable number of inaccuracies, and since we shall see that AR is an important witness to the Clonmacnoise group it is necessary to give here a detailed account of the MS and its text.[26] The MS was written by Brendan O'Conor, a Franciscan friar

---

24 Mc Carthy, 'Chronology', 209–12 (CS crucial witness).   25 Hennessy, *CS*, (edition); xlii–viii (uncertain marginal chronology). Mc Carthy, 'Chronology', 243 (Hennessy's accuracy). Mc Carthy, 'Synchronization', *s.a.* 336–1150 (reliable chronology).   26 MS descriptions: Bindon, 'Burgundian library', 491; Van der Gheyn, *Catalogue* vii, 48–9; Gleeson & Mac Airt, *AR*, 137–8,

who was sent from Louvain to Ireland in 1641 to collect historical material. It comprises thirty-three leaves measuring *c.*21.5×16 cm, and bears two paginations; the first, by O'Conor running pp. 1–65, was used by Gleeson and Mac Airt in their partial edition and will be used in this discussion; the second, a modern pagination running pp. 97–162, is needed for references to other texts in Bibl. Royale 5301–20. This volume consists of a compilation of over thirty Franciscan MSS, of which the first on pp. 1–70 is the only surviving copy of Mac Fhirbhisigh's *Fragmentary Annals* (FA), transcribed by Thomas O'Sheerin, John Colgan's successor in Louvain, followed on pp. 71–88 by his alphabetic index to these annals.[27] The text of AR on pp. 97–162 follows, and its range is *c.*Flood–AD 995, with lacunae at *c.*948 BC–AD 157, AD 252–335, 480–549 and 602–19. The annals for AD 336–58 and 441–79 are also displaced, probably as a result of mutilation of the exemplar. The text of AR, like that of FA, is followed on pp. 163–234 by an index that was compiled by O'Sheerin, in which all the personal names cited in AR following S. Patrick's *uenit* are arranged alphabetically and indexed by page number, and the chronology of events involving them is regularly tabulated 'juxta Annales Dungallenses'. Thus the whole context of AR's MS suggests an environment of intensive annalistic study. In his heading to the index for AR O'Sheerin identified 'Patrem Fratrem Brendanum Conorum' as the scribe of extracts, 'ex Annalibus Roscreensis seu Codice R.D. Cantwel', and this identification is confirmed by comparing the Latin handwriting of AR with a signed letter of O'Conor's, which is bound into the volume on pp. 89–96. There is no date on the text of AR, but as it happens we do know something of the activities of Brendan O'Conor over 1641–2.

On 10 July 1641 O'Conor, enroute for Ireland, wrote a letter in haste from London to James Ussher, then also in England, urging him to return to Ireland to rejoin Ware and other friends there so that they could study manuscripts together. In this letter O'Conor asked to be excused for the shaking of his hand indicating that he was about to mount his steed, and he also mentioned that he had just partly copied a 'Librum Annalium' which he had obtained from Finghín Mac Carthaigh, alias Florence Mac Carthy.[28] We shall see that AR was indeed copied in great haste, and that it is also an incomplete transcription of its exemplar, and so circumstantially it seems virtually certain that O'Conor copied AR in July 1641 from an exemplar provided by Finghín Mac Cárthaigh. Three months later, on 22 October 1641, a major uprising commenced in Ireland, and

141–2. 27 Radner, *Fragmentary annals* (edition). The hand of the indices to FA and AR is established by comparison with O'Sheerin's four signed letters to Francis Harold, MS Killiney D.5 pp. 9, 15–16, 177–8, 237. 28 Gwynn, 'Archbishop Ussher', 281–2 (letter now TCD 567 f.62), 282, 'Tertium, quod vrgeo, est, domum ad nostrum Waraeum et caeteros Philopolitas scribas, me in notis Tibi studiis promoveant codd' MSS. mecum communicent, … 2^m Librum Annalium a D'no Carthaeo obtineas, quem exscribere mihi non fuit integrum … Excusa P'r festinationem equu' ascendatis atq' Motam manu'. London. 10. Julii stylo nouo. 1641.'

in a subsequent letter written by O'Conor on 20 September 1642 to Hugh Bourke, superior of the Franciscans in Belgium, O'Conor asserted that he was under some obligation to participate in this uprising. His early participation in a leadership role is confirmed by Rory O'More, a general in the uprising, in a letter written also to Bourke on the same day, wherein he stated:[29]

> We the first undertakers have Father Brandon O'Cnoughour with us from the first day and afore ... He [was] so much imployed in our very temporall affayres to unite all and see us orderly proceed at home and abroad, whereof we have great need ...

Anticipation of this uprising may explain both O'Conor's urgency to proceed to Ireland in July 1641, and also the word with which he commenced his text of AR.

O'Connor began by writing with a flourish in double-sized letters the single word 'Jubuleu' at the centre top of the first page, which word has been subsequently emended to 'Jubileus', i.e. the Jewish cry of freedom. Above this title O'Conor subsequently added the description, 'Adversaria rerum Hiberni[ae] quae excerpta ex mutila historia D. Cantwelij', and his description of his exemplar as 'mutila' would explain why some of the annals he transcribed are out of sequence, as noted above. Furthermore, his description here of his transcription as 'adversaria rerum Hiberni[ae]', i.e. provisional memoranda or jottings of Irish affairs, accurately describes what follows for the subsequent sixty-five pages. O'Conor's transcription of 'mutila historia D. Cantwelij' was done in two phases, and in the first of these, leaving ample margins and a generous spacing between lines, he transcribed principally Irish items in either a rapid, cursive, flourishing Latin hand, or in an inclined, semi-cursive Irish hand, neither of which is attractive but both are readily legible, cf. plate 6. He continued thus leaving occasional blank spaces up to p. 23, which finished with a synchronism on the death of Conchobar mac Nessa, and then he left p. 24 blank except for the catch-word 'Patricius' for the following page.[30] On the following page O'Conor transcribed the entry for S. Patrick's *uenit*, and continued then with post-Patrician entries maintaining the same generous margins and line spacing through to p. 65, on the top of which he wrote a single entry, a Clonmacnoise obit for 995. Since this single entry would have readily fitted at the bottom of p. 64, the inference is that while his exemplar continued,

---

29 Historical Manuscripts, *Franciscan manuscripts*, 192–4 for both letters. Explaining his lack of progress in 'procuring monuments', O'Conor wrote of 'my charge to assist some of the generals which I cannot choose', and, 'If you blamed me ever for these wars, truly you wronged me; for it was God that stirred all; but afterwards, to tell you truly, mine endeavours were not found wanting.' 30 The synchronism, 'A morte quoque Concubhar mac Nessa 412 anni sunt', is nearly verbatim with CS 432.2.

O'Conor discontinued his transcription at this point, and thus AR represents a truncated edition of 'Historia Cantwelij'. This marks the end of the first phase of O'Conor's transcription.

O'Conor then returned to p. 1 and commenced phase two, where now writing with a finer nib and with greater haste, he commenced transcribing principally chronological criteria into the broad left-hand margin. Initially these comprised Biblical epochs and kalend counts and by p. 9 intermittently large 'K's appear, showing that kalends existed in his exemplar, and by p. 17 they included informal designations such as 'duobus annis' as well as the AD data '157' and '158'. After this these marginal criteria became more frequent, including on pp. 25–30 the monotone sequence of numbers: 26, 27, 29, 36, 38, 40, 43, 45, 51, 58, 59, [60], [61], 71, 78, 79, 84, 88, 95, 102. Following this on pp. 31–7 O'Conor inscribed chronological data informally, commencing with, 'sub seq^{ti} cum fig 5'.[31] Collation of the ensuing series of these numbers with AT/CS shows them to be ferial data, extending for 571–601 and 625–42 where they terminate just two years before the corresponding series in CS. An important observation here is that while these AR ferials correlate most closely with those of CS, they are in places noticeably better than either CS or AT. For example, CS lacks both kalend and ferial at 571 and ferial at 574, while AT's ferial 'u' at 574 is corrupt. But O'Conor's exemplar had the appropriate ferials, '5' and '2' respectively at both these years, showing that it had here preserved a better kalend+ferial apparatus than either CS or AT. Now if the differences between the successive figures of the monotone sequence are computed it will be found that with just one exception they lie in the range 1–7. This together with the fact that O'Conor transcribed ferial data over 571–601 and 625–42 suggests that the monotone sequence itelf derived from ferial data. At the very first of these data O'Conor wrote, AR §6 'Ab adventu Patrici ad hunc annum 6 K. ponuntur qui videntur per adiunctas figures computa[n]di 26 anni', and it is explicit from this statement that O'Conor mistook the ferial data at the preceding '6 K.' to represent kalend multipliers, and he thought that he was computing the total number of years, cf. '26 anni'.[32] In confirmation of this inference I consider O'Conor's next four marginal annotations which read: AR §8 'Precedentum K. quod facit 27'; AR §9 'Sequenti K. Cassianus obit quod facit 29'; AR §11 'Sub seq^{ti} K. quod facit 36'; AR §12 'Sub seq^{ti} K. quod facit 38'. It is clear from these

---

31 Gleeson & Mac Airt, *AR*, 145–7; (marginal criteria where '[60], [61]' represent restored readings due to the leading digits being concealed in the binding), 148 (cit.).   32 Our only other witness to ferial data over 433–8 is CS whose data when summed yield 7+1+[omitted] +3+5+6=22. The implication therefore of O'Conor's summation result of 26 is that the ferial omitted at CS 435 was 26−22=4; in this case the datum was both corrupt and sequentially impossible, and this may well explain its omission in CS. For CS ferial data see Mc Carthy, 'Synchronization', *s.a.* 433–38.

annotations that O'Conor took these years to be sequential, whereas in fact they refer to the years 439–40 (AR §§8–10) and 550–1 (AR §§11–12). For the years 439–40, 550–1 AT/CS witness the ferial series 1, 2, 7, 2 and these when accumulated to O'Conor's '26' do indeed yield his monotone sequence, viz. 26+1=27, 27+2=29, 29+7=36, 36+2=38.[33] From these mistakes, and the clumsy way in which he transcribed the whole chronological apparatus, it is apparent that O'Conor had no real understanding of the chronological apparatus of his exemplar.

In phase two over pp. 1–25 O'Conor also intermittently added non-Irish entries, usually marginally but occasionally interlinearly. However, on p. 27 he began to regularly insert these additional entries interlinearly and since the overall sequence of his entries, including these interlinear entries, matches very closely the sequence of entries in AT/CS, it is virtually certain that all these additions represent entries that he had omitted in the first phase of his transcription. On p. 37 he began mixing chronological criteria and increasing numbers of additional entries interlinearly, with the consequence that his text became chaotic, and he subsequently began to omit the chronological criteria. By p. 43, where nearly every interlinear space has received an additional entry, he had largely forsaken chronological criteria, and used instead large 'L'-shaped brackets to try to gather his accumulated entries under one year. He continued thus to p. 53, at which point he was evidently obliged to abandon phase two, for neither chronological criteria nor interlinear entries are found in pp. 54–65.

After O'Conor had finished transcription there was a third phase to his interaction with the MS for it is evident that he himself started to construct an index of it. This is clear because, leaving p. 66 blank, he took a fresh page and wrote the title, 'Index Annalium Roscreensium', across the top. Regarding this title O'Conor first inscribed it obliquely beside his heading 'Jubuleu' on p. 1 after completing phase one, but he subsequently cancelled this and then moving to the upper margin of p. 25 immediately above 'Patricius venit' he inscribed 'Annales Roscreenses' in a flourishing script about four times the size of his regular script. Now given O'Conor's evident respect for Ussher and Ware's annalistic scholarship and their repeated use of 'annales' to entitle Irish chronicles, and O'Conor's emphatic inscription of it, I suggest that this title was O'Conor's own invention inspired by Ussher and Ware's contemporary nomenclature.[34] Because of the final position of this title Gleeson and Mac Airt

---

33 Gleeson & Mac Airt, *AR*, 141–2 (Mac Airt was perplexed by O'Conor's monotone sequence and mistakenly concluded, 'the series can hardly have a chronographic importance'). 34 Ussher, *Whole works* xvii, this index to Ussher's work shows that in his *Veterum Epistolarum Hibernicarum Sylloge* published in 1632 he referred to 'Annales Dubliniensis', cf. iv 488, 517, and in his *Antiquitates*, published in 1639, he referred repeatedly to 'Annales Ultonienses', 'Annales Tigernaci', 'Annales Inisfallenses', cf. *Whole works* v–vi *passim*.

confined their edition only to the ensuing post-Patrician annals, but examination of the microfilm shows that the pre-Christian section incorporates both a substantial account of the Irish origin legend and also non-Irish entries cognate with those in CS/AI/AB. In these circumstances far more importance should be attached to O'Conor's acknowledgement at the very start of his transcription that his exemplar was 'historia D. Cantwelij'. Gleeson showed that the Cantwell family were established within twenty miles of Roscrea in county Tipperary from the time of the Norman invasion, and it appears from O'Conor's adopted title 'Annales Roscreensis' that he also had some grounds for associating 'historia D. Cantwelij' with Roscrea.

O'Conor had first foliated his text as ff. 1–29, but then cancelling that he paginated it as pp. 1–65 in large boldly written Arabic numerals and both of these show that he considered his transcription of 'historia D. Cantwelij' to be a unitary text. Then it is apparent that he had access to a number of chronicles, including FM, and that he collated his transcription with these sources. For, in seven places he marginally annotated AD dates and in each case attributed these to either, 'Quat. Mag.' or, 'Q. Mag', see plate 6. As well as these he made marginal interjections citing, 'Marianus Scotus', and 'Gordanum', and he also added un-attributed AD dates in both left and right-hand margins. This was as far as O'Conor's indexing progressed, and it was left to O'Sheerin to complete the job and he began by striking through O'Conor's index title, and writing underneath it:[35]

> extracta per Patrem Fratrem Brendanum Conorum ex Annalibus Roscreensibus seu Codice R.D. Cantwel hic digesta ordine alphabetico, praetermissis tamen iis quae praecesserunt missionem S. Patricii, annotatis ad marginem annis quibus quaeque occiderunt, juxta Annales Dungallenses.

It may be first noted that O'Sheerin described O'Conor's exemplar as 'codice R.D. Cantwel', and his introduction of 'R.' here suggests that 'D. Cantwel' was a 'Reverendus', or priest, and that O'Sheerin knew something of his person. From the form of this title it is unlikely that Cantwell was a Franciscan.[36] It should also be noted that O'Sheerin here explicitly acknowledged his decision to omit the pre-Patrician entries, further underlining the unitary character of 'codice R.D. Cantwel'. This heading is then followed by seventy-two pages of O'Sheerin's neat, carefully compiled index in which O'Conor's entries were substantially re-written and indexed by page number.[37] In the course of this

---

35 Gleeson & Mac Airt, *AR*, §§17, 19, 54, 55, 116, 122, 139 (FM attributions); §139 (Marianus Scotus); §29 (Gordonus); 143 n. 20 (cit.).   36 This point was made to me by Fr Ignatius Fennessy, the Librarian at Dún Mhuire, Killiney, Co. Dublin.   37 Both Bindon, 'Burgundian library', 491, and Gleeson & Mac Airt, *AR*, 138, 142–3 stated that the index was by O'Conor, but this is ruled out by both the handwriting, and O'Sheerin's title, which, while identifying O'Conor as the scribe of the 'extracta', implicitly acknowledges O'Sheerin's own work with 'hic digesta'.

O'Sheerin made a small number of marginal emendations and additions to O'Conor's text; for example on p. 25 he inserted the summation 440+80=520 beside AR §8 'Natiuitas sanctae Brigidae', evidently assigning Brigit's *natus* to 440 and allocating her an eighty year life span, and then computing the year of her obit. I have described this compilation process in considerable detail in order to try to correct a number of misapprehensions that arise from Gleeson and Mac Airt's published edition, specifically:[38]

a) Gleeson and Mac Airt were ambivalent regarding the relationship between O'Conor's designations 'Annales Roscreensis' and 'historia D. Cantwelij' and were evidently unaware of his cancelled inscription of 'Annales Roscreensis' on p. 1. Consequently, they chose to edit only the post-Patrician section of the text, i.e. pp. 25–65. However, examination shows that the range of O'Conor's exemplar, 'historia D. Cantwelij', included the Flood and extended beyond AD 995. O'Conor's relocation of his title 'Annales Roscreenses' immediately before S. Patrick's *uenit*, and this edition commencing at that same point are the result of a widespread misapprehension that the Annals commenced with the arrival of Christianity in Ireland.

b) Gleeson and Mac Airt described the interlinear entries as, 'entries or parts of entries which appear to us to have been interpolated in O'Conor's exemplar', and concluded that 'the transcript is an accurate one and certainly not abbreviated.' In this they passed over O'Conor's descriptions of his transcript as 'adversaria rerum Hiberni[ae]' and 'excerpta', and the fact that he indeed transcribed mainly Irish entries in phase one but included many non-Irish entries in phase two. Therefore their hypothesis that the interlinear position of these entries reflected an interpolated status in 'historia D. Cantwelij' is not sustainable. These interlinear entries were a consequence of O'Conor's two-phase transcription.

c) Gleeson and Mac Airt printed all of the material from the left-hand margin in a small font, implicitly suggesting thereby that it was written by another hand, whereas it was practically all written by O'Conor in the second phase. Incongruently, even though they regarded the material written in the right-hand margin to be that of a 'later annotator', they printed it in the standard size font.

d) Gleeson and Mac Airt concluded that 'there is no reason to think that our text of the "Roscrea Annals" is not a fair copy of the Cantwell exemplar.' However, close examination of the MS shows that O'Conor, working in haste, made only an incomplete and truncated transcription of his exemplar.

38 Gleeson & Mac Airt, *AR*, 137–44 (historical introduction), 145–70 (edition), 138, 143 (ambivalence regarding 'Annales Roscreensis'), 140–1 ('interpolated' entries), 143 ('accurate' transcription), 142, 144 (attribution of FM references to a 'later annotator'), 143 ('fair copy'). Mc Carthy, 'AU compilation', 77–84 (mistaken belief that AU commenced at 431).

Regarding the entries transcribed by O'Conor, it is remarkable that, notwithstanding his haste and late date, the orthography of some of them preserves some old details. For example, compare the orthography of S. Columba's name in AR §55 'Columbae Cille' with that of AU 573.2, 'Columbe Cille', normally considered to preserve the oldest annalistic orthography; these are the only two annals to retain both the Latin 'b' and 'e' of 'Columbae'. Moreover, some entries that in AR are entirely in Latin appear in AT/CS translated into Irish, e.g.:

> AR §180.2:   Exberect Christi miles in II Paschae die pausat.
> AT 729.1:   [Eicbericht] Ridire Crist do éc la casca ...

Regarding the chronological apparatus of AR, collation of AR with AT/CS shows that, despite labouring under the disadvantage of not understanding its chronological apparatus, O'Conor transcribed enough kalends and ferial data to show that his exemplar preserved a better kalend+ferial apparatus than that of AT/CS. These two considerations together show that 'historia D. Cantwelij' preserved features of the Clonmacnoise chronicle not transmitted by AT/CS. Moreover, examination of the lacunae of AR shows that its only substantial lacuna is that over c.948 BC–AD 157 and this closely corresponds with the range of Rawl. B. 502, viz. c.769 BC–AD 140, particularly at its later boundary. These three aspects taken together suggest the hypothesis that 'historia Cantwelij' in fact derived from a good copy of the now-missing sections of Rawl. B. 502.[39] This and its conservative orthography and accurate chronological data make it an important witness to the Clonmacnoise group, complementary in its content to Rawl. B. 502 and preserving many entries lost from AT/CS.

The purview of AR corresponds closely with that of AT/CS and certainly nothing in it suggests a Roscrea provenance. This was also Gleeson and Mac Airt's conclusion, viz., 'Their general tenor suggests a close affiliation with the Clonmacnoise group', and 'It would not appear ... that the collection had any particular association with Roscrea.'[40] In summary, it emerges that Bruxelles 5301-20 pp. 97–162, while at first sight an unattractive MS, appears on present evidence to preserve an independent witness to some of the now-missing sections of Rawl. B. 502, and hence to some sections of the Clonmacnoise chronicle at an earlier stage of its history than either Rawl. B. 488 or TCD 1292. The only edition of this MS is that published in 1958 by Gleeson and Mac Airt and as discussed above this is both acephalous and misrepresents a number of

---

39 Ó Cuív, *Catalogue*, 164 points out that f. 1ʳ and 12ᵛ of Rawl. B. 502 are 'dark and rubbed' whereas the 'inner pages show comparatively little discoloration', showing that ff. 1–12 have been long separated from the remainder of their codex.   40 Gleeson & Mac Airt, *AR*, 141 (cit.).

significant aspects of the MS. Thus an edition of the full text should be considered a priority.[41]

Cuana group

This group comprises AU/AI/AB and I will describe them in that order.

Annals of Ulster

AU is undoubtedly one of the most important witnesses to the Annalistic genre on account of its large number of entries, extensive range, conservative orthography, and unique chronological apparatus. There are six known substantial witnesses to it, but TCD 1282 with its myriad interpolations can be shown to be the ultimate source of most of the material in the other five, and so it is the primary witness. The most comprehensive description of this MS is by Mc Carthy in 2003; the earlier descriptions by the Revd Bartholomew Mac Carthy in 1901, and Abbot and Gwynn in 1921, are both incomplete and misguided as a result of their adopting the Revd James Todd's mistaken hypothesis that the first three leaves of the MS represented an interpolated 'fragment of an ancient copy of Tigernach'. Earlier descriptions also mistakenly asserted without justification that TCD 1282 was truncated.[42] The MS now consists of 120 vellum leaves measuring c.30.5×23 cm. arranged as fourteen gatherings foliated by James Ware as ff. 12–143. Their content is as follows: ff. 12–14 contain acephalous, truncated annals for AD 81–c.387; f. 15ᵛ contains an elegy in thirty-two quatrains to Feidhlim, brother of Cathal Óg Mac Maghnusa; ff. 16–143 contain annals for AD 431–1504 inclusive, but with two lacunae. Before Ware's time at least two leaves were lost, one before and one after the present f. 15, and since Ware's time twenty two leaves have been lost, viz. ff. 1–11, 64, 66–75. As a result, the present range is: ff. 12–14 for AD 81– c.387; ff. 16–63 for 431–1100; f. 65 for 1109–15; ff. 76–143 for 1163–1504. Because in c.1507 TCD 1282 served as the exemplar for most of Bodleian Rawl. B. 489 some of the former's lacunae can be restored by using the latter, viz. 1101–8 fully, and 1116–62 partially except for 1132–54 where Rawl. B. 489 itself has a lacuna.[43]

The compilation of TCD 1282 was undertaken by Cathal Óg Mac Maghnusa, a powerful cleric and political leader who lived at Seanadh, an island near the

---

41 The author gratefully acknowledges Bart Jaski's generosity in providing him with a copy of his transcript of pp. 1–24 of this MS on which numerous details of the above account are based. Hopefully this transcript will soon serve as the basis for a published edition of the remainder of the text.   42 Mc Carthy, 'AU compilation', 70, 87–93 (TCD 1282 description), 78–84 (Todd's hypothesis); Mac Carthy, *AU* iv, pp. i–xiii (TCD 1282 and other witnesses); Abbot & Gwynn, *Catalogue*, 20 (TCD 1282); O'Curry, *MM*, 517 (Todd citation).   43 Ó Cuív, 'Elegy', 261–8 (elegy on f.15ᵛ); Ó Cuív, *Catalogue*, 153–63 (Rawl. B. 489).

eastern shore of Upper Lough Erne.[44] Cathal Óg's obit at AU 1498.8 asserts that he 'projected and collected and compiled this book from very many other books', and this together with Mac Carthy's identification of Cathal as the principal interpolating hand (H[2]) has led most scholars to conclude that Cathal himself compiled the text of TCD 1282.[45] However, collation of the numeral and letter forms of the many interpolations by H[2] with Rawl. B. 489 ff. 1–32^{rao}, which was written by Ruaidhrí Ua Caiside, show that he was responsible for them. Ruaidhrí Ua Caiside †1541 was a member of a Fermanagh family of hereditary physicians, archdeacon of Clogher and vicar of Kilskeery in county Tyrone from c.1502, and compiler in c.1525 of the *Register of Clogher*.[46] Furthermore collation of Ua Caiside's many interpolated entries in TCD 1282 with the entries written *in prima manu* by the principal scribe Ruaidhrí Ua Luinín, a member of an erenagh family from Ard, Co. Fermanagh, particularly those containing Arabic numerals, chronological criteria, or ambivalent interjections, leads to the conclusion that it was Ua Caiside who constructed the exemplar which Ua Luinín then transcribed, as will be discussed in chapter 11, p. 313 ff. A singular feature of Ua Caiside's writing was his strong inclination to substitute Arabic numerals for Roman, and since the chronological apparatus of TCD 1282 is written uniformly in Roman numerals up to 1484 and erratically in Arabic numerals from 1485 onwards, it appears that Ua Caiside's primary source was an existing chronicle extending from Adam to c.1484. Into this Ua Caiside interpolated entries taken from numerous other sources, some of which he identified with interjections such as 'alios', 'Cuana', 'liber monachorum' or 'Duibh da Leithi'. Ua Luinín then carefully transcribed this primary source, including Ua Caiside's interpolations. Thus it emerges that Ua Caiside was the principal compiler of the text of AU, and Mac Maghnusa's role was confined to supplying the MS sources, furnishing the physical resources, and presumably remunerating Ua Caiside and Ua Luinín up until his death in 1498. One would expect in this situation that Mac Maghnusa maintained a supervisory role over the work of Ua Caiside and Ua Luinín, but to judge from the number of compilation and chronological errors found in the text Mac Maghnusa exercised no effective supervision of their work. Ua Caiside's role in the compilation of AU is registered in his obit at AU 1541.2, 'Ruaidhri O'Casside ... wrote this book for the great part.'

Most of the text, viz. ff. 12^r–129^v for AD 81–1489, except for the elegy on f. 15^v, was written by Ua Luinín, and from f. 16^r onwards he wrote in two columns

---

44 Ó Muraíle, *AU* i, [7–18] (Cathal Óg).   45 Mac Carthy, *AU* iii, 429 (cit.); Ware, *De scriptoribus*, 77; Mac Carthy, *AU* iv, pp. vii–viii; Gwynn, 'Cathal Mac Magnusa I', 230; Ó Muraíle, *AU* i, [6–7], [13–14] (All identify Cathal as compiler of AU). However, Mac Niocaill, *MIA*, 37 asserted that the 'text was compiled by Ua Luinín'.   46 Ó Cuív, *Catalogue*, 156–9 (Ua Caiside's contribution to Rawl. 489); Mc Carthy, 'AU compilation', 73–7 (Ua Caiside's contribution to TCD 1282);

using a very neat minuscule leaving blank lines between successive years. The entries are written continuously, virtually without paragraphing, except if the start of an entry coincides with a new line when the initial letter is sometimes enlarged and capitalized, and, like the 'K' of each kalend, offset into the margin. A distinctive feature of the text is the use of punctuation, with the textual and numerical elements of chronological criteria marked off with points, and when these points divide semantic units of entries they are often emphasized by an attached triangular ornament, cf. plate 7. From AD 431 onwards, Ua Luinín places either a point or semi-colon at the end of each last entry, and presumably the intention here was to clearly delimit the entries *in prima manu* from any subsequent additions in the blank space. But at AD 754 a noticeable development occurs when the semi-colon is doubled, thus ';;', and this termination is substantially sustained until AD 924, after which it becomes exceptional. The remainder of the text, ff. 130^r–143^v for 1489–1504 was written by Ua Caiside, so it is likely he that composed Cathal Óg's obit, and in these folios Ua Caiside's handwriting progresses from a crude to a convincing facsimile of Ua Luinín's hand.[47] It seems certain that there was an interval of at least six years between Ua Luinín concluding his writing at f. 129vb, in the middle of an obit for 1489, and Ua Caiside completing the obit on f. 130ra and concluding the text in *c.*1505. It seems likely that it was Cathal Óg's death in 1498 that caused this hiatus.

Regarding annotations in TCD 1282, as already indicated by far the most prolific contributor was Ua Caiside who repeatedly inscribed chronological criteria into the blank spaces left by Ua Luinín following the 'Kł.iań', and additional entries both interlinearly and into the blank space between years. Most but not all of these interpolations are found in Rawl. B. 489, which in *c.*1507 Ua Caiside and Ua Luinín jointly transcribed from TCD 1282 from AD 431–1504 with Ua Caiside producing a close facsimile of Ua Luinín's handwriting. Another, very distinctive interpolating hand, using light brown ink, inscribed the name 'Wıllıam o Carabuıl' in the middle of the otherwise blank f. 15^r, as well as repeated marginal instances of 'NB', and a substantial inscription on f. 136^v. Other hands are identifiable, including the separate foliations by Ware and Eugene O'Curry, but there has been no proper study of the marginalia of the MS.[48]

The first printed edition of AU was that published by the Revd O'Conor in 1826 for 431–1131 based upon Rawl. B. 489, which suffers from many inaccuracies. The next was by William Hennessy in 1887 who, omitting ff. 12–14, based his edition on ff. 16^r–59vb of TCD 1282 for 431–1056, with a

Nicholls, 'Clogher' (*Register of Clogher*).   **47** Mc Carthy, 'AU compilation', 73–7 (scribes and their contributions).   **48** Mc Carthy, 'AU compilation', 70 ('o Carabuil'), 89–93 (Ware and O'Curry foliations).

parallel English translation, in which edition he made no serious attempt to either distinguish the hands of Ua Luinín or Ua Caiside, or to document the parallel text of the other important witness, Rawl. B. 489. On the other hand, Mac Carthy's 1895–7 volumes for ff. 59vb–143^v employed Rawl. B. 489, where possible, to restore text lost in TCD 1282's lacunae, and also to extend the text to 1588. Mac Carthy's apparatus also registered Ua Luinín's hand as 't.h', i.e. 'text hand', and all other hands as 'n.t.h', i.e. 'not text hand', and as well he made an earnest attempt to document the parallel text in Rawl. B. 489 and other witnesses. In addition, notwithstanding the profound chronological deficiencies of the text, Mac Carthy made a heroic but misguided attempt to restore the chronological apparatus of his text to synchronism with Julian and Church calendars, cf. chapter 12, p. 349 ff. The first edition of the annals in ff. 12–14 was published by Whitley Stokes in 1897 in *Revue Celtique*, where, following Todd, he entitled it 'The Dublin Fragment of Tigernach's Annals'. Next in 1983 Seán Mac Airt and Gearóid Mac Niocaill published a re-edition of the annals in TCD 1282 ff. 12–14 subtitled 'Pre-Patrician', and ff. 16–63, 65 subtitled 'Post-Patrician', with the lacuna filled from, and their text extended to AD 1131, by using Rawl. B. 489. From AD 431 onward their apparatus systematically used 'H', 'H^1', and 'H^2' to identify the hands respectively of Ua Luinín transcribing, Ua Luinín emending his transcription, and Ua Caiside interpolating, and in this way a major deficiency of Hennessy's edition was made good. In their preface, however, 'H^2' was mistakenly identified with Cathal Óg Mac Maghnusa, and it was incorrectly asserted that 'the ms. is incomplete at the end'. Finally in 1998 a facsimile edition of Hennessy and Mac Carthy was published with a comprehensive introduction by Nollaig Ó Muraíle.[49]

Annals of Inisfallen

In the introduction to his edition of AI, the most substantial collection of annals for the province of Munster, Seán Mac Airt noted nine MSS containing all or part of the text.[50] However, of these, only Bodleian Rawl. B. 503 is earlier than the seventeenth century, and the first thirty eight leaves of it can be securely dated to the late eleventh century, while the remainder is approximately contemporaneous to the events it records up to 1326. Consequently, it has been regarded as the primary witness to AI. In 1933 R.I. Best gave a very detailed description of this MS, and Mac Airt ably supplemented this in the

49 O'Conor, *Rerum Hib.* iv, 1–398 (edition); Hennessy, *AU* i and Mac Carthy, *AU* ii–iii (edition); Stokes, *AT*, 450–66 ('Dublin Fragment'); Mac Airt & Mac Niocaill, *AU*, viii–ix (hands); Ó Muraíle, *AU* i, [1]–[73] (Introduction). 50 Mac Airt, *AI*, xi–xiii (nine MSS – cf. appendix 1). This work must be distinguished from the similarly entitled but unrelated 'Dublin Annals of Inisfallen' for which see Ó Cuilleanáin, 'Dublin Annals of Inisfallen'.

introduction to his edition of 1951, and Brian Ó Cuív has further augmented these in his catalogue of the Bodleian Irish MSS.[51] These three works provide the basis for the following account, together with some additional observations of my own.

Rawl. B. 503 now consists of fifty seven vellum leaves measuring c.24.8×17.8 cm., which are foliated ff. 1–57, apparently originally by Ware who evidently excerpted the MS in 1624 and who included it both in his earlier list of MSS of c.1625, and his published catalogue of 1648.[52] Ware certainly owned the MS by 1627, for that year he wrote to Ussher on 21 September asserting, 'I have now special occasion to use my Ulster Annals and the Annals of Inisfallen; I entreat your grace to send them me by this bearer.'[53] Moreover, it is virtually certain that Ware bestowed the title, 'Annals of Inishfallen' on the MS for along with his excerpts he wrote, 'I ghess the aforesaid Annales did belong to the priory of Inisfallen in Kerry from the often mention thereof therein.' It appears that four leaves were lost before Ware's foliation, viz. two before f.1 and two between ff. 6 and 7. Thus the present range is from God's promise to Abraham to AD 1326, with a lacuna at c.252–26 BC; it appears virtually certain, therefore, that before the loss of the four leaves the range extended continuously from Adam.[54]

Best identified that a total of thirty-nine hands had contributed annals to the MS, of which the first hand wrote ff. 1–29[r], now covering from Abraham to the middle of AD 1092 in an 'elegant symmetrical book-hand, clearly that of an expert scribe'.[55] Since the second hand adds entries for AD 1092–4, and the remaining thirty-seven hands of diverse quality continue incrementally adding annals, it has been accepted that the first scribe wrote c.1092 and the subsequent entries are for the most part approximately contemporaneous. Thus these annals are the most substantial example of institutional accumulation that we have. It has also been inferred that the initial transcription to 1092 was made either in Emly or Lismore in Munster, and that it was subsequently continued in one of these communities until sometime between 1130 and 1159, after which it was removed to a west-Munster monastery, probably that of Inisfallen.[56]

The text is mostly written in two columns, however ff. 12–36 are in three columns and ff. 38[r], 46[v] are in single columns. The offset enlarged kalends mark paragraphs and entries commence with a capital and end with a point. Both Best and Ó Cuiv remarked the use of the colours red, yellow, blue, pink, green and purple in the MS, principally used to decorate these enlarged 'Kl' and initial letters. However, they overlooked the placing of coloured cartouches about the

51 MS descriptions: Best & Mac Neill, AI facsimile, 1–25; Mac Airt, AI, x–xii, xxx–xli; Ó Cuív, Catalogue, 201–7 (descriptions).   52 O'Sullivan, 'Finding list', 71, 90 (Ware's ownership of AI). 53 Ussher, Whole works xvi, 461 (cit.).   54 Mac Airt, AI, xi–xii citing from BL Add. 4787 (Ware's identification of 'Inisfallen').   55 Best & Mac Neill, AI facsimile, 5–25 (hands).   56 Ó Cuív, Catalogue, 202 (AI's compilation locations).

headings of important epochs in the pre-Patrician annals. These cartouches now appear white or grey, with the exception of one on f. 5rb surrounding part of AI §171, viz. 'Incipit regnum Persarum', parts of which show that it was originally bright red. It appears certain from the reduction in the text height and the colour of this pigment that these cartouches were done by the first scribe along with his other decoration. From surviving traces of pigment it is clear that the other cartouches were likewise similarly brightly coloured, but most of their pigment has flaked away just leaving a bright line of previously protected vellum surrounding the heading. Some of these same headings were emphasized in the approximately contemporary Rawl. B. 502 by means of offsetting, enlarging and capitalizing their initial letters.[57] Cartouches appear therefore to be an eleventh-century introduction into the annals, cf. the attribution to Tigernach in plate 5c) and discussion in chapter 6, p. 191 ff.

Regarding annotations, Best identified fifteen hands altogether, which interpolations he dated from the fourteenth to the early seventeenth centuries, and the most substantial of these both consisted of sustained AD sequences as follows:[58]

1. Marginal AD system-A on ff. 18[rc]–31[vc] running for 979–1103 and written by 'an Anglo-Irish hand seemingly of the fourteenth century'. These are nearly always written as 'Ân Do' or 'Â D' followed by the year written substantially in medieval Arabic numerals, but the cursive Roman numerals 'M' and 'c' for 100 are unusual, see plate 8 for an instance of 'M°'.[59] Moreover, relative to the AD year implied by the ferial and epactal criteria, these system-A data are always one year *high*. Best also noted over twenty other inscriptions by this same hand.

2. Marginal AD system-B on ff. 8[vb]–18[rc] and 34[vc]–50[rb] running intermittently for 400–978 and for 1120–1282 all written by Ware. In contrast to system-A, Ware's data up to 978 are nearly always one year *low*. It appears Ware was collating the MS with AU, cf. his request to Ussher for both MSS in 1627, and, when he found common entries, he copied its AD year consequently introducing AU's one-year deficit.

The first printed edition published by the Revd O'Conor in 1825 from Rawl. B. 503 for the years *c.*428–1296 was marred by his characteristic inaccuracy.[60] By contrast Seán Mac Airt's edition of 1951, both accurately represents the text of Rawl. B. 503, with any restoration of text clearly identified, and provides many

---

57 Ó Cuiv, *Catalogue*, 205 and Best, *AI facsimile*, 6 (decorations). I have identified cartouches on ff. 4va–9va, about part of the following: AI §§138, 141–2, 156, 165 (bis), 171, 184, 191, 204 (bis), 335, 344, 386.   58 Best & Mac Neill, *AI facsimile*, 24–5 (interpolating hands).   59 Capelli, *Dizionario*, 413 (c), 417 (M°)   60 O'Conor, *Rerum Hib.* ii, 1–122 (edition).

useful bibliographic references. However, prompted by Paul Walsh's 1939 paper Mac Airt based his marginal post-Patrician AD chronology upon the AD chronology of AU, and consequently between AI 474 and AI 747a he was obliged to effectively interpolate seventeen and omit three kalends.[61] The result is very unreliable, and examination of AI's collation in the synchronized chronology shows that up to AD 676 it is nearly always in error, and sometimes substantially so, e.g. Iserninus' obit at AD 470 is placed at 465 by Mac Airt. However, from AI 779, where the first regular epactal criteria are cited, Mac Airt's marginal AD synchronize with both this and the subsequent ferial data. Thus his ensuing marginal AD chronology is much better, though it still requires validation from other sources.

Annals of Boyle

Four MSS of this text are known, of which three are seventeenth-century or later, while the fourth, BL Cotton Titus A. xxv, can be reliably dated to the earlier thirteenth century and is undoubtedly the primary witness to the text. Descriptions and accounts of the history of this MS have been given by the Revd O'Conor, Eugene O'Curry, Standish O'Grady, Martin Freeman and Robin Flower.[62] The earliest identifiable reference to the MS is by Ware in 1639 when he described it as, 'Anonymus Monachus coenobij Buelliensis appendicem adjecit annalibus rerum Conaciensium usq*ue* ad an. 1253. quo tempore vixit.'[63] Subsequently in his 1648 catalogue he listed a copy in his own collection and Cotton Titus A. xxv as, 'Exemplar Annalium Conatiensium, sive coenobij Buelliensis, usq*ue* ad annum 1253. Autographum extat in Bibliotheca Cottoniana, Westmonasterij.'[64] As can be seen in these Ware identified a Connacht purview, and considered them the annals of the monastery of Boyle in county Roscommon, and that an unknown monk of that monastery had added an appendix dealing with the contemporary affairs of Connacht extending to 1253. Some details of Ware's summary are however inaccurate. Cotton Titus A. xxv now consists of thirty-five vellum leaves measuring *c*.20.3×14 cm., bearing a modern pencil foliation running ff. 1–35, and showing evidence of trimming to the outer margins. Two earlier foliations by Ware in the upper margin make it clear that the original first folio was missing in his time, and also that the present f. 2 was then misplaced between ff. 8 and 9. In 1927 Freeman noted the following losses:[65]

61 Walsh, 'Dating AI', 677–82; Mac Airt, *AI*, xliv (marginal AD), 1–439 (edition). 62 MS descriptions: O'Conor, *Bibliotheca* i, 202–5; O'Curry, *MM*, 105–13; O'Grady, *Catalogue*, 4–14; Freeman, *AB* (1927), 336–9; Flower, 'Origin', 339–44. 63 Ware, *Scriptores*, 60 (cit.). 64 O'Sullivan, 'Finding list', 94 (cit.). 65 Freeman, *AB* 44 (1927), 338 (lost folios).

1. The original first leaf is lost and the present f.1 is an interpolation made, probably, like the aforementioned trimming, at the time of Cotton's binding. As a result, the text commences 102 years before the birth of Enos, which event it places at AM 335. It is apparent that an account of Adam and the subsequent 233 years occupied the lost first leaf.
2. Probably three leaves lost between ff. 28 and 29, with the resultant loss of AD 1202–23.
3. An uncertain number of leaves lost between ff. 34 and 35, with the resultant loss of AD 1239–50.

Consequently, the range of the text is AM 234–AD 1201, 1224–38, 1251–57, so Ware's accounts misrepresented the termination of these annals.

The text was written in a single column by the first scribe as far as f. 29^v, i.e. to AD 1228. He wrote Latin minuscule in an Anglo-Norman hand, even when writing Irish, and a feature of the text is its unique orthography for Irish passages, some of which were described by O'Grady as, 'furnishing a rude specimen of phonetic spelling'.[66] The remainder of the text was written by ten other scribes who nearly all maintained both the Latin minuscule and Anglo-Norman hand, as well as the unique orthography for Irish over the years 1228–57.[67] Hence Ware misjudged the number of hands responsible for the concluding 'appendix'. Both the incremental nature of these scribal additions, and the character of the entries themselves support the view that these entries are approximately contemporary to the events they describe. Thus these entries are an example of institutional accumulation. Since, after the last entry for 1257 there remained ample space at the bottom of f. 35^v, it is apparent that nothing has been lost from the end of the MS, but rather that accumulation simply ceased in c.1257.

The entries themselves are written for the most part as a continuous text, with no paragraphing or marginal offsetting of enlarged capital letters. On the other hand, each entry and personal name normally commences with a capital letter, and each entry concludes with a point. Another distinctive feature is the use between ff. 18^v and 25^r of enlarged capital letters coloured green in order to highlight events evidently considered significant; for example on f. 22^v the obit of 'Conchubur mac Tordelbaich U Conchubuir', and the foundation of Boyle abbey are highlighted in this way, see plate 9. Another feature is the frequent use between ff. 2^r and 20^v of red cartouches enclosing AM data. Between its quarto codex size, distinctive script, unique orthography, punctuation, use of capital letters and frequent cartouches, there is a profound contrast between this and

66 O'Grady, *Catalogue*, 5–12 (phonetic spelling).   67 Flower, 'Origin', 340, 'these almost annual references … are the record of events made from year to year in the house in which they occurred.'

all other Annalistic texts, which suggest that it represents a recension that has been compiled within a markedly different environment to all the others. In particular the abandonment of both Irish orthography and script suggest this compilation was made outside the mainstream of Irish scholarship. Regarding marginalia, there are a number of these in different hands, one of which was identified by O'Curry as that of Brian Mac Diarmada who added dates in Irish from which O'Curry inferred that it was in his possession at the end of the sixteenth century.[68] Mac Niocaill considered it certain that Mac Diarmada had employed it in the compilation of the L1 section of LC, see below.[69]

Many details of the entries identify the purview of the annals from $c.$ 1095 as Cistercian, and from 1148 specifically as that of Boyle abbey. However, in an entry for 1229 the purview suddenly and emphatically realigns with the ecclesiastical and political interests of the nearby Premonstratensian monastery of the Holy Trinity in Loch Cé, and it remains thus until the text terminates at 1257.[70] However, none of the other distinctive characteristics of the text such as script, orthography, punctuation, or paragraphing show any significant change over these last three decades. O'Dwyer drew attention to the trauma that affected the Irish Cistercian foundations over the years 1227–8 when the archbishop of Dublin, Henry of London, made an earnest attempt to 'enforce his conviction that the church which had been reformed by the Anglo-Normans must be free of Irish leadership.' Thus O'Dwyer concluded that the 'vernacular language of the monasteries had to change from Irish to French, and the organization and observance had to follow that of the Anglo-Norman foundations in Ireland. All of this was designed to cause a radical disruption of the Irish tradition and identity which prevailed in the monasteries of the Mellifont filiation.'[71]

As was outlined in chapter 1 and as will be discussed more fully in chapter 7, p. 217 ff., AB is based on Liber Cuanach, which in this compilation was adapted to Latin letters and a non-Irish orthography. This was then extended up to 1228 with entries of a Cistercian and specifically Boyle Abbey purview, as well as a Connacht secular purview. Thus up to 1228 it clearly represents a now lost Boyle chronicle. Furthermore, from the facts that this MS was written by a single hand up to 1228, and that the chronological apparatus is deficient immediately prior to the purview shift, with missing and misplaced kalends over 1224–7, I conclude that it is a transcript of that Boyle chronicle made shortly after 1228 by someone who both had access to it and a knowledge of its contents. Moreover, those near-contemporary chronological errors at 1224–7

---

68 O'Curry, *MM*, 108 (Mac Diarmada).   69 Mac Niocaill, *MIA*, 30–2, (Mac Diarmada).
70 O'Dwyer, 'Annals', 85–7 (purview shift).   71 O'Dwyer, 'Annals', 87–8 and *Conspiracy*, 16–19,
34–7 (conflict of 1227–8), 14 (cits.).

suggest that the latter part of this transcript was made under some pressure. It appears then that *c.*1228 the sympathies of a group of Boyle monks, trained in its scriptorium, realigned to identify henceforth with the ecclesiastical and political affairs of the nearby monastery of the Holy Trinity in Loch Cé. Shortly after 1228 these monks left Boyle monastery bringing this transcript with them, but they remained in the neighbourhood, most likely in Holy Trinity monastery. Over the next three decades, they added a contemporaneous end chronicle to their transcription which reflected both their identification with Holy Trinity and severance from Boyle. Their end chronicle continued most likely until they were too feeble to carry on, for the entries over 1252–7 are noticeably shorter than the preceding entries for 1229–51 and suggest a fading capability on their part to maintain the chronicle. Except for occasional entries in Irish script this end chronicle retained all of the distinctive script and orthographic features of the transcript, reflecting their Boyle training. But this occasional appearance of Irish script and the fact that characteristic Irish ferial data commence in 1233 suggests that the Cistercian cultural reform of 1227–8 had indeed played a significant role in the alienation of these monks from Boyle.[72]

The first published edition of the text was by the Revd O'Conor in 1825 from Cotton Titus A. xxv for the years *c.*420–1245 and is not satisfactory.[73] The complete edition was published by Martin Freeman in *Revue Celtique* over 1924–7, with separate English translation of the Irish passages. His edition accurately represents the entries, including the marginalia in footnotes, but does not identify any of the conspicuous graphic elements such as the enlarged or coloured initials or the many cartouches surrounding chronological data. However, his treatment of the chronological apparatus is not satisfactory for he gathered successive kalends together and represented them by just a single 'K' followed by a count in brackets. For example his AB §2 'K(37)' represents the MS sequence:

'k.k.k.k.k.k.k.k.k.k.k.k.k.k.k.k.KŁ.eñ.k.k.k.k.k.k.k.k.k.k.k.k.k.k.k.k.k.'

By levelling all MS instances of 'k' and 'KŁ.eñ' to 'K' Freeman obscured the link between these annals and AU and Liber Cuanach. More serious was Freeman's failure in AB §13–17 to recognize the first scribe's own shorthand for

---

72 O'Dwyer, 'Annals', 88 made the remarkable statement that, 'the only certain conclusion to be drawn from this [change in purview at 1228] is that there was both affinity in cultural interests and close contacts between the Cistercian monastery of Boyle and the Premonstratensian monastery of Holy Trinity.' O'Dwyer's conclusion overlooks both the character of the entry at 1229, AB §390, which describes from a Holy Trinity perspective a conflict between the two monasteries, and the ensuing silence regarding Boyle affairs.   73 O'Conor, *Rerum Hib.* ii, 1–48 (edition).

repeated kalends, which he introduced on f. 3^r as an enlarged 'KŁ', regularly placed between AM data in red cartouches. These AM data nearly all increment by nineteen, so that it is clear that here the scribe was employing it to represent nineteen kalends, thus:

$$KŁ = \text{'k.k.k.k.k.k.k.k.k.k.k.k.k.k.k.k.k.k.k'}$$

Freeman's solitary 'K.' thus effectively omits eighteen kalends. Similarly Freeman made no attempt to reproduce the textual details of numbers and in some cases misread them, e.g. his AB §329 'Mcxliii' misrepresents the MS '.M̄^{o}.c^o.xł.u^{o}i.', cf. plate 9, line 8.

Connacht group

The two members of this group are distinguished by their Connacht purview, their secular contexts, their associations with the Uí Duibhgeannáin of Roscommon and Leitrim, their late sixteenth-century dates of compilation, their distinctive chronological apparatus, and their derivation from a common source which Mac Niocaill considered to have been 'a text compiled by a member of the Uí Maoilchonaire, probably in the mid-fifteenth century.'[74]

Annals of Connacht

This work survives in three MSS, two paper copies from the seventeenth century which were copied by Maurice O'Gorman from the primary MS, a sixteenth-century vellum now RIA 1219 (C.iii.1), and descriptions of this have been published by the Revd O'Conor, O'Curry, Freeman and Mulchrone.[75] It consists of ninety-one leaves measuring c.28.4×20.3 cm., which are foliated ff. 1–90, f. 26* having been missed. The text commences with a conspicuously decorated 'K' and a protracted account of the achievements of Cathal Crobderg Ua Conchobair †1224, so it clearly represents the start of an important section and possibly is the original beginning of the text. The range of the chronicle is AD 1224–1544, with a later addition for 1562, and there are two lacunae arising from the loss of leaves which were probably conjugates, viz. 1379–83 and 1394–97. A third lacuna at 1428–32 is not caused by folio loss, but to judge from the disturbance in the chronological apparatus for 1424–34, it was a deficiency already in the exemplar, cf. chapter 9, p. 252 ff.[76] The title 'Connacht Annals' was employed in 1767 by Charles O'Conor of Bellanagare †1791 and subsequently

---

74 Mac Niocaill, *MIA*, 32 (cit.).   75 MS descriptions: O'Conor, *Biblioteca* i, 73–7; O'Curry, *MM*, 104–5,113–19; Freeman, *CT*, vii–xxiv; Mulchrone, *Catalogue RIA* fasc. xxvi, 3274–6. 76 Freeman, *CT*, ix, (lacunae).

repeated by his grandson the Revd Charles O'Conor as 'Annales Connaciae', and as a description of the text's purview it is broadly satisfactory.[77] However, it should be understood that the numerous references by both Ussher and Ware to 'Annals of Connacht' do not refer to this text. The text is written in two columns and was principally the work of three scribes whom Freeman, editor of the only complete edition, labelled A, B, and C, whose main contributions were as tabulated in Figure 2.

Scribe	ff.	AD range	Lacunae
A	1^r–61^v	1224–1468	1379–83, 1394–7, 1428–32
B	62^r–66ra	1468–1478	–
C	66ra–90rb	1479–1544	–

Figure 2. The sigla of the scribes of MS RIA 1219, their folio and AD ranges, and lacunae.

The style of annals written by scribes A and B resembles that of the primary MSS of AT, CS and AI, being written continuously with enlarged initials and 'K's offset into the left-hand margin. However, with scribe C a major style change takes place, for the enlarged initials cease, and he writes uniformly sized letters, while at the beginning of each year he systematically indents three lines to the right, cf. plate 10. It seems most likely that this indentation was intended to accommodate an oversize 'K' but that scribe C did not complete his transcription, since most kalends are missing their 'K's and no colophon follows his concluding entry at 1544. Such 'K's as there are appear to have been written subsequently, most likely by Charles O'Conor, and those on f. 69^v do indeed occupy three full lines.

Regarding the identity of these scribes Freeman was alone in proposing that they were members of the Uí Maoil Chonaire.[78] Earlier Paul Walsh identified scribe A with Páidín Ua Duibhgeannáin, who flourished at the end of the sixteenth century, and this was repeated by Kathleen Mulchrone, who also identified scribe C as Seán Riabhach Ua Duibhgeannáin. On f. 85va scribe C interjected 'Misi Sean ⁊ is misdi me gan Dolp agum', that is, 'I am Seán and I am at loss without Dolp', and both Walsh and Mulchrone pointed out that the rare 'Dolp' was an Ua Duibhgeannáin name.[79] Subsequently Mac Niocaill also drew attention to a number of entries featuring the Uí Duibhgeannáin that linked the MS to that family, and also the many textual correspondences with

77 Ward & Ward, Letters i, 222 and ii, 196, 198 (Connacht Annals); O'Conor, Bibliotheca i, 73 (Annales Connaciae).   78 Freeman, CT, xii–xiv, (Uí Maoil Chonaire scribes).   79 Walsh, 'O'Duigenan books', 23 and Walsh, 'O'Duigenan family', 4–5 (Páidín); Mulchrone, Catalogue fasc. xxvi, 3274–6 (Seán Riabhach).

LC whose Uí Duibhgeannáin provenance is beyond doubt.[80] There can be no reasonable doubt then that RIA 1219 is an Uí Duibhgeannáin compilation. Regarding its date of compilation, since scribe C's transcription continues to 1544 it must at least postdate that year. In LC 1578.13 the obit of 'Dolbh mac Dubhthaigh I Dhuibhgéanáin' is given, and so if Seán's aforementioned statement refers to this Dolbh we may date Seán's contribution to c.1578, which accords well with the date of LC derived below.

Turning to the chronological apparatus of CT we find that over 1224–1478 it provides by far the most substantial apparatus of any Irish annalistic text. Following most kalends come the ferial, epact, lunar cycle, AD, Indiction, solar cycle, and occasionally the bissextile. For 1224–1424 the embolismic/common years, Dominical letters, hendecas and ogdoads series are cryptically written in a unique notation as letters prefixed and post-fixed as superscripts to the initial 'Kl'.[81] A further idiosyncratic detail is the use for extended intervals of 'Kll' instead of 'Kl'. A distinctive feature of the epactal series is the systematic omission of the nineteen-year saltus, so that this series is asynchronous with the ecclesiastical calendar from 1235 onward. On the other hand collation shows that the kalend+ferial+AD series of this apparatus all maintain excellent synchronism with the Julian year over 1224–1478, and these represent indeed the most trustworthy Annalistic chronological apparatus over this interval, cf. chapter 12, p. 349 ff.[82] Since it is known that members of the Uí Maoil Chonaire served as hereditary ollamhs over this interval to the ruling Ua Chonchobair dynasty, the implication is clear that the compilation of this elaborate chronological apparatus was done by the Uí Maoil Chonaire. After 1424 the number of chronological series reduces and those retained become intermittent until at 1479 they all cease except for kalend+AD. Here, synchronized to scribe C, a completely new chronological apparatus suddenly takes over, numerically equivalent to AD but expressed largely in Irish words and designated 'bliadan ... aois an Tigerna'. The first instance reads:

CT 1479.1: Kl eñ nai mb*liadna* dec ar *tri* fic*h*tib ar ceithre ced ar mile aois an tig*er*n*a* an tan sin.

Note that the number of the year is written in words from the least significant digit 'nai', to the most significant 'mile', and the concluding element 'an tan sin' serves to emphasize that this is a new beginning. This apparatus continues until 1544 and since this section represents the Uí Duibhgeannáin contribution the

80 Mac Niocaill, *MIA*, 33 (Uí Duibhgeannáin entries).   81 Freeman, *CT*, frontispiece (scribe A); xiv–xx (discusses the chronological criteria but omits the kalends and his explanations of epactal and other errors in terms of Sacrobosco's computus are naïve).   82 Mc Carthy, 'Synchronization', *s.a.* 1224–1478 (synchronization of CT's kalend+ferial+AD with the Julian calendar).

implication is that both the 'Aois an Tigerna' apparatus and distinctive writing style of scribe C are both Uí Duibhgeannáin characteristics. On the other hand the traditional writing style and elaborate chronological apparatus transcribed by scribes A and B is associated with the Uí Maoil Chonaire compilation of the fifteenth century, identified by Mac Niocaill. This will be discussed in more detail in chapter 9, p. 249 ff. The introduction of the 'Aois an Tigerna' apparatus also had important implications for the compilers of LC as will be discussed below in relation to that text.

Regarding the history of the MS, the annotations 'Aois Xt 1471' and 'A.C. 1476' on the top margins of f. 63ᵛ and f. 65ᵛ respectively, in handwriting which corresponds both in style and appearance with that of Mícheál Ó Cléirigh's chronological apparatus in FM, suggests the MS was used by him. Ó Cléirigh in his preface to FM listed 'leabhar na muintire Duibhgendán' as having a range of AD 900–1563, and notwithstanding the substantial difference in range at the beginning, there are good reasons to believe that this MS is part of that tradition.[83] Subsequently it appears to have remained in the possession of the Uí Duibhgeannáin, for an inscription on f. 15ʳ indicates that it was in the possession of a 'Dominick Diggenan' in 1727. About two decades later Charles O'Conor signed it in 1744 on f. 70ᵛ, but he probably had obtained the MS by 1741 for on f. 1ʳ appears a computation in his hand of the number of years from the start of Toirrdelbach Ua Conchobair's reign to 1741. O'Conor's neat annotations appear frequently throughout the MS, and Freeman's ill-tempered descriptions of them as 'indiscriminate scribbling', 'a disaster', 'defaced the volume', 'attacks on the integrity of the text' are unjustified.[84] From Charles O'Conor the MS passed to his grandson, the Revd O'Conor, thence in c.1847 to the earl of Ashburnham, thence in 1883 to the British Government, and finally to the RIA.[85]

Regarding printed editions of the text, the first was that for AD 1317–1412 by Hennessy based upon the secondary MSS of CT, viz. TCD 1278 and RIA 986–7, with which he filled that lacuna in his 1871 edition of LC. In 1933–4 Martin Freeman published the annals of 1224–1412 from RIA 1219 in *Revue Celtique* without translation, and then in 1944 his edition of the entire text with parallel English translation and introduction was published by DIAS, and this was reprinted in 1970, 1983 and 1996. In general this is a fair representation of the entries and the chronological apparatus, however Freeman's systematic replacement of every 'Kl' and 'Kll', one of the most distinctive elements of Irish annalistic texts, with '*Calann*' was an extraordinary decision, and it appears

---

83 O'Donovan, *FM* i, pp. lxv–vi ('leabhar Duibhgendán').   84 Freeman, *CT*, x–xi (scribbling); Walsh, 'O'Duigenan books', 24 (defends O'Conor's annotations, stating 'the additions are mostly correct').   85 Ó Muraíle, *Celebrated antiquary*, 316 (MS history).

to reflect an attitude of superiority on his part towards the text and its scribes. Having omitted the kalends from his discussion of the chronological apparatus Freeman dismissed those of 1479–1544 as 'the meaningless vestigial *Calann Enair*', underlining thereby his complete lack of understanding of their role in the chronological apparatus.[86]

Annals of Loch Cé

The MS structure of the second member of the Connacht group is the most complex of all our texts. Rather than regard it as a unitary text it is more accurate to consider it as a series of four sections, with the unifying aspect that Brian Mac Diarmada †1592 was responsible for their compilation, and wrote part or all of each of them during the latter part of his life. At this time Mac Diarmada was chieftain of his clan and ruler of Magh Luirg, in north Roscommon, with his castle 'Carraig Mhic Dhiarmada' located on an island in Loch Cé. Consequently, the purview of these four sections represents the affairs of north Connacht and the Mhic Dhiarmada in particular, and for this reason the title 'Annals of Loch Cé' bestowed upon them by O'Curry in 1861 is appropriate to their provenance.[87] Only one copy of each of these sections exists, preserved in two MSS, viz. TCD 1293 (H.1.19) ff. 1–136, and BL Add. 4792, ff. 19–32, descriptions of which will be found in Abbot and Gwynn, O'Grady, O'Curry, Hennessy, and Walsh.[88] TCD 1293 preserves three of these sections for which Mac Niocaill employed the sigla L1, L2, and L3, and BL 4792 preserves the fourth section to which the sigla may be usefully extended by naming it L4.[89] Both MSS are written on either vellum or paper in a single column, with paragraphs marked by enlarged 'K's and capitals offset in the left-hand margin, cf. plate 11. The MS details and the range and lacuna of these four sections are tabulated in Figure 3.

Sect.	MS	Range	Lacuna
L1	TCD 1293 ff.1, 6–81	1014–1316	1139–69
L2	TCD 1293 ff. 95–101	1413–1461	–
L3	TCD 1293 ff. 103–36	1462–1577	1572–76
L4	BL 4792 ff. 19–32	1568–1590	1571–76

Figure 3. The sigla, AD ranges and lacunae of MSS TCD 1293 and BL 4792.

---

86 Freeman, *CT*, xx (cit.).   87 Walsh, 'O'Duigenan books', 16–17 and O'Curry, *MM*, 96, 100 (Brian Mac Diarmada and 'Loch Cé').   88 MS descriptions: Abbot & Gwynn, *Catalogue*, 66; O'Grady, *Catalogue*, 21; O'Curry, *MM*, 93–5; Hennessy, *LC* i, pp. lv–vii; Walsh, 'O'Duigenan books', 15–23.   89 Mac Niocaill, *MIA*, 32–5, 40 (L1, L2, L3 sigla).

These two MSS are both late sixteenth century, and the sections are discussed here in the order in which they were written. The oldest of the sections is L4 which was written on four vellum (ff. 21–4) and ten paper leaves of two different sizes, viz. ff. 19–24 are *c.*23×18 cm., while ff. 25–32 are *c.*25×18 cm., by a number of scribes, one of whom was Brian Mac Diarmada. Both the multiplicity of scribes and the nature of the entries support the conclusion that at least from 1577 onward these are records of contemporary events. Mac Diarmada's attitude towards scholars and scholarship is clearly indicated by his contemporary addition to the obit for Colbach Mac Domnaill †1581, where he wrote, 'the loss has pained the hearts of all Connacht, and especially it has pained the scholars and poets of the province of Connacht. And it has divided my own heart into two parts.'[90] Thus it is clear that by 1581 Mac Diarmada was himself involved in the world of scholarship and actively engaged with others in compiling annals of the affairs of his own principality, and also that this process continued to within two years of his death. It appears likely that the termination of this compilation was caused by his advancing years rather than his death for there was space on f. 32 for further entries after 1590. It is noteworthy that in this first compilation neither consistency of medium or folio size was maintained. Subsequently L4 was in Ware's possession for his distinctive annotations may be seen there, including an earlier foliation and his characteristic marginal AD data, and in his 1648 catalogue he described it simply as 'Rerum Hibernicarum Annales, ab anno Dom. 1579. us*que* ad annum 1590. Hibernicè.'[91]

The first section of the remaining compilation to be written was L2, which was written by Brian Mac Diarmada himself on seven paper leaves of size *c.*25×20 cm, and so incommensurate with those of L4. The annals themselves are very meagre, some years being without any entries, and Brian wrote these at two to five annals per page, generally spacing them equally regardless of whether the year had entries or not. This left ample blank space between years suggesting that while Brian's sources were sparse he had the hope of further supplementing them. There is no indication of a date on this section but from considerations given below it is likely that he wrote L2 not long before November 1588. The next section to be written was L3, whose range is continuous with that of L2, and this is written on thirty-four vellum leaves commensurate in size with L2, the last of which is so deeply discoloured that its verso is completely illegible. In an interjection on f. 114[r] the principal scribe identified his patron, himself, date of writing and place as follows:[92]

90 Hennessy, *LC* ii, 435 (Colbach's obit), cf. O'Curry, *MM*, 96.   91 O'Sullivan, 'Finding list', 94 (Ware's catalogue).   92 Walsh, 'O'Duigenan books', 18 (cit.).

I cease from this; may God grant to the man of this book, to return safe from the town of Athlone, i.e. Brian, the son of Ruaidhri Mac Diarmada; I am Philip who wrote 1588; the festival day of Brendan [November 29] exactly; and Cloonybrien is my place.

Note that in this, Pilip, as he called himself, both identified Brian with the work and expressed concern for his security. Pilip was identified by both O'Curry and Hennessy as a member of the Uí Duibhgeannáin, and by Walsh and Mac Niocaill specifically as 'Pilib Ballach Ó Duibhgennáin'.[93] Now examination of the MS shows that when Pilip started on f. 103^r he was not only transcribing the same sparse sources as Brian but that he also maintained Brian's distinctive principles of layout. That is for ff. 103^r–110^r Pilip cooperated with Brian and Dubthach Ua Duibhgeannáin to continue writing two or three equally spaced annals per page.[94] Thus it is clear that these two scribes were simply continuing on vellum the transcription of Brian's sparse sources in close cooperation with him. Therefore it is likely that Brian had completed L2 not that long before Pilip's interjection on 29 November 1588. However, upon the completion of the entries for 1496 on f. 110^r Pilip left the the verso blank, and on f. 111^r embarked on the annal for 1497, now writing continuously down each page. Moreover, the reason for the change is apparent, for the entries are now copious so that it is evident that another much more substantial source had been acquired and henceforth Pilip wrote annals continuously up to f. 122^r from whence Dubthach completed the transcription. Furthermore, these two scribes remained in the service of Brian after the completion of L3, for they both contributed to L1, with Pilip again the principal scribe. Thus sections L2–3 together show the start and development of the working relationship between Brian, Pilip and Dubthach. Regarding L3's lacuna, since the entries for 1571 are truncated and those of 1577 acephalous, it is clear that some leaves have been lost at this point, and it is remarkable that L4's lacuna corresponds so closely to this.

The section L1 consists of sixty-six leaves of vellum commensurate in size with L2–3, and the first of which, like the last leaf of L3, is so deeply discoloured that it is only legible with difficulty, so that a re-transcription of f.1^r made by S. Mac Conmidhe in 1698 has been inserted in the MS. However, the first kalend is clear enough and its 'K' is nearly fifty percent taller than that of subsequent kalends, and its associated chronological criteria are distinctively concluded by the emphasis 'in tan sin'.[95] Thus this folio indeed represents the

---

93 O'Curry, *MM*, 94, Hennessy, *LC* i, p. lvi, and Mac Niocaill, *MIA*, 33 (identification of Pilip and other scribes).   94 Hennessy, *LC* i, p. lvi (Dubthach Ua Duibhgeannáin).   95 Hennessy, *LC* i, p. xxxi, following O'Donovan, was mistaken about the start of the MS, writing: 'it is most likely, as O'Donovan says, that it [*sc.* TCD 1293] has "lost several pages at the beginning." The first page begins with a capital of the usual size, not with an enlarged or ornamental letter, as manuscripts generally do.'

original start of L1 by Pilip, and, at the bottom of f. 11ᵛ, he has again identified his patron, himself and date of writing as, 'Is im sgítheach do barc Briain Mhic Diarmada. A°.D°. 1589 Misi Pilip badł', cf. plate 11. This interjection was interpreted by O'Curry, Hennessy and Walsh to mean that Pilip was weary of writing Mac Diarmada's 'book'.[96] However, the word 'barc' means a 'vessel' or 'ship', and so it appears much more likely that here Pilip was again expressing his anxiety when waiting for Mac Diarmada and his vessel to return safely. Regarding the lacuna in L1, the entries for 1138 conclude without truncation on f. 24ᵛ, and those for 1170 commence on f. 31ʳ, with six blank paper leaves bound between them. From this it appears that annals for the years 1139–69 have not been lost, but were in fact never written, presumably because Mac Diarmada was unable to supply the exemplar. Pilip then transcribed 1170–1241 (f. 56ʳ) alone, and for 1242–1316 (f. 81ᵛ) he was assisted by two other scribes, one of whom was again Dubthach Ua Duibhgeannáin. Thus in the years 1588–9, just a year before L4 terminates, Pilip and Dubthach Ua Duibhgeannáin transcribed most of L3 and L1 for Brian Mac Diarmada. In these circumstances it seems likely that the ensuing lacuna 1317–1412 was the result of the compilation terminating incomplete in c.1590.

Thus it emerges that LC represents a series of increasingly ambitious compilations made by a clan chieftain with an interest in scholarship and history and Uí Duibhgeannáin support to document the affairs of his own kingdom in the final years of his life. First L4 documented Brian's own times, then in L2–3 he carried the chronicle back to 1413, and finally in L1 he endeavoured to extend the compilation back to 1014, but this was never completed, probably on account of his age. It appears that the sections L1–3 were subsequently bound as a single volume, almost certainly without boards since ff. 1ʳ and 136ᵛ are similarly discoloured, and the writing on f. 1ʳ was evidently obscure by 1698 when Mac Conmidhe re-transcribed it. With its disparate media of intermixed vellum and paper, its sparse layout for L2–3, its lacunae, and its incomplete binding, there is apparent a want of overall consistency and competence in the compilation of this volume, which likely reflect Brian's age and circumstances. It is probable that this volume remained in the possession of the Meic Diarmada well into the seventeenth century, for intermittent entries referring to their affairs for the years 1595–1648 were added to it. Subsequently it passed into the possession of Roderick O'Flaherty for he inscribed a considerable number of marginal identifications and chronological annotations. Then in 1724 William Nicolson described a 'Folio Volume, a Copy of the Annals of the old Abby of *Inch-Maccreen*, an Island in the Lake of *Loghkea* … this Book

---

96 O'Curry, *MM*, 94 misread Pilip's date as '1580', but Hennessy, *LC* i, p. 58 n. 4 and Walsh, 'O'Duigenan books', 17 transcribe it accurately.

commences at the Year 1013, and ends with 1571', in possession of John Conry in Dublin, and this description corresponds very closely with our text.[97] Finally, in 1766 Thomas Leland purchased the MS from the estate of Dr John Fergus †1761 for Trinity College, Dublin, where it still remains.[98]

Regarding the chronological apparatus, Mac Diarmada's Ua Duibhgeannáin compilers employed 'aois an Tigerna' from the very start of their compilation of L4 at 1568, and continued it until the conclusion at 1590. Then in 1588 Brian employed it for L2, and his Uí Duibhgeannáin compilers of L3 continued it for 1462–1577. Then in 1589 they substituted it for AD in L1, systematically providing a kalend+ferial+epact+'aois in Tigerna' apparatus for 1014–1221, cf. plate 11 and Figure 34, p. 247. From 1222, however, the AD series in Roman numerals found in CT replaces 'aois in Tigerna', and the epactal series omits every saltus and so reproduces CT's asynchronous series. While for 1231–1316 L1 normally includes the lunar, solar, and indiction series found in CT. Thus for 1222–1316 Brian's compilation reproduced much of the chronological apparatus of the Ua Maoil Chonaire compilation.

The only printed edition is that published by Hennessy in 1871 in which he provided a fair copy of the entries of all four sections. For the chronological apparatus he mostly translated into Irish words the AD years, which are often expressed in complex combinations of Roman and Arabic numerals, and Latin and Irish words, and he introduced commas and semi-colons in order to separate and clarify the other criteria. For example, 1014, the first year of L1 commences:

TCD 1293 f. 1ʳ: Kłł In*ar.for.*Aoine.u.i.xxᵗ.l.x.u.4°.bła.x.7.M.Aois.an.t*igherna*.in. t*an*.sin

LC 1014.1: Kłł. Ináir for aoíne, ui. xx.ⁱᵗ.l.; xu.; ceithre bliadna x. ocus mile aoís an Tigerna in tan sin.

Hennessy also filled the lacuna between L1 and L2 by using the two secondary MSS of CT, viz. TCD 1278 and RIA 986–7, and while he clearly indicated his source change in the margin, the result suggests a continuity that the MS does not possess.[99] In 1959 Gearóid Mac Niocaill published the text of the *prima manu* entries from MS H (TCD 1282) of AU and LC over 1014–1220 in parallel, remarking their close textual correspondence.[100]

97 Nicolson, *Historical library*, 243 (cit.).   98 O'Sullivan, 'Irish manuscripts', 235, 246 (Leland). 99 Hennessy, *LC* i, pp. lii–iiii (CT sources).   100 Mac Niocaill, 'Annála', 18 'chífear gur aon chroinic amháin, go bunúsach, atá iontu.'

Regnal-canon group

Here we have just MB/FM and I describe them in the order in which they were written.

Mageoghagan's Book

There are eight substantial and two fragmentary witnesses to this work and while short accounts of these were given by O'Curry and O'Grady, the only extensive study of them is that made by Sarah Sanderlin for her doctoral thesis of 1980.[101] From this in 1982 Sanderlin published an account of the eight substantial MSS in which unfortunately her conclusions mutually conflict, and they also silently contradict those of her doctoral thesis.[102] Since Sanderlin's conflicting conclusions bear upon the question of which MS should be regarded as primary, the matter must be considered in some detail here. In her thesis Sanderlin concluded that the oldest MS, Armagh Public Lib. (MS A) written in 1660 by an unidentified scribe, and MS BL Add. 4817 (MS B) written in 1661 by Domhnall Ó Súilleabháin of Tralee descended from a common ancestor. Whereas in her publication Sanderlin concluded that, 'B descended directly from A.' However, MS B has four prefatory items, viz. a title page, Mageoghagan's preface, bibliography, Ó Súilleabháin's preface, and two suffixed items, viz. eight annals in Irish for 425–1466 and Ó Súilleabháin's index. On the other hand MS A, which has lost folios at the beginning, has only Mageoghagan's preface and the eight suffixed annals in Irish. However, in 1685 when Tadhg O'Daly used MS A as exemplar for his copy, now TCD MS 673 (MS T), all four prefatory items were present. In this copy O'Daly reproduced not only text appropriate to the now missing folios, but also many of the annotations found in MS A. It is apparent therefore that MS A is an incomplete copy of Ó Súilleabháin's edition of Mageoghagan's work by an unidentified scribe, whereas MS B is a copy by Ó Súilleabháin himself.[103] Moreover, in his preface Ó Suilleabháin apologized that his index was not alphabetically arranged, for which he had been chided by 'some of my skillful friends in Chronology', and indicated that he would emend this deficiency in 'my next transcription'.[104]

---

101 In March 2007 Dáibhí Ó Cróinín discovered a ninth substantial MS in Leipig evidently transcribed by Lisa Stokes, daughter of Whitley, in 1894 in London. Her exemplar remains to be established but first indications suggest BL Add. 4817 is a likely candidate. The MS is registered in appendix 1. 102 O'Curry, *MM*, 130–9, and O'Grady, *Catalogue* i, 17–20 (earlier accounts). Sanderlin, *Conell Mageoghagan*, 11–39 surveys the substantial and fragmentary MSS, and Sanderlin, 'Manuscripts' 111–23 summarizes her earlier work. However, her stemma in 112 and 122 are inconsistent in details, and both conflict with that in her thesis at 39. I am grateful to Dáibhí Ó Cróinín for arranging access for me to the NUI Galway copy of Sanderlin's thesis. 103 Sanderlin, *Conell Mageoghagan*, 20–2 (MS A's lost folios), 33–4 (MS T). Sanderlin, 'Manuscripts', 112, 116, 122 (MS B descending from MS A). 104 O'Grady, *Catalogue* i, 19, and

These remarks, together with the existence of a copy of his preface from before 1660 show that Ó Suilleabháin was engaged in the production of a series of copies of Mageoghagan's work, one of which was used by the scribe of MS A. Furthermore, examination of MS B shows that as well as the integrity of its text and ancillary material, Ó Suilleabháin was a more accomplished scribe than that of MS A, reproducing English, Irish and Latin in a wide range of appropriate styles, including decorated initial capitals far more proficient and numerous than those in MS A.[105] Cognizance should also be given to Ó Suilleabháin's own assertions in his preface in respect of his handling of the text, wherein, having pointed out that the 'Translator [Mageoghagan]' and his source had anachronistically treated Heremon before his older brother Heber, Ó Suilleabháin stated:[106]

> ... beinge loath by alteration to disorder the industriousnesse of the obliedginge Translator I have inconfusedly and immutably transcribed his worke, onely the augmentinge of some marginalls for your good: & the compileinge of a confus'd yett accordinge to the pages somewhat orderly Index ...

Whilst the profuseness of Ó Suilleabháin's style does not make easy reading there can be no mistaking his assertion that, notwithstanding his own serious objections, he has 'immutably transcribed' the work, and he has also clearly identified his own ancillary additions to it. To summarize, in MS B we have a complete copy of the work of an accomplished scribe who has provided an account of his transcription, the details of which reconcile with his text. In MS A we have an incomplete copy by an unidentified scribe of an earlier transcription by Ó Suilleabháin. In these circumstances I conclude that while both MSS A and B share a common ancestor, the latter is at least one stage closer to that ancestor than the former, and so MS B should be considered the primary manuscript. MS A remains of course an important witness and sample collation with MS B show that they share many orthographical and textual features. Regarding the remainder of the MSS Sanderlin cited evidence that the other seventeenth-century MS descended from MS A, and that all four post seventeenth-century MSS descended from NLI 767 (MS N7). But her conclusions regarding the ancestry of MS N7 were inconclusive and further collation is needed to resolve this.[107]

Murphy, *AC*, 5–6, (Ó Suilleabháin's preface – Murphy's edition is garbled both by O'Daly's omissions of words and loss of a line by trimming). **105** MS BL 4817, ff 2[r], 3[r], 5[r], 11[r], 90[v]. 94[r], 113[v], 115[r] (decorated initials). **106** MS BL 4817 f. 2[r], cf. O'Grady, *Catalogue*, 19, and Murphy, *AC*, 5 (cit.). Sanderlin, 'Manuscripts', 116, 'O'Sullivan's low opinion of AClon, revealed in his preface' is a misjudgement; Ó Suilleabháin's concern was to draw attention to the anachronistic and partisan treatment of Heber and Heremon by both Mageoghagan and his source. **107** Sanderlin, 'Manuscripts', 121, 'It is not possible to be more precise about ... the complicated connections between A and N7.'

MS B was written on paper and consists of 175 folios comprising f. 2^r title page, ff. 3^r–4^r Mageoghagan's preface, f. 4^v Mageoghagan's bibliography and Ó Suilleabhán's preface, ff. 5^r–173^r text of MB, f. 173^r eight Irish annals, and ff. 174^r–175^r Ó Suilleabháin's index. Each page of the chronicle was ruled into two columns and a heading, with the narrower left-hand column used for Mageoghagan's chronological data and annotations regarding important persons or events. In the wider right-hand column the entries were written in paragraphs, each paragraph commencing with a conspicuous capital letter, and where chronological data or annotations were provided in the left-hand column the alignment between them and the intended paragraph is unambiguous, cf. plate 12. The chronological apparatus consists of two independent series. The older comprises a series of reigns and regnal years extending from the Fir Bolg king, Slánga mac Dela, to Máel Sechnaill Mór †1022, which will be discussed in chapter 10. The more recent is Mageoghagan's marginal AD series in the left hand column; this is sporadic before the seventh century and becomes annual at 637 though it is subsequently disrupted by numerous lacunae. Up to the eleventh century it is virtually always in arrears by up to seven years.

At the top of each verso-recto folio pair a print-style heading identifies the current king(s) of Ireland; for example on ff. 55^v–56^r, 'The Raigne of kcallagh and Congall | koyle kinges of Ireland.' The heading of each recto folio also includes a folio number between 1 and 170, and these numbers have been referenced both from Mageoghagan's genealogy of Randolph earl of Antrim, and from Ó Suilleabháin's index.[108] It seems obvious that Mageoghagan's page layout imitated that of a printed work but I have not been able to identify any appropriate source. In view of his contacts with James Ussher it is striking that the layout of Ussher's *Annales Veteris Testamenti* of 1650 is very similar to that of MB.[109] Apart from a few corrections MS B has no annotations whatsoever, in striking contrast to the multiple hands that have repeatedly annotated MS A, which annotations are comprehensively described by Sanderlin.[110] One of the most prolific of these was Roderick O'Flaherty who emended the text, made marginal and interlinear additions and many AD annotations, and it is virtually certain that his annotations of 'Cod. Cluan' in Mac Fhirbhisigh's copy of CS (TCD 1292) refer to this MS, and that he collated these two MSS together in the course of preparing his book *Ogygia* published in 1685.

The only published edition of MB is that of 1896 by Denis Murphy who stated in his own preface that he had used Tadhg O'Daly's 1685 copy, our MS

---

108 Murphy, *AC*, 210 and BL 4817 f. 110^v (genealogical folio reference – Ó Suilleabháin's foliation duplicates '8'). 109 Ussher, *Annales*, *passim* (layout), cf. Mc Carthy, 'James Ussher', 78 fig. 4 (reproduction of p.1 of the 1650 edition of Ussher's *Annales*.); Cunningham & Gillespie, 'James Ussher', 88–98 (Mageoghagan's contacts with Ussher). 110 Sanderlin, *Conell Mageoghagan*, 26–8 and 'Manuscripts', 114–15 (MS A annotations).

T, which Sanderlin described as 'a fairly good copy of A[rmagh]'.[111] However, O'Daly omitted the very first paragraph of the chronicle beginning, 'My Author omitteth to treate of Holy Scripture ...', found in both MSS B and A, and sample collation of passages shows that MS T frequently varies in text and orthography from the other two which usually agree. For example MSS A and B refer to Mageoghagan's source as the 'old Irish booke', whereas MS T calls it the 'ould Irish booke'. Moreover, regarding MS T's chronological apparatus, O'Daly made no serious attempt to reproduce the paragraphing of MS A, which matches that of MS B, with the result that the relationship between Murphy's prefixed AD data and the entries is compromised. Sanderlin also pointed out that 'Murphy silently supplied words, altered readings he considered unlikely, and on two occasions censored the text without proper indications silently.'[112] Her allusion to his censorship refers to two passages in his exemplar that Murphy omitted, apparently on account of their explicit references to sexual matters, in both cases acknowledging his omission with dots but giving no information. However, since these passages amount to only about one page of text, Murphy's edition does represent most of the known text of MB.[113] On the other hand Murphy omitted all of the notes and some of the chronological data given in Mageoghagan's left-hand column, and all of his page headings, while at the same time including many of the marginal and interlinear inter-polations made into MS A and transmitted by O'Daly's MS T. Thus Murphy's edition is a misleading representation of Mageoghagan's work and a re-edition based upon the witness of all the MSS is urgently needed.

Annals of the Four Masters

This text represents the last major annalistic compilation undertaken by Gaelic scholarship. It was executed under the leadership of the Franciscan brother, Mícheál Ó Cléirigh, with five secular antiquaries, and provides a substantial account of Irish history written entirely in Classical Modern Irish. In respect of the authorship of this work, I consider that Colgan's term 'Quatuor magistri', which he introduced merely to compliment the work and its principal compilers, has hindered the understanding of the compilation. Consequently, while retaining the siglum 'FM' I will assign authorship to Mícheál Ó Cléirigh for he was undoubtedly leader of the compilation. Of the manuscripts produced under his leadership four autograph volumes on paper survive as is tabulated in Figure 4.[114]

111 Sanderlin, 'Manuscripts', 117 (cit.).   112 Sanderlin, 'Manuscripts', 111 (cit.).   113 Murphy, *AC*, 134, 153 (omissions replaced by dots); Sanderlin, *Conell Mageoghagan*, 166, 217–18 for the missing passages, the second of which was also published by Dumville, 'Millennium', 104–5. 114 Colgan, *Acta Sanctorum*, [7] ('Quatuor Magistri'). MS H has usually been said to extend only

Sigla	Shelfmark	Size (cm)	Folios	Range
A	UCD OFM A 13	19×28	523	AM 2242–AD 1169
P	RIA 687–8 (23 P 6–7)	15×23	578	AD 1170–1616
C	RIA 1220 (C iii 3)	17×27	522	AM 2242–AD 1171
H	TCD 1301 (H. 2. 11)	19×28	c.478	AD 1334–1616

Figure 4. The MSS of FM with their sigla, folio size and count, and range in AM/AD.

Accounts of these MSS have been published by O'Curry and Ó Muraíle, and detailed descriptions are given in the catalogues of the manuscript collections of the RIA, Franciscan library Killiney, and Trinity College Dublin, and they have been recently discussed extensively by Bernadette Cunningham.[115]

While they were written by different scribes these MSS all exhibit a similar style, with the text in a single column, virtually all in Irish and written in an Irish minuscule script, with punctuation by capitals to commence entries and commas or a point to end them. Paragraphing is by means of enlarged initials offset into the left-hand margin, see plate 13. Ample space has been left between successive years, evidently for further additions, sometimes amounting to multiple blank pages. The primary chronological apparatus comprises a series of reigns and regnal years extending from the Fir Bolg king, Slánga mac Dela, to Máel Sechnaill Mór †1022, and this will be examined fully in chapter 10, p. 293 ff. The secondary chronological apparatus was computed by accumulating the regnal years and is arranged in two distinct sections, the first commencing at the Flood with 'Aois domhain 2242', which represents the Septuagint AM date for that event. This continues to 'Aois domhain 5199', which is followed by 'An céd-bhliadhain d'aois Chriosd', so that Aois Chriosd 1 = AD 1 = Aois domain 5200, i.e. the Septuagint AM date for the Incarnation. Mícheál Ó Cléirigh explained his reasons for preferring the Septuagint AM dating in the preface to his edition of LG completed just prior to commencing FM. This secondary AD apparatus continues to the end normally written 'Aois Criost' or 'Aois cř', and, as can be seen in plate 13, the year is written twice, first in Arabic numerals and then in Irish words. Note that not only does the designation 'Aois Criost' contrast with the Uí Duibhgeannáin 'Aois an Tigerna', but the Ó Cléirigh year is written from the most significant digit to the least significant, using the particle 'a'. This

---

to AD 1605, e.g. Ó Muraíle, 'Autograph MSS', 76. But examination of the MS shows the fragments of year headings for 1613–15, and an entry for 1616, cf. Ó Muraíle, idem, 87. **115** MSS descriptions: O'Curry, *MM*, 155–6; Ó Muraíle, 'Autograph MSS', 88–95; Duncan, *Catalogue RIA* fasc. xvii, 2112–14; Mulchrone, *Catalogue RIA* fasc. xxvi, 3276–82; Dillon et al., *Catalogue*, 24–7; Abbot & Gwynn, *Catalogue*, 82–3. Cunningham, *Making FM*, 155–90, 370–77 (discussion of MSS).

apparatus is sometimes followed by the numbered year of the current reign, all written in Irish words. Thus like MB this compilation has completely forsaken the use of 'KÍ'.[116]

As can be seen the range of these MSS is AM 2242–AD 1616, and thanks to the work of Walsh and Ó Muraíle we know that MSS A+P represent both a complementary pair and the final draft, while MSS C+H represent a preceding draft.[117] Walsh for example characterized the relationship of MSS A+P to C+H as follows:[118]

> There were ... two complete autograph copies prepared of the whole body of Annals. That which is now represented by C.iii.3 and H.2.11 was presented by the scribes to their patron Ferghal Ó Gadhra in recognition of his generosity. I consider it to have been the completed draft from which the final copy was made for transmission to headquarters at Louvain. This final copy now survives as the Franciscan MS [A 13] and its continuation in the Academy MSS 23.P.6 and 23.P.7 ...

This represents a useful summary of the relationship between these MSS, further details of which will be examined in chapter 10, p. 300 ff. However, Walsh's statement concerning the disposition of these MSS with respect to Fearghal Ó Gadhra and Louvain needs re-consideration and this will be done in chapter 11, p. 334 ff.

The prefatory material found in common to MSS A and C consists of a dedication to Fearghal Ó Gadhra, a short preface, and six testimonials. As well, MS P has two vellum leaves inserted between the years 1207–8 with a copy of the dedication followed by a longer version of the preface. The various copies of the dedication substantially agree, and in it Mícheál Ó Cléirigh praises Fearghal Ó Gadhra for his patronage, recites his genealogy, dedicates the work to him, and states that the compilation commenced on 22 January 1632 and was completed on 10 August 1636. The six testimonials in MSS A and C, which are dated between 2 November 1636 and 18 February 1637, also agree, and they purport to provide authoritative approvals of the compilation, though collation shows much textual dependency amongst them. The short and long prefaces which identify the compilers and their sources are both dated 10 August 1636, but they differ in many important details, and these differences have never been addressed. Paul Walsh, who was one of the few authors to acknowledge the existence of the short preface, simply stated that 'the compilers did not regard the form of their prefatory matter as final.' This matter and the questions

116 O'Curry, *MM*, 169, 172–3 (Ó Cléirigh LG & Septuagint AM).   117 Walsh, *Four Masters*, 10–14 (MSS A & P complementary); Walsh, 'MSS of FM', 81–3 and Ó Muraíle, 'Autograph MSS', 76–8 (A & P final drafts); Cunningham, *Making FM*, 155 (endorses Ó Muraíle). 118 Walsh, *Four Masters*, 12 (cit.).

concerning the history of the four MSS will be examined in detail in chapter 11, p. 334 ff. Regarding marginalia all except MS P have been annotated, MS C by a Henry Búrc in *c.*1655 and Charles O'Conor in the eighteenth century, MS H by Roderick O'Flaherty, and MS A by John Colgan in Louvain.[119] While not annotated by him it is certain that MS C was used by Dubhaltach Mac Fhirbhisigh to compile the regnal-canon for his Leabhar Genealach.[120]

Regarding the character of this compilation, collation of FM entries with the corresponding entries in their known sources shows that the compilers did not simply transcribe and translate their source material into Classical Modern Irish, rather they omitted many entries found in their sources, and those that they did include frequently show significant semantic changes. Exactly the same characteristic emerges in respect of the chronology of their compilation, for a sample collation up to AD 1000 shows repeated erratic divergences of up to at least nineteen years between the chronology of FM and its sources. For example FM place both the death of Illann Mac Dunlaing and Cath Luachra at 506, whereas the chronology of the Clonmacnoise chronicle places them both at 525. Thus Paul Walsh's statement, 'In earlier parts of the Four Master's Annals the margin of error is as much as five years', represents a serious understatement, cf. Figure 43, p. 299.[121] We must conclude therefore that, notwithstanding the impressive credentials of the compilers, the wide range of their sources, and the fulsome character of the testimonials, the compilation itself did not accurately reproduce either the content or structure of their sources. In these circumstances it is not surprising that within months a member of the Uí Maoil Chonaire, Tuileagna, should start a campaign to prevent the publication of the work on the grounds of its inaccuracy. For any chronographer with access to any of its sources must have quickly seen that FM repeatedly diverged semantically and chronologically from these sources. It is noteworthy that when Colgan emphatically praised the work and its compilers it was its piety and not accuracy he emphasized.[122] In 1631 Mícheál Ó Cléirigh, with the assistance of Fear Feasa Ó Maoil Chonaire, Cú Choigcríche Ó Cléirigh and Cú Choigcríche Ó Duibhgeannáin, completed a compilation of LG in Lisgoole, county Fermanagh, and in his preface Mícheál stated his objective very clearly. He wrote, 'I, the friar Michael O'Clery, have, by permission of my superiors,

---

119 Walsh, *Gleanings*, 71–80 reproduces dedication, short preface and testimonials from MS A, and these items were in MS C when it was copied in 1734–5 by Hugh O'Molloy. O'Donovan, *FM* i, pp. lv–lxxi reproduces the dedication and long preface from MS P. Walsh, *Gleanings*, 76 (cit.). 120 Ó Muraíle, *Book of Genealogies* iii, 4 and idem, *Celebrated antiquary*, 178 (Dubhaltach's use of MS C). 121 Walsh, *Four Masters*, 32 outlines FM's error margins, substantially following O'Conor, *Bibliotheca* i, 114 cf. O'Curry, *MM*, 151. 122 Walsh, *Genealogiae*, 131–4 (Tuileagna), cf. Jennings, *Michael O Clerigh*, 161–3, an unconstrained apologist for Mícheál, who summarily dismissed Tuileagna's campaign as, 'He was young, and evidently presumptuous'; O'Curry, *MM*, 144–5 (Colgan's praise).

undertaken to purge of error, rectify, and transcribe this old Chronicle called *Leabhar Gabhála ...*'[123] His authoritative and corrective attitude towards the text is very conspicuous and is incompatible with the verb 'transcribe', and since the same four men commenced work on their compilation of FM a mere month later it seems very likely that they maintained a similar attitude towards their Annalistic sources. Such an attitude would explain why their compilation exhibits so many divergences from their source material. The principal interest of the text today lies in those FM entries not found in other Annalistic sources, however we must accept that these FM-unique entries too have been subject to a similar arbitrary semantic and chronological treatment and consequently treat them with caution.

The first printed edition of the work was in 1826 by the Revd O'Conor from MS C for AM 2242–AD 1171, with a parallel Latin translation, both of which suffer from his customary inaccuracy. In 1846 Owen Connellan published an English translation of MS P for AD 1170–1616. In 1848–51 John O'Donovan published his monument of scholarship in seven volumes providing parallel Irish and English texts for AM 2242–AD 1616, systematically omitting however both the chronological apparatus in Arabic numerals and the entire apparatus for all those years without entries. Up to 1171 O'Donovan used O'Conor's edition collated with RIA 988–9 and TCD 1279, while for the remainder he used MS P collated with MS H. A facsimile edition of O'Donovan's edition was reissued in 1966. Earlier in 1882 Henri Lizeray published a French translation extending up to 432.[124]

Summary

Reviewing the ten accounts above it can be seen that considerable development took place in the compilation of the Annals between the eleventh and the seventeenth century. Textually they went from multiple columns with continuous text on vellum with enlarged ornamented capitals used to define paragraphs to uniformly-sized text with modest unornamented capitals written on paper in a single column using line breaks between years. The chronological apparatus went from kalend+ferial, to kalend+ferial+epact+AD, to kalend+'aois in Tigerna', to a bare 'Aois Criost'. Entry numbers increased from a couple per annum up to dozens. When the transitions in these conventions are examined some historical horizons appear, the arrival of Christianity in Ireland, the reign of Brian Bóruma, the Norman invasion and the battle of Kinsale. These horizons will reappear in the forthcoming chapters.

---

123 O'Curry, *MM*, 168 (cit.), cf. Jennings, *Michael O Clerigh*, 119–24.   124 Editions: O'Conor, *Rerum Hib.* iii; Connellan, *Annals of Ireland*; O'Donovan, *FM* i–vii; Lizeray, *Quatre maîtres*.

CHAPTER THREE

Annalistic literature

The purpose of this chapter is to review what conclusions scholarship has developed and maintained regarding the question of how these Annals were assembled into the form we now find them. Since the Annalistic genre was introduced at an early stage into the culture of Gaelic scholarship and it was there that it flourished, it is appropriate to begin by examining what Gaelic scholars stated concerning their origin and assembly. However, following the overwhelming of the remaining strongholds of Gaelic culture in Connacht and Ulster by the English armies following the battle of Kinsale in 1601, the manuscripts of many of the important Annals quickly transferred into the possession of Anglo-Irish scholars. Following this, in the enlarging English political and cultural domination of the British Isles, what those Anglo-Irish scholars thought and wrote about these Annals played a crucial role in determining the view of them by their contemporaries and immediate successors. Subsequently, from around the middle of the nineteenth century, scholars brought more modern techniques to the examination and analysis of these works. Hence this review is presented under the three headings, Gaelic, Anglo-Irish, and modern scholarship.

Gaelic Annalistic scholarship

It is in the nature of chronicles that they offer little scope for their compiler to document his sources from within his compilation. The customary place for such information is instead a preface, which arrangement was employed by Eusebius in his chronicle, where his first book, the *Chronography*, functioned as a preface wherein he identified and discussed his sources at length. These sources he then compiled in his second book, the *Chronological Canons*, into his innovative, parallel, synchronized chronicle of the Old World and its kingdoms, and to this he prefixed a further short preface giving an account of the compilation. Subsequently, Jerome, while dispensing with the *Chronography* and translating only the *Canons*, provided a preface into which he incorporated a Latin translation of Eusebius' short preface, adding a brief account of his own compilation.[1] In the case of the Irish Annals we have just three prefaces, viz.

---

1 Helm, *Hieronymus – die Chronik*, 1–19 (Jerome's preface); Schoene, *Eusebi Chronicorum* i, 1–296

those in CS, MB and FM, although since the primary MSS for AT, AU, AI and AB are all acephalous it is possible that prefaces may have been lost from them, but we have no evidence for this. As well as prefaces we sometimes find occasional interjections by the compiler in which he briefly remarks upon his source, usually simply citing the author's name. Finally, consideration of the larger characteristics of the MSS, such as their media and size, the skill of their scribes, and the quality of their decoration, reveals something of the status accorded them by the communities that commissioned and read them. These three aspects, the prefaces, interjections, and production of the Annalistic manuscripts will be considered.

The preface to CS immediately follows the title, which it explains, and it reads in translation as follows:[2]

> Understand, Reader, that for a certain reason, and plainly to avoid tediousness, what we desire is to make a short Abstract and Compendium of the History of the Scoti (*airisin na Scot*) only in this copy, leaving out the lengthened details of the Books of History (*leapar airisin*); wherefore it is we entreat of you not to reproach us therefor, as we know that it is an exceedingly great deficiency.

As can be seen while this briefly acknowledges the compiler's proposed abridgement of his source the primary purpose of his preface was to apologize for this abridgement. Regarding his compilation, collation does indeed show CS to contain an abridged version of the Irish origin legend and the Clonmacnoise chronicle, which this compiler has identified simply as 'History of the Scoti' and 'Books of History'. While these identifications are clearly of a very generalized character it does appear that the 'Scoti' qualification carried the connotation of authoritative, early northern history, for we find interjections elsewhere which attribute authoritative early northern material to the 'Scoti'. For example, the additional obit for S. Patrick in AU 491.1 reads, 'Dicunt Scoiti hic Patricium archiepiscopum defunctum fore.' This addition to AU synchronizes with the only obit for Patrick found in the Clonmacnoise chronicle at 491. A much more substantial source with a northern provenance is identified with the 'Scots' in AT in the well known interjections added to the entry which synchronizes Cimbáed's reign at Emain with the eighteenth year of Ptolomy [Soter]:[3]

> In anno .xuiii. Ptolomei fuit initiatus regnare in Emain Cimbæd filius Fintain, qui regnauit .xxuiii. annis. Tunc Echu Buadach pater Úgaine in Temoria regnase ab aliis fertur liquet praescripsimus ollim Úgaine imperasse. Omnia monimenta Scottorum usque Cimbæd incerta errant.

(*Liber prior – Chronography*). **2** Hennessy, *CS*, xxviii–xxix, 2–3 (cit.), cf. Ó Muraíle, *Celebrated antiquary*, 99 and O'Curry, *MM*, 127. **3** Stokes, *AT* i, 24 (cit.).

> In the eighteenth year of Ptolemy, Cimbáed son of Fintan, who reigned twenty-eight years, began reigning in Emain. While others have held that at this time Eochu Buadach father of Úgaine reigned in Tara, we have written that Úgaine reigned earlier. All the [written] monuments of the Scots until Cimbáed were [chronologically] uncertain.

In his first interjection this compiler has acknowledged the existence of a current conflict regarding the chronology of the kingship of Tara, cf. 'others have held' vs 'we have written'. Hence the context of his second interjection, 'All the monuments of the Scots until Cimbáed were uncertain', is chronological. Thus the uncertainty indicated was chronological, i.e. not *whether* these named individuals ruled, but *when* they ruled. Moreover, it is implicit that this compiler trusted the chronology of the 'monimenta Scottorum' for the regnal succession for Emain henceforth, because a sustained succession of kings of Emain ensues in AT from *c.*313 BC. On the other hand, the regnal succession of Tara does not commence in AT until AD 49. It is clear therefore that this compiler considered 'monimenta Scottorum' as authoritative for the regnal succession of Emain from Cimbáed on. It appears therefore that when the compiler of CS referred to his source as 'History of the Scoti', it was their authoritative early northern material that he wished to emphasize and he did this by entitling his compilation 'Chronicum Scottorum'.

Turning next to MB, the preface that Conall Mageoghagan addressed to Terence Coghlan and placed before his translation and dated 20 April 1627 is by comparison with that of CS very forthcoming, but too long to cite in full so a paraphrase must suffice. It commences with a panegyric on the accomplishments of Brian Bóruma †1014, and asserts that Brian had initiated the compilation at Cashel of 'the psalter of Cashell', which work is described as 'a booke containing all the Inhabitants euents and scepts that lived in this land from the first peopleing ... untill that present.' Copies of this, signed by Brian, bishops and prelates, were given to the provincial kings with the charge that, 'there should be noe credit giuen to any other Chronicles thenceforth, but [they] should be held as false, Disannulled & quite forbidden for ever.' Mageoghagan then states that since that time there were many, 'whose profession was to Chronicle and keep in memory the state of the K[ing]dome as well for the time past present & to come.' But now, i.e. in 1627, he says that because these historians 'cañot enjoy that respect & gaine by their said profession as heretofore they neglect their Bookes, and choose rather to put their children to learne eng[lish].' This last passage gives a graphic and convincing picture of the collapse of the profession of hereditary historians in post-Kinsale Gaelic society. Mageoghagan concludes by stating that it was Coghlan's interest in history that 'made me to undertake the translating of the ould Irish booke for you.'[4]

4 Murphy, *AC*, 7–9 (cits.).

Thus Mageoghagan's preface represents that a major compilation entitled the 'psalter of Cashell' initiated by Brian Bóruma and intended to supersede earlier chronicles had been distributed widely and authoritatively in Brian's time. Now Pádraig Ó Riain, in his careful assessment of the evidence concerning the compilation of the 'psalter of Cashel' regarded this attribution by Mageoghagan to Brian as the 'more likely, but as yet untested, view', than the traditional attribution of the Psalter to Cormac mac Cuileannán †908.[5] And indeed the examination of the development of the regnal-canon presented in chapter 10 confirms that its origins lay in a comprehensive early eleventh-century Munster compilation of Irish regnal series. Since this canon provided the chronological basis for MB and FM and the chronicles LG and CG, there are good grounds to accept the substance of Mageoghagan's account of its origin. As well as this Mageoghagan included effectively a second preface in which he identified the following list of authors whose works had been incorporated into his source, the 'old Irish booke'.[6]

> The names of the severall authors wch I have taken for this booke: Saint Colum Kill, sainte bohine, Collogh O'More Esqr, venerable Bede, Eoghye O'Flannagan arch dean of Ardmach and Clonfiachna, Gillernew Mac Con ne mboght, arch-priest of Cloniuckenos, Keilachar Mac Coñ alŝ Gorman, Eusebius[,] Marcellinus, [Moylin] O'Mulchonrye and Tanaige O'Mulconrye, 2 professed Chroniclers.

This list is arranged anachronistically, giving priority to the two saints, the first two abbots of Iona, followed by Collogh O'More, Mageoghagan's contemporary, and for the majority of the names listed there is independent evidence that they indeed served as contributors to the 'old Irish booke', as will be shown in chapter 10. Overall the details of Mageoghagan's prefatory material reconciles accurately both with his translation and the evidence we have concerning the development of the regnal-canon.

Turning next to the short and long prefaces of FM, these have already been mentioned above and will be discussed fully in chapter 11, p. 328 ff.[7] Regarding sources, they agree on the following list having been employed for the compilation extending to 1333: a) the book of Cluain-mic-Nois, blessed by S. Ciaran, son of the carpenter; b) the book of the Island of Saints, in Loch Ribh; c) the book of Seanadh Mic Maghnusa, in Loch Erne; d) the book of the Clann Ua Maelchonaire; e) the book of the O'Duigenans of Kilronan.[8] Of these sources

---

5 Ó Riain, 'Psalter of Cashel', 126–8 (Mageoghagan). 6 Murphy, *AC*, 10, but I read 'Moylin' and 'old' with BL Add. 4817 f. 4^v instead of Murphy's 'McOylyne' and 'ould'. 7 O'Donovan, *FM* i, pp. lxiv–v (long preface); Walsh, *Gleanings*, 75 (short preface). 8 Gwynn, 'Cathal Mac Magnusa', 370, 'the Book of Seanadh Mhic Mhaghuire is beyond any doubt the A-text [TCD 1282] of the Annals of Ulster'.

we can identify a) as a member of the Clonmacnoise group, c) as TCD 1282 of AU, and d–e) as members of the Connacht group, and the additional four sources listed in the long preface may be similarly identified. Considered together a common characteristic of these prefaces is that all three identify the compilation of sources which are never named as 'annals', but rather as 'history', 'books of history', or 'chronicles' Together they identify sources attributed to 'Scoti' which were regarded as authoritative for early northern history, another associated with the monastery of Clonmacnoise, another associated with the first abbots of Iona, and others associated with the Uí Maoil Chonaire, Uí Duibhgeannáin, and Meic Maghnusa. All these identifications can be shown to reconcile closely with medieval compilations whose existence is known independently.

Next we consider interjections into the entries, which may arise when a compiler wishes to identify or emphasize the authority of an entry, or to contrast two conflicting sources, as the above example of 'monimenta Scottorum' illustrates. Of all the Annals AT possesses by far the most such identifying interjections, attributing entries to the following authors: Josephus †*c.*100, Tertulian †*c.*225, Julius Africanus †*c.*240, Eusebius †*c.*340, Jerome †420, Orosius †*p.*417, Marcellinus †*c.*534, Isidore †636, Bede †735, and Tigernach †1088. As well as this the following Biblical authors are identified with interjections: Ezra, Judith, Isaiah (Essaias), Jeremiah (Heremias), Ezekial (Ezechal), Daniel, and Zachariah (Zacharias). The majority of these interjections are found in the first four folios of Rawl. B. 502, i.e. up to the time of Darius king of Persia, and most of them and their associated entries are found, virtually verbatim, in Bede's DTR cap. 66. Furthermore, since DTR cap. 66 also shows a corresponding decline in interjections synchronized to that in Rawl. B. 502, this was evidently a feature of their common source. Some of these interjections show that their compiler was critically comparing the chronology of his sources.[9] For example, consider the following, where Eusebius, Julius Africanus, and Jerome are all collated:[10]

> AT 13d: **Eusebius ait** annos .xxx. ab euersione Hierusalem usque ad initium Cirii Regis Persarum. **Iulius autem Africanus** .lxx. annos computat. **Hieronymus autem in tractatu Danielis ait:** Tradunt Ebrei huiusmodi fabulam usque ad septuagissimum annum …

---

9 These authors' interjections may all be located in Stokes, *AT*, by means of Index 3 in Ó Murchadha, *Index*, 199–214, and the parallel entries in Bede's DTR cap. 66 may be located by means of the index in Wallis, *Reckoning*, 465–79. Byrne, 'Ut Beda boat', 46–56 reproduces a substantial number of these interjections in full.   10 Stokes, *AT* i, 13 and cf. Jones, *CM*, 483 §150; cf. also O'Conor, *Bibliotheca* i, 193 n. 1.

However, not all of AT's interjections are found in DTR cap. 66, for example the following citations from Tertulian and Josephus are unique to AT:

AT 66:   Nero Iohannem apostulum in doleum feruentis olei missit, **ut Tertulianus ait** ...

AT 71:   Templum soló strauit. Regnum Iudeorum subuertit. Urbi undecies centum milia capta esse et ducta **Euseppus perhibet.**

While for its part DTR cap. 66 has interjections not found in AT, viz.,

DTR §149:   **Consentit his Iosephus in Antiquitatum libro scribens** ...
Huius Darii **Daniehl ipse ita meminit:** In anno primo Darii ...

Together these AT-unique and DTR-unique interjections show that both these texts are derived from a common source, which was more substantial than either of them. I have shown this source to be a compilation made by Rufinus of Aquileia †c.410, sometime between c.402 and 410, and this compilation will be discussed further in chapter 4, p. 125 ff.[11] Thus the interjections up to c.400 referring to the early Jewish and Christian authors up to and including Jerome are the work of Rufinus in the course of compiling his chonicle. Regarding the Annalistic interjections citing Orosius, Marcellinus, and Isidore we will see in the next chapter that their three chronicles provided a late seventh-century extension of the imperial succession from Valentinianus †375 to Heraclius †641. This imperial extension is found in both the Annals and Bede's chronicles, and some annals have interjections appropriately identifying some of the regnal citations. In the case of Orosius his regnal series was collated back into pre-Christian times and differences and identities noted with interjections and interpolations. It is important then to understand that the process of collation with and interpolation from the works of Orosius, Marcellinus and Isidore, took place *after* Rufinus' compilation and *before* Bede's compilation of DT in 703.

Regarding the Annalistic interjections referring to Bede the earliest that these are attested is in AT Rawl. B. 502, and since these interjections substantially influenced modern Annalistic scholarship, it is appropriate to examine them here. In Rawl. B. 502 there are seven such interjections, five incorporated into the text and two written interlinearly, all by the same scribe.[12] Of these, two retrieve chronological details and four retrieve passages either transmitted or composed by Bede, but omitted in the Annalistic transmission. The seventh

---

11 Mc Carthy, 'Status', 140–2 (Rufinus' chronicle).   12 Bedan interjections in Rawl. B. 502 and their source in DTR cap. 66: 1) AT 7b – DTR §128; 2) AT 11c – DTR §138; 3) AT 13c – DTR §149; 4) AT 1 – DTR §7; 5) AT 1 – DTR §268; 6) AT 7 – DTR §269; 7) AT 46 – DTR §284. Rawl. B. 488: AT 539 – not in DTR.

remarks a semantic conflict between AT and DTR cap. 66, and it consequently explicitly signals a process of critical collation.[13] And indeed collation of AT against DTR shows many interpolations from DTR, some of which have either duplicated or displaced imperial regnal entries. It is clear then that this major phase of interpolation took place *after* Bede's compilation of DTR in 725 and *before* Rawl. B. 502 was written in the late eleventh century. As has been mentioned already, it is clear that collation of Rawl. B. 502 and DTR cap. 66 was in progress at the time the MS was written, cf. the Bedan interjections reproduced in plates 2–3. Finally in AT 1088.2 we have the influential interjection 'Huc us*que* Tigernach scr*i*bsit o*cht*.ar.o*chtmogait* quieuit', and as will be discussed in chapter 6 this obit refers to Tigernach Ua Braein †1088, *comharba* of Ciaran and Comain, and its significance will there be examined in detail, cf. p. 191 ff.

Turning next to AU we find as well as the interjections referring to Marcellinus and Isidore it presents some unique interjections of its own that refer to Bede, Liber Monachorum, Cuana, and Dub dá Leithe, as well as many anonymous instances, e.g. 'secundum alios', or 'alii dicunt'. The Bedan interjections are mostly attached to entries registering the papal or imperial successions over the fifth and sixth centuries, and those attached to the former are demonstrably incorrect. For example:[14]

> AU 432.1: Patritius peruenit ad Hiberniam nono anno regni Teodosii Minoris, primo anno episcopatus Xisti xl.ii. episcopi Romane Æclesie. **Sic enumerant Beda 7 Marcillinus 7 Issiodorus in Cronicis suis.**

But neither Isidore nor Bede's chronicles register the papacy of Xystus. Similarly at AU 440 and 460 details of Xystus' and Leo's deaths are incorrectly attributed to Bede. These interjections then are not by a compiler identifying his sources, but rather they appear to be attempts to emphasize the authority of these papal entries. Two AU entries have interjections 'secundum Liber Monachorum', viz. AU 511.4 and 527.3, and since both entries are found nearly verbatim in the Clonmacnoise group there are good grounds to identify 'Liber Monachorum' with a copy of the Clonmacnoise chronicle.[15] Next I consider AU's unique series of thirteen interjections between AU 467 and AU 628 which reference either 'Cuana' or 'Liber Cuanach', cf. Figure 23, p. 198. Both their

---

13 Mc Carthy, 'Status', 128–9 (semantic conflict). The single additional interjection found in Rawl. B. 488, 'ut Beda boath', cf. Stokes, *AT* i, 96, attached to the notice of pope Vigilius' reign taken from *Liber Pontificalis*, is like some AU interjections erroneous since Vigilius is not found in either Bede's DTR cap. 66 or HE.   14 Marcellinus, Isidore and Bede interjections at AU 432, 440, 449, 456, 535, 565, 583, 616.   15 All AU editions render AU 527.3 as 'Librum Mochod', but examination of TCD 1282 shows that while indeed it has been retraced as 'Mochod', it was initially written by Ua Caiside as 'Monachorum' using the same suspensions as he employed for AU 511.4.

style and the fact that Ua Caiside made textual emendations to some of these interjections show that he had inscribed them into his primary source, from whence Ua Luinín transcribed them. One of them shows clearly that Ua Caiside was engaged in critically comparing the chronology of his primary source and Liber Cuanach, for he wrote:

> AU 602.3: Omnia quae scripta sunt in anno subsequente, inveni in Libro Cuanach in isto esse perfecta.

I have identified the compiler of this 'Liber Cuanach' as Cuán Ua Lothcháin †1024, and it appears that he compiled it in *c.*1022, which compilation will be discussed in more detail in chapter 7.[16] Regarding the interjections referring to Dub dá Leithe these are at AU 629, 962, 1003 and 1020, and Dub dá Leithe was identified by Mac Niocaill as the lector at Armagh for 1046–9 and *comharba* there for 1049–64, cf. Figure 28, p. 225.[17] Finally regarding the many anonymous interjections in Ua Luinín's hand in AU TCD 1282, collation with the interjections in Ua Caiside's many interpolated entries leads me to conclude that he is author of most of them. They arose because when compiling AU Ua Caiside interpolated entries into his primary source and included his characteristic interjection, and Ua Luinín subsequently copied these.

Next I consider the evidence implicit in the MSS themselves. The MSS of AI and AT, Rawl. B. 503 and 502, show that by the late eleventh and early twelfth centuries the Annals had attained a formidable status in the intellectual and cultural life of literate Gaelic society. For these volumes are very high-quality book productions, written and decorated by skilled scribes to a high standard. The entries are dense and the chronological apparatus of the Christian era, whilst apparently slight, is in fact subtle and precise, and with its repeated decoration was clearly celebrated by both the scribe and the informed readers alike. These productions are the confident statements of a mature and self-assured chronicling culture, regularly expressing the entries relating to Irish affairs in Irish, but equally competent in Latin, and confidently integrating Irish personal and placenames into this Latin.[18] In the fourteenth century, as represented by the Rawl. B. 488 MS of AT, the same production skill and self-assurance is evident, and although the pre-Christian text has suffered attrition and the Latinity has waned, the number of entries per annum and inclusion of secular events in the later centuries have increased very considerably. By the late

---

16 AU 467, 468, 471, 475, 482, 489, 544, 552, 598, 600, 602, 610, 628 (Cuana interjections); Byrne, 'Ut Beda boat', 57–67 (Cuana entries). Mc Carthy, 'AU apparatus 82–1019', 279–81 (identification of AU's 'Cuana' with Cuán Ua Lothcháin).   17 Mac Niocaill, *MIA*, 20 (Dub dá Leithe). 18 Dumville, 'Latin and Irish', 323–4, referring to personal names, 'in the great majority of cases (and from the very first) they [annalists] resorted to natural native forms of expression.'

fifteenth century, as represented by the part of TCD 1282 of AU written by Ua Luinín, the pre-Palladian text has been very significantly eroded and substantial spaces were left between the post-Palladian entries, suggesting that the compiler Ua Caiside considered their text to be incomplete. Moreover, kalend loss resulted in the AD chronology for AU 438–1012, 1193–1372 being in error from one to five years. Thus whilst the text was very skilfully written by Ua Luinín, and the scale of the manuscript impressive, the decoration is more modest, and there is evident a significant decline in both the status of their manuscript and the ability of the compiler. This decline is even more conspicuous in the character of the extensions to Rawl. B. 489 compiled during the later life of Ua Caiside over 1505–41, which cease shortly after his death. Subsequently, in the later sixteenth century, the writing, decoration, and size of the manuscripts of the Connacht group of annals all exhibit a very substantial decline. Finally, in the seventeenth century, MB and FM abandoned the kalend apparatus and FM introduced its own esoteric chronology, which is far inferior to that of any earlier annalistic text. Both have suffered severe attrition in the earlier Christian centuries, and FM entries are also often distorted semantically. These compilations are but pale shadows of the accomplished editions produced from the late eleventh to the fourteenth century.

Anglo-Irish Annalistic scholarship and its legacy

The two names that dominate Annalistic studies for the first six decades of the seventeenth century are James Ussher and James Ware. Both men were born into essentially English families that had settled relatively recently into sixteenth-century Dublin, and which families had established powerful ecclesiastical and secular connections in Ireland. Both men were educated at Trinity College, Dublin, and their subsequent scholarly interests played a crucial role in determining the ultimate fate of the majority of the most important Annalistic manuscripts, and scholarship's understanding of their significance.

James Ussher (1581–1656) was one of the first students at Trinity College when it opened in 1594, graduating in 1597, and taking his Master of Arts in 1600, whereupon he was appointed a Fellow and first Proctor to the College, and subsequently professor of Divinity in 1607. While there was religious division in his parents' backgrounds, Ussher grew up a deeply informed and ardent supporter of the Reformed Church, with a profound knowledge of early Christian texts and history. To this interest he brought a critical perception of both philological and chronological aspects of textual studies, and a willingness to apply the emerging disciplines of the Renaissance to his textual and historical studies. His instinct was to read widely across all sides of a subject, and, shortly after his appointment as Proctor, fate favoured him in an unexpected way, when, following the battle of Kinsale in 1601, the victorious English army donated the then enormous sum of £1800 to the nascent Trinity College for the development of its library. With this, Ussher, only in his early twenties, together with Dr Chaloner, spent the next decade acquiring books from all over Western Europe.[19] That for Ussher this campaign also included Irish books and manuscripts is made clear by his letter to his uncle Richard Stanihurst in Louvain, written evidently sometime before 1606, in which Ussher stated that he was engaged 'in gathering together the scattered antiquities of our nation; whereof I doubt not but many relics are come into your hands, which I would very willingly hear of.' To this Ussher added a request for a list of Irish historical books and a manuscript of a life of S. Patrick, a 'manuscript whereof I have much desired'.[20] As well as having access to substantial fiscal resources to realize these desires, Ussher had the further advantage of his powerful family connections, including his uncle Henry Ussher †1613, who was at the time archbishop of Armagh. Ussher's first published references to Irish Annals, and his first application of the word 'annales' to them, are found in his 'Corbes, Herenaches and Termon Lands', written in 1609, wherein he twice cited the 'Annales Ultonienses' in such a way as to show he had examined the text very carefully.[21] Details of his correspondence with David Rothe, the Catholic bishop of Ossory, show that he was using the TCD 1282 text of AU, and by 1619 he referred to this text as 'my Ulster annales'.[22] Thus less than two decades after Kinsale the most substantial collection of annals known to have been produced by fifteenth-century Gaelic scholarship had passed into Anglo-Irish possession.

Ussher's interest in the Annals was principally confined to their historical information and in his account of the early Insular Church published in 1639, *Britannicarum Ecclesiarum Antiquitates*, he cited many entries from AT, AU and AI.[23] In this Ussher brought to bear his formidable critical faculties to evaluate the reliability of the sources that he employed. In particular, Ussher cited the computation of the Jesuit chronographer, Dionysius Petavius, for the solar

19 Elrington, *Life of Ussher* in *Whole works* i, 23–9 (Ussher & Chaloner).   20 Ussher, 'Letters' in *Whole works* xv, 4 (cit.). The letter is not dated but was placed by Elrington before Ussher's letter to William Camden on 20 October 1606.   21 Ussher, 'Corbes' in *Whole works* xi, 423, 432–3 for AU citations which he annotated respectively 'ex Ultoniensibus annalibus' and 'Annal. Ulton'. In the former, Ussher correctly located the duplicate obits of Feichín of Fobhar at AU 664 and 667, and in the latter he correctly identified 'Imfeathna' (recte Fethgna) as the first-named *comharba* of Patrick in AU 868.3, and he also accurately summarized AU 920.1. His English paraphrase of AU 858.2–3 is, however, inaccurate in its details.   22 O'Sullivan, 'Correspondence', 11, 37 (Rothe).   23 Ussher, *Antiquitates*, in *Whole works* vi, AT: 145, 147, 235, 246, 610; AU: 146, 256, 261, 278, 416, 421–2, 430, 437–8, 444–5, 447, 484, 514–15, 532–4, 536, 540, 542, 610, 697; AI: 370, 401, 404, 470, 523, 538.

eclipse of 664 wherein he calculated that, when viewed from London, mid-eclipse had occurred at 4.12 pm on 1 May 664. This use by Ussher of a result from the emerging discipline of orbital mechanics, based upon the experimentally founded laws of planetary motion of Johannes Kepler †1630, was characteristic of him. It demonstrated on the one hand that the record of the date of this eclipse in the Irish Annals was accurate, and on the other hand it showed that Bede's account of this eclipse in his chronicles in DT and DTR, and his *Historia ecclesiastica*, were systematically incorrect. Ussher wrote:[24]

> Astronomical calculation shows that Bede was deceived in designating the eclipse which preceded this plague to that day [3 May], and that that darkness happened on 1 May as our Annals say.

Thus Ussher's contribution served in general to raise a serious question mark regarding the accuracy of Bede's chronology and his works on time, the authority of which had been accepted widely across Europe virtually since Bede's death in the eighth century. In particular, since in his *Historia ecclesiastica* Bede had repeatedly linked this eclipse with the synod of Whitby, Ussher's observation also raised a serious doubt regarding the accuracy of Bede's account of this synod, so crucial to the subsequent ecclesiastical history of the British Isles. On the other hand, Ussher's identification of the accurate Annalistic record of this eclipse pointed to the Irish Annals preserving accurate records of other early Insular events.[25] Thus even though Ussher expressed no interest in the history of the Annals themselves, his identification and use of them as an accurate historical source served to stimulate the interest of other scholars, and in particular that of his student at Trinity College Dublin, James Ware. Furthermore, in initiating both the collection of Irish historical MSS, and the critical study of their historical and chronological significance at Trinity College Dublin, Ussher founded a tradition there that has endured to the present day.

James Ware (1594–1666) graduated from Trinity College in 1616 and it seems certain that by this time he already shared both Ussher's friendship and interest in Irish history in general, and in the Annals in particular, because just four years later he wrote in familiar and affectionate terms to Ussher enclosing a list of Annalistic obits of bishops of Armagh. This list Ware had obtained from 'an ould M S. (wch as I take it might be fitly called the annals of the North, as treating thereof principally).'[26] This 'ould M S.' is readily identifiable as the Rawl. B. 489 transcript of TCD 1282, already in Ussher's possession, and it is

24 Petavius, *De doctrina*, 855–6 (eclipse calculation); Ussher, *Antiquitates*, 515–16 (citation translated by Dr Jennifer Moreton, pers. communication September, 1996.) 25 Mc Carthy & Breen, 'Astronomical observations', 12, 24–30, 41–2, and idem, 'Evaluation', 122, 128–32 (eclipse and synod of Whitby). 26 Ó Muraíle, *Celebrated antiquary*, 248–51, and O'Sullivan, 'Finding

clear from Ware's proposal of the title, 'Annals of the North', that he had absorbed Ussher's principles of Annalistic nomenclature but did not realize that his MS was largely a transcript of Ussher's copy, already named by him as the 'Annals of Ulster'. While it is not certain that Ware owned Rawl B 489 at this time, since its name does not appear in the first list of his MSS made in c.1625, in the subsequent years Ware accumulated a large library of valuable MSS, including many unique texts of enormous importance for the study of Irish history.[27] Thanks to Ware's notebooks and O'Sullivan's careful bibliographical research we can follow the sequence of this accumulation in some detail.[28] Restricting our attention to his collection of Irish Annals this shows that by c.1627 Ware was in possession of Rawl. B. 488, 489, and 503, i.e. primary MSS for AT, AU and AI, so that in his early thirties Ware owned the primary MSS for the most substantial Clonmacnoise and Cuana group texts. By 1648, when he published a comprehensive catalogue of his collection, he had further acquired Rawl. B. 502, the earlier text for AT, the L4 section of LC, a transcript of AB, Latin translations of AU from 431 to 1172, as well as many annalistic fragments, some now lost. That Ware himself placed very high value on his MSS of AU and AT, is suggested by his placing of Rawl. B. 489, 488 and 502 at positions two, three and five respectively in his list of fifty-five 'Libri Historici, Politici et Geographici'.

Ware's repeated annotations on these MSS show that he was no mere collector of chronicles but was deeply interested in their entries, and moreover he digested these into twelve books which he published over 1626–65, of which all except one dealt with Irish history. In most of these works Ware used his annals simply as historical sources, however in *De scriptoribus Hiberniae* published in 1639 he gave an account of authors who had flourished before 1600 and had written on Irish affairs. He was prompted, he wrote in his preface, 'Ut verò hanc, pro virili, ornarem Spartam, praeter libros impressos, multos etiam vetares codicis manuscriptos, qui ad rem facerent, non indiligenter evolvi.'[29] This work, together with his account of his own MSS in his 1648 catalogue, played a seminal role in subsequent Annalistic scholarship because in both of them Ware set forth briefly and clearly what he believed regarding the compilation of the most important Annalistic texts. Consequently, it is necessary to review what Ware stated in some detail. Regarding the annals in Rawl B 488 Ware wrote in *De scriptoribus*:[30]

list', 69–70 (Ware). Mc Carthy, 'AU compilation', 89–90 (Ware's letter of 20 Sept. 1620 to Ussher). 27 O'Sullivan, 'Finding list', 72 (counts ninety-three MSS), 78–83 (concordance of Ware's MSS). 28 O'Sullivan, 'Finding list', 71–2 (Ware's earlier MS lists), 84–99 (1648 catalogue). 29 Ware, *De scriptoribus*, [iii] (cit.). 30 Ware, *De scriptoribus*, 51 (cit.).

Tigernacus antiquitatum Hibernicarum diligens indagator, Scripsit *Hiberniae annales*, quos perduxit usque ad annum Domini 1088. Id quod ex authore vetusto, qui continuavit dictos annales liquet. Non possum non autumare hunc fuisse Tigernacum O Broin *Airenachum* sive Erenachum Clonmacnoisensem, quem eo anno obijsse produnt annales Ultonienses. Nam conveniunt & tempora & nomina. Annales ejus, & anonymi qui eos continuavit MSS[os]. habeo.

Thus Ware cited AU 1088.3 to identify 'Tigernacus' with Tigernach Ua Braein, whose death as erenagh of Clonmacnoise is recorded there, and he construed this Tigernach as the sole careful compiler ('diligens indagator') of all the entries in Rawl. B. 488 up to 1088, and ascribed the remainder to a singular anonymous author. This summary judgement regarding the compilation of the principal primary MS of the Clonmacnoise group rested on just four words in Rawl. B. 488 f. 19[r], 'Huc usque Tigernach scribsit', and it was to exert a powerful influence on the subsequent development of Annalistic scholarship. In his catalogue of 1648 Ware repeated this attribution, making it absolutely explicit that he believed Tigernach had compiled all the world history and pre-Patrician entries, writing:[31]

> Annales Tigernaci o Broin Erenachi Clonmacnoisenesis, in quibus Author historiam Universalem attingit usq; ad adventum S. Patricij. Inde verò res Hibernicas usq; ad annum Christi 1088. quo obiit, satis diligenter describit. Liber meus MS. caret principio, & incipit à morte Alexandri Magni.

Thus in these brief accounts Ware simply asserted that a major compilation of annals had been accomplished at Clonmacnoise by Tigernach and truncated by his death in 1088. On the other hand, his catalogue entry for the earliest MS of AT, Rawl. B. 502, stated: 'Annales ab Urbe condita ad imperium usque Anonini Pii Characteribus Hibernicis, in fol. membr. Caetera desunt in MS. meo. Huius Libri ignoratur Author.'[32] Both his statement here that no author was known for this MS, and his remark cited above in respect of Rawl. B. 488, 'Liber meus MS. caret principio', show that Ware had not recognized these as two descendants from a common source.

Regarding the compilation of AU, which he repeatedly employed and acknowledged in *De scriptoribus* as source for the obits of his writers, Ware was noticeably more vague. Citing 'Annal. Ulton.', he wrote of Cathal Mac Maghnusa, whose obit is recorded at AU 1498, as follows:[33]

> Carolus Magwirius patriâ Fermanachanus ecclesiæ Armachanæ canonicus, historicus insignis. Scripsit *annales Hiberniae* usque ad sua tempora. Obijt 20. Cal. April. anno Domini 1498. ætatis suæ 60.

---

31 O'Sullivan, 'Finding list', 87 (cit.).   32 O'Sullivan, 'Finding list', 87 (cit.).   33 Ware, *De scriptoribus*, 77 (cit.).

It appears that Ware considered Mac Maghnusa the scribe of AU up to his own time, and he must therefore have been thinking of TCD 1282 which shows a conspicuous change of hands at 1489; he could not have made such a statement in respect of Rawl. B. 489, since it does not exhibit any change of hand in Mac Maghnusa's time. Of Ruaidhrí Ua Luinín, whose obit and role in writing Rawl. B. 489 is recorded there at AU 1528, Ware had nothing to say. However, of Ua Luinín's colleague, Ruaidhrí Ua Caiside, he wrote, 'scripsit posteriorem partem annalium Ultonensium, una cum varijs interpolationibus prioris partis.' This description must also refer to TCD 1282, since only it exhibits diverse inter-polations in its first part, and the abovementioned change of hands at 1489 is to that of Ua Caiside.[34] Thus in 1639, Ware, while accurately describing Ua Caiside's scribal contribution to TCD 1282, was either uninformed about, or chose to pass over, Ua Luinín's role in the compilation of the two AU manu-scripts, both of which Ware had used but whose separate existence he did not acknowledge.[35] When in 1648 he came to catalogue Rawl. B. 489, he wrote:[36]

> Annales Hiberniae, partim Latinè, partim Hibernice, descripti, ab anno Domini 431 usq; ad annum 1541. quo obiit Rodericus Cassidaeus Archideaconus Clochorensis, qui scripsit dictorum Annalium partem posteriorem. Hi vulgò Annales Ultonienses appellantur, quia praecipuè continent res gestas Ultoniensium. in fol. membr.

Here Ware's first assertion can only refer to Rawl. B. 489, whose range commences at 431 and whose entries, except for lacunae, extend continuously to 1541, where indeed Ua Caiside's obit is found. However, Ware's subsequent con-tention that Ua Caiside was the scribe of the last part of this text shows that he had confused this MS with TCD 1282. Thus both of Ware's accounts of AU show confusion on his part concerning the compilers, their roles, and the two MSS.

Regarding Cuana and the role of 'Liber Cuanach' in the compilation of AU, Ware wrote:[37]

> In annalibus Ultoniensibus sæpe citatum invenio *Librum Cuana* al. *Cuanachi* usque ad annum Dom. 628. sed non posteà. unde conjicio eum authorem Chronici fuisse, & sub hoc tempore floruisse, si author recentior, forte vel *Cuana* ille fuit, qui in jam dictis annalibus *Cuana nepos Bessani scriba Treoit* appellatur & obijsse dicitur. an. 738. vel *Cuana* ille *sapiens & episcopus de Lugmai* qui in iisdem annalibus obijsse dicitur, anno 824. Sed de hac re nihil definio.

---

34 Mc Carthy, 'AU compilation', 75 (Ua Caiside as scribe). 35 Ware, *De scriptoribus*, 83 (Ua Caiside); Mc Carthy, 'AU compilation', 73–7 (scribes of TCD 1282); Gwynn, 'Lynch's *Praesulibus*', 46 (Ware's use of both MSS). 36 O'Sullivan, 'Finding list', 86–7 (cit.). 37 Ware, *De scriptoribus*, 19 (cit. with italic thus).

Thus all of Ware's hypotheses concerning 'Cuana' placed him in the Old Irish period, not later than the first quarter of the ninth century, which hypotheses, notwithstanding the complete absence of any justification and indeed Ware's *caveat*, 'nihil definio', have proved subsequently influential. Thus in these accounts of AT and AU Ware made a series of clear but unsupported statements regarding their compilation, which were to prove extremely influential on subsequent scholarship. Unfortunately, in respect of the roles of Tigernach, Cuana and Mac Maghnusa, Ware was seriously mistaken, as shall be discussed in due course.[38]

Regarding AI, because he had no putative author, Ware did not include mention of it in *De scriptoribus*, but in his catalogue of 1648 he did provide a brief account of its compilation, as follows:[39]

> Annales coenobij Inisfallensis in agro Kerriano, in quibus Author leviter attingit historiam Universalem, ab orbe condito usq; ad annum 430. vel circiter. Inde verò res Hibernicas usq; ad annum 1215. quo vixit, satis accurate describit. Hos Annales continuarunt alij usq; ad annum 1320. in 4. membr.

Here, having summarily assigned these annals to the monastery of Inisfallen on the basis of just twelve entries referring to that monastery distributed over two and a half centuries, Ware proceeded to attribute the compilation of these annals up to the year 1215 to a single 'Author' who lived up to that year, and then continued by others to 1320. He made no attempt to justify this hypothesis, which simply cannot be reconciled with the fact of the first hand continuing to 1092 followed by twenty-eight hands to 1214, and ten more thereafter to 1321.[40] Thus in a summary fashion, analogous to his account of AT, Ware naïvely attributed compilation of the entire sweep of AI from Biblical history to the thirteenth century to a single, relatively late author.

Thus it transpires that, notwithstanding the depth of his interest in Irish history and his unparalleled collection of Annalistic and historical manuscripts, many of Ware's hypotheses in respect of these three most important texts, AT, AU and AI, were mistaken or inaccurate. However, at the time and long after, on account of the prestige attached to his MS collection, his extensive publications based upon this collection, and his association with the scholarship of James Ussher, Ware's hypotheses were received with respect and repeated by

---

38 Mac Neill, 'Authorship', 30–8 (repudiation of Ware's attribution of AT to Tigernach); Mc Carthy, 'AU apparatus 82–1019', 259–60 (Mac Maghnusa), 279–81 (Cuana).   39 O'Sullivan, 'Finding list', 90 (cit.).   40 Ware's statement in BL Add. 4787, 'I ghess the aforesaid Annales did belong to the priory of Inisfallen Kerry from the often mention thereof therein', cf. Mac Airt, *AI*, xi–ii, rested upon references to 'Inis Faithlinn' in AI 1075, 1110, 1116, 1120, 1180, 1204, 1208, 1212, 1280, 1320. Best & Mac Neill, *AI facsimile*, 5–24, and Mac Airt, *AI*, xxx–xli (hands of AI).

other scholars. Indeed Ussher, in his own *Britannicarum Ecclesiarum antiquitates* published the same year as Ware's *De scriptoribus*, adopted Ware's nomenclature for both AT and AI, and in his concluding sentence he paid the following warm compliment to Ware and endorsed his contribution in respect of the Irish Annals:[41]

> a D. Jacobo Waræo Dubliniensi, equite aurato et regii apud nos ærarii rationali dignissimo, Hiberniæ nostræ annales, una cum patriorum scriptorum catalogo (e quibus eorum quæ hac in parte desiderantur non exiguum peti poterit supplementum) benevolus Lector expectabit.

However, in fact both men were deeply alienated from Gaelic scholarship by their effective illiteracy in Irish and their own cultural, social, and ecclesiastical affiliations.

In reviewing the Annalistic scholarship that followed the work of Ussher and Ware, it is out of the question to do so comprehensively on account of the amount of material. Thus for the most part I will concentrate on the views expressed in respect of AT and AU, since these are the most important members of their respective groups. I commence with Roderick O'Flaherty (1629–1718), alias Ruaidhrí Ó Flaithbheartaigh, who represents what survived of Gaelic scholarship into the later seventeenth century. O'Flaherty was of aristocratic background and a friend of, and partially educated by Dubhaltach Mac Fhirbhisigh, and he inherited some of Dubhaltach's MSS, including his own compilation of CS.[42] His major work, *Ogygia, seu, Rerum Hibernicarum Chronologia*, published in London in 1685, was undertaken in response to a request from John Lynch, archdeacon of Tuam, to resolve the Annalistic chronological conflicts highlighted by Ware's publication of *De Hibernia et antiquitatibus eius disquisitionis* in 1654. O'Flaherty's classical title *Ogygia*, which he reiterated throughout his work, he derived from William Camden's citation of Plutarch's 'insula Ogygia id est perantiquae'. O'Flaherty shamelessly misquoted Camden †1623 in order to make the extravagant claim that, 'The Irish date their history from the first aeras of the world ... the antiquity of all other countries is modern, almost in its infancy!'[43] O'Flaherty had substantial access to AT, CS, MB and MS H of FM, for MSS heavily annotated by him all survive. Nevertheless he based his own chronology principally upon MB so that *Ogygia* itself is a chronicle of the regnal-canon tradition. While O'Flaherty set forth his

---

41 Ussher, *Antiquitates* in *Whole works* vi, 545 (cit.).   **42** O'Flaherty, *Ogygia*, 13 referred to Dubhaltach as 'intimo nostro amico Dualdo Firbisio'.   **43** Hely, *Ogygia*, 34 (cit.), cf. O'Flaherty, *Ogygia*, 22, 'Nam Ogygiae titulum assumpsi, qua ratione apud Camdenum habetur; Non immerito haec Insula Ogygia, i.. perantiqua Plutarcho dicta fuit ... omnium gentium Antiquitas fit novitas, & quodammodo infantia'; Camden, *Britannia*, 756 (citation of 'Ogygia').

chronology in considerable detail it is marred by numerous computational errors.[44] Regarding AT O'Flaherty wrote, 'Tigernachus Cluanensis Anno 1088 mortuus in suo partim Latino, partim Hibernico Chronico sic aeram Mundanam cum nostra vulgari Dionysiona Latinè connectit: ... '[45] Thus here O'Flaherty simply repeated Ware's assertion that Tigernach Ua Braein was responsible for both the text and the chronology of the work. Regarding AU O'Flaherty wrote:[46]

> Nec multum à clarissimi viri Jacobi Waraei Equitis Aurati in suis Hiberniae Antiquitatib. discedo sententia ex annalibus, quibus ipse, & Usserius Ultoniensibus nomen impertierunt, qui à Colgano Senatenses vocantur, à Cathaldo Maguir de Senat-mac-Magnus in Fermanach agro scripti qui Ecclesiae Ardmachanae Canonicus, & insignis historicus anno 1498 vita defunctus est; & à Rodericus Casidaeo Archidiacono Clochorensi Anno 1541 mortuo antiquitatum patriae peritissimo recogniti, & continuati.

From this it is evident that O'Flaherty was simply paraphrasing Ware's account of AU, and noting that Ware and Ussher had imposed a name, 'Annales Ultonienses', which differed from Colgan's nomenclature. Therefore, notwithstanding his Gaelic education O'Flaherty gave no independent account of either of these texts, but simply repeated what he had read in Ussher, Ware and Colgan.

In 1697 E. Bernard, in his catalogue of the MSS of England and Ireland, gave a wildly inaccurate account of the range of Rawl. B. 489, stating that, 'Incipit ad An. Dom. 444. Explicit ad An. 1041. quo obit Rodericus Cassiddeus ...'[47] Both of Bernard's errors show up in subsequent accounts and add to the confusion regarding AU's two primary MSS. In 1724 William Nicolson, bishop of Derry, published his comprehensive *Irish Historical Library* which included a substantial account of Annalistic MSS, and his account of AT stated:[48]

> *Irish* Annals by *Tigernach*, an *Erenach* of *Clonmacnoise*, ending in the Year 1088 in which the Author died ... Primate *Usher* appeals to this Historian; as a better, as well as elder, Witness than *Joceline* of *Fourness*. This Annalist allows that *Omnia monumenta* Scotorum *usque* Kimbaoth ... *incerta errant.*

Thus Nicolson, repeating Ware's identification, made Tigernach a 'Historian' more reliable than Joceline on the authority of Ussher, and author of the impressive 'Omnia monumenta' interjection. With this account in Nicolson's

---

44 O'Flaherty, *Ogygia*, the additions used to obtain the following data are all erroneous: AM 3922, AD 279, 357, 405, 463, 534, 724, 863, 1002, 1684. Since the same errors are repeated in his recapitulation 'Ogygia Carmen' (443–60), they cannot be typographic in origin.   45 O'Flaherty, *Ogygia*, 7. This is followed by an apparent citation from AT given in italics, but collation shows it to be in fact a collation of conflated passages, cf. Stokes, *AT*, 12, 36.   46 O'Flaherty, *Ogygia*, 19 (cit.).   47 Bernard, *Catalogi*, 3 (cit.).   48 Nicolson, *Historical library*, 30–9, 243–4 (Annals MSS), 30 (cit.).

prestigious publication the legend of the learned Tigernach, 'erenagh' of Clonmacnois, was firmly established in Anglo-Irish scholarship. Regarding AU, Nicolson was aware of both MSS, and wrote of Rawl. B. 489, 'They begin at the Year 444, and end (not at 1041. as the printed Catalogues of our MSS. but) at 1541.'[49] Regarding TCD 1282, then in the possession of one John Conry in Dublin, Nicolson wrote:[50]

> An ancient Copy of the *Annales Senatenses*, written on Vellum and in a fair Character; but imperfect at the beginning and end: For it begins at the Year 454, ten Years later than the Duke of *Chandois's*, and ends (about 50 Years sooner) at 1492.

Thus Nicolson described the MS as deficient 'at the beginning and end', and stated explicitly that its range was substantially less than that of Rawl. B. 488. Virtually every one of these details was incorrect, and his error in the range was to have serious consequences.

Charles O'Conor of Bellanagare (1710–91) was descended from the O'Conor kings of Connacht, and his family retained a small part of their ancestral estates in Roscommon, where as a young man he received his early training in Gaelic scholarship, in which he displayed both interest and proficiency. He went on to be regarded as the foremost authority on Irish history and to collect a number of important Gaelic chronicles, including the MS of CT and MSS C and P of FM. He annotated some of these and was responsible for the production of a number of transcripts of them. In his historical publications he drew on these sources but expressed no interest in either the origin or inter-relationships of the Annals. In 1775 O'Conor edited and published Roderick O'Flaherty's *Ogygia vindicated*, but again in his preface displayed no interest in the history of the Annals.[51] On the other hand, his grandson, the Revd O'Conor (1764–1828), took a close interest in both the compilers and compilation of the Annals. The Revd O'Conor was educated in Rome and appointed in 1789 as parish priest of Kilkeevin, county Roscommon.[52] In 1798 the marquis of Buckingham, married to a Catholic, appointed him chaplain to the marchioness and librarian at Stowe in Buckinghamshire. O'Conor brought to Stowe his grandfather's valuable collection of Irish MSS where they were joined to the marquis' own collection. As librarian at Stowe, O'Conor also had access to most of Ware's valuable collection of Annals, much of it residing in the Rawlinson collection at the Bodleian library at Oxford, and in 1818 O'Conor published a catalogue of the marquis' collection in which he repeatedly referenced the Rawlinson MSS. Subsequently over 1825–6 he published the first printed editions of parts of AT,

---

49 Nicolson, *Historical library*, 37 (cit.). **50** Nicolson, *Historical library*, 243 (cit.). **51** O'Conor, *Dissertations* I & II, *passim* (Annalistic citations); idem, *Ogygia vindicated*, i–ix (preface). **52** Ó Muraíle, *Celebrated antiquary*, 315–16 (Charles O'Conor).

AI, AB, FM, and AU, and, while his inadequate textual skills resulted in many errors afflicting these, they were the only access to the Annals for many scholars and were consequently very influential throughout the nineteenth century.[53] Regarding AT, O'Conor wrote in his catalogue:[54]

> It has not been hitherto observed, that there are two Oxford copies, both imperfect; the first ... is marked Rawlinson, No. 502 ... The second copy of Tigernac in the Bodleian, [is] Rawlinson 488.

Thus O'Conor observed correctly that the two Rawlinson MSS derived from a common source, and he went on to consider the interjections found in the first four folios of Rawl. B. 502, writing:

> The quotations from Latin and Greek authors in Tigernac are very numerous; and his balancing their authorities against each other, manifests a degree of criticism uncommon in the iron age in which he lived.

So O'Conor explicitly made Tigernach the author of all these interjections. Subsequently, in the preface to his 1825 edition of AT, which he arbitrarily began at Cimbáed and terminated at 1088 thereby affording prominence to the two important interjections, 'Omnia monumenta ...' and 'Huc usque Tigernach scribsit ...', O'Conor wrote:[55]

> Glorior inter meos Majores extitisse antiquissimum omnium Historicorum Septentrionalium qui Annales Patrios lingua vernacula descripsere. Glorior etiam virum fuisse Sanctum, et doctum, qui bibliothecam instructissimam habuisse videtur, et Sacras literas impense coluit Saeculo ferreo. Obiit enim grandaevus anno 1088.

Thus O'Conor, echoing Nicolson's 'Historian' identification, now conjectured for him from the interjections the best furnished of libraries where the learned and saintly Tigernach diligently studied sacred literature until his death at a great age. No basis is evident for either Tigernach's supposed sanctity, or his great age at death, while the splendid library rested on the four words, 'Huc usque Tigernach scribsit'. Thus O'Conor, so far from critically assessing Nicolson's enlargement of Ware's naïve attribution of all of Rawl. B. 488 up to 1088 to Tigernach, instead very considerably inflated and glorified it. Regarding AU, O'Conor wrote of Rawl. B. 489 in his catalogue:[56]

---

53 O'Conor, *Bibliotheca* i–ii, (catalogue); O'Conor, *Rerum Hib.* ii–iv, (editions).   54 O'Conor, *Bibliotheca* i, 193 (cit.).   55 Mac Neill, 'Authorship', 33 (cit. – Mac Neill identified his source as 'O'Conor (vol. ii, p. 83)' but it is not found at p. 83 in either *Bibliotheca* ii or *Rerum Hib.* ii).   56 O'Conor, *Bibliotheca* i, 174 (cit.).

The Bodleian MS (Rawlinson 489) is called the original, because it is the *Matrix* of all the copies now known to exist. But it is not meant that there were not older MSS. from which *Cathal-Maguir* collected and transcribed them before the year 1498 ... *Maguir* died in 1498. *Cassidi* continued his transcript to 1541, and died in 1541 ... Nicolson says that 'the Ulster annals begin at 444 ...' He mistakes. They begin at 431.

Regarding TCD 1282 O'Conor cited Nicolson's account of 1724, mistakenly attributing it to Edward Llhwyd, writing:[57]

> Mr Ed. Llhwyd [recté William Nicolson] mentions a copy of these Annals which he calls *Senatenses*, which he had from Mr John Conry, written on vellum in a fair character, but imperfect at the beginning and end, for it begins, says he, at the year 454, ten years later than Duke of Chandos's, and ends about fifty years sooner, at 1492.

Thus it can be seen that O'Conor's mistake in calling Rawl. B. 489, 'the *Matrix* of all the copies known to exist', was a direct consequence of Nicolson's inaccurate description of TCD 1282's range falling within the range of Rawl. B. 489. As a result, O'Conor inferred the latter to be the most comprehensive MS of AU, and his assertion that 'They begin at 431' is the first of many iterations of this particular mistake, but to be fair full responsibility cannot be laid at his door, for Nicolson's range error had played a crucial role. These accounts by O'Conor of the compilations of AT and AU, juxtaposed as they were to the first printed editions of these texts, were enormously influential in shaping the views of subsequent generations of scholars.

The textual skills and the techniques of the scholars who succeeded O'Conor in Annalistic studies in general far exceeded his, so that it is convenient to broadly classify subsequent scholarship as modern. Before proceeding, however, it is worth identifying the important hypotheses concerning AT and AU that were established as a result of the work of Ussher, Ware and their successors. In respect of AT we have Ware's hypothesis of Tigernach Ua Braein's authorship of the entire text up to 1088, while for AU we have O'Conor's simple assertion that they commence at 431. Notwithstanding their extremely precarious basis, both of these appear repeatedly in the work of subsequent scholars and so it will be helpful to give each author's hypothesis a meaningful title. Thus we have Ware's *Tigernach* hypothesis, and O'Conor's *AU-431* hypothesis. In the case of Ware's *Tigernach* hypothesis, Nicolson and O'Conor made florid additions concerning Tigernach himself, and O'Conor correctly identified Rawl. B. 502 with AT, but the essence of all three was Ware's hypothesis that Tigernach had

---

57 O'Conor, *Bibliotheca* i, 174 (cit.).

compiled the entire text up to 1088. In the case of O'Conor's *AU-431* hypothesis it was a consequence of Nicolson's earlier mistake, but being the year given by Prosper of Aquitaine for Palladius' despatch by pope Celestine as the first bishop to the Irish believers in Christ, it possessed an epochal attraction for historically sensitive minds.

Modern Annalistic scholarship

The first scholar to bring more critical scholarship to bear on the Annals was John O'Donovan (1806–61), who with his editions of the annals of Dublin (1832), FM (1848–51), and FA (1860) made a huge contribution to Annalistic studies.[58] However, as can be seen, O'Donovan did not engage with any of the texts of the important Clonmacnoise or Cuana groups. Instead, the magnificence of his edition of FM had the effect of raising its status so that it eclipsed the other Annals for many years as Mac Niocaill observed in 1975, '[FM] to the layman is the "Annals" *par excellence* – many indeed have never heard of any other.'[59] In these editions O'Donovan did not discuss in any substantial way either AT or AU, so his work cannot contribute to the present review.

O'Donovan's older contemporary, Eugene O'Curry (1794–1862), made an important contribution to Annalistic studies when in 1861 he published a series of lectures on the manuscript materials for Irish history, which lectures he had delivered following his appointment as Professor of Archaeology and History in the Catholic University in Dublin in 1854. In this publication O'Curry effectively afforded first place to the Annalistic genre by devoting lectures III–VII to a survey of the MS sources for AT, AU, LC, AI, AB, CT, FM, CS, MB, which he himself listed in this order in his introduction.[60] In these lectures O'Curry undertook the first comprehensive review of the Annalistic manuscript evidence, and he set forth in detail what he believed regarding these and also the compilation of their texts, and his review is still valuable after 140 years, notwithstanding a sprinkling of textual and numerical errors. In assessing O'Curry's lectures it should be borne in mind that at the time the only printed editions of these texts available to him were O'Conor's partial editions of AT, AI, AB, FM and AU, and John O'Donovan's recent full edition of FM, which edition O'Curry welcomed with abundant praise for author and publisher alike.[61] It is also pertinent to remember that O'Curry was of humble background and self-taught, as he mentioned in his preface, and he clearly felt himself at a considerable disadvantage beside other formally educated scholars.[62] This is

58 Ó Muraíle, *Celebrated antiquary*, 318–31 (O'Donovan biography).   59 Mac Niocaill, *MIA*, 18 (cit.).   60 O'Curry, *MM*, 52–161 (lects. III–VII, lects. I–II were introductory), 52 (list). 61 O'Curry, *MM*, 160–1 (FM praise).   62 O'Curry, *MM*, v–vi (self-taught).

relevant because when we examine what O'Curry wrote concerning AT and AU, we find it influenced by his deference towards both the Revd Charles O'Conor, a Catholic priest educated in Rome, and the Revd James Todd (1805–69), a clergyman professor of Hebrew at Trinity College Dublin and an active patron of O'Curry.

Turning to consider AT, immediately following the above-cited list O'Curry wrote:[63]

> At the head of our list I have placed the Annals of Tighernach, a composition, as we shall presently see, of a very remarkable character, whether we take into account the early period at which these annals were written, namely, the close of the eleventh century, or the amount of historical research, the judicious care, and the scholarlike discrimination, which distinguish the compiler ...
>
> How far the arrangement of events and the chronology observed in most of our annals are to be ascribed to Tighernach, is a matter that cannot now be clearly determined. It is certain, however, that there were careful and industrious chroniclers and chronologists before his time, with whose works he was doubtless well acquainted.

Thus in this first paragraph O'Curry simply repeated both the substance and the tone of O'Conor's conclusions. His second paragraph, however, shows that while O'Curry was keenly aware that accomplished chronographers had preceded Tigernach in time whose careers he expounded in the ensuing pages, he was unable to relate their work to that of Tigernach. That done he continued:[64]

> Let us now return to Tighernach, whose name stands among the first of Irish annalists; and, as we shall see in investigating the portions of his works which remain to us, this position has been not unjustly assigned him. If we take into account the early period at which he wrote, the variety and extent of his knowledge, the accuracy of his details, and the scholarly criticism and excellent judgment he displays, we must agree with the opinion expressed by the Rev. Charles O'Conor, that not one of the countries of northern Europe can exhibit a historian of equal antiquity, learning, and judgement with Tighernach ...
>
> Tighernach himself was undoubtedly one of the most remarkable of all the scholars of Clonmacnois. His learning appears to have been varied and extensive. He quotes Eusebius, Orosius, Africanus, Bede, Josephus, Saint Jerome, and many other historic writers ...

Thus having enthusiastically endorsed all of the Nicolson/O'Conor extensions to Ware's *Tigernach* hypothesis, O'Curry then introduced another crucial hypothesis, writing:[65]

---

63 O'Curry, *MM*, 52–3 (cit.). 64 O'Curry, *MM*, 57 (cit.). 65 O'Curry, *MM*, 62 (cit.).

In the Trinity College Library there is however also preserved a fragment, consisting of three leaves of an ancient vellum MS., apparently of Tighernach, though it is now bound up with the vellum copy of the Annals of Ulster.

This identification presented by O'Curry of ff. 12–14 of TCD 1282, was, in fact, the work of his patron the Revd Todd, as O'Curry made clear by publishing Todd's letter of 6 October 1858 in full.[66] Critical examination of this letter shows that Todd's textual argument was inconclusive, demonstrating only that ff. 12–14 and AT share a common source, his chronology was confused, and he did not even examine TCD 1282 in the College library working instead from a transcript made by O'Curry.[67] But Todd's letter was also authoritative, asserting 'There can be no doubt that the sheets at the beginning [i.e. ff. 12–14] of the MS of the Annals of Ulster in Trin. Coll. contain a fragment of an ancient copy of *Tigernach*.' O'Curry respectfully repeated Todd's conclusion, writing, 'I can add nothing to the observations of the Rev. Dr Todd (in his letter printed *ante* Appendix XXXII), whose conclusion in the affirmative is, of course, entitled to the greatest weight.'[68] Thus O'Curry, despite obvious reservations, was responsible for adding Todd's mis-identification of ff. 12–14 to the complex gallery of misconceptions already gathered about AT.[69] This summary detachment by Todd of ff. 12–14 from TCD 1282, with what I shall call Todd's *AT-fragment* hypothesis, carried the important corollary for AU that its two primary MSS could then both be considered to commence at the signal year of 431. In this way O'Conor's *AU-431* hypothesis was maintained against the evidence of the MSS, and so O'Curry affirmed of AU: 'These Annals begin thus – "Anno ab Incarnatione Domini ccccxxxi., Palladius ad Scotos ...".'[70] When he turned to consider the compilation of AU O'Curry preferred the title 'Annals of Senait', and he wrote:[71]

> The reason why these annals are called the Annals of *Senait Mac Maghnusa* is, because they were originally compiled by *Cathal* Mac Guire, whose Clann or Chieftain title was *Mac Maghnusa*, and whose residence and property lay chiefly in the Island of *Senait* in Loch Erne ... The death of the original compiler is recorded by his continuator in these annals, at the year 1498 ...

Thus O'Curry followed Ware and O'Conor in regarding Cathal Mac Maghnusa as the compiler, but it should be noted that O'Curry avoided the ambiguity

---

66 O'Curry, *MM*, 517–19 (Todd's letter). 67 Mc Carthy, 'AU compilation', 77–9 (Todd's letter & O'Curry; Todd examined the full copy of TCD 1282 made for him in 1841 by O'Curry, now RIA 3.C.16–17). 68 O'Curry, *MM*, 534 (cit.). 69 Mc Carthy, 'AU compilation', 77–9 (Todd's mis-identification), 79–84 (consequences), 87–92 (evidence that ff. 12–14 are part of the original compilation of AU). 70 O'Curry, *MM*, 90 (cit.). 71 O'Curry, *MM*, 84 (cit.).

inherent in the use of the verb 'to write'. Then, when considering the matter of their continuation, O'Curry wrote:[72]

> After the death of *Mac Maghnusa*, the annals were continued by *Ruaidhridhe O'Caisidé*, or Rory O'Cassidy, down to the year 1537, or 1541, according to Ware. They were continued after this (I mean the Dublin copy) by some other persons, probably the O'Luinins, down to the year 1604, where they now end. I say probably by the O'Luinins, because the Dublin copy was transcribed by *Ruaidhrighe*, or Rory O'Luinin, as appears from two insertions which occur in that volume in a blank space, at the end of the year 1373. The first ... is immediately followed by these words: 'It is fitter to bestow it on the soul of Rory *O'Luinín*, who wrote the book well'.

This is a remarkably confused statement by O'Curry, for the 'Dublin copy' ends at 1504 so there is no question of speaking of its continuation from '1537, or 1541' or 'to the year 1604'. However, the latter part is the first correct identification of Ruaidhrí Ua Luinín as the main scribe of TCD 1282, and it was most unfortunate that this important identification was first presented in such a confused and contradictory context. In summary, O'Curry's contribution drew attention to the separate existence, importance and differences of the TCD 1282 text of AU, to which he correctly ascribed Ua Luinín as main scribe. However, the really unique part of TCD 1282, ff. 12–14, was immediately and mistakenly identified by Todd with Tigernach, to whom O'Curry attributed compilation of AT even more vividly than had Ware, Nicolson and O'Conor.

I next briefly note that while William Hennessy (1829–89) in the introduction to his valuable edition of CS published in 1866 did not discuss AT he did refer in passing to 'the monastery of Clonmacnois, where the more ancient and important Chronicle of Tigernach was also compiled.' This suggests then that Hennessy had fully accepted Ware's *Tigernach* hypothesis. Regarding AU of which in 1887 Hennnessy was editor of the first printed edition based upon TCD 1282 his brief preface simply anticipated a full introduction when the whole edition had been completed. Unfortunately Hennessy did not live to complete this, but his view of ff. 12–14 of TCD 1282 may be inferred from the facts that he commenced his edition at AD 431, prior to which he interpolated the pious invocation 'IHC, Mei est incipere, Tui est finire', and he subtitled his volume, 'A Chronicle of Irish Affairs from A.D. 431, to A.D. 1540.'[73] Together these make it clear that Hennessy had indeed adopted both O'Conor's *AU-431* and Todd's *AT-fragment* hypotheses, and in this way his edition of AU did not acknowledge in any way the presence of the pre-Palladian annals in the primary MS for the text.

---

72 O'Curry, *MM*, 85 (cit.).   73 Hennessy, CS, xxxiii. (Tigernach), and idem, *AU* i, p. iii (preface), 1 (invocation). Mc Carthy, 'AU compilation', 79 (interpolated invocation).

Turning next to Bartholomew Mac Carthy (1843–1904), his first publication dealing with chronological material was his discussion of the chronicle compiled by the Moville monk, Marianus Scottus †1082, in Mainz over 1069–76. In this Mac Carthy set forth his definite views on a number of the Annals, including AT and AU. Regarding the status of AT and its relationship to CS he referred to 'the fact that *Tigernach* and the *Chronicon Scottorum* stand in the relation of original and compendium.' Thereafter Mac Carthy cited a number of passages from both Rawl. B. 502 and 488, repeatedly identifying Tigernach as their author, from which it is clear that Mac Carthy accepted Ware's *Tigernach* hypothesis.[74] Mac Carthy's attitude towards Tigernach, however, contrasted greatly with that of his predecessors in that he considered Tigernach's scholarship low-grade. The reason for this lay in Mac Carthy's interest in chronological systems, together with his enthusiastic adoption of Todd's *AT-fragment* hypothesis. Mac Carthy described ff. 12–14 as, 'a fragment bound up with the Trinity College MS. of the *Annals of Ulster*, which he [Todd] (rightly, I believe) took to belong to *Tigernach*.'[75] Without adverting to the fact that neither Rawl. B. 502 nor 488 share any of the chronological data of ff. 12–14, Mac Carthy proceeded to evaluate the ferial and epactal sequence of the alleged 'fragment', and he concluded: 'In a word every lunar reckoning in the Fragment is five years wrong! ... In view of the foregoing, Tigernach can scarcely be regarded as the most trustworthy of the native annalists.'[76] Thus Mac Carthy's poor opinion of Tigernach was a direct consequence of Todd's *AT-fragment* hypothesis. Turning next to his own very substantial chronological reconstruction of AI for the years AD 433–56, Mac Carthy stated that, 'the years are marked in unbroken continuity by the luni-solar incidence of Jan. 1.' This statement, while true of Mac Carthy's reconstruction where he himself has supplied the ferial, epact and AD in virtually every year, i.e. the 'luni-solar incidence of 1 Jan.', is absolutely untrue of the text preserved in Rawl. B. 503. Nevertheless Mac Carthy concluded: [77]

> The ferial and epact were, in fact, the requisite criteria from which by computistic methods the incidence of Easter and of the other moveable feasts of the current year was determined. We have thus revealed the fundamental datum in reference to the native A.D. Annals.
>
> **The Paschal Cycle was the basis of the Irish Chronicle.**

The last sentence of this conclusion was separately paragraphed and printed in bold by Mac Carthy as shown here, and it clearly represented for him the

---

74 Mac Carthy, 'Palatino-Vaticanus', 250 (cit.), 251–5 (AT passages).   75 Mac Carthy, 'Palatino-Vaticanus', 252 (cit.).   76 Mac Carthy, 'Palatino-Vaticanus', 355–61 (evaluation of ff. 12–14), 357, 361 (cits.).   77 Mac Carthy, 'Palatino-Vaticanus', 352–3 (reconstruction of AI), 361 (cits.).

ruling principle of the chronological apparatus of the Irish Annals, and consequently determined many of his judgements and editorial decisions. As a result of this principle, depending entirely upon his own reconstruction of AI, Mac Carthy regarded the systematically erroneous epactal series of ff. 12–14 as proof of Tigernach's incompetence, and hence that he was untrustworthy.

AU, on the other hand, with its sustained AD series, and intermittent ferial and epactal series from 431 fulfilled Mac Carthy's principle admirably and consequently, when he was invited to continue Hennessy's edition of the text he relentlessly supplied the ferial, epactal and AD series, in many cases quite regardless of the MS readings.[78] When in 1904 Mac Carthy came to write the introduction anticipated by Hennessy in 1887 he began with a description of TCD 1282 in which he re-numbered the MS from f. 16, silently omitting ff. 12–15, evidently reflecting his belief in Todd's *AT-fragment* hypothesis. Mac Carthy considered the MS to be the work of five hands, only the fifth of which he described and identified as inscribing 'on the margins, a court hand, evidently of the Compiler (who else would have been at pains to record the birth-days of his children?) made entries. …' On the basis of this rhetorical question he subsequently identified this 'Compiler' as Cathal Mac Maghnusa, and described this in the following terms:[79]

> The sustained similarity between these and the other native Annals proves that the work of Mac Manus consisted in selection, mainly with reference to Ulster events, from the Chronicles he had collected. His well applied diligence in this direction merits ample acknowledgment.

Mac Carthy consequently attributed to Mac Maghnusa the interpolated ferial and epactal data of the text, and he registered his warm appreciation for this supposed contribution, writing:[80]

> Unlike O'Clery and his associates, he neither tampered with the text, vitiated the dating, nor omitted the solar and lunar notation, but, side by side with the chronological errors he was unable to correct, preserved the criteria whereby they can with certainty be rectified.

Thus Mac Carthy accorded Mac Maghnusa both a compilatory and a scribal role in TCD 1282, but he did not acknowledge the roles of either Ruaidhrí Ua Luinín or Ruaidhrí Ua Caiside.[81] On the other hand, when he discussed Rawl B

---

78 Mac Carthy, *AU* ii–iii, invariably supplied ferial and epactal data synchronized with his marginal AD data, regardless of the MS data, which he relegated to his apparatus. He also incorporated Ware's marginal Arabic AD into his text for AU 1263–1372, always writing it in Roman numerals, cf. *AU* ii, 334 n. b, 'Above the date a modern hand placed 1265.'   79 Mac Carthy, *AU* iv, p. ix (cit.).   80 Mac Carthy, *AU* iv, p. ix (cit.).   81 Mc Carthy, 'AU compilation', 73–7 (roles of Ua

489, on the basis of their obits therein and relative ecclesiastical status he identified Ua Caiside as the 'author of that recension' up to 1506, and asserted that Ua Luinín had acted as scribe for Ua Caiside.[82] Mac Carthy's introduction to AU, demonstrating his knowledge of Irish, Latin, Greek, ecclesiastical history, and his numeracy was very influential, notwithstanding its sternly authoritarian style and opaque and pretentious English. In it, Mac Carthy, with his insistence on the priority of ferials and epacts, his appreciative account of Mac Maghnusa's alleged skills, and his derisory account of Tigernach's supposed incompetence succeeded in establishing AU in a position of pre-eminence amongst the kalend tradition of Irish Annals. This achievement I shall refer to as Mac Carthy's *AU-priority* hypothesis. This together with the large range of the printed edition of 431–1588, the huge number of entries and their approximately contemporaneous orthography from *c.*750, and the easy access conferred by Mac Carthy's heavily restored AD apparatus, have made AU the principal Annalistic source cited in historical studies.

Between these two publications of Mac Carthy, Whitley Stokes (1830–1909), published in *Revue Celtique* over the years 1895–7 the first full edition of AT from Rawl. B. 502 and 488, together with the annals of TCD 1282 ff. 12–14. Stokes divided the joint text of Rawl. B. 502 and 488, up to 'Huc usque Tigernach scribsit' at 1088, into 'Fragments I–IV', and he entitled these 'The Annals of Tigernach'. The remainder of the entries from 1088 up to 1178 he entitled, 'The Annals of Tigernach – The continuation, A.D. 1088–A.D. 1178', and the annals from ff. 12–14 of TCD 1282 he entitled, 'The Dublin Fragment of Tigernach's Annals'. These titles show clearly that Stokes had adopted both Ware's *Tigernach* and Todd's *AT-fragment* hypotheses, and indeed the first sentence of his two-page preface identified this 'Tigernach' as, 'Tigernach hua Braein was a learned abbot of Clonmacnois who died in the year 1088.' Following this, Stokes turned to the matter of sources and simply asserted that 'the non Irish portions are, for the most part, compiled from the following works', and he then listed in order Jerome's chronicle, Orosius' *Historiarum libri septem*, Bede's DTR cap. 66, the Vulgate, Isidore's *Etymologiarum Libri XX*, a Latin translation of Josephus' *Antiquities of the Jews*, and, possibly, Julius Africanus' lost *Chronicon*.[83] Of these the latest by far was Bede's DTR cap. 66, compiled in 725, and this then provided a *terminus ante quam non* for those subsequent authors who accepted Stokes' uncorroborated identification. Thus, with no fuss or critical enquiry of any kind, Stokes quietly launched the hypothesis that the compilation of AT had relied on Bede's DTR cap. 66, to which I shall refer as Stokes' *Bedan-source* hypothesis.

Caiside and Ua Luinín). **82** Mac Carthy, *AU* iv, pp. ix–x (cit.). **83** Stokes, *AT* i, 4–5 (preface and cits.).

Stokes' hypothesis carried a very important corollary in respect of the inauguration of Irish contemporaneous chronicling and the year 725. For if one held that contemporaneous chronicling had commenced *before* that year, and Ussher's identification of the accurate record of the solar eclipse of 664 strongly suggested this to be the case, then one had also to accept that all of the world history entries supposedly derived from Bede's DTR cap. 66 had been prefixed to this contemporaneous Irish chronicle in a compilation at some date *after* 725. This hypothesis of a *prefix compilation* of a world-chronicle involving Bede's DTR cap. 66 became an important element of virtually all Annalistic scholarship that came after Stokes' publication. Of course for Stokes himself and those before him who simply attributed the entire compilation of AT up to 1088 to Tigernach Ua Braein there was no need to hypothesize any such prefix compilation. However, most scholars who came after Stokes adopted this prefix compilation hypothesis, with the consequence that their accounts of the compilation of AT in particular became considerably more complex than those of earlier scholarship. In 1998 I published an account of the impact of Stokes' *Bedan-source* hypothesis upon scholars' interpretations of the pre-Patrician annals, i.e. principally the world history entries.[84] The account given here, however, reviews the impact upon scholars' views of the compilation of both the world history and the contemporaneous Irish entries.

In 1910, not long after Mac Carthy had asserted the priority of AU, Tomás Ó Máille (1880–1938), published an important evaluation of the language of AU in which he began by citing Kuno Meyer's authority for the antiquity of their language. In his discussion of the MSS of AU he did not acknowledge the existence of ff. 12–14 of TCD 1282, but in a subsequent footnote he wrote:[85]

> I do not take account of the history previous to A.D. 431 in the first few folios of H. 1.8 [TCD 1282] which is in Irish not earlier than the eleventh century, and which was obviously added at a later time.

This was an important observation for it identified that the language of ff. 12–14 was appreciably later than that of the entries from 431 onwards, but on the other hand it also suggests that Ó Máille had adopted both O'Conor's *AU-431* and Todd's *AT-fragment* hypotheses. Regarding the language of the subsequent annals he began by stating, 'these Annals are taken from contemporary documents from the seventh century onwards, and represent more or less faithfully the Old and Early Irish sources from which they were compiled.' Then having given a substantial number of dated examples he wrote:

---

84 Mc Carthy, 'Status', 100–16 (earlier review).   85 Ó Máille, *Language of AU*, 2–3, (AU MSS), 10 n. 1 (cit.).

Thus we see that in these entries up to 700 we have a good many instances which can be shown to belong to the ninth century, some tenth or later, whilst others point to the eighth century and may go back to 700 or before it.

Subsequently he concluded, 'but I think if we begin with about A.D. 740 or 750 … that we shall be absolutely safe in concluding that we are dealing with *bona fide* contemporary language from that onwards.'[86] Thus Ó Máille's contribution suggested that contemporaneous compilation of Irish Annals had possibly begun in the seventh century, and had definitely begun by the mid-eighth century. But he also found that some later perturbation had resulted in the language of the entries from 431 to *c.*700 being spread from the late seventh to beyond the tenth centuries. Any hypothesis of the compilation of AU must take account of these results. Overall Ó Máille's work, based primarily on linguistic considerations, served to endorse both O'Conor's *AU-431* and Mac Carthy's *AU-priority* hypotheses.

The first scholar to discuss the prefix implication of Stokes' *Bedan-source* hypothesis in print was Eoin Mac Neill (1867–1945) who in 1913 presented a complex reconstruction of the compilation stages of AT up to 1178, and of AU, including ff. 12–14 of TCD 1282, up to 766. Mac Neill commenced with a review of the development of the attribution of AT to Tigernach Ua Braein, which he characterized as the 'legend of Tigernach', in which he compellingly identified the weakness of the successive elaborations of Ware's *Tigernach* hypothesis.[87] Next Mac Neill pointed out that over the range 489–766 AT and AU are, 'in the main identical, even as to phrasing', but over 975–1178 he asserted that they 'are quite independent chronicles.' This latter assertion by Mac Neill was a serious mistake, for scrutiny shows that AT and AU share many common entries with cognate language from 975 up to *c.*1055, but Mac Neill's assumption allowed him to conclude emphatically that 'Tigernach, then, was not the compiler of Fragment III [i.e. AT 489–766].' Having thus denied authorship to Tigernach of the third fragment Mac Neill proceeded to extend this result, writing, 'it is clear that, unless and until better evidence is discovered, we cannot pronounce Tigernach to be the author or compiler of the text represented in Fragments I and II [i.e. AT for *c.*769 BC–AD 318].'[88] With Tigernach accordingly rejected as compiler of AT up to 766, Mac Neill proposed instead that Irish contemporaneous chronicling had commenced in *c.*712 with a compilation that had been inspired by Bede's *De temporibus* written in 703. Adopting O'Conor's *AU-431* hypothesis Mac Neill proposed that this compilation commenced at 431 and extended to *c.*712, and he entitled this 'the

86 Ó Máille, *Language of AU*, 1, 18 (cits.).   87 Mac Neill, 'Authorship', 30–8 (review), 32 ('legend of Tigernach').   88 Mac Neill, 'Authorship', 40 (cit.).

Old-Irish Chronicle'. He regarded that AT and AU preserved distinct redactions of this, and stated that 'there is much variation in the sequence of events extending as far as A.D. 584.'[89] To explain AT's world history Mac Neill proposed that an Irish version of Jerome's chronicle had extended his parallel regnal series to *c.*606 and added an Irish regnal series. This he entitled 'the Irish "Chronicon Eusebii"', and he further supposed that this had been subsequently, 'freely supplemented … from the older version continued by Prosper, from Orosius, St. Isidore, and Bede'. Next, the 'false guise of annals was imposed on all this heterogenous and deranged material, by the artificial separation of the material into years, distinguished by the headings "K", etc.'[90] Then at some date, unspecified by Mac Neill, but implicitly falling between 725 and the twelfth century, an unidentified compiler combined this supplemented 'Irish "Chronicon Eusebii"' with the continuation of the 'Old-Irish Chronicle'. In this way Mac Neill construed that world history incorporating Bede's DTR cap. 66 was prefixed to a contemporary Irish chronicle. Apart from Mac Neill's mistake regarding the supposed independence of AT and AU from 975 onwards, the weakest part of his reconstruction was the remarkably elaborate compilation that he proposed for the 'Irish "Chronicon Eusebii"'. This latter ultimately rested upon the AT and AU entries at 608 reading respectively, 'Finis cronice Euséui' and 'Finis Cronici Iusebii', which terminate the papal succession compiled from Marcellinus' chronicle and the *Liber Pontificalis*. There is, however, no corroborating evidence for such a compilation.[91]

Mac Neill's reconstruction of the compilation stages leading to the surviving texts of AT and AU was very carefully considered and extensively documented, and he introduced a number of important new hypotheses into the subject, and these became key elements in subsequent scholarly studies. The essential hypotheses introduced by Mac Neill were:

1. An *Irish world chronicle* considered to have been assembled from a selection of the known Western chronographic sources consisting of the chronicles of Jerome, Orosius, Prosper, Isidore and Bede, to be termed Mac Neill's *IWC* hypothesis.
2. An *Irish inaugural chronicle* considered to extend from 431 to its date of inception, and to have been extended continuously thereafter, to be termed Mac Neill's *IIC* hypothesis.
3. A *prefix compilation* in which the Irish world chronicle was compiled with the Irish inaugural chronicle, to be termed Mac Neill's *Prefix-compilation* hypothesis.

89 Mac Neill, 'Authorship', 77 (dependence on Bede's DT), 73 (cit.), 73–92 ('Old-Irish Chronicle'). 90 Mac Neill, 'Authorship', 107 (cit.). 91 Mc Carthy, 'AU apparatus 431–1131', 67 (papal succession derivation from Marcellinus and LP).

Of these three hypotheses Mac Neill was least forthcoming about the third which he assigned to an unidentified 'pseudo-annalist' working in an unspecified location at an undetermined time bounded only by 725, the date of compilation of DTR cap. 66, and the twelfth-century date of Rawl. B. 502. As we shall see subsequent scholars endeavoured to refine the details of all of Mac Neill's hypotheses, and particularly this one. However, when Mac Neill came to consider the scholarship of the author of the prefix compilation he was much more forthcoming, describing the alleged perpetrator as, 'Our unknown pseudo-annalist, then, is an example of the worst effects of an evil time in the learning of ancient Ireland. His work is a combination of ignorance and effrontery.'[92] These remarks adversely influenced ensuing scholarly attitudes towards this Irish world history material so that it was regarded as low-grade beside the corresponding material found in DTR cap. 66.[93]

Subsequent scholars undertook to refine and emend the details of Mac Neill's reconstruction, so that in 1928 A.G. Van Hamel rejected Mac Neill's assumption of an Irish continuation of Jerome's chronicle to $c.606$ as the basis for an Irish world chronicle. Instead Van Hamel argued that the requisite prefix compilations for both AT and AI had been derived from separate interpolations from Prosper, Orosius, Isidore and Bede into Jerome's chronicle.[94] Then in 1945 R.A.S. Macalister (1870–1950) incorporated Mac Neill's *Prefix-compilation* hypothesis into his title, 'The sources of the preface to the 'Tigernach' annals', and he began by emphatically endorsing Mac Neill's rejection of Tigernach's authorship of AT, and his *IWC* and *IIC* hypotheses. Macalister asserted that AT 'can be divided into two sharply contrasted sections … [the first] is almost entirely in Latin, and is a summary of world-history … [the second] is almost entirely in Irish, and begins with the mission of St. Patrick.'[95] Thus Macalister just introduced the minor variations that his *IIC* commenced with Patrick, rather than Palladius, and he synchronized contemporaneous chronicling with the battle of Ocha in 482, considerably earlier than Mac Neill's $c.712$.[96] For his *IWC*, however, Macalister rejected Jerome's chronicle as a source and instead proposed the regnal series found in Isidore's *Etymologiae* v.39 and Bede's *De temporibus*, writing, 'I do not hesitate to claim it as proved that the scholar, who undertook to prefix the preface to the 'Irish Annals', began by copying out this short chronicle of kings … and with K at the left-hand of each line.'[97] In fact Macalister proved no such thing, but his claim makes explicit his adoption of

---

92 Mac Neill, 'Authorship', 108 (cit.).   93 Mc Carthy, 'Status', 102–3 (earlier evaluation of Mac Neill's paper).   94 Van Hamel, *Vorpatrizianische Annalen*, 249–50 (collation of AT and AI); Mc Carthy, 'Status', 104 (Van Hamel).   95 Macalister, 'Sources', 40 (cit.).   96 Macalister, 'Sources', 48 (Ocha – 'I concluded that the 'Irish Annals' began with that important battle').   97 Macalister, 'Sources', 51 (cit.).

Mac Neill's *Prefix-compilation* hypothesis. Regarding the matter of where or when this 'scholar' had undertaken this prefix operation Macalister was completely unforthcoming. However, his assertion that 'the few dates inserted here and there ... [are] those of Bede, taken from his larger chronicle contained in *De temporum ratione*', show that his proposed prefix compilation could not have been completed before 725. Thus both Van Hamel and Macalister's work mainly represent attempts to formulate an *IWC* hypothesis more plausible than that proposed by Mac Neill.

One year after Macalister, Thomas F. O'Rahilly (1882–1953) published a substantial discussion of the development of the early Annals in a chapter entitled 'Some questions of dating in early Irish annals'. In this O'Rahilly maintained all of Mac Neill's three hypotheses, varying only the dates and ranges of the proposed compilations, which he defined as follows:[98]

> My own views on these matters, summarily stated, are as follows.
>
> (1) The 'Ulster Chronicle', as I have ventured to call it, was compiled in East Ulster (probably in the monastery of Bangor) *ca.* 740, and was thereafter continued from year to year; it began with the arrival of Palladius in 431. The compiler drew most of his material from local Irish (including Scoto-Irish) records; but he also utilized certain foreign sources, e.g. the Chronicle of Marcellinus and a *Liber Pontificalis*. The compilation is best preserved (though in conflate form) in AU ...
>
> (2) At a later period, certainly not earlier than the ninth century, another East Ulster scholar compiled what may be called 'The Irish World-Chronicle', which began with the creation of the world and ended with A.D. 430, and was no doubt intended as a supplement to the Ulster Chronicle. It was compiled from various Latin sources, mainly Eusebius (the Latin version), Orosius and Bede ...

Thus O'Rahilly reiterated the same two Irish compilations, his Irish inaugural chronicle initiated in *c.*740 and again commencing at 431, his Irish world chronicle compiled 'not earlier than the ninth century' from Jerome, Orosius and Bede, and this latter 'intended as a supplement' to the first. Regarding the former he considered that it was best represented by AU and he echoed Mac Carthy's view that the earliest annals had employed lunar epacts, offering no evidence and simply stating that 'such was the system of dating employed in the original 'Ulster Chronicle' is beyond doubt'.[99] Regarding AT, again without considering any evidence, he simply asserted that 'In the so-called Annals of Tigernach ... the lunar notation has been discarded, but the ferials are given ... [and] they are often hopelessly confused.' These statements, and his use of

---

98 O'Rahilly, *Early Irish history*, 235–59 (chapter xiii), 253–4 (cits.). 99 O'Rahilly, *Early Irish history*, 238 (cit.).

'Ulster' in the title of his proposed Irish inaugural chronicle of *c.*740, and his statements in respect of the orthographical differences, show that O'Rahilly considered AT a poor representative of the earliest stage of Irish chronicling.[100] These, together with the specification of his *IIC* demonstrate O'Rahilly's adoption of both O'Conor's *AU–431* and Mac Carthy's *AU-priority* hypotheses. Finally, by using CS to represent AT over its lacuna for 489–973 O'Rahilly introduced his own hypothesis of Clonmacnoise chronicle/AU independence. He began by repeating Mac Neill's mistake concerning the supposed independence of AT and AU after 974, and wrote:[101]

> ... but when the text [of AT] resumes at 974 it is quite independent of AU. The point at which the divergence of Tig. from AU began is inferable from Chron. Scot. ... About the year 911 the connexion between Chron. Scot and AU ceases. The mutual relationship of these chronicles would deserve a closer study than the present writer has had time to give it; but one may infer, provisionally at least, that a copy of the Ulster Chronicle and its continuation reached Clonmacnois in the early years of the tenth century, and that a new recension of it, incorporating the local annals, was made at Clonmacnois at that time.

Now apart from repeating Mac Neill's mistake, O'Rahilly's statement in respect of CS and AU is simply untrue, for they share one textually cognate entry in common at 911 and 912, three at 913, two at 914, five at 915, and six at 916.[102] Moreover, CS and AU continue to share many textually cognate entries up to 1064 and beyond, cf. Figure 5, p. 104, and Figure 6, p. 106. Thus on the basis of two demonstrably false premises O'Rahilly invented yet another alleged compilation at Clonmacnoise, this time supposedly merging Clonmacnoise and Ulster entries. Furthermore, his admission of having given the matter inadequate attention, together with his characterization of his hypothesis as 'provisional', suggest that O'Rahilly was aware of at least some of these deficiencies. Notwithstanding these obvious shortcomings, what I shall term O'Rahilly's *Clonmacnoise-911* hypothesis, was to prove immensely influential with subsequent scholars.

Shortly after this in his 1951 edition of AI, Seán Mac Airt (1918–1959), when discussing the compilation of an Irish world chronicle repeated Stokes' *Bedan-source* hypothesis and its corollary, as: 'since quotations from Bede formed an integral part of it [the *IWC*] ... Thus the earliest possible date for the compilation lies in the first decades of the eighth century.' To this he added O'Rahilly's terminus of 'not earlier than the ninth century', for the requisite prefix compilation, showing thereby his reliance on O'Rahilly's work.[103]

---

100 O'Rahilly, *Early Irish history*, 240, 243 (AU vs AT orthography).   **101** O'Rahilly, *Early Irish history*, 258 (cit.).   **102** Mc Carthy, 'Synchronization', *s.a.* 911–16. (CS/AU common entries) **103** Mac Airt, *AI*, xviii (cits.).

Similarly in 1958–9 Liam Ó Buachalla's two papers dealing with the Irish annals over 429–550 relied largely on O'Rahilly. In these Ó Buachalla concluded that while most entries between 429 and 466 were 'late computations' but 'about half-a-dozen are possibly genuine contemporary records', from 467 onwards the entries represented 'genuine contemporary annals'.[104] This, the earliest proposed inauguration date for contemporary Irish chronicling, was virtually ignored by subsequent scholars. Regarding pre-Palladian annals Ó Buachalla simply stated as fact that a compilation, 'composed probably in the ninth century, giving an outline of world history taken from Bede and other foreign chronicles extending from the Creation to 430', had been 'prefixed to certain collections of Irish annals: Annals of Innisfallen, 'Tigernach' and Cottonian Annals [AB]'.[105] Thus Ó Buachalla maintained O'Conor's *AU–431* and all of Mac Neill's three hypotheses.

Next in 1963 John Kelleher published the first of his two discussions of the development of the Irish Annals. In this first publication he employed all three of Mac Neill's hypotheses, proposing additionally that at the time of the prefix compilation the earlier part of the *IIC* had been redrafted. Kelleher described the compilation of the *IWC* and the prefix compilation as:

> the Irish World Annals ... based on Bede's Chronicle, with additions from Jerome, Marcellinus, Prosper, and so on, contains Irish material from *Lebor Gabála, Do Fhlathiusaib Érenn* ... have entirely replaced the original annalistic texts up to about 590 and from then to 735 fit like a sleeve over what remains of the true annals.

For the subsequent annals he adapted O'Rahilly's *Clonmacnoise-911* hypothesis, guessing an association with Armagh, as follows:[106]

> Apart from interpolations it would appear that up to 910 all the annals are but selective versions of one common source, a text very likely composed in that year and ... My guess is that it was composed in some monastery associated with Armagh.

In his subsequent paper of 1971 Kelleher did not refer to his earlier hypothesis of the 'Irish World Annals', and presented instead a series of contradictory assertions resting upon vaguely defined entry counts. For example he endorsed O'Rahilly's *Clonmacnoise-911* hypothesis, writing:[107]

104 Ó Buachalla, 'Construction', 115 and Ó Buachalla, 'Notes', 77 (cits.). 105 Ó Buachalla, 'Construction', 104 (cit.). 106 Kelleher, 'Early Irish history', 125–6 (cits.). 107 Mc Carthy, 'Status', 110 (Kelleher's contradictory assertions); Kelleher, 'The Táin', 116–17 (cits.).

a) As has often been pointed out, the common source of the existing early annals ends in 911/912.

b) It is of interest that after 911 AU and the Clonmacnois Version texts also have a common source which, however, accounts only for a percentage of all entries varying from almost nothing in the years immediately after 911 to twelve or fifteen percent in some later decades.

The observation b) was the first accurate statement of the relationship between the Clonmacnoise group and AU, and an immediate repudiation of O'Rahilly's hypothesis, but in the face of Kelleher's preceding sweeping endorsement of that hypothesis in a), much of the value of his observation was lost. Overall the effect of Kelleher's enthusiastic but repeatedly contradictory mixture of guesses, opinions, and observations was to bring further confusion to an already badly compromised field of scholarly endeavour. The fact that he wrote from the prestigious office of professor of history at Harvard University merely added a further authoritative complication to the confusion.

Between these two papers, and in response to Kelleher's first paper, in 1967 Francis John Byrne published a valuable survey of the agreement between historical data preserved in seventh-century Irish texts and the Annals. This was in response to 'the scepticism which has been expressed as to the authenticity of the early annals', and Byrne's conclusion was that 'in fact we find that where they can be so checked, the annals emerge with their veracity vindicated.'[108] In this paper Byrne was amongst the first to draw attention to the important role of Iona in Annalistic compilation, writing: 'It has long been obvious that one of the most important strands in the annals is an Iona chronicle (which ceases in the 730s).' He also offered the opinion that 'my own reading of the annals inclines me to the view that the entries begin to be contemporary in the second half of the sixth century.' However, some of his comments also show that he had adopted Mac Carthy's and O'Rahilly's hypotheses, viz., 'the seventh century annals ([are] best represented by the original hand of the oldest manuscript of the *Annals of Ulster*)', and, 'The so-called *Annals of Tigernach* and the *Chronicum Scotorum* represent a Clonmacnois compilation of the early tenth century, from which date they diverge considerably from the *Annals of Ulster*.'[109] At the same time his characterization, 'diverge considerably', shows that Byrne was aware that the independence alleged by Mac Neill and O'Rahilly was incorrect.

In 1968 John Bannerman adopted as his starting point O'Rahilly's version of Mac Neill's *IIC* hypothesis, writing:[110]

---

108 Byrne, 'Seventh-century documents', 164, 178 (cits.). 109 Byrne, 'Seventh-century documents', 178–80 (cits.). 110 Bannerman, 'Scottish entries' in *Studies*, 9 (cit.).

That the *Ulster Chronicle*, as O'Rahilly has called it, contains entries which derive from Scotland, probably Iona, was recognised by both MacNeill and O'Rahilly, while O'Rahilly's dating of the *Ulster Chronicle* was partly determined on the evidence of these entries.

Bannerman justified the identification of the *IIC* with Iona by a careful evaluation of the purview of entries up to *c.*740 and, consequently he entitled those entries with an Iona purview collectively as the '*Iona Chronicle*'. In his paper he undertook to 'clarify the relationship of the versions of this [Iona] chronicle in AU and AT'. For this he conducted a careful and substantial survey of both of these texts and concluded that:[111]

> The precisely dated series of Scottish entries, beginning in 686, suggests more or less contemporary compilation down to the last of them in the year 740 ... All of the evidence so far presented suggests that the *Iona Chronicle*, as we have it now, came to an end about 740

Thus Bannerman derived his important hypothesis of an *Iona chronicle*, compiled contemporaneously in Iona from *c.*686, and continuing there until its cessation in *c.*740, which I shall call Bannerman's *Iona chronicle* hypothesis. This is in fact just a version of Mac Neill's *IIC* hypothesis, but in contrast to Mac Neill's and O'Rahilly's versions of *IIC* Bannerman's hypothesis was based on a very substantial and convincing examination of the purview and chronological performance of AT and AU entries over these years.

One year after Kelleher's second publication Kathleen Hughes (1927–77) published her widely cited book, *Early Christian Ireland: Introduction to the sources*, in which she devoted a chapter to discussing the development of the Annals.[112] Hughes began by examining the similarities and dissimilarities of AT and AU and introduced her own title for their common source, writing, 'both AU and *Tig.* go back ultimately to the same version. Let us call it the Chronicle of Ireland.' She then effectively reiterated O'Rahilly's *Clonmacnoise-911* hypothesis:[113]

> Up to 766 AU and *Tig.* are closely related. Then there is a gap in *Tig.* When *Tig.* resumes in 975 the two sets of annals are independent ... *CS*, as a faithful though much abbreviated, copy of a MS of *Tig.* will tell us when the two families of *Tig.* and *AU* diverged. After 913 (*AU*) the two texts separate ... To sum up, *AU* and *Tig.* represent a Chronicle of Ireland which must have been drawn up at some time before 913, for at this point the two families diverge. A copy was made then and was subsequently taken to Clonmanoise, where additions were inserted.

111 Bannerman, 'Scottish entries' in *Studies*, 10, 25 (cits.). 112 Hughes, *Early Christian Ireland*, 99–162 (chapter 4). 113 Hughes, *Early Christian Ireland*, 105–7 (cits.); 114–15 Hughes offered no justification whatsoever for choosing the year 913, but she did acknowledge that it differed from

Thus Hughes, without presenting any additional evidence or indeed acknowledging O'Rahilly, simply reiterated his invention of an early tenth-century Clonmacnoise compilation. Regarding the earlier history of this text Hughes, drawing on Bannerman, concluded that it was 'contemporary from about the 680s and that records were kept before this, even if they were not written up as formal annals until the later part of the century.'[114] Thus she considered contemporaneous chronicling commenced in *c.*680 and drew on earlier non-annalistic material, and it is evident that she believed that the Annalistic form commenced at *c.*585, for she wrote subsequently: 'My conclusion is that the Chronicle of Ireland had notes and marginalia on the period before 585; that a lot of the material before 585 in our present annals was added after 913 when the texts of *AU* and *Tig.* diverged.'[115] Thus it is implicit that Hughes believed that the world chronicle element of AT was prefixed after *c.*913 to an Irish inaugural chronicle initiated in *c.*680 and beginning at *c.*585. Hughes simply asserted that 'The Annals of Ulster start at 431', but did not seriously consider the world history material, so that her account constitutes in effect minor variations of O'Conor's *AU-431*, Bannerman's *Iona chronicle*, and O'Rahilly's *Clonmacnoise-911* hypotheses.[116]

In the same year in which Hughes' book appeared John Morris (1913–77) published the first critical appraisal of some of the world history passages found in common in AT/AI/DTR, focussing on those with interjections referring to Eusebius and Jerome. From these collations Morris deduced:[117]

a) That AT/AI preserved details of Eusebius' *Chronicle* not transmitted by either Jerome or Bede.

b) In some AT/AI passages which parallel Bede, the details showed that 'the Irish Annals did not here copy Bede; either Bede copied them, or both drew upon the same source.'

c) The existence of a 'critical editor' who 'knew Book I [the *Chronologos*] of Eusebius ... [and who] was probably the same editor who had used Jerome's commentaries to annotate the text.'

To explain this source behind AT/AI/DTR Morris adopted Mac Neill's *IWC* hypothesis to infer 'the probable existence, in the 7th and 8th centuries, in

Kelleher's date, writing, 'I find myself in agreement with his view about when the texts of *AU* and *Tig.* diverged (whether it is 910 or, as I have suggested, 913, really makes little difference).'
114 Hughes, *Early Christian Ireland*, 118 (cit. where her preceding assertion that 'from 686–740 there is a series of precisely dated entries' makes clear her debt to Bannerman's paper).
115 Hughes, *Early Christian Ireland*, 144 (cit.).   116 Hughes, *Early Christian Ireland*, 118 (cit.).
117 Morris, 'Chronicle of Eusebius', 85–8 (deductions).

Ireland and Britain, of a full Latin translation of Eusebius' Chronicle, different from any now extant.'[118] While Morris made no explicit statement on how or when the Latin translation of Eusebius had been converted to Annalistic form (kalends), his assertion concerning Bede that 'he had the means of acquiring copies both of the 607 edition of Eusebius, and of Annals that had made use of it', clearly required that Morris considered that the conversion to annalistic form had taken place before 725, and that Bede had used them in compilation of his DTR. Morris then concluded:[119]

> These considerations suggest that there was less originality in Bede's Chronicle than has often been supposed. The conclusion does not detract from the stature of Bede, for his fame and achievement owe relatively little to his Chronicle. But the analysis of the sources that he and the Irish used invite deeper enquiry.

Thus Morris' paper provided compelling grounds for serious doubt concerning the validity of Stokes' *Bedan-source* hypothesis, and consequently to challenge the prefix compilation hypotheses of Van Hamel, Macalister, Mac Neill and O'Rahilly that all depended upon it. However, in the twenty-five subsequent years Morris' paper was cited just once, where it was summarily dismissed.[120]

In the very same year as Hughes' and Morris' work appeared Alfred Smyth published a valuable survey and analysis of contemporaneous entries in AU. Smyth began by reiterating Mac Carthy's *AU-priority* hypothesis, writing that 'the common substratum' of all the major Annalistic texts up to the ninth century 'is preserved most faithfully within the compilation of the *Annals of Ulster*'.[121] Similarly his reference to AU, 'beginning at 431 A.D.' shows that he had adopted O'Conor's *AU-431* hypothesis. Then, having made a careful survey of all those AU entries that could be plausibly classified as contemporary, Smyth concluded that:[122]

> It has been found that the earliest contemporary entries within the compilation of *A.U.* date from about the middle of the sixth century, and that this phase also coincides with the earliest entries relating to the Ulaid and the Iona and Scottish area. Since Columba sailed to Iona in 563, there is now every reason for assuming that our earliest body of annals take their origins from the time of the saint himself ... An interest in chronology and the necessity of preserving paschal tables was the background out of which the earliest annals at Iona began to evolve ... Iona being the sole centre of monastic recording prior to the early eighth century.

118 Morris, 'Chronicle of Eusebius', 80 (cit.).   119 Morris, 'Chronicle of Eusebius', 89 (cits.). 120 Dumville, 'Ulster heroes', 53 instanced it as a study which failed 'to lay forth in detail and with full documentation all the evidence for the hypotheses' that it presented.   121 Smyth, 'Earliest Irish annals', 1 (cit.).   122 Smyth, 'Earliest Irish annals', 3–30 (evaluation of AU entries), 41–2 (cit.).

Thus, like Bannerman, Smyth concluded that the annals of AU up to the eighth century were compiled contemporaneously on Iona, but he pushed the starting date of this contemporaneous chronicling back to *c.*550. Regarding the annals before this date Smyth wrote that 'the annalist who began to keep his record at Iona in the 560s projected his chronicle back to the death of Patrick at *c.*490.' However, he considered that it was 'later compilers' who subsequently, 'projected backwards from *c.*490 to a *new* beginning at 431'.[123] Smyth did not discuss the world history material but implicitly placed its introduction to post 800 with the statement that 'claims for a chronicle at Clonmacnoise before 800 A.D. must be rejected'. Smyth's study, like Bannerman's, concentrated on establishing the detailed parameters of an Irish inaugural chronicle.[124]

In 1975 when Gearóid Mac Niocaill set out to review the early Irish Annals he began by citing the work of Mac Neill and O'Rahilly, by endorsing Bannerman's account of the Iona chronicle, and by accepting Smyth's rejection of a Bangor source contributing to the Annals. He accepted the mid-eighth century as the date of transfer of the Iona chronicle to Ireland, after which he postulated the existence in AU of 'two main annalistic streams. One is centred in the north, around Armagh ... [and] a second element which is centred in Meath, covering the period mid-eighth to mid-tenth century.' Further, Mac Niocaill agreed with Smyth that 'the most likely place of origin of this [second] element is Clonard'. In this discussion Mac Niocaill tacitly accepted Mac Carthy's *AU-priority*, writing that:[125]

> What is substantially the same text as that of *U* [AU] has, as noted above, been transmitted by other sets of annals. It is identifiable in *T* [AT] and *CS*, which demonstrably have a common origin, and with these *Clo* [MB] must also be classed. The transition point to independence in these – as a group – can be dated fairly closely: it begins to show signs of independence about the middle of the tenth century ... T.F. O'Rahilly (in *Early Irish history and mythology*, p. 258) suggested – rightly, in my view – that a copy of the text passed to Clonmacnoise about that time ...

Thus Mac Niocaill here adopted, either explicitly or implicitly, Mac Neill's three hypotheses, and O'Conor's, O'Rahilly's and Bannerman's hypotheses, and Smyth's interpretation of this latter. However, Mac Niocaill's vague statements that the alleged 'transition point ... can be dated fairly closely', and that the Clonmacnoise group 'begins to show signs of independence about the middle of the tenth century', show that despite apparently endorsing O'Rahilly's hypothesis, he had difficulty accommodating it to the actual texts.

123 Smyth, 'Earliest Irish annals', 44 (citation where the italic emphasis is Smyth's).   124 Smyth, 'Earliest Irish annals', 35–6 reviews Bannerman's study.   125 Mac Niocaill, *MIA*, 21–3 (cits.).

In 1979 David Dumville published the first of a series of challenging articles in which he discussed the inter-relationships and textual history of the Annals. This first article was prompted by Kelleher's second publication in 1971, and in his response Dumville pointed out a number of serious deficiencies in Kelleher's arguments, concluding 'the reasoning by which he has arrived at a date and a textual history for them seems to me to be lacking in cogency.'[126] He also pointed out a number of conflicts between the views of Hughes and Kelleher on the one hand, and Mac Niocaill on the other.[127] Dumville made the valuable observation that resolution of these conflicts required more careful examination and documentation of the evidence, writing:[128]

> The major difficulty in all this is of course that even on very basic points there is no agreement between experts as to the detailed relationship of the early Irish annalistic collections. Until there is more common ground on basic issues – and this will be achieved only by studies which lay forth in detail and with full documentation all the evidence for the hypotheses which they present (unlike the practice of a number of recent publications) – it will be impossible to give credence to larger theories such as those advanced in 'The Táin and the Annals'.

However, a number of his own assertions demonstrate that, notwithstanding this admirably critical approach to evidence, he had already absorbed a considerable number of the hypotheses of earlier scholars, which rested upon either non-existent or dubious evidence. For example his references such as:[129]

> a) the common annalistic stock which breaks off *ca*. A.D. 910–913 (as has been noted by a number of scholars) ...
> b) For these entries to have been part of the common stock to *ca* 910 ...
> c) At present, evidence seems to be lacking that they [Táin entries] formed part of a common stock of annals antedating *ca* 910.

all show that, despite having footnoted Kelleher's observation that 'AU and the Clonmacnoise group continue to have a small percentage of common entries, perhaps as far as *ca* 1050', Dumville had firmly adopted the year 911 from O'Rahilly's *Clonmacnoise–911* hypothesis as the point at which the Clonmacnoise group and AU diverged. Further, his assertions that:[130]

---

126 Dumville, 'Ulster heroes', 52 (cit.).   127 Dumville, 'Ulster heroes', 49–51 (conflicting views). 128 Dumville, 'Ulster heroes', 52–3 (cit. – it was unfortunate, however, that in p. 53 n. 43 Dumville chose to cite the valuable articles of Morris and Mac Niocaill's *MIA* as instances of such 'recent publications').   129 Dumville, 'Ulster heroes', 49, 50, 54 (cits.).   130 Dumville, 'Ulster heroes', 48, 50, 51 (cits.).

a) AU is not a witness until the fifth century ...

b) ... since the copy of AU in T.C.D. MS. 1282 (H. 1. 8) begins only with A.D. 431.

c) We are always brought back to the difficulty that AU have no pre-Patrician section.

together demonstrate that he had also adopted O'Conor's *AU-431*, and Todd's *AT-fragment* hypotheses. Finally his statement that 'The common stock of the pre-Patrician chronicle is datable after 725 (the publication of Bede's *De temporum ratione*) ...', shows that he had also adopted Stokes' *Bedan-source* hypothesis. These instances illustrate just how difficult it is for a scholar wishing to introduce more critical standards of evidence to escape from the weight of established hypotheses.

Dumville's next publication, a careful evaluation of the process of replacement of Latin by Irish in AU over 431–1050, was just such a study as he had called for in 1979.[131] This was a valuable contribution which highlighted a considerable number of linguistic characteristics of the work of the Annalists. However, in his opening and concluding discussions a number of statements regarding AU vis-à-vis the other texts show him maintaining the earlier hypotheses. For example:[132]

a) the *Annals of Ulster*, now preserved in manuscripts of the late fifteenth and earlier sixteenth century but generally held to represent accurately the results of eight centuries or more of contemporary annalistic recording.

b) In the period before 913, they [AU] embody one or more chronicles not available to the compilers of the other major texts.

c) In the course of this survey of bilingual usage in the *Annals of Ulster* we have found little reason to doubt that that text remains a fairly faithful representative of the work of the various annalists who contributed to its growth in the early Middle Ages.

All these effectively maintain Mac Carthy's *AU-priority* hypothesis. While his assertions:[133]

a) Close agreement between the *Annals of Ulster* and the other major compilations ends at 913.

b) Certainly by the tenth century, and perhaps before, we can point to the use of the chronicles of Eusebius-Jerome, Prosper, Sulpicius Severus, Marcellinus, Isidore and Bede in Irish 'historical' writing and to the employment of some of these in the extant annal collections.

---

131 Dumville, 'Latin and Irish', 323–32 (evaluation), 334–41 (comprehensive appendices). 132 Dumville, 'Latin and Irish', 320, 321, 332 (cits.). 133 Dumville, 'Latin and Irish', 321, 323 (cits.).

Here a) shows him adopting Hughes' year 913 for O'Rahilly's *Clonmacnoise-911* hypothesis, while b) shows his acceptance of both Stokes' *Bedan-source* and Mac Neill's *Prefix-compilation* hypotheses. The former of these prompted Dumville in his conclusions to examine his language results for possible verification of O'Rahilly's hypothesis. Noting first that the 'annals from 917 to 937 show a variety of entries expressing value-judgements, a feature uncharacteristic of the normally laconic annalistic genre', he asked the following question: 'If the end of this annalist's work is fairly well defined, can we say also when he began to write annals?' His answer to this was, 'A number of hints points to the 910s', and he distinguished six language variants over 905–37 and then concluded: [134]

> On these few criteria we might wish to suppose that this annalist took up his trade between 911 and 916. If that is right, it is curious that he appears just at the point at which Kathleen Hughes saw a major change in the text-history of the annal collections – in fact, where her 'Chronicle of Ireland' comes to an end.

Now while Dumville expressed this conclusion in very tentative terms, 'we might wish to suppose', and, 'If that is right', but the effect of his discussion was in fact to endorse Hughes' version of O'Rahilly's *Clonmacnoise-911* hypothesis.

Two years later Dumville commenced his incisive review of Mac Airt and Mac Niocaill's re-edition of AU by declaring in general of Annalistic scholarship, 'that here too lie acres of ignorance protected by high fences of misconception and false deduction.'[135] Nevertheless he proceeded to maintain his own support for Todd's *AT-fragment* hypothesis by writing in reference to ff. 12–14 of TCD 1282:[136]

> On the face of it, these are two separate works, joined together (in MS H) only because of their common genus; it is doubtful that the compilers of *AU* ever intended a world chronicle to be prefixed to their annals of the Irish Middle Ages.

Likewise his assertion that 'They [other Irish chronicles] attest the sequence of entries and annals which all texts hold in common to A.D. 911', shows no inclination to vault the high fence surrounding O'Rahilly's misconstruction of annalistic independence after 911.[137] Finally his 'One tends to think of the *Annals of Ulster* as embodying contemporary annals from at least the later seventh century', implicitly draws on O'Conor's *AU-431*, Mac Carthy's *AU-priority*, and Mac Neill's *IIC* hypotheses.

In 1984 Dumville, together with Kathryn Grabowski, published the only book devoted to a study of the textual relationships and history of the Irish

---

134 Dumville, 'Latin and Irish', 331 (cit.).   135 Dumville, 'Editing', 67 (cit., where he preceded this with a similar remark in respect of the Irish genealogies, hence his 'here too').   136 Dumville, 'Editing', 76 (cit.).   137 Dumville, 'Editing', 83, 85 (cits.).

Annals, and as such this warrants serious examination. The basis of the work was a careful collation undertaken by Grabowski of AI, AU, AT, and CS over 431–1092, in which she systematically identified unique and common entries. From a chronological point of view it was unfortunate that AI, on account of it having the oldest MS, was chosen as the reference text, for this imposed all the problems of AI's complex chronology upon the collation. Further, both O'Conor's *AU–431* and Todd's *AT-fragment* hypotheses, as well as O'Rahilly's *Clonmacnoise-911* hypothesis were deeply embedded assumptions in the collation process. Consequently, collation commenced wherever possible at 431, and was repeatedly divided at the year 911, and resulted in section headings such as, 'Unique material AI 431–911' and 'The unique material of AI 912–1000'.[138] In her introduction Grabowski's assertions repeatedly reveal her own adoption of O'Conor's, Todd's, Mac Carthy's, and O'Rahilly's hypotheses, for example:[139]

> a) There is little indication that this text ever included any 'pre-Patrician' sections as do both AI (Mac Neill's section A) and AT.
> b) The earlier date [431] represents the beginning of the 'common stock' which forms the basis of all our annalistic compilations including AI …
> c) … the evidence of the entries from the annals for 901–11 is discussed along with the ninth-century material. This was done in order to contain the 'common-stock' period in AI with a single discussion …

Citations a) and b) here implicitly affirm Todd's *AT-fragment* and Mac Carthy's *AU-priority* hypotheses, b) affirms O'Conor's *AU-431*, while c) derives from O'Rahilly's *Clonmacnoise-911* hypothesis. In respect of c) Grabowski devoted a section of her discussion in order to 'determine the point at which AU and the Clonmacnoise group diverge'.[140] Here she collated AU and CS fully for 910–11, and then summarized the collation for 912–14, emphasizing the small number of common entries and their disparate language and concluded: 'For three years in sequence, then, we have no clear evidence of a relationship between AU and the Clonmacnoise group. We can suppose that the texts diverge after the annal for 911, on the evidence which I have presented above.'[141] However, had she continued her discussion to the very next year she would have disclosed the following relationship between all five entries of CS, and the first, second, fourth, fifth and seventh entries of AU as shown in Figure 5.

---

138 Grabowski & Dumville, *Chronicles*, 94, 69 (cits.), 1–107 (Grabowski's collation).
139 Grabowski & Dumville, *Chronicles*, 5, 8 (cits.).   140 Grabowski & Dumville, *Chronicles*, 53–6 (discussion & citation).   141 Grabowski & Dumville, *Chronicles*, 55 (cit.).

CS 915	AU 914
1. *Oengus* ... mic *Maeilechlainn, Ridamna* *Eirenn* ... periit	1. *Oengus* h. *Mael Sechnaill, ridomna* Temrach ... *moritur*
2. *Domnall mac Aodha, Rí Ailigh*, post *penitentiam* periit	2. *Domnall m. Aedho, ri Ailigh*, ... in *penitientia moritur*
3. *Maolciarain mac Echucain, Princeps Cluana eois*, et Muccnama *Epscop Aird Macha* ... dormiuit	4. *Mael Ciarain m. Eochacain, princeps Cluana hAuis episcopus* Aird Macha ... [*moritur*]
4. *Sgannlan* Epscop *Tamlachta*, quieuit	5. *Scannlan*, airchinnech *Tamhlacta* ... *moriuntur*
5. Orgain Corcaige ... ó *Gentibh*	7. Tórmach ... *ghentibh* ... indred ... Muman

Figure 5. Collation of all CS and AU entries for AD 915 which record evident common events with cognate textual features; cognate text is shown in italic.

Thus entries describing all of the five events recorded in CS are found in identical sequence in AU, each with some cognate textual elements, here highlighted in italic. Now the probability that two annalists recording five events independently would arrange them in identical sequence is one in $1\times2\times3\times4\times5=120$. That they would independently use the same words in the same order significantly lessens this probability. Furthermore a glance at the comprehensive collation of CS/AU entries online will show that subsequently this common ordering, while not absolute, predominates. For example over the six years 957–62 all fourteen common CS/AU events are identically ordered and the probability of independent annalists achieving this is one in $(1\times2\times3\times4\times5)\times(1\times2)\times(1\times2\times3)\times(1\times2)\times(1)\times(1\times2)=1152$. On these grounds we are obliged to conclude that CS and AU transmit a common source and that the textual differences observed between them have arisen from subsequent editing during the transmission of either or both. It is completely out of the question to 'suppose' with Grabowski that these texts have diverged at 911, rather she imposed O'Rahilly's *Clonmacnoise–911* hypothesis regardless of the evidence. The situation illustrated by the above collation and discussion continues in fact until 1055, though thereafter the number of shared entries and their degree of textual correspondence reduces. Before 1055 however both transmit some closely corresponding entries, for example at 925:

CS 925.3: *Dubgall mac Aodha, Rídamhna Uladh, iugulatus est* ó Cinel Maeilchae.
AU 924.1: *Dubghall m. Aedha, ri Ulath*, a suis *iugulatus est*.

Moreover, it is certain that Grabowski was aware of this continued correspondence, for, having first insisted that the texts diverge at 911, she subsequently returned to the subject and asserted vaguely that:[142]

> From perhaps the middle of the tenth century, and lasting for about a century, a different relationship may be observed between AU and the Clonmacnoise group. Sufficient entries exhibit close similarity or identity to indicate either the use of a common source for the period or, perhaps more likely, contamination of an ancestor of AU by a Clonmacnoise-group text now lost ...

However, as the examples cited from 915, 925 and 957–62 demonstrate, this 'common source' relationship definitely did not commence in 'perhaps the middle of the tenth century', but it continues from 911 onwards.

Finally, and incongruently in view of the sustained relationship that she acknowledged existed between AU and the Clonmacnoise group texts into the eleventh century, she employed a textual correspondence that she identified between AT and AI at 1061 'to substantiate the suggestion that AI represent a version, albeit abbreviated, of a Clonmacnoise-group text like that which underlies AT.'[143] Thus both Grabowski's organization and interpretation of her collation was strongly conditioned by the hypotheses she had inherited from O'Conor, Todd, Mac Carthy, Stokes, Mac Neill, and O'Rahilly. In consequence, unfortunately, those of her conclusions which rest on their hypotheses cannot be sustained.

For his part of the book, which Dumville subtitled 'The Clonmacnoise redaction of the "Chronicle of Ireland"', he commenced by reiterating Grabowski's results. In this he again insisted that the 'common source' extended only to 911, while acknowledging evidence to the contrary, writing:[144]

> It is abundantly clear that AU and the hypothesised original of the Clonmacnoise group share a common source: in chapter I it has been argued that that source ended with the annal for 911, even though (presumably at a much later stage in the history of AU) another member of the Clonmacnoise group was subsequently lightly drawn on to provide some material for its years *ca* 950–1054.

Now examination of the Internet collation of AT/CS/AU shows the number of common entries between AT/CS and AU over the decades prior to and following Dumville's range 950–1054 to be as shown in Figure 6.

---

142 Grabowski & Dumville, *Chronicles*, 56 (cit.).   143 Grabowski & Dumville, *Chronicles*, 66 (cit.).
144 Grabowski & Dumville, *Chronicles*, 111 (cit.), 109–226 (Dumville's chapters II–IV).

AD range	940–9	950–9	1045–54	1055–64
Common entry count	21	27	17	17

Figure 6. Decadal counts of entries found in common between AT/CS and AU over 940–59 and 1045–64.

Consequently, it is absolutely impossible to justify Dumville's specified range '*ca* 950–1054' for a common source. Indeed when he acknowledged a common source over this interval, it is very difficult to believe that he was unaware that effectively the same relationship was sustained over 911–50. This question of the relationship between the Clonmacnoise group and AU in the centuries following 911 will be re-examined in chapter 8, p. 241 ff. Regarding world history Dumville wrote of 'the undoubted major accessions to the Clonmacnoise chronicle' as follows:[145]

> A much greater international flavour – anchoring the notices of Irish history securely within a European context – is provided by some forty borrowings (often of a substantial size) from Bede's *Chronica maiora* …

making it clear that he accepted Stokes' *Bedan-source* hypothesis. Regarding the location of the compilation, despite his choice of title having already in effect determined this, he wrote:[146]

> It has been generally agreed (albeit without any detailed study having been devoted to the question) that this recension was effected at Clonmacnoise. In O'Rahilly's view, the work was undertaken 'in the early years of the tenth century'.

Thus it is explicit that he was merely repeating O'Rahilly's *Clonmacnoise–911* hypothesis, while at the same time acknowledging it to be unsubstantiated. Regarding the world history element of AT Dumville wrote candidly that 'It seems most likely to be an integral part of the 'Clonmacnoise Chronicle', but very little attention has been devoted to it as yet and the conclusion is scarcely more than a guess.'[147] Finally, in seeking to establish a date for 'the work of recension which created the "Clonmacnoise Chronicle" he again invoked O'Rahilly's hypothesis to assert that 'it was executed no earlier than A.D. 911', while to obtain a *terminus post quem non* he made an extensive collation between the common entries found in the Irish Annals and the *Annales Cambriae*.[148] From this collation he concluded:[149]

145 Grabowski & Dumville, *Chronicles*, 112 (cit.).   146 Grabowski & Dumville, *Chronicles*, 122 (cit.).
147 Grabowski & Dumville, *Chronicles*, 156 (cit.).   148 Grabowski & Dumville, *Chronicles*, 209 (cit.);
Phillimore, *Annales Cambriae*.   149 Grabowski & Dumville, *Chronicles*, 226 (cit.).

> The certain dating of AC (A) [i.e. the A text of *Annales Cambriae*] not later than the third quarter of the tenth century (and probably not later than the 950s) provides a *terminus ante quem* for the creation of the 'Clonmacnoise Chronicle' ancestral to AT/CS and their relatives. We may suspect that AC were compiled in the early 950s. We may therefore give to the composition of the 'Clonmacnoise Chronicle' the dates 911×954 with some confidence that they cannot be undermined.

The confidence expressed in this final sentence is, alas, belied by Dumville's reliance on earlier hypotheses all resting on inadequate grounds. While enormous effort went into the collations presented in this book, both the organization and interpretation of these collations were conditioned from the outset by the hypotheses of O'Conor, Todd, Mac Carthy, Stokes, Mac Neill, and especially O'Rahilly, none of which can be shown to rest on valid grounds. Consequently, and sadly, most of the conclusions obtained by Grabowski and Dumville in this book are likewise invalid.

In 1982, just two years before Dumville and Grabowski's publication, the *AU-431* and *AU-priority* hypotheses received perhaps their most authoritative endorsement when the RIA published volume eight of its *New history of Ireland* series. This volume entitled *A chronology of Irish history to 1976*, with the three formidable editors of Theodore W. Moody, Francis X. Martin, and Francis J. Byrne, actually enshrined both the *AU–431* and *AU-priority* hypotheses into its chronology with the entry *s.a.* 431, '"Annals of Ulster" begin'. In the introduction to the section 432–1169, compiled by Francis J. Byrne and Charles Doherty, the only MS discussed was TCD 1282 and of this it was then asserted:[150]

> We have given all duplicate entries made by the primary hand of A.U. (as at 457/61, 562/3) but have ignored the numerous interpolations by later hands; we have also indicated the variant dates implicit in *Ann. Inisf.* [AI] as supplied by Mac Airt ...

Thus absolute priority in Byrne and Doherty's chronology was accorded to AU, including its many duplicates, compounded with the further discrepancies introduced by Mac Airt's marginal AD in his edition of AI. The result consequently reflects all of the chronological confusion of the Cuana group over the

---

150 Moody et al., *A Chronology*, 9, 16 (cits.), 16–71 (chronology for 432–1169). The principle however was not systematically followed, e.g. '461/3 Death of Lóeguire' cf. AU 462 & AI 463; '467/9 Ailill Molt ... Feis Temro' cf. AU 467 & 470, & AI 469; '483 Assassination of Cremthann', cf. AU 483, AI 485 & 487. Furthermore on pp. 8–9 it was stated 'from 482 to 1013 ... we have followed the now generally accepted convention of adding one year throughout this period', whereas collation over 482–90 shows that in fact they followed the convention adopted in Mac Airt & Mac Niocaill, *AU*, xi and incremented only from AU 488.

fifth, sixth and seventh centuries. Similarly in the subsequent section 1169–1534, whilst nothing was stated in its introduction, the chronology of Mac Carthy's edition of AU was reproduced and so his anachronisms over 1193–1223 and 1263–65. Hence this prestigious publication relied unequivocally upon AU for its chronology of early and medieval Ireland, and confronted its readers with most of its inherent chronological problems.

Next in 1997 Annette Kehnel gave a substantial discussion of the Clonmacnoise annals in her book examining the monastery of Clonmacnoise and its properties. However, in this she repeated the conclusions of principally Hughes, Dumville, and Grabowski, so that both the *AU-priority* and *Clonmacnoise–911* hypotheses are prominently asserted and assumed when comparative interpretations of Annalistic entries are made.[151]

Finally, Thomas Charles-Edwards published in 2006 what was essentially a conflate edition of English translations of AU/AT/CS extending over 431–911. He entitled this edition the '*Chronicle of Ireland*' which title had been invented by Hughes in 1972 and cited repeatedly by Dumville in 1984 in his book with Grabowski.[152] Charles-Edwards' adoption of the range of 431–911 without any discussion or acknowledgement demonstrated just how firmly O'Conor's and O'Rahilly's hypotheses had become established in the mind-set of Annalistic scholarship, for this range implicitly invoked their *AU–431* and the *Clonmacnoise–911* hypotheses. In the introduction to his edition Charles-Edwards explicitly endorsed nearly all of the hypotheses that had been introduced since the time of O'Conor as follows:[153]

AU-priority: He asserted without qualification that 'in the Annals of Ulster we have the best text of the early annals'.

AT-fragment: He wrote that the 'so-called 'Dublin Fragment' … is generally thought to have been in origin a separate manuscript bound together with the Annals of Ulster in Trinity College Dublin MS H.1.8 at a later stage.' Here he omitted the attribution to Tigernach but retained the 'fragment' hypothesis, and while he acknowledged the existence of an argument showing the 'fragment' to be part of AU he declined to consider the evidence.

Bedan-source: He wrote that for 'the subsequent period [from 527] up to 725 Bede's *Chronica Maiora* were the principal external source.'

---

151 Kehnel, *Clonmacnois*, 4–14 (discussion), 4, 246–96 (*AU-priority*), 4–5, 9–11 (*Clonmacnoise-911*). 152 Hughes, *Early Christian Ireland*, 101 (invention of title); Grabowski & Dumville, *Chronicles*, 111 ff. (citations of title). 153 Charles-Edwards, *Chronicle of Ireland* 1, 1–59 (Introduction), 7 (*AU-priority* cit.), 3 n.2 (*AT-fragment* cit. and acknowledgement of Mc Carthy, 'AU compilation'), 52–7 (*Bedan-source* cit.), 3 (*Prefix-compilation* cit.).

Prefix-compilation: He adopted Mac Neill's *IWC, IIC* and *prefix-compilation* hypotheses in the following single sentence: 'The Irish World Chronicle has, however, a different textual history from the Chronicle of Ireland, in that it can only be shown to have been prefixed to the Chronicle of Ireland in a daughter chronicle compiled in the monastery of Clonmacnois.'

Thus in his introduction Charles-Edwards either implicitly or explicitly embraced most of the misguided hypotheses of the Annalistic scholarship of the preceding two centuries, and naturally reflected these in his edition.[154] Here by a combination of indentation, italic font and parentheses he endeavoured to represent whether entries or parts thereof appeared in AU and/or the Clonmacnoise group.[155] In this presentation the *AU-priority* hypothesis was repeatedly and conspicuously expressed in two different ways. First, all text unique to AU was printed in the plain Times font used as the primary font for the edition, whereas all text unique to the Clonmacnoise group was printed in italic Times font. Thus all entries unique to the Clonmacnoise group were represented as abnormal in terms of their font. Second, Charles-Edwards' own AD chronology for the edition was prefixed to each kalend as a bare number and this series followed the MS AD of AU identically for 431–85. He then effectively inserted a kalend at 486, and for 487–911 incremented the MS AD of AU by one year; thus his editorial AD reflected only the chronological structure of AU.[156] However, the assertion that his translation 'gives an editorial AD date for each annal which is the corrected date of the edition by Mac Airt and Mac Niocaill' is not correct since their editorial AD effectively inserted the additional kalend at 488.[157] Rather by inserting a kalend effectively at 486 Charles-Edwards adopted the solution to AU's chronological problems proposed by Mac Carthy in 1901.[158] One serious consequence of this relentless maintenance of the *AU-priority* hypothesis was the reproduction of all of AU's duplicates, some of which were augmented to become triplicates as a result of Charles-Edwards representing Clonmacnoise group entries separately.[159] In summary, Charles-Edwards'

---

154 He did not however endorse Ware's *Tigernach* hypothesis, and he emended Bannerman's *Iona chronicle* hypothesis to commence contemporaneous chronicling shortly after S. Columba's arrival on Iona, cf. p. 8.   155 Charles-Edwards, *Chronicle of Ireland* 1, 58–9 (representation of text). 156 Charles-Edwards, *Chronicle of Ireland* 1, 78 (insertion *s.a.* 486 where the reader is referred to pp. 35–8 for the 'chronological problem', but no account of this insertion is given either there or elsewhere in the Introduction).   157 Charles-Edwards, *Chronicle of Ireland* 1, 37–8 (cit.); Mac Airt & Mac Niocaill, *AU*, xi (discussion), 54 (insertion at 488).   158 Mac Carthy *AU* iv, pp. xcvii–xcix (Mac Carthy's solution); xcix ('the chronology to 485, inclusive, is correct; 486 is wanting; thenceforward, to 1013, the dates are one year in advance').   159 Charles-Edwards, *Chronicle of Ireland* 1, (triplicates – e.g. *Natus Brigidae s.a.* 439, 452, 456; *Feis Temhra s.a.* 467, 469, 470; *Bellum Bregh Ele s.a.* 473, 475, 478.)

conflate edition of AU/AT/CS represents a valiant but misguided effort to compile an edition of these annals conforming to the mistaken hypotheses of modern scholarship.

Reviewing the history of scholarly discussion of the origin and development of the Annals, it is clear that from and beginning with Ware's summary hypothesis that Tigernach was the compiler of Rawl. B. 488 up to 1088, a long series of hypotheses was introduced with either no reference, or inadequate reference to the MSS themselves. The later hypotheses of Mac Neill and O'Rahilly depended on the earlier hypotheses of Ware, O'Conor, Mac Carthy and Stokes, and the result has been a labyrinth of interconnected hypotheses none of which are supported by the evidence of the MSS. Indeed in modern times this labyrinth has been maintained against the evidence of the MSS. Overall there is apparent an involuntary reflex amongst scholars educated to respect the importance and priority of Bede's works on time, including his chronicles, to consequently 'explain' both world history entries and the phenomenon of the Irish Annals as a consequence of Bede's influence and his work. In fact examination of Bede's works on time shows that he drew heavily on Irish source material, as Charles Jones, editor of those works, acknowledged sixty years ago: 'The bulk of the Northumbrian computistical material came from the Irish ... Bede's sources were Irish.'[160] Jones' assertion has been fully demonstrated by Dáibhí Ó Cróinín's publications demonstrating the composition and transmission of Irish computistical texts from Ireland to both Northumbria and the Continent in the seventh century.[161] Bede's own account of the introduction of Christianity into Northumbria under King Oswald in HE iii.1–6 emphasizes that Oswald brought it from Iona. This Irish origin for Northumbrian seventh-century Christianity, and its *computistica* in particular, which was never acknowledged by any of the above scholars, would strongly imply that both the world history entries and the chronicle tradition itself flowed from Iona to Northumbria.[162] Only John Morris realized this. For the others, all who considered the world history material were trapped by the myth of a late Clonmacnoise compilation, first instituted by Ware's attribution to Tigernach Ua Braein and 1088, and subsequently moved to *c.*911 by O'Rahilly, where it was sustained against the evidence of the MSS. Only the work of Bannerman and Smyth, who both focussed their efforts on identifying the characteristics and parameters of Irish contemporaneous chronicling, escaped

---

160 Jones, *BOT*, 131 (cit.).   161 Ó Cróinín, 'Bede's Irish computus', 212 'research carried out since Jones' path-breaking discovery of 1937 indicates that his verdict in BOT, that Bede owed almost all he knew in the field of computistics to the Irish, has been thoroughly vindicated'; cf. Wallis, *Reckoning*, lxxvii–viii.   162 Mc Carthy, 'Bede's source', *passim* (demonstration that Bede's world chronicles in DT/DTR derive substantially from a copy of the Iona chronicle).

the consequence of this myth. But their judgments were still adversely influenced by the hypotheses of O'Conor, Todd and Mac Carthy, which imposed on them the supposed priority of AU's textual authority, and the misguided time horizon of the year 431 for its alleged beginning.

To complete this review it seems appropriate to include an account of my own articles that address Annalistic matters, since this will clarify where I have adopted and subsequently rejected the hypotheses of earlier scholars. In cases where the substance of these articles is to appear in subsequent chapters just a brief synopsis will be included here. My first such article was published in 1994 and examined the chronological apparatus of AU for 431–1131, in which I tried to resolve the asynchronism between the kalend+AD chronology written largely in the first hand of Ua Luinín, and the ferial+epact chronology written largely in the second hand. In the paper I concluded that the asynchronism was the result of the use of two different AD conventions, viz. one changing the AD on 25 March, and the other changing the AD on 1 January, together with the loss of one kalend. Subsequent research has shown that this conclusion was mistaken, and this research was published in 2003. The chronological summary given in the conclusion of the 1994 article shows clearly that I had adopted most of the existing scholarly hypotheses relevant to AU, such as its assumed priority, its beginning at 431, its dependence on DTR cap. 66, and Mac Neill's three hypotheses. With hindsight the most useful element of the paper was the tabulation of the papal succession, which showed that with just two exceptions it had been compiled from the chronicle of Marcellinus and the *Liber Pontificalis*, and that the entry 'Finis Cronici Iusebii' had been inserted in order to truncate LP's papal succession prematurely.[163]

Next in 1997 two papers were published jointly with Dr Aidan Breen which examined the astronomical entries in the Annals, one with an astronomical emphasis appeared in *Vistas in Astronomy*, the other with a textual emphasis appeared in *Peritia* and was the more relevant to Annalistic studies. The survey was based upon the chronology of AU, and the conclusion that of all the Annals, 'AU preserves the most records and the most accurate with respect to both their description and their chronological details', remains valid. However, the statement that 'Until *c.*912, when they diverge from AU, they preserve practically identical material, except when lacunose, but thereafter they either record different events or, as at 1023, the same event differently', shows the influence of O'Rahilly's *Clonmacnoise–911* hypothesis. The collation of the texts of the entries highlighted contrasts and correspondences between AU, AT, CS,

---

163 Mc Carthy, 'AU apparatus 431–1131', 58 (1 Jan. vs 25 Mar. AD), 77–9 (final summary), 67–70 (papal succession). Mc Carthy, 'AU apparatus 82–1019', 269–73 (re-evaluation of AU).

and AI, and examination of the language and distribution of the entries disclosed that an eschatological motive lay behind the observation and recording of astronomical extremes.[164]

As a result of searching for astronomical entries in AT and CS I became aware of their common ferial series, and in 1996 I began to collate this data together with brief tokens of each entry, using the table structure in Word. It soon became clear that the kalend+ferial chronology of their common source could be recovered over AD 1–664, and when this was collated against AU 431–663 it was obvious that AU's chronology was both later and derivative, and consequently the priority claimed for AU by Mac Carthy was mistaken. An account of this work was published in the PRIA in 1998 in which the entire ferial sequence of AT/CS over those years was tabulated, as well as the full collation at the five points where AU possessed an additional kalend. Calibration of the joint kalend+ferial sequence disclosed that AT/CS was missing seven kalends for 425–31, and a further six kalends between 612 and 664. Comparison with AU showed however that only five kalends had been restored between 575–648, leaving a deficit of one kalend. This then was the cause of the one year deficit in AU's AD chronology to 1013. Furthermore AU's chronology over the interval 492–536 was seen to be severely disturbed and, because this interval synchronized with interjections referring to 'Cuana' or 'Liber Cuanach', this suggested the hypothesis that Cuana was the author of this disturbed chronology. Collation with AI showed that, while its chronology was quite severely corrupted, it possessed elements of AU's chronological emendments, showing that they shared a common source.[165] This paper demonstrated beyond all reasonable doubt that Mac Carthy's *AU-priority* hypothesis was mistaken, and the cogent ferial series of AT/CS extending from AD1 to 644 also strongly suggested that Mac Neill's three prefix hypotheses were also mistaken. However, re-examination of the paper shows that I still clung to a number of the other received hypotheses, such as Stokes' *Bedan-source*, and Todd's *AT-fragment* hypotheses, as well as my own earlier hypothesis that AU had used two different AD conventions.[166] In March 1999 the table of chronological and entry tokens synchronizing the principal Annalistic texts was made available on the Web* along with an explanatory introduction, and this provided the first substantial synchronization of the principal Annals over the years AD 306–722. By

---

* www.irish-annals.cs.tcd.ie

164 Mc Carthy & Breen, 'Evaluation', 117–38, and Mc Carthy & Breen, 'Astronomical observations', 39 (cits.), 21–3 (eschatological motivation).   **165** Mc Carthy, 'Chronology', 245–50 (AT/CS kalend+ferial collation), 251–4 (AU's five restored kalends), 225–9 (calibration and missing kalends), 232–5 (Cuana), 238 (AI).   **166** Mc Carthy, 'Chronology', 228, 230, 233, 238 (Bedan source), 209, 242 ('Dublin fragment'), 230, 235–6 (Annunciation AD).

September 1999 this had been extended to AD 1–722, by September 2000 to AD 1–1178, and by March 2005 to AD 1–1590.

The collation of AT and CS had shown that the earliest chronological apparatus had consisted of just kalend+ferial extending at least from AD 1 to 644, and an obvious question was, when and where had this been compiled? In an effort to answer this I began collating the entries of AT and DTR cap. 66 over the years AD 1–358, and it quickly became apparent that Stokes' *Bedan-source* hypothesis was unsustainable, and this provided the basis for the paper 'Status of the pre-Patrician Irish annals'. Here detailed comparison of the Roman imperial succession from Octavian to Trajan showed that Eutropius' *Breviarum ab urbe condita* had been used as a source, but that more of Eutropius had been transmitted in AT than in DTR cap. 66. Similarly, collation of AT/DTR entries that conflicted semantically showed that AT had regularly transmitted more of the earlier sources than DTR. Thus Morris' conclusion that AT and DTR shared a common source was independently and emphatically confirmed. Next, examination of the Alexandrian episcopal succession in AT showed that it preserved both textual and chronological details in common with Rufinus' translation of Eusebius' *Ecclesiastical history*. Moreover, errors in the construction showed that Rufinus himself was the most likely author of it, and this hypothesis received strong support from the substantial and admiring treatment accorded to Origen, Rufinus' chief spiritual inspiration. As well as this, collation of Bede's series of rulers for his Third Age with the parallel entries in AI showed that they corresponded, and that whenever they diverged from Jerome's chronicle Bede had preserved interjections by the compiler that could most plausibly be attributed to Rufinus.[167]

It consequently emerged that the most likely author of the world history chronicle up to *c.*400 in AT, AI and DTR was Rufinus of Aquileia, and he compiled it between the completion of his *Ecclesiastical History* in *c.*402 and his death in 410. Regarding transmission of this chronicle to Ireland, a series of chronological emendments together with entries referring to S. Martin and S. Hilary suggested that it had travelled via Sulpicius Severus in southern Gaul. Sulpicius was the author of the *Vita* of S. Martin, a correspondent of Rufinus, and author of the *latercus* or 84-year Paschal cycle followed in Iona until 716. The hypothesis thus emerged that the most plausible origin for the inauguration of the Irish Annals was that they simply represented a continuation of Sulpicius' continuation of Rufinus' chronicle, so that Mac Neill's prefix hypotheses, based upon Stokes' *Bedan-source* hypothesis, were all mistaken.

---

167 Mc Carthy, 'Status', 116–25 (imperial succession), 126–30 (semantic conflict), 131–8 (Alexandrian succession), 138–40 (Origen), 142–8 (Third Age).

Between them, these two papers raised many serious problems for the current scholarly account of both the origin and the development of the Irish Annals, and further problems arose when collation of AT, CS and AU from 900 to 1178 was completed in September 2000. This collation showed that these texts all transmitted a diminishing number of common entries virtually until AT's termination, so that Mac Neill's assumption of their independence and O'Rahilly's *Clonmacnoise-911* hypothesis were both unsustainable.

In 2000 I published a study of the chronology of S. Brigit, and the textual and chronological characteristics of Brigit's entries in AU and AI confirmed my earlier observation that these texts shared a common source. Furthermore collation of the chronology of fifth and sixth-century individuals found in both the Annals and Brigit's *Vita prima* showed that, while these chronologies were independent, they agreed, which implied the existence of an agreed chronology for early Christian Ireland from considerably earlier than the date of *c.*550 deduced by Smyth for the start of contemporaneous chronicling in Iona.[168]

In 2001 a summary review of the arguments and results of the two 1998 papers was published in *Early medieval Europe*. The only new element in this paper was an additional argument based upon dislocations in the papal and imperial successions which proposed that both compilation of the papal succession and the removal of the thirteen kalends had taken place between 716 and 720.[169] Also in 2001 I presented at the DIAS *Tionól* a paper dealing with the chronology of S. Columba in which I presented the evidence supporting the AT/CS chronology for him, viz. *natus* at 520, *navigatio* at 562 and obit at 593.[170] In particular I pointed out that a series of contemporary famine, mortality and plague entries located at 538, 540, 550 and 553 were all closely and correctly synchronized with the dendrochronological record of the Irish climate for the years 538–53.[171] The synchronism of these two independent multi-event series suggested that a substantial capacity for contemporary chronicling existed in the Irish monastic world by 538, and implied thereby that this chronicling had commenced earlier than this date.

By 2002 I had come to harbour serious doubts concerning Todd's hypothesis that ff. 12–14 of TCD 1282 was a 'fragment of Tigernach', firstly on account of the complete lack of correlation between its chronological apparatus and that of AT/CS, and secondly because of the close correspondence in incidence between its annals and those of AB over the years 81–387. Consequently, with

---

168 Mc Carthy, 'S. Brigit', 258–62 (Brigit's entries), 270–8 (*Vita prima* collation).   169 Mc Carthy, 'Chronology & sources', 329–30 (additional argument).   170 Mc Carthy, 'S. Colum Cille', at www.dias.ie/english/tionol/tionol1.html.   171 Mc Carthy, 'S. Colum Cille', slide 4 (annals–dendrochronology synchronism); Baillie, 'Dendrochronology', 215 fig. 3 and Baillie, 'Patrick', 70 figure 1 (European and Irish dendrochronological series).

assistance I collated codicological and palaeographic aspects of ff. 12–14 with those of ff. 16–143. From this examination, and supported by textual and chronological evidence, it emerged that the acephalous and truncated annals of ff. 12–14 are indeed part of the original compilation of the text. Moreover, the codicological evidence implied that originally these pre-Palladian annals had continued to AD430, and had extended back deep into pre-Christian times, almost certainly originally commencing at Adam. Thus it transpired that Todd's *AT-fragment* hypothesis was absolutely unsustainable. Furthermore, in the course of the palaeographic examination I observed that the Arabic numerals used to interpolate most of the chronological data between 432–1014, and in many marginal and interlinear entries throughout, corresponded precisely with those that Brian Ó Cuív had identified as written by Ruaidhrí Ua Caiside in the ff. 1–32^r Rawl. B. 489 transcript of the text. Consequently, I concluded that Ua Caiside was the author of all those interpolations, and also that he had completed the original writing of ff. 130^r–143^v of TCD 1282 in *c.*1505. Thus it emerged that Mac Carthy's identification of Cathal Mac Maghnusa as the scribe of these interpolations was mistaken. Rather, I concluded that Ua Caiside was responsible for the chronological organization of the compilation and Ua Luinín was the principal scribe, while Ua Caiside took over as scribe from f. 130^r onwards and subsequently interpolated many chronological annotations and entries.[172] This paper was published in *Studia Celtica* in 2004.

Having established that ff. 12–14 constituted part of the original compilation of the text by Ua Caiside and Ua Luinín and aware that the ferial and epactal elements of ff. 12–14 corresponded both textually and computationally with those from f. 16 onwards, I undertook an examination of these data. This showed that ff. 12–14 had been fitted with a formidable and accurately synchronized chronological apparatus consisting of kalend+ferial+epact+AM. As well, a series of six synchronizations identify an '[Anno] ab Incarnatione secundum Dionissium' (AI$_{Dion}$), with the equation AI$_{Dion}$ I = AM 4205, and indeed an Incarnation entry 'secundum Dionissium' is found at this year located in the middle of the third century at AD 254. The compiler of this apparatus arranged his ferial and epactal sequence so that for this year these corresponded precisely with the Dionysiac criteria for AD I. To achieve synchronism with the Dionysiac AD required that 253 kalends be interpolated following this year, and, in fact, when these annals truncate in *c.*387 at the time of S. Jerome in Jerusalem, 171 kalends were interpolated. The implication of these observations was that by 431 the compiler had achieved complete synchronism between his chronological apparatus and all the Dionysiac criteria. Thereafter he

---

172 Mc Carthy, 'AU compilation', 87–9 (codicological and palaeographic comparison), 73–5 (Ua Caiside's Arabic numerals), 75–7 (roles).

re-sequenced a considerable number of events in 438–550, and he restored only five of the six kalends missing between 612 and 664, with the consequence that his chronological apparatus henceforth was one year in arrears. Thus ff. 12–14, so far from being a 'fragment of Tigernach', actually represent our most important witness to the introduction of Anno Domini and Dionysiac epactal data into the Irish Annals. Various chronological details imply that this compilation was made in *c.*1022 and suggest that it represented the 'Liber Cuanach' cited repeatedly in AU. This together with onomastic details prompted the hypothesis that Cuán Ua Lothcháin †1024 was the author of 'Liber Cuanach'.[173] This work was published in *Peritia* in 2002.

Summary

When the evolution of Annalistic scholarship is examined it can be seen that there was virtually no continuity between the Gaelic scholars who compiled and maintained the Annals, and the Anglo-Irish scholars who took over much of the corpus in the early seventeenth century. Rather it was the nomenclature and novel hypotheses formulated by Ussher and Ware that provided the basis for all subsequent scholarship. Consequently the influential hypotheses subsequently proposed by Ware, O'Conor, Todd and Stokes in respect of AT and AU can be shown either to rest upon entirely inadequate MS evidence, or indeed to actually conflict with it. Nevertheless these hypotheses have been accepted as authoritative by modern scholarship and used to propound an account of the genesis of the Irish Annals with the following essential features:

a) AU best represents the archetype of the Irish inaugural chronicle and it commenced at 431.
b) An Irish world history chronicle was compiled from Bede's DTR cap. 66 and earlier Western chronicles.
c) The Clonmacnoise chronicle was compiled in the early tenth century by prefixing the world history chronicle to the Irish inaugural chronicle.

Since the hypotheses upon which this account is based are unsustainable, these supposed features are all misconceptions and the account itself is profoundly misguided and misleading.

Rather, critical examination of the MS evidence together with the chronological apparatus shows that it is the archetype of the Clonmacnoise

173 Mc Carthy, 'AU apparatus 82–1019', 265 fig. 1 (six synchronisms), 266 (Incarnation 'secundum Dionissium'), 268–9 (253 interpolated kalends), 269 (synchronism with Dionysiac criteria), 278–81 (Cuana).

group known as the Clonmacnoise chronicle which best preserves the form and content of the Irish inaugural chronicle. Moreover, this Clonmacnoise chronicle was simply the Irish continuation of an early fifth-century world history chronicle compiled initially by Rufinus of Aquileia. Bede also received a continuation of Rufinus' chronicle in the form of a copy of the Iona chronicle, and he used this as the basis for his DT cap 16–22 and DTR cap. 66, so that these works and the Annals share common world history material. Finally AU, which when originally compiled commenced not at 431 but at Adam, is based on a redaction of the Clonmacnoise chronicle made by Cuán Ua Lothcháin in c.1022 in which he introduced both Dionysiac epacts and AD. It is the purpose of the following chapters to establish as precisely as possible the genesis and evolution of the Irish Annals by following the sequence of compilation stages starting from Rufinus and continuing to Mícheál Ó Cléirigh.

CHAPTER FOUR

World history in Insular chronicles

Historians employ the term *world history* to describe chronicle entries that refer to the affairs of the Old World dynasties which flourished in the Middle-East and about the Mediterranean in the millennia prior to and that following the time of Christ. The principal Christian source for such entries was the chronicle of Eusebius of Caesarea which he compiled in *c.*303 as two books. In his *Chronography* he first discussed his sources, and then in his *Chronological canons* he tabulated in parallel columns the regnal series of the Old World dynasties, affording particular prominence to the Hebrew and Judean successions from the time of Abraham's birth up to the Captivity of the Jews in Babylon. These parallel regnal series then provided the chronological apparatus for his short entries recording Biblical and secular events. In *c.*380 Jerome translated Eusebius' *Chronological canons* into Latin, and extended them up to AD 378, incorporating an end chronicle with a Roman purview. Jerome's chronicle became the principal world history source used by most subsequent Western chronographers such as Orosius, Prosper, Hydatius, and Isidore, all of whom compiled their own continuations of it. However, as we shall see, while the Insular chronographers had access to these works they also drank from another fountain.[1] In the British Isles world history is found in the Irish Annals and in Bede's two chronicles embedded in his works on time, viz. his *De temporibus* cap. 16–22 and his *De temporum ratione* cap. 66, otherwise known as his *Chronica minora* and *Chronica maiora* respectively. Bede's best known chronicle, his *Historia ecclesiastica*, treats primarily the history of Christian England.[2] Now as discussed in chapter 3 earlier scholarly studies of the world history in the Annals simply assumed that correspondences between Bede's chronicles and the Annals were the result of the Annalists having copied either DT or DTR. However, in 1972 Morris demonstrated on textual grounds that this was not the case and suggested instead that they had both drawn on a Vulgate source. Then in 1998 I confirmed Morris' demonstration on both

---

1 Bede DTR 67.5, translated Wallis, *Reckoning*, 239, 'we, who drink from the pure fountain of Hebrew Truth.'   2 Mommsen, *Bedae chronicae*, 247–327 (parallel critical editions of DT and DTR chronicles); Jones, DTR, 463–535 (copy of Mommsen's DTR 66); Jones, DT, (copy of Mommsen's DT 16–22); McClure & Collins, *Bede*, 307–40 (translation of DTR 66 §§268–593); Wallis, *Reckoning*, 157–237 (full translation of DTR 66), xcvii–xcix (published editions of DTR); Colgrave & Mynors, HE (edition).

chronological and more extensive textual grounds, and proposed that Rufinus of Aquileia †410 was the principal compiler of this source.[3] It is the purpose of this chapter to examine these works and to establish the details of their inter-relationships.

I commence by summarizing in Figure 7 the world history found in the Annals and Bede's two chronicles, indicating for each text the appropriate paragraphs, their temporal range, and the regnal series that they reproduce.

Chronicle[4]	Range	World history regnal series
AB §1–128	c.Adam–c.AD 361	Hebrew, Judean, Persian, Alexandrian and Roman.
AI §1–562	Abraham–c.AD 575	Hebrew, Judean, Persian, Alexandrian, Roman and Byzantine; also lacunose Assyrian, Argive, Egyptian, Athenian, Israelite, Latin, and Medean.
AT 5c–77d	c.770 BC–AD 358	Judean, Persian, Alexandrian and Roman; also Israelite, Athenian, Macedonian, Lydian, Egyptian, Assyrian, Medean and Chaldean.
AT 80a–187d	AD 489–720	Byzantine.
AU §1–206	AD 81–c.387	Lacunose Roman.
AU 431–719	AD 431–720	Byzantine.
DT cap. 16–22	Adam–AD 703	Hebrew, Judean, Persian, Alexandrian, Roman and Byzantine
DTR cap. 66	Adam–AD 725	Hebrew, Judean, Persian, Alexandrian, Roman and Byzantine

Figure 7. Tabulation of the temporal range and regnal series of world history found in Insular chronicles.

Regarding the Annalistic sources it is clear that by far the most comprehensive world history regnal series are to be found in the first two sections of AT, and indeed collation of these with the parallel entries in AB, AI and AU shows that

---

3 Morris, 'Chronicle of Eusebius', 86 (Bede–Annals relationship); Mc Carthy, 'Status', 125 (Annals and Bede's Vulgate source), 135–42 (Rufinus' authorship).   4 Vestigial Roman regnal series are also found in CS, AR and MB.

they all represent acephalous and truncated abridgements of a Vulgate source. Notwithstanding this loss it is also clear from the above table that between them all the Annals provide a continuous regnal series extending from *c.* Adam (AB §1) to AD 720 (AU/AT), which when taken together include the essential Biblical and Christian chronological series of Hebrew, Judean, Persian, Alexandrian, Roman and Byzantine dynasties. Turning to Bede's two chronicles it may be seen that not only does their range correspond very closely with the collective range of the Annals but also that their primary chronological apparatus likewise comprises the regnal series of Hebrew, Judean, Persian, Alexandrian, Roman and Byzantine dynasties. Furthermore these chronicles divide all time into six

Interval	Annals[5]	Bede DT[6]	Isidore[7]	Jerome[8]
Age 1	1756	HV – 1656		
		LXX – 2242	2242	2242
Age 2	292	HV – 292		
		LXX – 942	942	942
Age 3	942	HV – 942		
		LXX – 942	940	940
Age 4	473	HV – 473		
		LXX – 485	485	486
Age 5	589	HV – 589		
		LXX – 589	586	588
Ages 1–5	HV – 3951	HV – 3951		
	LXX – 5189	LXX – 5198	5195	5198

Figure 8. A collation of the number of years for Ages 1–5 separately and collectively as found in the Annals, Bede's DT, and Isidore and Jerome's chronicles. The Annals and DT/DTR all cite '[H]ebreos' / 'Hebraica veritatis' = HV, and '.lxx. Interpretes' = Septuagint = LXX, as the authorities for their regnal data. Where the intervals are not cited explicitly by Jerome and Isidore they have been computed from their *Anno Abrahami* and *Anno Mundi* respectively.

5 For Annals Ages 1) AB §14; 2) AB §21; 3) AI §89.2; 4) AI §89.4; 5) AI §165.3, AT 12b, AT 36b; 1–5) HV AT 36c (Stokes misreads 3955) & AI §205 (3952-1), LXX AT 36c & AI §205 (5190-1). 6 Jones, DT, 600–7; for Ages 1–5 cf. DT 16.2–18 and 1) 17.2–3; 2) 18.2–3; 3) 19.2; 4) 20.2–3; 5) 21.2; 1–5) 22.3–4 (3952-1 & 5199-1). 7 Mommsen, *Isidori chronica*, 428, 431, 439, 445, 454 for Ages 1–5. The intervals are computed from Isidore's AM data as: Age 2 = 3184–2242; Age 3 = 4124–3184; Age 4 = 4609–4124; Age 5 = 5195–4609. 8 Helm, *Hieronymus*, 174, 174, 67a, 90a, 169 for Ages 1–5; Ages 3–5 are computed from Jerome's *Anno Abrahami* = AA as follows: Age 3 = AA 940; Age 4 = AA 1426–940 = 486; Age 5 = AA 2014–1426 = 588; Age 1–5 = AA 2014+2242+942 = 5198. Eusebius cited the same data for Ages 1–2 in his preface according to Jerome's translation, cf. p. 15.

Ages as follows: Age 1 = Adam to the Flood; Age 2 = Sem to Thare; Age 3 = Abraham to Saul; Age 4 = David to Sedecias; Age 5 = Ezechiel to Augustus 41; Age 6 = Incarnation to the end of time. These correspondences imply that the Annals and Bede's chronicles share a common source, and this implication is further corroborated by collation of their structural details against each other and other Western chronicles. Isidore also divided his chronicles into these Ages, and Jerome in his chronicle cited the first two, apparently following Eusebius. It is instructive therefore to compare the years of these Ages in different chronicles, and since Bede's second chronicle in DTR reproduces virtually the same structural features as that of his earlier DT it is sufficient to tabulate DT. Thus in Figure 8 the number of Annalistic years for Ages 1–5 is collated with those in Bede's DT, and Isidore and Jerome's chronicles.

Regarding this figure, it may be seen that Jerome, Isidore, and Bede's LXX series all represent the Septuagint chronological tradition, and all these intervals reconcile to within ±3 years. On the other hand the Annals' and Bede's HV series provide a significantly shorter chronology based essentially upon the Hebrew Bible whose Latin translation by Jerome was earlier known as the 'Hebraica veritatis', and later as the 'Vulgate'. It should be emphasized here that in DT and DTR, while Bede cites both the Septuagint and Vulgate total years for each Age, his actual regnal years and hence chronology conform to his Vulgate totals, and that the Annals likewise conform to Vulgate chronology.

Now regarding this HV series in modern times it has been simply assumed that Bede was responsible for the construction of it. For example, in the preface to his critical editions of DT and DTR Mommsen was absolutely explicit as to who compiled their Vulgate chronology, for he commenced his discussion of it as follows:[9]

> In chronologia operas maioris (nam libellus minor …) Beda per duas primas mundi aetates numeris chronicorum Eusebianorum ab Hieronymo retentis substituit eos, quos idem Hieronymus posuerat biblia sacra ad Hebraicum textum vertens eosque c.273 ad ipsum Eusebium Beda refert: ita ab Adamo ad Noe computantur anni non 2242, sed 1656 …

Then in 1913 Mac Neill, referring to DT, wrote of Bede's 'introduction of a quite new reckoning of the age of the world, differing by more than a thousand years from any older reckoning.' Similarly Jones wrote in the introduction to his 1943 edition, 'In DT, Bede had promulgated a new *annus mundi* of his own computation', and in 1983 Ó Cróinín likewise referred to 'the new, "revolutionary" dating of Bede'. More recently Wallis asserted, 'In *On Times*, Bede replaced the

9 Mommsen, 'Bedae chronicae', 230.

Eusebian-Septuagint chronology of the first two World-Ages with a new chronology based on Jerome's translation of the Hebrew text of the Old Testament.'[10] Modern discussions of this supposed 'new chronology' have concentrated on Ages 1–2 where the discrepancies between Vulgate and Septuagint are the greatest, cf. Figure 8.[11] But construction of this alternative chronology for these first two Ages required simply the substitution of the Septuagint *genuit* data by the Vulgate figures, and this alternative compilation had been considered already by Eusebius.[12] However, critical examination of all the Ages shows that by far the most complex analysis was required for Age 3 for which both DT and DTR affirm 942 years by either computation. This complexity arises for the following reasons:

a) The Vulgate version of Exodus 12.40–1 asserts that the Hebrews spent 430 years in Egypt and this conflicts with its assertion in Exodus 6.18–20 that, 'Kohath, son of Levi, ... was born in the land of Canaan, lived for 132 years, and his son Amram the father of Moses for 137 years, and Moses himself was 80 years old at the time of the departure from Egypt, and obviously the sum of these years cannot amount to 430.' The Septuagint, on the other hand, provides no chronology for the Hebrews in Egypt and it must be deduced from its statement in Exodus 12.40 that they dwelt in 'Egypt and Canaan 430 years'.[13]

b) The Vulgate includes Achialon with ten years in its regnal succession, while the Septuagint omits him entirely.

c) Neither Vulgate nor Septuagint supply any regnal chronology for Iosue, Samuhel or Saul.

d) The Vulgate and Septuagint versions of 1 Kings 6.1 both impose the chronology that Solomon commenced work on the Temple in his fourth year, which was in the 480th year after the Exodus. Since the reigns of Iosue, Achialon, Samuhel and Saul *all* fall within this interval, this places a limit on their overall summation.

As a result of these conflicts diverse numbers of years were assigned to the problematical intervals in different chronicles as is tabulated in Figure 9.

10 Mac Neill, *Authorship*, 76; Jones, *BOT*, 133; Ó Cróinín, *Sex Aetates Mundi*, 139; Wallis, *Reckoning*, 358 and cf. also 359, 'why did Bede revise the standard chronology of the *annus mundi* so radically in *On Times*, shaving nearly 1200 years off the conventional age of the world.' 11 Wallis, *Reckoning*, 355 for example, 'The dates for the period after Abraham are established by the regnal lists ... The first two Ages are much more problematic', which overlooks the repeated chronological conflicts in DT/DTR for Ages 3–5, cf. Figure 9 and Figure 12. 12 Helm, *Hieronymus*, 14, Jerome's translation of Eusebius' preface states: 'Itaque manifestum est Abraham Nini aetate generatum, iuxta eum tamen numerum, quem contractiorem editione uulgata sermo praebet Hebraeus.' 13 Wallis, *Reckoning*, 166–7 (cits., translating Bede DTR cap. 66 §46).

Interval	Bede DT	Isidore	Jerome	Δ
Hebrews in Egypt	145[14]	144	144	+1
Iosue	26	27	27	−1
Achialon	10	−	−	+10
Samuhel & Saul	32	40	40	−8
Age 3	942	940	940	+2

Figure 9. Collation of the data found in Bede DT, Isidore, and Jerome for the conflicting Vulgate and Septuagint intervals over Age 3. The column Δ registers the differences between DT and Isidore/Jerome.

As can be seen Isidore followed Jerome, but Bede's chronology in DT cap. 19 extended Age 3 by two years by means of four adjustments, and of all five differences Bede acknowledged only that of Achialon's ten years as, DT 19.18 'Achialon ann ·x·; hic in ·lxx· interpretibus non habetur.'[15] But had Bede himself as a young man aged about thirty compiling his first chronicle actually been responsible for the computation of these data, all of which contradict the long established authority of the chronicles of Jerome and Isidore, then he was surely obliged to justify the remaining four differences, most especially the reduction of Samuhel and Saul's joint reign by eight years? Instead, at the very start of the following chapter he immediately countermanded his assignment of thirty-two years to Samuhel and Saul, writing, DT 20.4–6 'Salomon ann ·xl·, qui templum aedificauit anno ·cccclxxx· egressionis ex Egypto, ex quo apparet Samuhel et Saul ·xl· annis praefuisse.'[16] Since the reduction of Samuhel and Saul's reign from forty to thirty-two is the principal means by which the introduction of Achialon's additional ten years is offset, this rejection by Bede shows both that *he* was not responsible for the assignment of thirty-two years and nor did he understand its function. Rather it is apparent from Bede's ambivalence and his silence with respect to the other differences that Bede was summarizing the chronology of a source that he did not properly understand. We shall see a further instance of this when we examine Age 4 below. A glance at Mommsen's *apparatus fontium* for DT will show that in it Bede repeatedly cited Isidore's *De natura rerum* and his minor chronicle found in Book V cap. 38–9 of his *Etymologiae*, debts that Bede also did not acknowledge. However, whenever

14 Jones, DT, 603 reads with Mommsen 'CXLVII' for the Hebrews in Egypt, against two of their MSS with 'cxlv' which value conforms to the Vulgate total of 942.   15 Jones, DT, 604 with number representations restored to the MS tradition.   16 Jones, DT, with number representations restored to the MS tradition.

Bede's chronology in DT diverges from that of Isidore it corresponds closely with that found in the Annals, cf. Figure 8, p. 120, and Figure 11, p. 126. It emerges therefore that Bede was in fact collating another chronicle which already provided Vulgate chronology with Isidore's minor chronicle, and when they diverged he followed the Vulgate. I shall refer to this source for the present as the 'Vulgate source'

Notwithstanding Bede's silence regarding the construction of the chronology of his DT, such has been his international reputation as a scholar that he has been accorded not only full responsibility for it but also the accolade that he wrote it to 'correct' his antecedent chronographers. For example, Jones referring to DT asserted that, 'Bede wrote primarily as a teacher, as a corrector and adaptor', while Wallis likewise considered that, 'We may hypothesize, then, that in *On Times* Bede revised Eusebius' chronology in the interests of what he saw as historic accuracy.'[17] But these conjectures regarding Bede's motives simply cannot be reconciled with the Byzantine chronology of the later seventh century in DT, for this exhibits repeated conflicts with the established imperial chronology, as is demonstrated in Figure 10.

DT Byzantine reigns	*The Byzantine Empire*
22.69: Heraclius ann ·xxxvi·	610–41 Heraclius [r. 31 y].
22.70: Eraclonas cum matre sua Martina ann ·ii·	–
22.71: Constantinus filius Eracli mens ·vi·	641 Constantine III and Heraclonas.
22.73: Constantinus filius Consantini ann ·xxviii·	641–68 Constans II [r. 27 y].
22.75: Constantinus filius Constantini superioris ann ·xvii·	668–85 Constantine IV [r. 17 y].
22.76: Iustinianus filius Constantine ann ·x·	685–95 Justinian II [r. 10 y].
22.79: Leo ann ·iii·	695–8 Leontius [r. 3 y].

Figure 10. Collation of the seven penultimate Byzantine reigns in DT 22 with the Byzantine chronology of J.M. Hussey (ed.), *The Byzantine Empire* (1966) 776. Numbers in DT have been restored from Mommsen's capitalized version to their MS tradition.

As can be seen this chronology in DT, which extends over the lifetime of Bede and his older contemporaries – his abbot Ceolfrith †716 was born c.642 – presents repeated conflict with respect to its nomenclature and chronology with the Byzantine chronology resolved by modern scholarship. Regarding nomenclature, DT registers Constans II as 'Constantinus f. Constantini', with

17 Jones, *BOT*, 131 (cit.); Wallis, *Reckoning*, 361 (cit.). Mommsen, *Bedae Chronicae*, 226 simply stated that Bede compiled DT by augmenting and modifying Isidore's minor chronicle, 'chronica minora Isidoriana a Beda hic illic aucta et mutata'.

the result that three successive emperors are named 'Constantinus', and Leontius whose reign ended just five years before Bede wrote DT, is named 'Leo'. Regarding chronology, DT assigns an additional five years to Heraclius, assigns Heraclonas joint reign with his mother Martina for two years instead of less than one year with Constantine III, places Constantine III *after* Heraclonas instead of making them joint, and assigns twenty-eight years to Constans II instead of twenty-seven. These errors of nomenclature and chronology extend to within five years of Bede's compilation of DT so that there can be no possible grounds on which to bestow upon him accolades for either his 'correction' or 'historic accuracy'. Rather virtually every one of these erroneous and idiosyncratic features of DT's Byzantine succession is found in the Annals, cf. Figure 13, p. 135. I submit therefore that Bede did not compile either the Vulgate chronology of Ages 1–5 or the Byzantine chronology of Age 6. Rather he took these from a source which has also been transmitted in the Irish Annals. Since no other copy of this Vulgate source is known to exist our next task is therefore to reconstruct its essential features by collation of the Annals with Bede's chronicles.

Reconstruction of the Vulgate source for Insular world history

When collating our Insular world history sources to identify the content and characteristics of the Vulgate source we are in the fortunate position that Bede made two separate and very distinct recensions from it, both of which have survived in many early MSS. Although the two most important Annalistic MSS of AT and AI are almost four centuries younger than the earliest Bedan MSS, nevertheless collation of these together throws a great deal of light on the content and organization of this Vulgate source. As already mentioned the most substantial Annalistic source is the Rawl. B. 502 MS of AT, and this commences in the second year of Iotham who is the thirteenth ruler of Age 4. Before this the much more abbreviated and textually inferior AI provides the best Annalistic representative commencing with Abraham in Age 3. Since all our sources exhibit division into Ages it is worthwhile to survey a complete Age and so Age 4 is the first such where we may employ AT, and Age 4 also has the advantage of being wholly Biblical in character. That is, the Bible provides an account of all the rulers of Age 4, and it is also important to note that the Vulgate and Septuagint give conflicting regnal years for three of the twenty reigns of this Age, viz. Athalia, Amon and Iosias. I commence therefore by collating in Figure 11 example entries including these three reigns taken from this Age as transmitted by AI/AT and DT.

AI/AT	DT cap. 20
AI §89: Finit tertia aetas mundi … incipit quarta aetas (mundi quae continet) annos .cccclxxiii. [blank space]	20.1: **Quarta aetas continet annos iuxta Hebreos ·cccclxxiii·; ·lxx· translatores ·xii· adiciunt.**
AI §90: Kl. Dauid primus rex regnauit de *tribu Iuda* annis .xl. …	20.2: David ann ·xl·
AI §117: K. Otholia mater Azarias annis .ui. …	20.12: Athalia ann ·vi·
AT 5d: K. Achaz filius Iotham rexit *Iudam* annis .xui. … K×13	20.17: Achaz ann ·xvi·
AT 6a: K. Osse filius Hela rexit *Israel* annis .ix., qui fuit nouissimus decim tribuum rex.	–
AT 7b: K. Achaz mortuus est.	–
AT 7b: In hoc tempore, **ut Eusebius ait,**[18] regnum defecit *.x. tribuum* … [a] Salmanasar rege Caldeorum et translatae sunt in montes Medorum. [cf. Jerome & Armenian chr. *s.a.* Achaz 11.]	20.18: Israhel in Medos transfertur
AT 7b: Ezecias filius Achaz rexit *Iudam* annis .xxix. … K×4	20.18: Ezechias ann ·xxviiii·
AT 7c: K. Nunc incipit captiuitas *.x. tribuum.* Sexto Ezechiae anno Salminasar rex Assiriorum capta Samaria transtulit *Israel* in Assirios … [cf. II Kings 18.10–11.]	–
AT 10a: K. Ammon filius Mannasse rexit *Iudam* annis duobus **iuxta Ebreos. secundum uero .lxx. Interpretes** annis .xii. …	20.20: Amon ann ·ii·
AT 10a: K. Ammon a seruis suis interficitur.	–
AT 10a: K. Iosias filius Ammon rexit *Iudam* annis .xxxi. Hic mundata Iudea et Hierusalem … .xuiiiº. anno regni sui. …	20.21: Iosias ann ·xxxi·
AT 10c: K×17 … **Hoc anno ut praescripsimus** Iosias mundata Iudea, **et reliqua** …	–
AT 12b: **Finit quarta aetas. Incipit quinta, quae continet annos .dlxxxix.**	21.1: **Quinta aetas continet ann ·dlxxxviiii·**

Figure 11. A sample of entries from the Judean and Israelite (.x. tribuum) dynasties for Age 4 taken from AI, AT and DT, including the reigns of Athalia, Amon and Iosias for which Vulgate and Septuagint chronology conflict. The dynastic identifications and source interjections have been emphasized in italic and bold respectively, and DT number citations have been restored from Mommsen's capitalized versions to the MS tradition.

18 Because the scribe of Rawl. B. 502 f. 1ʳ placed a point after the word 'ait' Stokes suffixed this

The most conspicuous feature of DT is the remarkable brevity of its entries, with regnal entries comprising simply a name and number of regnal years linked by the abbreviation 'ann', exactly as in Isidore's minor chronicle. On the other hand Annalistic entries are relatively prosaic and their most distinctive feature is the many 'K' or 'Kl' representing 'kalendae Ianuarii' distributed amongst them, and it will be demonstrated below that both the prosaic style and these kalends derive from the Vulgate source. Regarding their overall structure it is clear from their appearance in both AI/AT and DT that the Vulgate source was divided into numbered Ages, each of which commenced with a summation of years for that Age. Furthermore from DT it is apparent that when the Vulgate and Septuagint chronology differed both summations were cited, the former identified here as 'Hebreos' and the latter as '.lxx. interpretes', or as '.lxx. translators'. While AI does not explicitly reproduce this latter, space has been left for it in the MS. Both AI and AT attest that each Age began appropriately with an 'incipit' and ended with a 'finit' which Bede has omitted. Regarding the regnal successions both AI and AT provide multiple parallel successions, cf. Figure 7, p. 119, of which just two are illustrated here and these are nearly always explicitly identified as 'Iudam' or 'Israel/.x. tribuum'. In most cases too the Annalistic entries identify the ruler's immediate antecedent or tribe. In DT, on the other hand, rulers are normally identified with just a single word and neither their antecedents nor dynasty is cited. Regarding the representation of numbers, in the Annals and in the MSS of Bede's chronicles these are written in lower case letters and are normally delimited with two points that are usually raised in Bede's chronicles, thus '·xl·', as Jones represented in all of his own editions of Bede's works. However, Mommsen, in his editions of Bede's two chronicles, systematically capitalized all Roman numerals and lowered both points, and he regularly suffixed the initial point to the preceding word, thus misrepresenting 'David añ ·xl·' as 'David ann. XL.' Unfortunately Jones silently reproduced all these misreadings in his CCSL editions of the chronicles of DT and DTR, but in all citations from these works here the MS tradition has been restored. The editors of the Annals on the other hand have generally reproduced the MS form of the numbers accurately.

A distinctive feature of DT's treatment of the difference between Vulgate and Septuagint chronology is that while these are always registered in the Age summations, the reigns that contribute to these differences are never themselves identified. Thus whereas in Age 4 the Vulgate assigns Athalia 6, Amon 2 and Iosias 31 years, where the Septuagint assigns them respectively 7, 12, and 32

interjection to the obit of Achaz. However, since Eusebius does not register rulers' obits and he agrees with II Kings 16.2 regarding Achaz' reign of sixteen years, but is in chronological conflict with the accounts of the Captivity in II Kings 17.6 and 18.11, it is clear that this interjection in fact *prefixes* the account of the transfer of the ten tribes to the Medean mountains, and it explains the subsequent parallel account at AT 7c.

years, DT only registers the total of the additional twelve years. In contrast to DT it can be seen that AT 10a has explicitly identified the second of these differences and since Amon's obit is given under the following kalend it is apparent that the compiler has in fact adopted the Vulgate chronology of two years. In the cases of Athalia and Iosias, while AI/AT do not identify the Vulgate/Septuagint difference, in both instances they cite the Vulgate regnal years and their kalend chronology reflects these. Finally an important feature of the Vulgate source that may be identified from Figure 11, p. 126, is that not only did its compiler systematically identify the discrepancies between Vulgate and Septuagint chronology, he also registered chronological discrepancies found in other chronicles of antiquity. One instance of this is shown above where an interjection at AT 7b registers that Eusebius had located the termination of the Israelite dynasty at the end of Achaz' reign, asserting that the Israelites were then transferred by a Chaldean king to the Medean mountains. Since this assertion is indeed found in both the Jerome and Armenian translations of Eusebius' chronicle at the eleventh year of Achaz, this identification and interjection are absolutely correct.[19] However, II Kings 18.10–11 asserts that it was in the sixth year of Achaz' successor, Ezechias, that the Assyrian king, Salmanasar, captured Samaria and transferred the Israelites into Assyria. Thus as well as the conflicts in their narratives there is a difference of eleven years in their chronology. The entries at AT 7 b–c show that while the compiler of the Vulgate source has registered both chronologies he has clearly opted for the Biblical chronology since the entry is preceded by the statement, 'Nunc incipit captiuitas .x. tribuum.' In DT, on the other hand, by placing 'Israhel in Medos transfertur' under the reign of Achaz Bede followed the Eusebian chronology against the Biblical chronology for the start of the Israelite captivity. Thus it can be seen from this collation that the compiler of the Vulgate source registered not only Vulgate and Septuagint chronological conflicts, but also conflicts with other authoritative sources such as Eusebius' chronicle.

While this collation has examined only Age 4 the observations made above will be found to apply generally to all of pre-Christian DT. Thus in summary we conclude that in DT Bede transmitted only the skeleton of the Vulgate source, abandoning all Age incipits and finits, all kalends, all dynasties except the essential sequence Hebrew, Judean, Persian, Alexandrian, Roman and Byzantine, and in imitation of Isidore's minor chronicle he reduced each regnal entry to its textual minimum. This was indeed how Bede himself described the work when writing of it to Plegwine some five years later: 'These are the things which, according to the faith of Holy Scripture, I was solicitous to summarize for myself, and for those of my circle who asked me, in a concise and simple manner, as I believe and think.'[20] The Annals, on the other hand, have transmitted

19 Helm, *Hieronymus*, 88a, and Karst, *Armenischen Übersetz*, 182 (First Captivity).   20 Wallis, *Reckoning*, 408 (cit.).

128

AI/AT	DTR cap. 66
AI §89: **Finit tertia aetas mundi ... incipit quarta aetas (mundi quae continet) annos .cccclxxiii.** [blank space]	§81: **Quarta mundi aetas** non solum **cum inchoato gentis Iudeae imperio,** sed et cum innouata promissione quae patribus olim data est imperii Christiani sumit exordium ...
AI §90: Kl. Dauid primus rex regnauit de *tribu Iuda* annis ·xl· ...	§82: ·ii̅ dccccxxx· Dauid primus ex *tribu Iuda* rex an ·xl·
AI §117: K. Otholia mater Azarias annis.ui ...	§108: ·ii̅i̅lxxi· Athalia mater Azariae an ·ui· ... **In ·lxx· interpraetibus** ·uii· an regnasse Athalia narratur.
AT 5d: K. Achaz filius Iotham rexit *Iudam Iuda* annis ·xui· ... K×13	§124: ·ii̅i̅ccxxiiii· Achaz filius Ioatham an ·xui· ...
AT 6a: K. Osse filius Hela rexit *Israel* annis .ix., qui fuit nouissimus decim tribuum rex.	–
AT 7b: K. Achaz mortuus est.	–
AT 7b: In hoc tempore, **ut Eusebius ait,** regnum defecit .*x. tribuum* ... [a] Salmanasar rege Caldeorum et translatae sunt in montes Medorum. [cf. Jerome & Armenian chr. *s.a.* Achaz 11.]	–
AT 7b: Ezecias filius Achaz rexit *Iudam* annis .xxix. ... K×4	§128: ·ii̅i̅ccliii· Ezechias filius Achaz an ·xxuiiii·
AT 7c: K. Nunc incipit captiuitas .*x. tribuum.* Sexto Ezechiae anno Salminasar rex Assiriorum capta Samaria transtulit *Israel* in Assirios ... [cf. II Kings 18.10–11.]	Huius anno sexto Salmanassar rex Assyriorum capta Samaria transtulit *Israhel* in Assyrios ...
AT 10a: K. Ammon filius Mannasse rexit *Iudam* annis duobus iuxta **Ebreos.** secundum uero .**lxx. Interpretes** annis .xii. ...	§133: ·ii̅i̅ cccx· Amon filius Manasse an ·ii· **In Hebraica Veritate** duobus annis, in ·lxx· legitur regnasse ·xii·
AT 10a: K. Ammon a seruis suis interficitur.	–
AT 10a: K. Iosias filius Ammon rexit *Iudam* annis .xxxi. Hic mundata Iudea et Hierusalem ... .xuiii°. anno regni sui ...	§136: ·ii̅i̅ cccxli· Iosias filius Amon an ·xxxi· Hic mundata Iudea et Hierusalem ... ·xuiii· anno regni sui ...
–	§139: **In Hebreo** ·xxxi· an regnasse Iosias, in ·lxx· **interpretibus** ·xxxii· legitur; sed et **Eusebius** inter regnum eius ... Verum quid **Veritas** habeat, **Hieremias** pandit ...
AT 10c: K×17 ... **Hoc anno ut praescripsimus** Iosias mundata Iudea, **et reliqua** ...	–
AT 12b: **Finit quarta aetas. Incipit quinta, quae continet annos .dlxxxix.**	§143: **Quinta mundi aetas** ab exterminio **coepit** regni Iudaici, quod iuxta prophetiam Hieremiae ·lxx· annis permansit.

Figure 12. The same sample of AI/AT entries for Age 4 shown in Figure 11 are here collated with Bede's DTR cap. 66. Again dynastic identifications and source interjections have been emphasized in italic and bold respectively, and DTR number citations restored to the MS tradition.

the kalends, prosaic entries, the parallel dynasties, and some but not all of the interjections registering the chronological conflicts between the Vulgate and Septuagint and other authoritative chronicles.

Next, turning to Bede's second recension of Age 4 in DTR cap. 66, in Figure 12 I collate it with the identical sample of AI/AT entries given in Figure 11. The most conspicuous development apparent from this collation is that in DTR Bede replaced DT's cryptic entries with prosaic entries that textually closely approximate the corresponding Annalistic entry. In particular his Judean regnal entries now systematically cite either the tribe or ancestor, cf. DTR §82, 108, 124, 128, 133, 136. To these regnal entries Bede has prefixed an AM which, following that of Isidore, anachronistically registers the final year of each reign.[21] That in fact the Vulgate source had a chronological apparatus which registered every year can be seen from the Annalistic account of Iosias' purification of Judea and Jerusalem in his eighteenth year. This purification is related in some detail anachronistically immediately following Iosias' regnal entry, and both the Annals and DTR have transmitted this account, cf. AT 10a, DTR §136. However, *only* the Annals have located this purification appropriately seventeen kalends later in Iosais' eighteenth year, cf. AT 10c, and the interjection there of 'Hoc anno ut praescripsimus … et reliqua' shows that both entries were written by the same author. This then implies that this same author also inscribed the intervening seventeen kalends that correctly locate this entry, all of which Bede has omitted. Likewise, as in DT, he has omitted from Age 4 all successions except the Judean succession. Furthermore in DTR §128 he silently relocated the start of the captivity of the Israelites from the reign of Achaz where in DT it agreed with Eusebius' chronology, to the sixth year of Ezechias so that it now agrees with II Kings 18.10–11 and synchronizes with the Annals. This correction is yet another verification that in *c.*703 when Bede was composing DT he did not fully comprehend the chronology of his Vulgate source. Finally Bede has moved all the contrasting summations of Vulgate and Septuagint chronology from the start of each respective Age to DTR §2–7, and instead at DTR §81 he has restored an Age incipit. However, since this incipit now incorporates an anachronistic reference to Christian rule it is clearly Bede's own interpolation. On the other hand in DTR §108, 133 and 139 Bede has transmitted all three interjections registering the conflict between the Vulgate and Septuagint regnal chronology for Athalia, Amon and Iosias. Moreover, in DTR §139 he has transmitted a discussion which employs Jeremiah 25.1 to support the Vulgate chronology against that of Eusebius, all of which has been lost from the Annals.

Overall we conclude from this examination of Age 4 that the Vulgate source of the Annals and Bede's chronicles included:

21 Mc Carthy, 'Status', 124 n. 70 (anachronism of Isidore and Bede's AM).

a) A primary chronological apparatus of kalends.
b) A comprehensive set of Eusebius' dynastic successions distributed over these kalends.
c) Prosaic regnal entries providing substantial accounts of the rulers and current events.
d) Substantial interjections providing critical assessments of the chronological conflicts principally between the Vulgate and Septuagint, but also other early chronicles. These assessments favoured Vulgate chronology, and this was reflected in the kalend chronology.

Of these four constituents only the Annals have transmitted them all in part; in DT Bede transmitted *only* the Vulgate chronology of d), but in DTR he transmitted mostly prosaic entries and more of the interjections than have been transmitted by the Annals. Thus by collating the Annals with Bede's two recensions we can reconstruct the form and content of their Vulgate source for Age 4 in some detail. While these conclusions have been based upon a consideration of Age 4 alone, examination of the other pre-Christian Ages shows that they apply equally to them. For Ages 1–2 our only Annalistic source, AB, is evidently quite abbreviated and corrupted, nevertheless it clearly preserves both the kalends and the Vulgate chronology, cf. Figure 8, p. 120. For Ages 3–5 AI transmits corrupt and lacunose versions of the kalends, prosaic entries and Eusebian dynastic successions, but no interjections, while AT transmits all these features for the latter part of Age 4 and all of Age 5. Of particular interest are the accumulated interjections transmitted by AT and DTR in which the compiler explicitly cites the following authors and works: '[H]ebreos', '·lxx· Interpretes', 'Josephus', 'Josephus in Antiquitatum', 'Josephus in primo contra Appionem', 'Africanus', 'Julius Africanus', 'Eusebius', 'Cronicam Eusebii', 'Eusebius in temporum libri', 'Eusebius in cronicis suis', and 'Jerome in Danielis'. These interjected attributions and their associated chronological discussions are most important for they show the compiler of the Vulgate source to have been critically collating a broad spectrum of Christian and non-Christian sources extending at least from the Jewish Josephus' *Antiquitates* of *c.*94 to Jerome's *In Danielem* of *c.*406. In these discussions the compiler, with just one exception, favours the Vulgate chronology against that of the Septuagint, the works of Josephus †*c.*100, Julius Africanus †*c.*240, Eusebius and Jerome, whenever these are in conflict. The exception is in Age 3 as discussed above, where the compiler points out that the Vulgate chronology of 430 years for the Hebrews in Egypt contradicts its own account of the Hebrew succession, and concludes that the Septuagint chronology must be followed. This critical collation of the Vulgate, Septuagint and antique chronicles is very impressive for it implies a very comprehensive reading and understanding of both Biblical and early chronicle material.

The credit for this compilation has been mistakenly accorded to Bede who in fact merely twice edited his copy of the Vulgate source, omitting many of its most singular textual features but reproducing and highlighting its Vulgate chronology. The textual character of the Vulgate source has rather been best preserved in the Annals, most particularly in AI and AT, though because these lack the first two Ages their Vulgate chronology is not so conspicuous. Critical examination of AT and AI discloses citations from the translation of Eusebius' EH by Rufinus of Aquileia, and these together with details of the imperial and Alexandrian episcopal successions reveal that Rufinus himself was in fact the author of this Vulgate source. Rufinus, a monk and scholar literate in Latin and Greek, studied in Egypt and Palestine in his earlier years, was a close friend of Jerome from *c.*367 until their breach in *c.*393, and between his return to Italy in 397 and his death in 410 in Sicily he was author and translator of about twenty historical and Biblical works.[22] To Rufinus then is due the credit for the construction of the Vulgate chronology which he established using Jerome's Latin translation of the Hebrew Bible, the Septuagint, and an impressive array of the chronicles of antiquity.[23]

Regarding when Rufinus wrote his chronicle, the latest source he cited was Jerome's *In Danielem* written *c.*406, so Rufinus compiled it within the last four years of his life. As regards the question of how Rufinus' chronicle travelled to the British Isles we have no direct information. However, we do know that a letter from Sulpicius Severus in southern Gaul seeking chronological information was sent to Rufinus in 403, and also that Sulpicius subsequently compiled his eighty-four year *Latercus* using the Latin translation of *De ratione paschali* cited by Rufinus in his translation of EH. Sulpicius' *Latercus* was the Paschal tradition followed by many of the Insular churches from the fifth to the eighth centuries, and so circumstantially it appears likely that Sulpicius and his *Latercus* provided the conduit by which Rufinus' chronicle reached the British Isles.[24] Regarding the range of Rufinus' chronicle AB, DT and DTR all show that it commenced at Adam, while the details of the AT/CS ferial series indicates that he brought it to *c.*398. But his Byzantine succession extended only to the last complete reign in Jerome's chronicle, namely Jovian †364. However, a colophon exists in AI at *c.*422 which suggests that Rufinus' chronicle had received a small extension before arriving in the British Isles. It reads, 'Now ends this little work collected from the beginning of the world out of various sources, that is not from one particular exemplar.'[25] Thus it appears that

22 Mc Carthy, 'Status', 125 (Annals and Bede's Vulgate source), 135–42 (Rufinus' authorship); Murphy, *Rufinus, passim* (Rufinus' life and works).   23 Mc Carthy, 'Bede's primary source', 18–19 (Rufinus' knowledge of Vulgate chronology).   24 Mc Carthy, 'The *latercus*', 40–1 (Sulpicius' letter & Rufinus' connections); Mc Carthy & Breen, *De ratione paschali*, 117–18, 138–41 (Rufinus' citations of *De ratione Paschali*).   25 Anderson, *Kings*, 5 (translation), cf. AI §344.

Rufinus' chronicle had received an extension of just over two decades, and the presence of a natus, floruit, and obit for S. Martin to whom Sulpicius was devoted suggest that the extension was the work of either himself or someone in his circle.[26] Notwithstanding this uncertainty, because we shall see in chapter 5 that the monastic tradition of Sulpicius and his *Latercus* played a crucial role in the introduction of chronicling in Ireland, I shall refer to this extension of Rufinus' chronicle to *c.*422 as the 'Rufinus-Sulpicius chronicle'.

Finally, one important element of the chronological apparatus of the Christian era of Rufinus' chronicle should be mentioned here. At nineteen year intervals commencing at the Incarnation there were three-way synchronisms between the Septuagint AM, the Vulgate AM and the 'anno ab Incarnatione' i.e. AD. These have only survived in the Annals and in AT they commence at AD 1 and continue to 324 with two lacunae; for example AT 48a: 'K.ui. Ab initio mundi .u.*m*.cccix. *secundum* lxx, *secundum* Ebreos .iiii.*mc*. Ab Incarnatione .cxu.' Regarding Rufinus' use of AD here, since he wrote these well over a century before Dionysius Exiguus compiled his influential Paschal table in 525, clearly Dionysius did not invent 'Anno Domini' as has been invariably asserted in modern times. Rather I have argued elsewhere that Eusebius himself was the originator of reckoning years 'ab Incarnatione Domini', and Rufinus merely reproduced Eusebius' data here in his chronicle.[27] The presence of this AD in the Rufinus-Sulpicius chronicle proved as influential with Bede as did Rufinus' Vulgate AM chronology there, for when Bede came to write his chronicle of Christian England, he employed the AD intermittently throughout HE and systematically in his recapitulation in HE 5.24. This then raises the question of the route taken by the Rufinus-Sulpicius chronicle between the Irish Annalists and Bede, and this is best addressed by investigating the Christian section of the chronicle.

The Insular evolution of the Rufinus-Sulpicius chronicle

In general considering the matter of the evolution of Christian texts in the British Isles I may first observe that the relative proximity of these islands each to the other, and their close cultural links, readily facilitated the movement of texts between them. Thus a text originating at A may be readily copied and transported to B and there emended, and if subsequently this emended version, or a descendant, be returned to A and collated with the original or a descendant then some or all of the emendations may find their way back to the original or a descendant. Two examples of this process are found with the world history in

26 Mc Carthy, 'Synchronization', *s.a.* 327 (Martin's natus), 367 (floruit), 398 (obit).
27 Mc Carthy, 'Emergence of AD', 44–6 (three-way synchronisms), 49 (Eusebius' invention).

the Insular chronicles. Now given the quantity of world history in the Christian era of the Annals and Bede's chronicles it is quite out of the question to fully examine the material here. However, as the imperial succession plays an important structural and functional role in our chronicles then we may use it to explore questions of textual descent. Consequently, in Figure 13 I collate details of the Byzantine succession from Theodosius r. 408–50 to Leo r. 717–41. I choose this succession since it must certainly represent an extension to the succession in the Rufinus-Sulpicius chronicle and the objective is to try to establish from its textual details who compiled it and when.

S	AU reigns	AU inc.–obit	AT~ AU	AT~ DTR	DT & DTR regnal incipits
M1	Teodosius imperator uiuendi finem fecit	lac.–**449.1**	lac.	lac.	DT 22.55: *Theodosius minor 26.* DTR §477: *Theodosius minor Arcadii filius 26.*
M2	Marcianus imperator 6y 6m	**449.1–456.2**	lac.	lac.	DT 22.56: *Marcianus 7.* DTR §488: Marcianus et Valentinianus 7.
M3	Leo Senior imperator Leone Iuniore a se iam Cessare constituo … 17y 6m.	**456.2–473.1**	lac.	lac.	DT 22.58: *Leo maior 17*; *Leo minor 1.* DTR §494: Leo 17.
M4	Zenon Augustus 17y 6m	**473.1–490.1**	490.1	–	DT 22.60: *Zenon 17.* DTR §498: *Zenon 17.*
M5	Anastasius imperator 27y 2m 29d	**490.2–517.1**	518.3	*491.1*	DT 22.61: *Anastasius 27.* DTR §505: *Anastasius 28.*
M6	Iustinus imperator 9y 2m	– **526.3**	525.5	*519.1*	DT 22.62: Iustinus 8. DTR §509: *Iustinus senior 8.*
M7	Iustinianum ex sorore sua [Iustini] nepotem	**526.3** –	525.5	*AM526.1*	DT 22.63: Iustinianus 39. DTR §515: **Iustinianus Iustini ex sorore nepos 38.**
I1	*Iustinus Minor 11*	*565.3* –	–	*563.1*	DT 22.64: *Iustinus minor 11.* DTR §521: *Iustinus minor 11.*
I2	*Tiberius* Constantinus 7	*576.2* –	–	*AM575.1*	DT 22.65: *Tiberius 7.* DTR §525: *Tiberius* Constantinus 7.
I3	*Mauricius 21*	*583.2* –	–	*582.1*	DT 22.67: *Mauricius 21.* DTR §528: *Mauricius 21.*
I4	*Foccas 7*	*604.3* –	–	*AM603.1*	DT 22.68: *Focas 8.* DTR §533: *Focas 8.*
I5	*Eraclius 26*	*612.4* –	–	*AM611.1*	DT 22.69: *Heraclius 36.* DTR §538: *Heraclius 26.* →

	AU reigns	AU inc.–obit	AT~ AU	AT~ DTR	DT & DTR regnal incipits
Κ1	Eraclas cum matre sua Martina 2	638.7 –	–	$^{AM}641.1$	DT 22.70: Eraclonas cum matre sua Martina 2. DTR §542: Heraclonas cum matre sua Martina 2.
Κ2	Constantinus filius Eraclii 6m.	641.3 –	–	$^{AM}643.1$	DT 22.71: Constantinus filius Eracli 6m. DTR §545: Constantinus filius Heracli 6m.
Κ3	Constantinus filius Constantini 28	642.6 –	–	$^{AM}644.1$	DT 22.73: Constantinus filius Constantini 28. DTR §547: Constantinus filius Constantini 28.
Κ4	Constantinus filius superioris Constantini regis 17.	672.6 –	–	–	DT 22.75: Constantinus filius Constantini superioris 17. DTR §556: Constantinus filius Constantini superioris regis 17.
Κ5	Iustinianus Minor filius Contantini 10	689.5 –	690.6	$^{AM}673.1$	DT 22.76: Iustinianus filius Constantini 10. DTR §563: Iustinianus minor filius Constantini 10.
Β1	–	–	–	$^{AM}683.1$	DT 22.79: Leo 3. DTR §568: Leo 3.
Β2	*Tiberius* Cesar 7	*701.5 –*	–	$^{AM}686.1$	DT 22.79: Tiberius dehinc 5. DTR §571: Tiberius 7.
Β3	*Iustinianus secundus cum Tiberio filio 6*	*709.8 –*	*710.5*	*693.1*	DTR §576: Iustinianus secundo cum Tiberio filio 6.
Β4	–	–	–	*699.1*	DTR §579: Philippicus 1 m. 6.
Β5	–	–	–	$^{AM}701.1$	DTR §582: Anastasius 3.
Β6	*Teodorus 1*	*719.4 –*	*720.4*	$^{AM}704.1$	DTR §587: Theodosius 1.
Β7	–	–	–	$^{AM}705.1$	DTR §591: Leo 9.

Figure 13. Textual collation of the Byzantine succession transmitted by AU, DT and DTR showing their nomenclature and regnal years given in Arabic numerals to conserve space. Those entries that are substantially verbatim citations from Marcellinus', Isidore's or Bede's chronicles are identified in bold, italic, and italic-bold respectively. The first column identifies AU's source as M=Marcellinus, I=Isidore, X=not identified, B=Bede. The columns headed 'AT~AU' and 'AT~DTR' separate AT entries into those cognate with AU and with DTR respectively, while a superscript 'AM' prefix shows that an AM accompanies the latter.

When considered in terms of its sources in AU this succession divides into four separate sections and these have been identified by the sigla in column one. The first seven reigns originate in citations from Marcellinus' chronicle and hence are labelled M1–7; the next five reigns all originate from Isidore's major chronicle, as is identified by the 'Minor' in I1, and hence are labelled I1–5; the next five reigns are by an as yet unidentified compiler and hence are labelled X1–5; the last seven reigns are the work of Bede in the course of his own extensions, first in DT (Leo and Tiberius), and subsequently in DTR, and hence these are labelled B1–7. Considering first the series M1–7 we see that in DT Bede provided the briefest possible epitome of the series, normally transcribing the regnal entries from Isidore's minor chronicle. In DTR Bede slightly expanded these except in the case of M7 where he substituted an epitomized citation from Marcellinus. Since it simply is not plausible that an annalist expanded Bede's orderly Isidorean epitomes into unsystematic but accurate citations from Marcellinus, I submit that here the sequence of compilation was as follows. First an annalist abstracted the imperial succession from Marcellinus' chronicle which Bede then subsequently collated with Isidore and epitomized, except for M7 which entry he partly transcribed. Moreover, the Annals preserve interjections remarking the source or chronology of these entries, cf. AU 449.1 'ut Marcillinus dicit', 456.2 'ueluti Marcillínus docent', 490.1 'Hi sex menses … quem non numerant Cronica', while another registered the end of Marcellinus' chronicle, viz. AU 535.1 'Hucusque Marcellinus perduxit Cronicon suum.' All of these are in accordance with Annalistic compilation of M1–7. Regarding next the series I1–5, the brevity of Isidore's regnal entries makes it impossible to decide on textual grounds whether the annalist or Bede was the compiler. However, we note that just as in the case of Marcellinus the Annals preserve an interjection at 615 registering the end of Isidore's chronicle, viz. 'Usque hunc annum scripsit Isiodorus Cronicon suum …', and the citation which follows is from the first edition of Isidore's major chronicle.[28] All of this is in accordance with the 'Minor' in I1. Note also that the word 'Constantinus' in reign I2 does *not* occur in Isidore, but it does resonate with the reigns X2–5 as we shall see. Next, while the author of reigns X1–5 is unidentified we note that in AU all are noticeably prosaic and that also in DT, in complete contrast to all his other extremely cryptic regnal entries, Bede has all of these prosaic regnal entries virtually verbatim. In these circumstances it is not credible that Bede compiled this series X1–5. Moreover, the name 'Constantinus' appears in four of these reigns, at least once incongruently, and as mentioned this name has been interpolated into the reign I2. Taking these

---

28 The interjections at AU 565.3 and 583.2 making attributions to 'Beda' and 'Beda & Isiodrorus' are subsequent additions.

details with the tradition of prosaic regnal entries in the Annals I submit that the compiler of X1–5 was an annalist, and he also compiled M1–7 and I1–5, whereas Bede in DT and DTR has constructed two epitomes of the annalist's succession, normally but not always substituting Isidore for Marcellinus. On the other hand the final series of reigns B1–7 are clearly the work of Bede when appending end chronicles to his Annalistic source, first in 703 and again in 725. On the other hand the reigns B2–3 and B6 in AU have been copied from Bede's DTR by a subsequent compiler as will be discussed below.

I have not included in this analysis the six reigns between Jovian r. 363–4, the last complete reign of the Rufinus-Sulpicius chronicle, and Theodosius (M1) because AI, our best Annalistic source in this interval, is here severely corrupt and lacunose. However, collation of it with DT and DTR shows that these six reigns were abstracted by an annalist from Orosius' chronicle for which Bede again subsequently either epitomized or substituted Isidore's entries. Thus the overall picture which emerges is that an annalist used the chronicles of Orosius, Marcellinus, and Isidore and his own knowledge to extend Rufinus' Byzantine succession from Jovian to Justin Minor (X5) r. 685–95. It appears therefore that this annalist brought the succession up to his own time, and since Bannerman and Smyth have established that in the seventh century the Annals were maintained and compiled on Iona, it is there that we should look to identify their author. Now Adomnán †704 was abbot of Iona for 679–704 and hence the reign of Justin Minor fell entirely within his abbacy, so I conclude that Adomnán was responsible for the compilation of the entire extension of the Byzantine succession from Jovian to Heraclius (I5) using the chronicles of Orosius, Marcellinus and Isidore, and the continuation (X1–5) to Justin Minor was his own work. Regarding the low-grade chronology of this section X1–5 that has been documented in Figure 10, p. 124, examination of Adomnán's *Vita Columbae* confirms that he had an extremely sanguine attitude as regards chronological accuracy.[29] As well as constructing this Byzantine regnal extension I suggest that Adomnán also extensively collated Orosius over the immediate pre- and post-Christian sections of the Rufinus-Sulpicius chronicle. For collation of AT/DTR reveals about fifty interpolations from Orosius, with some of those in AT marked with interjections similar to those that identify his use of Marcellinus and Isidore.[30]

The next question to consider is how did Adomnán's extension to the Rufinus-Sulpicius chronicle reach Bede in Northumbria? Now as it happens Bede himself in HE 5.15 has provided us with a detailed account of the

29 Mc Carthy, 'S. Colum Cille', *s.v.* Adomnán.   30 AT 17d, 18a (pre-Christian citations from Orosius entries with interjections); Wallis, *Reckoning*, 182–218 identifies forty-four Orosius citations in her apparatus, a few more survive only in AT.

transmission of documentary Biblical material from Adomnán in Iona to Northumbria sometime in the years 686–8. For here Bede recounts how Adomnán took down a detailed account of the sacred places referenced in the Bible from a Gaulish bishop called Arculf, from which he wrote a book entitled *De locis sanctis*. Adomnán subsequently made two visits to Northumbria over 686–8 and on one of these visits, most likely the latter, he presented a copy of this book to Aldfrith, king of Northumbria for 686–705, whom he described as 'my friend King Aldfrith'.[31] Bede in his Life of S. Cuthbert asserts that a year before Ecgfrith's death in 685 Aldfrith 'was then on the island which is called Iona', and subsequently twice states that Aldfrith had pursued his studies 'among the islands of the Irish', and 'for some considerable time ... in the regions of the Irish'. The anonymous Life of S. Cuthbert also states explicitly that Aldfrith was in Iona.[32] It seems likely therefore that Aldfrith had studied in Iona under Adomnán's abbacy and it was this, together with their friendship and Aldfrith's recent elevation to the Northumbrian kingship that prompted Adomnán's present of a copy of his *De locis sanctis* to him. Bede tells us that Aldfrith circulated this book and at least by *c.*703 this had reached Bede for at about that time he himself made an epitome of it.[33] In HE 5.15 Bede accorded great praise and respect to Adomnán's book, and HE 5.16–17 comprise simply extracts based upon it which contribute nothing to his history of the English church and which disrupt the chronology of his account of early eighth-century Northumbria. Now Aldfrith's interest in and ability for Biblical studies are well attested, and Adomnán's present of *De locis sanctis* provided him with a detailed spatial map of the important Biblical sites.[34] The world history found in common in the Annals and Bede's chronicles provides a correspondingly detailed temporal map of Biblical events. The circumstances and synchronism of Bede's compilation in *c.*703 of both his own epitome of *De locis sanctis* and DT suggest then that in *c.*687 Adomnán had also presented Aldfrith with at least a copy of the world history in the Iona chronicle which registered the Byzantine succession up to and including Justinian's accession in 685. Furthermore that Aldfrith had likewise circulated this chronicle so that it reached Bede by *c.*703 and he similarly made an epitome of its world history in his DT. The incongruity of Bede's prosaic regnal entries X1–5 as compared with all his other cryptic regnal entries in DT suggests that he knew and respected his source, for indeed Adomnán was still alive when Bede wrote DT.

Bede's complete silence with regard to his Iona chronicle world history source is readily understood in terms of the ecclesiastical relationship then

---

31 Sharpe, *Adomnán*, 46–8 (Adomnán's two visits to Northumbria), 203 ('my friend'). 32 Colgrave, *S. Cuthbert*, 105, 237, 239 (cits.), 329 (Aldfrith); Ireland, 'Aldfrith', 73–7 (Aldfrith's scholarship).   33 Bieler, 'Adamnán', 175–234 (edition); Fraipont, 'Bede', 249–80 (edition); Foley & Holder, *Bede Miscellany*, 1, 5–25 (date and translation).   34 Ireland, 'Aldfrith', 73–4 (citations

prevailing between Iona and Northumbria, for since at least the synod of Whitby in 664 Iona and its Paschal tradition had been classified by the Northumbrian church as schismatic. In citing Biblical chronology from a chronicle from Iona Bede was playing with ecclesiastical fire, and it comes as no surprise that members of Wilfrid's party should subsequently criticize him. While Bede's *epistola ad Pleguinam* in 708 represents that this criticism arose simply from his substitution of Vulgate for Septuagint chronology, their knowledge of his actual source for this Vulgate chronology must surely have helped fan the criticism directed against him.[35] On the other hand, Bede's over-emphatic acknowledgement and recognition accorded to Adomnán for his *De locis sanctis* in HE 5.15–17 may be read as expressing his silent gratitude for Adomnán's role in providing him with a chronicle authoritatively reflecting the chronology of Jerome's Vulgate. Since no schismatic controversy attached to the spatial distribution of Biblical sacred sites Bede could express his appreciation for Adomnán's literary contribution to Northumbrian Christian scholarship more safely by praising his *De locis sanctis*. But for Bede to have publicly acknowledged the source of his Vulgate chronology in DT, and later DTR, would have been to invite a Roman ecclesiastical anathema. In the event, notwithstanding Bede's enormous contribution to English scholarship, he would not ascend the scale of sanctity beyond the 'Venerable'. Next, to understand how three reigns (B2–3, 6) of Bede's own Byzantine extension were copied back into the Iona chronicle we need to consider how the relationship between Iona and Northumbria changed dramatically in 716.

The Annalistic papal chronicle and reform of the Iona chronicle

A unique feature of world history in the Insular chronicles is the chronicle of papal affairs in the Annals extending over AD 431–608, which includes a continuous papal succession from pope Xystus r. 432–40 to Sabinian r. 604–6. In DTR Bede, notwithstanding his enthusiasm for the papacy reflected in his many citations from LP, made no attempt to reproduce LP's papal succession. This Annalistic papal chronicle is unique therefore and it is best preserved in AU where its sources may be readily identified as the chronicles of Prosper and Marcellinus, LP and DTR. The succession itself was compiled by taking extracts from Marcellinus and LP, and since the edition of LP employed extended for at least a further five reigns as far as Honorius r. 625–38, it is apparent that the interjection 'Finis Cronici Iusebii' at 608 marks the truncation of this papal succession.[36] As well as the celebration inherent in systematically

from Bede, Eddius Stephanus and Alcuin praising Aldfrith's learning).   35 Jones, 'Ep. ad Pleguinam', 613–26 (edition); Wallis, *Reckoning*, 405–15, 405 (English edition, criticism).   36 Mc Carthy, 'AU apparatus 431–1131', 66–7 (papal succession), 68–9 (truncation). The edition of LP

registering the succession of bishops of Rome, a number of other features show that this papal chronicle was intended to perform an important polemical role in the Annals. The first is that this papal chronicle is positioned precisely between the seven consecutive kalends that were deleted over 425–31, and the six non-consecutive kalends that were deleted over 612–64 as part of the reform of the Iona chronicle in the eighth century.[37] While we have no direct evidence concerning what entries were removed with these deleted kalends it appears likely from their synchronization with the papal chronicle that they are related. In particular the absence of all account of the *Latercus* of Sulpicius, or its arrival in Ireland, or the Insular Paschal controversy of the seventh century, suggest that the deletions over 425–31 erased the record of the *Latercus'* arrival, while those deletions over 612–64 erased Iona's account of the Paschal controversy. Thus the papal chronicle and these deletions can be seen to be precisely complementary in both polemical and chronological terms. The second noteworthy feature is the character of the very first entry of this papal chronicle which is drawn from the notice in Prosper's chronicle recording pope Celestine's ordination and despatch of Palladius as bishop to Ireland together with the consuls for the following year. To this has been suffixed Bede's synchronism with the eighth year of Theodosius. I set forth all the entries below:[38]

> AU 431.1: Palladius ad Scotos a Celestino urbis Romae episcopo ordinatus episcopus, Ætio et Ualerio consulibus, primus mittitur in Hiberniam ut Christum credere potuissent, anno Teodosi uiii°.
> Prosp. §1307: Ad Scottos in Christum credentes ordinatus a papa Caelestino Palladius primus episcopus mittitur.
> Prosp. §1308: CCCCV Aetio et Valerio.
> DTR §482: Ad Scottos in Christum credentes ordinatus a papa Caelestino Palladius primus episcopus mittitur anno Theodosi octauo.

Here, while Prosper asserted that pope Celestine had sent Palladius to serve as the first bishop to the Irish believers in Christ (*ad Scottos in Christum credentes*), this compiler emended the entry to assert that Celestine, bishop of Rome, had despatched Palladius as the first bishop to the Irish so that they might believe in Christ (*in Hiberniam ut Christum credere potuissent*). Into this emendation he anachronistically interpolated the consuls 'Aetio et Valerio', who are the consuls given by Prosper for the following year with Anno Passionis 405 = AD 432. To this he further suffixed Bede's synchronism of Palladius' despatch with the eighth year of Theodosius, and conflicting therefore with the consuls. Thus this

---

used by Bede contained a further twenty-three complete papal reigns beyond Sabinian. **37** Mc Carthy, 'Chronology', 229, 239–40 (reformed Iona chronicle). **38** Mommsen, 'Prosperi chronicon', 473 (§1307–8); Jones, DTR, 516 (DTR §482).

reforming compiler emphatically assigned a papal origin to the very beginning of the Christian faith in Ireland, whereas Prosper had acknowledged that the faith had already preceded Palladius. Subsequently this compiler further underlined the pre-eminent role he attributed to the papacy by interpolating Bede's version of an imperial decree of papal primacy derived from LP:[39]

> AU 605.3: At the request of Boniface, he [Emperor Phocas] decreed the See of Rome and of the Apostolic Church to be head of all churches, because the Church of Constantinople was wont to describe itself as the premier church.

As in his Palladian entry he here again cited DTR, so that it is clear that this reforming compiler wrote after 725 and he was in complete accordance with Bede regarding the primacy of the papacy and its role in the inauguration of the Insular churches.[40]

Regarding the question of the identity of this reforming compiler, from his kalend deletions and this papal chronicle it is apparent that he must have been a person occupying a position of high authority in Iona after 725 with complete liberty of access to their chronicle. His cultural affiliation is suggested by the presence in the Annals of an Anglo-Saxon chronicle which, as it extends over 611–718, it is, like the truncation of his papal chronicle at 608, closely synchronised to the kalend deletions commencing at c.612. This chronicle was described in detail by Bannerman and it comprises twenty-two entries referring to eighteen members of Anglo-Saxon royalty, of whom fourteen were Northumbrian.[41] The synchronization of both this Northumbrian end chronicle and the polemical papal chronicle with the kalends lacunae, and the access to the Iona chronicle required for the kalend deletions all combine to suggest that the author of this reform was the Northumbrian nobleman and monk Ecgberht †729.[42]

As a young man Ecgberht crossed to Ireland in search of learning and in HE Bede gives a comprehensive and admiring account of his life and work there. Having survived the plague of 664 in Rath Melsigi he initiated the Christian mission to Frisia by Willibrord in c.692, and in 716 Ecgberht persuaded the Iona community to abandon the eighty-four year Paschal *Latercus* of Sulpicius Severus and to follow the Roman Paschal tradition. Two years later the Annals record that the coronal tonsure was imposed on the community at Iona, thereby further extending the Roman reform, and Ecgberht died there eleven years later.

---

39 DTR §535, cf. Mommsen, *Liber Pontificalis*, 164 (Phocas' decree). 40 DTR §331 and HE 1.4 (Pope Eleuter bestows Christianity on king Lucius and the Britons), cf. AT 172.3. 41 Bannerman, 'Scottish entries', 21–3 (Anglo-Saxon entries with correction of his AT chronology). 42 I wish to record my gratitude to Colin Ireland for his assistance with the orthography of Anglo-Saxon names.

Ecgberht is the only known authoritative figure on Iona with an ecclesiastical and cultural background appropriate to the papal and Northumbrian chronicles found in the Iona chronicle over 431–718. Hence I submit that it was Ecgberht who reformed the Iona chronicle sometime between 725 and his death in 729, and since he employed DTR for his papal chronicle it was likely he who copied three of Bede's reigns (B2–3,6) while compiling his Northumbrian end chronicle.[43] While textually the papal entries interpolated by Ecgberht have been best preserved in AU his reformed chronological apparatus has been best preserved in AT/CS, which both show that he corrupted the ferials from 433 onwards and abandoned them from *c.*644 onwards, leaving the apparatus as a bare kalend thereafter.[44]

There is a second series of important entries closely linked to Ecgberht's papal succession and while these are not world history they may be most conveniently examined here. These are the ten Patrician entries extending from a natus at 336 to an obit at 458, and two of these entries are textually integrated with Ecgberht's papal succession. The first of these papal-Patrician entries is that at 432 registering Patrick's arrival in Ireland:[45]

> 432: Patrick arrived in Ireland in the ninth year of the reign of Theodosius the Less and in the first year of the episcopate of Xistus, 42nd bishop of the Roman Church. So Bede, Marcellinus and Isidore compute in their chronicles.

Now we first observe here how the very first regnal incipit of the papal succession has been integrated with the notice of Patrick's arrival. Secondly we note that while this entry simply asserts that he 'arrived in Ireland', and so can be equally identified with his arrival in Ireland as a captive aged sixteen as narrated in his own *Confessio*, the subsequent impressive synchronisms with the reigns of Theodosius and pope Xystus suggest a more momentous arrival. This suggestion is further emphasized by the following interjection alleging that the synchronism is represented in the chronicles of Bede, Marcellinus, and Isidore, though in fact only Marcellinus registers Xystus' papacy. However, all ambiguity regarding which of Patrick's two arrivals in Ireland was intended is swept aside by the subsequent series of three entries as follows:[46]

---

43 Mc Carthy, 'AU apparatus 82–1019', 270 where my attribution of the revision and interpolation of Prosper's Palladius entry to the 'Dionysiac Computist' was mistaken.   44 Mc Carthy, 'Chronology', 227–8 (corrupt ferials), 250 (abandoned ferials).   45 Patrician entries, cf. Mc Carthy, 'Synchronization', *s.a.* 336 (*natus*), 341 (*baptisus*), 352 (*captiuus*), 358 (*a captiuite*), 367 (*Germanus*), 432 (*uenit*), 438 (*apostulus*), 441 (*probatus*), 443 (*florens*), 458 (*dormitatio*). The cit. is of AU 432.1 as this preserves the best textual reading as may be established by collation with CS 432.2, AR §1, AI §390–1, AB §144, MB 65a.   46 The citations are: AI 439 (Secundinus et al.); AR §89 (Leo); AU 443 (*floruit*).

438: Secundinus, Auxilius and Isserninus are sent to help Patrick; nevertheless, not they, but Patrick alone held the apostleship.

441: Leo was ordained the forty-third bishop of Rome, by whom Patrick was approved in the Catholic Faith and [also] by the succeeding bishops of Rome.

443: Bishop Patrick flourishing in the fervour of the Faith and in the doctrine of Christ in our province.

These three entries emphatically assert that: Patrick was the sole apostle to Ireland; his Catholic faith was endorsed by pope Leo and his successors; he had episcopal status; his Christian mission in Ireland was successful. As can be seen the assertion of Patrick's papal approval is integrated with the incipit of pope Leo's reign again taken from Marcellinus' chronicle, just as Patrick's *uenit* was integrated with the incipit of Xystus' reign taken from Marcellinus. I submit that the integration of these two papal-Patrician entries was the work of the original compiler, and having identified Ecgberht as the author of the papal succession he must also be taken as the author of these Patrician entries. Now the most likely source for the Patrician elements in these entries is Muirchú's *Vita S. Patricii*, compiled sometime between 661 and 700, during which period Ecgberht was resident in Ireland.[47] In cap. 8–10 of book I Muirchú relates in turn the consecration of Palladius by pope Celestine and his brief and unsuccessful mission to Ireland, immediately followed by Patrick's episcopal consecration and that of Auxilius and Iserninus and others to lower orders and their embarkation for Ireland. The Annalistic entries over 431–43 should be compared with Muirchú's summary of this, and also the success of Patrick's apostolate and his orthodoxy, 'when Patrick came the worship of idols was abolished and the Catholic Christian faith spread over our whole country.'[48] Muirchú's emphasis upon pope Celestine's ordination of Palladius, Patrick's education by bishop Germanus, and his episcopal consecration by Amathorex make certain his support for Roman episcopal orthodoxy. I submit therefore that because Ecgberht shared Muirchú's Roman ecclesiastical outlook, he used Muirchú's *Vita* to construct a Romanised account of Patrick for the reformed Iona chronicle. In these circumstances it is also necessary to consider Muirchú's chronology of Patrick.

Muirchú's chronological apparatus consists of a series of time intervals and derived ages for Patrick, and initially these follow the chronology of Patrick's own *Confessio*, viz. captivity aged sixteen followed by his release six years later aged twenty-three.[49] To this Muirchú added Patrick's visit at age thirty years to Germanus, bishop of Auxerre, with whom he spent a further thirty years

---

47 Bieler, *Patrician Texts*, 2 (date of compilation), 61–123 (Muirchú's *Vita*). 48 Bieler, *Patrician Texts*, 77 (cit.), 72–7 (Muirchú book I, cap. 8–10). 49 Bieler, *Libri Patricii*, 56 (Conf. §1 – captivity), 66 (Conf. §17 – release); Bieler, *Patrician Texts*, 66–9 (Muirchú I.1 – captivity & release).

studying before embarking aged sixty on his mission to Ireland immediately upon hearing of the failure of Palladius' mission there.[50] Finally Muirchú asserted that Patrick died on 17 March aged 120 years, thereby according him a Mosaic life span which is consonant with the many other Mosaic parallels in his *Vita*.[51] Now while Muirchú's chronology for Patrick's sixty year mission conform to the Annalistic *uenit* and obit at 432 and 491, the most obvious difficulty is the inherent implausibility of any real mission lasting for sixty years to an age of 120. A further problem is that Muirchú described Benignus as a 'small boy', and asserted that Patrick identified him as his successor, but Benignus' Annalistic obit at 469 antedates Patrick's obit at 491 by over two decades.[52]

Next, bearing in mind Muirchú's distinctive Patrician chronology I turn to consider the question of what obit Ecgberht gave to his own Patrician compilation in the Iona chronicle. Now it is the case, when all the Annals are collated, just two Patrician obits emerge, viz. 'Patricius' on 17 March at 491, and 'senis Patricius' at 458.[53] Parenthetically I may observe here that AU's duplicate obits at 461.2 and 492.4 served to virtually double the complexity of Patrician chronology for all those scholars who accepted the *AU priority* hypothesis. Had Ecgberht chosen the obit at 491 then in following Muirchú we should expect to find a natus at *c.*371, but none is to be found there. Rather at 336, that is 122 years before 458, there is a natus witnessed by AT/CS/AU/AI, and followed by three entries registering Patrick's captivity, release and visit to Germanus. When these are collated against Muirchú's chronology we find the situation that is tabulated in Figure 14.[54]

Notwithstanding the minor deviations between Muirchú's and the computed Annals' ages it is clear that these five entries essentially reproduce Muirchú's chronology. I conclude therefore that Ecgberht intruded his own obit for Patrick retarded to 458 and then interpolated these four entries from Muirchú referred to it. As a result Ecgberht's interpolation of Muirchú's account of Patrick into the Iona chronicle retained most of Muirchú's structural features but he reduced Patrick's mission from sixty to thirty-six years and retarded his obit to 458. Thus I conclude that it was Ecgberht who invented the 'early' chronology

50 Bieler, *Patrician Texts*, 70–3 (Muirchú I.7 – Germanus). The only MS witness to Muirchú here states the interval ambiguously as 'some say forty years, others say thirty (*alii quadraginta alii triginta annis*)', but clearly the capitulum has been emended since the chapter headings anticipate a statement of his age, viz. p. 70 'De etate eius quando uisitauit [per] eum angelus ut ueniret ad hiberniam', cf. p.64. However, this age is now lost, but most derivatives of Muirchú cite this interval as thirty years, e.g. Byrne & Francis, 'Two Lives', 35 for the *Vita Secundum* and *Vita Quarta*. 51 Bieler, *Patrician Texts*, 116–19 (Muirchú II.7 – 120 years); Byrne & Francis, 'Two Lives', 17 (Mosaic parallels). 52 Bieler, *Patrician Texts*, 100–3 (Muirchú I.28 – Benignus). 53 Mc Carthy, 'Synchronization', *s.a.* 458, 491 (Patrician obits). 54 Collation shows that the best readings of these are: AU §163 (natus); AU §173 (captivity); AU §181 (release); CS 367.2 (Germanus); AU 457.2 (obit). The first three AU entries are all followed by a later interjection rejecting the entry, viz. 'but this is incorrect', hence the ellipses.

Muirchú's Age	Annals Age	Annals AD	Patrician entry
–	–	336	According to some, Patrick was born here ...
16	16	352	Patrick was brought as captive to Ireland ...
23	22	358	Patrick was released from captivity ...
30	31	367	Patrick [went] to Germanus.
:	:	:	:
120	122	458	Repose of the elder Patrick as some books state.

Figure 14. The Annalistic Patrician chronology tabulated against that of Muirchú.

for Patrick and it seems clear that one of his motives for this was to resolve the aforementioned anachronism regarding Patrick's alleged 'successor' Benignus. For Benignus now appeared to have an eleven year reign until his obit at 469 where he is indeed described as 'successoris Patricii', and then followed by Iarlathi's obit at 481 where he is described as 'tertii episcopi Ard Machae'.[55] Since these succession qualifications are *only* chronologically possible when Patrick's obit is made to precede that of Benignus it seems likely to me that it was Ecgberht who added them.

But an obvious question to ask is why did Ecgberht select the specific year 458? I believe that here, just as at 432 where he adapted an existing Annalistic entry registering Patrick's arrival as a captive to purport that Patrick's Christian mission commenced at that year, so at 458 he adapted a then existing entry registering Patrick's mission to purport an obit. My reasons for this belief are:

a) The year 458 falls twenty-six years after Patrick's captivity at 432 and hence it conforms closely with their relative chronology as given by Patrick in his *Confessio*, viz. that his mission commenced thirty years after an offence committed when he was nearly fifteen.[56] This then placed his mission about twenty-nine years after his captivity at sixteen, but since Patrick himself expressed uncertainty as to whether he had reached fifteen when he offended and the 'thirty years' is itself likely a rounded figure, so that some margin must be admitted.

55 CS 469.1 (Benignus), AU 481.1 (Iarlathi).   56 Bieler, *Libri Patricii*, 73 (Conf. §27 – mission).

b) Independent sources exist which place the incipit to Patrick's mission at about this time.[57] Namely a British chronicle prefixed to the B MS of the *Annales Cambriae* locates the entry, 'sanctus Patricius monente anguelo Hiberniana petit' five years after the Council of Chalcedon which took place in 451, i.e. in 456.[58] Likewise, a synchronism in the Book of Leinster genealogies asserts that Baetán mac Sineall established his church in the fifth year of Faelán mac Colmán, king of Leinster, and the 182nd year after the coming of Patrick. Since Faelán defeated his predecessor at Ath Goan in 636, Patrick's arrival is implicitly located at 636+5–182=459.[59]

Thus these sources imply that Patrick's mission commenced at *c.*458 and hence I conclude that Ecgberht located his obit there as a result of substituting it for the then existing incipit of Patrick's mission. These conclusions regarding Ecgberht's emendations then suggest that the earlier Annalistic chronology for Patrick was: *c.*416 natus, 432 captivity, *c.*438 release, *c.*458 mission, 491 obit aged about seventy-five. Regarding the chronological relationship between Patrick's Irish arrivals and the kings of Tara, the seventh-century accounts by Muirchú and Tirechán both represent that Laoghaire mac Neill was king at the start of his mission. Muirchú simply states that 'In the days when this took place there was in those parts a great king ... by name Loíguire son of Níall.' Tirechán, on the other hand, asserts precisely but opaquely that, 'Here are the latest of his wondrous deeds, accomplished and happily performed in the fifth year of the reign of Loíguire son of Níall.'[60] However, examination of the Annalistic Tara regnal succession shows that the earliest version is transmitted by the Clonmacnoise group and was established only in the middle of the eighth century, cf. the Moville chronicle discussed in chapter 6. This succession placed Laoghaire's regnal incipit at AD 429 and obit at 462, and hence located Patrick's captivity at Laoghaire 4, and his mission at Laoghaire 30, so that both of Patrick's arrivals indeed fell within the reign of Laoghaire.

Now two questions may well be asked at this point. Firstly, what was Ecgberht's motive in introducing Muirchú's account of Patrick into the Iona chronicle? Well, Bede in HE 5.22 makes it clear that Ecgberht's mission to Iona in *c.*716 was to reform their Paschal tradition to orthodoxy with the Roman tradition. Furthermore, at least since Cummian's letter of *c.*633 Patrick's Paschal tradition had been accorded priority by those who considered the 84-year *Latercus* of Sulpicius as schismatic. Cummian, writing to Ségéne abbot of Iona amongst others, listed the Paschal cycles known to him as follows:[61]

57 Carney, *The problem*, 7 (British chronicle), 18–20 (Baetán).   58 Carney, *Studies*, 342–3 (British chronicle).   59 O'Sullivan, *Book of Leinster* vi, 1547–8; Carney, *The problem*, 18–20 (Baetán m. Sineall).   60 Bieler, *Patrician Texts*, 75, 127 (cits.).   61 Walsh & Ó Cróinín, *Cummian's Letter*, 85–7 (cit.), 6–7 (date of letter), 29–35 (discussion of Patrick & Anatolius).

The first is that which holy Patrick, our bishop, brought and followed, in which the moon is regularly observed from the fourteenth to the twenty-first, and the equinox from March 21st. Secondly I found Anatolius (whom you extol) who says that those who observe a 'cycle of eight-four years can never arrive' at the correct reckoning of Easter.

Here Cummian, by placing Patrick first and calling him 'holy' and 'our bishop' identified him and his Paschal principles with orthodoxy, while at the same time subordinating Anatolius and using him to dismiss from orthodoxy all those who followed a cycle of 84-years. However, we know that Cummian's argument did not prevail in Iona until the arrival of Ecgberht there, whereupon, Ecgberht, nearly a century later, by deleting all references to Sulpicius' 84-year *Latercus* and by establishing Patrick in the Iona chronicle as 'founder' of Irish Christianity, followed Cummian in ascribing primacy to Patrick and his ecclesiastical traditions. Secondly, it may be asked why, when Ecgberht was reforming the Iona chronicle, did he not delete the Annalistic obit at 491? The answer to this I would suggest is that Ecgberht's objective was to create as much chronological confusion around Patrick as he could in order to obscure the reality that Patrick was a second-generation Christian missionary to Ireland. By deleting kalends, by introducing but retarding Muirchú's Mosaic chronology, and by retaining the obit at 491 Ecgberht succeeded in distributing his papally approved, episcopal, Catholic saint ambiguously over most of the fourth and fifth centuries. To observe just how well Ecgberht succeeded in his enterprise one has only to glance at the Patrician literature bristling with conflict that was published over 1942–62 by such accomplished scholars as Bieler, Binchy, Carney, Grosjean, Gwynn, Mac Airt, O'Rahilly and Ryan.[62] The postscript to Ecgberht's obit at 729 in AT describing him as 'the Bearded Foreigner, he who was wisest in his time (*in Gall Ulcach, fear as glicca bai na aimsir*)', shows that a keen awareness of his intellectual capability endured amongst the Annalists.

In his reform Ecgberht inflicted grievous damage on the historical and chronological integrity of the Iona chronicle that profoundly disrupted all early Irish historiography, and which challenges historians and chronographers even to the present day. Moreover, there is a malevolence apparent in his reform, for he not only deleted entries that he evidently considered schismatic, but he wantonly obliterated their associated kalends as well. There is too mendacity in Ecgberht's distortion of Prosper's record of Palladius' mission, in his use of Muirchú's Mosaic chronology for Patrick to construct a completely fallacious, papally endorsed, patriarchal 'founder' of Irish Christianity, and in his specious

---

62 Patrician conflict: Bieler, *Life and legend*; Binchy, 'Patrick'; Carney, *The problem*; Grosjean, 'S. Patrice á Auxerre'; Gwynn, 'S. Patrick'; Mac Airt, 'The Chronology'; O'Rahilly, *Two Patricks*; Ryan, 'Two Patricks'.

invocation of the name of 'Eusebius' to justify his own truncation of a papal succession he transcribed largely from LP. The character of Ecgberht's reform, with its sustained emphasis upon episcopacy, whether papal or Patrician, make him the likely inspiration if not author of the title 'episcopus' interpolated into nearly every Christian obit of the fifth century. All of this has contributed to the misapprehension that the foundation of Irish Christianity was episcopal in character, whereas it was in fact monastic as will appear in chapter 5.[63] Ecgberht's performance also makes him the likely author of the Annalistic interjections misrepresenting concurrences between papal and regnal entries with Bede, cf. AU 431.1, 440.1, 460.1, 565.3, 583.2.

The final compilation of Annalistic world history

The final compilation that introduced further substantial world history into the Annals is explicitly indicated by the interjections referring to Bede and excerpts from DTR in Rawl. B. 502, cf. plates 1–2. For indeed collation of AT with DTR shows that many of Bede's own emendations and interpolations in the Christian era, particularly those taken from LP, were subsequently interpolated into the Clonmacnoise chronicle. In the pre-Christian era of DTR Bede himself made numerous deletions but very few additions to the Rufinus-Sulpicius chronicle, but upon arriving at the Incarnation at the start of Age 6 Bede himself turned editor as a glance at Mommsen's *apparatus fontium* will show. For it is the case that over half of the thirty or so sources identified by Mommsen were written after Rufinus' death in 410, though of course most of the regnal citations copied from Orosius, Marcellinus and Isidore had already been made by Adomnán in his compilation of *c.*687. Of the remainder by far the most intensively used source was an edition of *Liber Pontificalis* (LP) that continued to *c.*716 and Bede's fifty-six citations from this work extend from AD *c.*108 to *c.*716, viz DTR §310–589, so there can be no question but their inclusion was indeed the work of Bede. Examination of this substantial corpus of citations shows that Bede's purpose was *not* to reproduce LP's papal succession but rather to underline papal sanctity as proven by martyrdom, to identify instances of papal authority and generosity, to emphasize the papal and civil contributions towards the provision of ecclesiastical architectural splendour, and to identify the primacy of the papacy. These LP citations, together with much smaller numbers from Augustine's *De ciuitate Dei*, Prosper and Isidore's chronicles, and the works of pope Gregory †604, were the means by which Bede placed his recension of world history based upon Adomnán's extension to the Rufinus-Sulpicius chronicle firmly within the tradition of

63 Ó Cróinín, *Early medieval Ireland*, 147 (episcopal to monastic transformation).

Roman ecclesiastical orthodoxy. To this Bede added a Northumbrian end chronicle in the form of nine entries referring to Northumbrian persons and events between c.596–716. Since Ecgberht in fact transcribed only a few of Bede's additions in DTR this left a substantial discrepancy between the quantity of world history in the Christian era in DTR and the Annals. In these circumstances it was inevitable that eventually some annalist would seek to redress this imbalance, and indeed in the Clonmacnoise group we find substantial numbers of Bede's Christian world history additions. As these additions are *not* found in the Cuana group we may use the differences between these two groups to infer the character and approximate date of this secondary compilation.

Since the number of these Bedan world history additions is too great to deal with comprehensively, in order to obtain some insight into this compilation I return to consider some further details of the Byzantine succession tabulated in Figure 13, p. 135. When AT's Byzantine entries are examined it is found that they fall into two disjoint groups, the first comprising entries textually cognate with AU entries and the second comprising entries textually cognate with DTR. In Figure 13 these are separated into the two columns headed respectively, AT~AU and AT~DTR. Of the former four (M4–7) derive from Marcellinus' regnal entries interpolated by Adomnán, and two (B3,6) derive from Bede's regnal entries interpolated by Ecgberht. All of the remainder of AT's entries have been copied from DTR, and, as well as their textual correspondence, these entries are distinguished in every case by their occupying the first position immediately after the kalend. Moreover, most of these Bedan regnal entries have an AM datum either marginally or interlinearly. Thus in AT these entries copied from DTR represent a major but clumsy attempt by an annalist to replace Adomnán's prosaic imperial succession entries with Bede's more cryptic entries and associated AM, as may be seen in Figure 13 above. The result was disastrous because the seventeen-year reign of Constantine IV (Constantinus filius Constantini) was omitted, resulting both in some duplicate reigns and in all of the subsequent interpolations taken from DTR falling back by *circa* seventeen years. For example Justinian Minor's ten-year reign is registered at AT 690.6 (Adomnán's original) and duplicated at AT 673.1 (DTR copy), cf. Figure 13. This compiler also revised Ecgberht's papal succession, which mostly comprised a single entry incorporating a papal reign plus obit, into two separate regnal incipit and obit entries. This final compilation from DTR has been best preserved in AT but largely omitted from the other two members of the Clonmacnoise group; however, the appearance of the anachronistic regnal entries for Justinian Minor, Justinian II and Philip in AR §139.2, §153.2 and CS 699.1 shows that they too descend from this compilation.

Regarding when this final world history compilation took place, since none of these DTR entries are found in the Cuana group it must postdate Cuán's compilation of *c.*1022, and it must also precede the writing of the late eleventh-century Rawl. B. 502. Since throughout the eleventh century the Clonmacnoise chronicle was maintained in Clonmacnoise this compilation must have been undertaken either by or with the acquiescence of the superior at the monastery. In chapter 6 we shall see the evidence that Tigernach Ua Braein †1088 was the *comharba* at Clonmacnoise for 1071–88, and that he did indeed introduce some major revisions into the Clonmacnoise chronicle. In these circumstances Tigernach appears to be the most likely candidate for this compilation of DTR world history entries. It was the presence of these DTR interpolations in AT which prompted Stokes' *Bedan source* hypothesis, with its inevitable corollary of a prefix-compilation. Had Stokes collated AT and DTR more critically he would have found that both preserve independent earlier entries from the Rufinus-Sulpicius chronicle, and that most of the entries identifiably transcribed from DTR lie within the Christian era.

Summary of the evolution of world history in Insular chronicles

It may be helpful to summarize here for the reader in chronological sequence the evolution of the world history in the Insular chronicles:

Circa **410** – Rufinus compiled his chronicle with its kalend+ferial apparatus extending to *c.*400, introducing Vulgate chronology and with an imperial succession extending to Jovian †364. In the Christian era Rufinus included at nineteen-year intervals a series of three-way equivalences commencing at the Incarnation that synchronized Septuagint AM, Vulgate AM and AD. This is the earliest known usage of AD in a Latin chronicle.

Circa **422** – Either Sulpicius Severus or one of his circle extended the kalend+ferial apparatus to *c.*422 and interpolated some Martinian entries, and this Rufinus-Sulpicius chronicle was carried to Ireland by *c.*425, where its kalend+ferial apparatus was continued and Irish entries added.

Circa **562** – S. Columba carried a copy of this extended chronicle to Iona where he and his successor abbots continued the apparatus and added Irish and Scottish entries annually.

Circa **687** – Adomnán extended the Byzantine succession inherited by the Iona chronicle from the Rufinus-Sulpicius chronicle by using successively the chronicles of Orosius, Marcellinus and Isidore, viz. from Valentinian I to Arcadius and Honorius using Orosius, from thence to Justinian I using Marcellinus, and from thence to Heraclius using Isidore's *Chronica maiora*. Adomnán then extended it from Heraclius to his own time, viz. Justinian Minor r. 685–95, introducing his own idiosyncratic chronology.[64] In *c.*687 Adomnán

---

64 Adamnán's chronology placed the start of Justinian Minor's reign at AD 690 whereas in fact it commenced at 685.

sent a copy of his continuation of the Iona chronicle to king Aldfrith together with his *De locis sanctis*, and by 703 these works had reached Bede.

Circa 703 – Bede collated Adomnán's compilation with Isidore's minor chronicle to compile his DT cap. 16–22 in which he omitted all kalends and included only cryptic regnal entries for those successions essential to Biblical and Christian chronology. In this way Bede compiled an epitome of all the main features of Rufinus' Vulgate chronology and Adomnán's idiosyncratic Byzantine succession, which he extended to his own time, viz. the reigns of Leontius and Tiberius.

Circa 725 – Bede compiled his DTR cap. 66, this time reproducing extensive citations from Adomnán's copy of the Iona chronicle, but again omitting all kalends and retaining only Biblically essential successions, and extending the Byzantine series to the eighth year of Leo r.717–41. Bede reckoned the years of the successions using an anachronistic AM imitated from Isidore, and expanded the Christian era with many LP citations, and smaller numbers from other Christian works including Augustine's *De civitate Dei*, Prosper's chronicle, Gildas' *De excidio* and Gregory's *Dialogi*. In this way the Christian era of DTR strongly expressed the orthodoxy of the Roman church.

Circa 727 – The Northumbrian nobleman and monk Ecgberht, having earlier persuaded the Iona community to conform to the Roman Paschal and tonsure traditions, reformed the Iona chronicle. In his reform Ecgberht deleted the seven consecutive kalends from 425 to 431, and six non-consecutive kalends between 612 and 664. Between these two series of deletions Ecgberht interpolated a papal chronicle emphasizing the primacy of the bishop of Rome and misrepresenting pope Celestine as the founder of the Irish church. With this papal chronicle Ecgberht also interpolated a series of entries closely reproducing the Patrician chronology of Muirchú's *Vita S. Patricii*, to which he added an emphatic papal endorsement of Patrick's mission. Immediately following his papal succession Ecgberht interpolated an end chronicle of Anglo-Saxon nobility, mostly Northumbrian, between 611 and 718. The damage that Ecgberht inflicted upon the integrity of the Iona chronicle created complex problems for all subsequent Irish historiographers and chronographers.

Circa 731 – Bede compiled his HE and in it employed the AD chronological apparatus introduced by Rufinus in his chronicle, and Bede used this to locate many events of his chronicle of the English church, notably in his recapitulation HE 5.24. The success of Bede's HE contributed significantly to the adoption of AD in European historical writing.

Circa 1071 – It was likely Tigernach Ua Braein, *comharba* at Clonmacnoise 1071–88, who revised the Clonmacnoise chronicle by collating their then existing chronicle with DTR and introducing many of Bede's additions over the

Christian era. As part of this an attempt was made to substitute Bede's imperial succession at least from Anastasius I †518 onwards, but on account of the inadvertent omission of the seventeen-year reign of Constantine IV †685 all subsequent transcriptions from DTR are retarded by *circa* seventeen years.

CHAPTER FIVE

The Iona chronicle

The term 'Iona Chronicle' used as a title was introduced by John Bannerman in his important paper of 1968 dealing with the Scottish entries in the Irish Annals. Bannerman wrote that, 'recently Dr Isabel Henderson has suggested new grounds for believing that a Scottish annalistic record was compiled in Iona about the middle of the eighth century. For convenience of reference it may be cited henceforth as the *Iona Chronicle*.'[1] Remarkably, just one year earlier, Francis John Byrne had used the very same term, but not in the form of a title, viz., 'It has long been obvious that one of the most important strands in the annals is an Iona chronicle.'[2] However, Bannerman's use of italics and capitals, together with his careful analysis of the material, gave the term an identity that has endured, and it has been often repeated by subsequent scholars. Because the term succinctly identifies an important phase in the development of the Annals I employ it here, though not in title form but following Byrne's usage. Bannerman's work, together with the studies published by Smyth and Hughes contributed a great deal towards identifying the distinctive features of the Annals from the sixth to the middle of the eighth centuries, and establishing their relationship with the monastery in Iona. However, in every case these authors' evaluation of the origin and early development of this material was misguided by the pervasive *Bedan-source* hypothesis, as can be seen implicitly in Bannerman's repetition of Henderson's assertion that the, 'annalistic record was compiled ... about the middle of the eighth century.' On the other hand the discussion in chapter 4 has identified a completely different origin for Insular chronicling, viz. the Rufinus-Sulpicius chronicle that arrived with monastic Christianity sometime in the third decade of the fifth century. Consequently, it is the purpose of this chapter to consider the implications arising from this revised source history for those annals that have been associated with the monastery of Iona.

The monastery on Iona was founded by S. Columba, and the earliest association between him and the island is found in the Annals which record that he sailed there in 562 when he was aged about forty-two, and then his death in 593 aged about 73, so that he was born *c*.520.[3] These details and this essential

1 Bannerman, *Studies*, 9 ('*Iona Chronicle*').   2 Byrne, 'Seventh-century documents', 179 (cit.). 3 Mc Carthy, 'Synchronization', *s.a.* 520 (natus), 562 (navigatio), 593 (obit); Mc Carthy, 'S. Colum

chronology are all recited by Bede in HE 3.4, along with synchronisms between Columba's arrival on Iona and the Byzantine emperor Justinian Minor and the Pictish king 'Bridius the son of Malcolm'. From these it appears that the copy of the Iona chronicle received by Bede included at least some Irish and Pictish entries. Bede also described in some detail the distinctive monastic tradition established by Columba at Iona and its dependent monasteries, and he emphasized its purity and asceticism, its commitment to Biblical study and learning, its rejection of episcopal rule and adherence to a Paschal tradition celebrating on luna 14–20 and employing an eighty-four year cycle.[4] Now these features are all consistent with what we know of the monastic tradition of Sulpicius Severus, the author of the Paschal *Latercus* followed by Columba.[5] These correlations suggest therefore that having reached Ireland *c.*425 the Rufinus-Sulpicius chronicle passed through monasteries run by monks loyal to the monastic tradition of Sulpicius, until it reached Columba sometime in the earlier sixth century. Thus I commence by reviewing what can be discerned regarding the Rufinus-Sulpicius chronicle in the fifth and earlier sixth centuries.

Evolution of the Rufinus-Sulpicius chronicle in early Christian Ireland

As we have no direct information regarding where or how this chronicle was maintained in the decades following its arrival in Ireland we must try to deduce this from an examination of the Annals themselves. Ó Buachalla was the pioneer here with his 1958 study of the Irish annals over 429–70. He demonstrated that when all entries showing any evidence for retrospection were eliminated the six remaining entries have a predominantly Leinster provenance.[6] These entries comprised the ecclesiastical obits of Secundinus †447, founder of Dunshaughlin in Meath, Auxilius †459, founder of Killashee in Kildare, and Iserninus †470, founder of Kilcullen in Kildare and Aghade in Carlow, together with the obit of Bresal †436, king of Leinster, and two battles involving a victory and a defeat for the Leinstermen at 446 and 453. Now the consistent Leinster provenance of these secular entries combined with the Kildare foundations of Auxilius and Iserninus together suggest that it was in one of these monasteries that the Rufinus-Sulpicius chronicle was first continued. While from these few entries the continuation appears to have been quite intermittent, as we do not know how many early entries were deleted by Ecgberht's reform we cannot be certain about the original level of coverage. These three clerics are considered to have

---

Cille', (Columba's chronology). 4 Bede HE 3.4 (cit.); HE 3.4 (Columba & his monastic tradition); HE 2.2, 2.4, 2.19, 3.3, 3.4, 3.17, 3.25, 3.28, 5.21 (luna 14–20); HE 2.2, 5.21 (84-year cycle). 5 Stancliffe, *S. Martin*, 48–54 (origins of Sulpicius' monastic tradition), 265–96 (ascetic–episcopal conflict); Mc Carthy, 'The *latercus*', 39–40 (Sulpicius' compilation of the *Latercus*). 6 Ó Buachalla, 'Construction', 109 (three secular Leinster entries), 114 (three Leinster-Meath

come from Gaul and in the Patrician hagiography they are always made subordinate to him and his mission.[7] However, in fact Secundinus was dead before Patrick commenced his mission, Auxilius died about the time it began, while Iserninus survived it for only about a decade. But their very inclusion in the Patrician hagiography affirms the success of their Christian missions, and moreover I suggest that the appearance of their obits in the Annals requires that their foundations were all in the monastic tradition of Sulpicius. They were *not* episcopal foundations as has been inferred by the title 'episcopus' later interpolated into the obits of Auxilius and Iserninus. In particular they were *not* followers of Palladius and his episcopal tradition as has been conjectured.[8] Adomnán tells us that Columba studied 'divine wisdom' in Leinster under one Gemmán, and we know that Columba's younger contemporary Columbanus (*c.*543–615) also studied in Leinster and in *c.*603 he likewise identified his Paschal tradition with the 'reckoning of eighty-four years and with Anatolius'.[9] Thus these accounts confirm the presence in Leinster, less than one century after Secundinus et al., of well-established monasteries transmitting the tradition of Sulpicius.[10] De Paor pointed out that their foundations at Dunshaughlin, Killashee and Kilcullen were all proximate to and overlooked by the powerful contemporaneous strongholds of Tara, Naas and Dun Ailinne, from which it is clear that long before Patrick's mission commenced the principal secular dynasties of the central east coast had adopted Christian monastic foundations in the tradition of Sulpicius.[11]

However, the provenance of the annals subsequent to 470 did not remain thus, and Ó Buachalla's subsequent study of annals over 471–550 identified the emergence of a south-eastern Ulster provenance.[12] Since there can be no serious doubt but that the chronicle was maintained in a Christian context this effect can be best demonstrated by chronologically listing the provenance of all Christian obits over the fifth century, and these are tabulated in Figure 15.

As can be seen a significant Armagh-Down provenance appears in the second half of the fifth century, and with this must be reckoned the evidence of the secular entries which deal principally with the kings of Tara. These taken together indeed support Ó Buachalla's suggestion that recording of the chronicle had moved northwards from Leinster into closer proximity with Meath, Armagh and Down. While we have very little evidence on which to base a judgement as to which monastery the chronicle moved, three details prompt me to tentatively suggest that it was the monastery of the British monk Mochta †533 at Louth,

obits). Ó Buachalla employed a mixed AU/AI chronology and actually cited the range as '429–66.'
7 De Paor, *Patrick's world*, 43 (Gaulish origin).   8 Ó Cróinín, *Early medieval Ireland*, 22, and de Paor, *Patrick's world*, 43 (conjecture).   9 Walker, *Columbani opera*, xxxvi (date), 19 (cit.).
10 Sharpe, *Adomnán*, 174 (VC 2.25 – Gemmán), 11 (Columbanus).   11 De Paor, *Patrick's world*, 41.   12 Ó Buachalla, 'Notes', 74–5 (Ulster obits).

AD	Irish Christian obits	Provenance
447	Secundinus	Meath
459	Auxilius	Kildare
469	Benignus	Armagh
470	Iserninus	Kildare
479	Brendainn of Armagh	Armagh
481	Iarlathi	Armagh
487	Mel of Ardagh	Longford
488	Ciannán of Duleek	Meath
489	Mac Caille	Offaly
491	Patricius	Armagh-Down
496	Mac Cuilinn of Lusk	Dublin
497	Mo Chae of Nendrum	Down
497	Cormac	Armagh

Figure 15. List of all Irish Annalistic Christian obits for the fifth century, but omitting Ecgberht's duplicate of Patrick (Senis Patricius). In the Annals all except Secundinus, Ciannán and Mo Chae are entitled as 'episcopus'.

about seven miles south-west of Dundalk. The first is that this location between Meath and Ulster fits the provenance of the ecclesiastical and secular entries very well. The second is that Mochta was selected by Adomnán to prophesy Columba's fame 'through all the provinces of the ocean's islands', and this implies that Adomnán perceived some continuity of tradition between Mochta and Columba.[13] The third is that Mochta is the earliest Christian in Ireland to whom an Annalistic entry is explicitly attributed, namely the entry at AU 471.1 'Praeda secunda Saxonum de Hibernia ...' is attributed to him as 'ut Maucteus .i. Mochtae dicit'. On these grounds I provisionally propose that it was in Mochta's foundation at Louth that the chronicle was continued. Regarding when this move took place we may note that by 470 Secundinus, Auxilius and Iserninus were all dead, and indeed the abovementioned interjection citing Mochta is found in the year immediately following Iserninus' death. In any case the concentration of northern ecclesiastical obits over 479–91 suggests that by c.490 the move northwards had occurred. Regarding the question of the route taken by the chronicle from this northern location to Columba we may first note that even if the hypothesis concerning Mochta is correct it is not plausible that Columba acquired it directly from him, for at Mochta's death in 533 Columba was a youth of only about thirteen years. However, various details suggest that a monastic neighbour of Mochta in county Louth may have served as the conduit.

13 Sharpe, *Adomnán*, 105 (cit.), 244 (discussion); idem, 'S. Maucteus', 85–93 (Mochta).

As an educated follower of the monastic tradition of Sulpicius the most likely place for Columba to have learned of the existence of the chronicle was from his Christian teachers.[14] As well as Gemmán in Leinster Adomnán in his *Vita S. Columbae* twice asserted that Columba's teacher in Ireland was a 'bishop Uinniau', but provided insufficient information to identify him decisively.[15] However, in a series of articles Pádraig Ó Riain has persuasively argued that 'Uinniau' is to be identified with Finnian of Moville †577 rather than Finnian of Clonard †550, and this identification is also supported by a number of details of the Annalistic entries.[16] First, in the Annals Finnian of Moville's name is consistently registered as 'Uinnianus episcopi' which form and title correspond more closely with Adomnán's usage, whereas Finnian of Clonard is systematically registered as 'Finnia moccu Telduib'. Second, Finnian founded two monasteries, one at Droimín in Louth about eight miles south of Mochta's monastery, and the other at Moville in Down, and both of these locations reconcile closely with the provenance of the later fifth and earlier sixth-century Annalistic entries. Clonard, on the other hand in south-west Meath does not reconcile with the Ulster provenance. Third, as will be demonstrated in the next chapter, when the Iona chronicle returned to Ireland in the mid-eighth century it was to Finnian's monastery in Moville that it went. Since it was by then a comprehensive chronicle of Ireland's affairs it was an extremely valuable compilation, and so that it went to Moville in itself suggests some special relationship existed between the Iona chronicle and Moville's founder Finnian. Fourth, the Columban literature contains an explicit account of Columba obtaining a book from Finnian at Droimín. The well-known story is found in *Betha Columb Chille* by Maghnus Ua Domhnaill, and in a much more summary form in *Foras Feasa* by Keating, and it recounts how Columba while visiting Finnian at Droimín borrowed and surreptitiously copied a book (*lebhair*) belonging to him. When Finnian learned of this he accused Columba who defended his action and referred the matter for judgement to Diarmait Ua Cearbhaill, king of Tara, who then made his famous ruling, 'To every cow her young cow ... and to every book its transcript.' This judgement Columba rejected and he threatened Diarmait with punishment, and this then furnished the motivation for the battle of Cúl Dreimne in 560.[17] Now of course this narrative may be simply rejected on the grounds of its lateness, but the

---

14 We know of either Columba or his Iona foundation that they espoused Sulpicius' Paschal tradition, the *latercus*, his preference for abbatial control over episcopal, and his emphasis on the study of history and chronology.   15 Sharpe, *Adomnán*, 154, 208 (VC 2.1 & 3.4 – Columba's teacher), 110 (VC 1.1 – Columba lives with Uinniau), 11–12, 317 n.210 (uncertain identity); Dumville, 'Gildas & Uinniau', 207–14 (Uinniau).   16 Ó Riain, *Feastdays*, 68 'saint Finnian [of Moville] ... is the man stated by ... Adomnán to have taught Columba'; cf. Ó Riain, 'Finnian or Winniau'; idem, 'Finnio and Winniau'; idem, 'Finnio: priority'.   17 O'Kelleher & Schoepperle,

following considerations lead me to accept its substance. The story places Columba, the premier saint of the Uí Néill, in a most dishonourable light, for not only does he betray the trust of his own teacher but when challenged he defends his betrayal, and then proceeds to vengefully reject a judgement he himself has invoked. Even Adomnán writing a century after Columba's death was obliged to acknowledge that his saintly hero had been excommunicated and exposed to public censure, so that it is clear that Columba had committed some serious transgression in the eyes of his Christian contemporaries.[18] Given the saintly status accorded to Columba from soon after his death the complete invention of such a shameful narrative seems quite improbable, and I conclude that this account reflects a real event in Columba's life. In chapter 6, p. 173 ff., I shall present the evidence that suggests that after leaving Iona in c.740 the Iona chronicle moved to Finnian's other foundation at Moville. The delivery of the Iona chronicle to Moville in the mid-eighth century can then be understood as the execution of Diarmait's judgement 'to every book its transcript', albeit with a two century delay. Thus while acknowledging the evidence to be circumstantial I conclude that Columba acquired his copy of the Irish continuation of the Rufinus-Sulpicius chronicle in an irregular fashion from his teacher Finnian at Droimín. Then Adomnán's prominent references to S. Uinniau and Columba at the start of each book of his *Vita Columbae* can be read both as Adomnán's acknowledgment of Columba's debt to Finnian, and as a denial of any misdemeanour on Columba's part.

Regarding when Columba acquired his copy of the chronicle Ó Buachalla remarked and Smyth systematically demonstrated that post c.550 two profound changes occur, namely the Annalistic provenance expands to include all provinces of Ireland and contemporaneous Irish entries are found in virtually every year.[19] There can be no serious doubt but that Columba was responsible for both of these developments and hence that he had acquired the chronicle by c.550 when he was aged about thirty. Having acquired it he proceeded to develop it into an annual ecclesiastical and political survey of the provinces of Ireland and her neighbouring islands, and this very expansion of purview seems to be remarked in Maghnus Ua Domhnaill's account of Columba defending his copying of Finnian's book, 'I declare that it was right for me to copy it, ... seeing it was my desire to give the profit thereof to all peoples.'[20] In summary then from the limited evidence available to us it appears that the Rufinus-Sulpicius chronicle was first continued intermittently in the Kildare monasteries

Colaim Chille, 176–9 (Finnian's book); Comyn & Dinneen, *Foras Feasa iii*, 88 (Keating's version from 'Leabhar Dubh Molaga'). **18** Sharpe, *Adomnán*, 207 (VC 3.3 – Columba's excommunication of which Adomnán's account is self-contradictory). **19** Ó Buachalla, 'Notes', 74 (expansion of purview); Smyth, 'Earliest Irish annals', 10 (annual record). **20** O'Kelleher & Schoepperle, *Colaim Chille*, 179 (cit.).

of Auxilius or Iserninus, but in the later fifth century it moved northwards, possibly to Mochta's monastery at Louth. Subsequently it appears likely to have passed into the possession of Finnian of Moville in his monastery at Droimín in Louth, and it was here in *c.*550 that Columba irregularly acquired a copy of it.

On the reliability of Irish chronicling prior to 550

The near complete acceptance by scholarship of Stoke's *Bedan-source* hypothesis and its prefix compilation corollary meant that scholars were obliged to regard all early Irish entries as profoundly retrospective and hence as historically untrustworthy. Conservative historians just took the date of Bede's compilation of DTR in 725 as their *terminus ante quam non*, but more critical scholars realized that the existence of such as unique and accurate astronomical observations from the seventh century implied a much earlier terminus.[21] Smyth undertook a comprehensive survey of years without Irish entries and demonstrated conclusively that annalistic chronicling had commenced by *c.*550. However, while annalistic chronicling does indeed imply close contemporaneity, intermittent chronicling does *not* necessarily imply non-contemporaneity. The test of contemporaneity ultimately lies in the entries themselves, not in their frequency.[22] But as there never was a prefix compilation and non-annual chronicling may still incorporate contemporaneous records there are in my view insufficient grounds to reject *all* entries prior to *c.*550 as implicitly retrospective. Of course some such as Ecgberht's Patrician interpolations are certainly retrospective and deeply misleading, but I submit that unless there are *prima faciae* grounds for suspecting manipulation then entries should be assumed contemporaneous and their chronology trustworthy. In support of this principle I wish to present accounts of two investigations which independently demonstrate that a monastic capacity for the accurate recording and transmission of records of Irish events indeed existed from the fifth century.

The first investigation arose from the dendrochronological record for the width of annual growth rings of Irish oak trees for the last seven thousand years assembled by Mike Baillie of Queens University, Belfast. Baillie's tree-ring index for 534–52, together with the averaged tree-ring index for oaks from fifteen other European sites and the mean annual growth are plotted in Figure 16. This shows that over the sixteen years 536–51 the growth of all European oaks was severely

---

21 Byrne, 'Seventh-century documents', 180 ('the second half of the sixth century'); Hughes, *Early Christian Ireland*, 118, ('from about the 680s'); Ó Cróinín, *Early medieval Ireland*, 26 ('nothing in our native annals can be taken at face value in the period before the mid-sixth century at the earliest'). 22 Smyth, 'Earliest Irish annals',10, 'the number of blank years which occur before 550 is large enough ...The only satisfactory explanation of this phenomenon is to hold that the period prior to *c.*550 was never covered by contemporary annalistic documentation.' Smyth

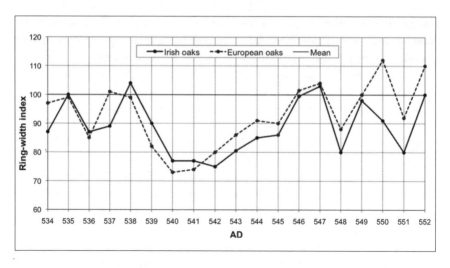

Figure 16. Tree-ring index for Irish oaks, and the averaged index for fifteen other European sites, plotted as solid and broken lines respectively for the years AD 534–52, with the mean annual index shown as a horizontal continuous line, after Baillie, 'Patrick', 70. For most years between 536 and 551 all oaks exhibited severely diminished annual growth, with Irish oaks showing substantially less growth than the European average.

retarded below mean values, with the growth of Irish oaks substantially lower than the European average. In particular over the eleven years 536–7, 539–45, 548 and 551 growth rates, and hence temperatures, dropped to levels experienced extremely rarely. Indeed analysis of the parallel data from a North American foxtail pine chronology showed that it registered 536 as the second coldest year in the last two millennia.[23] The Irish oak record therefore speaks of eleven years of intense cold in Ireland at a level which represented a hazard to most higher life forms. Now it is known from both European and Chinese records that in this interval severe famine and plague were widespread across both of these areas, Procopius providing a graphic account of the devastation caused by the Justinian plague in the eastern Mediterranean commencing in 542. From China there is evidence that in 536–8 between seventy to eighty percent of the people starved to death.[24] When we examine the Annals for entries registering social stress we find the four entries tabulated in Figure 17.[25]

Now social stress that is caused by climatic deterioration must obviously occur shortly after the climatic extremes, and it is apparent that these four

never considered the possibility that 'blank years' may arise from chroniclers choosing to record entries intermittently or from entry loss by attrition in transmission.   23 Baillie, 'Dendrochronology', 213 (second coldest year).   24 Baillie, 'Marker dates', 234 (Procopius & Chinese evidence).   25 Mc Carthy, 'Synchronization', *s.a.* 538, 540, 550, 553 (chronology); Stokes, *AT*, 136–7, 141–2 (cits.).

AD	Annalistic entries registering social stress
538	Perditio panis. [AU 535.3, 538.1]
540	Mortalitas magna quae blefed dicitur, in quá Mo-Bí Clarineach, cui nomen est Berchan, brecanó poeta, periit. [AU 544.1]
550	Mortalitas magna .i. ín Crom Conaill nó in Buidhe Chonnaill, in quo isti sancti pausauerunt .i. Findia mac húi Tellduib ⁊ Colum mac Crimthaind ⁊ Colam Indse Cealtra ⁊ Sineall mac Cenandain ab Cilli Achaidh Drumfada, ⁊ Mac tail Chilli Cuilind, qui nominatur Eogan mac Corcrain. [AU 548.3]
553	Pestis quae uocatur Samtrusc. [AU 553.2]

Figure 17. Annalistic entries registering social stress in the mid-sixth century; the citations are from AT with parallel AU entries listed in brackets. The AD years should be compared with the years of the onset of severe cold indicated in Figure 16.

annalistic entries fall either one or two years after the onset of periods of extreme cold, and consequently all are appropriately synchronized to the climatic events. It appears certain therefore that the substance of these four entries was recorded contemporaneously together with accurate chronological information, and they thereby demonstrate that a capacity for accurate chronicling in the most difficult of circumstances existed in an Irish monastic context by 538. This conclusion is further supported by the additional personal information recorded in respect of the names of two of the victims, Mo Bí and Mac Tail. Moreover, it should be noted that all of the victims whose names are recorded were from a monastic context, and most were monastic leaders, viz. Mo Bí was the principal teacher at Glas Nóíden (Glasnevin), Finnian was founder of Cluain Iraird (Clonard), Colum mac Crimthaind was prominently associated with Tír dá Glas (Terryglas), Mac Tail with Cell Cuilind (Kilcullen), and Sineall was abbot and founder of Cell Achaid (Killeigh).[26] The purview of these names shows that this chronicle of the catastrophe was monastic in origin, and the number and prominence of these men who perished is a measure of the extent of the devastation wrought by the disaster. Of particular interest is Mo Bí, for whom is given his origin 'Clarineach', his alternative name 'Berchan', and his profession 'poeta', for he is described in the twelfth-century *Betha Coluim Cille* as the teacher in the monastery of Glasnevin in Dublin of a number of prominent sixth-century monastics, including Ciarán of Clonmacnoise, Comgall of Bangor, Cainnech of Aghaboe, and Columba himself. In this *Betha* it is also

26 Smyth, 'Earliest Irish annals', 15 (identifications).

related how Columba survived an inundation at Glasnevin and subsequently Mo Bí instructed all the students to leave the monastery on account of a forthcoming plague in which he himself then perished.[27] The physical details of this *Betha* account reconcile correctly, therefore, with the record of extreme climatic and social conditions preserved in the dendrochronological series and the Annals, affording a remarkable verification of the *Betha*.

Thus it is apparent that between them Finnian of Moville and Columba managed to maintain an accurate chronological record of famine, plague, and widespread mortality through a global social catastrophe which endured for at least sixteen years. Now given the nature and scale of this disaster it is simply not plausible that this monastic chronicling capacity commenced just at the very start of these events. Rather accurate chronicling was a well-established capacity within this monastic community long before the disaster, for it was a capacity that had arrived in Ireland with the Rufinus-Sulpicius chronicle and the monastic tradition of Sulpicius, and it was maintained thereafter. We may here also note that the independently-confirmed chronological accuracy of these four entries provides us with a basis on which to judge the chronological performance of AU over these years. As can be seen from Figure 17 above, AU duplicates 'Perditio panis' at 535 and 538, the first of which anachronistically precedes the climatic deterioration, it retards 'Mortalitas ... blefed' by four years to 544, it anticipates 'Mortalitas ... Crom' by two years at 548, and it accurately locates only 'Pestis ... Samtrusc' at 553. Thus AU has seriously dislocated three of these four entries, and duplicated one of them anachronistically, and these errors presented major obstacles to Baillie's discussion of the Irish record, which account he based entirely upon the chronology of AU.[28] These four entries then verify for us simultaneously the chronological and semantic reliability of the record transmitted by the Clonmacnoise group and the chronological unreliability of that transmitted by AU.

As my second investigation I examined the evidence of the accuracy and extent of monastic chronicling in the later fifth century in relation to the life of S. Brigit. While the Annals simply register Brigit's natus at 439 and her obit at 524, the seventh-century *Vita prima S. Brigitae* recounts her interactions with twenty-four named individuals of whom eleven appear in the Annals. When the Annalistic references are collated with the *Vita prima* narratives, some of which give implicit age relativities between the individuals, then they are found to be fully consistent both chronologically and topologically. In particular the account of Patrick shows him as a contemporary of both Mel and Mac Caille, cf. Figure 15, p. 156, but a generation older than Brigit, and this is indeed consistent with

27 Herbert, *Iona*, 192 (date), 228–30 (Mo Bí), 218–47 ('Betha Coluim Cille'), 248–69 (translation).
28 Baillie, 'Dendrochronology', 212, 215 (discussions of AU).

the *natus* of *c*.416 established for Patrick in chapter 4. Whilst we have no evidence regarding the remaining thirteen individuals who are not registered in the Annals, there are no apparent grounds to doubt the chronological accuracy of them in the *Vita prima*. Neither are there any indications that the chronology of the *Vita prima*, which effectively registers floruits, or its topology, have been derived from the Annals which effectively record just obits and battles. Consequently, it appears that there existed in the seventh century, available to the author of the *Vita prima*, a comprehensive account of all these individuals and their lives which provided an accurate chronology and topology for them consistent with that of the Annals. I conclude, therefore, that not only did the monastic community maintain and accurately extend the Rufinus-Sulpicius chronicle through the fifth century, but they also maintained a much more substantial body of accurately dated records than has survived in the Annals. These records were available to the author of the *Vita prima* when it was originally compiled, most likely by Ultan of Ardbraccan †656.[29] The astronomical entries over 594–764 which record precise observations are another instance of an early accurate source, but many of these are displaced typically by one year, showing them to have been inserted into the chronicle after 764 as will be discussed in chapter 6, p. 188 ff. This conclusion corresponds essentially therefore with that of Ó Buachalla, who, on the basis of the Annalistic political entries over 431–70 proposed that, 'they must be regarded as going back to a genuine contemporary chronicle.' Ó Buachalla's conclusion however was ignored, except by Smyth who dismissed it merely on the grounds that it did not fulfil his unwarranted assumption of continuity.[30]

Contribution of Columba and his successors to the Iona chronicle

The review above of the evidence for early Irish chronicling shows that in *c*.550 Columba acquired from Finnian of Moville a chronicle that had been maintained since the inception of Irish monasticism at *c*.425. From *c*.550 until Columba's death in 593 the purview of these annals is dominated by Irish political developments, and it specifically emphasizes the emerging dominance of Columba's relatives in the northern Uí Néill. To this is added a broad sample of secular events from all of Ireland, as well as Scotland and Pictland, together with a similarly broad sample of ecclesiastical obits. From these it is clear that Columba's interests covered the secular and ecclesiastical affairs of all of Ireland and extended well into Scotland and Pictland. The extent and character of this

---

29 Mc Carthy, 'St Brigit', 267 (Brigit's chronology), 270–8 (*Vita prima* vs Annals). Mc Carthy, 'Topographical', 248–56 (*Vita prima* topography), 264–9 (*Vita prima* author and origin). **30** Ó Buachalla, 'Construction', 109 (cit.). Smyth, 'Earliest Irish annals', 11 (assumption of continuity), 13 (rejection).

expansion have some interesting implications regarding Columba's communications infrastructure and his priorities. First, the breadth of the provenance of his
entries implies the existence of a co-extensive network of observers corresponding
with him on a regular basis, and it seems likely that these were a judicious
selection of fellow abbots distributed through the expanding network of monasteries. It is interesting to note that this communication process was in no way
inhibited by his move to Iona in 562. Second, the extent of Columba's secular
and specifically political interest shows that notwithstanding his reputation for
sanctity he was deeply involved with the flux of secular power around him.
Third, it seems likely that the extensive information of all kinds gathered by
Columba provided invaluable intelligence for his political allies.[31] However,
conspicuously few references to Iona itself from Columba's period are found,
half of them being the references to Columba himself which were likely entered
following his death.[32] While such entries in a simple sense might be described
as 'retrospective', in the context of a community that maintained dated accounts
of its affairs this does not imply that such entries are arbitrary or of uncertain
chronology. His *navigatio* in 562, for example, almost certainly left a trail of
correspondence that could serve his successor as a reliable source for this entry.
Likewise his *natus*, often considered a most unreliable category of entry, was
surely based upon an informed evaluation of his personal history and its
synchronisms.

After Columba's death this enlarged provenance was sustained by his
successor abbots with an increasing coverage of Scottish events up until their
sudden reduction at *c.*740. Bannerman summarized this as follows, 'Scottish
events are recorded from the beginning of the sixth century with progressively
greater frequency and detail down to 737. Immediately thereafter they become
comparatively sparse and concise.'[33] Bannerman underlined his observation
regarding the sudden decline of the Scottish purview from the Annals by an
analysis of the direction of verbs of motion used in some entries. This showed
that whereas from 670 to 730 individuals either went to (*pergit ad*) or returned
from (*venit de/revertitur de*) Ireland, but from 754 to 766 they came or returned
to (*venit in/ reversio in*) Ireland.[34] The clear implication is that between 730 and
754 the place of recording moved from Iona to Ireland. Further analysis of
other details of the entries over this interval led Bannerman to conclude, 'All
the evidence so far presented suggests that the *Iona Chronicle*, as we have it now,
came to an end about 740.'[35] Smyth's detailed study of the AU ecclesiastical
entries over 550–800 confirmed this result, and he further noted that from *c.*740,

31 Smyth, *Warlords*, 95–7 (Columba's relationship with kings).   32 Bannerman, *Studies*, 13 (Iona references).   33 Bannerman, *Studies*, 11 (cit.).   34 Bannerman, *Studies*, 11–12 (verbs of direction).   35 Bannerman, *Studies*, 25 (cit.).

'the Leinster and midland record shows an expansion from this time forward.'[36] Thus there can be no doubt that *c.*740, about thirteen years after Ecgberht had effected a major reform of the Iona chronicle, it was abruptly terminated and henceforth it was continued in Ireland.

A remarkable fact about this sudden decline of the Scottish provenance in the Iona chronicle and its relocation to Ireland is that there appears to be no contemporary record either in the Annals or elsewhere, which explains what circumstances precipitated the move. Bannerman drew attention to victories over Scottish Dal Riada by the Pictish king Oengus mac Fergus in 734 and 736, and to the entry in AU at 741, 'Percutio Dal Riatai la hOengus m. Forggusso', and posed the question, 'Were some or all of the contents of the Iona scriptorium taken to Ireland for safety about this time?'[37] Bannerman did not answer this but there is one singular entry in the Annals at 744, which, while clearly retrospective, appears to offer a possible answer to his question. In AT it reads:[38]

> A strange sign was manifested in Boirche, in the time of Fiachna, son of Aed Ron, king of the Ulaid, and in the time of Eochaid, son of Bresal, king of the Húi Echach, to wit, a whale which the sea cast to land with three golden teeth in its head and fifty ounces in each of these teeth; and one of the teeth was taken, and remained on the altar of Bennchor for a long time.

Now this is clearly not a contemporaneous annalistic entry and it is normally just considered an example of a medieval *mirabilis* entry, but as it stands it does affirm the arrival in *c.*740 of valuable, indeed sacred objects on the Boirche coast, which is the coast of county Down south of Strangford Lough. Furthermore, in a monastic context the role of a whale to transport these objects is suggestive, since in the *Book of Jonah* 1:17 the Lord appointed a whale to transport the prophet Jonah safely to dry land. Subsequently, in *Matthew* 12:40, Jesus himself cited this passage as an analogy in anticipation of his own crucifixion and resurrection. Thus from a Christian Biblical perspective a whale as a transport mechanism is heavily charged with significance. Moreover, we know that whales do not have teeth, and in particular they do not have 'golden teeth', and these features then suggest that the entry is in fact allegorical. In this case, given that we know that at just about this time the Iona chronicle was indeed relocated to Ireland, we should consider the possibility that the 'three golden teeth' may represent valuable books being transported from Iona. Now Pádraig Ó Riain has in fact already proposed that the *Martyrology of Tallaght*

36 Smyth, 'Earliest Irish annals', 24–6 (ecclesiastical entries), 34 (cit.).   37 Bannerman, *Studies*, 26 (cit.).   38 Stokes, *AT*, 206–7. A clearly related medieval account in the history of the descendants of Ir states that Fiachna m. Aed received the teeth and gave one to an architect who assisted him to build bridges, and 'two of them to make shrines for the province [*sc.* Ulaid]', cf.

originated in a martyrology which, having left Iona *c.*740 'spent some time in a north-east Ulster monastery', and arrived in Tallaght by 828. As regards which 'Ulster monastery' it first reached, following a comprehensive review of the evidence, Ó Riain concluded: 'only Bangor qualifies for serious consideration as the Irish church most likely to have first received the Iona martyrology, probably before 752.'[39] Thus Ó Riain's proposed itinerary conforms closely to this allegorical account of valuable items having come ashore on the Down coast, one of which 'remained on the altar at Bangor for a long time', and then implicitly moved somewhere else thereafter. For indeed, since a martyrology registers the feastdays of saints to be celebrated on each day of the year, the altar is exactly the appropriate location to maintain such a work. These correlations then support the inference that the 'golden teeth' were intended to represent volumes considered valuable, and hence, given the chronology, that they included also the Iona chronicle. A third candidate 'tooth' would be the psalter known as the *Cathach* regarded as approximately contemporaneous with Columba and believed by some to be written by him.[40] From both the approximate internal dating of the events as 'in the time of Fiachna [†789] son of Aed Ron [†735] and in the time of Eochaid [†?] son of Bresal [†750]', and from the construction, 'remained ... for a long time', it is clear that this allegory was composed a long time after the events it reflects. However, its presence in both the Clonmacnoise group and AB §235.2 suggests that it was inserted in the Clonmacnoise chronicle *before* Cuana's compilation of *c.*1022. While this entry long postdates the actual transfer of the Iona chronicle to Ireland it does nevertheless come from a context which was maintaining and extending that chronicle, and it is reasonable to believe that the Annalists themselves transmitted a history of their own Annals. The veiled, allegoric form of this entry itself suggests that this was specialist knowledge intended only for the initiated. If the above interpretation of this entry is correct then it supports Bannerman's hypothesis that 'some or all of the contents of the Iona scriptorium taken to Ireland for safety about this time.' It also suggests that the Iona chronicle left Iona in irregular circumstances, and this may explain both the precipitate nature of the transfer and the Annalistic silence concerning it.

Summary of the evolution of the Iona chronicle

In this chapter, based principally on the purview of the Annals, I have inferred the following sequence of compilation stages following the arrival in Ireland of the Rufinus-Sulpicius chronicle:

Circa 425 – The Rufinus-Sulpicius chronicle was brought from Gaul to Leinster.

Dobbs, 'Descendants of Ir', 80–3.   **39** Ó Riain, 'Martyrology', 21 nn. 11, 113 (cit. 'Ulster monastery' & 828); idem, *Feastdays*, 71 (cit.).   **40** O'Neill, *Irish hand*, 2–3 (*Cathach*).

Circa 425–490 – The Rufinus-Sulpicius chronicle was continued in the monastery of Auxilius or Iserninus in Kildare.

Circa 490–533 – The chronicle was continued in a location proximate to Meath and south Ulster, possibly in Mochta's monastery at Louth in county Louth.

Circa 533–550 – The chronicle was continued most likely by Finnian of Moville in his monastery at Droimín in county Louth.

Circa 550 – An irregular copy of Finnian's chronicle was made at Droimín by Columba and retained by him against the judgement of Diarmait Ua Cearbhaill.

Circa 550–561 – Columba expanded the provenance of his continuation to include all Ireland, and added both ecclesiastical and secular entries on an annual basis.

Circa 562–593 – Columba continued the chronicle on Iona, now including a Scottish and Pictish provenance.

Circa 594–687 – Columba's abbot successors at Iona continued the chronicle, steadily expanding its Scottish provenance.

Circa 687 – Adomnán substantially expanded the world history content with many interpolations taken from the chronicles of Orosius, Marcellinus and Isidore, extending the Byzantine succession to Justinian r. 685–95, and sending a copy of this to king Aldfrith.

Circa 687–727 – Adomnán and his successors continued the chronicle on Iona.

Circa 727 – Ecgberht reformed the Iona chronicle by deleting thirteen kalends, together with the chronicle of the founding of Irish monasteries in the tradition of Sulpicius 425–31, and the chronicle of the Paschal dispute in the seventh century, replacing them with Patrician, papal, and Anglo-Saxon chronicles.

Circa 727–740 – Ecgberht's reformed chronicle was continued on Iona.

Circa 740 – The Iona chronicle was precipitately removed from Iona to Ireland, probably in irregular circumstances.

CHAPTER SIX

The Moville and Clonmacnoise chronicles

Bannerman's careful study of the Annals over AD 431–*c*.800 showed that *c*.740 their place of recording had shifted from Iona to Ireland, and the crucial question that arises is, to whence did they go? O'Rahilly was one of the first to consider this issue when he formulated his hypothesis of an 'Ulster Chronicle', writing, 'The "Ulster Chronicle", as I have ventured to call it, was compiled in East Ulster (probably in the monastery of Bangor) *ca*. 740.' O'Rahilly offered absolutely no evidence in support of this tentative Bangor hypothesis, which he had simply adapted from an earlier suggestion made by Mac Neill.[1] Nevertheless in 1968 Bannerman, pointing to the known relationship between Columba and Comgall, repeated the hypothesis, writing, 'the known contacts between Bangor and Scotland make it a likely depository of Scottish annal entries in Ireland.'[2] Then, four years later Smyth, without presenting any evidence, expressed certainty regarding O'Rahilly's hypothesis concerning Bangor, writing, 'it is the conclusion of this study that at *c*.740 a copy of the Iona annals reached Bangor, which were afterwards continued there to provide the nucleus that later grew into the compilation of *A.U.*' Smyth subsequently emphasized this 'conclusion' by referring to, 'the fact that the copy of the annals was transcribed *c*.740 at Bangor.'[3] However, Smyth did not consider that Bangor remained the principal recording site, for, following a substantial discussion of the post-740 purview of AU's Leinster entries, he wrote:[4]

> ... the increase of documentation *c*.780 which involved Leinster sites with a predominantly northern distribution was due to the commencement of an annalistic record most likely centred on Cluain Iraird.

Thus Smyth, having first confined his survey to Leinster, concluded that *c*.780 the recording site had shifted from Bangor, 'most likely' to Clonard, although he also considered Kildare a possibility. At about the same time Hughes, pointing to the agreement between the Bangor abbatial list in the seventh-century *Antiphonary of Bangor* and the joint AT/AU list, cautiously endorsed O'Rahilly's hypothesis, writing, 'On the whole I am inclined to believe in a

1 O'Rahilly, *Early Irish history*, 253 (cit.), 253 n. 1 (adaptation from Mac Neill, 'S. Secundinus', p. 130). 2 Bannerman, *Studies*, 25 (Iona chronicle move *c*.740), 14–15, (cit.). 3 Smyth, 'Earliest Irish annals', 34, 41, 43 (cits.). 4 Smyth, 'Earliest Irish annals', 29, 21–30 (discussion), 32 (exclusion of

168

Bangor Chronicle. We have that very rare thing, a complete seventh-century list of abbots, and we know that Bangor had a *scriptorium* in the seventh century.'[5] The only voice to dissent from the Bangor hypothesis was that of Mac Niocaill, who wrote:

> It can be fairly argued that the links of Iona with Bangor are sufficient to account for the Bangor material ... In short, I can find no convincing evidence to support the theory of a Bangor chronicle as an element of the Irish annals.

Instead of Bangor Mac Niocaill proposed both Armagh and Clonard as locations of simultaneous recording, citing Smyth in support of the latter but adducing no compelling evidence.[6]

Thus while there has been a small but hesitant consensus in favour of O'Rahilly's tentative suggestion of Bangor as the recording and compilation site from *c*.740, the only evidence presented for this has been the sustained sequence of abbatial obits for that monastery. However, obits of the abbots of important monasteries are a stereotype of the Annals, for in the same way that the headlines of newspapers virtually everywhere tend to register the elections of American presidents and British prime ministers, these Bangor abbatial obits merely reflect the power attached to that particular office. In these circumstances I submit that the issue has not yet been adequately examined, and that what is required is an objective survey of the Annalistic evidence which will reliably disclose the locality of recording post 740.

The Moville chronicle and the purview of the Annals over 740–66

I commence from the premise that whenever and wherever in Ireland the Iona chronicle was continued, its purview post 740 must reflect something of the provenance and perspective of the compiler. Regarding the character of the entries around this time Colmán Etchingham has shown by an extensive survey of the years 731–900 that they are dominated by ecclesiastical events, and moreover these ecclesiastical events themselves are dominated by the obits of the ecclesiastical leaders.[7] These are mainly the obits of monastic abbots, but for some monasteries obits of bishops and abbesses also occur, and this prominent monastic emphasis requires therefore that the Annals continued to

Clonmacnoise).   **5** Hughes, *Early Christian Ireland*, 121 (cit.), 122–3 (Bangor abbots).   **6** Mac Niocaill, *MIA*, 20 (cit.), 22 (Armagh and Clonard). Curiously on p. 19 he attributed to Smyth the view, 'that the evidence for Bangor is shaky', whereas in fact Smyth was the only author to express certainty regarding Bangor.   **7** Etchingham, *Viking raids*, figures 4–5, 7 on pp. 12, 15, 51 show that in the interval 791–900 the Annals typically register about fifty ecclesiastical obits and ten non-obit ecclesiastical events per decade, as against about twenty two secular obits and twenty five non-obit secular events per decade.

be maintained in a monastic context. In these circumstances I suggest that those entries which refer explicitly to named monasteries are best able to provide us with a reliable index to the provenance of their compilers. Regarding the coverage of the post 740 years, examination of the synchronized collation shows that AT, until its lacuna at 767, and AU provide by far the most substantial coverage of events. They have many entries in common which are normally arranged in identical sequence, and each has some unique entries. For simplicity of presentation and because AT's monastic coverage is slightly greater I will survey AT's entries citing specific monasteries over the years 740–66 inclusive. These twenty-seven years are sufficient to give a clear impression of both the character of the entries, and the spatial distribution of the favoured monasteries in the compilation of this part of the Annals. However, to ensure that my choice of AT is not skewing the result I will also include a summary of AU's coverage.

Ó Murchadha's valuable index of place and tribal names for AT makes it straightforward to establish which monasteries receive coverage over these years, while Mac Carthy's splendid index for AU likewise registers its coverage for these monasteries. The table in Figure 18 records counts of entries for all twelve monasteries which are cited in AT more than once over 740–66. The entries have been classified into three mutually exclusive groups, viz. 'Leader obits', registering obits of abbots, abbesses and bishops, 'Other obits', registering all

Monastery	Leader obits	Other obits	Non-obit entries	AT total	AU total
Clonmacnoise	4	2	3	9	9
Kildare	5	–	–	5	5
Clonard	3	1	1	5	4
Clonfert	4	–	1	5	4
Lismore	4	–	1	5	4
Bangor	2	–	2	4	4
Louth	3	–	1	4	2
Ferns	3	–	–	3	3
Fore	2	–	1	3	3
Moville	3	–	–	3	3
Armagh	1	1	–	2	2
Clones	2	–	–	2	2
Totals	36	4	10	50	45

Figure 18. Counts of entries in AT referring explicitly to the listed monasteries over 740–66, with entries classified into obits and non-obits, and the obits divided into leader and non-leader obits. The monasteries have been ranked by AT's totals, and AU's totals are listed for comparison.

other obits, and 'Non-obit entries', registering all other entries. Totals for these counts are given under 'AT total', and, for comparison, the entry count for citations of that monastery in AU are given alongside under 'AU total'.

I now consider three different aspects of this data, namely the type of entries, their spatial distribution and the pre-eminent monastery. Regarding entry type, with the exception of Clonmacnoise, leader obits clearly dominate the monastic entries with 72% (36/50) of entries falling into this category. Regarding spatial distribution, this extends from Bangor in the north to Lismore in the south, and from Ferns in the east to Clonfert in the west, so it covers a substantial part of Ireland. However, the fact that the first three monasteries, Clonmacnoise, Kildare and Clonard, fall within the central midlands and account for 38% (19/50) of the total entries for twelve monasteries shows that the spatial distribution is skewed towards this central area. What is more, when the nearby midland monasteries of Clonfert, Louth and Fore are included these six account for 62% (31/50) of total entries, all of which originate from within the central triangular area defined by Clonfert-Kildare-Louth. Regarding the pre-eminent monastery, this is clearly Clonmacnoise with either nearly or more than twice as many entries as all the other monasteries, and it dominates them both in terms of its total entry count and the diversity of its entry types. Moreover, the correlation in both the value and the rank of both AT and AU totals show that this conclusion does *not* depend upon the choice of AT as the survey basis, for the identical conclusion emerges from AU's counts. Furthermore these counts show that *none* of the monasteries that have been hitherto proposed as post 740 recording sites, viz. Bangor, Clonard, Kildare and Armagh, are plausible locations for the compiler who continued the Iona chronicle. Regarding Bangor, one of its non-obit entries is the allegorical whale entry, which, as discussed in chapter 5, is clearly retrospective and thus should be excluded, so Bangor should in fact be ranked at best seventh after Louth.

Next, in order to examine the textual relationship between the Clonmacnoise entries and those of other monasteries I list in Figure 19 all of its nine AT entries, followed by second ranked Kildare's five entries. Considering first the Clonmacnoise entries we see that they regularly supply either specific details or unusual events, viz.: temporal details 'in .xii. kl Aprilis'; locative details, 'do Conmaicnib', 'de Corcelig', 'thibrat Fingen', 'im-Moin Coisse Baái', 'do Síl Cairpri', 'do Luaignib'; unusual events, viz. 'ancorita ... mortus', 'Gorman ... adbath a n-ailithri', and two monastic battles.[10] On the other hand the four obits of the abbots and abbesses of Kildare are substantially stereotypic, and only the murder of bishop Eachtigirn by a priest in the oratory there registers an unusual event. Thus whether assessed simply in terms of entry counts, or in terms

10 Hughes, *Early Christian Ireland*, 105 considered the 'Gorman' entry 'a later comment', but as its omission will not alter the conclusion it has been included to simplify the discussion.

AD   AT Clonmacnoise entries for 740–766

740 Bass Cellaigh maic Secdi .i. o Buidemnaigh do Conmaicnib, ab Cluana maic Nois.
753 Quies [Lucrid] de Corcelig ab Cluana maic Nois.
755 Combustio Cluana maic Nois in .xii. kl Aprilis.[8]
756 Aelgal ancorita Cluana ... [et alii] mortui sunt.
758 Gorman comurba Mochta Lugbaidh .i. athair Torbaig comurba Patraig, isse
     robai bliadain for usci thibrat Fingen a Cluain maic Nois, 7 adbath a n-ailithri
     i Cluain.
760 Cath eter muintir Cluana 7 muintir Biror im-Moin coisse Blái.
762 Quies Cormaic ab Cluana maic Nois, 7 do Sil Cairpri do.
764 Q. Ronan ab Cluana maic Nois, do Luaignib do.
764 Cath Argamain iter familiam Cluana maic Nois 7 Durmuig, ubi cecidit
     Diarmuit mac Domnuill. [AU 763.6 identifies Durrow's losses of 200 and a
     Clonmacnoise victory]

AD   AT Kildare entries for 740–66

743 Mors Aifricci, banab Cille dara.
748 Dormitatio do Dimoc ancorite abbad Cluana hIraird 7 Cille dara.
752 Cathal mac Forandain, abb Chille dara ... [et alii] mortui sunt.
758 Martha filia Maic Dubain, dominatrix Cille dara, obit
762 Occisio Eachtigirn episcobi a sacerdote a nderthaigh Cilli dara.[9]

Figure 19. Chronological listing of all Clonmacnoise and Kildare entries from AT over
740–66 from Stokes, *AT*, 203–22.

of the information content of the entries, the Annalistic treatment of
Clonmacnoise events is distinctive, and underlines the pre-eminent status
accorded to this monastery over this interval.

However, when we consider the temporal distribution of the Clonmacnoise
entries over 740–66 a conspicuous feature is that, while there is only one entry
recorded in the thirteen-year interval 740–52, there are eight entries recorded
in the fourteen-year interval 753–66. Now this brief burst of entries focussed
upon Clonmacnoise would not in itself demonstrate that the entries were
compiled there, for they could conceivably be the work of an enthusiastic
Clonmacnoise supporter writing from another monastery. However, if this rate
of coverage were sustained for the working lives of several consecutive annalists
then it would effectively require that the entries must have been compiled
institutionally in Clonmacnoise. In Figure 20 therefore is shown a comprehensive survey of the composite coverage of Clonmacnoise provided by

---

8 This entry is duplicated under the same kalend.   9 This entry is duplicated together with a
retrospective addition at AD 760.

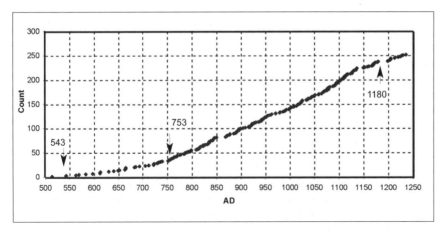

Figure 20. The cumulative count of all entries in AT/CS/AU/MB referring to Clonmacnoise versus AD. Note that entries common to more than one source are counted only once, and the arrows at 543 and 1180 identify respectively the foundation of Clonmacnoise and the arrival of the Normans in its vicinity.

AT/CS/AU/MB, by plotting the cumulated count of entries referring to Clonmacnoise against AD. As the rate of coverage increases so the plotted count must rise more steeply, and we see that from its foundation in 543 up to *c.*740 the coverage of Clonmacnoise is sporadic but steadily increasing.

However, this rate changes significantly at 753 when a much more intense coverage of Clonmacnoise is suddenly initiated, and this is effectively sustained until *c.*1227. There is no other Irish monastery which receives this level of sustained Annalistic coverage of its affairs extending from the mid-eighth century to Norman times. I submit that the only reasonable explanation of this coverage is that over *c.*753–*c.*1227 these Clonmacnoise entries were written by annalists working in Clonmacnoise. Figure 20 also discloses a number of relatively brief cessations in the Clonmacnoise entries appearing as lacunae in the plot of the cumulated entry count, and the last of these over 1180–97 is closely synchronized to the time at which the district in which the monastery lies was overrun by the Normans. It seems likely therefore that the advent of the Normans precipitated instability in the affairs of the monastery that ultimately ended the maintenance of the Clonmacnoise chronicle there, as shall be discussed below. Of the remaining lacunae I can only discuss here that already remarked over 741–52 which suggests that during this interval chronicling was conducted at some other location. In order to identify possible candidate monasteries in Figure 21 are tabulated the ranges covered by the entries over 740–66 referring to the monasteries listed in Figure 18 above.

Monastery	AT total	AD range	Monastery	AT total	AD range
Kildare	5	743–62	Ferns	3	742–63
Clonard	5	745–65	*Fore*	*3*	*740–50*
Clonfert	5	749–65	*Moville*	*3*	*743–49*
Lismore	5	746–60	Armagh	2	750–59
Bangor	4	744–60	*Clones*	*2*	*746–51*
Louth	4	758–59			

Figure 21. Tabulation of the counts and ranges of entries referring to the specified monasteries in AT over the years 740–66. Monasteries whose last reference falls before 753 are highlighted in italic.

As can be seen the only monasteries whose entries *all* fall in the interval 740–52 are Fore, Moville, and Clones, and of these Moville is the most singular in that in AU its entries exhibit a very large lacuna both prior and subsequent to this interval.[11] These Moville entries, all obits of its abbots, are as follows: Sillan †619, Colman †736, Affiath †743, Cuanan †747, Liber †748, Flannabra †825. Thus after a lacuna of 116 years we suddenly find obits for four Moville abbots in just thirteen years, three of whom fall in the 741–52 interval, and these are followed by a further 77 year lacuna. There are other indications that point to Moville in this context for we have shown already in chapter 4 that there are a number of reasons to associate the continuation of the Rufinus-Sulpicius chronicle with Columba's teacher, Finnian of Moville. In the eleventh century we know that Marianus Scottus of Mainz was a monk at Moville until 1056, following which he moved to Germany where he wrote a substantial world chronicle that is distinguished textually by the presence of marginal verses in Old Irish, to which subject I shall return below.[12] Thus there is independent evidence pointing to Moville as a monastery with a chronicling tradition, and this then suggests the following sequence. The Iona chronicle arrived in Ireland in *c.*740 and was then brought to Moville in execution of Diarmait mac Cerbaill's judgement 'to every book its transcript'. There the obit of their recently deceased abbot Colman was inserted, and over the next decade the chronicle was maintained in Moville and the obits of abbots Affiath, Cuanan and Liber were added. I shall refer to this compilation as the Iona-Moville chronicle and to its author(s) as the Moville compiler. Then in *c.*753 a copy of this Iona-Moville chronicle was made and brought to Clonmacnoise where it

11 The corresponding precedent and subsequent lacunae are: Fore – nine and twenty years; Clones – thirty and twenty seven years. 12 Mac Carthy, *Palatino-Vaticanus*, 4–9 (Marianus), 20–31 (Irish verses), 29 (Old Irish).

was maintained thereafter to provide the source for all our surviving Annals. From the slightly increased rate of coverage observed between 723–40 it appears likely that the Clonmacnoise annalists inserted a Clonmacnoise end chronicle retrospectively over this interval. Another indication that the year 753 was regarded as a significant year in the history of the Annals is the fact that when Ua Caiside interpolated a copy of the allegorical whale entry into TCD 1282, he relocated it from 744 to the year 753, and he also interpolated the AD year explicitly into the entry, cf. AU 752.13.

The most important conclusion which emerges from this examination of the purview of Annalistic entries over the middle of the eighth century is that after a brief sojourn in Moville the Moville-Iona chronicle was continued in Clonmacnoise from c.753 onwards. Thus Ware's *Tigernach* hypothesis in which he proposed that Tigernach Ua Braein had compiled the entire Clonmacnoise chronicle up to 1088, and O'Rahilly's *Clonmacnoise-911* hypothesis in which he proposed that the Clonmacnoise compilation postdated 911, are in error by approximately 335 and 160 years respectively. A particularly misleading consequence of both of these hypotheses has been that subsequent scholars have assumed that Clonmacnoise entries from the eighth to the early tenth centuries must have been inserted retrospectively, and thus that their historical value was questionable. For example Smyth having adopted the *AU priority* hypothesis in the first sentence of his paper simply asserted without any evidence that, '[a] great deal of the expanded entries in the Tigernach or Clonmacnoise group of annals are borrowed from hagiographical sources such as the *Lives* of Ciarán the founder, or of Cóemgen of Glenn dá Locha.' Smyth never seriously considered the possibility that these *Lives* had themselves drawn on a Clonmacnoise chronicle, and he argued simply from Annalistic silence regarding small monasteries in order to dismiss the possibility of 'a chronicle at Clonmacnoise before 800 A.D.'.[13] However, I submit that we must now regard most Clonmacnoise entries in the Clonmacnoise group of texts from c.753 onwards as having been composed in Clonmacnoise contemporaneously with the events which they record. Their status therefore as historical witness is exactly the same as all other contemporaneous Annalistic entries. However, before examining this matter in more detail I wish first to consider whether the Moville compiler made any further contributions to the chronicle.

The Moville chronicle and its verse, regnal successions,
and the Irish origin legend

A distinctive feature of the early annals of AT/CS/AR/AU/AI/AB is the intermittent appearance of verses, nearly always quatrains, written entirely in

---

13 Smyth, 'Earliest Irish annals', 1 (*AU priority*), 32 (cits.).

Irish in the metre known as *deibide*.[14] Since Latin is the dominant language of the early Annals and most of these verses refer to events already registered by an entry in Latin, it seems certain that the verses are subsequent additions to the text. Furthermore in character these verses stand in high contrast to the detached, anonymous Annalistic entries, for they usually emphasize emotive and dramatic aspects of the events, and they are quite frequently attributed in stereotyped Latin to known historical figures. For example, at 514 AT/CS/AU record a battle at Druim Dergaighe followed by a quatrain attributed to Cenn Faelad mac Aililla †679 of the Cenél nEógain. The version in CS reads:[15]

[Bellum] Droma Dergaige for Foilgi mBerraide ria Fiacaigh mac Nell, unde campus Mide a Lagenis sublatus est, ut Céndfaoladh cecinit:–	Battle of Druim Dergaighe gained over Foilge Berraidhe by Fiachaidh, son of Niall, on account of which the plain of Midhe was taken from the Lagenians, as Cendfaeladh sang:–
Diogal Dia seacht mbliadna Bassídigde a cride, Cath a nDromaibh Dergaige Ba de do cer Magh Midhe	The seven years' vengeance of God It was that tamed his heart; The battle in the Droma Dergaighe – By it the plain of Midhe was lost.

It seems obvious from these language and mood contrasts that this quatrain represents a quite distinct and later historiographic tradition, and so an important issue to resolve is when were these verses interpolated into the Annals. In an effort to gain insight into this matter I surveyed these verses up to AD 1000 in AT/CS/AR/AU/AI/AB, the results of which are tabulated in appendix 2. This survey shows that the distribution of these verses is non-uniform both temporally and textually. Regarding the verses in the Clonmacnoise group it is a close approximation to say that they effectively commence at the Flood and discontinue abruptly at 738. On account of AT's lacuna over the first four Biblical Ages most of the pre-Christian verses have survived only in CS/AR of the Clonmacnoise group, and these are paralleled by corresponding verses in AI/AB of the Cuana group. In the Christian era however AT preserves the most verses, though several additional quatrains are found in CS. Given that AT continues to 766 and that CS extends continuously from 804 to 1150, this cessation at 738 is significant and it has the consequence that nearly all the verses found in the Clonmacnoise group are confined to the range of the Iona chronicle. I further consider that the verse in AU over 491–743, most of which closely parallels the verses in AT/CS/AR and which was inscribed by both Ua

---

14 Knott, *Irish syllabic poetry*, 4, 18–19, and Smith, *Gilla Cóemáin*, 85–6 (*deibide* metre).
15 Hennessy, *CS*, 38–9 (cit.); AT's entry is semantically similar, but expressed nearly entirely in Irish, while its quatrain differs only in its orthography. In AU 516.3 Ua Caiside duplicated both Ua Luinín's entry and quatrain at AU 515.1.

Luinín and Ua Caiside marginally into TCD 1282, was copied by them from the now-missing continuation of Rawl. B. 502, and hence represents the Clonmacnoise tradition. I believe this because: a) On f. 10rb Ua Caiside annotated Rawl. B. 502 showing he used this MS; b) AU frequently provides better readings than AT/CS/AR for the verses. Consequently, I conclude that the AU-unique verses over 491–743 simply represent verses of the Clonmacnoise tradition lost in the transmission of AT/CS/AR. For example the quatrain at 662 now found only in AU 661.1 laments the 'deaths of this year … Mael Dún, Béc son of Fergus, Conaing, and Cuiméne the Tall', but *only* AT records obits for all these four individuals. After 743 verse continues in AU but it changes significantly in character with a much broader range of themes and infrequent attributions.

The themes found in these Annalistic verses over the pre-Christian era reflect Vulgate Age chronology and a small number of powerful world chronicle rulers. On the other hand in the Christian era up to 743 the verses refer mostly to battles and the deaths of Irish political leaders and prominent Christians, and they do not focus specifically on the affairs of the Uí Néill. Linguistically they are written in Old Irish, and thus have been composed approximately between the early eighth and the early tenth century.[16] However, these verses of the Christian era exhibit a distinctly secular and northern purview with only ten of sixty-two instances referring to specifically Christian events, of which only one celebrates a southern event, viz. the obit of Brendan of Birr †572. The secular events are nearly all battles or assassinations with a northern emphasis which veers towards the Cenél nEógain with no less than three separate verses attached to the already prolix and passionate Annalistic entry for the battle of Ath Senagh in 738. This battle was won by the Cenél nEógain king Áed Allán †743, to whom the third verse is attributed. Furthermore the verse at 743 attached to his own obit is described as Áed Allán's 'last stanza', suggesting a contemporaneous designation. Moreover, there is evident an interest in Áed Allán's Cenél nEógain ancestors with verses celebrating Áed's great, great grandfather Muirchertach mac Ercae, his sons Fergus and Domnall, Domnall's son Áed Uaridneach, and his grandson Fergal mac Máele Dúin. In particular the obit of Fergal, Áed Allán's father, is celebrated with six quatrains.[17] Finally notable is the number of attributions that have northern associations, e.g. Patrick, Columba, Ninnine Eces and Cú Bretan of Airgialla, Cenn Faelad and Áed Allán of the Cenél nEógain, Bec Boirche king of Ulaid, and Adomnán of the Cenél Conaill.[18] Simply on the features noted above it is not plausible that these verses

---

16 I am grateful to Colmán Etchingham, Bart Jaski, Tomás Ó Concheanainn and Peter Smith, who all offered views on this question, however they are not responsible for my conclusions.   17 See verses at AD 532 (Bádudh Muircertaig), 565 (C. Gabra Life), 610 (C. Odhba), 722 (C. Almuine); cf. Byrne, *Irish kings*, 283–4 (Áed Allán's ancestors).   18 I am grateful to Bart Jaski for bringing this detail to my attention.

up to *c.*743 were composed and inserted into the Iona chronicle while it was in Iona. On the other hand since these verses also exhibit no discernible Clonmacnoise purview neither can they be plausibly attributed to the Clonmacnoise annalists who continued from *c.*753. Rather the northern provenance and attributions to northern authors and termination at 743 all lead me to conclude that these verses represent a collection of predominantly northern mainland Irish *seanachas* that the Moville compiler interpolated into the Iona chronicle shortly after its arrival there in *c.*740. Moreover, the prominence afforded to Áed Allán and his affairs at the end of this sequence makes it likely that he exerted some influence over this process; he was after all probably the most powerful individual in the northern half of Ireland after his victory in 738. In these circumstances I conclude that in *c.*753 the Clonmacnoise annalists simply transcribed these verses from the Iona-Moville chronicle wherein they had only recently been interpolated.

The quatrain mentioned above from AU 661.1 shows that some verses were written in response to the then existing Annal entries, obits in this case. However, much of the secular verse celebrating heroic regnal deeds and deaths has been excerpted from poems then already existing, as evidenced by the attributions to poets such as Cenn Faelad who was dead long before *c.*740. Now the introduction of so many heroic verses, all of them necessarily in Irish except for a stereotyped introduction in Latin, e.g. 'ut dixit/cecinit', represented an important development in the Annalistic tradition towards accommodating the secular, vernacular learned tradition. For it expanded the role of Irish in the Annals from merely representing proper nouns to that of celebrating society's most influential individuals, whether secular or Christian. This immediately raises a question in respect of the pre-Patrician Irish regnal successions in the Annals, for these successions just like the verses are heroic in theme and written entirely in Irish apart from the stereotyped regnal incipits in Latin. In particular at AD 352 one of the verses is integrated with the regnal incipit of Eochaid Muigmedon, suggesting thereby that verse and incipit share a common origin.

Collation of the regnal successions in the pre-Patrician Annals shows unmistakeably that AT has transmitted by far the most substantial and earliest version of these successions.[19] It comprises two separate series as follows: a) The Emain Macha succession of thirty-two reigns extending from Cimbáed at *c.*313 BC to Fearghus Fogha at AD 253, is followed by Emain's extinction at 329; b) The Tara succession of eighteen reigns extending from Lugaid Réoderg at AD 49 to Laoghaire mac Néill at 429.[20] The arrangement of these successions

---

19 Bart Jaski, personal correspondence 12 Dec. 2002, was the first to state this conclusion when, referring to the Emain and Tara successions, he wrote, 'the list in AT is the oldest witness to a precursor of *Réim Rígraide.*'   20 Emain incipits at AT 24b, 25d, 26b, 27d, 28d, 30a, 32a, 32b, 32c, 32d, 33b, 33d, 34a, 34c, 34d, 35c, 40a (bis), 41b, 46a, 47c, 48c, 49a, 51a, 52c, 54b, 56c, 58b, 59d,

consists of a stereotyped regnal incipit in Latin citing the ruler's name and the number of his regnal years, followed in many cases with the ruler's obit in Irish, often describing the circumstances of his death. The regnal incipits of the Emain succession also include the name of the dynasty as 'in Emain' in Rawl B 502, but in Rawl. B. 488 the dynastic names have been translated to the Irish 'a n-Emain'. On the other hand in the Tara succession the dynastic name 'Temoria' or 'a Temraig' is nearly always omitted and must be inferred from earlier reigns of the succession.[21] Analysis of the kalends shows that with the few obvious scribal corruptions emended the correlation between the cited regnal years and the count of intervening kalends is excellent, so it is clear that both these successions have been very carefully interpolated.[22] These successions commence in AT with the well-known interjection synchronizing Cimbáed in Emain with the eighteenth year of the Egyptian Ptolemy as follows:[23]

In anno .xuiii. Ptolomei fuit initiatus regnare in Emain Cimbáed filius Fintain, qui regnauit .xxuiii. annis. Tunc Echu Buadach pater Úgaine in Temoria regnase ab aliis fertur liquet praescrípsimus ollim Úgaine imperasse. Omnia monimenta Scottorum usque Cimbáed incerta erant.

In year eighteen of Ptolemy Cimbáed son of Fintan, who reigned twenty-eight years, began reigning in Emain. It is held by others that at this time Eoch Buadach father of Úgaine reigned in Tara, however we have written above that Úgaine reigned earlier. All the records of the Scots until Cimbáed were [chronologically] uncertain.

The second sentence here is important for it shows that this compiler was specifically considering chronological conflict and he differed from 'others' in believing that Úgaine's reign at Tara preceded that of Cimbáed. Thus my insertion of the word 'chronologically' qualifying 'uncertain' in the translation. The compiler's final sentence then dismissed the chronology of all Scots' records before Cimbáed as uncertain, and hence it explains his omission of all preceding dynastic successions. This final sentence is also important since with 'omnia monimenta Scottorum' this compiler acknowledges his knowledge of a substantial corpus dealing with the pre-history of the Scots prior to Cimbáed. His Emain succession follows systematically from Cimbáed, but his Tara

---

61a, 61b, 62a, 74a. Tara incipits at AT 41d, 44d, 46b, 48a, 49a, 50d, 51c, 53a, 56a, 64b, 67c, 73a, 73b, 76b, and the last four incipits at CS 362, 378, 406 and 429 because of AT's lacuna over 359–487. **21** Examples: AT 26b, 27d, 49a (in Emain); AT 41d, 51c (in Temoria); AT 51a, 62a (a n-Emain); AT 67c (a Temraig). **22** Emain: AT 32b cites 'lxv' for Fiac m. Fiadchon but he is assigned 14 kalends, and with the 'l' emended the number of kalends over 313 BC–AD 329 differs from the sum of regnal years by just one year. Tara: AT 67c cites 'xxuii' for Fiach Roibtine but he is assigned 36 kalends, and CS 362 cites 'u' for Cremthann m. Fidaigh but he is assigned 16 kalends; with 'x' supplied to both the number of kalends over AD 49–429 differs from the sum of the regnal years by one year. **23** AT 24b (cit.); the regnal incipit for Úgaine is preserved in AB §86; cf. Mac

succession does not commence until over three centuries later and both this Tara lacuna and his choice of initial Tara ruler are indicative of his provenance, for he began his Tara succession as:[24]

Lugaid Réoderg mac na trí Find n-Emna regnauiti n Temoria annis xxui. Trícha ríg do Leith Chuind óthá Lugaid co Diármait mac Cerbaill.	Lugaid Réoderg, son of the three Finds of Emain, reigned in Tara twenty-six years. Thirty kings from Conn's half from Lugaid to Diarmait mac Cerbaill.

Thus this compiler explicitly linked the first king in his Tara succession to both Emain and to Diarmait mac Cerbaill, the king who gave judgement for Finnian against Columba in the matter of the copy. Evidently this compiler also had access to a substantial succession of Leinster kings over *c.*313 BC–AD 166 for he wrote at *c.*74 BC:[25]

Trícha ríg robói de Laignib for Herind óthá Labraid Loingsech co Cathaer Mór.	Of Leinster there were thirty kings over Ireland, from Labraid the Exile to Cathaer the Great.

Nevertheless he chose instead to present his regnal successions with the emphasis firmly placed upon Emain, the oldest and most powerful kingdom of east Ulster. Thus this provenance would be entirely appropriate to a compiler in Moville, about forty-five miles north-east from Emain, who was intruding heroic verse celebrating the deeds of northern Irish kings into the Iona chronicle. I conclude therefore that it was the Moville compiler who interpolated these Emain and Tara successions and also the verses into the Iona chronicle sometime in the period *c.*743–53. This material in AT/CS/AR is important because it gives us a good view as to how the Emain and Tara regnal lists stood in the middle of the eighth century, and shows us that by then substantial regnal successions had been compiled for the pre-historical period for the principal kingdoms of Emain, Tara and Leinster. The compiler's opening interjections regarding Cimbáed also show us that there was then no consensus regarding the detailed chronology of these regnal lists, and indeed the Emain and Tara successions transmitted in the Cuana group show significant modifications relative to the arrangement of the Clonmacnoise group.[26]

The preceding discussion has argued that the pre-Patrician regnal succession was interpolated into the Iona chronicle by the Moville compiler, and, since it is scarcely plausible that he terminated his Tara succession at Laoghaire mac

Carthy, *Palatino-Vaticanus*, 251-54, 280 (Cimbáed). **24** AT 41d (Irish citation, Stokes' translation emended by myself). **25** AT 32c (cit.). **26** Byrne, *Irish kings*, 254, 276–7 (seventh-century Tara successions); Ó Riain, *Corpus*, 276–7 (Emain successions).

Néill in 429, it is important to also carefully consider the post-Patrician succession. In fact comprehensive collation of the Clonmacnoise and Cuana groups for the twenty-eight reigns from Laoghaire mac Néill †463 to Áed Allán †743 shows that they too have been defined in most instances by a regnal incipit followed by the ruler's obit. These regnal incipits are not stereotyped but vary textually, and the following is a comprehensive survey of these twenty-eight reigns ranked by count and identified by citing the appropriate year in the synchronized collation from whence they may all be located. The letter 'X' represents the regnal name and 'N' the regnal years:

9 × 'X regnare incipit' – cf. AD 510, 543, 610, 665, 672, 675, 695, 705, 710.
5 × 'X regnauit/regnat' – cf. AD 572, 613, 630, 728, 734.
5 × Incipit is omitted – cf. AD 569, 644, 657, 723, 724.
4 × 'Initium regni X' – cf. AD 464, 485, 584, 596.
2 × 'X regnauit annis N' – cf. AD 533, 603.
2 × ' ... cui successit/successerunt X' – cf. AD 563, 565.
1 × 'X regnum Hiberniae tenuit' – cf. AD 429.

These incipits are all in Latin with the exception only of five AT entries where they have been translated to Irish as 'X gabail rigi n-Erenn', cf. AD 510, 543, 584, 644, 728. On the other hand in AU they have frequently been omitted but then subsequently restored by Ua Caiside (H²), most probably from the now-missing section of Rawl. B. 502 since textually his restorations always agree with the Clonmacnoise group, cf. AD 464, 485, 510, 533, 610, 630, 710, 734. Like the pre-Patrician Tara succession in most cases the dynastic name has not been given, and this together with the repeated textual variations and lacunae in the regnal incipits suggest that this post-Patrician succession up to Áed Allán is indeed also the work of the Moville compiler. This conclusion is supported by the presence of heroic quatrains accompanying the obits of nine rulers, cf. AD 463, 484, 532, 584, 602, 671, 695, 722, 743. A singular feature however is his occasional use of the word 'Hibernia' as a dynastic name, which is almost certainly his work since it appears consistently in multiple members of both the Clonmacnoise and Cuana groups. The three instances are:

CS/AI/AB s.a. 429: Loegare tenuit **regnum Hiberniae**. [AI §387]
AT/CS/AR/AU s.a. 643: Mors Domnaill m. Aedha **regis Hiberniae** in fine Ianuari. [AU 641.1]
AT/CS/AR/AU/AB s.a. 703: Bellum Corainn in quo cecidit Longseach m. Aongusa **rex Hiberniae**. [AR §161]

The Moville compiler's anticipation here of a singular omnipotent ruler of Ireland is consistent with late seventh-century instances in Muirchú's *Vita*

Patricii and Adomnán's *Vita Columbae*.[27] Regarding the question of how the Moville compiler constructed this post-Patrician succession it appears that he first selected the obits of twenty-eight rulers that he considered pre-eminent in their time. To eight of these he interpolated a dynastic title of either 'rex Temoria' (cf. AD 584, 610, 671, 695, 710, 734) or 'rex Hiberniae' (cf. AD 643, 722), and in nine instances he interpolated heroic quatrains in their obits as mentioned already. For twenty-three of the reigns he then interpolated a regnal incipit for the following reign in the subsequent year. In some instances it is apparent from these incipits that the Moville compiler was uncertain as to who should be considered the pre-eminent ruler, for in five instances he named two rulers in these regnal incipits (cf. AD 563, 569, 596, 644, 657). In one of these he interjected that other historiographers considered that no less than four individuals had ruled together:

> AT/CS/AR/AU/AB *s.a.* 644: Hic dubitatur quis regnauit post Domhnall. Dicunt alii historiagraphi regnasse .iiii. reges, .i. Cellach 7 Conall 7 duo filii Aedho Slane, .i. Diarmait 7 Blathmac, per commixta regna. [AU 642.7]

This interjection is of considerable interest as it implies the Moville compiler considered himself a historiographer and also that he was familiar with the work of others of that profession. Moreover, just as in his interjection to the incipit for Cimbáed cited above, the Moville compiler here reported the views of others and expressed his own uncertainty. Regarding this uncertainty it should also be noted that the late seventh-century regnal succession known as *Baile Chuind* also differs from both the regnal succession of the Moville compiler and that of 'alii historiagraphi' at this point.[28] From this it is clear that the mid eighth-century historiographers were in disagreement regarding the succession of pre-eminent Irish kings for the seventh century. Needless to remark, when they were uncertain about the succession one hundred years before their time, it would be naïve to regard their compilations for the fifth and sixth centuries as reliable. Nevertheless the series compiled by the Moville compiler was destined to become by far the most influential succession of Irish historiography since it was used as the basis for the Irish regnal-canon in the early eleventh century as will be discussed in chapter 10. Regarding the historicity of his succession I submit that its only reliable element was the obits that he inherited from the Iona chronicle since these were recorded contemporaneously. While it is indeed likely that such obits referred to influential individuals, it would clearly be naïve to infer either that these individuals were necessarily pre-eminent rulers, or that

27 Byrne, *Irish kings*, 254–5 (Muirchú and Adomnán references to a 'king of Ireland').
28 Murphy, 'Two dates', 146–7 (*Baile Chuind* edition), 149–51 (date); Bhreathnach & Murray, 'Baile Chuinn', 73–94 (*Baile Chuind* edition).

they remained even influential for the entire interval from their incipit to their obit. More realistic is to recognize that political pre-eminence circulates amongst a number of powerful individuals. Indeed the Moville compiler's inclusion of six reigns with multiple rulers and his omission of five incipits represent a tacit acknowledgement by him of the unstable passage of power from generation to generation.

Finally I turn to consider those accounts largely in Irish of the successive invasions of Ireland that are found in both the Clonmacnoise and Cuana groups, and which purport to explain the origin of the peoples living in Ireland. In these the successive invasions by Cesar/Berba, Partholón, Nemed, the Fir Bolg, the Tuatha Dé Danann, and the Meic Miled are preserved in CS/AR/AI/AB, with vestiges in AT. All of these MSS exhibit substantial lacunae but collation shows that all of these invasions except that of Nemed are attested by at least one Clonmacnoise and one Cuana group source.[29] As well as these entries explicitly identifying invasions there is a larger corpus of entries common to the Clonmacnoise and Cuana groups which recount events associated with these invasions, especially the Milesian, such as the route taken from Scythia, invader's deaths, subdivisions of Ireland, and the eruption of lakes and rivers. The existence of this substantial corpus of what are normally called *Irish origin legend* entries that are common to both the Clonmacnoise and Cuana groups requires that they were incorporated into the Clonmacnoise chronicle before *c.*1022 as will be discussed below and in chapter 7.[30] Now this account of Ireland's prehistory is well known from MSS from the twelfth to the seventeenth centuries where it is entitled 'Lebor Gabála' (LG) and is found in four major recensions. However, I cannot here embark upon the complex matter of the historical development of this Irish origin legend which itself represents an enormous field of study and is the subject of intensive, ongoing research.[31] Consequently, it must suffice to say here that having considered the question carefully I have come to the conclusion that these Annalistic origin legend entries were interpolated into the Iona chronicle over *c.*743–53 by the Moville compiler along with the Annalistic verse and regnal successions. In support of this I submit a brief summary of the principal grounds for this conclusion:

a) Modern scholars have agreed that the Irish origin legend was well established by the late seventh century, and in consequence it provided the

---

29 Invasions: CS 2d (Cesar/Berba); AR 1a, AB §14 (Cesar); CS 4c, AR 1d, AB §22 (Partholón); CS 8b (Nemed); CS 8c, AR 2d, AI §24, AB §32 (Fir Bolg); CS 8c, AR 3a, AI §31, AB §35 (Tuatha De Danann); CS 10a, AR 3b, AI §35, AB §36 (Meic Miled); AT 17b (Vestige, 'Ab ingressu Scottorum') cf. AI §179, AB §82. 30 Carey, *Origin-legend, passim*; Jaski, 'Irish origin legend', *passim*. 31 Macalister, *LG i–v*, (LG edition); Scowcroft '*LG* I', (guide to Macalister's edition); idem, '*LG* II', (evolution of LG); Carey, *Lebor Gabála* (introduction to LG); Jaski, 'Aeneas & Fénius', 415–60

historiographical context in which the Moville compiler worked when incorporating Irish heroic verse and dynastic successions into the pre-historical section of the Iona-Moville chronicle. His own 'Omnia monimenta Scottorum' acknowledged this and the origin legend furnished the appropriate background for his dynastic successions. Had he omitted it his successions would have commenced in a vacuum.[32]

b) Historiographically the Milesian invasion is by far the most important of these invasions in that it supplies the genealogical basis for all of Ireland's medieval regnal dynasties, and Bart Jaski has shown that the oldest version of the Milesian invasion was synchronized by reference to the epoch of the Biblical Exodus.[33] All of AT/CS/AR/AI/AB implicitly locate the Milesian invasion very shortly after the Exodus, and CS/AR/AI explicitly locate it just over thirty years after the drowning of the Pharaoh at the very commencement of the Exodus. Thus all the annals of the Clonmacnoise and Cuana groups reflect this earliest Milesian synchronism. Otherwise the earliest known instance of this Exodus chronology is the now lost eighth-century work *Cín Dromma Snechtai* which located the Milesian invasion just two years after the Exodus. Subsequently Nennius in his early ninth-century *Historia Britonnum* also referenced the Exodus epoch, but introduced a delay of 1002 years.[34]

c) The very first invasion of the origin legend is that by Cesar/Berba who came to Ireland with 150 maidens and three men, and John Carey has shown that this account, particularly that of CS, most closely parallels that of *Cín Dromma Snechtai*. He has concluded that the underlying basis for it was a pre-Christian drowning legend concerning Berba. Thus both this Cesar/ Berba invasion and the Exodus synchronism of the Milesian invasion represent versions of the Irish origin legend dating from the eighth century or earlier.[35]

d) The *Historia Brittonum* account of the Irish origin legend is followed by a relative chronology of the Incarnation, Patrick's *uenit*, Brigit's obit and Columba's *natus*. This requires that around the beginning of the eighth century Nennius was using a chronicle which combined the Irish origin legend with the Incarnation, Patrick, Brigit and Columba. This is precisely the compilation we now find in the Clonmacnoise and Cuana groups.[36]

(LG research bibliography to 2005, interspersed). **32** Early evidence for the origin legend: Carey, *Lebor Gabála*, 3 n.6; Jaski, 'Irish origin legend', 3–4; Scowcroft, '*LG* II', 9–11, 19; Macalister, *LG* i, pp. xxvi–xxxiv. **33** Exodus synchronism: Jaski, 'Irish origin legend', 35–6; idem, 'Invention of tradition', 37–8. **34** CS 12a, AR 4c, AI §35 (Milesian invasion *c.*30 y. after Exodus); AB §36 (Invasion 6 kalends before Moses' obit); AT 17c (Scotti arrive in Egypt *c.*1524 BC = AM 2428, cf. Exodus at AM 2453); Mommsen, 'Historia Brittonum', 156–8 (Exodus epoch). **35** Carey, 'Cesair legend', 38–40 (*Cín Dromma Snechtai* & Annals), 48 (pre-Christian element). **36** Mommsen, *Historia Brittonum*, §13–16, 154–9 (Origin legend & relative chronology).

Principally then on these grounds I conclude that in *c.*743–53 the Moville compiler interpolated into the Iona chronicle an early version of the Irish origin legend, together with heroic verse and Emain and Tara regnal successions. In particular it should be noted that in accordance with his rejection of the chronology of 'omnia monimenta Scottorum' before Cimbáed this compiler's invasion entries supply no regnal chronology for any of the rulers of any of the invasions. Of the four surviving Annalistic versions of the origin legend that of AI preserves the oldest orthography, and also what appear to be some older structural details than the Clonmacnoise group. For example, AI asserts that Mil had four sons but it names five sons, while AR both asserts and names seven, whereas CS/AR/AI all only identify birthplaces for four sons. On the other hand only the Clonmacnoise group include Nél m. Fenios and details of Partholón's residence in Ireland.[37] It seems likely therefore that some later development of the origin legend has taken place in the Clonmacnoise group versions. However, exploration of this matter belongs properly to research into the evolution of the origin legend, not that of the Annals.

In summary then I conclude that *c.*743–53 the Moville compiler interpolated a substantial amount of Irish material into the Iona chronicle shortly after it arrived in Moville. This material furnished a Classical origin for the people of Ireland congruent with the Biblical account of the origin of all races. It also supplied a pre-history for the dominant dynastic successions of the northern and eastern parts of Ireland, Emain and Tara, and a celebration in verse of principally northern kings and saints over the years 353–743. It thus marked the introduction of a substantial corpus of the works of secular Irish scholarship into the Annals. Ó Riain has recently documented an analogous process of interpolation of substantial Bangor and Moville material into the martyrology received in Bangor from Iona 'probably before 752'.[38]

The Clonmacnoise chronicle and the importance of AT and AU as its witnesses

The survey of AT and AU over 740–66 given in Figure 18, p. 170, shows that AT transmits about ten percent more entries relating to the named monasteries than does AU. On the other hand the list of AT's Clonmacnoise entries given in Figure 19, p. 172, shows that in respect of the singular entry at 764 recording a battle between the monasteries of Clonmacnoise and Durrow, AU has transmitted significantly more information regarding the outcome of that battle which itself indeed suggests the entry was compiled in Clonmacnoise. The

---

37 AI §35 (p.6), CS 12b, AR 4d (Mil's sons); CS 4b, AR 3a (Nél m. Fenios); CS 4c–8b, AR 2a–c (Partholón's residence).　38 Ó Riain, *Feastdays*, 65–9 (Bangor & Moville material), 71, (cit.).

presence of entries, or parts of entries, unique to one or the other of these sources naturally prompts the question as to whether these unique elements are to be regarded as subsequent additions to the text in which they do appear, or as subtractions from the text in which they do not appear? In general, except for assuming as retrospective all Clonmacnoise entries in Clonmacnoise group annals prior to *c*.911, scholars have tended to consider the differences as subtractions, sometimes making perceptive observations in support of this. For example Hughes pointed out that to obtain an Annalistic succession of Bangor abbots that corresponds with that given by the *Antiphonary of Bangor* it is necessary to combine AT with AU.[39] However, no comprehensive evaluation of this situation has been published and in these circumstances I am grateful to Colmán Etchingham for both providing me with a copy of his detailed thematic analysis of the AT and AU unique entries over the years 701–66, and for his permission to present the following summary of his survey and conclusions. In Figure 22 are given Etchingham's counts of those entries unique to AT and to AU classified thematically by region and content.[40]

Thematic classification	AT	AU
Northern ecclesiastics and churches	4	14
Northern politics and magnates	3	10
Southern Uí Néill ecclesiastics and churches	4	10
Southern Uí Néill politics and magnates	4	11
Scottish/Iona/English ecclesiastics	6	2
Scottish politics and magnates	9	17
Connacht ecclesiastics and churches	5	3
Connacht politics and magnates	4	7
Leinster/Ossory ecclesiastics and churches	1	3
Leinster/Ossory politics and magnates	11	5
Munster ecclesiastics and churches	2	2
Munster politics and magnates	8	2
Natural and supernatural phenomena	1	11
Persons/places of unspecified/obscure status	17	65
Imperial	–	1
Totals	**79**	**163**

Figure 22. Counts of entries unique to AT and AU over 701–66 classified by Colmán Etchingham thematically according to their region and content.

39 Hughes, *Early Christian Ireland*, 122 (Bangor abbots), 102–3 (where she points out that AI sometimes confirms particular entries otherwise unique to AT or AU).   40 Colmán Etchingham, pers. correspondance 28 Nov. 2000. In his survey Etchingham indicated uncertainty in respect of his identifications of six AT-unique entries and eight AU-unique entries. Since these few

The first point to be made about these fifteen classifications is that they apply with equal relevance to the material found in common to AT and AU, so that there is nothing about the themes found in unique material to distinguish them from those of the common material. However, there are clearly differences in the emphases of unique material found in each text. In particular AT provides significantly more unique entries than AU which refer to Scottish/Iona/English ecclesiastics, and to Leinster/Ossory and Munster politics and magnates. For its part AU provides substantially more unique entries referring to Northern and Southern Uí Néill ecclesiastics and politics, Scottish politics, natural and supernatural phenomena, and to persons/places now found to be obscure. Together these result in AU providing in total more than twice as many unique entries than AT. However, it is most important to note that while the identifiable regional emphasis of the unique material corresponds in each case with the traditionally regarded provenance, viz. AT with Clonmacnoise and hence Leinster, Ossory, Connacht and Munster, and AU with Ulster and the Uí Néill, but in both cases each text provides unique entries dealing with regions remote from its regional emphasis. Namely AT provides unique entries with a Northern and Scottish provenance, and AU provides unique entries with a Leinster, Connacht and Munster provenance. It was these observations which led Etchingham to conclude that AT and AU, 'are in some sense incomplete but complementary witnesses to a larger body of contemporary annalistic records for the period up to 766.' Thus it emerges that if we wish to obtain a more accurate picture of the original content of the Iona chronicle up to c.740, and the Clonmacnoise chronicle from c.753 onwards, then we must take the combination of AT with AU. Although Etchingham's survey extended only up to the point of AT's lacuna at 767, collation of the Clonmacnoise-group with AU repeatedly shows that they all preserve common entries in identical sequence up to 1178, and this therefore strongly suggests that the other members of this group are, likewise, 'complementary witnesses to a larger body of contemporary annals'. Thus the texts of AT/CS/AR/AU/AI/FM/MB should all be used together to derive a more accurate picture than just AT/CS/AR of the original content of the Clonmacnoise chronicle. In particular, David Dumville has highlighted the value of the CS-unique entries as witness to the Clonmacnoise chronicle over the range 974–1150, and he has usefully listed all CS-unique entries.[41] Indeed these unique elements of CS will prove crucial when we come to consider the question of the relationship between the historical 'Tigernach' and the annals in Rawl. B. 502 and 488. Before that, however, I turn to review the evolution of the Clonmacnoise chronicle.

uncertainties have no effect on the overall conclusions, to simplify the presentation I have reckoned all these uncertain identifications as certaintities. 41 Grabowski & Dumville, *Chronicles*, 155–83 (discussion), 184–9 (CS-unique entries).

The evolution of the Clonmacnoise chronicle c.753–c.1227

A survey of the Clonmacnoise group post 753 shows that in the ensuing centuries the bare kalend of Ecgberht's reform of the Iona chronicle remained the chronological apparatus up to c.1022. The provenance of the entries while effectively covering most of Ireland has a discernible emphasis on the affairs of the central midlands. The ecclesiastical entries deal predominantly with the affairs of the well-established monasteries with an emphasis naturally on Clonmacnoise, cf. figures 18–20 above, pp. 170, 172, 173. The secular entries similarly monitor the affairs of the principal provincial dynasties but with an emphasis on the Uí Néill kings. In particular the Clonmacnoise annalists continued the Tara succession, maintaining for the most part the Moville compiler's incipit-obit definition of the reigns. However, from Domhnall mac Murchadha †763 on they made the dynastic title the norm, introducing the forms 'ri h-Erenn uile' in 862 and 'ardri Erenn' in 980. But following the decline in Uí Néill power with the death of Máel Sechnaill mac Domnaill in 1022 the Clonmacnoise annalists were less interested in representing the shifts in hegemony amongst the Uí Briain and Uí Lochlainn as a regnal succession. In summary, the result of the combined activity of the Moville compiler and Clonmacnoise annalists was to invest the Clonmacnoise chronicle with a sustained and well defined Tara succession extending from Lugaid Réoderg †75 to Máel Sechnaill †1022.

A third category of entries requiring some discussion at this point are the phenomenological entries. These are terrestrial and astronomical entries recording such events as meteorological and agricultural extremes, earthquakes, plagues, volcanic clouds, eclipses, comets, aurorae and assorted sky observations. These commenced in the time of Finnian and Columba with their records of famine, plague and the resultant mass mortality over 538–53, cf. Figure 16, p. 160, and Figure 17, p. 161, while the Irish astronomical observations commence with a record of the solar eclipse of 23 July 594, and these continue until 1133. Circa 687 Adomnán transcribed some Byzantine earthquake, comet and eclipse records from Marcellinus, but these are readily distinguished from the Irish observations.[42] Now while textual and observational analysis of the astronomical entries has shown that these were indeed unique and accurate Irish observations of the phenomena of eclipses, comets and aurorae, a most perplexing fact is that up to and including the solar eclipse of 764 many of these entries are displaced in the Annals. That is the event is accurately recorded but the entry is located under the incorrect year. Nearly all of these displacements are by one year but

---

42 Mc Carthy & Breen, 'Evaluation', 121–26 (astronomical entries); idem, 'Astronomical observations', 10–19 (astronomical entries). Mc Carthy, 'Synchronization', s.a. 442, 466, 496, 498,

the eclipse of 594 is antedated by five years, and no plausible explanation has ever been given for these discrepancies.[43] Since it is scarcely credible either that so many records were entered contemporaneously under the incorrect year, or that they were subsequently deliberately dislocated, then some other explanation is required. However, examination of all phenomenological entries over 538–773 shows that in virtually every case these entries are either the very first or the final entry under the year in question. While this may not be considered significant in the fifth century where the entry count per year rarely exceeds three, by the seventh century we typically have about nine entries per year so that the initial and final positions of these entries is indeed singular. Furthermore it seems quite improbable that the abbots annually compiling these entries would systematically place such entries in either just the first or final position, and indeed from 777 onwards these entries are distributed randomly amongst the other entry types. On the other hand it is the case that when entries that have been written marginally beside the kalend are incorporated into the main text in a subsequent transcription they tend to be written either in the first or final position. Moreover, there is an inherent ambiguity of one year regarding such marginal entries since it is often unclear as to whether the interpolated entry was intended as an addition to those entries preceding, or those succeeding the kalend. These considerations then suggest that the phenomenological entries up to 773 were first written marginally into the Clonmacnoise chronicle, and then subsequently transcribed into the main text resulting in many of them being displaced by one year. This in turn implies that the transcript of the Moville-Iona chronicle made by the Clonmacnoise annalists did *not* incorporate phenomenological entries but rather there was at that time a separate chronicle containing these entries. However, in *c.*777 it was evidently decided in Clonmacnoise to combine the two chronicles and so the phenomenological entries over 594–773 were all transcribed into the margin of the Clonmacnoise chronicle, while all subsequent phenomenological records were entered directly. As a consequence when all of these marginal entries were eventually transcribed into the main text many were either ante or postdated by one year. This mechanism then explains satisfactorily how so many accurate astronomical observations came to be displaced in the Clonmacnoise chronicle, with the exception only of the five-year antedating of the solar eclipse of 594. However, when it is recalled that Ecgberht had removed six kalends over 612–64, then it seems very likely that it was this substantial asynchronism that caused the singularly large displacement of the eclipse entry for 594.

512, 518 (Marcellinus' entries).   43 Mc Carthy, 'Synchronization', *s.a.* AD 676, 688, 691, 744, 745 (one year postdating); AD 719, 726, 763, 764 (one year antedating); AD 664, 734, 735, 753, 773 (accurate dating).

The most significant development in the life of the Clonmacnoise chronicle was c.1022 when Cuán Ua Lothcháin †1024 used it as the basis of his compilation of Liber Cuanach as discussed in chapter 7.[44] This was done when Muiredhach mac Mugróin was *comharba* over 1015–25, and a number of details suggest that Cuán had the support of the *comharba* and community at Clonmacnoise. The first of these is the appearance intermittently in AT over 1019–66 of Cuán's distinctive chronological apparatus of kalend+ferial+epact, written in close agreement with the arrangement employed in Liber Cuanach. For example compare AT 1022 'Kł.ii.feria.luna.xx.iiii.' and AU 1022 'Kł.Ian.ii.f.l.xxº.iiii.'. Furthermore, sometimes the kalend was explicitly identified with January and the AD was included written in Roman numerals, which data had both been introduced by Cuán, cf. AT 1041, 'Kł.Enair.u.feria.M.xli.' and AU 1041 'Kł.Ian.u.f.l.xx.iiii.Anno Domini.Mº.xlº.iº'. The fact that Cuán's chronological apparatus was incorporated into the Clonmacnoise chronicle, and so promptly after its introduction, surely requires that Cuán was working closely with the Clonmacnoise annalists. The second detail suggesting a constructive working relationship between them is the positive coverage accorded in the Clonmacnoise group to the affairs of Máel Sechnaill mac Domnaill †1022, the Uí Néill high king to whom Cuán was chief poet, particularly when it is observed how this contrasts with the coverage given to his contemporary Brian Bóruma †1014.[45] It appears that in the conflict between Máel Sechnaill and Brian, the Clonmacnoise community sided with the former, and taken together these details suggest that Cuán's attempt to restore the chronological integrity of the Iona section of the Clonmacnoise chronicle, and to impose his own kalend+ferial+epact+AD chronological apparatus across the whole chronicle was supported by the Clonmacnoise community.

Next I consider the question of when the Clonmacnoise chronicle concluded. Figure 20, p. 173, shows that the relatively intense rate of coverage of Clonmacnoise affairs initiated in c.753 was effectively maintained up to the year c.1227. Historically it is apparent that c.1180 the political milieu of the monastery was changing rapidly from Irish to Norman domination. For military incursions into the Clonmacnoise area by Myles de Cogan in 1177 and Hugo de Lacey in 1178 were followed in 1180 by the marriage alliance of Hugo with the daughter of Ruaidrí Ua Conchobair †1198, king of Connacht. After c.1227 Clonmacnoise entries become so intermittent that it is not plausible to consider that the entries were written there. However, before this year some Clonmacnoise entries show such significant details as precise dates and locations, and, as Kehnel pointed out, other entries describing raids on Clonmacnoise 'are so

44 Mc Carthy, 'AU apparatus 82–1019', 279–81 (Cuán and Liber Cuanach).   45 Mc Carthy, 'Synchronization', *s.a.* 1013–22 (Máel Sechnaill vs Brian purview – see 'Remarks').

detailed and vivid that we must take them as eyewitness accounts. Clearly the nature of the surviving annalistic accounts strongly suggests that contemporary history in Clonmacnois was still recorded even after the Anglo-Norman invasion, perhaps down to the year 1227.'[46] Now it is of this year that Mícheál Ó Cléirigh, in both his short and long preface to FM, asserted, 'neither the book of Cluain, nor the book of the Island, were [carried] beyond the year of the age of our Lord, 1227.'[47] Thus both the distribution of the surviving Clonmacnoise entries and Ó Cléirigh's observation agree that the Clonmacnoise chronicle concluded at about 1227. Consequently, I take *c.*1227 as the final year of the Clonmacnoise chronicle, and as we shall see in chapter 9 this makes the Clonmacnoise chronicle chronologically complementary to the Connacht chronicle. Regarding the conspicuous lacuna over 1180–97 in Figure 20, p. 173, this is a consequence of the truncation of Rawl. B. 488 at 1178, and that Mageoghagan also interjected that his source, the 'old Irish book', was lacunose at this point.[48] However, examination of FM over the interval 1180–97 discloses four unique Clonmacnoise entries consistent in style with those both preceding and succeeding, so that the lacuna in Figure 20 does not therefore imply a cessation of chronicling at Clonmacnoise over these years but is rather the result of lacunae in the sources of AT/CS/AU/MB.

Finally I briefly consider the relationship between the MSS Rawl. B. 502 and 488. Since the former was written in Clonmacnoise about the end of eleventh century it must represent contemporaneous work by the annalists there not long after the death of Tigernach Ua Braein. It is most unfortunate for us therefore that it truncates at such an early date as AD 140, well before the Irish historical period. On the other hand, while Rawl. B. 488 lacks the obits of nearly all the Clonmacnoise *comharbai*, as is dicussed below, it contains a very substantial account of the affairs of the later Uí Chonchobhair kings of Connacht.[49] Since the scribe of Rawl. B. 488 was clearly carefully transcribing his exemplar it is not plausible that he was responsible for this secular edition of the Clonmacnoise chronicle. Rather we will find in chapter 9 that these changes have been the result of the transfer of the Clonmacnoise chronicle to a secular environment in Connacht. Hence we must posit at least one copy between these two MSS wherein these changes were introduced.

Tigernach's contribution to the Clonmacnoise chronicle

As discussed in chapter 3 the name 'Tigernach' has been associated with the annals of Rawl. B. 488 ever since 1639 when Ware attributed compilation of all

---

46 Kehnel, *Clonmacnois*, 162–7 (Norman invasion), 165 (cit.).   47 O'Donovan, *FM* i, p. lxv (cit.).
48 In chapter 2 p. 24 I give my reasons for believing that O'Flaherty possessed the now missing continuing folios of Rawl. B. 488; Murphy, *AC*, 215 (interjection).   49 Kehnel, *Clonmacnois*,

the annals up to 1088 to Tigernach Ua Braein, 'Erenachum Clonmacnoisensem'. However, following Mac Neill's challenge to this identification in 1913 modern scholars have usually prefixed such as 'so-called' to this attribution.[50] But in light of what has been established regarding the primacy of the Clonmacnoise group it seems worthwhile to re-examine the issue here. Ware's attribution rested entirely upon an entry under 1088 on f. 19^r of Rawl. B. 488, which is reproduced in plate 5c. This entry may be transcribed as, '[Huc us*que* Tigernach scr*i*bsit o*cht*.ar.o*chtmogait* quieuit ([To here Tigernach wrote, eight on eighty he died)', but the character '[' preceding this entry was omitted by Stokes from his edition and it has never been discussed. However, examination of the cartouches normally encircling AM data shows that the first scribe initiated their left-hand end in black ink and the illuminator subsequently completed them in red ink, cf. plate 5a. Occasionally however they were left incomplete by the illuminator as in plate 5b. Thus it is clear that the character preceding Tigernach's obit is the left-hand end of an incomplete cartouche, and that in the exemplar this 'obit' appeared in fact as a heading surrounded by a cartouche. Indeed it is the case that all illumination ceases in this MS at f. 14vb.[51] Hence this obit and incomplete cartouche are definitely not the invention of the first scribe of Rawl. B. 488, but rather he incompletely transcribed them from his exemplar, and they show that an earlier compiler believed that an annalist named 'Tigernach' had written the annals prior to this point and that he had died in the year 1088.[52] Let us refer to this earlier compiler as the 'Tigernach-admirer'. Moreover, Tigernach-admirer felt sufficiently strongly about these details to interpolate them as this completely unorthodox entry into his compilation as a heading, replete with a cartouche. Thus this singular entry itself, so far from being contemporaneous with the death of 'Tigernach', was certainly composed long afterwards and consequently is open to question on this count alone. In order to try to resolve its significance I will consider first of all the question of who was this 'Tigernach' and what office may have been held by him, and then what annals he may have compiled.

When all available annals are examined three others provide obits for an individual called Tigernach in the year 1088 as follows:

CS 1088.4: Tigernach H. Braín, do Sil Muiredhaigh, comarba Ciarain Cluana M Nois ocus Comain, quieuit.

AU 1088.3: Tighernach H. Broein airchinnech Cluana M. Nois in Christo quieuit.

FM 1088.3: Tighernach Ua Braoin, ard-chomharba Chiaráin & Chomáin, d'ecc i n-Iomdhaidh Chiaráin. Suí leighind & senchusa ésidhe.

167–72 (Uí Conchobhair kings). **50** Ware, *De scriptoribus*, 51 (attribution); Mac Neill., 'Authorship', 30–5 (challenge); Walsh, 'Dating Irish Annals', 355 ('so-called'), cf. idem, 'Annals attributed', 154–9. **51** Ó Cuív, *Catalogue*, 145 (illumination cessation). I am grateful to Dr Barker-Benfield of the Bodleian Library for his crucial assistance with identifying the cartouches in Rawl. B. 503 and subsequent discussion. **52** The meaning of the element '·o·aro·' preceding

As can be seen while all sources agree that this Tigernach belonged to the Uí Braein, they are in conflict regarding his office, CS and FM making him *comharba* of Ciaran of Clonmacnoise and also of Comain (Roscommon), while AU makes him simply 'airchinnech (erenagh)' of Clonmacnoise. Hitherto the *AU-priority* hypothesis has ensured that the CS entry has been dismissed merely as the result of subsequent emendation, which had propagated to FM. However, we now should regard CS as the primary witness.[53] Moreover, AU is the *only* source to make reference to the office of erenagh at Clonmacnoise and its three such references are distributed over nearly three centuries, viz. AU 796.2, 893.3, 1088.3. On the other hand CS, supported by AU/MB/FM, provides a substantial series of obits of Clonmacnoise principals described as holding the office of either *comharba* of Ciaran (cb. C), and/or *comharba* of other monastic familia. This CS *comharba* series begins in 954 and continues to 1093, and the fifteen individuals and their designated offices are:[54] Celecair cb. C. †954, Cormac cb. C. & Comain & Tuama Gréine † 966, Tuathal cb. C. †971, Dunchad cb. C. †989, Maolfinnia cb. C. †992, Maol Poil cb. C. †1001, Flannchadh cb. C. †1003, Flaithbertach cb. C & Finian †1014, Muiredhach cb. C. †1025, Bresal cb. C. †1030, Loingsech cb. C. & Comain †1042, Echtigern cb. C & Comain †1052, Ailill cb. C. †1070, Tigernach cb. C. & Comain †1088, Ailill tainaise abbadh C. & cb. Cronan † 1093.

Thus so far from Tigernach appearing as the only known 'erenagh' of Clonmacnoise over the tenth and eleventh centuries, he emerges in the Clonmacnoise group as one of a long line of holders of what must have been in those centuries one of the most influential ecclesiastical offices in Ireland. Indeed Tigernach, like some of his predecessors was also *comharba* of Comain, and I submit that this succession series recorded in Clonmacnoise is much more trustworthy and accurate than that found in AU which has in fact demoted him. Hence I conclude that Tigernach Ua Braein was indeed *comharba* of Ciaran and Comain for 1071–88, and consequently an extremely powerful individual in late eleventh-century Ireland, commanding the monastery whose scriptorium gave us such splendid MSS as *Lebor na hUidre* and Rawl. B. 502 f. 1–12. That from such an office Tigernach was able both to access the Clonmacnoise chronicle

'quieuit' has been disputed, but since marginal annalistic AD annotations regularly employ truncated Irish number words marked off with raised points and using the particle 'ar', and this is the year 1088, I consider Hogan's reading '*ocht ar ochtmogait*' beyond doubt, cf. Stokes, *AT*, 312. 53 For example, Mac Neill, 'Authorship', 31, 'Thus "do Shíl Muiredhaigh" is merely an obvious amplification by the compiler'; 34, 'the known contemporary evidence goes no farther than to say that Tigernach was *airchinnech* of Clonmacnois.' 54 This series is taken from CS with the exception of Dunchad †989, who is recorded in both MB and AU. All the others except Cormac †966 are also recorded in AU and FM, though sometimes with differences in the specification of their office, cf. Kehnel, *Clonmacnois*, 260–4.

and to determine what entries were inserted annually seems beyond all reasonable doubt. Indeed the concluding assertion in FM 1088.3 explicitly identifies his expertise in history.

It is also important to note in respect of this *comharba* succession that with the exception only of Tigernach none of the above listed *comharba* obits is registered in AT, so that it is clear that they had all been omitted from both the exemplar used by the scribe of Rawl. B. 488 and that used earlier by Tigernach-admirer. Thus it can be seen that the earlier interpolation by Tigernach-admirer was simply restoring the obit of Tigernach to his copy of the text. Moreover, from the fact that Tigernach-admirer placed this interpolation between the entries 'Indradh Corcomruadh …' and 'Dub Choblaith … mortua est', which is just exactly where it is positioned in CS, it seems clear that he was collating his exemplar against a corresponding but more complete Clonmacnoise group text that had retained the *comharba* obits. Thus Tigernach-admirer's 'Huc usque' referred to the position of Tigernach's obit in his Clonmacnoise group exemplar, *not* to Tigernach's hand appearing in his exemplar which, since it lacked all the *comharba* obits could not possibly have been the manuscript maintained at Clonmacnoise. Hence examination of the Annalistic obits for Tigernach Ua Braein shows us that Tigernach-admirer had indeed excellent grounds on which to base his restoration of an obit for Tigernach at this particular point.

This being so I next turn to the question of what annals Tigernach Ua Braein may have written as is implicit in Tigernach-admirer's words, 'Huc usque Tigernach scribsit.' Since these words suggest that he wrote up to 1088 the obvious annals to examine are those compiled when Tigernach was *comharba* over 1071–88. What we find at 1071, for the very first time in the entire text of AT, is that the kalends ferial is expressed in Irish, viz. 'Kł. Enair for Satharnn', thereby using the preposition 'for' and the Irish weekday 'Satharnn' to represent the ferial. Hitherto in this text the ferial was nearly always expressed simply in Roman numerals, thus at 593 'Kł.iiii.', though after 1019 the Latin 'feria' was sometimes suffixed to it, thus at 1020 'Kł.ui.feria', and also occasionally the number was replaced by its Latin word equivalent as at 1021, 'Kł. prima feria'. But these are all written in Latin and so the ferial at 1071 expressed in Irish as a weekday represents a sudden derogation from a very long tradition. Moreover, this Irish ferial at 1071 is followed, likewise for the first time, by the epact expressed in Roman numerals followed by an Irish prepositional pronoun referring to 'Kł. Enair', thus 'Kł. Enair for Satharnn .xx.ui. fuirri (Kalends January on Saturday and 26 thereon)', so that no meaning is explicitly attributed to the number 'xx.ui'. Hitherto the epact had nearly always been expressed explicitly by prefixing the Latin word 'luna' to the epact written in Roman numerals. These changes, while transmitting essentially the same chronological data as the Latin version, represent much more than a simple translation of the Latin elements into Irish, for they constitute a break from an Annalistic chronological style that had been established at least by the early fifth century and that was still used in the eleventh century for Paschal tables and their computations. Furthermore this Irish chronological apparatus, synchronized to Tigernach's assumption of the office of *comharba*, was sustained not only over the remainder of his tenure, excepting only the latter years 1083, 1086–7, but it was substantially maintained for the remainder of AT/CS up to their terminations at 1178 and 1135 respectively.

It thus emerges that there are very good grounds to believe that Tigernach was responsible for introducing this new Irish chronological style into the Clonmacnoise chronicle upon his accession to the office of *comharba* in 1071, and that his innovation remained the standard chronological apparatus in the Clonmacnoise chronicle thereafter. Furthermore it should be noted that in the two Connacht texts, LC and CT, this style was used virtually continuously between 1206 and 1478, while in AI it was used continuously from 1001 to 1321, and in AB from 1236.[55] There can be no question therefore but that Tigernach's innovation played an important role in the writing of the Annals from 1071 onwards. In these circumstances it is not surprising that Tigernach-admirer, whose exemplar systematically omitted obits of all the *comharbai* at Clonmacnoise, should have chosen to restore Tigernach's obit to his copy and also to acknowledge his contribution to the writing of Clonmacnoise annals.

Tigernach's action in reforming the chronological apparatus of the Clonmacnoise chronicle points to his having had an interest in chronological matters, and this is the principal basis for the suggestion made in chapter 4 that he was responsible for the attempt to replace Adomnán's prosaic Byzantine succession with DTR's stereotyped regnal succession including an AM, cf. Figure 13, p. 135. Intrinsically linked to this by the omission of the seventeen-year reign of 'Constantinus filius superioris Constantini' are the many citations from DTR found in the Clonmacnoise group over the Christian era. Since neither this interpolated succession nor the many DTR citations are found in the Cuana group they must have been incorporated into the Clonmacnoise chronicle *after* 1022 when Liber Cuanach was compiled, but *before* Rawl. B. 502 was written around the end of the eleventh century. In these circumstances it seems to me that Tigernach is the most likely author of these additions from DTR which, to judge from their appearance in Rawl. B. 502 were made marginally, cf. plates 1–2, and henceforth I shall identify him as their author.[56]

55 The appearance in AI of chronological data in Irish at 1001 does not predate their use in AT, but rather the Emly compiler of the exemplar of Rawl. B. 503 writing *c.*1068–81 was influenced by the Clonmacnoise usage to introduce this Irish style retrospectively into his compilation, cf. chapter 7, p. 211 ff.   56 The fact that the citations of DTR §529–31 at AT 582.2–3 have been translated into Irish also suggests Tigernach's authorship.

Moreover, since the marginal AM data interpolated by Tigernach from DTR were regularly surrounded by a cartouche and he himself introduced a completely new Irish chronological style, it was indeed appropriate that Tigernach-admirer should have acknowledged this by both surrounding his obit with a cartouche and by partly registering the AD in Irish.

Thus it can be seen, when the evidence is carefully assessed, that the title 'Annals of Tigernach' can be applied accurately *only* to the annals over 1071–88 and the excerpts from Bede's DTR which were compiled during Tigernach Ua Braein's term as *comharba*. Even over this interval he may well have delegated the task of compilation of some of them to subordinates, as the chronological apparatus reversions to Latin in his last two years suggest. This is a far cry indeed from the sweeping compilatory claims advanced on his behalf by Ware, O'Conor, O'Curry and Stokes; indeed the seventeen-year anachronism caused by his omission of the third Byzantine Constantinus is enough to discredit any claim of great 'accuracy' on Tigernach's behalf. On the other hand, the subsequent endurance of Tigernach's Irish chronological apparatus in the Clonmacnoise group texts, and its continuation in the later Connacht group surely does warrant recognition. When carefully restricted to this Irish chronological apparatus and the annals over 1071–88, and the Bedan AM and his Christian additions it does seem to me fitting to retain an association between Tigernach's name and the MSS Rawl. B. 502 and 488.

Summary of the evolution of the Moville and Clonmacnoise chronicles

Circa 740–752 – The Iona chronicle was brought to Moville and there obits for its abbots added over these years. As well a large number of verses relating predominantly to northern political conflict were interpolated over the years 352–743, together with Emain regnal successions for *c.*313 BC–AD 329 and Tara successions from AD 49 onward. These successions were preceded by an early version of the Irish origin legend. These Moville interpolations represent the first substantial introduction of the vernacular, secular learned tradition into the Annals. *Circa 753* – A copy of the Iona-Moville chronicle was made and brought to Clonmacnoise and a brief Clonmacnoise end chronicle over 723–40 incorporated. *Circa 753–1022* – Annals with an Irish provenance but midland emphasis and a monastic and Uí Néill purview were accumulated institutionally at Clonmacnoise continuing the bare kalend chronological apparatus of the Iona chronicle. In *c.*777 entries from a separate phenomenological chronicle from Iona was transcribed marginally into the Clonmacnoise chronicle, and henceforth phenomenological entries were entered with ecclesiastical and secular entries. *Circa 1022* – The Clonmacnoise chronicle was used by Cuán Ua Lothcháin as the basis for his compilation of Liber Cuanach.

Circa 1022–1071 – Institutional accumulation continued at Clonmacnoise but the chronological apparatus now systematically included the feria, and intermittently the epacts and AD introduced by Cuán Ua Lothcháin.

Circa 1071–1088 – Tigernach Ua Braein reformed the chronological apparatus to an Irish written form, interpolated Bede's DTR Byzantine succession over *c.*491–720 and their associated AM, but omitted one seventeen-year reign, and also interpolated many of Bede's own additions to the Christian era of DTR taken from LP.

Circa 1100 – A prestigious copy of the Clonmacnoise chronicle was made retaining Tigernach's Bedan interpolations, and a substantial fragment of this survives as Rawl. B. 502 ff. 1–12 and this constitutes the first section of AT.

Circa 1088–c.1227 – Tigernach's reformed chronological apparatus was effectively maintained at Clonmacnoise until chronicling ceased there at *c.*1227.

CHAPTER SEVEN

Liber Cuanach and its descendants

The evidence for Liber Cuanach

The only evidence associating annals with a person called 'Cuana' is the thirteen interjections found in AU citing either 'Liber Cuanach' or 'Cuana' as their authority. It is important therefore to examine this evidence carefully to determine the significance of these interjections, and also to assess the role of their author. Accordingly all thirteen entries are reproduced in Figure 23.[1]

AU	Entries citing Cuana/Liber Cuanach
467.2:	Cena Temhra la h-Ailill Molt ^{mc. Dath I mc. Fiachrach mc. Eathach Muidhemhon}. **Sic in Libro Cuanach inueni.**
468.2:	Bellum Dumai Achir, .i. for Oilill Molt **sicut in Libro Cuanach inueni.**
471.1:	Praeda secunda Saxonum de Hibernia, ut alii dicunt, in isto anno deducta est, ut Maucteus ^{.i. Mochtae} dicit. **Sic in Libro Cuanach inueni.**
475.1:	Bellum ^{alias dorndghal} Breg h-Eile re n-Ailill Molt for Laighniu. **Sic in Líbro Cuanach inueni.**
482.1:	Bellum Oche, ^{.i. la Lugaid mc. Laegaire 7 la Muirchertach Mc. Earca} in quo cecidit Ailill Molt.
482.2:	A Conchobro filio Nesae usque ad Cormac filium Airt anni .ccc.uiii. A Cormac usque hoc bellum cxui., **ut Cuana scripsit.**
489.2:	Bellum Cinn Losnado ^{I Ceall Losnaigh i Maigh Fhea} ubi cecidit Oengus filius Nat Fraich ^{ri Mughan}, **ut Cuana scriphsit.**
544.3:	Diarmait ^{mc. Fergusa Cerrbheoil mc. Conaill Cremthainne mc. Neill Naoighiallaigh} regnare incipit **secundum Librum Cuanach.**
552.2:	Mors Craumthain mc. Briuin. **Sic in Libro Cuanach inueni.**
598.2:	Quies Cainnigh Acaidh Bó, **ut Cuana docet.**
600.3:	**Sic inueni in Libro Cuanach. Bellum Slenne 7 bellum Cule Coil; 7 pausa Comghaill 7 mors Oddach m. Aedha in isto anno** *perfecta esse.*[2]
602.3:	**Omnia quae scripta sunt in anno subsequente, inueni in Libro Cuanach in isto esse perfecta.**
610.3:	Quies Colmain Elo. **Sic est in Libro Cuanach.**
628.3:	Uel bellum Fedho Euin ubi ceciderunt nepotes Aedain, Rigullon, Faelbẹ.
628.4:	Mors Echdach Buidhe, regis Pictorum, filii Aedain. **Sic in Libro Cuanach inueni.**

Figure 23. The thirteen AU entries citing either 'Liber Cuanach' or 'Cuana', with Ruaidhrí Ua Caiside's interjections into his primary source all shown in bold, and his subsequent interpolations in TCD 1282 (H²) shown in superscript. Ua Luinín's own subsequent addition to AU 600.3 as H¹ is shown in italic.

1 Mac Airt & Mac Niocaill, *AU, s.a.*, cf. Byrne, 'Ut Beda boat', 57–67 who usefully cites these and parallel entries from other annals.   2 Mac Airt & Mac Niocaill, *AU*, 98 attribute these two words

Now in chapter 2 I briefly identified that Ruaidhrí Ua Caiside was the effective compiler of TCD 1282, and that his primary source was a chronicle extending from Adam to c.1484. In chapter 11, p. 316 ff., I will show by a comprehensive survey of the attributive interjections in AU that Ua Caiside was responsible for the great majority of these, including those referrring to 'Cuana' and 'Liber Cuana'. The same situation prevails with the analogous interjections making attributions to 'Duibh da Lethe', cf. Figure 28, p. 225. Thus Ua Caiside was the author of all of these Cuana interjections and they show that as well as his primary source he also had another source he knew as 'Liber Cuanach' and that he was collating the two of these together. Along with these interjections he transcribed a total of seventeen entries from Liber Cuanach, and these comprise the only direct information we have regarding the content and structural organization of this chronicle. Considering first the entries we see that linguistically, apart from the proper nouns in Irish, they were all written entirely in Latin. Specifically, and in contrast to the corresponding entries in the Clonmacnoise group, the principal defining word is always in Latin, viz. 'cena', 'praeda', 'bellum'×7, 'anni', 'regnare', 'mors'×2, 'quies'×3, 'pausa'. Thus in this respect they exhibit the very same linguistic relationship to the Clonmacnoise group entries as do the other contemporaneous entries of AU. Furthermore when these seventeen entries are collated semantically with those of the Clonmacnoise group it is found that just four provide identical semantic content, while the remaining thirteen Cuana entries all represent a reduction of the corresponding Clonmacnoise entry. Thus in both their linguistic and semantic character these Cuana entries exhibit exactly the same relationship to the Clonmacnoise group entries as do the other contemporaneous AU entries. Moreover, seven of these Cuana entries are duplicated elsewhere in AU and collation of these shows numerous textual and orthographic correspondences, as the collation in Figure 24 demonstrates.

The cryptic form of most Cuana entries here suggests that Ua Caiside has abbreviated them in transcription, while the unique orthography of his 'Oddach' seems likely to be his own invention, for he was not an accurate copyist. Nevertheless these correspondences are sufficient to show that Liber Cuanach and Ua Caiside's primary source both shared a common textual origin. In particular their two accounts of 'Bellum Feda Euin', cf. AU 628.1,3 represent but separate parts of the much longer account preserved in the Clonmacnoise group, cf. AT:[3]

to '? *add* H', tentatively suggesting them to be by Ua Luinín transcribing, but examination of TCD 1282 shows clearly that Ua Luinín subsequently added them in lighter ink after his earlier concluding ';'. Hence they must be considered an emendation by him as H[1]. **3** Byrne, 'Ut Beda boat', 66; cf. Stokes, *AT*, 140–1.

Cuana entries	AU duplicate entries
475.1: *Bellum* ^{alias dorndghal} *Breg h-Eile* re n-Ailill Molt for Laighniu.	478.1: *Bellum Bregh h-Eile.*
598.2: *Quies Cainnigh* Acaidh Bó, ...	599.1: *Quies Cainnigh* sancti ...
600.3: *Bellum Slenne* ⁊ *bellum Cule Coil*; ⁊ pausa *Comghaill* ⁊ *mors* Oddach *m. Aedha* ...	601.1–4: Quies *Comghaill* Bennchair; *Bellum Slenne* in quo Colman Rimidh, rex Generis Eugain, uictor erat, ⁊ Conall Cuu m. Aedho m. Ainmirech fugitiuus alias fugitiuus euasit; *Bellum Cule Coil* in quo Fiachna m. Demain fugit. Fiachna m. Baetan uictor erat; *Mors* h-Uatach *m. Aedho.*
628.3: ... *bellum Fedho Euin* ubi ceciderunt nepotes Aedain, Rigullon, Faelbę.	628.1: *Bellum Feda Euin* in quo Mael Caich m. Scannail, rex Cruithne, uictor fuit. Dal Riati ceciderunt. Conid Cerr, rex Dal Riati, cecidit.

Figure 24. Collation of Cuana entries against AU duplicate entries wherein all textual and orthographic correspondences have been highlighted in italic.

AT 632.1: Cath Fedha Éoin in quo Mael Caith mac Scandail rex Cruithniu uictor
erat. Dal Riada cecidit. Condadh Cerr rí Dal Riada cecidit ⁊ *Dicull mac
Echach, rí ceneoil Cruithne cecidit* et nepotes Aedan ceciderunt id est
Rigullan mac Conaing ⁊ Failbe mac Eachach ⁊ *Oisiric mac Albruit,
rigdomna Saxan cum strage maxima suorum.*

The italic text here shows the passages omitted by both Liber Cuanach and Ua
Caiside's primary source, and as can be seen they have abandoned the obits of
both Dicull and Osiric.

Turning next to consider chronological aspects of these Cuana entries we
first note that the chronological apparatus of Ua Caiside's primary source
comprised kalend+ferial+epact+AD, though in many instances the principal
scribe, Ruaidhrí Ua Luinín, deliberately omitted transcription of the ferial and
epact data, leaving instead a blank space for them. Subsequently Ua Caiside
transcribed many of these data into these blank spaces, cf. plate 7. Regarding
the chronology of the Cuana entries we find that three of Ua Caiside's
interjections explicitly identified relative temporal issues, cf. AU 471.1, 600.3
and 602.3 in Figure 23 above, and regarding these we observe that:

a) At AU 471.1 his 'Praeda secunda' entry from Liber Cuanach synchronizes precisely with the corresponding Clonmacnoise group entry at AD 471.

b) Ua Caiside's interjections and duplications over AU 598–603 show that the Liber Cuanach entries were all one year in advance relative to his primary source.

From the information Ua Caiside gives we may reconstruct the structural character of Liber Cuanach and some of its content over these years as shown in Figure 25.

Ua Caiside's primary source for AU	Liber Cuanach reconstruction
Kł.Ian.5.f.l.29.AD.598. 1. Ailither p. 2. Q. Cainnigh Acaidh Bó **ut Cuana docet**. ←	Kł.Ian.5.f.l.29. – 1. Q. Cainnigh Acaidh Bó.
Kł.Ian.6.f.l.10.AD.599. 1. Q. Cainnigh sancti …	Kł.Ian.6.f.l.10. –
Kł.Ian.1.f.l.21.AD.600. 1. Terremotus … 2. Mors Brendain … 3. **Sic inueni in Libro Cuanach**. Bellum ← Slenne 7 bellum Cule Coil, 7 pausa Comghaill 7 mors Oddach m. Aedha **in isto anno perfecta esse**.	Kł.Ian.1.f.l.21. – 1. Bellum Slenne … 2. Bellum Cule Coil … 3. Pausa Comghaill … 4. Mors Uatach m. Aedha.
Kł.Ian.2.f.l.2.AD.601. 1. Quies Comhghaill … 2. Bellum Slennae … 3. Bellum Cule Coil … 4. Mors Huatach m. Aedho … 5. B Echrois. ←	Kł.Ian.2.f.l.2. – [B. Echrois.]
Kł.Ian.3.f.l.13.AD.602. 1. Quies Finntain … 2. Bellum Echrois … 3. **Omnia quae scripta sunt in anno** ← **subsequente, inueni in Libro** **Cuanach in isto esse perfecta**.	Kł.Ian.3.f.l.13. 1. Iug. Colmain … 2. Iug. Aedho Slane … 3. Iug. Aedho Roin … 4. Aed Buidi … 5. Mors Chonaill … 6. Cuu cen Mathair …
Kł.Ian.4.f.l.24.AD.603. 1. Iug. Colmain … 2. Iug. Aedho Slane … 3. Iug. Aedho Roin … 4. Aed Buidi … 5. Mors Chonaill … 6. Cuu cen Mathair …	Kł.Ian.4.f.l.24. –

Figure 25. A reconstruction of Ua Caiside's primary source and Liber Cuanach in parallel for the years AU 598–603 showing the chronological relationship between the Cuana entries transcribed by him into his primary source as indicated by the '←', and the same entries already present there.

As can be seen at 598, 600 and 602 Liber Cuanach's entries have antedated those in Ua Caiside's primary source by one year, and in the first two instances he has transcribed these acknowledging that they come from Liber Cuanach. In the third instance, probably on account of the greater number of entries involved, Ua Caiside instead made his interjection reference the subsequent year in his primary source. Because in the first two instances essentially the same entries occurred in the primary source in the following year this has resulted in duplication of these entries, all of which Ua Luinín dutifully copied into TCD 1282. Indeed there are good reasons to suspect that Ua Caiside also transcribed the two-word entry AU 601.5 'Bellum Echrois' from Liber Cuanach, but he omitted any interjection, because just like these other Cuana duplicates this entry is a substantially reduced version of that following at AU 602.2. Furthermore when all of the forty-five duplicates over AU 435–673 written by Ua Luinín are collated it is found that virtually all of them are in Latin and one a reduction of the other, and some of them incorporate an interjection referencing Cuana, *alia* or *uel*.[4] I therefore submit that Ua Caiside was responsible for nearly all of these duplicates in the course of collating his primary source with Liber Cuanach and other sources. In 1998 I proposed this hypothesis based upon the synchronism between the Cuana interjections and the anachronistic chronology observed in AU relative to the Clonmacnoise group, and consider that the textual evidence discussed above confirms that the hypothesis was essentially correct.[5] Thus Ua Caiside's collation process and his weak grasp of historical chronology generated many duplicates in his compilation of TCD 1282, and these when combined with the *AU-priority* hypothesis have caused serious chronological problems for historians. Finally, the reasons for including ferials and epacts in the Liber Cuanach reconstruction of Figure 25 above are twofold. Firstly, Ua Caiside needed to use some criteria additional to kalends in order to synchronize his two sources. Secondly, he himself transcribed ferial+ epactal series either into the year or proximate year of *all* his Cuana attributions, showing that he was using these data as his basis for synchronization.[6]

Now considering Figure 25 we can see that even though Ua Caiside has only given us a brief section of Liber Cuanach there is enough to show that in terms of its language, orthography, content, structural arrangement, and chronological apparatus that it was cognate with his primary source. Thus these two chronicles were both descendants from a redaction of the Clonmacnoise chronicle made at a time before Irish had replaced Latin in it, and in this redaction a substantial apparatus of kalend+ferial+epact replaced the simple apparatus of kalend+ferial that the Clonmacnoise chronicle had inherited from

---

4 Mc Carthy, 'Chronology', 255 (table of AU duplicates).   5 Mc Carthy, 'Chronology', 255 the 'duplicate(s) are interpolations from another source, most probably the Book of Cuanu.'   6 Ua Caiside's ferial+epactal series are continuous over AU 458–71, 475–6, 481, 486–504, 510–37,

the Iona chronicle up to this point. These features are important, most particularly the epacts, because they are all found in the annals of the Cuana group, and hence I conclude that AU, AI and AB are all descendants from Liber Cuanach. While our only direct evidence concerning Liber Cuanach is the collection of seventeen entries and thirteen interjections interpolated by Ua Caiside into his primary source, we may infer more about the structure and content of Liber Cuanach from a critical examination and collation of AU/AI/AB. In particular it is important to try to establish other salient characteristics of Liber Cuanach, viz., its chronological apparatus, the range of its coverage, the date of its compilation, its chronological accuracy, and the identity of 'Cuana'.

The chronological apparatus and range of Liber Cuanach

Considering first of all the chronological apparatus of AU/AI/AB over the post-Palladian period we find that of both AI and AB constitute a degradation of that of AU. Consequently, I conclude that the kalend+ferial+epact+AD chronological apparatus of AU best represents that of Liber Cuanach. Of these four series the kalend+AD run uniformly over AU 431–1012, but at least over AU 663–1012 these are in arrears by one year, i.e. the MS AD is low by one year. This asynchronism arose because in the course of his compilation Cuana restored only five of the six kalends deleted by Ecgberht over 612–64. On the other hand the ferial+epact series transcribed by both Ua Luinín and Ua Caiside are synchronous with the kalend+AD over AU 431–81, but they are postdated by one year over AU 486–1012. It is apparent therefore that in Ua Caiside's primary source a misguided attempt had been made to rectify the one-year asynchronism caused by the missing kalend by postdating the ferial+epact apparatus over AU 486–1012. However, Ua Caiside's collation of Liber Cuanach with his primary source shows that Liber Cuanach's ferial+epact apparatus had undergone no such postdating, cf. Figure 25. On these grounds therefore I conclude that the post-Palladian chronological apparatus of Liber Cuanach consisted originally of a comprehensive series of synchronized kalends, ferial, epact and AD data extending continuously from 431 to at least the early eleventh century. Now since the AD apparatus in AU extends uniformly from 431 to 1012 then this implies that this was all the work of a single compiler working after 1013.[7] However, detailed collation of the parallel series of ferial and epactal data and entries in AU/AI/AT over 431–1022 imply rather that Liber Cuanach had originally extended to c.1019 and Cuana had completed this compilation shortly after 1022.[8]

545–53, 563–604, 608–54, cf. Mc Carthy, 'AU apparatus 431–1131', 64.   7 Mc Carthy, 'AU apparatus 82–1019', 273–4 (post 1013 terminus of the compilation of Liber Cuanach).   8 Mc Carthy, 'AU apparatus 82–1019', 274–7 (c.1022 date of the compilation of Liber Cuanach).

Regarding the pre-Palladian chronological apparatus of Liber Cuanach AB is our only witness to the immediate post-Creation period, and this shows an apparatus comprising AM+kalend+ferial+epact, though only the kalends were written continuously. For examples, AB §4 'Kł.eñ.vii.f.', AB §5 'Anni ab initio mundi d.l.x.Kł.eñ.' AB §12 'M.xxx.vu.Kł.eñ.', AB §24 'Kł.iª.f.l.xx.', AB §49 'Kł.eñ.ii.fª.l.xviª.'. The textual correlation here with AU's apparatus is unmistakable, cf. AU §2 below. As well as this where sequences of AB's kalends are uninterrupted by entries they were repeatedly written in groups of nineteen.[9] This apparatus continues up to the Incarnation at AB §93 but with all except the kalends becoming infrequent after Abraham. The post-Incarnation apparatus of Liber Cuanach is best preserved in AU, and examination of ff. 12–14 of TCD 1282 has shown that it is intrinsically linked to the apparatus from 431 onwards. That this pre-Palladian apparatus was a formidable construction may be seen from the entry for AU's first surviving complete year:[10]

AU §2: .ꟾꟾꟾꟾxxxiiii.Kł ē.ui.f.l.xx. Fiacha Findamnas mac Ireil Glunmair regnauit i nEmain di eis a athar annis .xx.

This apparatus thus consists of an AM+kalend+ferial+epact, and it is thus cognate with that of AB. Analysis shows that all the components of this apparatus in AU, which extends for 489 kalends, are virtually precisely synchronized throughout. The assembly of this extended, complex structure represents a remarkable computational and inscriptional achievement on the part of Cuana, and reveals that he was a most accomplished computist.[11] However, when we consider the accuracy of the historical chronology of Cuana's compilation some very serious problems quickly emerge. The initial, acephalous entry can be shown to refer to the year AD 82, and indeed the emperor Domitian's death is registered appropriately just thirteen kalends later in AD 95; at the end of the surviving text the very last entry records S. Jerome's preaching in Bethlehem, where he was living by 386. Thus it is clear that historically these entries cover about three centuries from the late first to the late fourth century. On the other hand, 489 kalends from AD 82 should bring the chronicle into the later sixth century, so that it is apparent that there must be an excess of approximately two hundred kalends. Resolution of this conundrum discloses Cuana to be the author of the most extraordinary chronological invention to be found in the Irish Annals.

---

9 Cf. Freeman, *AB*, 302–8, but the cited examples are taken from the MS Cot. Titus A xxv since Freeman does not accurately reproduce the apparatus; AB §9 (19-year groups). 10 Mc Carthy, 'AU apparatus 82–1019', 261–9 (pre-Palladian apparatus), 272–3 (relationship between the pre- and post-Palladian apparatus). 11 Mc Carthy, 'AU apparatus 82–1019', 265, (Cuán's skill), 265 n.29 (lists all apparatus errors, nearly all scribal).

The key is provided by an Incarnation entry located at AM 4205 and reading:

> AU §96: .iiiiccu Kł ē.uii.f.l.xx. Hic est annus Incarnationis Christi secundum Dionissium, quia secundum eum secundo anno ciclo magni Paschalis natus est, qui annus habet .u. concurrentes 7 .xuii.

This Incarnation 'secundum Dionissium' is placed nearly thirty years after Origen's *claruit* at AM 4176 and thus in the middle of the third century AD, in fact at AD 254. This enormous asynchronism is the consequence of Cuana having followed an earlier doctrine proposing the introduction of 253 years between the Hebrew AM 3952 and the Incarnation 'secundum Dionissum'. This doctrine can be traced to a ninth-century appendix to the *Chronicon breve a mundi exordio usque ad annum Christi dcccx*, both of which have been attributed to the ninth-century Irish scholar, Dúngal of St Denis †*p*.825. This doctrine was also followed by the late eleventh-century Irish chronicler Marianus Scottus †1082, who attributed it to Bede, writing:[12]

> Hoc autem dicit Beda, ut ostendat damnum 261 annorum, qui desunt in cronicis de predicta summa secundum Ebreos, ab ipso anno, in quo contigit dominica nativitas secundum supputationem predictam, qui est annus 253 ante incarnationem iuxta Dionisium usque ad annum 9 incarnationis secundum eundem Dionisium, qui est annus nativitatis dominice secundum Bedam ... Ab Adam usque ad Christum, hoc est in annum 253 ante incarnationem iuxta Dionisium 6 indictione, anni sunt 3952 ...

Thus Marianus believed that Bede's words had shown that there were 261 years missing between AM 3952 and the ninth year of the Incarnation 'iuxta Dionisium', and consequently 261−(9−1)=253 years to be restored between AM 3952 and the year of the Incarnation 'iuxta Dionisium'. Hence in his own chronicle completed at Mainz in 1076 Marianus resolved this by placing the Eusebian Incarnation in the forty-second year of Augustus, effectively at AM 4183, and then introducing his own 'Incarnatio secundum Dionisium', just twenty two years later.[13] Cuana, on the other hand, introduced his 'Incarnatio secundum Dionissium' entry retarded by 253 years from the Eusebian Incarnation, thereby placing it anachronistically in the middle of the third century AD. Thirty three years later at AM 4238 he inserted a corresponding 'Passionis Christi secundum Dionissium', and these two profoundly anachronistic entries in the middle of the third century establish beyond question that,

---

12 Van der Brincken, 'Marianus Scottus, 227 (cit.); cf. idem, 'Universalhistoriker', 996; Migne, *PL* civ, cc. 607–10 (the appendix); Verbist, 'Marianus Scottus', 284–6 (Marianus' life), 287–96 (his development of the doctrine), 291–2, (attribution of both chronicle and appendix to Dúngal).
13 Waitz, 'Mariani Scoti', 500–1, 502, 505 (two Incarnation and Passion entries).

not withstanding his remarkable computational skills Cuana had a very weak grasp of historical chronology.[14] Even more remarkably, and as if to underline his disregard for historicity, Cuana inserted a further two Incarnation entries at this time. The first at AM 4183 registers the Incarnation according to those who believed in Resurrection on vi Kł. Apr. (27 March), the other at AM 4212 registers the Incarnation that he attributed to 'Bede'. Cuana's three additional Incarnation entries are all accompanied by his corresponding Passion entries at respectively AM 4216 'Resurrectionem .ui. Kł Apr.', AM 4238 'secundum Dionissium', and AM 4246 'secundum Bedam'.[15]

Next, Cuana synchronized the Dionysiac ferial and epactal data to his Incarnation at AM 4205, so that his ferial 'uii.f' and annalistic epact 'l.xx' at this year correspond precisely with Dionysius' ferial and epactal data for AD 533, and hence also for his AD 1.[16] Finally, having retarded Dionysius' AD 1 by 253 years in historical terms, Cuana proceeded to interpolate 253 additional kalends following his Incarnation 'secundum Dionissium', in order to synchronize his later chronicle. In the surviving fragment we can identify 171 of these kalends between AM 4205 and 4522, so that instead of representing 4522–4204=318 years as it purports, it actually represents only 318–171=147 historical years, and the chronology of all Cuana's entries between AD 254 and 386 has been seriously distorted by these interpolated kalends. Moreover, his rate of kalend interpolation ensured that by AD 431, the year of pope Celestine's despatch of Palladius as bishop to the Irish Christians, a total of 253 additional kalends had been interpolated, and all of the elements of his chronological apparatus were accurately synchronized both with those of Dionysius' Paschal table and also historically.[17]

This extraordinary procedure by which Cuana introduced Dionysiac criteria into his redaction of the Clonmacnoise chronicle, relocating Christ's life to the third century and distorting the historical chronology of all the entries between AD 254 and 430, show him to have been a chronological reformer in a position to fearlessly introduce large-scale and draconian revisions. This fact alone suggests that he occupied a position of great power. Regarding their consequence, Cuana's pre-Palladian revisions were so obviously bizarre and conspicuous that they could be easily detected by any serious historical chronographer. However, his post-Palladian chronological apparatus introduced further revisions far more insidious on account of their inconspicuous character. These first appear in the

---

14 Mc Carthy, 'AU apparatus 82–1019', 265–7 (detailed examination of these Incarnation and Passion entries).   15 Verbist, 'Marianus Scottus', 295 (Marianus reproduces the Incarnation and Passion attributed to Bede).   16 Mc Carthy, 'AU apparatus 82–1019', 266 (identity with Dionysius' data).   17 Mc Carthy, 'AU apparatus 82–1019', 268–9 (details of these interpolated kalends). These interpolations are readily discernible in Mac Airt & Mac Niocaill, *AU*, 20–37 as extended sequences of repeated 'Kł'.

fifth and sixth centuries where collation with the chronology of the Clonmacnoise chronicle show that Cuana had revised the chronology of the entries of numerous events, particularly those relating to prominent early Irish Christians. His most substantial revisions of this kind are those associated with S. Brigit whose *natus* he moved from 439 to 452, and her obit from 524 to 523 in order to reduce her lifespan to exactly seventy years.[18] Other significant revisions by Cuana were: Benignus †469 by two years, Iserninus †470 by two years, Mac Nissi †511 by five years, Ciarán's *natus* in 514 by three years, Comhgall's *natus* in 517 by two years, Cainneach's *natus* in 518 by eight years, Columba's *natus* in 520 by two years, and Tigernach †544 by four years.[19] Since the modern chronology for early Irish Christian history has mostly been taken from AU, it usually incorporates these distortions of Cuana. But his most pervasive and elusive revision occurred when he extended his apparatus over 574–664, for here Cuana restored only five of the six kalends missing from the Clonmacnoise chronicle over 612–64. This then had the consequence over AU 574–612 that his apparatus was one year in advance with respect to the entries, and that his subsequent apparatus over 664–1019 was one year in arrears.

In this way Cuana's ambitious project to restore chronological integrity and bring ecclesiastical orthodoxy to his redaction of the Clonmacnoise chronicle resulted in a chronological apparatus, which, whilst ecclesiastically orthodox and impressive in appearance, introduced errors of far greater magnitude than those caused by the thirteen missing kalends inherited by the Clonmacnoise chronicle from the Iona chronicle. In particular it is clear that the uncertainty regarding the location of the kalend omitted by Cuana from the mid-seventh century raised serious chronological problems for the Irish Annalists that they never resolved.[20] For the effect of Cuana's sweeping chronological revision was to present yet further difficulties for all subsequent Annalists, since they now had the problem of deciding between two profoundly disparate chronologies, which both presented serious but inconspicuous chronological errors. Examples of the confusion induced by Cuana's chronology over 431–*c.*1019 are: Ua Caiside's interpolated duplicates in AU, and his repeated ferial and epactal interpolations and AD emendments; Ua Luinín's repeated ferial and epactal omissions; AI's duplicate Palladian and Patrician entries, its extremely intermittent ferial and epactal apparatus, and its badly damaged kalend apparatus; AB's seriously incomplete kalend apparatus, and its resultant severely damaged historical chronology.

18 Mc Carthy, 'S. Brigit', 258–64, 281.   19 Cf. Moody et al., *A Chronology*, *s.a.* 467/8 (†Benignus), *s.a.* 465/8 (†Iserninus), *s.a.* 507/9 (†Mac Nissi).   20 The situation was clarified only in 1998 in Mc Carthy, 'Chronology', 225, 251–4 by the collation of the Clonmacnoise chronicle [AT/CS] chronology for events against their independently known chronology, and this revealed that six kalends were missing between 612 and 664. Collation with AU disclosed that Cuana's first restored kalend at AU 574 was about forty years too early, and his four subsequent restorations at AU 634, 640, 647 and 654 had left a deficit of one kalend.

The identity of Cuana

Regarding the identity of 'Cuana', the attribution to him of a compilation which continued to *c*.1019 necessarily locates his *floruit* in the early eleventh century. Thus all those identifications which replaced the tenth-century orthography of 'Cuana' with its Old Irish equivalent of 'Cuanu', and then searched AU for individuals of this orthography are unsustainable.[21] It is in fact the case in AU, whose name orthography was considered contemporaneous by Ó Máille from 740 onwards, that the forms 'Cuana' and 'Cuanu' cease after 825 and are replaced by 'Cuan'. However, that the earlier forms were both known and still used by later authors is demonstrated by the occurrence of all three forms used as synonyms in the *Corpus genealogiarum sanctorum Hiberniae*.[22] In a specifically annalistic context the name of the Holy Roman emperor Conrad II was Gaelicised as 'Cuana' and 'Cuanu' respectively, cf. AU 1023.8 and 1037.3. Furthermore, it is apparent that the annalist's Gaelicization was based upon the 'Con' element of 'Conrad', showing that in his mind 'Con', 'Cuanu' and 'Cuana' were all synonyms. It is clear then that by the eleventh century, while the form 'Cuan' had long been customary usage, the then archaic forms 'Cuanu' and 'Cuana' were both known, and, what is most significant, they were regarded by the annalist as appropriate forms to use for the supreme figure of authority in Western Europe. It is clear from these instances that these archaic forms were used to express respect towards the person so named.

When we search the Annals for individuals named 'Cuan' who were plausibly alive in *c*.1022, the only candidates are: Donncuan ua Machainen, who was killed by Gilla Ciarain, king of Mugdorna in 1062, cf. AU 1062.5, and Cuán Ua Lothcháin who was murdered in 1024. Of these Donncuan, a member of the Mugdorna ruling dynasty, is implausible by the form of his name, his background, and late date. On the other hand, Cuán Ua Lothcháin is described in Annalistic obits variously as: AT 'primsenchaidh Erenn 7 a primeolach'; CS 'prim hécius Erenn ocus saoi senchusa'; AU 'primeices Erenn'; AI 'ardfile Herend 7 senchaid'; AB 'priméches Erend'; LC 'prímh-éigess Erenn'; MB 'prince poet of Ireland, a great chronicler and one to whome for his sufficiencie the causes of Ireland were written to be examined and ordered'; FM 'primh-écces Ereann, & saoi-senchaidh'.[23] All of these entries accord Cuán the highest

---

21 For example Ware, *De scriptoribus*, 19; Kelleher, 'The Táin', 122; Ó Mórdha, 'Cuanu', 189–91. In particular Byrne, 'Ut Beda boat', 65–7, on the assumption that Cuana's use of the title 'rex Pictorum', cf. AU 628.4, was anachronistic hypothesized that 'Cuanu' was Cuanu Lugmaidh †825. But the title 'rex Pictorum' occurs 15 times elsewhere over AU 579–877, leaving no basis for this hypothesis. 22 Ó Riain, *Corpus*, *s.v.* 'Cuan', 'Cuana', 'Cuanu'. Mc Carthy, 'AU apparatus 82–1019', 279–80 (AU and *Corpus Genealogiarum* occurrences). 23 Annalistic orthography normally has this personal name as 'Cuan', O'Brien *Corpus genealogiarum*, 575–6 has 'Cúán' whereas Byrne apud Ó Cróinin, *New history* i, 860, 869, 877 has 'Cuán', which I follow. For poems

Plate 1 (*overleaf*). MS Bodleian Rawl. B. 502 f. 10ʳ was written at Clonmacnoise around the end of the eleventh century and represents our best example of the Annalistic genre near the climax of its monastic phase, and in particular note the fine writing and decoration on good quality vellum. In the fourth line of the left-hand column note the series of fourteen successive kalends ('K's) followed by the illuminated, enlarged 'M' of 'Maria' registering the birth of Mary. Lower, an enlarged 'S' emphasizes the start of the Sixth Age, followed seven lines lower by an enlarged 'K' recording the year of Christ's Incarnation. In the third line of the right-hand column an illuminated 'M' marks the obit of Cuchuland 'fortissimi herois Scottorum', and six lines below four successive 'K's are each followed by a ferial datum. The last two lines of this column record the obit of Archelaus, son of Herod. The kalends, ferials, Mary's birth, Sixth Age, Incarnation and Archelaus' obit are all inherited from Rufinus' chronicle, Cuchulann's obit was added by the Moville compiler, and additions taken from and attributed to Bede may be seen both incorporated into the main text and as marginal additions. Reproduced with the permission of the Bodleian Library, University of Oxford.

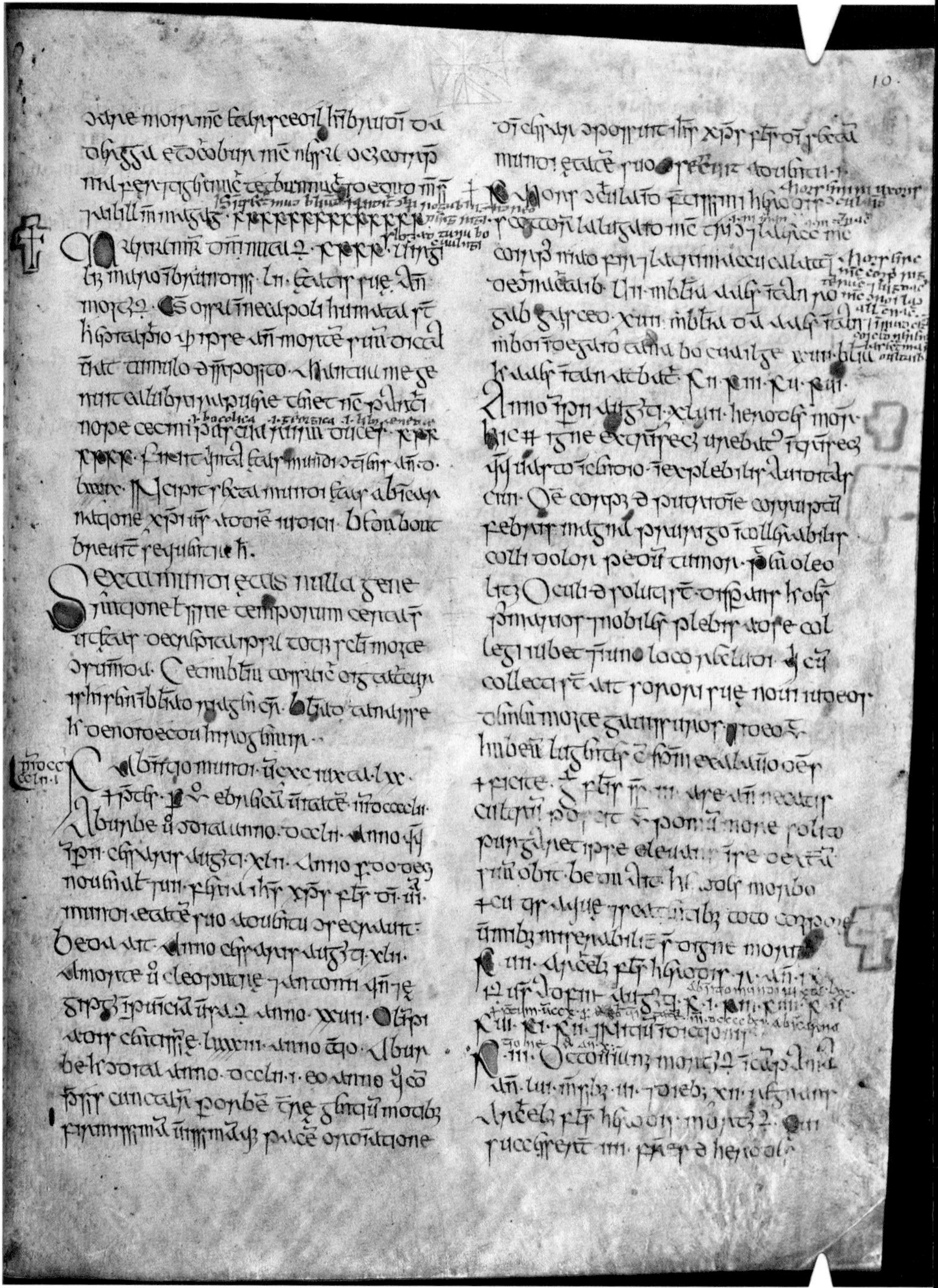

Plate 1

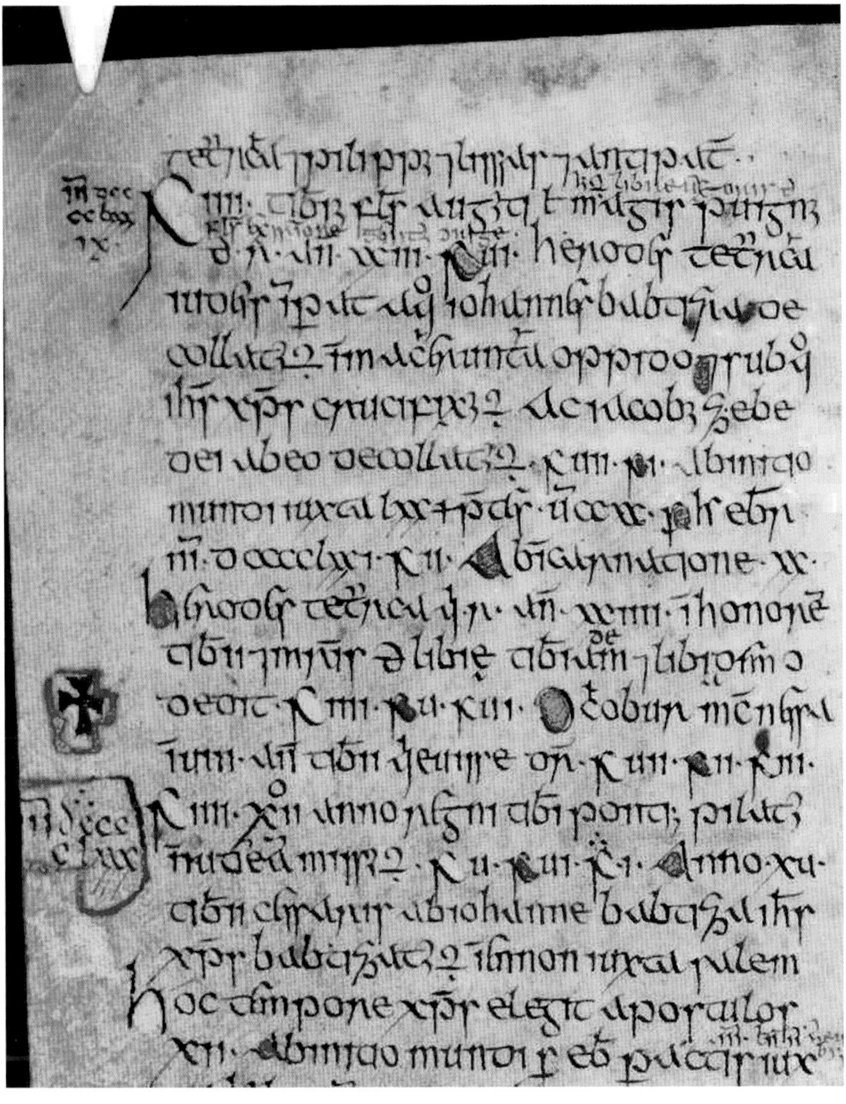

Plate 2. AT – Detail of MS Bodleian Rawl. B. 502, f. 10va for AD 15–28, cf. Stokes, *AT*, 38. Note the illuminated kalends 'K' followed by the ferial, paragraphing by enlarged, offset marginal capitals, punctuation by points, and the two marginal cartouches with Vulgate AM. The AM 3989 prefixed to the second line marks the reign of Tiberius, and like the interlinear addition is taken from Bede's DTR §270, cf. plate 3. The AM 3980 is linked by a '∴' to 'K.i.', the year of Christ's baptism, see also plate 1. Reproduced with the permission of the Bodleian Library, University of Oxford.

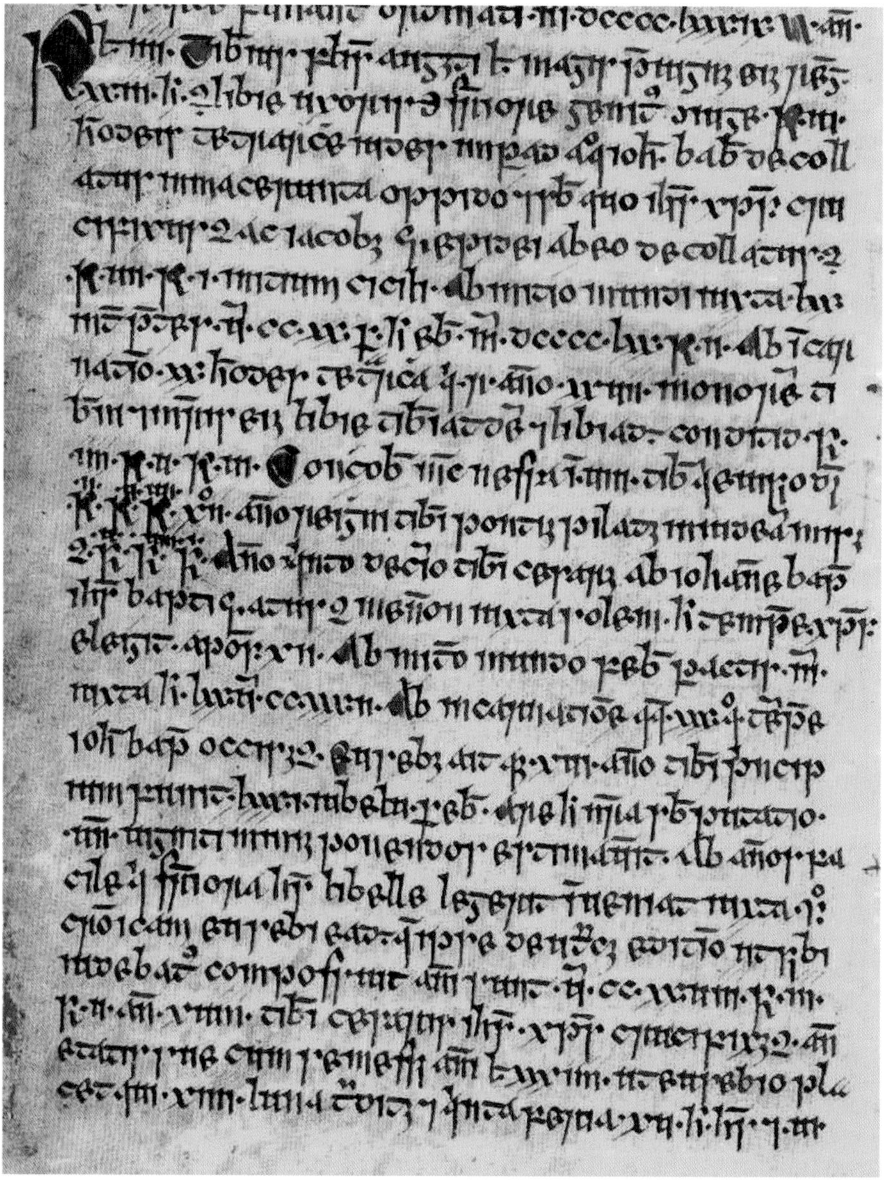

Plate 3. AT – Detail of MS Bodleian Rawl. B. 488, f 3ra for AD 16–33, cf. Stokes, *AT*, 38–9. The excerpt begins at the reign of Tiberius and so parallels that of plate 2. Decorated kalends and paragraphing remain but the text is much more dense with less ornament. Collation with plate 2 shows numerous textual variations including lost kalends, and also that interlinear passages and marginal AM from Bede's DTR cap. 66 are now incorporated. The last three lines register the Crucifixion and note the lack of emphasis suggesting a secular context. Reproduced with the permission of the Bodleian Library, University of Oxford.

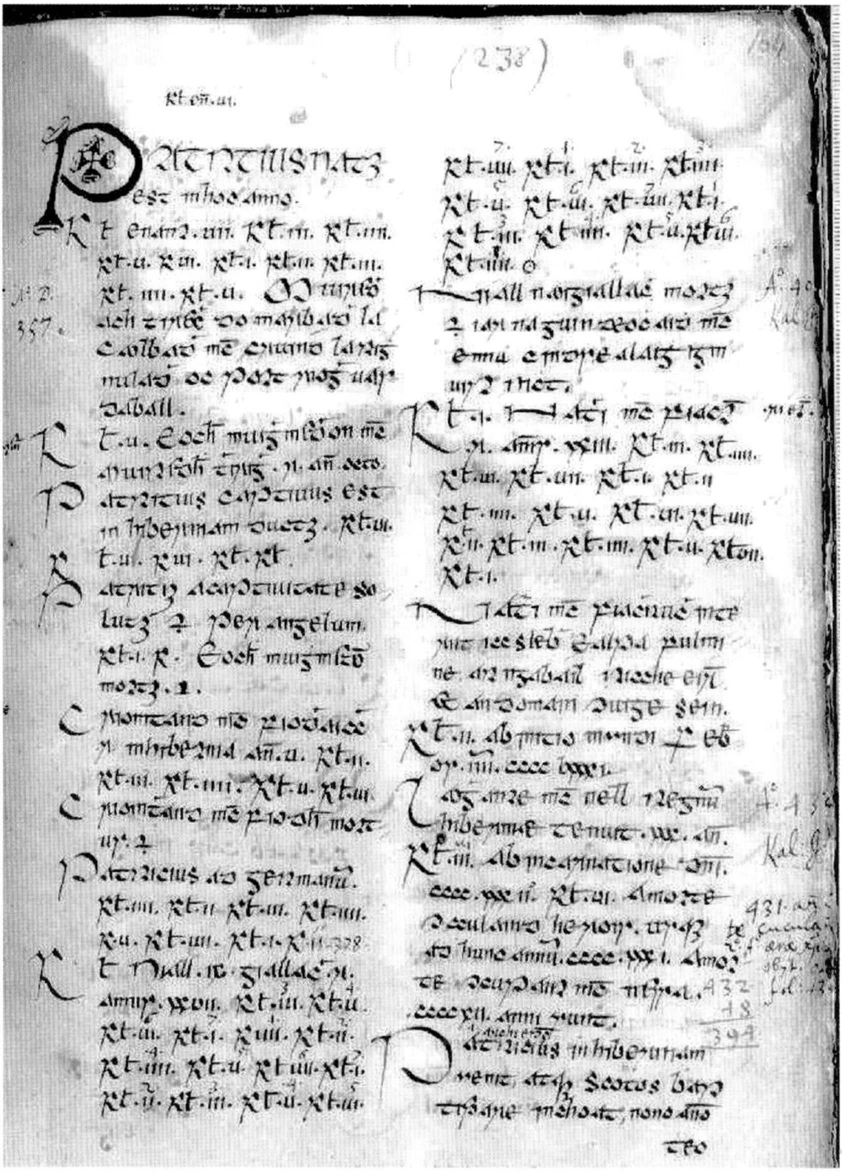

Plate 4. CS – TCD 1292 f. 164ʳ for AD 336–432 written by Dubhaltach Mac Fhirbhisigh *c.*1640. Note the text in two columns, the kalend+ferial chronological apparatus, the large, decorated initial of 'Patritius', the frequent paragraphing defined by enlarged offset initials, and Roderick O'Flaherty's marginalia. Reproduced with the permission of the Board of Trinity College, Dublin.

a) 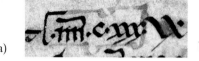 b)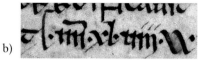

c)

Plate 5. Details of MS. Rawl. B. 488:

a) A cartouche at f. 4^va1 in black and red ink surrounding the AM ·iiii*m*·c·xxx·

b) An incomplete cartouche at f. 4^ra5 preceding the AM ·iiii*m*·xl·u*iii*·, where the first scribe has drawn the left-hand end '[', but the illuminator even while rubricating the double strokes has failed to complete the central and right-hand parts of the cartouche.

c) An excerpt from f. 19rb for AD 1088 showing the notice of Tigernach's authorship and his obit on the third line. Note the character '[' with which the scribe commenced the entry, which thus represents the left-hand end of a cartouche in his exemplar and which, like that in b), was left incomplete by the illuminator. The entry has been highlighted by the marginal index hand of a later annotator. Reproduced with the permission of the Bodleian Library, University of Oxford.

Plate 6 (*opposite*). AR – Bruxelles Bibl. Royale 5301–20 p. 123 (olim p. 27), cf. Gleeson & Mac Airt, AR §16–29. Phase one – note O'Conor's generous margins and line spacing, and his flowing, cursive script. Phase two – with a finer nib and writing more rapidly he ·has added chronological criteria in the left-hand margin, beginning, ' eodem anno cum preced^ti', followed by his summation of ferial data, '43, 45, 51, 58 …'. Interlinearly he has added the non-Irish entry 'Pelagius P*a*P*a* natione Romanij sedit annis xi diebus 8.' Phase three – following the completion of his transcription he has collated his text with FM and added two references to 'Quat. Mag.' in the upper right margin, and a *floruit* for Brendanus 'iuxta Gordonum' in the bottom margin. In the top right-hand corner his bold pagination '27' was written above his cancelled foliation '14', beside which is the modern pagination '123'. MS 5301–20, p. 123 copyright Bibliothèque royale de Belgique, Bruxelles and reproduced with their permission.

eodem anno mors bcc onc & Prophete.

Quæ Mag. referunt mortem Cronthani huius Ao 547

eodem eti ano Mors Cptuumacani mc bprhn
—i. in hunc mundu

hub heg li K. 43 Natuitas mo lca mc hr octo
fait 43.

heg hub K. 45 Catbat m frzza Epus Acard crn R. 20.

Hanc referunt Quæ z Magri ad an. Roi 548, germuit

Centesimo . l . anno ætatis suæ obiit

1 hub heg K. Pelagius PP nasc Romanus sedit annis 71 diebz

eodzcupd. Jhm colmayn tori

8 heg 6 K. koc mc bach hr dar ann.

eodem anno nisrau te prror z pausat

hub heg K.   Jugulao colmayn more mc dignuta
            in cuuu suo odrbloto hnr iptica
            Eua Brauchoyn fundata e

hub heg K.   Vpeanynd eua am e trana fra fundauit

eodz anno   Ascensio Vpeanzm in cuuu suo in acie.

hub heg K.   Cena postrema tlmpu la dignaroo mc
            cogboll

Brandanus flo. An. 560 mctu Gerdomi

taidg umail ruanaid dudallud kł uefedf
fot .i. Grrac iðubneoil .kł. Bliaðai natcatan
nida .kł. Mathelage ðoipoð aeðiarmair mic
ricaða . Mʒ mic felan rnarurail rmic mŭc gor
mai ðumarbuð leffiŭ rmic gilli mo colmo cðu
dalluð fof leir . Gʒ xł ii. Conftructio meʈ .kł
Conċub ualbai arð mumán .m.ʒ. Anno ðũi
co icarnatioi .G.ʒ.xł. iii. kł Murcað uamail
feʒ . ðeugabail latordelbac uacóċub irigimidr
ðurabairr ðucóċub ðanic. Gilla engula ua
clumai olluʒeres .m.ʒ. kł Conċubra mctor
delbaic ucóċub ri mიდi .o.ʒ. kł Anu abi
uo mundi . Ai ccc xł iii. kł Tigernan ua
ruairr guloclong ubi ocūð grʒp ii fula fueri
yef cóbulir. Maiðm nacleri arā luði kł ʒa
Bualað righnai uruairr rco flac rordelbaic
uóċub . kł Malacias uamongau legarʒ
rcd hibΒ rig uir feiffimʒ mulril miraclir icla
raualle irʒ deu . Abbia ðebuellio h ano fun
ðaraʒ . Aʒʒoð ominico icaʒ .G.ʒ. xł uii. kł
kł . Maurici uaðubrhaiʒ rdeyf onacre ii.ʒ. q.
Oðnall mc mic ðonaill uóċub .o.ʒ. Adaiʒ fia
caire ʒfa ðuibe

Plate 9 (*opposite*). AB – BL Cotton Titus A. xxv, f. 22ᵛ cf. AB §325–36. Note the single column in an Anglo-Norman hand, distinctive kalends, unique orthography, enlarged initials coloured green in the MS emphasizing the obit of 'Conchubur mac Tordelbaich u Conchubuir' and the foundation of 'Abbatia de Buellió', both of which are immediately followed by additional chronological data. Reproduced with the permission of the British Library.

Plate 10 (*overleaf*). CT – RIA 1219 (C.iii.1) f. 66ʳᵃ⁻ᵇ cf. CT 1478–81. In column a scribe B completes the entries for 1478 in traditional Annalistic style, cf. plates 1–3. Scribe C follows writing uniformly-sized script with no offset capitals, and indenting the first three lines of each year to the right, thus leaving space for an oversize 'K', never completed. Note the missing 'K's at 1480 and 1482, while those at 1479 and 1481 were added by Charles O'Conor according to Freeman. Reproduced with the permission of the Royal Irish Academy © RIA.

1479

1479

148

Plate 10

Plate 11 (*overleaf*). LC – TCD 1293 f. 11ᵛ cf. LC 1057–61. Note the single column of uniformly written text, except for the enlarged 'K' of each 'Klł' preceding the year identified as 'a.ın.t.', i.e. 'aois in Tigerna'. The entries for each year are written continuously with a blank line between successive years, and on the last line may be seen Pilip Ua Duibhgeannáin's interjection, 'Is im sgítheach do barc briain mhic diarmada. .A°.D°. 1589 Misi pilip badł'. Reproduced with the permission of the Board of Trinity College, Dublin.

Plate 12 (*opposite*). MB – BL 4817 f. 56ʳ cf. MB 105c–106b for AD 658–61. Note the two ruled columns, with Mageoghagan's AD apparatus and annotations of significant persons and events entered in the left-hand column, and the clearly paragraphed entries in the right-hand column. At the top the heading identifies the current kings of Ireland and the folio number. Reproduced with the permission of the British Library.

56

Flidibor kinge off ffrance died

656. Fynian mc Rivta Bushop died. Colman of Gleannida-
logh died. and Danill of kingary died
Cahagh mc Blathmac son off L. Hugh Slane died
Conel fron davona died. Eoanan mc Tuahallain died
Foylan kinge off Ultey was killed by the Leinstermen
Aillill mc Donogh mc Hugh Slane, died

657. Comyn abbott and Bushop off Aedmagh, died.
Comyng o Daint abbott of Imleagh Ivor, died.
Comyn abbott came to Ireland this yeare
Magopec mc Slawa, died

658. Comyn Foda in the seaventy two yeare of his age, died
Sagan o eigh   Sant Saran mc Credan died
raptain.
Moylowyn sonn off Hugh Breaman died
The battle off y Gawyn att kinorbadan, when Conyng
mc Conoyle mc Hugh Slane was killed and Ultam
mc Ernany kinge off kinnaghty was fought, in which
kinge Blathmarko was quite overthrowen by y the
army off Diermott mc Hugh Slane, and Duchowe
mc Saram were the thiefe actors.
Moynvagh mc Fynin kinge of Mounster, died
Scanlan Abbott of Louth, died

The generall Co   The generall Councell off Constantinople was held
uncell of Consta   onder Pope Agatho. and Constantine the kinge, and
ntinople.
was the Siath Oniversall Synod consisting off one
hundred and fiftie Bushoppes, wch there assisted together

1   The first generall Councell was the Nicene in the
Cittie of Bithinia, where there was a Congregation off
three hundred and eighteene fathers in the time off
Pope Julius against Arrius in the presence off
Emer Constantine.

2   The Second in Constantinople off one hundred
and fiftie fathers against the heresies of Macedon=
=ius

Plate 12

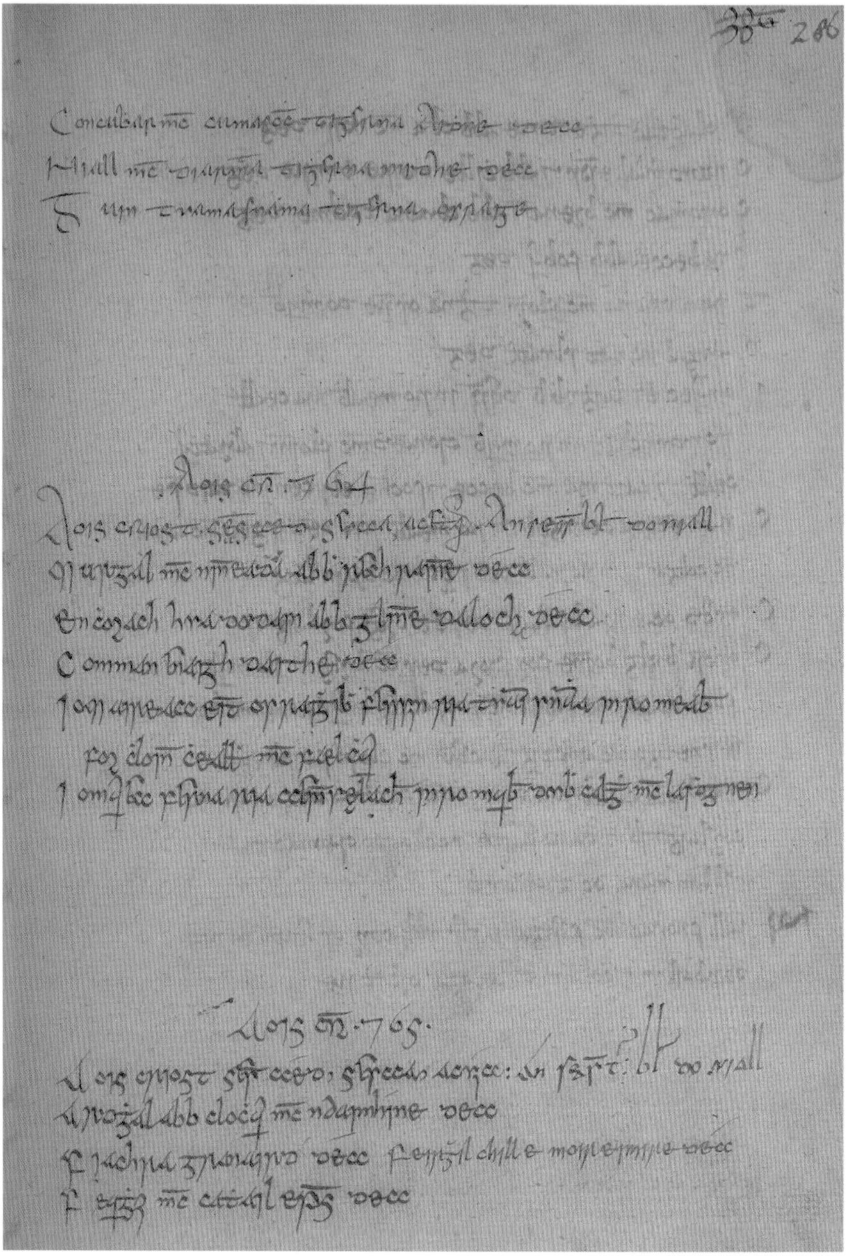

Plate 13. FM MS C – RIA 1220 (C.iii.3) f. 286ʳ for AD 763–5. Written in a single column with substantial space left between years. The chronological apparatus 'Aois Chriost' is indented and written first in Arabic numerals then in Irish words followed by the year of the current king of Ireland. Each entry commences on a new line with an offset capital. The scribe here is Conaire Ó Cléirigh with an addition by Mícheál Ó Cléirigh on the second last line. Reproduced with the permission of the Royal Irish Academy © RIA.

intellectual status on a national level, some specifically describing him as a 'historian (*senchaid*)', a 'chronicler' and a corrector of the 'causes of Ireland'. Cuán is also known outside of the Annals from his poem on Tara and his tract 'Geasa agus Buadha Riogh Eireann', which is prefixed to *Leabhar na gCeart*. According to O'Donovan Cuán was, 'chief poet to Maelseachlainn (Malachy) II, monarch of Ireland, who died in 1022. After the death of this monarch … we are informed that Cuan O'Lochain and Corcran Cleireach were appointed governors of Ireland'[24] It is certain then from these survivals and accounts that Cuán was indeed a successful poet and author, and politically an extremely powerful man. The Annalistic descriptions of him are all appropriate to record the death of a man who had but recently compiled a national chronicle reaching from Adam to *c.*1019, and for all of these reasons I propose that Cuán was indeed the author of Liber Cuanach, which he completed shortly before his murder in 1024. Indeed, when one considers the controversial character of his pre-Palladian chronology and his revisions to early Irish Christian chronology, it would not be surprising if it were these that precipitated his murder. Regarding the matter of why subsequently Ua Caiside referred to him as 'Cuana', the Annalistic references to the emperor Conrad II as 'Cuana' and 'Cuanu' themselves suggest an explanation. For when the annalist chose to render the 'Con' element of Conrad by the then long archaic forms of 'Cuana' and 'Cuanu', he clearly considered these forms both appropriate and respectful of the emperor and his office. I suggest that, likewise, in order to express respect for the man and his compilation, the archaic name 'Cuana' was used to identify Cuán Ua Lothcháin, and thus his book was identified using the corresponding genitive 'Cuanach'.

The descendants of Liber Cuanach

The discussion of manuscripts in chapter 2 has already supplied brief justification for placing AU, AI and AB in the Cuana group, and now having established the range, chronological apparatus and character of Liber Cuanach we are in a position to enlarge on those discussions. The purpose of the following is, therefore, to outline the relationship between the chronological apparatus and entries of these surviving texts to the structure and content of Liber Cuanach. Additionally, for AI and AB I shall provide a short account of what is known of their sources and history after 1019.

Regarding AU, the chronological apparatus of its surviving pre-Palladian section is our best witness by far to Cuán's work, and the relatively small

---

attributed to him see: Gwynn, *Metrical Dindsenchus*, i 14–26, 38–, iii 286–90, iv 30–4, 42–56, 146–62; Todd, *Cogadh Gaedhel*, 54–6; Best et al., *Book of Leinster* i, 144–54; Meyer, 'Mitteilungen', 21–3. I am grateful to Bart Jaski for all of these.   24 O'Donovan, *Leabhar na g-Ceart*, xlii (cit.), xlii–xlviii (Cuán Ua Lothcháin), 2–25 ('Geasa agus Buadha'); cf. Murphy, *AC*, 173a; Petrie, 'Tara

number of scribal errors show that it has been accurately transmitted. On the other hand the historical accuracy of this apparatus is so conspicuously in error, it is truly remarkable that it was still being copied nearly five centuries after Cuán's compilation. One senses that this was out of respect for the authority of Cuán Ua Lothcháin rather than the material itself, for it is noticeable that Mageoghagan's seventeenth-century obit for him has very considerably expanded the account of Cuán's accomplishments. Regarding AU's post-Palladian apparatus, it is evident that its kalend+AD series for AU 431–1012 accurately reflect Cuán's compilation, whereas AU 1014–19 represents a subsequent correction to his work. Likewise all the ferial and epactal data inscribed by Ua Luinín at AU 872–85, 939–42, 954–5, 999–1019 are later corrections, as are Ua Caiside's intermittent ferial, epactal and AD inscriptions over AU 486–1012.[25] Thus in AU much of Cuán's post-Palladian ferial+epactal series has been either deleted or corrected.

Regarding AU's pre-Palladian entries, an important point to note is its loss of nearly all the imperial regnal series, for the few surviving entries deal mainly with the Christian aspects of imperial affairs. However, these occasional survivals, together with the fact that AI transmits a virtually continuous imperial series, some of which AU retains, e.g. AU §158, 160 record Constantine's death and the subsequent rule of his sons, show that Cuán had retained most of the imperial series from the Clonmacnoise chronicle. The longer and older versions of these are still found in AT. Turning to AU's post-Palladian entries we find a more complex situation. We know that Ua Caiside restored some entries from Liber Cuanach, and this alone proves that Ua Caiside's primary source transmitted an incomplete version of Cuán's compilation. We also know that Ua Caiside supplied entries from other unidentified sources which he acknowledged with interjections such as 'alii libri dicunt'. Almost certainly he also interpolated further entries without adding any identifying interjection. Thus there is the problem of distinguishing Ua Caiside's interpolations from Liber Cuanach with those he took from other sources; possibly systematic evaluation of the entries' name orthography may help separate these different origins. However, it is not likely that Ua Caiside's restorations and additions extended far beyond AU 642 at which point interjections *in prima manu* such as 'ut alii dicunt' effectively cease. Furthermore, from the mixture of orthographical ages of the entries in AU from the fifth to the seventh centuries identified by Ó Máille, it appears that over 432–654, as Cuán chronologically relocated entries from the Clonmacnoise chronicle, he also sometimes emended their orthography using forms distributed in date from the sixth to the tenth centuries. However, after

---

Hill', 143–9 (Cuán's poem on Tara).   **25** Mc Carthy, 'AU apparatus 82–1019', 271–2 (ferial, epactal & AD data).

Cuán had restored his last kalend at AU 653, from the fact that the sequence of AU entries nearly always corresponds exactly to that of the Clonmacnoise group, it appears that thereafter Cuán continued simply transcribing his selection of the entries of his Clonmacnoise chronicle source. This chronicle at that time clearly retained both Latin functional words and a contemporaneous name orthography, and these Cuán transcribed accurately into his compilation.

However, it is not the case that all AU entries hereafter simply derive from Liber Cuanach, for at least three categories of entries clearly do not. The first category consists of the large number of entries commencing at *c.*790 that refer to the affairs of Armagh, cf. Figure 27, p. 223. The second category comprises those entries commencing at *c.*908 which refer to Derry affairs. The third category consists of those entries from *c.*978 up to 1022 which refer to the affairs of Brian Bóruma and Máel Sechnaill, for examination shows that in AU these latter speak regularly more favourably of Brian than Máel Sechnaill.[26] Given that at the time of his compilation Cuán was poet to Máel Sechnaill, it is not plausible that he composed these entries in the form we now find them. These three categories are not the work of Cuán but of a mid eleventh-century Armagh compiler and a late twelfth-century Derry compiler, as will be discussed in chapter 8. On the other hand, that Cuán added an end chronicle in the tenth and early eleventh centuries relating to Meath, its kingship, and Máel Sechnaill seems virtually certain, but likely now to be mostly lost.

Turning to consider AI I first note that the only section of this work relevant to Liber Cuanach is that surviving part over Abraham–1092 written by the first scribe. Furthermore the textual evidence of some of the immediately following entries by the second scribe over 1092–4 indicates that the first scribe had completed his work by 1093.[27] Many modern scholars have remarked both the attrition of Iona chronicle entries and the emergence and eventual pre-eminence of entries with a Munster provenance, which Munster emphasis is first evident in the mid-sixth century and grows to pre-eminence in the early ninth century. Most scholars have also identified that the monasteries of Emly and Lismore feature prominently amongst these Munster entries, with the most comprehensive evaluation being the exemplary survey made by Grabowski.[28] This shows Emly pre-eminent amongst Munster monasteries in AI from its first entry at 708 until 1081, but with a detectable decline from *c.*1065 and Lismore prominent over 814–1092. Considered simply it might be thought that this long Emly pre-eminence could be used to argue that the compilation of AI over Abraham–1092 was undertaken in that monastery, and indeed Best did propose

26 Mc Carthy, 'Synchronization', remarks *s.a.* 978–1022. 27 Best & Mac Neill, *AI facsimile*, 9 and Mac Airt, *AI*, xxxii (first scribe completed by 1093). 28 Iona chronicle attrition, Munster/Emly/Lismore prominence: Best & Mac Neill, *AI facsimile*, 9, 26–9; Mac Airt, *AI*, xxii–vii; Hughes, *Early Christian Ireland*, 108–15; Grabowski & Dumville, *Chronicles*, 1–81.

this.[29] However, Mac Airt was the first to identify the serious obstacle to this hypothesis in that over 1080–9 there are five important Emly events that are missing from AI. A further obstacle clearly documented and identified by Grabowski is the emerging prominence of Killaloe relative to Emly over c.1065–85.[30] These observations together preclude the possibility that these latter decades of AI are simply the result of an Emly compilation. To these obstacles must be added the further observation by Mac Airt that for 'the period 1092–1130 the weight of this [provenance] evidence indicates Lismore [as the place of compilation]'. These considerations led Mac Airt to tentatively assume that 'the transcript (up to 1092) was made from 'Emly' documents to the order of the Lismore monastery.'[31] With this hypothesis Mac Airt envisaged in effect two compilation stages, the earlier in Emly followed by a 'transcript' made from this for Lismore. However, I submit that the resolution of the conflicting Emly-Lismore provenance evidence requires that there actually occurred two quite separate compilations in close succession, the first in Emly over c.1068–81 followed by a second in Lismore in c.1092. It was this latter that yielded Rawl. B. 503 ff. 1–29[rc] covering Abraham–1092.

The most conspicuous evidence for this earlier Emly compilation is the distinctive chronological apparatus over 1068–78 that consists of kalend+ferial+epact+AD criteria written predominantly in Irish with Latin intermingled. Here the kalend is always written linguistically mixed as 'Kl. Enair', the ferial as the weekday in Irish preceded by the particle 'for', and the epact as the Dionysiac lunar age in Roman numerals followed by 'furri/fuirri', e.g. AI 1068.1 'Kl. Enair for Mairt 7 .xxiii. furri'. The AD for 1068–69, 1073–78 is written predominantly in Irish but with the tens expressed in Roman numerals, e.g. AI 1068.1 'Ind ochtmad bliadain .lx. ar míle ó Inchollugud Crist', except for 1070–1 where it is written predominantly in Latin, e.g. AI 1070.1 'lxx. annus ar mile ab Incarnatione Domini', and AI 1072 where it is omitted. The fact that here these four chronological series are perfectly synchronized shows that their compiler possessed complete mastery over all of them. Moreover, this kalend+ferial+epact series in mixed Irish-Latin extends backwards to 996, with two further instances of the Irish 'ó Inchollugud Crist (from the Incarnation of Christ)' at 1032 and 1054, all series maintaining synchronism throughout. Prior to 996 the 'Enair' is omitted and the apparatus is written entirely in Latin, and prior to 973 the ferial+epact series become quite intermittent, but nevertheless these two series maintain synchronism right back to 779. Notwithstanding one additional and three missing kalends this apparatus also includes intermittent

29 Best & Mac Neill, *AI facsimile*, 9 'It is not improbable that this first portion [to 1092] was produced at Emly.' 30 Mac Airt, *AI*, xxvi (missing Emly events); Grabowski & Dumville, *Chronicles*, 83–4, 93 (Emly vs Killaloe). 31 Mac Airt, *AI*, xxviii (cits.).

but accurate Dionysiac concurrents, identifications of the first year of the Dionysiac cycle (*Initium circuli*) and two bare AD data.[32] The first point to note about this accurate chronological apparatus extending over 779–1078 is that it is clearly the work of a single compiler extremely competent in all aspects of the Dionysiac cycle. Second, it is important to note that it corresponds closely in extent with the pre-eminence of Emly entries over 708–1081 in AI.[33] The third point is that while employing the same four criteria in the same order as Liber Cuanach it has none of the latter's asynchronisms over this interval. The fourth point is that the distinctive Irish AD series 'ó Inchollugud Crist' comes to an absolute end at 1081.[34] Fifth we note that synchronized to this cessation of 'ó Inchollugud Crist' is the obit for the Emly lector, AI 1081.2 'Fland Cuilleain, fer legind Imlecha Ibair, quieui(t).' Thus at the very point at which an accurate apparatus co-extensive with Emly entries ceases we find an obit for an Emly man of learning. Now in AI the *fer legind* obits are distributed over a relatively narrow range of years, namely of a total of twenty-seven such obits twenty-two are over 1020–1122, and seventeen are over 1020–81. Thus the lives of all seventeen of these *fir legind* must have either intersected or immediately preceded that of Flann Cuilleain. Furthermore the predominant spatial distribution of the *fir legind* obits preceding that of Flann is significant, namely five Clonmacnoise, four Emly, three Armagh, and three Tuamgreney obits. For this distribution suggests that the Emly *fir legind* maintained relationships with their learned colleagues in both Clonmacnoise and Armagh, the two principal monasteries engaged in chronicling in the eleventh century. While the prominence afforded to the Tuamgreney *fir legind* suggests that Emly maintained a learned relationship with this monastery located on the west bank of the Shannon just about eight miles from Killaloe.[35] On the other hand not one Lismore *fer legind* obit is recorded in AI. Hence there is considerable evidence that over *c.*1068–78 Flann Cuilleain, *fer legind* of Emly, compiled a substantial chronicle of Munster and especially Emly affairs extending back to the mid sixth century. To this Flann fitted a continuous kalend and intermittent ferial+epact+AD apparatus extending accurately at least as far back as 779. That he embedded this Munster chronicle in Liber Cuanach is shown by their common ferial+epact series over AI 433–54, the textual and chronological characteristics for S. Brigit entries, and the Irish regnal series at AI §345–86 to

---

32 Mac Airt, *AI*, AI 804a (additional kalend); AI 827, 970–1 (missing kalends); AI 954, 963, 973, 977 (concurrents); AI 779, 798 (*Initium*); AI 963, 978 (AD), cf. xlii–iii (chronological criteria).   33 Mac Airt, *AI*, xliii remarks that notwithstanding kalend omissions 'the sequence of Kalends is fairly reliable after 704', cf. the first Emly entry at 708.   34 Entries employing the bare 'ó Inchollugud' are found at AI 1102–3, 1114, 1125–6, 1129, but these all show other significant textual differences from those over AI 1032–81.   35 Regarding the prominence of these Tuamgreney obits it is worth noting that Cormac Ua Cillin †966 was simultaneously chomarb of Clonmacnoise, Comáin and Tuamgreney thus linking all three monasteries.

be discussed below.[36] Now the five Clonmacnoise *fer legind* obits in AI extend over 1022–70, suggesting that Flann and his immediate predecessors had maintained a particularly close relationship with their colleagues in that monastery.[37] Indeed we note that Flann's employment of the Irish ferial+epact style synchronizes closely with its introduction into the Clonmacnoise chronicle by Tigernach Ua Braein, cf. chapter 6, p. 194 ff. Moreover, Grabowski has documented the presence in AI of Clonmacnoise entries extending as far as 1065, further suggesting that Flann maintained a working relationship with those responsible for the Clonmacnoise chronicle. This observation led Grabowski to conclude that:[38]

> ... the period 1068 to 1081 probably represents the beginning of that period when the Clonmacnoise-group text underlying AI was finally abbreviated and conflated with Munster sources, thus giving us AI as we know it today.

However, the abbreviation remarked here by Grabowski cannot credibly be attributed to Flann Cuilleain. In particular the omission of twenty kalends over 432–971 cannot plausibly be the work of a compiler who erected an accurate multi-series chronological apparatus extending over 779–1081. Indeed the omission of the two kalends at 970–71 alone would be sufficient to destroy the integrity of all the earlier part of that apparatus. Certainly the fact that the transition in the ferial+epact apparatus from intermittent to continuous is synchronized to these two omitted kalends suggests that the intermittency is the result of omission by a later compiler. Moreover, the ferial errors at AI 817, 874, 908, 931 are all clearly scribal in origin since in each case they involve the misreading of 'u' as 'ii'. These scribal and omission errors must therefore be assigned to the subsequent Lismore compiler who copied but certainly did *not* accurately transcribe the Emly compilation. This Lismore compiler, while writing 'an elegant symmetrical book-hand, clearly that of an expert scribe', plainly did not possess any of the chronological capabilities and interests of his recently deceased Emly predecessor, and he relentlessly abbreviated both the apparatus and the entries of the pre-Emly section over 432–*c*.700, frequently mutilating the sense of entries.[39] Given his own affiliation it is likely he that inserted the solitary seventh-century Lismore entry registering its foundation at AI 638,2. And similarly that he subjected the later Emly entries over *c* 1068–81 to attrition so that over this interval Killaloe entries now predominate.[40] This succession of a constructive compilation in Emly followed by a reductive

---

36 Mc Carthy, 'AU apparatus 82–1019' 274–6 (AI's apparatus); idem, 'S. Brigit', 258–63, 281 (Brigit entries).   37 Mac Airt, *AI*, AI 1022.5, 1034.6, 1038.2, 1054.6, 1070.7 (Clonmacnoise *fir legind* obits).   38 Grabowski & Dumville, *Chronicles*, 62–6 (AI/AT/CS common entries), 66 (cit.).   39 Best & Mac Neill, *AI facsimile*, 5 (cit.).   40 Grabowski & Dumville, *Chronicles*, 83–4, 93 (Emly/Killaloe entries).

compilation in Lismore satisfactorily explains the omission of important Emly events over 1080–9, already mentioned, and concerning which Grabowski perceptively observed:[41]

> These important omissions from AI's entries on Emly would seem to rule out the possibility that the extant manuscript of AI was written at that house. They do not, however, rule out the possibility that an Emly source, including Clonmacnoise-group entries, is incorporated in AI.

Grabowski also made pertinent observations regarding the synchronous distribution of the 'ó Inchollugud Crist' apparatus and Killaloe entries, and the appearance of briefer entries over *c.*1065–92. However, because she unfortunately truncated her discussion at exactly 1092 she did not perceive or identify the abridging influence of the subsequent Lismore compiler, but instead tentatively proposed a transfer of the chronicle from Emly to Killaloe in *c.*1068.[42]

Regarding AI's pre-Munster section it does retain one further chronological component which I consider to derive from Liber Cuanach, and that is its list of Irish kings whose reigns intersected Christianity in Ireland. This list, AI §345–86, is located immediately before the commencement of the reign of the first of these kings, that of Loegare mac Neill, and it is preceded by a heading enclosed originally in a red cartouche and reading, 'Nunc de regibus Hiberniae ex tempore Patricii incipit.'[43] It lists the durations and names of the holders of forty-two reigns, which series concludes with the nine-year reign of Máel Sechnaill who died in 1022. Thus the chronological range of this list is precisely in accordance with it having been compiled by Cuán in *c.*1022, following Máel Sechnaill's death.[44] That Cuán, who in 'Geasa agus Buadha Riogh Eireann' was in a position to prescribe duties and rights for the high king of Ireland (*rig Erend*), should also have compiled a list of the historical holders of that high kingship, is surely appropriate.[45] This regnal list does not appear in TCD 1282, our best MS for AU, but as one folio has been lost between the pre- and post-Palladian annals it is not possible to be certain whether it was omitted by the compilers, or has since been lost on the missing folio.[46]

Regarding AI's entries prior to the regnal list at AI §345 it must be acknowledged that there is no compelling evidence that they were taken from Liber Cuanach. For none of the extensive ferial+epact+AM apparatus of AU is found, nor the duplicate Incarnation and Crucifixion entries, nor the

41 Grabowski & Dumville, *Chronicles*, 84 (cit.).   42 Grabowski & Dumville, *Chronicles*, 86–7, 93 ('inchollugud', Killlaloe, brief entries & tentative hypothesis of an Emly to Killaloe transfer). 43 Mac Airt, *AI*, 42–4 (regnal list); Mc Carthy, 'AU apparatus 82–1019', 276–7 (cartouche). 44 However, Bart Jaski has pointed out the possibility that since Máel Sechnaill had no agreed successor as high king this termination may just reflect that reality.   45 Mc Carthy, 'AU apparatus 82–1019', 280–1 (Geasa).   46 Mc Carthy, 'AU compilation', 88–9 (regnal list & missing folios).

additional 253 kalends between AD 254 and 431. In these circumstances and given that the Emly compiler had access to the Clonmacnoise chronicle entries up to 1065 it seems much more likely that the pre-Palladian section of AI derives directly from the Clonmacnoise chronicle. Indeed this joint source may explain the duplicate *Patricius uenit* entries in AI where that at AI §390.1 is cognate with CS 432.1 and is followed by 'Finit', whereas that at AI §391.3 is cognate with AU 432.1 and is preceded by 'Kł. Enair'. In this pre-Palladian section the Clonmacnoise world history entries have been generally retained, although in common with the post-Palladian AI entries inherited from Liber Cuanach these have been regularly severely abbreviated by the Lismore compiler, sometimes resulting in serious loss of sense. For example, AI §216 '[Gaius Caligula] regnauit annis .iii.^{bus} 7 Agripa Iudeos', has omitted both Gaius' *name*, and that Agripa *ruled* the Jews *for seven years*. On the other hand many Irish pre-history entries have been abandoned in AI. In contrast to this after 432 it is the world history entries that have been substantially abandoned in AI and only severely abbreviated versions of Liber Cuanach's Irish entries have been transmitted, commonly just one entry per year up to c.720 after which Munster entries progressively displace entries from Liber Cuanach.[47] A particularly diagnostic entry is AI 721.2 where a destructive incursion into Meath by Cathal m. Finguine and Murchad m. Brain, and exactions of tribute and hostages on Leinster by Fergal m. Maile Dún, cf. AU 720.6, 8 and AT 721.3, 5, have been conflated into an attack on Meath by Cathal alone, now entitled *rí Muman*, and a consequent submission to him by Fergal, now entitled *rí Temrach*. This conflation is followed by an anachronistic list of five Munster kings, including Cathal, alleged to have ruled Ireland (*.u. rig ro gabsat Herind iar cretim*). Since all but one of these five kings belonged to the Eóganacht Glendamnach in whose territory Lismore lay it seems clear that this uncharacteristically prolix eighth-century entry was the work of the Lismore compiler, showing that he brought a polemical agenda to his compilation.[48] In the following years AI transmits a diminishing number of Liber Cuanach entries, though occasional entries from it survive as late as the tenth century.

As regards AI's post 1092 textual history Seán Mac Airt has given the best account of the relationship of AI's entries to the principal monasteries and dynasties of Munster, and I can do no better than to summarize his conclusions here. He concluded that after the compilation had been continued in Lismore over c.1093–1130 the recording location had moved westwards in Munster,

---

47 Grabowski & Dumville, *Chronicles*, 96–100 list all AI-unique entries in full, and they generally average about five per decade or more from 720 to 769; from 770 onwards they average over ten per decade. Nearly all these unique entries relate to Munster. 48 Byrne, *Irish kings*, 172–3 (Eóganacht Glendamnach territory), 293 (Eóganacht Glendamnach kings), 177 (Emly controlled by Eóganacht Airthir Chliach), 208 (discusses AI 721.2).

possibly but by no means certainly to the monastery of Inisfallen. However, he considered the entries over 1280–3 as 'original, being made at Inisfallen perhaps in 1284', and the entries for 1325–6 on the final folio to be 'the work of Inisfallen scribes'.[49] It seems likely that it was the prominence of these later entries at the end that prompted Ware to misguidedly assign the title 'Annals of Inisfallen' to this chronicle. In view of the conclusions derived above a title such as 'Annals of Emly-Lismore' would more accurately describe the work.

Next I consider AB's chronological apparatus, which, since it lacks any reference to Palladius, must be referred instead to Patrick. In the pre-Patrician apparatus we find the following distinctive features: kalends repeatedly presented in groups of nineteen, e.g. AB §1–13; intermittent 'Kl' suffixed with 'eñ'='enair', e.g. AB §2 'Kl.eñ'; intermittent ferial data suffixed with 'f'='feria', e.g. AB §4 'Kl.eñ.iiii.f'; very occasional Dionysiac epacts prefixed by 'l'='luna', e.g. AB §24 'Kl.iª.f.l.xx.'; intermittent AM prefixed to the kalend, in the earlier part mostly given at intervals of nineteen kalends, for example:

AB §7: 'dxc.ix.Kłeñ.kkkkkkkkkkkkkkkkkk.dcxv.iii.Kłeñ.kkkkkkkkkkkkkkkkkk.'

AB therefore presents a sample of all of the elements of Cuán's pre-Palladian chronological apparatus in a textual arrangement corresponding very closely to that found in AU. As well, Cuán's interpolated Incarnation 'secundum Dionissium' is found at AB §93, practically verbatim with that of AU §96. However, in AB this entry has been relocated back to the time of Augustus, the other three Incarnation entries have been deleted, and all of Cuán's 253 interpolated kalends have been removed. Indeed since AB §126–8 register events spanning AD 180 to 337, i.e. 158 years, and only eight kalends separate these entries, it is clear that the deletion of Cuán's interpolated kalends was taken much too far. Furthermore Cuán's use of Dionysius' name to confer orthodox status on his chronology has been sustained, with intermittent AM synchronisms attributed to him; for example, the first of these, AB §91 'Anni ab initio secundum Dionisium vM.clxxxviii', is located twelve kalends before the AB §93, 'incarnationis Christi secundum Dionisium'. Since the cited AM 5188 plus the twelve kalends locates this Incarnation entry at AM 5200, it is apparent that it is actually a Septuagint AM that has been introduced at this point, and four more such follow at AB §96([Passion]), §147(S. Martin), §162(S. Patrick), §280(Brian Bóruma). This Septuagint AM dating does not of course come from Liber Cuanach, but represents a later interpolation by the Boyle compiler. The post-Patrician apparatus following Patrick's *uenit* at AB §144 consists of an incomplete sequence of kalends, the aforementioned intermittent AM 'secundum Dionisium', a solitary AD 800 at AB §243, intermittent AD from 1013 to 1081, and then from 1148 onwards AD accompanying events associated with Boyle itself. Thus in post-Patrician AB Cuán's ferial and epactal series have been completely abandoned, and his AD series nearly so, and only the kalend series retained, and, just as in AI, the integrity of this kalend series has been badly damaged.

Regarding the entries of AB, in 1998 Kari Maund made a comprehensive examination of the world history entries, and I have collated all its entries for AD 1–740 against the other annals.[50] Commencing then with the pre-Patrician entries we find that where we have AU, viz. from AD 82 to 387, that AB registers virtually the identical sequence of entries, as Maund also noted, requiring therefore that the two texts must closely derive from a common source.[51] This is useful as it helps us to fill out our view of both the extent and the character of the material lost from pre-Palladian Liber Cuanach. In particular AB shows us that Cuán's compilation extended back to Adam and that his AM, kalend, ferial and epactal series all commenced from there.[52] Most of AB's earlier pre-Patrician world history entries derive ultimately from the Iona chronicle, so that the discussion of chapter 4 identifies the relevant sources; unfortunately here most of Maund's conclusions rest upon the *Bedan-source* hypothesis and hence are unsustainable. However, Maund did demonstrate a textual relationship between some AB entries and passages in Iohannis Beleth's *Summa de ecclesiasticis offices* written in *c.*1150.[53] Although the parallel passages themselves would allow for borrowing in either direction Maund simply assumed that AB's compiler had drawn on Beleth. However, with Marianus Scottus working earlier on the Irish Annals in Cologne, Fulda and Mainz, the possibility that Beleth borrowed from the Annals needs to be examined.[54]

AB's post-Patrician entries represent a relatively small sample of those found in AU and some few are found only in the Clonmacnoise group, but no comprehensive study of their inter-relationships exists. However, sample collation of entries indicates that up to 1200 the readings and semantic content of AB's common entries usually correspond most closely with AU, as might also be expected from the close correlation of their pre-Patrician entries. The following collation represents the typical relationship:

> AT 560.1: Cath Chuile Dremni for Diarmuid mac Cerbuill. Forgus ⁊ Domnall, da
> mac Muirchertaig maic Earca, ⁊ Ainmiri mac Sedna ⁊ Nindidh mac
> Duach ⁊ Aed mac Eachach Tirmcharna ri Connacht uictores errant per
> orationem Coluim cille dicentis ...

50 Maund, 'Cottonian annals', 153–76 (world history entries); Mc Carthy, 'Synchronization', *s.a.* 1–740. 51 Maund, 'Cottonian annals', 166, 'AU*p* and AB are very closely related.' 52 Mc Carthy, 'AU compilation', 92 (use of AB to judge material lost from AU). 53 Maund, 'Cottonian annals', 158, 165–6, 171–5 (Beleth). 54 Verbist, 'Marianus Scottus', 284 (worked at Cologne, Fulda and Mainz over *c.*1056–1082).

AB §180:   Cath Culi Dremne for Diarmait mac Cherbaill. Fergus 7 Domnall da
mac Erca 7 Ainmere mac Setnai 7 Nainnaid mac Duach et Aed mac
Echach rí Condacht uictores errant per orationes Coluim Chille.

AU 560.1: Bellum Cuile Dreimne for Diarmait mc. Cerbaill. Forggus 7 Domnall, da
mc. Mc Ercae, 7 Ainmire mc. Setni 7 Nainnid m. Duach uictores errant, 7
Aedh m. Echach ri Conacht. Per orationes Coluim Cille uicerunt.

Here, while AB has the principal word 'Cath' of the Clonmacnoise group, its
name orthography is generally closer to that of AU; it is noteworthy though that
AB does not share AU's misplaced 'uictores errant'. Whilst this correspondence
is typical it is also the case that intermittently AB has entries now found
otherwise only in the Clonmacnoise group.[55] Furthermore, over 1179–86
occasional world history entries suddenly appear unkown in other annals, cf. AB
§365.2, 367.4, 369.3, 371.6, 372.4. These considerations then suggest that it was
the Armagh-Derry[+] chronicle, to be discussed in chapter 8, that served as the
principal source for the compilation of the Boyle annals, to which the compiler
has added Cistercian, Boyle and world history end chronicles.

At what date was this Boyle compilation made? When the entries referring
either explicitly to Boyle or to Cistercian events in the later twelfth century are
isolated, we find the entries shown in Figure 26.

AD	AB Boyle/Cistercian entries
1148:	Abbatia de Buellió **hoc anno** fundata est. **Anno dominice incarnationis Mcxlviii.**
1153:	**Eodem quoque anno** sanctus Bernardus .i. abbas Clare Uallis quieuit. … **Anni dominice incarnationis Mcliii.**
1161:	Abbatia Buellensis **hoc anno** fundata est iuxta Buellium. **Mclxi. Ab initio uero mundi viM.ccclx. Primo** incepit esse apud Grellach da Iach. **Secundo** apud Druim Connaid. **Tertio** apud Bun Finni. **Quarto** apud Buellium. In primo loco **primus** abbas Petrus úa Mórda fuit. In secundo Aed ua Maccain **per duos annos. Post** eum Marucius in eodem loco **per vi annos** et apud Bun Finni **per duos et dimidium.** In Buellio uero abbatisauit **xiii et dimidio.**
1174:	Murgius ua Dubtaich **primus** abbas Buelli 7 **tertius** secundum antiquitatem domus quieuit.
1195:	Flórint mac Ríagain ú Máilrúanaid **tertius** abbas Buellí et **postea** Elifinensis episcopus quiet in Christo. **Anno dominice incarnationis Mcxcv. Ab initio uero mundi viM.cccxciiii.**
1197:	Conchubur mac Diarmata rí Mugi Luirc et Artig apud Buellium in habitu monachali mortuus est.

Figure 26. A chronological list of all AB entries that either explicitly cite Boyle (*Buellium*),
or Cistercian events following the foundation of Boyle in 1148. Interjections implying
retrospectivity are shown in bold.

55 Mc Carthy, 'Synchronization', *s.a.* 485, 510, 520, 525, 533, 564, 584, 613, 630, 636 for AB entries

As can be seen these entries all employ Latin, except for names, and all except the last entry include elements clearly identifying that the entries were composed retrospectively. As well, the distinctive phrases 'Anno dominice incarnationis' and 'Ab initio uero mundi' are repeatedly used to specify AD and AM synchronisms with these Boyle events. These chronological formulae are also found at 1013, 1046, 1086, 1142, 1145, 1153, 1156, 1157, 1167 attached to the obits of leading dynasts, or conflicts involving them. There are then excellent grounds to conclude that all these entries were composed by a single author after 1195, the date of the last entry showing retrospectivity. Regarding how much later, there is no indication of contemporaneity in the entries over 1196–1200, and unfortunately a lacuna then interposes over 1201–23. However, when the annals resume at 1224 the entries are written in very distinctive Irish, and these indeed appear to be contemporaneous and they remain so until the first hand ends at 1228, after which the provenance moves to nearby Holy Trinity monastery in Loch Cé. I conclude therefore that the Boyle compilation was made sometime between 1201 and 1223. The magnificent abbey church at Boyle was consecrated in 1220, and the most likely scenario is that these annals were prepared around that time in order to memorialize those abbots who had played leading roles in the enormous undertaking of establishing Connacht's first Cistercian abbey.[56] A date of *c.*1220 also accords well with the issues arising from the entries common to AT and AU over the later eleventh and twelfth centuries as will be discussed in chapter 8, p. 233 ff.

The situation following the change of hand at 1228 in BL Cotton Titus xxv, and the transfer of the provenance of the annals to nearby Holy Trinity in 1229 is very interesting, for the entries of these and some following years again show clear signs of retrospectivity as follows: AB 1228 'isin bliadain sein'; 1229 'eodem anno' and 'in fine eiusdem anni'; 1231 'eodem anno'; 1232 'hoc anno'; 1234 'isin bledin sen'. It appears from these interjections that, following the conflict between the two monasteries in 1229, the transcription of the Boyle annals made in that year was brought to Holy Trinity, but writing was not resumed until after 1234. When it did resume it is noticeable that the scribe who wrote the extended account of the conflict of 1229 wrote Latin in a style closely resembling the earlier Boyle entries. Thus it may well be that the compiler of the original Boyle annals departed in 1229 to Holy Trinity with a transcript made under some pressure as discussed in chapter 2, with the result that our text exhibits both late chronological errors over 1224–7, and some remarkable omissions. For example, the obit of both the second abbot of Boyle, and abbot Maoil Breanainn †1225 were omitted. Thus it appears that *c.*1235 this compiler

only otherwise found in the Clonmacnoise group over 431–642; this represents about one entry every twenty one years.   56 Freeman, *AB*, §299, 328, 335, 339, 343, 347, 360, 369, 379, 381 (Cistercian

220

helped to bring the text up to date. In summary then, the annals in AB up to 1228 represent entries compiled in Boyle some time in the early thirteenth century, probably *c.*1220, using principally the Armagh-Derry chronicle, combined with an end chronicle of Cistercian and Boyle material recorded over 1179–1228. The remaining AB entries over 1229–57 represent entries compiled in Holy Trinity over *c.*1235–57.[57]

Regarding the possible identity of this Boyle compiler there is one conspicuous obit in AB after 1235, namely:[58]

> AB 1236: Aed O Gibelláin, sacerdos of Cell Rotáin and finally a canon of Trinity Island, mortuus est, at Christmas and was waked in the choir that night until the next day's Mass, and buried honourably on that day.

Now the funeral details given in this obit are quite remarkable, and they are nearly all repeated in CT 1236.20 and LC 1236.32, so Aed was remembered into the sixteenth century at least. While nothing in the obit suggests that Aed was learned, it is the case that obits of subsequent bearers' of this name are remarked for their learning; at LC 1287.2 'Floirint .H. Gibeallán, airchideochain Oilefinn, feallsom fessa ⁊ eoluis ⁊ intlechta, ⁊ chleirchechta, quieuit in Cristo', and LC 1328.12 'Muiris .H. Gibillan, ard maigistir Eireann a ndlighidh nua ⁊ a sendligidh, h-i canoin ⁊ i lex, fellsom fesa agus fireolais … in Cristo quieuit.' Thus there are some grounds to propose that Aed Ua Gibelláin may have been a member of a learned Connacht family and thus a possible compiler of the annals of Boyle in *c.*1220 and subsequently in Holy Trinity in *c.*1235 just prior to his death in 1236; certainly following his death the Latin style of the earlier Boyle entries does not recur. Obviously this is a speculative identification, but nevertheless one I consider worth making in the hope that further research into Uí Gibelláin history will serve to either confirm or to reject the hypothesis.

In summary, examination and comparison of AU, AI, and AB helps us to reconstruct something of the character and extent of their common source, Liber Cuanach. In the pre-Palladian era it is necessary to effectively take the sum of their respective chronological apparatus and entries in order to appreciate the scale, complexity and idiosyncrasy of Cuán's compilation. In the post-Palladian era, in each case in the centuries prior to and beyond the conclusion of Liber Cuanach in *c.*1019, we find that each text incorporates entries reflecting the provenance of its later compiler. Munster material in the case of AI, Connacht and Cistercian material in AB, and Derry and Armagh material in AU as will be discussed in chapter 8.

---

and Boyle entries).   57 O'Dwyer, 'Annals', 84–7 discusses the relationship between AB (Cotton Titus xxv) and its exemplar.   58 Freeman, *AB*, 382 (translation).

Summary of the evolution of Liber Cuanach

In this chapter, based upon examination of the thirteen Cuana entries in AU and a critical comparison of the chronological apparatus and content of AU/AI/AB I have derived the following sequence of events:

Circa 1022 – Cuán Ua Lothcháin compiled Liber Cuanach from the Clonmacnoise chronicle introducing nineteen-year Dionysiac epacts and with an AM+kalend+ferial+epact apparatus over Adam–Palladius. From Palladius onwards he substituted for his AM an AD which he referred to his additional Incarnation entry 'secundum Dionissium' located at AD 254, and he interpolated 253 additional kalends over 254–430 to synchronize his post-Palladian apparatus. This together with Cuán's revision of the Clonmacnoise chronicle chronology over 431–664 gave Liber Cuanach a severely perturbed chronology over much of 254–664, and his omission of one kalend over 612–64 antedated all his AD data over *c*.664–1019.

Circa 1050 – Dub dá Leithe †1064, abbot of Armagh, used Liber Cuanach as his principal source together with Armagh material over *c*.790–1050 to compile the Armagh chronicle, retaining most of Liber Cuanach's idiosyncratic chronological features, see chapter 8.

Circa 1068–81 – Flann Cuilleain †1081, *fer legind* of Emly, embedded a substantial Munster end chronicle in Liber Cuanach, substituting his own accurate kalend+ferial+epact apparatus from 779 onwards and his AD as 'ó Inchollugud Crist' from 1068. He and his predecessors evidently maintained a relationship with learned colleagues in Clonmacnoise and Flann drew his pre-Palladian and post-1022 entries directly from the Clonmacnoise chronicle.

Circa 1092 – A Lismore compiler severely abridged Flann's Emly compilation, omitting numerous kalends and entries and regularly mutilating others. This Lismore compilation survives as Rawl. B. 503 ff. 1–29^{rc} and constitutes the first section of AI.

Circa 1093–1130 – AI was maintained and extended in Lismore.

Circa 1130 – AI was moved to west Munster, perhaps to Inisfallen, and continued there to *c*.1326.

Circa 1220 – A Boyle compiler, possibly Aed Ua Gibelláin, compiled a chronicle for the abbey using an expanded recension of the Armagh-Derry chronicle as his principal source, to which he added Cistercian and Boyle end chronicles.

Circa 1229 – A copy of the Boyle chronicle was made that suffered from some omissions of chronological apparatus and abbatial obits over its last few years.

Circa 1235–57 – The copy of the Boyle chronicle was brought to Holy Trinity monastery and extended over 1229–34 and then continued incrementally up to 1257. This work survives as BL Cotton Titus A. xxv and constitutes AB.

CHAPTER EIGHT

The Armagh and Derry chronicles

The Armagh chronicle and Dub dá Leithe †1064

Even a cursory examination of AU discloses that it contains many entries that refer to the church of Armagh and its affairs, and this together with the known importance of that church has prompted some scholars to suggest that a chronicle had been maintained there.[1] To consider this matter I will first examine the distribution of those entries that refer explicitly to Armagh or its personnel, then the level of detail presented by some of those entries, and finally the significance of interjections found in the text. From Mac Carthy's index for AU *s.v.* 'Ard-Macha' we find over three hundred references to entries that mention Armagh over 500–1250, and when these are ordered chronologically their cumulative count provides a measure of the distribution of the coverage of Armagh recorded in AU. When this count is plotted against AD the steepness of the plot provides a graphic indication of the intensity of the coverage of Armagh, cf. Figure 27.

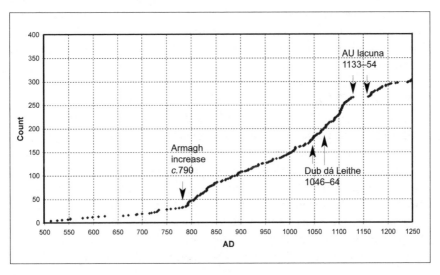

Figure 27. Plot of the cumulative count of AU entries referring explicitly to Armagh or its personnel for AD 500–1250 as registered by Mac Carthy AU iv pp. 20–4, versus AD.

1 Armagh chronicle: Mac Niocaill, *MIA*, 21–4; Gwynn, 'Cathal Mac Magnusa', 376.

As can be seen the coverage of Armagh over 500–750 is very moderate with just twenty-eight entries in 250 years, an average of one entry about every nine years. But at *c.*790 a profound change occurs and thereafter there is intense coverage of Armagh reaching at times a rate greater than one entry every year, which intense coverage is sustained up to AU's lacuna of 1133–54, and then continued until *c.*1200. After this a steady decline is observed until a complete cessation of Armagh entries is found over 1216–39, and thereafter they become quite intermittent with twenty five entries over 1240–99, three over 1300–99 and eleven over 1400–99. In summary Armagh receives a detailed coverage in AU extending over *c.*790–1200, after which it declines to a cessation at 1216, and then resumes intermittently from 1240. This sequence may be compared with the corresponding coverage for Clonmacnoise which extends effectively over *c.*753–*c.*1227, cf. Figure 20, p. 173.

Regarding the level of this coverage there are many exceptional details found in these Armagh entries of which I will instance just one, the terms employed in AU to designate Armagh clerical offices. Namely the terms, *ab/abbatis/ abbas/abbad/apadh, equonimus, princeps, tanuse abad, adbur abbad, airchinneach, fos-airchinnech, sacart/sacerdos/sacardd, secnap, uasal sacart, episcopus/espoc, uasal espoc, ardespuc, comharba/heredis Patrici, primaith, fer leigind, ard-fer leigind, scriba, sapiens, ard-ollam, toisech m. leighinn, anchorita,* are all applied in AU to Armagh ecclesiastics.[2] Whereas only the terms: *abbas, airchinnech, equonimus, comharba, fer leighind, uasal-shaccart* are applied in AU to Clonmacnoise clerics. Since Armagh and Clonmacnoise were monastic institutions of comparable scale one would expect a comparable system of office designations, so that this remarkable diversity of Armagh terms of office alone suggests that these entries were compiled in Armagh.[3]

Next I list in Figure 28 a series of interjections entered into TCD 1282 by both Ua Luinín and Ua Caiside which attribute entries to a certain Dub dá Leithe. First we note the textual correspondence of these interjections with the Cuana interjections viz., 'Sic in Libro Duibh da Leithi' vs 'Sic in Libro Cuanach'. Moreover, in this instance the interjections are written partly by Ua Luinin and partly by Ua Caiside, and consequently I suggest that evidentially they have a similar significance. Namely Ua Caiside first collated a chronicle he knew as 'Liber Duibh da Leithi' with his primary source and interpolated into this primary source some entries and interjections which Ua Luinín dutifully transcribed into TCD 1282.[4] Then subsequently Ua Caiside further collated

---

2 Pettiau, 'Armagh officials', 122–7 (review of Armagh offices).   3 Jaski, *Irish kingship*, 252, 254–5, 275 (*equonimus*), 60, 101, 116, 178 (*comarba*), 223, 252, 255 (*fer leighinn*); and *passim* for critical reviews of many civil offices.   4 Jaski, 'Psalter', 299 lists five tales in Rawl. B. 512 which also cite Liber Dub Dá Leithe as their source.

AU	Interjection	Hand and location
629.3	Uel sic in Libro Duibh da Lethe narratur: [Followed by a more detailed version of the battle of Leithirbhe than AU 629.1]	Ua Caiside in l.h. margin.
962.1	[Transport of ships to Loch Aininne]. Sic in Libro Duibh da Leithi.	Ua Luinín part incorporated, part r.h. margin.
1003.5	[The battle of Craeb Tulcha.] Sic in Libro Duibh da Leithi.	Ua Luinín in l.h. margin.
1021.3	[An emended detail of conflict in Lethderg.] uel sic in Libro Duibh da Leithi narratur. ['Aenaig Macha' emended interlinearly to 'uel Aird Macha'.] Sic in Libro da Leithi.	Ua Caiside in r.h. margin. Ua Luinín interlinear, and incorporated.

Figure 28. The interjections in AU that refer to 'Liber Duibh da Leithi', indicating also their scribe and textual status; cf. the 'Cuana' interjections given in Figure 23, p. 198.

this transcription with Liber Dub dá Leithe and added another two inter-jections. Second, the last interjection at 1021 appears verbatim in LC, and its text confirms the emendation of 'Aenaig Macha' to 'Aird Macha', suggesting that TCD 1282 and LC share a common source for that part of LC, cf. LC vs AU in Figure 38, p. 262. Third, Liber Dub dá Leithe extended at least over the range AU 629–1021. Fourth, regarding the identity of Dub dá Leithe, clearly his obit must postdate 1021, and the intensity of Armagh coverage illustrated in Figure 27 above, and the diversity of ecclesiastical offices employed both suggest an Armagh ecclesiastical association. The 'Duibh da Leithi' of these interjections was identified by Mac Niocaill as, 'doubtless the lector at Armagh from 1046 to 1049, and abbot (not without opposition) from 1049 to 1064', that is Dub dá Leithe mac Máel Muire †1064.[5] In support of Mac Niocaill's iden-tification we note that there is a significant increase in Armagh coverage synchronized to Dub dá Leithe becoming lector in 1046, cf. Figure 27 above. Furthermore, interjections located at 1040–1 provide convincing evidence that a compilation extending at least to 1041 was completed at about Dub dá Leithe's time. That at 1041 reads:[6]

5 Mac Niocaill, *MIA*, 20 (cit.). While Dub dá Leithe became abbot (*apdaine*) in 1049, from 1055 onwards he is described as 'comarba Patraic', giving him effectively an all-Ireland remit.
6 Hennessy, *AU* i, 579 took this interjection to refer only to the forthcoming entries of 1041, but

AU 1041.1: The events indeed are numerous, killings and deaths and raids and battles. No one can relate them all, but a few of the many are given so that the age in which the [various] people lived may be known through them.

This interjection clearly acknowledges the existence both of an abundance of records of death and conflict available to the compiler, and that he has only reproduced a sample of them in order to convey to his reader the general tenor of earlier ages. The other interjection is at the very beginning of 1040 wherein the Anno Domini has been reiterated, viz., 'AD 1040. This is the one thousand and fortieth year from the Incarnation of the Lord.' Both this and the subsequent interjection appear to be the work of a compiler nearing the conclusion of his protracted task, and explaining that he has not fully transmitted his sources on account of their prolixity. Finally we note that an earlier interjection at AU 1014.10 expresses in identical words a similar outlook on the large quantity of available material, viz.,'Numerous indeed are the events of this year.'[7] Thus there are compelling grounds on which to conclude that a substantial compilation extending to at least 1041 was completed at some date subsequent to that year. The synchronization of this compilation with Dub dá Leithe's *floruit* in Armagh, and with the increased coverage of Armagh affairs strongly supports Mac Niocaill's identification of 'Liber Dub da Leithi' with this man. I conclude therefore that sometime after 1041 Dub dá Leithe compiled a substantial chronicle representing the affairs of the people of Ireland, and especially the affairs of Armagh. The substantial increase in the Armagh coverage from the year of Dub dá Leithe's appointment as lector suggests that he likely undertook his compilation in *c.*1046, cf. Figure 27 above. Dub dá Leithe was a prominent member of Clann Sínaig, a powerful Armagh dynasty which possessed extensive territory about Armagh, and from at least the ninth century drew political and military support from their liaison with the northern Cenél nEógain. By 965 this family had achieved control of the church of Armagh and they filled the office of the 'successor of Patrick (*comharba Patraicc*)', in a virtually unbroken sequence from then until 1134. Thus the office was held in turn by Dub dá Leithe's great uncle, father, brother, himself, and then his nephews. These secular connections and Armagh's ecclesiastical possessions distributed widely across Ireland made Dub dá Leithe an extremely powerful political figure in eleventh-century Ireland. Regarding learning, Clann Sínaig provided a number of poets and authors of historical works, and actively supported the office of *fer léigind*, i.e. lector, and the school at Armagh. Dub dá Leithe himself held the office of *fer léigind* from 1046 to 1049, so that it is clear that as well as holding immense political power he was also a well-educated man.[8]

this cannot be reconciled to the reference to 'aesa na ndoene'. 7 Cf. AU 1014.10 'At imda tra airisi na bliadna-sa' and AU 1041.1 'At imdha thra na airisi eter ...'. 8 Ó Fiaich, 'Church of Armagh', 84–5 (Clann Sínaig), 87–95, 124 (*comharba*), 111–15 (scholarship).

Liber Dub dá Leithe vs the Clonmacnoise group to 1064

The aspects of Dub dá Leithe's compilation relevant to this present discussion are, what chronological apparatus and what sources did he employ for it? Regarding the chronological apparatus it is implicit that Dub dá Leithe used the apparatus of Liber Cuanach, but with its ferial, epact and AD data corrected from 1014 onwards. Regarding his sources it is clear from Figure 27 that Dub dá Leithe had to hand an Armagh chronicle, substantial in its coverage from *c.*790 onwards. It does not seem fruitful to spend time here speculating upon the form of that earlier Armagh chronicle, but it is worth noting that it had commenced less than forty years after the corresponding chronicle in Clonmacnoise. Regarding his treatment of this earlier Armagh chronicle it is important to note that examination shows that Dub dá Leithe occasionally edited these entries. For a simple example consider, AU 788.8: 'A quarrel in Ard Macha, in which a man was killed in front of the stone oratory.' The uncharacteristic anonymity of both assailant and victim here is in striking contrast to the precise location of the deed, suggesting that Dub dá Leithe has suppressed the identity of either or both protagonist, and we shall see further instances of his editing below. With regard to his use of Liber Cuanach, since this was based upon the Clonmacnoise chronicle we can form some view by examining his transmission of entries which referred to Clonmacnoise. Thus in Figure 29 are shown the cumulative count of AU's references to Clonmacnoise and the cumulative count of all available Clonmacnoise entries already plotted in Figure 20, p. 173.

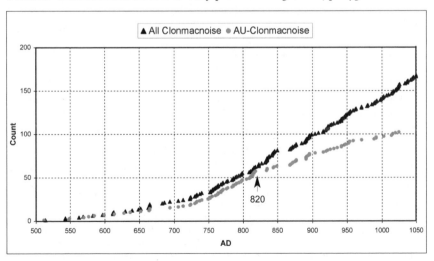

Figure 29. Comparative plot of cumulative counts of all Clonmacnoise references from AT/CS/AU/MB, and those found *only* in AU over AD 500–1050, based upon Mac Carthy *AU* iv, pp. 78–9.

As can be seen, up to *c.*820 Dub dá Leithe transmitted virtually all of the available Clonmacnoise entries, but thereafter he increasingly omitted them, so that by 1020 he had abandoned about forty percent of the Clonmacnoise entries likely to be available in Liber Cuanach.[9] Thus he significantly diminished the available Clonmacnoise representation in AU from the mid-ninth century onwards, and so ensured that Armagh entries substantially dominated his compilation. This observed reduction is also in accordance with his interjections at 1014 and 1041 remarking the prolixity of his sources and acknowledging that he had omitted some entries. In general, when considering entries found in common in the Clonmacnoise group and AU, scholars have believed that, 'their common substratum is preserved most faithfully within the compilation of the *Annals of Ulster.*'[10] However, Figure 28 and the interjection at 1041 show that Dub dá Leithe subjected his source material to substantial editing, and this then raises the question of in what other ways have his priorities influenced his compilation?

One simple index to a compiler's special interests is the length of his entries, and examination of this aspect of AU discloses a series of prolix accounts of battles beginning in the early tenth century, and culminating with the battle of Clontarf in 1014, which account is by far the longest of these entries. Collation of these with the Clonmacnoise group shows that they too have many of these entries but that, particularly in the early eleventh century AU often provides variant accounts and includes additional material, which suggests that these variants and additions are Dub dá Leithe's work. To explore this I examine those AU entries over 999–1014 which recount the expansion of Dál Cais power and consequent erosion of Ua Néill power. We first note that AU has a series of additions or unique entries which positively associate Armagh with the extension of Brian Bóruma's political hegemony. The first of these is in 1005 when both the Clonmacnoise group and AU agree that Brian left twenty ounces of gold on the altar at Armagh, but AU alone adds that Brian returned, 'bringing the pledges of the men of Ireland'.[11] The following year both assert that Brian brought his army via Tír Conaill and Tír Eógain to Bealach Dúin but AU alone adds that, 'the full demand of the community of Patrick and of his successor i.e. Mael Muire was granted'; the Máel Muire here is of course Dub Dá Leithe's father. Next in 1013 AU alone asserts that Máel Sechnaill, at the

9 Since Liber Cuanach was effectively a revision of the chronological apparatus of the Clonmacnoise chronicle, it is most unlikely that it was Cuán who abandoned so many of the later Clonmacnoise entries.   10 Smyth, 'Earliest Irish annals', 1 (cit.); cf. Byrne, *Irish kings*, 256 'the earliest annals, represented most reliably by the conservative *Annals of Ulster*'; Dumville, 'Latin and Irish', 320 'the *Annals of Ulster* ... [are] generally held to represent accurately the results of eight centuries or more of contemporary annalistic recording.'   11 It was apparently on this occasion that Brian's secretary, Máel Suthain, inscribed Brian's endorsement of Armagh's claim to Patrician churches (*totum fructum laboris sui*) on f. 16ᵛ of the Book of Armagh, at the same time adopting the title 'Imperator Scottorum' for him, see Gwynn, 'Brian in Armagh', 42–4 and Ó Cróinín, *Early medieval Ireland*, 291.

request of Máel Muire and Brian, 'made a raid on Conaille in revenge for the profanation of Patrick's *Finnfiadech* and the breaking of Patrick's staff.' Finally in 1014 AU alone states that, following the battle of Clontarf, 'Mael Muire … with his venerable clerics … brought away the body of Brian … the body of his son Murchad, and the head of Conaing and the head of Mothla, and buried them in Ard Macha in a new tomb.'[12] These AU-unique additions or entries positively identify the church of Armagh, and specifically Máel Muire, Dub dá Leithe's father, with the expansion in Brian's political hegemony into the northern half of Ireland. Furthermore, the common entries in the Clonmacnoise group and AU regularly exhibit subtle differences which in AU support the favourable Ua Briain perspective asserted by the abovementioned AU-unique entries. For example, the Clonmacnoise group state that in 999 a great victory over the foreigners of Dublin and the Laigin at Glen Mama was gained by both Máel Sechnaill and Brian, whereas AU 998.8 attributes the victory to Brian alone. The following year both the Clonmacnoise group and AU record the emergence of aggression by Brian towards Máel Sechnaill, and it is revealing to fully collate these two accounts together as shown in Figure 30.

AT 1000.8[13]	AU 999.7
Sluaigedh la Brian mac Cendeitigh ⁊ la Descert Chondacht co n-Osraigi ⁊ co **Laignib** ⁊ co n-**Gaillaib** Atha cliath do thorachtain Temrach acht do-chotar na Goill cath marcshluaigh **rompo a Magh m-Breagh conus-tarraidh Mael Sechlainn** ⁊ tucc a n-ár. **Do**-deachaidh **Brían** iarsin co m-bái a **Ferta Nemi a Muigh regh**, ⁊ luidh foro **chulu cen cath cen índrudh** cen daigh n-derg.	**Slogad la Brian** co **Ferta Nime** i **Maigh Bregh**. Do-lotar **Gaill** ⁊ **Laigin** crech **marcach rempu i Magh Bregh conus-taraidh Mael Sechlainn**, ⁊ pene omnes occisi sunt. **Do-luidh Brian** tra **fora chulu cen chath ce(n) indriudh,** cogente Domino.
A hosting by Brian, son of Kennedy, and by the south of Connaught, with Ossory and Leinster and the Foreigners of Dublin, to proceed to Tara. But the foreigners with a battalion of cavalry went before them into Magh Breg, and (there) MaelSechlainn overtook them and slaughtered them. Brian afterwards marched on till he was at Ferta neme in Mag Breg, and he went back without a battle, without ravaging, without red fire.	Brian made a hosting to Ferta Nime in Mag Breg. The foreigners and the Laigin, with a raiding party of horsemen, came before them into Mag Breg, and Mael Sechnaill came upon them, and they were nearly all killed (*pene omnes occisi sunt*). Brian then retreated without giving battle or making incursion – by the Lord's insistence (*cogente Domino*).

Figure 30. Parallel collation of AT and AU's account of Brian's hosting to Ferta Nime in 1000 showing all common passages in bold and AU's Latin passages repeated in the translation in parentheses and highlighted in italic.

12 Mac Airt & Mac Niocaill, *AU*, AU 1004.7, 1005.4, 1012.1, 1014.2, 1020.5 (Máel Muire citations).
13 CS and FM correspond closely with AT, and MB gives a summary translation of these.

Except for the Latin phrases indicated in AU, these two narratives contain many verbatim elements in Irish, but they present radically different accounts of events. AT and CS, supported by MB and FM, represent that Brian had formed a major alliance to attack Tara, which attack he abandoned upon Máel Sechnaill's successful destruction of the preliminary cavalry party, whereupon Brian simply visited Ferta Nimhe and then withdrew. AU however represents that Ferta Nime was actually his destination, identifies no alliance between Brian and the foreigners and Laigin, is ambiguous regarding who was killed in the conflict, and credits the Lord with dissuading Brian from battle. Thus while the Clonmacnoise group and AU agree that Brian withdrew from conflict with Máel Sechnaill, the former represents the withdrawal as a consequence of Máel Sechnaill's military success, whereas AU's first Latin passage makes that success ambivalent, and its second Latin passage attributes the withdrawal to divine influence. In particular it should be noted that the two phrases responsible for the principal contradiction between the two accounts are AU's Latin intrusions into the Irish. I conclude therefore that here the Clonmacnoise group provide a cogent, consistent narrative, and that AU shows clear evidence of deliberate emendation by an author intent on obscuring the details of Brian's intended act of treachery against Máel Sechnaill. As such these emendations are consistent with the AU-unique entries concerning Brian, and I propose that they are all the work of Dub dá Leithe. They show that Dub dá Leithe was determined that his compilation should record Armagh's mutually favourable relationship with Brian, and express its approval for Brian's military and political achievements, but wished to tone down the record of conflict between Brian and Máel Sechnaill. The need for these emendations arose because Dub dá Leithe's primary source for the conflict, Liber Cuanach, consistently expressed Clonmacnoise's more favourable attitude towards Máel Sechnaill. I have spent considerable time examining these Máel Sechnaill-Brian Bóruma entries because they disclose to us both that Dub dá Leithe was engaged in making major emendations to his source material, and also something of his methods.

These conclusions raise a serious question with respect to all those other entries found in common between the Clonmacnoise group and AU, as to which version most closely represents their common source? As noted above, hitherto AU's preponderance of Latin and more conservative name orthography have been taken to infer that its entries best represent the common source. However, in fact neither Latin nor conservative name orthography guarantees the semantic integrity of annalistic entries, and Dub dá Leithe's deliberate use of Latin to emend the meaning of an entry means that AU's Latin cannot safely be taken as a index of its reliability.[14] I turn now to review the wider textual and

AT/CS/FM add an interjection remarking that this was Brian's first revolt (*cét-impodh*).
14 Dumville, 'Latin and Irish', 320–41 (survey of Latin in AU).

semantic relationship between the entries common to the Clonmacnoise group and AU. Collation of the common entries of AT/CS/AR/MB/AU shows that up to 911 we may make the broad generalization that they all nearly always agree upon the semantic content of *parts* of the same original source text. That is, while they have all *lost* parts of entries, there has been no systematic *addition* of text to their entries. Regarding language, AT/CS regularly transmit high frequency words in Irish, e.g. *bas, cath, mac, ri*, whereas from 431 onwards AU usually transmits such words in Latin. However, collation with AR shows that at an earlier stage in its history the Clonmacnoise chronicle likewise had such words in Latin. The following entries recording the battle of Magh Cuilinn in 703 illustrate both the phenomena of partial transmission, where words in square brackets identify lost text, and translation to Irish shown in italic:

AT 703.1: *Cath* Campi Cuilínd a n-Aird Hua n-Echach *eter* Ulltu 7 Briton[es ubi cecidit] filius Radhgaínd, aduersaries ecclesiarum Dei. Ulaith uictores erant.

CS 703.1: *Cath Maighe* Culinn in Aird Ua nEcdach, inter Ulltoibh et Britones, ubi cecidit filius [Radgaind] aduersarius ecclesiarum Dei. Ulaidh uictores erant.

AR §161: Bellum Campi Cuilinn [in Airdd nepotum nEchdaigh] inter Ultu et Brittones [ubi cecidit filius Radgaind aduersarius ecclesiarum Dei.]. Ulaid victores [errant].

AU 702.1: Bellum Campi Culind i nAirdd nepotum nEchdaigh inter Ultu 7 Britones, ubi filius Radhgainn cecidit, [aduersarius] eclesiarum Dei. Ulaith uictores erant.

MB 111d: The battle of *Moy*gullyn [in Ard ua nEchdach] was fought between Ulster and Brittans where the sonn of Ragainn the adversary of the Church of God was slaine and Ulstermen victors.

While all five sources have lost parts of the original entry, with AR losing over half the text, it is AR which confirms that the common source of the Clonmacnoise group was originally in Latin, viz. 'Bellum Campi Cuilinn'. Thus we see that it is AU which has most accurately transmitted the original entry, and up to 911 this is often the case. However, there are also many exceptions to this, so that no general pronouncement regarding the 'original' form of an entry can be convincingly made without collating *all* of the available texts. The exceptions are often entries that refer to the affairs of Clonmacnoise and Armagh monasteries and to the activities of Uí Néill kings, and the following account of internecine Uí Néill conflict illustrates the typical character of Dub dá Leithe's emendations:

CS 868.6

AU 867.4

Cath Cille h. nDaigre re nAodh <u>Finnliath</u> <u>mac Nell</u> <u>ri Teamrach</u> 7 <u>re Concupar mac</u> <u>Taidg rí Connacht .i. uiii. Id. Septembir</u> oc Cill h. nDaigre for Aibh Nell Breg 7 for Laignib 7 for slúgh mór do Gallaibh .i. tri ced no ní as uille; <u>coig míle do Flann</u> <u>mac Conaing</u> 7 <u>aen míli d'Aedh Finnliath</u>; in quo <u>bello</u> ceciderunt Flann mac Conaing rí Bregh uile et Diarmaid mac Eidirsceli rí Locha Gabar et Gaill iomdha do marbadh ann 7 Factna mac Maeiliduin rigdomna an Fhochlai do-rocair a frithguin an catha.	Bellum re n-Aedh m. Neill oc Cill Oa n-Daighri for Ou Neill Breg 7 for Laighniu 7 for sluagh mor di Ghallaib, .i. tri cét *uel eo amplius,* in quo ceciderunt Flann m. Conaing rig Bregh n-uile, 7 Diarmait m. Etersceili, ri Locha Gabhor; 7 *in isto bello plurimi gentilium trucidati sunt* 7 Fachtna m. Maele Duin, righdomnai ind Fochlai do-rochair i frithguin in catha, 7 *alii.*

Here Dub dá Leithe's Latin translations are in italic and his omissions are underscored in the CS version. Regarding his Latin, the first and second passages render Irish passages, and his additional 'in isto bello' both replaces the 'bello' he omitted after 'in quo', and serves to emphasize the number of foreigners killed. Regarding omissions, his first reduces the proper name of Aodh, while his second omits Aodh's title 'ri Teamrach', and such proper name reductions and omissions of regnal titles occur quite frequently in AU. Following this he omits the participation of the Connacht king, Concobhar mac Taidg, thereby leaving the Cenél nEógain king, Áed mac Neill as the sole victor, which may be compared with his omission of Máel Sechnaill from the battle of Glen Mama in 999. Following this he omits the date of the battle and the tally of Fland and Áed's forces, thereby reducing the precision of the account. In summary, the identifying characteristics of Dub dá Leithe's editorial incursions before 911 are, brief Latin intrusions, reduction of proper names, omission of regnal titles and numerical details, and selective omissions of participants, and these are most likely to appear in entries referring to the affairs of the Uí Néill. However, sweeping generalizations regarding the relative value of the regnal entries of selected annals such as that of F.J. Byrne:[15]

> The Clonmacnoise annals and those which derive from them (notably the Four Masters) have been subject to interpolation from the official regnal lists which favour the Uí Briúin. The *Annals of Ulster* and the *Annals of Inisfallen* are uncontaminated ...

15 Byrne, *Irish kings*, 237 (cit., where no evidence whatsoever was adduced to support the assertion).

effectively represent just reiterations of the *AU-priority* hypothesis. Such simplified assertions have led historians to misjudge the Annalistic evidence, and I would emphasize that any serious enquiry must first fully collate all of the available witnesses in order to arrive at an informed conclusion.

At a per annum level an important property shared by all these sources up to 911 is that, except for AU over 431–543, their common entries are virtually always arranged in identical sequence.[16] It is thus evident that up to 911 Dub dá Leithe diligently transcribed his selection of entries from Liber Cuanach, preserving for the most part their orthography, semantic content, and sequence. However, in the following year, 912, a profound change takes place as may be seen by collating the text of the only entry AU has in common with the Clonmacnoise group for that year:[17]

CS 912.1

AU 911.3

Saruccadh Aird Macha o Cernacan mac
Duiligen .i. cimidh do breith as in
cill et a marbadh is Loch Cirr fria Ard
Macha anair. Cernachán do bádhadh
la Niall mac Aodha rig ind Oclai in
eodem lacu i ccinaidh saraigte Padraicc.

Cernachan m. Duilgein,
rigdomna na n-Airther, occisus est
in lacu crudeli o Niall m. Aedho.

The profanation of Ard-Macha by
Cernachan, son of Duligen, viz., a captive
was taken out of the church, and killed
at Loch Cirr, to the east of Ard-Macha.
Cernachan was drowned by Niall, son of
Aedh, King of the Fochla, in the same
lake, for the offence of the profanation
of Patrick.

Cernachán son of Duiligén, heir
designate of Int Airthir, was
killed in a cruel lake by Niall
mac Aedh.

The AU entry, which omits all reference to Cernachan's profanation of Armagh, is a very brief summary of CS, whose account is supported by those of MB and FM.[18] However, there can be no serious doubt but that Dub dá Leithe has deliberately suppressed this profanation, for his characterization of the lake as 'cruel (*crudelis*)' acknowledges that the lake held some additional but unexplained significance. He has however added the information that Cernachan was of Airthir royal stock, and this may well explain why he has

16 Mc Carthy, 'Synchronization', *s.a.* 1–911 (identical sequence); over 431–534 AU preserves the chronological revisions of Liber Cuanach. 17 Mac Airt & Mac Niocaill, *AU*, 359, and Hennessy, *AU* i, 424–5 (cits.); neither editor translated 'in lacu crudeli' both considering the text corrupt, but clearly the adjective 'crudelis' qualifies the 'lacus' in which Cernachán died. 18 Cf. FM 907.6 and MB 145a (Cernachan entry).

suppressed the crime because two of his nieces were married to the king of Airthir.[19] In a similar way Dub dá Leithe omitted Clonmacnoise entries recording acts of profanation by Brian in 977, and Máel Sechnaill in 986 and 988. In the six years following 912 the relationship between the common entries of CS/MB and AU sustains the change seen at 912 in that significant textual and semantic differences are found between common entries, and the order of these entries in AU differs, cf. Figure 5, p. 104. One of the principal reasons for the textual variation is the prominence accorded by Dub dá Leithe to the military career of the man who killed Cernachan, the Cenél nEógain king Niall mac Áeda †919. At 914 Niall is designated 'king of Ailech', and at 916, on the death of Flann mac Máel Sechnaill, 'king of Tara', and at 917 'king of Ireland'. In a series of twelve entries, those recounting his battles being very prolix and far exceeding the corresponding Clonmacnoise group entries, Dub dá Leithe has provided an account of Niall's regnal career which considerably exceeds in scope the parallel account in CS.[20] In places we find Dub dá Leithe's characteristic intrusion of Latin, for example for Niall's renewal of the fair of Tara in 916:

> CS 916.6–7: Níall Glundup, mac Aodha, regnare incipit. Oenach Taillten d'atnuaghadh la Niall.
>
> AU 915.5: Niall m. Aedha i r-righe Temrach 7 Oenach Tailten do aighe lais, **quodh multis temporibus pretermisum est.**

It thus emerges that the reason for the sudden change in relationship between the Clonmacnoise group and AU at 912 is that Dub dá Leithe shifted his attention from his regular transcriptions from Liber Cuanach to that of celebrating Niall's regnal and military career. At this point it may be as well to dispose of the possibility that this sudden change in the textual and semantic relationship between the Clonmacnoise group and AU at 912 could rather be the work of Cuán, and that Dub dá Leithe was simply copying from Liber Cuanach? However, the Armagh and Clann Sínaig sensitivities conspicuous in AU's emended account of Cernachan's death, at the very point of the textual departure, speak for an Armagh rather than a Meath compiler. Furthermore the fact that these selfsame Armagh sensitivities are still conspicuous a century later when Máel Sechnaill and Brian are under consideration, leaves no doubt but that Dub dá Leithe was responsible for the significant divergences between the Clonmacnoise group and AU over 912–1019.

Following Niall's death in 919 Dub dá Leithe gives a similarly expanded account of his son Muirchertach, from his first battle in 921 to his death as 'king of Ailech and Hector of the western world' in 943. Following Muirchertach's

---

19 Ó Fiaich, 'Church of Armagh', 89 (Dub dá Leithe's nieces and the king of Airthir). 20 AU 907.1, 909.2, 911.3, 912.6, 913.3, 913.6, 913.7, 914.3, 915.5, 916.3, 917.6, 918.3 (Niall's entries).

death Dub dá Leithe turns his attention in turn to celebrating the regnal careers of Niall's grandson Domnall mac Muirchertaigh 945–80, and then for 998–1014 Brian Bóruma, as discussed already. Neither is it difficult to see why Dub dá Leithe wished to celebrate these particular Uí Néill kings, for they were all of the Cenél nEógain, with whom Clann Sínaig had maintained a mutually constructive relationship from the ninth century. On the other hand the two high kings of Ireland who preceded Niall mac Áeda, Máel Sechnaill mac Maíle Ruanaid †862 and Flann mac Máel Sechnaill †916 were both Clann Cholmáin kings of the southern Uí Néill.[21] In this interval 912–1019 collation of the common entries shows that Dub dá Leithe continued taking entries from Liber Cuanach but repeatedly modified them textually. For example compare the Clonmacnoise account of Muirchertach's incursion into Leinster and Munster in 940 as given by CS and verified by MB and FM, with that in AU:

> CS 940.1: Sluaighedh la Donnchadh h. Maoileclainn et la Muircertach mac Nell co Laignibh is go fira Muman gur gabsad a ngíalla.
>
> FM 938.10: Slóigheadh lasan righ, Donnchadh, 7 la Muirchertach, mac Néill, go Laighnibh, 7 co Fiora Mumhan, co ro gabhsat a n-gialla.
>
> MB 151c: King Donnogh o'Melaghlyn and Mourtaugh m^cNeale went over all Munster and Leinster and took their hostages.
>
> AU 939.1: Slogad la Donnchad 7 la Muirchertach co Laighniu 7 co Muimnechu co tucsat a n-giallu dib linaibh.

Here as demonstrated earlier, Dub dá Leithe simplified the personal names and destinations, and he has added emphasis to Donnchad and Muirchertach's military success. However, in pointing out Dub dá Leithe's editorial contribution to the text of AU it should also be made clear that I have found no evidence of any substantial deliberate misrepresentation on his part, and the instance of Brian's intended treachery in 1000 discussed above is exceptional in my observation. Rather the hallmarks of Dub dá Leithe's editing are judicious omissions, ambivalence, and adjusting the tone of the narrative. While I have no information regarding the source of his additions to the regnal narratives it should be noted that with his grandfather Eochaid Ua Flannacáin †1004 a historian, and his great uncle, father and brother as *comharbai* before him, there is good reason to believe that Dub dá Leithe had access to the best of Armagh sources. Furthermore he was certainly skilful enough to make good use of them. Therefore in judging entries that Dub dá Leithe may have emended the principal issues to consider are his Armagh, Clann Sínaig and Cenél nEógain priorities.

---

21 Byrne, *Irish kings*, 282 (Clann Cholmáin kings), 284 (Cenél nEógain kings).

Regarding the relationship between the Clonmacnoise group and AU common entries after the termination of Liber Cuanach in *c.* 1019 and over Dub dá Leithe's lifetime, collation shows that up to 1064 typically around two entries per annum are in common, which are nearly all obits, cf. Figure 6, p. 106. Since each source has typically about ten entries per annum these common entries represent a significant percentage of both chronicles. However, the textual correspondence in the common entries is seldom protracted, often being confined simply to parts of the personal and place names, and when there are more than two common entries their sequences rarely correspond. To illustrate the character of the relationship I collate in Figure 31 the three entries with common textual elements found in AT and AU at 1041, with these common elements highlighted in bold.

AT 1041	AU 1041
1. **Muirchertach mac Gilla Patraic,** leith-rí Osraige, **do marbadh do h-Úib Caelaidhe** dia muintir fen per dolum.	4. **Muirchertach** mc. **Gilla Patraicc do marbad do h-Ui Chaillaidhe** a mebhail.
6. **Mac Ainmere aird**-bretheam **Aird Macha** 7 tuile eolais **Erenn** obít.	2. Mac Beathad m. **Ainmere** ard-ollam **Ard Macha** 7 **Erenn** archena.
7. **Gilla Comgaill mac Duind Chuan maic Dunlaing do breith ar eicin a Cill Dara** do Murcad mac Dunlaing, 7 **a marbadh** airm ar' saraigh comurba Brigde.	7. **Gilla Comgaill** m. **Duinn Cuan** m. **Dunlaing do breith a Cill Dara ar eicin** 7 **a marbad** iarum.

Figure 31. Parallel collation of AT/AU entries for 1041 showing common text in bold.

While there are significant textual correspondences, particularly in item seven, the sequence of these two series of entries do not agree, and there are also considerable textual and semantic differences between each entry. Thus it appears unlikely that these common entries found in AU over *c.* 1019–64 could be the result of Dub dá Leithe drawing either directly or indirectly on the Clonmacnoise chronicle. Furthermore when one considers the superfluity of entries that Dub dá Leithe remarked in his interjection at the beginning of this very year it seems quite improbable that he would also incorporate in his compilation contemporaneous entries from another monastery. For indeed his editing performance shows that he himself was fully capable of composing whatever entries were required to continue his Armagh chronicle. Finally, and in my view conclusively, collation of AU against the Clonmacnoise group over 1065–1178 shows that common entries continue to occur throughout this interval as will be discussed shortly.

Thus the evidence indicates that Dub dá Leithe, within about thirty years of Cuán's compilation of Liber Cuanach, used it as the basis for the re-compilation of an existing Armagh chronicle that had commenced at about 790. Dub dá Leithe's compilation was both analogous and approximately contemporaneous with that of the Munster compiler of AI, with the important difference that Dub dá Leithe took care to reproduce accurately the chronological apparatus of Liber Cuanach. Otherwise there are striking similarities between the two compilations: both employed Liber Cuanach as their source of world and early Irish history, and from virtually the same point in the eighth century both progressively displaced Liber Cuanach entries with end chronicles reflecting their preferred provenances of respectively Armagh and Munster. What became of Liber Dub dá Leithe after his death in 1064? It is clear from Figure 27, p. 223, that Dub dá Leithe's enthusiasm for the accumulation of Armagh annals was maintained up until c.1174. Indeed a graphic index of the subsequent Armagh enthusiasm for their chronicle is that the seventh quinion of TCD 1282 covers the years 1020–1115, i.e. 96 years, whereas the following quinion, although now missing, did cover the years 1116–62, i.e. only 47 years, so it is apparent that Armagh's annual coverage of events doubled over 1116–62.[22] However, after 1174 there is apparent a steady decline in Armagh coverage until it effectively ceases at 1216. What were the circumstances that led to this sudden decline in a chronicling process which had been sustained so vigorously over c.790–1174?

By far the most likely development to affect the orderly process of affairs in Armagh was the arrival of the Norman forces in Wexford in May 1169, from whence in the following three years they extended their military and political presence at least over extensive parts of Leinster, Meath and Munster. Whilst the Normans did not reach either Armagh or its neighbouring territories until 1177, the fact that the church at Armagh was then the head of an extended *paruchia* of churches across Ireland meant that its relationship with all those churches lying within Norman controlled regions was disturbed.[23] Thus Armagh's affairs and ecclesiastical control were disrupted from shortly after the commencement of the Norman invasion. In the event, in February 1177 John de Courcy invaded Down and seized Dún da Lethglaisse, and proceeded to make a series of attacks along east Down and Antrim. The consequences of these attacks for the monastery and town of Armagh are registered in a series of entries in AU recording serious destruction there in the years following 1177.[24]

22 Mc Carthy, 'AU compilation', 91 table 1 (quinions & years).   23 Duffy, 'John de Courcy', 2–3 (de Courcy); Ó Cróinín, *Early medieval Ireland*, 162, 'the principal churches (Armagh, Bangor, Clonmacnoise, Kildare, etc.) all claimed jurisdiction over daughter-houses scattered across Ireland.' 24 Mac Carthy, *AU ii*, AU 1177, 1179, 1184–5, 1189, 1196 (Armagh invasion and destruction; cf. Orpen, *Normans* ii, 8).

It is thus apparent that from 1177 onwards the church of Armagh was itself under siege, and its personnel laboured in conditions of personal insecurity, military threat, and political instability. In these circumstances it is not surprising to find that the chronicle of their annual affairs should decline. However, as can be seen from Figure 27, p. 223, it did not cease altogether until 1216 and so the question to be next addressed is, what happened to the Armagh chronicle after 1177?

The Derry chronicle

When AU is examined over the four decades following 1177 it quickly emerges that for at least part of this interval entries were being recorded in the monastery of Derry, as was first pointed out by Gwynn in 1959.[25] The evidence for this comprises the concentration of entries referring to Derry over 1121–1219, the level of detail included in these entries, and the occasional use of the directional verb, 'to come'. The first of these may be clearly demonstrated by displaying the cumulative count of all the references to Derry given by Mac Carthy in his index to AU against the year, and this is plotted in Figure 32 for the years 850–1350.

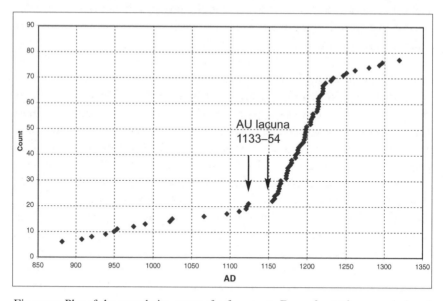

Figure 32. Plot of the cumulative count of references to Derry for AD 850–1350 indexed by Mac Carthy AU iv, 107–8, versus AD.

25 Derry compilation: Gwynn, 'Cathal Mac Magnusa', 372–3; Mac Niocaill, *MIA*, 29–30.

This shows that over 850–1100 Mac Carthy found just twelve references to Derry, an average of about one entry every twenty-one years. Thereafter a sudden increase is seen at 1121 which is unfortunately disrupted by AU's lacuna over 1133–54. But following that a total of forty-three entries is found over 1155–1218, i.e. an entry about every 1.5 years. Thus over 1155–1218 AU's coverage of Derry affairs increased by a factor of fourteen over the pre-1100 rate, only to revert to the earlier rate thereafter. Regarding the character of these Derry entries over 1155–1219 they frequently exhibit a detailed local knowledge, for example:[26]

> AU 1204.1: Doire was burned from the Cemetery of Martin to the Well of Adomhnan.
>
> AU 1213.5: Domnall Ua Daimin was killed by the sons of Mac Lachlainn at the door of the Monastery of Daire of Colum-cille.

both of which precisely locate their respective events. Finally some entries from 1196 onwards imply by their verb that they were composed in Derry:

> AU 1197.1: Then Roitsel Fitton came (*táinic*) on a foray to the Port of Daire …
>
> AU 1212.4: Thomas, son of Uchtrach with the sons of Raghnall, son of Somarle, came (*do thaidhecht*) to Daire of Colum-cille …
>
> AU 1214.3: Ua Cathain and the Men of Craibh came (*do thiachtain*) to Daire …

It is thus apparent that an earnest effort was made to chronicle Derry affairs over 1155–1218, and furthermore that at least some entries over this interval were composed in Derry, and these together justify our speaking of a Derry chronicle. We may note also in passing that a considerable number of these Derry entries, like the abovementioned reference to Liber Dub dá Leithe at AU 1021.3, served as source for LC over these years.[27]

In his discussion of the Derry entries Aubrey Gwynn pointed out the close relationship that existed between the monasteries of Derry and Armagh during the twelfth century, and the role of Gilla Meic Liac, *comharba* in Derry from 1121, and then in Armagh from 1137 to 1174. Gwynn went on to remark the reciprocal relationship between Armagh and Derry entries in AU, writing:[28]

> On the other hand, whilst the entries concerning Armagh cease after the year 1189, entries concerning Derry become exceptionally frequent and detailed for the next twenty-five years … I think it probable that in these troubled years, when

26 The chronology of Mac Carthy, *AU* ii over AU 1193–1223 is antedated by one year, cf. Mc Carthy, 'Synchronization', *s.a.* 1192–1222 and chapter 12, p. 349 ff.   27 LC 1021.3 (Dub dá Leithe); LC 1173.1, 1174.3, 1178.4, 1180.2–3, 1188.3, 1188.10, 1189.10, 1195.13, 1196.16, 1196.20, 1203.10, 1211.7, 1213.6, 1213.7–8, 1215.9, 1217.2, 1218.12 (Derry entries).   28 Gwynn, 'Cathal Mac Magnusa', 372–3 (Gilla Meic Liac), 376–7 (cit.).

the Normans under John de Courci were obtaining their first foothold in Down and Armagh and when the churches of Armagh were in danger of destruction, the old book which is the basis of Cathal's Annals concerning Armagh and Derry down to the end of the twelfth century [*sc.* AU's source] was taken for safety from Armagh to Derry in 1189 or 1190; and that the numerous entries concerning Derry from 1189 to 1223 were made in Derry at the end of the older Armagh book.

Now while reference to Figure 27, p. 223, shows Gwynn's assertion that Armagh entries 'cease after the year 1189' was inaccurate, his inference that it was the threat posed by de Courcy to the security of Armagh that precipitated the transfer of their chronicle to Derry is almost certainly correct. Regarding the year of this transfer, Gwynn's overstatement regarding 1189 prompted him to identify this or the following year, however there is in fact evidence that AU's entries were still being composed in Armagh in 1195, as the following shows: AU 1196.2 'Howbeit, the Cenel-Eogain of Telach-oc and the Airthir came (*tangatur*) to the Plain of Ard-Macha ...', and a major battle involving the Normans took place there. As shown in the collation above, an entry in the following year AU 1197.1 records that 'Roitsel Fitton came on a foray to the Port of Daire', so that it appears more likely that the Armagh chronicle was brought to Derry in the wake of the battle fought in 1195 on the plain of Armagh.

Regarding the extent of this Derry chronicle, as can be seen in Figure 32 above, the first increase in Derry entries occurs at 1121 and therefore synchronizes with Gilla Meic Liac's appointment there as *comharba* of Colum Cille. However, it is evident that these Derry entries up to 1195 were recorded in the Armagh chronicle because a distinctive characteristic of many of them is that they have received subsequent additions emphasizing their Derry association. For example all seven references to 'comarba Coluim Cille' over 1155–64 have been glossed with some variant of '.i., la Flaithbertach, mac in espuic h-Ui Brolcain'.[29] At 1178 an account of a storm 'which prostrated a very large portion of woods and forests ...', has an addition stating its specific impact on Derry, 'It prostrated also six score oaks, or a little more, in Daire of Columcille.' Examination of the Derry entries over 1121–95 leads me to conclude that they were either written in Armagh or added retrospectively in Derry after 1195. However, for 1196–1218 the entries all appear contemporaneous and to have been written in Derry, whereas thereafter, with just nine entries over the following century, it is not plausible to consider that a chronicle was maintained in Derry. The years *c.*1196–1218 therefore represent the period over which the Derry chronicle was compiled in Derry.[30]

29 AU 1155.2, 1158.3, 1161.2, 1162.1, 1163.4, 1164.2, 1164.6, 1178.4, 1178.4 (glossed Derry entries).   30 The subsequent Derry entries at AU 1220.1, 1223.1, cf. Mac Carthy, *AU* ii, 266–7, 270–1, both show evidence of retrospectivity.

Regarding the question of who may have compiled this Derry chronicle we first note that of the seventeen Derry entries over 1196–1218 fourteen of them refer in some way to the monastic community at Derry. It seems certain therefore that the chronicle was maintained in a monastic context and that the compiler(s) were in offices of ecclesiastical authority in Derry, and indeed two such offices are identified by these entries, the *comharba* of Colum Cille and the erenagh of Derry. Two entries refer to the office of *comharba*, viz. at 1196 the accession of Gilla Críst Ua Cernaigh, while at 1219 the obit of Fonachtan Ua Bronáin is followed by a protracted account of conflict showing evidence of retrospection. However, if either of these men had been responsible for the Derry chronicle it is remarkable that neither the departure of the first, nor the accession of the second is recorded. On the other hand regarding the erenagh of Derry there is recorded a clear succession of members of the Uí Daigre throughout the period of the chronicle, viz. Mac Craith †1180, Máel-Ísu †1218 and Geoffrey †1233. Thus it can be seen that Máel-Ísu Ua Daighri was erenagh for nearly forty years and his term of office included all the contemporaneous years of the Derry chronicle. While his own obit does not attribute learning to him in the following year his successor as erenagh Geoffrey Ua Daighri contended for the lectorship, suggesting thereby that Máel-Ísu had previously occupied that office. Moreover, his obit does underline his long term in office and his contribution to the community of Derry, viz.:

> AU 1219.5: Mael-Isu Ua Daighri, herenach of Daire of Colum-cille – forty years was he in the herenachy – after doing every goodness to both clergy and laity, by a good ending rested in peace on Sunday, the 6th of the Ides of December.

There are therefore good grounds to conclude that it was Máel-Ísu who received the Armagh chronicle in *c.*1196, who augmented its existing entries referring to Derry, and then continued it in Derry until his death. After this there are just two entries referring to Derry, the first of which recounts at length a complex power struggle in 1219 among the community of Derry in which the erenagh, Geoffrey Ua Daighri, Máel-Ísu's successor, conflicted unsuccessfully with the *comharba*, Muirchertach Ua Millugain, for the lectorship. The second entry at 1222 recounts a profanation in Derry. It appears that the Uí Daigre suffered a serious loss of power in the conflict of 1219 with the result that at that time the Derry chronicle effectively terminated.

Entries common to the Cuana and Clonmacnoise groups after 1064

The mistaken assertion by Mac Neill in 1913 that over 975–1178 AT and AU 'are quite independent chronicles' proved very influential, resulting ultimately in O'Rahilly's *Clonmacnoise-911* hypothesis as discussed in chapter 3, p. 92 ff. Both scholars and indeed most subsequent scholarship simply ignored the existence of a substantial corpus of entries common to AU and the Clonmacnoise group over 915–1178, cf. Figure 5, p. 104, and Figure 6, p. 106.[31] One exception however was David Dumville who wrote, '(presumably at a much later stage in the history of AU) another member of the Clonmacnoise group was subsequently lightly drawn on to provide some material for its years *ca* 950–1054.'[32] But he did not seek either to justify these terminal years or to establish at what date this 'later stage' had occurred. However, in fact small numbers of common entries are found in virtually every year over the surviving range of the Clonmacnoise chronicle. To make the nature of these clear and because the witness of AB is useful on account of its relatively early date I tabulate in Figure 33 the three entries found in common in AU/AT/AB at 1126, highlighting in italic AU/AB passages found in AT:

AU 1126	AT 1126	AB §316
1. *Ennai mc. mc. Murchadha ri Laigen* mortuus est.	1. Enna mac Dondchadha maic Murchadha, ri Laigin, dé'c.	1. *Enna mac Murcada ri Laigin* moritur.
2. *Sluagadh la Tairrdelbach H. Conchobuir* i l-Laighnibh co ro ghaibh a n-giallu.	2. Sluaiged la Tairrdelbach Húa Concobair, la rig nErenn do denom rig al-Laignib iarsin ... [8×lines] ...	
7. Righ-therus Toirrdhelbaigh H. Conchobuir *co h-Ath Cliath* co tard *righi* Atha Cliath ⁊ Laigen dia *mac .i. do Conchobur.*	Feacht lais co hAth cliath, co ndernsat Gaill a oigreir ⁊ cor' facaib a mac a righe and .i. Concobur ... [8× lines].	3. *Tárdelbach ua Concubair* do dul in *n-Ath Cliath corofagib Concubar a mac and.*
6. *Domnall H. Dubhdai do badhudh iar* n-denam *creichi i Tir Conaill.*	3. Domnall Find Hua Dubda, ri O n-Amalgaidh ⁊ O Fiachrach ⁊ Cera, do bathadh ac tabairt crecche a Tir conaill .i. an duine nach tuc éra ar neach riam.	2. *Domnall Find ua Dúbda* mersus est.

Figure 33. Parallel collation of AU/AT/AB entries for 1126 with AU/AB textual elements common to AT highlighted in italic.

---

31 Mc Carthy, 'Synchronization', *s.a.* 915–1178 (common entries).　32 Grabowski & Dumville, *Chronicles*, 111 (cit.), 109–226 (Dumville's chapters II–IV).

From this it is apparent that AU and AB independently transmit either in abridged form or paraphrase the three entries found more extensively in AT. It is conspicuous that all these entries relate to kings, two of whose kingdoms lay in the province of Connacht. Moreover, examination of the corpus over 915–1178 shows that this regnal, Connacht and abridged character prevails throughout. Now both the Connacht emphasis and the abridgement imply that the transmission has been from the Clonmacnoise to the Cuana group. Further, the continuation to 1178 at which point AT truncates implies that the transmission occurred *after* that year. Just how long after 1178 may be inferred approximately by considering AB, for its regnal entries common with AU continue to 1200.[33] Moreover, we know that the Boyle chronicle was compiled by 1228 so that the insertion of these entries common to AU/AB must have occurred between 1201 and 1228. In the circumstances that their common source, the Armagh-Derry chronicle terminated at 1218 I conclude that very shortly thereafter it was collated with the Clonmacnoise chronicle and regular but frequently abridged entries were transcribed into it. It was this expanded recension of the Armagh-Derry chronicle, enlarged with frequently abridged regnal entries mainly from Connacht that then served as the primary source for the Boyle compiler in *c.*1220, around the time of the consecration of the abbey there. When it is necessary to emphasize that it is the expanded recension that is intended I shall use the notation Armagh-Derry[+]. Later in the fifteenth century the Uí Chianáin compilers also employed this recension in order to extend their Fermanagh chronicle back to Adam as will be discussed in chapter 9. Of course it seems quite likely that in the course of collating the Clonmacnoise and Armagh-Derry chronicles in *c.*1220 that some entries then unique to the latter were also transcribed into the former. Such entries are not readily apparent however, and to establish this issue would require a more detailed analysis of the common entries than has been thus far possible.

Summary of the evolution of the Armagh and Derry chronicles

Circa 790 – The keeping of records of monastic offices commences in Armagh.
Circa 1046 – Dub dá Leithe compiled the Armagh proto-chronicle with the Liber Cuanach, employing Cuán's chronological apparatus but correcting it from 1014 onwards. Up until 911 Dub dá Leithe transcribed a selection of Liber Cuanach entries for the most part accurately except for occasional emendations to entries dealing with Uí Néill affairs, but after 911 he used Liber Cuanach principally as the basis for his expanded account of the Cenél nEógain kings of Ireland and Brian Bóruma up to 1019.

33 Common regnal entries: AB §378.1 – AU 1194.1; AB §382.1 – AU 1199.1; AB §385.1 – AU 1201.1.

Circa 1046–1195 – Dub dá Leithe's compilation was continued at Armagh.

Circa 1195 – The Armagh chronicle terminated as a consequence of the instability arising from the Norman presence in Ireland.

Circa 1196–1218 – The Armagh chronicle was transferred to Derry where it was likely the erenagh, Máel-Isu Ua Daighri, who augmented Derry entries in the existing chronicle and continued it up until his death in 1218.

Circa 1218 – The Derry chronicle terminated, most likely as the consequence of the power struggle of 1219 in which Máel-Ísu's successor, Geoffrey Ua Daighri, lost control of the lectorship.

Circa 1220 – The Armagh-Derry chronicle was collated with the Clonmacnoise chronicle and numerous regnal entries, often abridged, referring to the major Irish kingdoms particularly Connacht were transcribed into it. This expanded compilation, the Armagh-Derry[+] chronicle, then served as the primary source for the compiler of the Boyle chronicle.

CHAPTER NINE

The Connacht and Fermanagh chronicles

Between the synod of Rathbreassail in 1111 and the terminations of the Clonmacnoise and Derry chronicles in *c.*1227, and *c.*1218 the ecclesiastical and political arrangements in Ireland were transformed. Ecclesiastically the Irish monastic system of an extended *familia* subject to a parent monastery linked to a primary Irish saint was replaced by monasteries of the European monastic orders of the Augustinians, Cistercians and Premonstratensians, now embedded within a diocesan administrative structure. Thus the Irish monastic institution that had nurtured the development of the Annals from the fifth century onwards was no longer. Politically by 1218 the Normans had established direct control over much of the island, with the notable exception of Connacht which was still held by an Irish king, Cathal Crobderg Ua Conchobair †1224, though by charter from the Crown. Examination of CT/LC for the decades following the termination of the Clonmacnoise and Derry chronicles reveals two important developments in Irish chronicling. First, their provenance is emphatically that of Connacht, and second there is an unmistakable shift towards secularization both of chronicle content and its authors. Gone are the myriad obits referring to monastic offices including that of the *fer leighinn*, who is now replaced by a professional historian, the *ollamh*, holding a secular office patronized by a ruling family. In the thirteenth century it is clear that in Connacht it was these secular ollamhs who successfully took over the task of maintaining and extending the earlier monastic chronicles. Thus the institution sustaining the chronicle changed from a powerful monastery to those ruling families of Connacht who patronized the ollamh.[1] This development brought important changes to the purview of the chronicle, for it now followed the political imperatives of the patron family. As Norman modes of warfare were adopted these imperatives frequently resulted in violent conflict of both increasing scale and duration, and the entries recording such conflict sometimes expand to a more narrative form. Following the death of Cathal Crobderg in 1224 protracted conflict ensued between other members of the Uí Chonchobair

---

1 For the medieval ollamh: Mac Cana 'Schools', 126–46; Paul Walsh in O'Lochlainn, *Irish Men of Learning, passim*; Ó Muraíle, *Celebrated antiquary*, 1–52 (Dubhaltach Mac Fhirbhisigh); Simms, 'Ó Luinín family', 273–4; Comyn, *Foras Feasa* i, 70–3 (Keating's seventeenth century account of the Gaelic professions, including ollamhs, their books, their fiscal support and their numbers).

and the Normans led by Richard de Burgh, and accounts of this conflict are a feature of the Connacht continuation.[2] It is the purpose of this chapter both to identify as far as possible the compilers responsible for this Connacht chronicle and what was the sequence and extent of their contributions. Before commencing however it is worth recalling that the examination in chapter 2 of the primary witnesses of the Connacht group, CT/LC, shows they are not of equal authority. CT is a transcript of a formidable chronicle by three scribes highly competent in the annalistic genre. LC is an assembly of four separate compilations, L1–4, written for the most part by competent scribes but led by Brian Mac Diarmada, a clann chieftain with no apparent annalistic training. We must also note regarding AB that since it has a Connacht provenance from the founding of Boyle Abbey in 1148 to its termination in 1257, it clearly qualifies as a Connacht chronicle. This is in fact a Connacht end chronicle with an ecclesiastic purview and subsequently much of its Connacht material was transcribed by the secular compilers and so is found in CT/LC.[3] However, it is also apparent that this ecclesiastical chronicle did not flourish; in particular its unorthodox orthography, its faltering termination at 1257, and its relatively limited coverage of Connacht events over 1148–1257, all mark it as a largely unsuccessful endeavour to translate into the newly imported European monastic context a chronicle mode that had evolved within the Irish monastic tradition.

The Clonmacnoise origin of the Connacht chronicle

The scholars who commenced compilation of the Connacht chronicle in the earlier thirteenth century did not work in a vacuum for the tradition of annalistic compilation had flourished in Ireland over the preceding eight hundred years. It is helpful therefore to briefly review what has been already established concerning the availability of chronicles in c.1227. We have:

1. The Clonmacnoise chronicle extending to c.1227, located in Clonmacnoise.
2. The Armagh-Derry[+] chronicle extending to c.1218 and located in Derry to that time, but of uncertain location after its collation with the Clonmacnoise chronicle in c.1220.
3. The Munster chronicle maintained in west Munster since c.1130, possibly Inisfallen.[4]
4. The Boyle chronicle compiled c.1220, a copy of which was continued in Holy Trinity from c.1229 to 1257.

---

2 Orpen, *Normans* iii, 158–89 (Uí Chonchobair-de Burgh conflict).   3 Mac Niocaill, *MIA*, 30–1 (AB and CT/LC).   4 Best & Mac Neill, *AI facsimile*, 14–20 and Mac Airt, *AI*, xxix–xxx (AI's Munster location).

Of these four the Clonmacnoise chronicle with its substantial coverage of the Uí Fhiachrach, Uí Briúin and Uí Chonchobair kings offered a Connacht compiler by far the most Connacht material as background. By comparison the Connacht coverage of the Boyle-Holy Trinity chronicle commencing only in 1148 was relatively limited and expressed an ecclesiastical purview. On the other hand the Armagh-Derry+ and Munster chronicles either had no or minimal coverage of Connacht affairs over the tenth, eleventh and twelfth centuries. On these grounds alone one would expect any Connacht compiler to choose the Clonmacnoise chronicle as his starting point. That this is what in fact happened is confirmed by an examination of the language and distribution of the principal series of the chronological apparatus of AT/CT/LC/AU, thereby including our best representatives of the Clonmacnoise, Connacht, and Cuana chronicles. The language and distribution of their most important chronological series over 1000–1600 are shown in Figure 34.

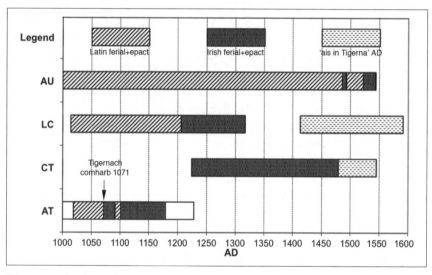

Figure 34. A schematic view of the language of the principal chronological series of AT/CT/LC/AU identifying those ferial+epact in Latin, ferial+epact in Irish, and AD in Irish expressed as 'ais in Tigerna'. Note that in order to simplify this presentation: data variations over five years or less, lacunae in AU/LC/CT arising from folio loss, LC's parallel 'ais in Tigerna' series over 1014–1225, and LC's parallel Irish ferial+epact series over 1547–90 have all been omitted. Any instances of mixed Irish/Latin criteria have been reckoned as Irish. On the other hand AT's lacunae over 1000–18 and 1179–c.1227 are shown outlined.

As may be seen the use of the ferial+epact series remained a feature of the Annals throughout the medieval period. However, as discussed in chapter 6, p. 191 ff. the representation of the series in the Clonmacnoise chronicle was changed by Tigernach Ua Braein from Latin to Irish in 1071, whereas the Armagh-Derry[+] chronicle retained the Latin form of its Liber Cuanach progenitor. Thus we have, AU 1071.1 'Kł.Ian.uii.f.l.xxui.' but AT 1071.1 'Kł.En. for Satharnn 7 .xx.ui. fuirri'. Tigernach's reformation was indeed an important development in the annalistic apparatus, even though his immediate successors did not systematically maintain his Irish reform. For as may be seen in Figure 34 above, while the apparatus of AT reverted to Latin over 1091–1100, from 1101 onward it was effectively continued systematically in Irish.[5] Unfortunately as a result of folio loss this series is now truncated in AT at 1178, but there are good grounds to believe that it originally continued thus up to the termination of the chronicle at c.1227. For indeed when CT commences at 1224 it begins, 'Kł.Enair for Luan & sechdmad uathad esca fuirri ...', and this tradition was effectively continued in CT until 1478, cf. Figure 34 above. Thus the language and style change instituted by Tigernach persisted for over four centuries. Moreover, another feature of the chronological apparatus of the Clonmacnoise chronicle after 1020 was the occasional inclusion of other chronological criteria such as the bissextile incidence, the AD, or the year of the lunar cycle, cf. AT/CS over 1020–24. Subsequently this practice continued in Clonmacnoise and these additional criteria became more frequent while still occurring randomly. For example over 1101–78 AT records the bissextile incidence twenty one times, the AD five times, and the lunar cycle thrice.[6] All of these additional criteria are in Irish except the AD which is in Roman numerals, and the randomness in the occurrence of these criteria, and indeed the occasional missing ferial or epact, are clear evidence for the contemporaneous character of this entire apparatus. Turning to CT, in the early years we likewise find similar additional criteria in Irish expressed in a style closely resembling those of AT. For example:

> AT 1158.1: Kl. enair for cétain . xx. uííí. fuirre, 7 bliadan deridh naedhecdha.
> CT 1234.1: Kł Enair for Domnach 7 vii.mad xx.it fuirri. Bliadain deridh noidecda hi ...

Here both record in Irish the kalend, ferial, epact and additionally the year of the lunar cycle in identical order and terms. These correspondences in their chronological apparatus, together with the continuity and expansion of their Connacht purview lead to an important conclusion regarding the Connacht chronicle, namely that the Connacht chronicle was the continuation in a secular environment of the Clonmacnoise chronicle. For indeed if we had the now-

---

5 Mc Carthy, 'Synchronization', s.a. 1086–7, 1091–4, 1096–7, 1100, 1110, 1112–13, 1116, 1127, 1173 (Latin criteria); these brief variations do not register at the resolution of Figure 34.   6 The bissextile incidence is the number of years from the last bissextile year.

missing final fifty years of AT whose Clonmacnoise entries may be partly recovered from copies surviving in MB/FM, and whose Irish ferial+epact apparatus partly survives in LC over 1208–24, cf. Figure 34 above, then we would see that together the Irish ferial+epact chronological apparatus and Clonmacnoise/ Connacht provenance of AT/CT form a continuum over 1071–1478. Furthermore, when the epactal series of the Connacht continuation is examined we find that the saltus, which every nineteen years increases the lunar age by one day, was omitted from 1234 onwards. Consequently, henceforth from 1234, when the first insertion of the saltus *after* the conclusion of the Clonmacnoise chronicle was required, the epacts of this Connacht chronicle steadily diverge from Dionysiac epacts. This systematic omission of the saltus, together with other epactal irregularities at 1341 and 1416, provide additional and compelling evidence that this chronicle was maintained in a secular context from 1234 on. For it is not plausible that generations of ecclesiastics, annually celebrating the moveable feast of the Pasch whose date was determined by the epact, could ignore the conflict between their chronicle data and their celebration. I next turn to consider the question of where and by whom in Connacht the Clonmacnoise chronicle was continued.

The location and identity of the Connacht compilers

While it is obvious from the vast number of Connacht obits from *c.*1227 onwards that the Clonmacnoise chronicle was continued in Connacht it is desirable to establish as precisely as possible the circumstances of this continuation. Consequently, we look for entries about this time that show evidence of being contemporaneous, and here we find in CT/LC over 1224–50 an elaborate and detailed narrative of the conflict in Connacht that shows every sign of being contemporaneous.[7] Its use of the verbs to come and go, and its adverbs of direction place its author in north Connacht, and this prompted Aubrey Gwynn to propose that the narrative had been compiled in the Augustinian monastery of Cong.[8] Subsequently O'Dwyer identified weaknesses in Gwynn's argument and remarked the prominence afforded to Clarus Mac Mailin †1251, archdeacon of Elphin and founder of four Premonstratensian monasteries in north Connacht, including that of Holy Trinity on Loch Cé, and so proposed Clarus as author. Mac Niocaill however firmly rejected both of these hypotheses and proposed instead that the compilation had been made 'in north Connacht – approximately the Boyle/Loch Cé area', and he designated it simply as the

---

7 Discussions of the conflict narrative: Mac Niocaill, *MIA*, 33; O'Dwyer, 'Annals', 89; Gwynn, 'Cong', 5; Orpen, *Norman* iii, 160.   8 Cong hypothesis: Mac Niocaill *MIA*, 33; Gwynn, 'Cong', 1–9.

'North Connacht Chronicle' in his stemma.[9] But if we search the thirteenth-century annals for possible compilers of this 'North Connacht Chronicle' only one plausible candidate family emerges and that is the Uí Maoil Chonaire, cf. Figure 37, p. 259. In support of this hypothesis we note that the first reference in the Annals to a member of the Uí Maoil Chonaire is an obit at 1136 in AT/FM for a Neidhe Ua Maoil Chonaire 'the historian (*in senchaidh*)'. Although nothing further is known of this man the entry itself implies that the Uí Maoil Chonaire were professional historians nearly a century before the termination of the Clonmacnoise chronicle.[10] The next Annalistic reference to the family records the death of 'Duinnin h. Maelconaire ollam Sil Muredaig Muillethain meic Fergusa' at 1231. This entry therefore identifies Duinnin as the first recorded ollamh to the Uí Chonchobair, the principal protagonists in the conflict described in the narrative entries of CT/LC over 1224–50. Moreover, in the following year is recorded Maoleoin Bodhar Ua Maoil Chonaire's possession of Cluain Plocáin, later Ballymulconry, in north Connacht, followed by his obit in 1266 as the second recorded 'ollam Sil Muredaig'. Since Maoleoin's life extended over the period of these conflict narratives, which deeply involved his patrons the Uí Chonchobair, surely the most plausible interpretation is that Maoleoin compiled them in Cluain Plocáin in his role as ollamh? Certainly Cluain Plocáin's situation on the west bank of the Shannon about three miles south of Boyle/Loch Cé and two miles north of Rath Cruachain, the ancient capital of Connacht, and heartland of the Síl Muiredaig dynasty, progenitors of the Uí Chonchobair, coincides with the perspective of these conflict narratives.[11] Moreover, the close relative timing of Duinnin's emergence as ollamh to the Uí Chonchobhair by 1231 with the termination of the Clonmacnoise chronicle at *c.*1227, suggests that before his death Duinnin had acquired access to it, and either he or his successor Maoleoin used it as the basis for their continuing account of the Uí Chonchobair and of Connacht. The presence of Maoleoin's descendants in Cluain Plocáin/Ballymulconry recorded as ollamhs to the Síl Muiredaig three hundred years after his establishment in 1232, certainly points to the foundation there of a formidable chronicle tradition.[12] Consequently, I conclude that the huge number of Connacht entries that emphasize the affairs of the Uí Chonchobair and which were recorded in the two centuries following the appointments of Duinnin and Maoleoin are the work of themselves and successive members of their family.[13] I shall use the term 'Uí Maoil Chonaire-I'

---

9 O'Dwyer, 'Annals', 94–100 (Clarus hypothesis); Mac Niocaill, *MIA*, 33 (cit.), 33–4 (rejections). 10 Mac Eoin, 'Interpolator', 44–5 (evidence that a member of the Ua Maoil Chonaire had connections with both Clonmacnoise and Cathal Crobderg in the thirteenth century).   11 Walsh, 'O'Maelconaire family', 46–8 (Cluain Plocáin/Ballymulconry location).   12 CT 1519.9, LC 1551.4 (ollamh Síl Muiredaigh); Walsh, 'O'Maelconaire family', 46–7 (Uí Maoil Chonaire in Cluain Plocáin).   13 Walsh, 'O'Maelconaire family', 34–48 (Uí Maoil Chonaire).

to designate the chronicle accumulated by the Uí Maoil Chonaire ollamhs in the two centuries following 1224, though of their individual contributions little detail is readily discernible apart from that implied by the sequence of their obits.

Regarding the year at which Uí Maoil Chonaire-I should be considered as commencing it seems clear from the remarkable emphasis given to the obit of Cathal Crobderg in 1224 that this was the year to which the Síl Muiredaig ollamhs looked. Cathal's long reign and his survival in the complex world of post-Norman Ireland made him a particularly suitable icon for the Uí Chonchobair. Moreover, the fact that in CT this emphasis is all concentrated at his obit suggests that the Síl Muirdaig ollamhs did not choose to extend their chronicle back over the coverage of the Clonmacnoise chronicle. Furthermore in both CT and AU the kalend of this year receives conspicuous emphasis by means of enlargement. Finally, I conclude that it was the emergence of the secularized chronicle tradition of the Uí Maoil Chonaire that explains the secular character and emphatic Uí Chonchobair purview found in Rawl. B. 488, when it is compared with other members of the Clonmacnoise group. For it is evident that a member of the Uí Maoil Chonaire prepared a secularized edition of the Clonmacnoise chronicle in order to complement their own Uí Maoil Chonaire-I. Here, by making suitable additions to entries referring to the Uí Chonchobair kings, particularly over the twelfth century, he highlighted the deeds of his patron's ancestors while at the same time by omitting the series of Clonmacnoise *comharba* he diminished the ecclesiastical status of the chronicle.[14] While there is no obvious way to date the compilation of this secular version of the Clonmacnoise chronicle, given the intensity of the coverage of the Uí Chonchobair over the second quarter of the thirteenth century this does seem the likely period for it. In Rawl. B. 488 we have a copy of this secular Connacht edition of the Clonmacnoise chronicle, while Rawl B. 502 represents the surviving remains of the Clonmacnoise chronicle that served as source.[15]

While Figure 34 is still proximate it is appropriate here to consider the character of the earlier sections of LC. In 1959 Mac Niocaill, following Hennessy and Ryan, emphasized and demonstrated the close textual relationship between LC and AU over 1014–1220, and this relationship is also apparent in LC's chronological apparatus.[16] For LC's ferial+epact series follows the Latin series of AU up until 1207, but thereafter switches to the Irish form which then continues until 1316, cf. Figure 34, p. 247. It appears therefore that when Pilip Ua Duibhgeannáin was compiling the L1 section of LC he also had available to him the closing two

14 Grabowski & Dumville, *Chronicles*, 171 (Uí Chonchobair entries).   15 Grabowski & Dumville, *Chronicles*, 158, 163–4, 182 (AT's secular character).   16 Mac Niocaill, 'Annála', 18 (LC/AU – Hennessy & Ryan), 19–25 (demonstration); idem, *MIA*, 29.

decades of the Clonmacnoise chronicle and transcribed its apparatus. As already noted this piecemeal character is a feature of the compilation of LC, cf. Figure 38, p. 262. I next turn to consider the longer-term evolution of Uí Maoil Chonaire-I.

The fifteenth-century recompilation of Connacht chronicles

I commence with Mac Niocaill's conclusion regarding the question of the primary source for CT/LC:[17]

> The two chief Connacht sets of annals for the later middle ages, *Conn* and *L1–L3*, both derive from a text compiled by a member of the Ó Maoilchonaire family, probably in the mid-fifteenth century. The evidence for this is the stress placed in both on the first occupation of Cluain Plocáin, later Ballymulconry in Roscommon, in 1232 by Maoileoin Bodhar Ó Maoilchonaire; the prominence accorded to succession to the ollavship of Connacht, e.g. by Tanaidhe Mór Ó Maoilchonaire in 1270; and the quotations strewn through the text, e.g. in 1233, 1274, 1278, 1293, from a poem on the kings of Connacht attributed to Donnchadh Losc Ó Maoilchonaire (†1404). That both present substantially the same text has long been recognised …

Mac Niocaill was certainly correct here in identifying that a fifteenth-century Uí Maoil Chonaire compiler was responsible for compiling the ultimate source of CT/LC, but he located this compilation just approximately as 'probably in the mid-fifteenth century'. However, an examination of the chronological apparatus of our texts reveals further details of this compilation and helps to date it more precisely. For both CT and LC show that upon taking over the Clonmacnoise chronicle the Uí Maoil Chonaire maintained and extended its Irish kalend+ferial+epact apparatus, and these series were carried forward in both texts over 1224–1478, though the epactal series is asynchronous from 1234 onwards as mentioned above. Indeed having inherited a chronicle with such an elaborate apparatus extending over *c.* 1071–1227 and accurately synchronized with the Julian calendar, it would be remarkable should they emend it at that time in any essential way. However, both CT and LC also show that subsequently a member the Uí Maoil Chonaire did very substantially augment the chronological apparatus of their Connacht chronicle. These additional chronological criteria systematically identify in Latin the AD, Indiction, lunar and solar cycles, embolismic and common years, Dominical letters, and the hendecas and ogdoads, and they will be designated here collectively as 'addimenta'.[18] This

---

17 Mac Niocaill, *MIA*, 32–3 (cit.).   18 Freeman, *CT*, xv–xix discusses all these criteria which together with the epacts he attributed to Patin Ua Maoil Chonaire †1506; neither this attribution nor his identification of BL Add. 27589 as source for the epacts, solar cycle and embolismic data is plausible.

remarkable chronological apparatus far exceeds in scale any other annalistic apparatus, and indeed any practical chronicle requirement, and the primary purpose of these addimenta was clearly just to impress the reader. Of the chronological criteria continued from the Clonmacnoise chronicle, the kalend and ferial both maintain close synchronism with the AD and the Julian calendar, as will be discussed further in chapter 12, p. 349 ff. Examination of the distribution and language of these chronological addimenta in CT provides a basis for inferring their approximate date and likely author, and so these are illustrated in Figure 35.

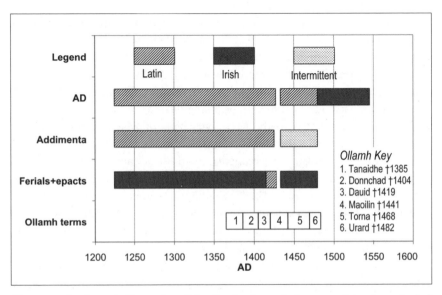

Figure 35. A schematic illustration of the distribution and character of the chronological apparatus of CT, distinguishing ferial+epact in Latin and Irish, AD in Latin (Roman numerals) and Irish ('ais in Tigerna'), and systematic and intermittent addimenta. The bottom row shows the terms of the Uí Maoil Chonaire ollamhs over 1385–1482, and the key lists their names and obits from CT.

The most conspicuous disruption to orderly compilation in CT is the lacuna over 1428–32 which it must be recalled is *not* the result of folio loss from RIA 1219. This lacuna is preceded by another disruption in that the ferial+epact series which was written systematically in Irish over 1224–1414, is in Latin over 1415–23. Thus after an Irish series sustained for over three centuries, someone suddenly reintroduced Latin, though since the Irish ferial+epact series resumes over 1424–7 and 1433–78 this reintroduction did not endure. However, the presence of the Latin ferial+epact series over 1415–23 shows that there existed a compiler about this time who favoured the use of Latin over Irish for chronological criteria. In regard to this use of Latin it must be emphasized that the vast majority of the addimenta over 1224–1423 were also written in Latin; the few exceptions occur near the beginning and these represent transcriptions from Uí Maoil Chonaire-I. The linguistic correspondence of this enormous series of Latin addimenta with the Latin ferial+epact series over 1415–23, and the subsequent cessation of systematic addimenta taken together indicates then that they were all the work of the same compiler. It emerges therefore that *c.*1423 the Uí Maoil Chonaire-I was subject to a very substantial recompilation over 1224–1423.

Before considering the question of who executed this compilation we need to first consider briefly the Connacht sources available in *c.*1423, and the character of the Connacht material in the Cuana and regnal-canon groups. Regarding known Connacht material, as well as Uí Maoil Chonaire-I itself we also have accounts of the Uí Duibhgeannáin ollamhs. They like the Uí Maoil Chonaire were professional historians, being ollamhs to the Síl Maolruanadh and Conmhaicne, that is to the Meic Diarmada of Magh Luirg, the Meic Donnchada of Tirerril, and the Uí Fheargaile of Annaile.[19] The first two of these territories cover the areas immediately south and north of Loch Cé, and Annaile approximately corresponds to county Longford to the east of it. The earliest annalistic reference to the Ua Duibhgeannáin in this role is the obit at 1340 of Pilib Ua Duibhgeannáin 'ollamh Conmaicne', and thereafter their obits repeatedly assert their contribution to learning and specifically to history. The principal learned branches of the family were established at Kilronan in county Roscommon from 1339, and in Castlefore in county Leitrim from *c.*1400. Since Kilronan and Castlefore are respectively about five miles north-east and twelve miles east of Loch Cé, these two learned Uí Duibhgeannáin branches were located close to the Uí Maoil Chonaire in Cluain Plocáin, which is about three miles south of Loch Cé. Given this and their common profession as historians it seems likely that the families associated in some way. While no explicit account of this is given in the Annals we shall see that there is good evidence for their joint cooperation. Thus there is good reason to believe that by 1423 the Uí Duibhgeannáin had accumulated a chronicle of the affairs of their patrons extending at least over *c.*1339–1423. These Uí Maoil Chonaire and Uí Duibhgeannáin compilations, together with Connacht material in the Boyle-Holy Trinity chronicle, i.e. AB over 1148–1257, represent the main corpus of known Connacht material in existence in 1423. Next we need to consider the character of Connacht material in the Annals from the other groups, for

19 Walsh, 'O'Duigenan family', 1 (Uí Duibhgeannáin ollamhs).

substantial quantities are found in AU/MB/FM. Now when we collate AU with CT/LC we find that they share numerous textually cognate entries each year over 1224–1422, and the table in Figure 36 illustrates the level of Connacht entries in AU at sample years over this interval.

AD	1224	1300	1358	1400	1410	1416	1420	1421	1422	1423–34
Common	4/8	8/9	8/10	1/12	3/3	10/14	5/8	7/11	4/6	0/5–24

Figure 36. For the given year the count of the textually cognate entries found in common between AU and CT over 1224–1434 are given by the first number, while the second gives the total number of AU entries. No entries are found in common over 1423–34 while AU entry numbers range over 5–24.

Thus this shows that over 1224–1422 the majority of AU entries under most years were derived from the secular Connacht chronicle, but that this ceases suddenly at 1423 and does not resume thereafter. Thus the range of these Connacht entries in AU is 1224–1422 and so corresponds virtually identically with the Latin addimenta in CT over 1224–1423.[20] Moreover, we note that the range of the corresponding material in MB is 1224–1408 and hence covers all but the final fifteen years of the interval. Thus the implication is clearly that this recompilation over 1224–1423 provided an important source for the compilers of both AU and MB as will be discussed further below. Furthermore when the provenance of these common entries in AU/MB is examined it quickly becomes clear that it includes Mac Diarmada, Mac Donnchada, Uí Fheargaile and Boyle material. Consequently, we are obliged to conclude the recompilation over 1224–1423 gathered *all* of the then available material for Connacht and proximate regions into the one chronicle and furnished it with the most imposing of all Irish chronological apparatus. This was indeed a most important development in Connacht chronicling for it resulted in the most formidable of all Irish chronicles with thirty or more entries found in the years 1225, 1404, 1411, 1416, 1419, 1422.[21] This far exceeded the coverage in any earlier known Irish chronicle and so it is not surprising to find it subsequently employed by later compilers.

20 Gwynn, 'Cathal Mac Magnusa' i, 377–8 and Mac Niocaill, *MIA*, 34–5 both identified this AU/CT relationship but restricted it to the thirteenth and fourteenth centuries', viz. Gwynn 377, 'From the beginning of the thirteenth to the end of the fourteenth century', and Mac Niocaill 35, 'for the greater part of the thirteenth and fourteenth centuries'.   21 The distribution of years in CT in which the entry count equals thirty or more is as follows, with the count suffixed to the year: 1225/37, 1404/32, 1411/31, 1416/33, 1419/34, 1422/30, 1461/40, 1464/53, 1466/31, 1468/40, 1471/36, 1473/49, 1478/30, 1536/34. As may be seen these entry concentrations cluster towards the end of Uí Maoil Chonaire-I at 1423, and Uí Maoil Chonaire-II at 1478.

Regarding who this compiler may have been all the evidence points to the Uí Maoil Chonaire, as Mac Niocaill identified. The regnal quatrains attributed to Donnchadh Losc, the emphasis accorded to the Uí Maoil Chonaire over this interval, and their relative seniority in Connacht chronicling, cf. Figure 37, p. 259, all support this identification. Indeed since 1423 marks the conclusion of the second century from 1224 it is tempting to propose that this major recompilation may have been an Uí Maoil Chonaire celebration of this anniversary. Regarding which of the Uí Maoil Chonaire may have been responsible, the 'Ollamh terms' shown in Figure 35, p. 253, are simply based upon the obits of those persons identified in CT as an ollamh of the Síl Muiredaig. But it is of course quite naïve to consider that each ollamh continued compilation of the chronicle up to the year of his death, for in the ordinary way the infirmities of old age usually impose that the successor effectively takes over well before his predecessor's death. In particular the obit of David †1419 states that he died in 'his own house (*ina tig fein*)' in Kilmorebrannagh which is in county Kildare.[22] In these circumstances it seems probable that his brother Maoilín †1441 took over before David's death, and therefore that it was he who was responsible for the reversion to Latin of the epact+ferial series over 1415–23. In any case it is clear that most of this series must have been recorded after David's death. Now since Latin was Maoilín's preference this suggests that he also constructed and inserted the substantial series of Latin addimenta over 1224–1423. However, to accomplish this insertion in practical terms would certainly require that the whole chronicle over 1224–1423 be rewritten, as would the inclusion of the substantial Uí Duibhgeannáin and Boyle material. Consequently, I conclude that Maoilín was responsible for this recompilation in *c.* 1423 of the chronicle accumulated by his Uí Maoil Chonaire predecessors over the previous two centuries. In support of this identification I would remark the choice of Donnchadh Losc's regnal quatrains, for Donnchadh †1404 was Maoilín's brother and David's predecessor as ollamh to Síl Muiredaig, and consequently a highly appropriate source for Maoilín to employ. Furthermore I note that when Mageoghagan acknowledged in his preface to MB the 'names of the severall authors wch I have taken for this booke', he concluded with 'Moylin O'Mulchonrye and Tanaige O'Mulchonrye, 2 professed Chroniclers'.[23] Since, as we shall see in chapter 10, p. 286 ff., Mageoghagan's 'old booke' derived from this Uí Maoil Chonaire recompilation, his acknowledgement here supports the proposed identification. For Mageoghagan's description of 'Tanaige' and 'Moylin' as '2 professed Chroniclers' can only reasonably be taken to refer to Tanaide Ua Maoil Chonaire †1385 and his son Maoilín †1441, both celebrated

---

22 Walsh, 'O'Maelconaire family', 36 (location of Kilmorebrannagh).   23 Murphy, *AC*, 10 (cit., but I read 'Moylin' with BL Add. 4817 f. 4[v] instead of Murphy's 'McOylyne').

in their obits as ollamhs to the Síl Muiredaig. Of these two of course only Maoilín could undertake a recompilation in *c.*1423. Consequently, when referring to the Uí Maoil Chonaire contribution to Connacht chronicling it is necessary to distinguish between their Uí Maoil Chonaire-I accumulated over 1224–1423 as a continuation of the Clonmacnoise chronicle, and their secondary chronicle compiled by Maoilín over 1224–1423 also incorporating Uí Duibhgeannáin and Boyle material, to which I shall refer as 'Uí Maoil Chonaire-II'.

The foregoing discussion of Maoilín's recompilation of Connacht material found in CT/LC has necessarily focussed on the years 1224–1423. However, it seems obvious that such a major recompilation would not simply commence at 1224 as CT now does. Rather we have already seen that Uí Maoil Chonaire-I represented a continuation of the Clonmacnoise chronicle that had been adapted to the secular environment of the Uí Maoil Chonaire. When we examine the origins of MB in chapter 10 we will see evidence that Maoilín undertook further development of this antecedent Clonmacnoise chronicle to furnish his Uí Maoil Chonaire-II with a substantial account of Irish prehistory. Having completed the initial compilation of Uí Maoil Chonaire-II it appears that Maoilín withrew from the field of chronicling for the Irish criteria reappear at 1424 and addimenta disappear at 1425, the lacuna over 1428–32 ensues and is followed by Irish ferial+epact series and very intermittent addimenta, cf. Figure 35, p. 253. The explanation for these disruptions over 1424–33 within Maoilín's lifetime possibly lies in the time and energy required for the compilation of Uí Maoil Chonaire-II and his age. For his obit states that he was over eighty when he died, implying therefore that in 1433 he was well over seventy so that possibly an amanuensis was responsible for compiling the years 1424–7. In any case it is clear that the continuation of Uí Maoil Chonaire-II was neglected over the latter part of Maoilín's life.

After Maoilín it was Torna †1468 who succeeded as ollamh and while he systematically used Irish ferial+epact series, he was quite indifferent regarding addimenta since with the exception of the AD these were all recorded very intermittently, cf. Figure 35, p. 253. Urard †1482 succeeded Torna as ollamh and he maintained the same style. While there is no clear evidence to tell us what was done with Uí Duibhgeannáin records over this period it seems likely to me that they were incorporated by the Uí Maoil Chonaire, for references to the Meic Diarmada, Meic Donnchada, and Uí Fheargaile abound. For example over 1434–78 there are a total of fifty-five references to the Ua Feargaile in CT. However, from 1479 a major development in the chronological apparatus of this Connacht chronicle took place when the ferial+epact series, a feature of all annals of the kalend tradition from *c.*1022, was suddenly abandoned and thereafter the AD alone was used, but now expressed in Irish as 'ais an Tigerna', i.e. the era of the Lord, cf. Figure 34, p. 247, and Figure 35, p. 253. This it may be noted is *not* a translation of 'Anno Domini', and furthermore the number of the year, hitherto written in Roman numerals, was now written in Irish commencing from the least significant digit, viz. –

> CT 1479: Kł.Enair. Nai mbliadna dec ar tri fichtib ar ceitri ced ar mile aois an Tigerna an tan-sin.

It is most unlikely that this profound change was the work of the Uí Maoil Chonaire ollamh at the time, Urard, for it occurred just three years before his death. Moreover, it is also the case that the year 1479 has no entries and the subsequent years have small numbers of relatively brief entries which are not particularly directed towards the affairs of either the Uí Chonchobair or Connacht. Thus as well as a profound change in the chronological apparatus an effective lacuna in Uí Chonchobair/Connacht affairs intrudes at 1479, and from this it appears that Uí Maoil Chonaire accumulation of Uí Maoil Chonaire-II terminated in 1478. Furthermore, as was noted in chapter 2, both the script style and the paragraph style changes profoundly with the commencement of scribe C at 1479. In sum therefore we have evidence of both the termination of Uí Maoil Chonaire annalistic chronicling by 1478, and of the introduction of a profoundly different chronological apparatus and script style from 1479 forward. These together suggest therefore that the annals from 1479 onwards in CT were compiled by scholars trained in a very different learned tradition. Now as Mac Niocaill concluded and as was discussed in chapter 2 all the evidence shows that the MSS of CT and LC were substantially written by members of the Uí Duibhgeannáin. There is absolutely no doubt that this 'ais an Tigerna' style was employed by the Uí Duibhgeannáin in the sixteenth century. For example Brian Mac Diarmada and his Uí Duibhgeannáin colleagues used it for the first of his compilations, L4, from *c.*1577 onwards, and they also employed it over 1413–1577 for L2 and L3 in 1588, and in the following year they substituted it for the AD in L1 over 1014–1225. The earliest dated instance of it that I have found is in the fragment of annals in Edinburgh Adv. 72.1.2 probably written by Ruaidhrí Ua Luinín in *c.*1507, where the apparatus for the year 1362 reads:[24]

> Kalendas Ianuarii. Dha bhliadhain ar thri fichit air .ccc. ar mhile Ais an Tiagherna

This Irish AD style is also found marginally in: Rawl. B. 488 from f. 15[r] onwards, cf. marginal AD system-B, p. 23; in a number of colophons written by David Ua

---

24 Mac Niocailll, 'Cáipéisí', 36 (cit.); all other years except 1363 employ kalend+AD, and the fact that their readings and chronology correspond with those of Rawl. B. 489, rather than TCD 1282, suggests that these annals were written by Ua Luinín between 1505 and 1507. Mac Niocaill, *MIA*, 35 refers to this Edinburgh MS simply as 'some fragmentary annals for the years 1360 to 1402'.

Duibhgeannáin in the seventeenth century; without 'ais an Tigerna' in dates interpolated into the Holy Trinity section of AB in Cotton Titus A xxv; with 'Áois an Tighearna' introducing each of the short annals of Leinster transcribed in 1668 by Eoghan Mac Conmhail.[25] A survey of the references to members of these families found in the Annals suggests that the *floruit* of the Uí Duibhgeannáin commenced about one century later than that of the Uí Maoil Chonaire, as may be seen in Figure 37.

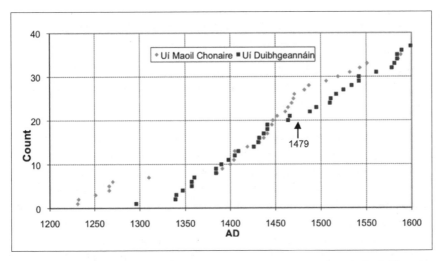

Figure 37. Accumulative counts of the references to members of the Uí Maoil Chonaire and Uí Duibhgeannáin families found in CT/LC/AU/MB. Attributions of quatrains to members of the Uí Maoil Chonaire have been omitted from the survey since they are clearly retrospective additions.

This shows that apart from the solitary entry in AT/FM at 1136 the record of the Uí Maoil Chonaire commences at 1231 and extends to 1588, though a significant reduction is evident following 1479, evidently reflecting the decline of their role in annalistic compilation. On the other hand the Uí Duibhgeannáin record in effect commences at 1339 and continues to 1599 and is noticeably more vigorous following 1479. It appears from this that there was a reciprocal relationship between the annalistic contribution of the Uí Maoil Chonaire and Uí Duibhgeannáin through the fifteenth century, the former progressively waning while the latter waxed, and indeed they flourished well into the seventeenth century. Thus these observations together with the synchronous

25 Ó Cuív, *Catalogue*, 144 (Rawl. B. 488 marginal 'ais an Tigerna' dates); Walsh, 'O'Duigenan family', 7 (colophons); Freeman, *AB*, *s.a.* 1228–9, 1233–5 (date annotations); Ó Muraíle, *Irish leaders*, 55 (P. Walsh's edition of the short annals of Leinster).

textual and chronological transformations observed at 1479 lead me to conclude that the entries in both CT and LC from that year forward were in fact the work of members of the Uí Duibhgeannáin. Closely synchronized to this year a further textual change is found in those entries, usually obits, that commence with a bare surname which is followed by '.i.', followed by the forename(s). Such entries are very occasional before 1478, but thereafter instances, sometimes multiple, are found in nearly every year, for example:[26]

> CT 1478.27: H. Cobthaig .i. Murcertach Losc mortuus est.
> CT 1478.30: Mag Samradan .i. Cathal mac Donnchada Ballaig 7 int Epscop Mag Samradain mortui sunt.
> CT 1480.3: Mac Maghnusa d'ecc .i. Cathal Occ.
> CT 1481.3: O Nell .i. Conn do gabail an bliadain-si.
> CT 1481.4: Mac Con Midhe .i. Conchobar Ruad, saí re dan, do dul d'ecc an bliadain-si.

The gap at 1479 is the consequence of there being no entries for that year, but the sustained character of the style thereafter, combined with the very occasional instances hitherto suggest that this was Uí Duibhgeannáin literary style.

Regarding the question of which of the Uí Duibhgeannáin may have been responsible for the continuation of Uí Maoil Chonaire-II over 1479–1544, Mulchrone succinctly reviewed the evidence that scribe C of CT had been a Sean Riabhach Ua Duibhgeannáin who wrote on f. 85ᵛ, 'I am Seaan and I am at loss without Dolp (*Misi Seaan 7 is misdi me gan Dolp*).'[27] Mulchrone also remarked on the emphasis accorded by Sean Riabhach to the obituary of Duibgeand mac Dubhthaigh Ua Duibhgeannáin at 1542, wherein he is described as, 'ollam sochraidh saoircerdach re senchus'. Now the Dolbh mac Dubhthaigh Ua Duibhgeannáin who died in 1578 appears to have been a brother of this man, so Duibgeand may well have been responsible for the Uí Duibhgeannáin compilation over 1479–*c.*1542. For then Sean Riabhach's remark, 'I am at loss without Dolp', may be understood to refer to his problem of completing the chronicle up to an *annus praesens* of *c.*1578. In the event Sean Riabhach was only able to bring it to 1544 on f. 90ʳᵇ, leaving the remainder of f. 90 blank, so these details suggest that CT was completed *c.*1578. Regarding the year at which the Uí Duibhgeannáin chronicle terminates it certainly must at least be considered to extend to the end of L3, i.e. 1577. Before considering the matter of at what year the Uí Duibhgeannáin chronicle began it will be helpful to first examine the overall provenance of its entries. For not all the later material in LC has a

---

26 Freeman, *CT*, (cits., and where the earlier instances of '.i.'are at 1365, 1419, 1422, 1460, 1462, 1464, 1466, 1469 and 1473).   27 Mulchrone, *Catalogue RIA* xxvi, 3274–5 (cit.).

Connacht provenance, some of it exhibiting a sustained interest in events in and around county Fermanagh, and it is to this issue that I next turn.

The Fermanagh chronicle

In 1975 Mac Niocaill discussed at some length the provenance of the common and unique material found in CT/LC/AU/AB/MB over the twelfth to sixteenth centuries.[28] Amongst other matters his discussion identified that from the fifteenth century AU and LC contain common material relating to the Uí Raghallaigh of Bréifne, the Meic Mathghamhna of Airgialla, and the Meig Uidhir of Fermanagh. Earlier Gwynn had identified the extension in AU's provenance from Connacht to include Fermanagh over the thirteenth to fifteenth centuries and he conferred the title 'Fermanagh chronicle' on these entries, and since modern county Fermanagh straddles medieval Bréifne and Airgialla it is indeed an appropriate title.[29] Just how far back in time this Fermanagh chronicle extended Gwynn did not say, but the Meig Uidhir and Meic Mathghamhna are key protagonists in it and their account begins in earnest at c.1350, cf. Figure 46, p. 321, for the Meig Uidhir. Since 1350 closely approximates the resumption of ferial data in AU at 1338, I will provisionally take this latter year as the start of the Fermanagh chronicle and return to the matter below. Mac Niocaill also showed that CT/LC/AU contain substantial material of a provenance at considerable variance with that asserted by their customary title or classification. For example, the *Annals of Ulster* contain substantial Connacht material over the thirteenth and fourteenth centuries, while LC, classified as a Connacht chronicle, contains extensive Armagh, Derry and Fermanagh material. CT also transmits much of the fourteenth-century Fermanagh material. Mac Niocaill's treatment of these relationships is very impressive, resting as it did on his detailed knowledge of the Annals and the peoples and territories referenced by them. However, these relationships are complex and consequently his account makes difficult reading, so that it seems worthwhile to summarize his conclusions graphically in terms of the various chronicles and their ranges.[30] Accordingly Figure 38 sets forth the distribution of these dominant source chronicles in CT/LC/AU.

28 Mac Niocaill, *MIA*, 30–7 (provencance discussion). 29 Gwynn, 'Cathal Mac Magnusa', 378–80 (Fermanagh chronicle). 30 Mac Niocaill, *MIA*, 30–7; the difficulties partly arise from the complexity of the material and partly from some errors and omissions. For example his collation in fig. 4, p. 32 contains a considerable number of errors, cf. Mc Carthy, 'Synchronization', *s..a.* 1195–7; his discussion makes no references to his stemma in figures 5–6 on pp. 35–6; he refers to 'some fragmentary annals for the years 1360 to 1402', but does not identify these which are evidently Edinburgh Adv. 72.1.2 ff. 79, 88.

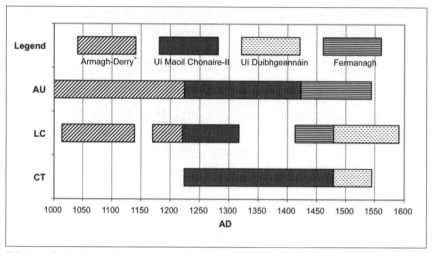

Figure 38. A schematic representation showing the dominant chronicle sources for CT/LC/AU over 1000–1600 based upon Mac Niocaill *MIA* 30–7, Freeman *CT* xxi–ii, and my own collations. The sources are identified by the legend as the Armagh-Derry[+], Uí Maoil Chonaire-II, Uí Duibhgeannáin, and Fermanagh chronicles. All small lacunae and those arising from folio loss have been omitted in order to simplify the presentation.

This figure shows graphically that CT comprises a combination of the continuation of Uí Maoil Chonaire-II chronicle to 1478, followed by part of the conclusion of the Uí Duibhgeannáin chronicle. By contrast the piecemeal character of LC is clearly demonstrated to comprise four separate sections, only two of which are of Connacht provenance and which are separated by a section of the Fermanagh chronicle. Finally it can seen that AU incorporates a substantial section over 1224–1422 principally derived from Maoilín's Uí Maoil Chonaire-II. When AU and LC are viewed in this way it can be seen that they exhibit a very similar overall structure, namely Armagh-Derry[+] then Uí Maoil Chonaire-II then Fermanagh chronicles; it is really just LC's concluding Uí Duibhgeannáin section that justifies its Connacht classification. Furthermore the decision by the Uí Duibhgeannáin compilers of LC to prefix the Armagh-Derry[+] chronicle to Uí Maoil Chonaire-II and to displace its later section with the Fermanagh chronicle demonstrates that these Uí Duibhgeannáin annalists' purview was directed much more strongly towards Bréifne and Airgialla than to Connacht. Consequently, it seems very likely that it was the Uí Duibhgeannáin who transmitted the Fermanagh material that Maoilín incorporated in Uí Maoil Chonaire-II. In these circumstances it is also of interest to identify the textual relationship between the Armagh-Derry[+] chronicle in AU and LC. From my own collations and those published by Mac Niocaill it appears that AU and LC are independent abstractions from a common source, each transmitting unique entries and passages and introducing their own individual errors, but this matter needs further critical analysis.[31] Incidentally the collation of LC against AT/AU/AB for 1126 shown in Figure 39 indicates that it was the expanded Armagh-Derry[+] chronicle that served as the principal source of LC over 1014–1224, and this LC/AU collation may be compared with the corresponding AU/AT/AB collation in Figure 33, p. 242.

LC 1126	AU 1126
1. *Enná mac Murchada, rí Laigen,* mortuus est.	1. *Ennai mc. mc. Murchadha ri Laigen* mortuus est.
2. *Slóighedh la Toirrdhealbach O Conchobair* a Laighneibh, gurro ghabh i n-gialla.	2. *Sluagadh la Tairrdelbach H. Conchobuir* i l-Laighnibh co ro ghaibh a n-giallu.
7. Rí-thurus Toirrdhealbaigh h-I Conchobair *co h-Ath Clíath,* go d-tard *righe* Atha Clíath 7 Laighen día *mac, .i. do Conchobar.*	7. Righ-therus Toirrdhelbaigh H. Conchobuir *co h-Ath Cliath* co tard *righi* Atha Cliath 7 Laigen dia *mac .i. do Conchobur.*
6. *Domhnall .H. Dúbhda do bháthad* iar n-denam *creiche a Tír Conaill.*	6. *Domnall H. Dubhdai do badhudh* iar n-denam *creichi i Tir Conaill.*

Figure 39. Parallel collation of LC/AU for 1126 showing in italic all textual elements found also in AT.

Here italics indicate the text that AU/LC share with AT which provides substantially longer versions of the three Connacht entries, showing the versions in AU/LC to have been summary additions to the Armagh-Derry chronicle taken from the Clonmacnoise chronicle. On the other hand the identical entry sequence and close textual correlation between AU and LC shows that here they both transmit faithful facsimiles of their common source.

In view of the trust that historians have reposed in the authority of AU as a result of the adoption of the *AU-priority* hypothesis it is worth examining AU's transmission of Uí Maoil Chonaire-II. I shall first consider the chronological and then the textual/semantic issues. The kalend+AD apparatus of LC/AU are asynchronous by one year over 1192–1223 and in 1901 Mac Carthy identified two entries which he asserted 'proved' that AU was correct against LC, and subsequent scholarship has accepted his verdict.[32] His first proposed 'proof' depended on his own assumption that the obit in question fell on a Sunday, while his second relied upon AU 1219.5's unique assertion that Ua

---

31 Mac Niocaill, 'Annála', 25 (AU/LC relationship).   32 Mac Carthy, *AU* ii, 240 n.2 (Obit assumed to fall on Sunday); idem, 264 n. e-e (AU alone asserts 'Domhnach'); Mac Niocaill, 'Annála', 18 n. 2 (citing AU 1219 vs LC 1218 asserts, 'Ag *AU* atá an ceart').

Daighri's death occurred on '8 December on Sunday (*.ui. id. December i n-Domhnach*)'. But since this date is unique to AU the cited weekday may just as easily be a subsequent computation based upon the cited AD of 1219. Furthermore in basing his judgement on just these two details Mac Carthy chose to ignore the facts that the independently attested deaths of both Ruaidhrí Ua Conchobair in 1198 and king William of Scotland in 1214, and also the inauguration of his son Alexander, are all accurately dated in LC but are one year late in AU.[33] In these circumstances I submit that the weight of evidence shows that LC's chronology is accurate over 1192–1223, but that AU has an additional kalend interpolated into AU 1192 and has omitted a kalend following AU 1223.[34] It is obvious that in fact this kalend omission served to synchronize AU 1224 precisely with Uí Maoil Chonaire-II's obit for Cathal Crobderg Ua Conchobair.

Next I turn to examine the chronological apparatus of AU over 1224–1484 and it must be noted that all references to AU here are specifically to its primary MS, TCD 1282, because significant changes were subsequently introduced to the chronological apparatus in Rawl. B. 489. I begin with the observation that the continuous presence in AU over 431–1484 of either the Latin ferial+epact+AD series or an appropriate blank space left for them shows that the compiler of Ua Caiside's primary source intended to extend the Latin apparatus of the Armagh-Derry[+] chronicle over the entire extent of his own compilation.[35] Since we know that Uí Maoil Chonaire-II provided an accurately synchronized kalend+ferial+AD apparatus over 1224–1423 this should have been simply a matter of translating the ferials from Irish to Latin. However, what in fact we find is that the chronological series transcribed by Ua Luinín exhibit either enormous lacunae or serious asynchronism over the period of Uí Maoil Chonaire-II. Namely the ferial series lacuna extends over 1169–1337, while the epactal series lacuna extends effectively over 1233–1484.[36] Now the start of this epactal lacuna at 1233 is just the year before the missed saltus at 1234 in Uí Maoil Chonaire-I discussed above. It is apparent therefore that the compiler of Ua Caiside's primary source was aware of the problem and here abandoned his campaign for Latin epacts and, more importantly, never returned to complete either them or the ferials over 1169–1337. Next, regarding AU's kalend+AD series over the period of Uí Maoil Chonaire-II, it is the case that between 1234

33 Mac Carthy, *AU* ii, 230 n.3 (Ua Conchobair), 259 n.1 (William & Alexander). 34 Mc Carthy, 'Synchronization', *s.a.* 1192, 1223. Mac Carthy, *AU* ii, 219–71 (AU 1192–1223); in his footnotes here Mac Carthy repeatedly noted that AU's interpolated entries synchronized with LC, but since these were transcribed by Ua Caiside based upon AU's AD they naturally synchronized. Mac Carthy pointedly ignored the many entries by Ua Luinín that are one year in arrears in AU relative to their cognates in LC. 35 In TCD 1282 Ua Luinín left part of the AD blank over 924–82 which Ua Caiside completed. 36 AU's only epacts after 1232, those over 1352–65, are all profoundly asynchronous.

and 1378 six kalends were omitted and one was interpolated. Consequently, AU exhibits an asynchronism varying from one to five years over 1263–1378 so that, for example, the entries at AU *s.a.* 1373 refer to events that occurred in AD 1378.[37] Now the AD series over 1343–78 as transcribed by Ua Luinín is highly erratic; for example it commences 1310, 1340, 1341, 1343, ..., and it duplicates 1352, 1355, 1360, 1365, while omitting 1342, 1351, 1354, 1358, 1364. But since Ua Luinín was an excellent scribe it is not plausible to attribute these incongruities to him, rather they show us that the kalend+AD series of Ua Caiside's primary source was seriously deficient. Subsequently Ua Caiside emended the series to remove most but not all of the incongruities.[38] The implication of all these kalend disruptions and consequent AD asynchronism is that the kalend+AD apparatus of Ua Caiside's primary source was in disorder over 1263–1378 and that Ua Caiside was unable to rectify it. On the other hand the kalend+AD series over 1379–1484 are synchronous, while the ferial series over 1338–1484 is substantially so.[39] The fact that this ferial series which resumes at 1338 is accurately synchronized and reflects none of the disruptions of the kalend+AD series over 1263–1378 shows it to be an entirely independent series. Now the year 1338 corresponds closely with the commencement in AU of specifically Fermanagh entries which were *not* in Uí Maoil Chonaire-II and hence this suggests that the compiler of Ua Caiside's primary source was using the Fermanagh chronicle to restore Fermanagh entries that had been omitted by Maoilín. It appears therefore that these ferials in AU from 1338 represent part of the original compilation of the Fermanagh chronicle. This Fermanagh chronicle evidently had a kalend+ferial apparatus extending over 1338–1484 and a reliable AD apparatus over 1379–1484. It appears in fact that this compiler was using Uí Maoil Chonaire-II to bridge the gap between the Armagh-Derry[+] and the Fermanagh chronicle but he was unable to synchronize them where they overlapped. Consequently, he did not transcribe the kalend+ferial+AD series of Uí Maoil Chonaire-II either accurately or completely, and it was these omissions that resulted in the extensive series of blank spaces and asynchronisms in AU over 1263–1378.

Turning next to the actual entries transcribed from Uí Maoil Chonaire-II by this compiler, collations of these with the parallel entries in CT/LC/MB shows that in AU many entries were either omitted or textual emendations introduced, including substantial abbreviation. In the following examples all significant textual and semantic differences have been shown in italic.

---

37 Mc Carthy, 'Synchronization', *s.a.* 1263, 1266, 1272, 1286, 1371, 1373 (kalend ommisions), 1314 (kalend interpolation).   38 Mac Carthy, *AU* ii, 474–561 further emended Ua Caiside's work to obtain a linear series over 1340–73 but his apparatus only identified the very last of Ua Caiside's emendations, cf. *s.a.* 1373, p. 560 n. b; cf. also Mc Carthy, 'Synchronization', *s.a.* 1343–78.   39 The only asynchronism of ferials after 1338 are those over 1356–67 which are one year in advance.

AU	CT	LC	MB
1300.1	1300.1	1300.1	258c.1
Teboit Buitiller, barun mór, úasal, mortuus est.	Teboit Butiler barun uasal mortuus est.	Tepóid Buitilér, barún mor uassal, mortuus est.	Theobald Buttler, a noble Barron, died.
1300.2	1300.2	1300.2	258c.2
h-Eoan Prinndregas do marbadh *le* mac Fiachra h- Ui Fhloínn.	Ioan Prendergas do marbad do mac Fiachra h. Flainn in hoc anno.	Ioan Prendarcass do mharbad do mac Fiacra h-I Fhloinn in hoc anno.	John Prendergrasse was slaine by the sone of ffiaghra o'fflynn.
1300.3	1300.9	1300.9	258c.4
Adam Sdondun, *barun mor aile, quieuit in Christo.*	Addam Stondun tigerna Cera mortuus est.	Adam Sdóndún, tigerna Cora, mortuus est.	Addam Stonton, Lord of *Beara,* died.

Here can be seen that the compiler transcribed nearly verbatim the first two entries of his source, but then skipped to the ninth entry where he omitted Adam's title 'tigerna Cera', but he implicitly acknowledged this omission with 'another great baron (*barun mor aile*)' referencing Teboit, and then substituted 'quieuit in Christo' for 'mortuus est'. In other cases this compiler introduced serious semantic errors as the following example shows:

AU 1301.3	CT 1301.3	LC 1301.2	MB 258c.3
Cairpri mac Cormaic h- Ui Mail-echlainn, do marbadh *tre fherghal*[at] [fhorghail] *a brathair fein*, mac Airt h-Ui Mail- echlainn.	Cormac mac Cormaic h. Mailsechlainn do marbad la mac Airt h. Mailsechlainn .i. mac derbrathar athar fein.	Cormac mac Cormaic h-I Mhaoilshechlainn do mharbad la mac Airt h-I Mhailsechlainn, .i. mac a derbbrathar a athar fein.	Cormack m^cCormach o'Melaghlenn was killed by the sonne of Art o'Melaghlen, *who was his one Cozen German,* his fathers brothers sone.

Here CT/LC/MB all agree against AU that the victim's name was 'Cormac' and that he was killed by Mac Airt, his father's brother's son; on the other hand AU's account makes his assailant Mac Airt his own brother. Moreover, in AU the word 'fherghal' is corrupt and this has resulted in an interlinear emendation by Ua Caiside endeavouring to restore sense.[40] In this instance the compiler of

40 Mac Carthy, *AU* ii, 396 nn. 3–5 (corruption & emendation).

Ua Caiside's primary source has substantially destroyed the meaning of the entry. Finally on encountering prolix entries this compiler frequently either omitted them or briefly summarized them as the following example shows:

AU 1338.2	CT 1338.4
Mac Iarla Uladh do ghabail d'Emonn a Burc 7 a chur *i* l-Loch *Oirbsen. Uilc mora 7 cagadh coitchenn i Connachtaibh trid sin.*	Emand a Burc .i. mac Iarla Ulad do gabail le hEmann a Burcc 7 cloch do chur fa braigit & a cur a Loch Mesca iar sin. Et tanicc milled Gall Condacht 7 a chinid fein trit-sin. Et do gab Toirrdelbach h. Conchobair nert Connacht iar sin 7 do hinnarbad Emann mac Uilliam Burcc a Connachtaib amach & do milled tuatha 7 cella Iarthair Connacht uli; 7 ro tinol Emand a Burc coblach mor do longaib 7 do barcaib ro bai ar olenaib na farrci re hed ciana. Lugni 7 in Corand do folmagad 7 do fassugad 7 a tigernus do gabail da n Gaidelaib duthcusa budein ar ndichur a nGall esib.

Semantically CT agrees with MB 292c both that Edmond de Burgh was put into Loch Mask with a stone about his neck and with its account of the ensuing widespread conflict in Connacht. However, in AU the stone has been omitted, the Loch has been changed to 'Oirbsen', i.e. Loch Corrib, and the conflict summarized as 'Great evils and general war in Connacht through that.' We are obliged therefore to conclude that the compiler of Ua Caiside's primary source made in effect a hasty précis of Uí Maoil Chonaire-II, omitting or summarizing longer entries and introducing textual and semantic emendations in the process. His transmission of the entries of Uí Maoil Chonaire-II is in fact as deficient as his transmission of its chronological apparatus. In these circumstances no priority of authority whatsoever can be given to AU's version of Uí Maoil Chonaire-II, rather before accepting them it is essential to first collate them against the parallel entries in CT/LC/MB. Parallel entries may also occur in FM but in these instances, since AU(MS H) was used in FM's compilation, agreement with FM alone cannot be taken as confirmation of the accuracy of AU's entry.

Finally I turn to consider the extent and origin of the Fermanagh chronicle. Here it must be emphasized that while the Fermanagh chronicle is illustrated in Figure 38, p. 262, as commencing in AU at 1423, this refers to the year at which Fermanagh entries become the dominant component of AU because transmission of Uí Maoil Chonaire-II ceased. In LC the Fermanagh chronicle is the dominant source from the very start of L2, i.e. from 1413. However, 1413 does not represent the start of this chronicle either, for in AU over 1338–1422 there are many entries unique to AU which predominantly refer to Fermanagh or its environs. From this it is evident that the compiler of Ua Caiside's primary source combined the Fermanagh chronicle with his précis of Uí Maoil Chonaire-II. When the purview of these Fermanagh entries is examined two institutions emerge conspicuously, the first the Meig Uidhir clan, cf. Figure 46, p. 321, and the second the monastery of Lisgoole (*Lis Gabhail*). This monastery is about one mile south of Enniskillen and was an abbey of Augustinian canons from the early twelfth century to the late sixteenth century. That by the fifteenth century there was a close connection between these two institutions is shown by AU's record of the burials of four Mag Uidhir in Lisgoole abbey, Cathal †1419, Domnall Ballach †1447, Piarrus bishop of Clogher †1450, Tadhg †1450, that Uilliam Mag Uidhir †1483 was abbot of Lisgoole, and that in *c.*1580 it was under Mag Uidhir control when Cú Connacht Mag Uidhir bestowed it upon the Franciscans.[41] Moreover, in the latter half of the fourteenth century the Annals register strong associations between Lisgoole abbey and the learned family of the Uí Chianáin. The earliest is Giolla na Naomh Ua Cianáin †1348, who is described in AU/FM as 'abbot of Lisgoole'. A generation later Ádhamh †1373 is described in CT/LC/FM as 'a learned historian', while his own colophons identify him as scribe of that part of the MS NLI G2–3 which was described by James Carney as 'the earliest surviving compilation of traditional material after the Book of Leinster, and antedates considerably the books of Lecan, Ballymote, Uí Maine, etc.'[42] Finally Ruaidhrí †1387 is described in CT/LC/MB/FM as 'chiefe Chronicler of the territory of Uriell (*ollamh Oirghiall le seanchas*)'. Thus we have three Uí Chianáin whose working lives extend over much of the fourteenth-century section of the Fermanagh chronicle in AU, two of whom were closely associated with Lisgoole and two of whom were historians. Circumstantially then there are good grounds to associate the founding of the Fermanagh chronicle and its compilation over 1338–1400 with the Uí Chianáin and Lisgoole. It seems very likely that it was an association between the Uí Chianáin and Uí Duibhgeannáin that led to the incorporation by Maoilín of many Fermanagh chronicle entries in his compilation of Uí Maoil Chonaire-II. In the fifteenth century the identification of the Uí Chianáin with history continues with Giolla na Naomh †1405 described in CT/LC/FM as 'ollamh of Fermanagh in history', followed by Maol Muire †1459 and Tadhg †1469 described in AU respectively as 'one who was to be professor of history and poetry' and 'the eminent historian'. Finally, an Uí Chianáin historian who lived contemporaneously with the compilation of Ua Caiside's primary source was Ruaidhrí mac Tadhg Ua Cianáin †1483 who is described in AU(MS H)/FM as 'ollam of Mag Uidhir in history (*ollam Meg Uidhir re senchus*)'. Now the only other person in AU to be accorded this title is Ruaidhrí Ua Luinín, the principal scribe of MS H, and taking this together with the close synchronism

41 Ó Muraíle, 'Ó Cianáin', 396 (Lisgoole).   42 Carney, 'Ó Cianáin', 123 (cit.).

of the death of Ruaidhrí Ua Cianáin with the termination of Ua Caiside's primary source I conclude that he was the probable compiler of it.[43] The one-year difference between Ruaidhrí's death in 1483 and the termination of the Latin chronological apparatus does not represent a serious obstacle to this identification since anyone such as an amanuensis to Ruadhrí Ua Cianáin may have extended the chronological apparatus in Latin by one year. In summary it appears that Ruaidhrí Ua Cianáin started with the Armagh-Derry[+] chronicle, and with the Uí Chianáin Fermanagh chronicle compiled by his ancestors, and he undertook to combine these two using Uí Maoil Chonaire-II to bridge the intervening gap. His intention was to maintain a Latin kalend+ferial+epact+ AD apparatus throughout but he never completed this, and his summary transcriptions of both the apparatus and entries of Uí Maoil Chonaire-II introduced numerous errors and problems into the chronicle. As a consequence the reliability of AU in terms of reproducing the chronology and semantics of its sources is variable. Since Ruaidhrí Ua Caiside was subsequently unable to rectify Ruaidhrí Ua Cianáin's chronological errors the result is that AU's chronological apparatus over much of 1192–1378 is seriously in error.

Summary of the evolution of the Connacht and Fermanagh chronicles

Circa 1220 – The Boyle chronicle was compiled in the Cistercian abbey at Boyle using the Armagh-Derry[+] chronicle together with Cistercian and Boyle records and it continued to 1228.

Circa 1228 – A copy of the Boyle chronicle was made and removed to nearby Holy Trinity where it was continued until it terminated at 1257, and this work survives as AB alias BL Cotton Titus A. xxv.

Circa 1231 – The Connacht chronicle was initiated at Cluain Plocáin by Uí Maoil Chonaire ollamhs for their Uí Chonchobair patrons as a continuation of the Clonmacnoise chronicle, maintaining its Irish ferial+epact apparatus. Their chronicle Uí Maoil Chonaire-I commenced with an eulogistic obit for Cathal Crobderg at 1224, and successive ollamhs continued this compilation up until *c.*1423. At some stage in this period a member of the Uí Maoil Chonaire compiled a secular version of the Clonmacnoise chronicle by enhancing some of the existing Uí Bhriúin and Uí Chonchobair entries, and omitting all the Clonmacnoise *comharba* series, and Rawl. B. 488 is a lacunose copy of this and constitutes with Rawl. B. 502 our AT.

Circa 1340 – The Uí Duibhgeannáin emerge as ollamhs to the Síl Maolruanadh and Conmhaicne and commence compiling a chronicle of their patrons, the Meic Diarmada, Meic Donnchada, and Uí Fheargaile.

---

43 Ó Muraíle, 'Ó Cianáin', 396 (Giolla na Naomh †1348), 397–402 (Ádhamh), 402–4 (Ruaidhrí †1387), 406–8 (Giolla na Naomh †1405, Tadhg, Ruaidhrí †1483).

Circa 1387 – The historian Ruaidhrí Ua Cianáin 'ollamh Oirghiall' initiated compilation of a chronicle centred on Fermanagh that commenced at *c.*1338 and accorded prominence to the affairs of the Meig Uidhir.

Circa 1423 – Maoilín Ua Maoil Chonaire undertook a major recompilation of Uí Maoil Chonaire-I together with the Boyle-Holy Trinity, Uí Duibhgeannáin and Uí Chianáin chronicles, in which he incorporated substantial Latin chronological addimenta into the chronological apparatus. For the pre-1224 compilation of Uí Maoil Chonaire-II see chapter 10, p. 289 ff.

Circa 1432–78 –Uí Maoil Chonaire-II was continued by ollamhs Torna and Urard Ua Maoil Chonaire normally omitting the addimenta.

Circa 1483 – A Fermanagh compiler, most likely Ruaidhrí Ua Cianáin, combined the Armagh-Derry[+] chronicle, Uí Maoil Chonaire-II and his ancestors' Fermanagh chronicle to obtain what was to serve Ruaidhrí Ua Caiside as the primary source for AU.

Circa 1542 – A member of the Uí Duibhgeannáin, possibly Duibgeand mac Dubhthaigh, extended the continuation of Uí Maoil Chonaire-II over 1479–*c.*1542. In this continuation the chronological apparatus was reduced simply to a kalend+'ais an Tigerna'.

Circa 1578 – Páidín Ua Duibhgeánnain and another, with the assistance of Dolbh, Duibgeand's brother, transcribed Uí Maoil Chonaire-II and the Uí Duibhgeannáin chronicle over 1224–1544, and their work survives as RIA 1219 which constitutes CT.

Circa 1577–90 – The Uí Duibhgeannáin with Brian Mac Diarmada recorded Magh Luirg events over 1568–90, and also made partial transcriptions of the Armagh-Derry[+], Uí Maoil Chonaire-II, Fermanagh and Uí Duibhgeannáin chronicles over 1014–1577. This work survives as TCD 1293 (H.1.19) ff. 1–136, and BL Add. 4792, ff. 19–32 and this constitutes LC.

CHAPTER TEN

The regnal-canon chronicles

In chapter 1 MB and FM were placed together in the regnal-canon group in recognition of the fact that their primary chronological structure consists of a virtually identical sequence of reigns of the 'king of Ireland (*rí hErenn*)'. This series commences deep in Irish legendary prehistory with Slainghe m. Deala, the first Fir Bolg king, and continues unbroken to Maolsechlainn Mór m. Domhnaill †1022. This is then followed by a series of kings characterized as the 'king of Ireland with opposition (*rí Herend co fressabra*)' extending from Diarmait m. Mael na mBó †1072 to Ruaidhrí Ua Conchobhair †1198. The questions to be addressed in this chapter are therefore, where and when and from what sources was this regnal-canon constructed, and how was it incorporated into MB and FM?[1]

Construction of the regnal-canon

The essential features of the regnal-canon of MB and FM are found in the following works:

a) The two poems *Rig Themra dia tesband tnú* and *Rig Themra toebaige iar tain* by Flann Mainistrech †1056, *fer leginn* in the monastery of Monasterboice in county Louth. These two poems recite the regnal-canon from Eochaidh Feidhleach to Maolsechlainn Mór, but only very occasionally cite regnal years. Complementary to Flann's two poems is the unattributed poem *Ereamhón is Eber ard* which recites the canon from Ereamhón to Eochaidh Feidhleach citing regnal years.[2]

b) The two poems *Hériu ard inis na rrig* and *At-tá sund forba fessa* by Gilla Cóemáin whose *floruit* is placed at 1072 by the *annus praesens* given by him in a third and related poem *Annálad anall uile*. In these two poems he recited the regnal-canon from Slainghe to Brian Bóruma citing regnal years for all except Modh Corb's reign.[3]

---

1 Useful background for this chapter will be found in Mc Carthy 'Irish regnal canon', *passim*. 2 Best et al., *Book of Leinster* iii, 504–15 (*Rig Themra dia tesband tnú*, and *Rig Themra toebaige iar tain*); Smith, 'Irish historical verse', 340 n. 91 (Flann's regnal years); Mulchrone, *Book of Lecan*, fac. ff. 14ᵛ–15ᵛ, 33ʳ⁻ᵛ (*Ereamhón is Eber ard*); Smith, 'Irish historical verse', 326–41 (a helpful survey of the development of Irish historical verse). 3 Smith, *Gilla Cóemáin*, 100–203 (critical editions

c) The *a* and *m* recensions of LG, which Mark Scowcroft, who has provided the most comprehensive analysis of the structure and development of the text, has dated between 1072 and 1166. In these two recensions the regnal-canon, including regnal years, is embedded in narrative accounts of the reigns which extend from Slainghe to Dathí m. Fiachrach †428. Recension *a* then continues from Laoghaire m. Néill to Maolsechlainn Mór followed by the kings with opposition to Ruaidhrí Ua Conchobhair.[4]

d) Amongst a series of fourteen canons in the composite MS now Laud Misc. 610 ff. 112^r–116^v, seven canons list the reigns and regnal years from Slainghe to Maolsechlainn Mór. This MS was written by Seaan Buidhi Ua Cléirigh and Gilla na Naem Mac Aedagáin in 1453–4 for Émann Mac Risderd Buitler *alias* Edmund McRichard Butler. While this MS long postdates a–c) above Mac Aedagáin states in a colophon that their exemplar was the Psalter of Cashel whose compilation will be discussed below.

The correspondence of the essential features of the regnal-canon in these works, viz. the names of their reigns, their order and regnal years, is demonstrated comprehensively in appendix 3. Regarding the form of the regnal-canon in these sources, in a–c) it is integrated with either prose or versified historical narrative to which it is subordinate, whereas in d) it appears in canon form together with other ancillary canons replete with interval summations, synchronizing equations and identifications of contemporaneity. This contrast alone provides grounds for proposing that these Laud canons preserve the regnal-canon at an earlier stage of its development than do the other versions. As we shall see this hypothesis is well supported by other independent considerations.

Kuno Meyer published an edition of these Laud canons in 1913, and references here to the text will be by his page and line numbers. In 1915 Eoin Mac Neill published his careful analysis of them which showed that the two scribes had transcribed the canons in anachronistic order, and had reduced some parallel canons to single columns.[5] Mac Neill showed that the canons nevertheless provided a virtually continuous sequence of reigns and regnal years of Irish kings together with some Mediterranean and ecclesiastical dynasties extending from Slainghe to Maolsechlainn Mór. The arrangement and content of these canons can most concisely be exhibited by numbering them sequentially

with translations), 136 (Modh Corb); cf. Best et al., *Book of Leinster* iii, 471–503 (*Hériu ard, Atá sund* and *Annálad anall uile*), 483 (Modh Corb).   4 Macalister, *LG* i–v, (the oft criticized but only substantial published edition of the text; his recension sigla R^1, R^2, R^3, Min. = Scowcroft *a, b, c, m*); Carey, *Lebor Gabála*, 7–19 (a succinct but comprehensive account of LG and its scholarship up to 1993); Scowcroft, '*LG* I' and '*LG* II' *passim* (analysis), and 'LG I' 85–7 (recensions), 96–7 (dates), 140 (LG *a*'s canon), 132–3, 141 (LG *m*'s canon).   5 Meyer, 'Laud synchronisms', 471–85 (edition); Mac Neill, 'Laud 610', 81–96 (analysis).

§1–14 and tabulating each canon according to the range of years into which it falls. This is shown in Figure 40.[6]

Range	Canon serial number and dynasty
c.1262 BC–c.995 BC	1. Fir Bolg, Tuatha de Danaan, **Hebrew**, and Assyrian kings.
c.980 BC–c.433 BC	4. Parallel canons of a) Assyrian kings, b) **Judaean kings/ Christ's ancestors**, c) Irish kings.
c.413 BC–c.40 BC	3. Persian kings, **Christ's ancestors**, and Irish kings.
c.44 BC–c.AD 33	2. Roman emperors, **Christ's ancestors**, and Irish kings.
c.AD 38–c.450	5. Parallel canons of a) Roman emperors, b) **Popes**, c) Irish kings.
c.AD 429–763	6. Parallel canons of a) Tara kings, b) **Armagh bishops**, c) Cashel kings; 7. Dál nAraide kings; 8. Mide kings; 12. Connaught kings; 13. Aileach kings; 14. Ulaid kings.
c.AD 764–1022	9. Tara kings; 10. **Comharba Patraic**; 11. Cashel kings.

Figure 40. The fourteen canons of Laud 610 ff. 112^r–116^v arranged in chronological order following Mac Neill *ZCP* x (1915) 87–93. Dynasties with a spiritual connotation are shown in bold.

The anachronistic order of these canons as written by the scribes can be seen in the sequence 1, 4, 3, 2, 5, 6:7:8:12:13:14, 9:10:11 where contemporaneous canons are here separated by colons. Their continuity can be seen in the virtually continuous sequence of ranges from 1262 BC to AD 1022, and consequently a virtually continuous series of Irish/Tara kings is found in the series of seven canons 1, 4c, 3, 2, 5c, 6a, 9.[7] Regarding their form, each of the canons 4, 5, 6 is arranged as a triple of parallel canons written in three columns, and Mac Neill pointed to convincing evidence that canons 1, 2, 3 had formerly also been written in parallel columns.[8] The arrangement of the surviving parallel canons and the content of formerly parallel canons show that the principle determining their construction was to have a central 'spiritual' dynasty flanked on either side by a secular dynasty. The series of spiritual dynasties

6 The canons are printed in continuous lines except for a poem that intrudes between canons 3 and 4 at 474.14–17, and detached fragments of canons 1 and 3 given by Meyer in 471 n.1. The following table cites the serial number and starting line of each canon: 1) 471.1; 2) 472.1; 3) 473.6; 4) 474.18; 5) 476.29; 6) 478.27; 7) 480.1; 8) 480.11; 9) 480.28; 10) 481.9; 11) 482.6; 12) 482.30; 13) 483.23; 14) 484.11. Meyer's heading 'kings of Cashel' at 482.9 belongs at 482.6, his 'kings of Ulster' at 482.30 should read 'kings of Connaught', and a heading 'kings of Ulaid' is needed at 484.11.   7 Meyer, 'Laud synchronisms', has misread at least eight regnal years and those affecting Irish/Tara kings are: 476.7 'Núado Finn Fáil, .xlx.' recte .xl.; 478.29 'Laegaire mac Neill, .xix.' recte .xxx.; 480.37 'Áed Findlíath, .lxvii.' recte .xvii.   8 Byrne, *Irish kings*, plate 36 opp. p. 175 (reproduces Laud 610 f. 114^v i.e. canon 5); Mac Neill, 'Laud 610', 81–3 (parallel canons).

comprised the Hebrew kings, Judaean kings, Christ's ancestors, Popes, Armagh bishops/chomarba, and these are shown in bold in Figure 40 above. The flanking secular dynasties comprised a Mediterranean and an Irish king until the arrival of Christianity in Ireland, and thereafter the kings of Tara and Cashel. These two kings ruling respectively Leth Cuinn and Leth Moga form symmetrical secular dynasties with the central spiritual dynasty of Armagh. Consequently, the term 'synchronism' that has been repeatedly applied to these canons is misleading. For the primary purpose of these canons was to present a harmonious balance between the southern and northern secular polities and the Christian church. Their primary motivation therefore was emphatically political and has nothing whatsoever to do with chronology or time as will be discussed further below. Obviously the canons of provincial kings 7:8:12:13:14 do not belong within this scheme and must be considered a subsequent accretion to canon 6, as is also indicated by canon 7 entirely lacking regnal years.

Regarding the compilation of these canons Mac Neill observed that the canons 6a–c all terminated within the years 743–63, and that canons 9:10:11 represent continuations of these. Based upon these observations Mac Neill proposed that they had been compiled in two phases the first of which he dated to 742, and the second had been continued 'by a later redactor down to the beginning of the eleventh century'.[9] In 1946 T.F. O'Rahilly convincingly rejected Mac Neill's dating of the first phase of compilation by pointing to errors and later features in canons 1–6 that implied they had been compiled much later, and instead O'Rahilly proposed 'probably not earlier than the latter half of the tenth century'.[10] Thus both these scholars considered that canons 1–6 had been compiled well before the time of either Flann Mainistrech or Gilla Cóemáin. Furthermore regarding the relationship between these canons and the works of Flann Mainistrech and Gilla Cóemáin, Mac Neill and O'Rahilly pointed to evidence that both poets had based their compilations upon an earlier version of these canons. Mac Neill wrote that a 'version of the Laud list was a principal source of the versified list of the kings of Mide by Flann Mainistrech', while O'Rahilly wrote that in 'the eleventh and twelfth centuries these Irish regnal lists provided a quarry for "historians" like Flann Mainistrech and Gilla Coemáin, who busied themselves in turning the lists into verse.'[11] These observations, together with the extensive structural correspondences demonstrated in appendix 3, constitute good reasons to conclude therefore that the canons transcribed into Laud 610 are closely related to the source used for the abovementioned poems of Flann Mainistrech and Gilla Cóemáin.

---

9 Mac Neill, 'Laud 610', 92 (cit.), 93 (compilation date).   10 O'Rahilly, *Early Irish history*, 418 (cit.).   11 Mac Neill, 'Laud 610', 94–5 (cit.); O'Rahilly, *Early Irish history*, 418 (cit.) and n. 2 where he cites examples.

Regarding the exemplar used by the scribes of Laud 610, fortunately Mac Aedagáin, having completed canon 14 and before he commenced the following text, inscribed a colophon in which he wrote:[12]

> We have in this book of the Ráith everything that we can find in the old book, the Psalter of Cashel, and whoever shall read and understand it, everything that is lacking at the end is supplied in the middle or at the beginning. The year of the Lord today is one thousand four hundred and forty and fourteen years more.

Now while Mac Aedagáin here wrote in general terms of 'this book of the Ráith', his acknowledgment of the disorderly sequence of their transcription correlates closely with their actual arrangement of these canons. This and their juxtaposition suggest then that his colophon applies especially to these canons. In any case it is absolutely explicit that the Psalter of Cashel had served as their exemplar for this text, so we next must turn our attention to this work. While the Psalter of Cashel was often cited as a source by medieval authors, particularly in genealogical works, unfortunately no copy of the work has survived leaving the questions of its contents, place and date of compilation, and author(s) surrounded by considerable uncertainty. However, in 1989 Pádraig Ó Riain published a valuable survey of the available evidence bearing on these matters and this showed that the most usual attribution was to Cormac mac Cuileannáin †908, the king and bishop of Cashel.[13] Now examination of these Laud canons 1–6 does indeed disclose a number of distinctive Munster features. Firstly a specifically Cashel provenance is implicit in canon 6c where the Cashel kings alone were tabulated in parallel with the kings of Tara and Armagh bishops. During the eighth century it was 'the Munstermen who evolved the doctrine of two equal hegemonies of Leth Cuinn and Leth Moga. An elaborate parallelism was worked out between the traditions of Dál Cuinn and Eóganacht.'[14] In canon 6 this doctrine was implemented with the Cashel kings representing Munster. Secondly examination of canon 4c shows that most of these Irish kings have also been given a provincial association with one of the tribes, 'a Mumain', 'a Temraig', 'a hUltaib', or 'do Corco Láidi', that is two tribes each from Leth Cuinn and Leth Moga. The genealogists assigned as ancestors to these tribes the four sons of Míl, viz. Éber, Éreamhón, Ír and Lugaid m. Ítha, and these are given exactly as thus by Cormac in his introduction to a genealogical collection for the whole of Ireland.[15] Thirdly a specifically

---

12 Dillon, 'Laud 610', 153 (cit.) and O'Sullivan, 'Three notes', 144 n. 32 (the sequence of marginalia xciii and xciv). The inference at *idem*, 151 that these two marginalia 'were probably written in after the completion of the manuscript' is not correct, for textual displacement shows they were written at the same time as the text.   13 Ó Riain, Psalter of Cashel, 116, 126 (Cormac).   14 Byrne, *Irish kings*, 202 (cit.).   15 Byrne, *Irish kings*, 202 (Cormac's introduction), 202–29 (Leth Cuinn vs Leth Moga and Éber et al.).

western Munster provenance is found in canon 6c where Cashel kings of the Uí Énnai affiliation and the death of Ailbhe of Emly are noted. Finally Cormac is distinguished by being the only individual in these canons whose death is precisely dated, viz. 'Cormac m. Cuilennáin. Laigin romarb I n-íd Septimbir 7 i mairt 7 i tres.'[16] Taking these four points together with the medieval attributions to Cormac that cannot be lightly set aside I conclude that he is indeed the most likely author of canons 1–6. While doubts have been expressed regarding Cormac's authorship of the genealogical material identified with the Psalter these have arisen because of the presence of specifically northern elements considered inappropriate to Cormac.[17] But in canons 1–6 there is no such northern intrusion, indeed in canons 2–3 twice as many Munster kings are explicitly noted as for Leinster, Tara or Ulster. Consequently, I consider the attribution of canons 1–6 to Cormac mac Cuileannáin as trustworthy.

I next turn to consider the sources that Cormac used for this compilation, focussing principally upon his series of Irish/Tara kings since it was these that subsequently furnished the basis for the Irish regnal-canon. I commence with canon 6a, comprizing twenty-nine Tara kings extending from Laoghaire m. Néill r. 429–62 to Domnall m. Murchada r. 744–64 and observe that:

a) The Laud regnal names correspond closely with the Annalistic names, cf. Laud 'Laegaire mac Néill … Ailill Molt … Lugaid mac Laegaire', with AU 'Laegaire filii Neill … Ailill Molt … Lughdach filii Laeghaire'.
b) The Laud regnal sequence corresponds with the Annalistic Tara series with just a solitary exception noted at a) below.
c) The start of canon 6 is closely synchronized with the commencement of Annalistic chronicling in Ireland at c.429, while the final three reigns of 6 a–c all commence shortly before 753. Namely Domnall m. Murchada r. 744–64, Céle Petair r. 751–8, and Cathassach m. Etersceoil r. 742–58.

Based upon these correspondences I conclude that it was the Moville chronicle compiled from the Iona chronicle in Moville at c.753 as discussed in chapter 6, p. 175 ff., that served as Cormac's primary source for canon 6. Since this terminus of 753 is also observed by the additional canons of 7:8:12:13:14 that all refer to dynasties of the northern half of Ireland and many of the obits of these kings are found in the Annals, I also infer that the Moville chronicle was an important source for their compilation. Of course Cormac also used other sources, particularly for the Cashel series of canon 6c and for the years of each final reign, but the Moville chronicle was unmistakably the most important

16 Meyer, 'Laud synchronisms', 482 (cit.). 17 O'Sullivan, 'Three notes', 147–51, and Ó Riain, 'Psalter of Cashel', 118–19 (northern elements).

source that he used in the compilation of the Christian Tara regnal series. It is consequently important to determine how accurately Cormac reproduced the chronology of his source, and collation of canon 6a against the Annalistic Tara succession shows as follows:

a) Cormac reversed the order of the reigns of Ainmire m. Setna and the joint reigns of Eochaidh m. Domnaill and Baodan m. Muirchertagh, and this is the solitary sequence discrepancy mentioned above at b).

b) Of Cormac's twenty-nine reigns only seven preserve regnal years identical with their Annalistic source, eight show a difference of one year, and fourteen show differences ranging from two to thirteen years. Thus nearly half of Cormac's reigns manifest substantial divergence from his Annalistic source.

c) The total inclusive interval from Laoghaire m. Néill r. 429 to Domnall m. Murchada †763 is 335 years, while the sum of canon 6a's regnal years is just 319 years, leaving an anachronism of sixteen years.

In these circumstances we are obliged to conclude that Cormac made no serious endeavour to reproduce accurately the chronology of his primary source, and the consequences of this for anyone who used his canon 6a were profound. To underline this point I tabulate in Figure 41 in parallel with their Annalistic source the four Laud reigns over the later sixth century wherein the anachronism is the most severe.[18]

Annals – reigns and obits	Laud 610 – line numbers and reigns
Ainmire m. Setna r. 3y., †568.	10. Baetan ⁊ Eochu .i. meic Muirchertaig [no regnal years cited]
Eochaid m. Domnaill ⁊ Baodan m. Muircertigh r. 3y., †571.	12. Anmere m. Sétnai .iii.
Baodan m. Nindeadha r. 13 y., †584.	13. Baetán .i. m. Ninnida ..., blíadain.
Aodh m. Ainmirech r. 12 y., †596.	15. Áed m. Anmerech, .xxu.

Figure 41. Parallel collation of Annalistic and Laud 610 reigns over the later sixth century showing their anachronisms in regnal sequence and years.

Here can be seen Cormac's reversal of the first two reigns, his near elimination of the third and his more than doubling of the fourth. Since these features were transmitted with only minor adjustments through all the descendants of Cormac's canon their chronological basis for the entire later sixth century was

18 Mc Carthy, 'Synchronization', *s.a.* 568, 571, 584, 596 (reigns); Meyer, 'Laud Synchronisms', 479 (reigns).

profoundly distorted. A comparable distortion exists also in the later seventh century as a result of Cormac reducing the regnal years of Finnechta m. Dunchadha from the Annalistic twenty to just eight years. However, unlike the preceding distortions this was not in general transmitted to the later editions of the canon.[19]

Having demonstrated the character of Cormac's compilation of the Tara succession for the post-Patrician period I turn to briefly examine his corresponding compilation for the pre-Patrician period, i.e. his canon 5c. Here we observe that:

a) Cormac commenced canon 5c with the reign of Lugaid Reóderg so that it is synchronized to the very first Tara reign of the Moville chronicle.

b) Canon 5c comprises twenty-nine reigns from Lugaid Reóderg to Dathí m. Fiachrach and these consist of the entire series of eighteen Tara reigns from the Moville chronicle merged with four of its Emain reigns, plus an additional seven reigns including three Leinster reigns.

Now in this process of supplementing the Moville chronicle's Tara succession with reigns from other dynasties Cormac made no attempt to maintain the chronology of the Tara succession. Thus whereas in the Moville chronicle this succession extends from Lugaid Reóderg r. 49 to Dathí m. Fiachrach †428, a total of 380 years, the summation of the regnal years of canon 5c is 462 years implying an asynchronism of eighty-two years. Hence we find that over the entire Christian period Cormac's canons of Tara kings were in severe chronological conflict with the Moville chronicle that he used as his primary source.

Finally I briefly consider Cormac's compilation of the pre-Christian Irish regnal succession in canons 1, 4c, 3, and 2. Here, with the exception only of the inceptions of the Fir Bolg, Tuatha de Danaan and Milesian dynasties these regnal successions were not included in the Moville chronicle before the reign of Cimbáed m Fintain. Rather the Moville compiler's assertion that 'All the records of the Scots until Cimbáed were uncertain' shows that he considered all earlier sources as chronologically unreliable as was discussed in chapter 6, p. 178 ff. Following Cimbáed however the Moville compiler supplied the Emain succession to Fergus Fogha †AD 253 and he located the Incarnation at year 27 of the Emain king Concobur m. Nessa and synchronized his death with the year of the Crucifixion. Cormac on the other hand supplied comprehensive successions from an unidentified source for the Fir Bolg, Tuatha de Danaan and Milesians extending to the Crucifixion in canon 2. Here he explicitly synchronized

---

19 Mc Carthy, 'Irish regnal canon', Table 3 reign 168 where the value is found effectively only in Ua Caiside's poem.

the Incarnation with year three of Eochaid Feidhleach and also with year 27 of Concobur m. Nessa, showing thereby that he was indeed using the Moville chronicle as a reference.[20] Cormac also placed the Incarnation at AM 3952 showing that he was assuming the Vulgate chronological tradition, and he located the arrival of the Milesians 1275 years after the Flood. Since the summation of his regnal years from the Milesians to the Incarnation is 1309 years Cormac's total for the period Flood–Incarnation is 1275+1309=2584, and this exceeds the Vulgate chronology of 3952−1656+1=2297 by 287 years.[21] Regarding the non-Irish entries in these canons there can be no doubt from their names, regnal years, summations and some synchronizing equations that up to c.AD 378 these were taken from Jerome's chronicle, excepting only Christ's ancestors who were taken from Matthew's Gospel 1.12–16.

In summary it emerges from this examination of the sources used by Cormac for his Irish regnal succession that for the Christian period his primary source was the Moville chronicle. However, Cormac made no attempt to reproduce its chronology, but rather his effort was directed towards the assembly of asynchronous tripartite secular and spiritual successions. For the pre-Christian period the summation of his regnal years is in serious conflict with that of Vulgate chronology. Thus over its entire range from the mythological to the historical Cormac's canons show repeated anachronisms and conflicts with both Biblical and Annalistic chronology. The conclusion appears inevitable that Cormac possessed an inadequate knowledge of and an extremely naïve approach to chronology. The consequence of this for anyone who adopted his regnal-canon was a labyrinth of irresolvable anachronisms, and that is indeed what transpired.

Next turning to canons 9:10:11, whose final reigns comprise Brian r. 1002–14, Mael Muire r. 1002–20 and Maolsechlainn Mór r. 1015–22 respectively, obviously these cannot have been finally completed before 1022. Consequently, they must be the result of a subsequent phase of compilation that has extended Cormac's canons. Now in his preface to MB Mageoghagan gave an alternative attribution for the Psalter of Cashel, which is unique in many respects and worth citing at length:[22]

> Amongst all the worthie and memorable deedes of King Brian Borow sometime kinge of this Kindome, this is not of the least accoumpt … after settinge himself in the quiet possession thereof … He assembled together all the Nobilitie of the Kingdome as well Spirituall as Temporall to Cashell in Mounster, and caused them to compose a booke containing all the inhabitations, euents and Septs that lived in this Land from the first peopling, inhabitation and discoverie thereof after

---

20 Meyer, 'Laud synchronisms', 472.10–12 (Incarnation synchronisms & Eochaidh Feidhleach).
21 Meyer, 'Laud synchronisms', 472.5 (AM 3952), 471.3 (Fir Bolg), 471.11 (Tuatha de Danaan), 471.25 (Milesians & Flood).   22 MS BL Add. 4817 ff. 3ʳ⁻ᵛ cf. Murphy, *AC*, 7–8 (cit.).

the Creation of the World untill that present, which booke they caused to be
called by the name of the Psalter of Cashell, signed it with his owne hand together
with the handes of the Kings of the five Provinces, and alsoe with the hands of all
the Bushoppes and Prelates of the Kingdome; caused severall copies thereof to bee
given to the Kings of the Provinces, with straight charge, that there should be noe
credit giuen to any other Cronicles thenceforth, butt should bee held as false,
disannulled and quite forbidden forever. Since which time there were manie Septs
in the Kingdome that liued by itt and whose profession was to Chronicle ...

In this passage Mageoghagan asserted that following Brian's achievement of
supremacy in the kingship he instigated the compilation of the Psalter of
Cashel. Now since Brian achieved supremacy in *c.*1002 and died in 1014 this
attribution fits very closely with the terminal dates of canons 9:10:11. Indeed
all but the final entries of these three canons could have been compiled within
the years 1002–14. Furthermore the appearance of Brian's name at the
conclusion of *both* the Tara and Cashel canons is climactic and underlines in a
dramatic way his achievement of national hegemony. Additionally, when Ó
Cléirigh's sources are examined below it will emerge that Mageoghagan was in
possession of a substantial body of historical material so that when he wrote of
those 'whose profession was to Chronicle', he was speaking also of himself, so
that he was therefore well placed to know something of the origin of his own
chronicle tradition. I conclude therefore that Mageoghagan's assertion that Brian
instigated the compilation of the Psalter of Cashel after achieving supremacy
over Maolsechlainn Mór is correct, and as part of this earlier canons compiled
by Cormac mac Cuileannáin were extended up to Brian's time.[23] It is also likely
that at this time the provincial canons 7:8:12:13:14 were added. Thus the
attributions to Cormac and to Brian may be regarded not as conflicting but as
complementary.

However, it is not possible to accept Mageoghagan's other assertions that
multiple copies of the Psalter of Cashel were issued to the five provincial kings
each endorsed with the signatures of Brian, the provincial kings, and many
bishops, together with an edict that other chronicles be suppressed. Firstly there
is absolutely no independent evidence for the existence of such a formidable and
authoritative production, and indeed Ó Riain remarked the absence of evidence
for it having circulated even in Munster in the interval 1350–1450. Secondly Ó
Riain pointed out that while the secular genealogies repeatedly cite the Psalter of
Cashel the version that actually circulated represented an Armagh revision of an
earlier Cashel version. Thirdly the existence of AT/CS/AR/AU/AI/AB/
CT/LC witnesses the substantial survival of other chronicle traditions. How

23 Jaski, 'Psalter', 301 '... it is possible that Brian updated and expanded material already gathered
by Cormac who, as its bishop and king, had a clear connection with Cashel.'

are these considerations to be reconciled? O Riain's survey of the content of the Psalter of Cashel showed that its scope was very substantial indeed, including secular and ecclesiastical genealogies and dynasties, *dinnsheanchas*, and Nennius' *Historia Brittonum*.[24] Since the evidence of these Laud canons indicates that the compilation of even a Tara-Armagh-Cashel canon in parallel form extending to Brian's time was not finalized, I suggest that compilation of the other Psalter components was also incomplete at the time of Brian's unexpected death at Clontarf in 1014. Thereafter the political impetus to complete a Munster-oriented compilation was lost and, with the reversion of the kingship to Maolsechlainn Mór, the scholarly initiative moved northwards and a copy of Brian's incomplete Psalter with it. This carried the authority of both Cormac and Brian, and was evidently welcomed as authoritative in Armagh where Brian was buried. Subsequently it was drawn upon by northern scholars such as Flann Mainistrech, Gilla Cóemáin, and the compilers of the Armagh recension of secular genealogies.[25]

In the foregoing discussion I have referred to the 'Laud canons', whereas Meyer published them under the title of 'The Laud synchronisms', and this has been used widely by scholars ever since. Unfortunately Meyer did not explain to which element the word 'synchronism' referred, though his use of it in the title naturally suggested that it applied generally to these canons. Subsequent scholars have understood 'synchronism' to qualify the canons tabulated in parallel columns, although Meyer himself designated these simply as 'parallel lists'. For example, Mac Neill's use of the terms 'synchronic columns', 'synchronic tabulated history', 'synchronic table', and O'Rahilly's 'columnar synchronization' and 'synchronistic columnar arrangement' show that both considered the parallel canons to be 'synchronized'.[26] However, examination of all the parallel canons shows that in fact reigns placed collinearly are simply very approximately contemporaneous. For example, canons 4a and 4b were taken respectively from the Assyrian and Judaean columns of Jerome's chronicle, and consider the reigns 'Offratalus .xx.' and 'Ioram mac Iosaphath .uiii.', which Cormac placed collinearly. Jerome's chronicle commences Offrataeus' reign of twenty years at AA 1066 and Ioram's reign of eight years at AA 1107, so that these two reigns do not even nearly run concurrently.[27] Thus these reigns cannot possibly be described as 'synchronized'. Moreover, if the regnal years in each column are summed then large anachronisms will be repeatedly found; for example, Offratalus to Offratanes = 20 years, Ioram to Ioas = 15 years, Eochaidh Faebarglas to Énna Airgdech = 78 years, where these three first and

---

24 Ó Riain, 'Psalter of Cashel', 112–13 (secular genealogies), 116–17 (circulation), 122–3 (content). 25 Jaski, 'Psalter', 329 cites independent reasons to conclude that Laud's regnal canons 'belonged to the Psalter as it was *c.*1015'.   26 Mac Neill, 'Laud 610', 81 (cits.); O'Rahilly, *Early Irish history*, 413 (cits.).   27 Meyer, 'Laud synchronisms', 475.3 (cits.); Helm, *Hieronymus*, 74a (Offrataeus), 77a (Ioram).

three last rulers appear collinearly. Indeed reflection shows that in general it is impossible to synchronize the *reigns* of concurrent dynasties, only the *years* of the reigns may be synchronized once the reigns are reduced to integral years, as Eusebius demonstrated. Thus the repeated designation of these Laud canons as 'synchronisms' was inaccurate and represents a misinterpretation of them. In particular Mac Neill's assertion that 'the whole tract followed the Eusebian model' represents a misunderstanding on his part of the structure of Eusebius' canons.[28] At most the collinear reigns of Laud's parallel canons may be described as very approximately contemporaneous, and their construction demonstrates an extremely simplistic approach to chronology on the part of Cormac. Rather than 'synchronisms', the primary motivation of these parallel canons was political, intending to present a balanced, tripartite image of approximately contemporaneous spiritual and secular dynasties. I should add that a relatively small number of genuine synchronisms do occur through the text, which I would prefer to term 'synchronizing equations'. For example, the Milesian invasion is synchronized with Solomon 2, the Incarnation with Eochaidh Feidhleach 3 and Conchobur m. Nessa 27, and the Crucifixion with Conaire Mór 4, and these synchronizing equations help to identify the evolution of the regnal-canon.[29]

Transmission of the Cashel regnal-canon

Following Brian's continuation of Cormac's compilation, which I shall term the 'Cashel regnal-canon', there is clear evidence that it was quickly regarded as authoritative by some northern scholars. The earliest such instances known to me are the two poems *Rig Themra dia tesband tnú* and *Rig Themra toebaige iar tain* by Flann Mainistrech †1056. In these poems Flann listed seventy-eight reigns corresponding in both regnal names and sequence to that of the Cashel canon, in both cases identifying the reigns in his opening lines as the 'kings of Tara (*rig Themra*).'[30] It seems likely from his omission of nearly all regnal years, and of any synchronization of the reigns of either Eochaidh Feidhleach or Conaire Mór with the life of Christ, that Flann had rejected the chronology of the Cashel canon. Flann also wrote three other poems reciting the regnal successions of Mide, Aileach and Brega, and their regnal years, together with a series of seven poems reciting the regnal successions of the Eusebian Mediterranean dynasties.[31] Collation of his Mide and Aileach poems with the

---

28 Mac Neill, 'Laud 610', 95 (cit.; this usage of 'synchronism' long precedes Mac Neill, cf. O'Curry, *MM*, 53–5). 29 Meyer, 'Laud synchronisms', 471.26 (Milesians), 472.10–12 (Incarnation), 473.4 (Crucifixion). 30 Mc Carthy, 'Irish regnal canon', Tables 2–3, reigns 113–91 (Flann's reigns). 31 Mac Airt, 'Middle-Irish poems', *passim* (Mediterranean dynasties); Mac Neill, 'Flann Mainistrech', 48 (qq. 1–14 Ailech kings), 82–4 (qq. 1–22 Mide Kings).

Laud canons 8 and 13 shows that he drew on the Cashel canon incorporating sequence and textual errors found identically in Laud.[32] Flann was thus very productive in the versification of regnal-canons and his work serves to demonstrate that within a few decades of its continuation by Brian the Cashel regnal-canon had achieved authoritative status in the eyes of some eleventh-century northern scholars.

The next citation of the Cashel regnal-canon is in the two poems of Gilla Cóemáin in which he recited the whole sequence of Irish and Tara kings together with their regnal years. In these he instituted a number of modifications which, because his version served as an authoritative source for later scholars, it is important to note here. The first of these is that he explicitly identified his entire canon with the kings of 'Ireland', cf. 'Hériu ard inis na ríg' and 'fer nHérend cen ancessa, remes cech ríg'.[33] Thus it appears that the progressive displacement of 'Temorie' by 'Erenn' seen in both the Clonmacnoise and Cuana groups reflected the terminology used by Gilla Cóemáin by c. 1072. This terminology is a consequence of Brian's achievement of national hegemony being projected anachronistically onto earlier provincial kings. Secondly, collation of Gilla Cóemáin's regnal-years against those of the Cashel canon show that whilst the great majority are identical, when differences occur his are nearly always the greater, and these differences are not readily explained by scribal error. For example Gilla Cóemáin assigns Conaire Mór seventy years against Laud's fourteen years. While these differences could represent an attempt by Gilla Cóemáin to rectify the chronological deficiencies of the Cashel canon this is not supported by analysis of his data. For example, in the second and fifth quatrains of *Annálad anall uile* by placing the Flood at AM 1656 and Incarnation at AM 3952 Gilla Cóemáin made it explicit that, like Cormac, he was assuming the Vulgate chronological tradition. But summation of his intervals and regnal years from the critical edition of *Hériu ard* yields a total of 3280 years from the Flood to Laoghaire 4, i.e. to Patrick's *uenit*.[34] However, Vulgate chronology allocates only $(3952-1656+1)+432 = 2729$ years from the Flood to AD 432 inclusive, so that Gilla Cóemáin's compilation has an excess of 551 years over this interval. This represents a considerable increase over the total excess of 354 years exhibited by the Cashel canons and shows that Gilla Cóemáin's chronology exhibits even greater anachronisms with respect to Biblical and Annalistic pre-Patrician chronology than did the Cashel canon.[35]

---

32 O'Rahilly, *Early Irish history*, 416–17, and Mac Neill, 'Laud 610', 95 (errors).   33 Smith, *Gilla Cóemáin*, 100, 162 (cits.), cf. Best et al., *Book of Leinster* iii, 471, 491.   34 Smith, *Gilla Cóemáin*, 100–57 (regnal years), 136 (Modh Corb), cf. Best et al., *Book of Leinster* iii, 471–90 (regnal years).   35 Mc Carthy, 'Irish regnal canon', *s.v.* 'Laud 610 synchronisms' computes discrepancies of 287 years over Flood–Incarnation, and 77 years over Incarnation–Dathi m Fiachrach †428, thus totalling 354 years.

Examination of the post-Patrician period reveals a similar situation. In a concluding quatrain of *At-tá sund* Gilla Cóemáin himself cites a total of 615 years from Laoghaire to Brian Bóruma, while the critical edition's total of 618 for all the reigns is within three years of this. However, by Gilla Cóemáin's own synchronism for Patrick's *uenit*, Laoghaire's reign must commence in 429 and Brian died in 1014, an inclusive interval of $1014-429+1 = 586$ years, which is twenty-nine years less than the interval actually stated by Gilla Cóemáin.[36] His chronology for the entire post-Patrician period consequently represents a substantial anachronism. Furthermore, collation of Gilla Cóemáin's forty-three reigns against Annalistic chronology shows that they agree exactly for only nineteen reigns, are within two years for twelve reigns, and differ significantly by up to seventeen years for twelve reigns. These anachronisms are absolutely fatal to the authority of Gilla Cóemáin's chronology, but this did not prevent it achieving a remarkably high status amongst some of his successors as witnessed by its repeated citation. In these circumstances O'Curry's admiring conclusion that:[37]

> ... the writings of Flann and *Gilla Caemhain* are quite sufficient to show that they were familiar with a large and extensive range of general history; and their chronological computations, parallels, and synchronisms, prove that they must have industriously examined every possible available source of the chief great nations of antiquity.

must be qualified since their industrious examinations of antique sources did not include Rufinus' chronicle embedded in their own Moville, Clonmacnoise and Connacht chronicles. Moreover, 'their chronological computations, parallels, and synchronisms', based upon the Cashel canon, are naïve and deeply flawed. It also completely overlooks their lack of critical judgement and competence in dealing with the chronology of their own kings. This situation rather points to a serious want of critical judgement with respect to historical chronology prevailing amongst the Cashel compilers, Flann Mainistrech, Gilla Cóemáin, and their peers, and probably also to powerful political pressures influencing these scholars' accounts of historical kingship.

It appears to have been the versified versions of the Cashel canon such as Gilla Cóemáin's with its brief accounts of each reign that helped to inspire the compilation of the mixed prose and poetic version of the regnal-canon known as *Lebor Gabála*.[38] The pre-Patrician sections of LG *a* and *m* are distributed

---

36 Smith, *Gilla Cóemáin*, 162–73 (regnal years), 178, quatrain 36 (615 years), 192, quatrain 33 (locates Patrick's *uenit* twenty-seven years after the death of Niall Noíghiallach, and since Dathí's intervening reign lasts twenty-three years, the *uenit* must fall in Laoghaire's fourth year). Cf. Best et al., *Book of Leinster* iii, 491–3 (regnal years), 495 ll. 15399–403 (615 years), 500 ll. 15536–9 (Patrick's *uenit*). 37 O'Curry, *MM*, 56 (cit.). 38 Macalister, *LG* i–v, (edition); Carey, *Lebor*

over a regnal-canon virtually identical with that of Gilla Cóemáin's *Hériu ard*, cf. appendix 3. Indeed the poem is recited in both recensions.[39] On the other hand LG *a*'s post-Patrician section has drawn upon a later version of the regnal-canon, *Ériu óg inis na naem*, by Gilla mo Dutu Ua Caiside *fl.* 1143–8 in which he recites the reigns and regnal years from Laoghaire to Maolsechlainn Mór, and then reigns only to Toirrdhealbhach Ua Conchobhair.[40] All recensions of LG appropriately commence at Creation and continue with an account of the 'Wanderings of the Gaedil' up to the arrival of Míl in Spain, and they then embark on the 'Invasions of Ireland' which necessitates a return to the Flood for the first invasion. Since the arrival of Míl in Spain long postdates the Flood they all consequently present a major chronological discontinuity at this point. The very presence of this discontinuity shows that the compilers of LG, like Gilla Cóemáin himself, were quite indifferent to matters of chronological precision. On the other hand LG's account of these Invasions and the reigns of their Milesian descendants have expanded Gilla Cóemáin's chronicle by the inclusion of both poetic and prose accounts of the kings and their lives up until the reign of Dathí m. Fiachrach. The non-secular material found here consists of Biblical settings for some secular narratives and synchronisms for the invasions. Indeed it was the anachronisms between these that were largely responsible for the subsequent LG *b* and *c* recensions.[41] With the arrival of Christianity in Ireland a profound change takes place in the narrative content of LG, for now are found cryptic extracts from Annalistic entries registering both ecclesiastical and secular events. These Annalistic extracts are gathered serially following the announcement of each reign, and these extend in both LG *a* and *c* from the reign of Laoghaire to that of Ruaidhrí Ua Conchobhair. These Annalistic extracts are preserved in three important MSS, the Books of Leinster, Lecan, and Ballymote, and collation of them reveals a body of extracts common to all three, implying therefore that they have all been derived from a common source. An important characteristic of these extracts in all three MSS is their sustained emphasis upon Patrick and Armagh, and to illustrate this I list below the first ten ecclesiastical extracts from the Book of Leinster:[42]

> [1] Loegaire mac Néill .xxx. annos regnum Hiberniae post aduentum **Patricíí** tenuit. [2] **Ard Mach** fundata est. [3] **Secundinus** ⁊ Senex **Patricius** quieuerunt ... [4] Quies **Benigni** secundi episcopi. [5] Quies **Iarlathi** tertii episcopi ... [6] Lugaid mac Loegairi .xxu. co torchair i nAchud Forcha **tre mírbail Pataic** ...

Gabála, 7–19 (succinct account); Scowcroft, '*LG* I' and '*LG* II', *passim* (analysis).   **39** Macalister, LG v, 354–5 (poem CXV=*Hériu ard*); Scowcroft, '*LG* I', 140–1 (poem CXV).   **40** Scowcroft, '*LG* I', 96–7 (Gilla Cóemáin), 100 (stemma), 129–30 (Ua Caiside).   **41** Scowcroft, '*LG* II', 29–31 (inconsistencies), and idem, '*LG* I', 101–15 (recensional divergences), 125–9 (synchronisms in *b*). **42** Best et al., *Book of Leinster* i, 94 (cits.).

[7] **Patricius** Scottorum episcopus quieuit. [8] Cormac primus abbas [**Aird Macha**]. [9] Quies **Ibari** episcopi. [10] Dubthach abb **Aird Macha** quieuit.

As can be seen items 1, 3, 4, 5, 6, 7, 9 refer either explicitly to Patrick or his supposed episcopal associates and successors, and items 2, 8, 10 refer to Armagh and its abbatial succession. This Armagh succession is sustained throughout and is evidently based upon the Cashel canons 6a and 10, which it extends up to Gilla m. Liac †1174.[43] In contrast to this prominent account of the Armagh church there is total silence regarding all other Irish ecclesiastical foundations including Clonmacnoise. Thus the compiler of the post-Patrician section of LG, despite having access to a comprehensive annalistic source clearly deriving from the Clonmacnoise chronicle, exercised a completely partisan approach in his selection of ecclesiastical extracts. Collation of LG's regnal years for the pre-Patrician period with those of Gilla Cóemáin shows that they are essentially identical except for a few small differences readily explained as scribal errors.[44] For the post-Patrician period the regnal years show frequent divergences from Gilla Cóemáin's *At-tá sund*, some of which appear to be the result of collation with Ua Caiside's poem, cf. appendix 3. The effect of these modifications was to further exacerbate the problems of LG's chronology for the historical period, and this degradation shows that the eleventh century want of competence in historical chronology continued unabated amongst twelfth-century scholars. However, as we shall see, these serious deficiencies did not deter subsequent scholars from drawing repeatedly upon LG in their historical writing. Indeed, as Ó Corráin pointed out:[45]

> [LG] became the sheet anchor of the genealogical tracts, a vast web of kinship, binding together all the dynasties of Ireland and linking them with the great of past times, with all the nations of the earth, and tracing them in an unbroken line of descent from Adam.

In summary, LG recensions *a* and *m* represent a compilation of secular and ecclesiastical historiographical material, based upon Gilla Cóemáin and Ua Caiside's versions of the Cashel canon by compilers who identified closely with Armagh.

Mageoghagan's Book

Before considering the relationship between MB and the regnal-canon it is desirable to first clarify the circumstances of Mageoghagan's compilation. In his

---

43 O'Rahilly, *Early Irish history*, 417 (Armagh bishops). 44 Mc Carthy, 'Irish regnal canon', Tables 1–3, (regnal year columns 'GC' and 'LG'). 45 Ó Corráin, 'Creating the past', 203 (cit.).

preface addressed to Terence Coghlan and dated 20 April 1627 Mageoghagan clearly stated that his purpose was, 'the translating of the old Irish booke for you'. Immediately following this and subsequently in several interjections in his translation Mageoghagan emphasized that this book was old, illegible in places and had lost leaves. In these interjections Mageoghagan normally referred to his source simply as the 'old booke', and since this source is our primary interest I will retain Mageoghagan's distinctive designation for it.[46] In the course of his translation Mageoghagan also inserted many interpolations and these must obviously be isolated in MB before the content of the old booke can be reliably identified. Fortunately in many instances Mageoghagan himself marked these interpolations by an introductory interjection, sometimes by addressing himself to 'Brother', 'Reader', or 'you', by making reference to 'mine author' or 'my history', by writing in the first person singular, by referring to English versus Irish meanings, or by simply placing brief interpolations within parentheses.[47] By examination of these clearly marked interpolations it is possible to establish Mageoghagan's interests and his *modus operandi,* and hence to at least partially separate the existing text of MB into Mageoghagan's translation of the old booke and his own interpolations. The systematic identification of these is a major desideratum of any future edition of MB.[48] These interpolations show that Mageoghagan was literate in Irish and English, able to read Latin, had access to contemporaneous printed books, was deeply interested in genealogy and the folklore of early Christian history, and was quite well informed regarding the textual history of both the regnal-canon and the old booke. On the other hand there is clear evidence of both a lack of interest and competence on his part regarding chronology. For instance, Mageoghagan was responsible for the addition of the marginal AM and AD data and the latter of these are completely unreliable until the early eleventh century. He also supplied page titles citing the current reign and most of the annotations in the left-hand margin, cf. plate 12.

The range of MB is Adam–AD 1408, though with numerous lacunae, some arising from folios either missing or illegible in the old booke, but others may be a result of deliberate omissions by Mageoghagan, as the following italicized interjections demonstrate:

46 Murphy, *AC*, 9 (cit.), 9, 215, 258 (illegible/lost folios). MS BL Add. 4817 consistently writes 'old booke', not 'ould Booke' as per MS TCD 673 and hence Murphy, *AC*, 7, 51, 215, 220, 258 (ould [Irish] Booke).   47 Murphy, *AC*, 7–9, 10, 14, 18, 25, 51bis, 58, 66, 68, 96, 112, 124–5, 136, 156, 165, 171, 183, 206, 207, 209–13, 215, 218, 220, 228, 258, 259, 266–7, 304, 308, 324, 328 (examples of Mageoghagan's interjections).   48 Sanderlin, *Conell Mageoghagan,* 113–30, 161–71, 209–30, 252–70 identified a number of Mageoghagan's interpolations but they cannot all be relied upon. For example at 116–19 she assumed that he had used the Book of Leinster. Sanderlin, 'Manuscripts', dealing with MB's MSS is the only part of the thesis to have been published, albeit with emended conclusions.

MB 125b: The o'Kellyes of Brey was the chiefe name of that Race, though it hath manye other names of by-septs, *which for brevityes sake I omit to particulate ...*

MB 165d: Bryan Borowa tooke the kingdome and government thereof out of the handes of king Moylseachlin in such manner *as I doe not Intend to Relate in this place.*

MB 220c: These and many other reproachful wordes my author layeth down in the old booke *which I was loath to translate ...*

Indeed the ambivalent words with which Mageoghagan concluded his translation, 'Here endeth this Booke', suggest that he possibly truncated his translation of the old booke before it had concluded.[49] His repeated references to this 'old booke' throughout suggest that except for the aforementioned folio losses it represented an integral and unitary source for him.[50] However, some of his references imply that he was not that familiar with it, for example:

MB 215c: There are soe many leaves lost or stolen out of the old Irish booke which I Translate, *that I doe not know how to handle it,* but to satisfie your request I will translate such places in the book as I can read ...

This suggests that the old booke was not his own property or that he had only recently acquired access to it, and I will pursue this matter below.

Regarding the authorship of the old booke Mageoghagan prefixed to his translation a list of eleven names whom he characterized as its 'seuerall Authors' as follows:[51]

The names of the seuerall Authors which I haue taken for this Booke.

Saint Colme Kill and Sainct Bohine. Calloch o'More Esquire. Venerable Bede. Eoghie o'Flannagan Archdeane of Ardmach and Clonfiaghna. Gillernew m^c Conn ne Mbocht archpriest of Clonvickenois and Keilleachar m^c Conn alias MacGorman. Eusebius. Marcellinus. Moylin o'Mulchonry and Tanary o'Mulchonry two professed Chroniclers.

This statement makes it absolutely clear that Mageoghagan was aware of the accumulative compilation of the contents of the old booke, and hence that his repeated allusions to 'mine Author' throughout do not refer to the actual compiler of the old booke itself. This list extends in time from Eusebius †c.340

---

49 Murphy, *AC*, 125, 165, 220, 328 (cits., which have all been collated and emended by reference to MS BL Add. 4817).   50 Because Mageoghagan interpolated 'Finis' following the completion of the Norman invasion Sanderlin, *Conell Mageoghagan*, 8 mistakenly concluded this represented 'an end to AClon itself'. But after 'Finis' Mageoghagan, having interpolated genealogies of three contemporaries, resumed his translation with the words 'In the year 1170 last mentioned', cf. Murphy, *AC*, 208 ('Finis'), 209–13 (genealogies), 213 ('year 1170').   51 From BL Add. 4817 f. 4v, cf. Murphy, *AC*, 10.

to Calloch O'More †1618 and it is conspicuously anachronistic in its order, clearly reflecting Mageoghagan's aforementioned indifference to chronological matters. When the list is re-arranged in chronological order we find that the obits of all but two of these 'Authors' pre-date 1408, the concluding year of MB, and it therefore provides an indication as to who may have been responsible for the actual compilation of the old booke.[52] These two are Maoilín Ua Maoil Chonaire †1441 and Calloch O'More †1618, and of these only Maoilín could have compiled a book extending to 1408 that could have been plausibly described as 'old' in 1627. Hence critical examination of Mageoghagan's own preface uniquely identifies the very individual whom on independent textual and chronological grounds we have already identified as the compiler in *c.*1423 of Uí Maoil Chonaire-II, cf. chapter 9, p. 252 ff. Either this compilation or any near contemporary copy of it would have been about two hundred years old in 1627, and would hence conform to Mageoghagan's repeated allusions to the 'old booke'.

Moreover, when we collate the content of MB over 1224–1408 with CT, which we have already concluded is based upon Uí Maoil Chonaire-II over these years, cf. Figure 38, p. 262, we find that MB repeatedly transmits in translation essentially the same entries in the same order. MB's entry counts are much less than those of CT, normally just a selection from near the beginning and the end of CT, suggesting thereby that Mageoghagan translated only a sample of the entries from each year. Furthermore in chapter 9 we concluded that the Uí Maoil Chonaire Connacht chronicle represented a continuation of the earlier Clonmacnoise chronicle extending to *c.*1227, and when we collate MB with AT/CS/AR over their common range of 432–1178 we again find that MB transmits in translation substantially the same entries in the same order.[53] When we turn to examine the lacuna in our sources for the Clonmacnoise chronicle over 1179–1227 we find in this interval in MB a total of fourteen Clonmacnoise entries, some of which clearly represent chronicling at Clonmacnoise. Consider for example the following account of an attack in *c.*1202:

> MB 219b: The Englishmen of Milick and Sile Anmchye accompanied with the 2 families of Moyntyr Kenay, and Moyntyr Milchon came to Clonvicknose upon the feast day of Saint Gregory, preyed and spoyled the church, Sanctuary, and towne of Clonvicknowe; the next friday the said company came to Clonvicknose and tooke the like spoyles from thence, and though the first spoyles were much, yett the second were farr greater ...

---

52 Chronological order: Eusebius †*c.*340, Marcellinus †*c.*534, Columba †593, Baoithín †596, Bede †735, Eochaid Ua Flannagáin †1004, Celechair m. Cuinn na mBocht †1134 and Gillernew m. Conn na mBocht held senior ecclesiastical offices at Clonmacnoise over 1067–1134, Tanaidhe Ua Maoil Chonaire †1385, Maoilín Ua Maoil Chonaire †1441 and Calloch O'More †1618.   53 Mc Carthy, 'Synchronization', *s.a.* 432–965.

Here as well as the verb 'came' we have details of the dates of the attacks, the attackers, and their targets, so that there are good grounds to conclude that this entry was recorded in Clonmacnoise and has been transmitted via Uí Maoil Chonaire-II. Thus I conclude that over 432–1227 MB transmits in translation entries from the Clonmacnoise chronicle that had been incorporated by Maoilín into Uí Maoil Chonaire-II. However, when we turn to examine MB's regnal succession over this same interval significant differences emerge between it and the Clonmacnoise chronicle. For we find that MB systematically provides regnal incipits including regnal years for the succession, and that these are substantially arranged in accordance with the regnal-canon. For example:

MB 88d: Boydan mᶜAnynnea raigned one yeare.
MB 90b: Hugh Mᶜ Ainmyreagh succeeded in the kingdom & Reigned 25 years.

As can be seen these reproduce the identical radical adjustments reducing Baodan m. Nindeadha's reign from thirteen to one year, and expanding Aodh m. Ainmirech's reign from twelve to twenty-five years, cf. the Laud/Annalistic collation above at p. 277. These were the changes that were introduced by the Cashel regnal-canon and essentially maintained subsequently by Gilla Cóemáin and LG. Indeed the majority of MB's regnal years over 432–1022 correspond identically with those of LG and such divergences that exist appear to be scribal errors.[54] Moreover, following the death of Maolsechlainn in 1022 MB reproduces a succession of kings extending from Diarmait m. Mael na mBó †1072 to Ruaidhrí Ua Conchobhair †1198 who ruled 'without a crown', which closely parallels the kings of Ireland with opposition (*co fressabra*) in LG.[55] Thus it emerges unmistakably that LG's regnal-canon had been interpolated into the post-Patrician section of the old booke. We also find in MB over 432–734 intermittent lists of the provincial kings of Scotland, Ulster, Leinster, Munster, Connacht and Ossory, corresponding to those found in the synchronisms of LG *b*.[56] These two features show that over 432–1198 the content of the old booke was a combination of that of the secularized Clonmacnoise chronicle and LG, and I conclude that this conflation was made by Maoilín as part of his compilation of Uí Maoil Chonaire-II.

When we turn to examine the content of MB before AD 432 we find that the relationship with the Clonmacnoise chronicle suddenly ceases and that it now substantially consists of citations from LG systematically incorporating the regnal-canon from Slainghe to Dathí m. Fiachrach. Thus it is apparent that the

---

54 Mc Carthy, 'Irish regnal canon', Table 3, reigns 148–191 (scribal errors).   55 Murphy, *AC*, 173 (cit.); Mc Carthy, 'Irish regnal canon', Table 3, reigns 192–7 (kings with opposition).   56 Murphy, *AC*, 69, 80–1, 97, 100–1, 115–16 (provincial kings); Scowcroft, '*LG* I', 130–1, points out that these synchonisms were omitted by Macalister but published by Thurneysen, 'Synchronismen', 81–99.

entire pre-Patrician section of the Clonmacnoise chronicle has been replaced
by Maoilin with an adaptation of LG to chronicle form that exhibits the
following features:

a) It commences with the Biblical succession from Adam to Noah based upon
   LG *c*, but it presents Vulgate chronology rather than LG *c*'s Septuagint
   chronology.[57]

b) Its account of the 'Wanderings of the Gaedil' is derived from LG *b*, but this
   has been relocated between the end of the Fir Bolg reigns and the arrival
   of the Milesians in Ireland. Thus it has, so far as is possible, minimized the
   chronological discontinuity between LG's account of the 'Wanderings of
   the Gaedil' and the 'Invasions of Ireland'.[58]

c) The summation of the inter-regnal intervals and regnal years between the
   Flood and the sixteenth year of Fachtna Fathach, with which the Incarnation
   is synchronized amounts to *c.*2296 years, which corresponds very closely
   with the Vulgate total of 3952–1656+1=2297 years.[59]

As may be seen these differences are such as to substantially improve upon the
chronological arrangement of LG's account of both the antediluvian period and
the 'Wanderings of the Gaedil', and to bring its chronology into correspondence
with Vulgate chronology. Since these improvements have drawn upon LG it is
evident that the pre-Patrician section of the old booke must also be regarded
as having been derived from LG. More extensive evaluation of the pre-Patrician
section leads to the conclusion that in fact it represents the result of a
substantial and critical collation of the major recensions of LG. When making
this evaluation Mageoghagan's interpolations must be taken into account since
he has in places revised the chronology of the old booke to accord with his own
views of LG.[60] Collation of MB's regnal years with those of Gilla Cóemáin and
LG again suggest that LG was used as the primary source. However, when
MB's regnal years are unique they are often substantially less than LG's, and
these reductions appear to be the result of Maoilín's earnest endeavour to bring
the chronology of his compilation into conformity with Vulgate chronology. In
MB two synchronisms for the Incarnation are given as follows:

---

57 Murphy, *AC*, 11 (Adam–Noah); Macalister, *LG* i, 96–102 (Adam–Noah), 104 (Septuagint vs
Vulgate vs LG).   **58** Wanderings: Murphy, *AC*, 19–20 cf. Macalister, *LG* ii, 32–8 (§118–27).
59 Mc Carthy, 'Irish regnal canon', *s.v.* 'Mageoghagan's Book' (Flood–Fachtna 16 summation).
60 For example Mageoghagan has both prefixed and suffixed interjections to the account from the
old booke of the 'Wanderings of the Gaedil' in order to synchronize the arrival of the Milesians
with the destruction of Troy. Murphy, *AC*, 18 'It is fitt that I shall put the Reader in Remembrance
… that about this time Paris of Troye ravished …', followed by the LG *b* account of Míl, then,
'The most part of our Ireish Cronacles agree that the sonns of Miletus came to this land in the
beginning of the destruction of Troy …', idem, 21.

MB 47a: Faghtna Fahagh was K. 24 yeares ... Some of our writers affirm that our Saviour Jesus Christ, the onely Begotten sonn of God almighty, was borne of the spotless Virgin Mary about the 16th year of this kings raigne ... [reigns of four kings] ...

MB 48b: Conary was K. 60 years ... Jesus Christ was crucified in his time, but some of the antiquarists affirm that our Saviour Jesus Christ was borne in the Raigne of K. Eochy Feyleagh, & not in the reign of Fagha fathagh & crucified by Tiberius Caesar in the raigne of Edersgall, K. of Ireland.

The former is evidently that used by Maoilín while the latter clearly derives from the Cashel regnal-canon and may be an addition by Mageoghagan. Together they show that six hundred years after the compilation of the Cashel canon the fundamental datum of Christian AD chronology was still completely unresolved.

Thus examination of the content of MB supports the conclusion that Mageoghagan's old booke was Maoilín Uí Maoil Chonaire's compilation of c.1423, and that in this Maoilín had replaced the pre-Patrician section of the Clonmacnoise chronicle with an account of Irish prehistory drawn from LG. In the post-Patrician section he had retained the Clonmacnoise chronicle material but had systematically interpolated into it LG's regnal-canon and also intermittent provincial king lists taken from LG. Hence from this I infer that Uí Maoil Chonaire-II was a most formidable compilation, extending from Adam to c.AD 1423. In retrospect this introduction by Maoilín of LG into the Annals is not surprising for we know that by the fifteenth century LG played a key role in supporting the genealogical constructs of the ollamhs. In this circumstance the brief and discontinuous account of Ireland's prehistory introduced by the Moville compiler and preserved in the Clonmacnoise chronicle was completely inadequate. Also we know from the surviving MSS of LG that the Uí Maoil Chonaire were deeply involved in their production so it is only to be expected that eventually they would supplant the Moville compiler's version of Ireland's prehistory with their own version of LG.[61]

Finally I consider the question of from whence Mageoghagan had obtained the old booke. He gives no explicit information concerning this but his inclusion of the name 'Calloch o'More' in his list of authors is singular on several counts. This name is the only one to which Mageoghagan appended a contemporary title, 'Esquire', and moreover he twice cited Calloch's authority for chronological details of Irish prehistory. In the first of these Mageoghagan cited Calloch for the period Ireland was waste after Partholón's death. In the second he referred to him as 'a uerie worthy gentleman and a great searcher of Antiquities', and he compared Calloch's date for the Milesian invasion of

---

61 Scowcroft, 'LG I', 85–6 (Uí Maoil Chonaire LG MSS).

Ireland with that in Philip O'Sullivan's 'printed book Dedicated to Phillip the 4th, King of Spaine'.[62] Now O'Sullivan's book was published only in 1621, and the contemporaneous nature of Mageoghagan's comparison and the terms of his reference to Calloch strongly suggest that he too was a contemporary, and indeed that Mageoghagan knew and admired him. Calloch O'More, alias Calbach Ua Mordha †1618, was son and heir of Ruaidhrí Caoch Ua Mordha of Noughaval in county Laoighis, slain in 1567. In 1574, in recognition of the services rendered by his father to king Edward VI, Calloch was granted the manor of Ballina in Carbury barony in the north-west of county Kildare, so that he had lived only about thirty miles from Mageoghagan in Lissmoyne, county Westmeath. In 1590 Calloch demonstrated his patronage for Irish scholarship when he provided accommodation for Risdeard Ua Conchobhair while he transcribed the Irish translation of the medical tract *Lilium Medecinae*. Finally, and most significantly, the manuscript of the Book of Leinster shows clear evidence that in 1583 Calloch was the owner of it, and also that earlier in the fifteenth century it was associated with his family. As owner of this valuable MS Calloch was possessed of substantial leverage to gain access to other rare and valuable sources.[63] Now Mageoghagan described Calloch both as 'a great searcher of Antiquities' and as an 'Author' of the old booke. This suggests then that it was Calloch who had obtained the old booke and that he had annotated it in places, for certainly by naming him as an 'Author' Mageoghagan closely associated him with the work. Of course at the time he was translating the old booke Calloch had been dead for some nine years, and since Mageoghagan appears to have been unfamiliar with the work it seems likely that he had gained access to it from Calloch's heir.

Michéal Ó Cléirigh's regnal-canon chronicles

Between 1630 and 1636 Michéal Ó Cléirigh with the assistance of other scholars compiled no less than three chronicles based upon the regnal-canon. These were *Seanchas Riogh Eireann* (SR) completed at Athlone, county Westmeath on 4 November 1630, *Leabhar Gabhála* completed in Lisgoole, county Fermanagh on 22 December 1631, and FM compiled at Bundrowes, county Donegal between 22 January 1632 and 10 August 1636.[64] Collation of these three compilations shows that they all share identical versions of the regnal-canon.[65] This is an important result for it establishes that Ó Cléirigh had resolved the regnal chronology of

---

62 MS BL Add. 4817 f. 13ʳ; Murphy, *AC*, 14, 25 (Calloch cits.); O Sullevenus, *Historiae Catholicae*, f. 32ʳ (tom. i, lib. iv, cap. i – Milesian invasion date).   63 Walsh, *Gleanings*, 123–4, 130, 146 (patronage); Best et al., *Book of Leinster* i, xiv–xv (Uí Mordha).   64 Walsh, *Genealogiae*, 1–36 (*Seanchas Riogh*); Macalister & Mac Neill, *Gabhála Érend*, (part LG); O'Donovan, *FM*, lxi (dates).   65 Mc Carthy, 'Irish regnal canon', *s.v.* 'SR', 'LG' and 'FM' (identical versions).

FM about fifteen months before he commenced compiling it, and for this reason it is essential to first identify the characteristic features of SR.

Fortunately UCD OFM MS A16 ff. i–lii^r preserves the compilation of SR in Ó Cléirigh's own hand, complete with signed and dated testimonials in the hands of Br. Seoirse Díolmhain, Guardian at Athlone, and Conall Mhag Eochagáin, alias Conell Mageoghagan of Lissmoyne. In SR Ó Cléirigh listed the kings of Ireland from Slainghe to Maolsechlainn †1022, followed by six kings with opposition up to Ruaidhrí Ua Conchobhair †1198. For each king Ó Cléirigh gave his genealogy, his regnal years, and a brief account of his death, so that SR represents a substantial regnal chronicle. It is important to note that with just one exception all of the AM and AD data printed by Walsh in his published edition of SR were inserted later either marginally or interlinearly by Conaire Ó Cléirigh.[66] Collation of SR's regnal sequence with those of LG and Gilla Cóemáin shows beyond all doubt that Ó Cléirigh based his compilation as far as Maolsechlainn Mór upon Gilla Cóemáin's poems *Hériu ard* and *At-tá sund*, and he employed LG only for his six kings with opposition.[67] We can be certain about this because Ó Cléirigh included in SR the reigns of Fiachaidh m. Muiredhaig, Badbchadh m. Eathach and Maolsechlainn's second reign to 1022, which are all interpolations found *only* in the later manuscripts of these poems, cf. Figure 42 below.[68] Moreover, there is abundant evidence of Ó Cléirigh's interest in Gilla Cóemáin's poems in the form of his three full copies of *Hériu ard* and his full copies of *At-tá sund* and *Annálad* found in RIA 1080 ff. 101^v–111^v (L^1), ff. 4^r–10^r (O), and Bruxelles Bibl. Royale 4640 ff. 10^r–15^r (Br^1). As well as this Ó Cléirigh made significant annotations on a fourth copy of *Hériu ard* which, as we shall see, served as the primary source for his compilation of SR. This copy is preserved in Bruxelles Bibl. Royale 4640 ff. 94^r–99^r (Br^2) in a hand that has not hitherto been identified. I cite here the sigla L^1, O, Br^1, Br^2 employed by Peter Smith in his critical edition.[69] Examination of a microfilm of Bruxelles 4640 shows that this hand has written most of the secular historical and genealogical material recorded in ff. 18–101, which folios were originally paginated 1–164, and that Ó Cléirigh himself has both annotated this material and constructed an index to its poems using this pagination, now prefixed to the collection at ff. 16^{r-v}. While this hand shows considerable variation over pp. 1–164 collation of it with Seoirse Díolmain's signature on his testimonial

---

66 Walsh, *Genealogiae*, 11–35 (AM and AD data); examination of UCD OFM A16 shows that except for 'cúicc céd & tri mile bł. 3500' on f. xxii^r the remainder is either marginal or interlinear. I gratefully acknowledge Dr Bernadette Cunningham's assistance in identifying the interpolating hand.   67 Mc Carthy, 'Irish regnal canon', Tables 1–3 (reigns 1–197, cf. GC/LG/SR regnal years).   68 Smith, *Gilla Cóemáin*, 128 (Fiachu), 134 (Badbchad), 172 (Maolsechlainn), 49–56 (interpolations), cf. Walsh, *Genealogiae*, 20 §49 (Fiachu), 22 §73 (Badbchad), 35 §44 (Maolsechlainn).   69 Smith, *Gilla Cóemáin*, 20–1 (sigla L^1, O, Br^1, Br^2); Fitzpatrick, *Catalogue RIA*, 3021–9 (L^1, O); Van den Gheyn, *Catalogue*, 46–8 (Br^1, Br^2).

prefixed to SR leads me to conclude that he was the principal copyist responsible for it.[70] Thus Díolmhain was the copyist who provided Ó Cléirigh with a substantial number of his working copies of this secular material. It was appropriate therefore that Ó Cléirigh should undertake the compilation of SR in the convent of which Díolmain was Guardian, and that he should testify to Ó Cléirigh's industry. Furthermore I suggest that it was Mageoghagan who had provided Díolmain's exemplars, because:

a) In his own testimonial Mageoghagan wrote that, 'I have seen the originals of this book.'[71]

b) In September 1644 the Franciscan friar Pól Ó Colla transcribed a substantial series of texts from copies owned by Mageoghagan in his house at Lissmoyne, and in his preface Ó Colla described Mageoghagan as, 'the industrious collecting Bee of everything that belongs to the honour and history of the descendants of Milesius and of *Lugaidh*, son of *Ith*, both lay and ecclesiastical, as far as he could find them.'[72] Thus fourteen years after the compilation of SR the Franciscans were still making copies of Mageoghagan's collection.

c) In MB when Mageoghagan's regnal names are anomalous they regularly correspond to those of Br², compare for example his 'Adamar', 'Ionamar' and 'Dahye' with the readings given by Br² in Figure 42 below.[73]

Thus there are good reasons to believe that Mageoghagan was the immediate source of a substantial quantity of Ó Cléirigh's working materials. Regarding the detailed chronological structure of SR a conspectus in Ó Cléirigh's hand is suffixed to his final copy of *Hériu ard* (Br¹ f. 15ᵛ), and in this he summarized the salient features of some chronological conflicts he found in different versions of Gilla Cóemáin's *Hériu ard*, noting that:

a) Some versions of *Hériu ard* locate the arrival of the Fir Bolg [recte Partholón] 311 years after the Flood, whereas others cite 278 years.

b) Some versions of *Hériu ard* locate the death of Dathí 126 years later than others.

c) If Siorna's reign would be made 150 years [rather than Gilla Cóemáin's 21 years] then the discrepancy in b) would be reduced to three years, [i.e. 150–126–21=3].

---

70 Compare MS Bruxelles 4640 ff. 96ʳ, 97ᵛ with the signature to Díolmhain's testimonial at UCD OFM A16 f. xiiiʳ, though Mícheál Ó Cléirigh appears to have written the testimonial itself. However, Díolmhain did not write all of pp. 1–164 or even *Hériu ard*, cf. f. 94ʳ ll.5–16.   71 Walsh, *Genealogiae*, 144 (cit.).   72 O'Curry, *MM*, 163 (cit. – O'Curry mistakenly attributes this preface to Ó Cléirigh).   73 Murphy, *AC*, 45–6, 64 (cits.).

Examination of SR shows that Ó Cléirigh based his compilation upon Díolmain's copy of *Hériu ard* and exploited all of these alternatives. This may be demonstrated by comparing a selection of SR's anomalous regnal readings with those from Ó Cléirigh's other MSS, and the Book of Leinster and these are collated in Figure 42.

Hériu ard - Smith	L	L¹	Br²	O	Br¹	SR
5. Flood to Partholón	311	*311*	311	*311*	*278*	[278]
17A. Flood to Fir Bolg	–	–	*$-^{1056}$*	*1056*	*1024*	[1024]
55. Ghedhe	21	*21*	12	*12*	*12*	*12*
60. Siorna	21	*21*	21*$^{l\,150}$*	*150*	*150*	*150*
80A. Fiachaidh Tolgrach	–	–	10	*10^{8}*	*10^{8}*	*10*
92A. Badbchadh	–	–	1½ d.	*1½ d.*	*1½ d.*	*1½ d.*
103. Amathair	Amathair	*Amatair*	Adamair	*Adamair*	*Adhamair*	*Adhamair*
104. Eochaidh Ailtlethan	14	*14*	17	*17*	*17*	*17*
112. Fintait Már	Fintait Már	*Fintait Mar*	Ionnatmar	*Ionnatmar*	*Innattmar*	*Ionnatmar*
134. Conn Cedcathach	20	*20*	20*$^{l\,35}$*	*35*	*35*	*35*
149. Nath Í	Nath Í	*Nathi*	Datí	*Datí*	*Dathi*	*Dathi*

Figure 42. A selection of anomalous regnal years and names from SR collated with Ó Cléirigh's MSS of *Hériu ard* (L¹, Br¹, O, Br²) and that in the Book of Leinster (L= TCD 1339 ff. 127ʳ–129ᵛ). Column one gives the quatrain number and reading from Smith's critical edition. All items shown in italics were written by Ó Cléirigh, and those shown in superscript he wrote either interlinearly or marginally. The entries under SR for quatrains 5 and 17A have been deduced from FM and hence are encased in brackets.

As may be seen, even though Ó Cléirigh had transcribed L accurately into L¹, in SR he chose to follow the readings of Br² except in the cases of Partholón, the Fir Bolg, Siorna and Conn Cedcathach, all of which he had deliberately modified by the time he wrote Br¹. Comprehensive collation of Br²'s readings with the other earlier MSS of *Hériu ard* suggests that it is a descendant of the version written by Ádhamh Ua Cianáin †1373, now NLI G 2–3 ff. 36ʳ–42ʳ.[74] Ó Cléirigh also introduced an unprecedented seven-year inter-regnum after Tigernmas' reign, and by these means he made a number of important changes to Gilla Cóemáin's regnal chronology as follows:

[74] Ní Shéaghdha, *Catalogue NLI*, 12–28:22 and Carney, 'Ó Cianáin', 122–3 (Adhamh Ua Cianáin).

a) Septuagint chronological tradition. The only AM date personally inscribed by Mícheál Ó Cléirigh in his original compilation of SR was AM 3500, his date for the invasion of the Milesians. This exact mid-millennial date suggests contrivance on his part and it also shows that he had adopted Septuagint tradition against Gilla Cóemáin's Vulgate tradition. We can show this since in Br[1] Ó Cléirigh assigned 1024 years from Flood to the Fir Bolg, cf. Figure 42 above, and in SR he assigned thirty-seven years to Fir Bolg reigns and 197 years to Tuatha de Danaan reigns, and these together imply that the Flood occurred at AM $(3500–1024–37–197) =$ AM 2242, which is indeed the Septuagint AM date for the Flood.

b) Synchronization of Patrick's *uenit*. As a result of Ó Cléirigh's adoption of Septuagint chronology and his increases to Siorna and Conn Cedcathach's reigns, cf. Figure 42, and a small number of other minor adjustments, Dathí m. Fiachrach's obit was relocated to AM 5627 $=$ AD $(5627–5199) =$ AD 428. Hence Laoghaire 4 and Patrick's *uenit* were located at AD 432, and in this way Ó Cléirigh eliminated Gilla Cóemáin's asynchronism of 552 years for this interval, and he precisely synchronized Patrick's *uenit* with the Clonmacnoise chronicle date of AD 432.

c) Relocation of Brian Borúma's obit. Between Laoghaire's reign and Brian's death Ó Cléirigh significantly reduced Gilla Cóemáin's regnal years for Domhnall m. Aodha (16 vs 30), Conall and Ceallach mm. Mael Cobo (17 vs 22), Cenn Faolad (4. vs 7). These reductions together with a number of smaller modifications advanced Brian's death to AM 6212 $=$ AD $(6212–5199) =$ AD 1013, thereby reducing Gilla Cóemáin's twenty-nine year asynchronism to just one year.[75]

By these means Ó Cléirigh's SR synchronized the Milesian invasion with AM 3500 and eliminated or substantially reduced the most conspicuous of Gilla Cóemáin's asynchronisms, bringing Patrick's *uenit* and Brian's obit into close correspondence with their Clonmacnoise chronicle chronology. But it must be emphasized and clearly understood that Ó Cléirigh's emendments were directed to just these few events, and he made no attempt whatsoever to harmonize the regnal years of the remainder of the post-Patrician reigns with their Clonmacnoise chronicle chronology. As a consequence SR's post-Patrician regnal chronology is normally significantly advanced with respect to Clonmacnoise chronicle chronology, reaching a maximum of seventeen years in the case of Baodan m. Nindeadha †584, cf. Figure 43, p. 299. As we shall see all of these characteristics were maintained in Ó Cléirigh's two subsequent compilations.

---

75 Walsh, *Genealogiae*, 15 (Milesians), 12 (Fir Bolg), 14 (Tuatha de Danaan), 29 (Dathí), 30–5 (post-Patrician reigns).

Turning next to O Cléirigh's compilation of LG, he wrote in the preface that his purpose was 'to purify, compile, and re-write the ancient honoured Chronicle which is called the Book of Invasions', clearly signalling that he intended to make major revisions to the work. He began by explicitly identifying his assumed Biblical chronological tradition, 'We give the computation of the Septuagint.'[76] Following this he omitted all of LG's antediluvian material and commenced instead at Ceasair's arrival immediately prior to the Flood. Structurally he relocated the 'Wanderings of the Gaedil' immediately before the arrival of the Milesians, exactly as in Mageoghagan's old booke, thereby minimizing the chronological discontinuity it caused. For the remainder of LG he reproduced identically the reigns and regnal years of SR. While in his preface Ó Cléirigh emphasized his use of the Septuagint chronological tradition he did not introduce any AM apparatus into his edition of LG. The few AM data to be found in the partial edition by Macalister and Mac Neill were written marginally or interlinearly and are evidently subsequent additions taken from FM.[77]

Finally turning to FM, both of Ó Cléirigh's prefaces to this work, to be discussed further in chapter 11, show that for its compilation he assembled at least nine important Irish chronicles as sources, and had the assistance of at least five other scholars whom he described as 'chroniclers and learned men'.[78] Collation of FM with SR shows that Ó Cléirigh employed its regnal-canon as his primary chronological apparatus and he reproduced its regnal years exactly.[79] To this he added first a Septuagint AM series commencing with Ceasair and the Flood at AM 2242, which apparatus he wrote as, 'AOIS DOMHAIN .2242. Aois domhain gus an m-bliadain-si na dileand, da mhile, da chéad, da fichet & da bhliadhain'. He continued in this style to the seventh year of Criomhthann Nia Nair, headed 'AOIS DOMHAIN .5199.', which he followed with, 'D'AOIS CHRIOSD .1. An céd-bliadhain d'aois Críosd, & an t-ochtmadh bliadhain do righe Chriomhthaind Niá Náir'.[80] Thus it is explicit that he maintained the Septuagint Flood tradition at AM 2242 and the Incarnation tradition with AM 5200 = AD 1, and then he continued this AD series to 1616. These AM and AD data correspond with those interpolated by Conaire Ó Cléirigh into UCD OFM A16. In this way FM inherited most of the anachronistic regnal chronology of Gilla Cóemáin, modified only by Ó Cléirigh's adjustments needed to adopt Septuagint chronology, and to synchronize Patrick's *uenit* with AD 432 and Brian Borúma's death mistakenly with AD 1013.

76 O'Curry, *MM*, 169, 172 (cits.), cf. Macalister & Mac Neill, *Gabhála Érend*, 3.   77 Macalister & Mac Neill, *Gabhála Érend*, 134, 250 (marginal AM).   78 O'Donovan, *FM* i, p. lxiv (cit.); Fennessy, 'Patrick Pearse', 86–7, n. 2–3 (FM bibliography).   79 Mc Carthy, 'Irish regnal canon', Tables 1–3 (regnal years).   80 MS UCD OFM A13 ff. 1ʳ, 177ʳ⁻ᵛ (cits.), cf. O' Donovan, *FM* i, 1, 92. Neither O'Donovan, *FM* i, nor its electronic descendant at www.ucc.ie/celt/ reproduce FM's chronological apparatus fully, for from AM 3266 onwards Ó Cléirigh recorded every year and its regnal year, regardless of whether other entries existed or not. Cunningham, *Making FM*, 8–9 remarks this omission.

Since, as already mentioned, this regnal chronology differs by up to seventeen years from the chronology of the Clonmacnoise chronicle, it is important to determine the effect of this asynchronism upon the chronology of FM's non-regnal entries. In order to illustrate this I have tabulated in Figure 43 the chronology of all events common to FM and the Clonmacnoise chronicle over the interval of FM's greatest regnal dislocation, i.e. from Diarmait m. Cerbeoill †563 to Aodh m. Ainmirech †596.

Clonmacnoise chronicle	FM	Δ	Clonmacnoise chronicle	FM	Δ
562 Mo Laisse †	563	−1	582 Feargus Scandal rí †	580	2
563 Diarmait m. Cerbuill †	**558**	5	582 Feargusa eps. †	583	−1
563 Colman m. Coirpre †	576	−13	582 Mo chaeme ab †	584	−2
565 Domnaill m. Muirc. †	**561**	4	583 Maic nisse ab †	589	−6
567 Demain rí†	565	2	**584 Baedan m. Nindeadha †**	**567**	17
568 Ainmire m. Setna †	**566**	2	585 Cath Bhealaig	572	13
569 Fergus m. Nelline †	568	1	585 Daigh m. Cairill †	586	−1
569 Aenu ab †	569	0	586 Cairillan eps. †	587	−1
569 Ite Cl. Credil †	569	0	586 Senaigh eps. †	587	−1
570 Maenu eps. †	570	0	586 Aedh Dubh †	592	−6
571 Baetan ₇ Eochaid †	**563**	8	587 Aedha m. Bric †	588	−1
572 Cath Femin	571	1	587 Aedha m. Brenuinn †	585	2
572 Brenaind ab †	571	1	588 Feidlimidh rí †	586	2
572 Cath Tola	571	1	588 Cath Muighe	586	2
573 Conaill m. Comgaill †	572	1	588 Lughdach †	588	0
574 Brenaind m. Briain †	573	1	591 Gregorius †	590	1
575 Brenaind Cl. Ferta †	576	−1	592 Cath Eudhuind	590	2
575 Aed m. Eachach †	574	1	592 Seanchain †	590	2
576 Etchen eps. †	577	−1	593 Aed Cerr †	591	2
577 Cairech †	577	0	593 Colum Cille †	592	1
578 Cath Droma	579	−1	595 Cumascaigh †	593	2
579 Aed m. Suibne †	581	−2	595 Cath Sliebe	593	2
579 Baedan m. Cairill †	585	−6	595 Tibruide †	593	2
581 Fearadhaigh †	582	−1	**596 Aedh m. Ainmireach †**	**594**	2

Figure 43. Comparison of the chronology of all events in common to the Clonmacnoise chronicle and FM for AD 562–96, where Δ=Clonmacnoise chronicle–FM. The events are given in the orthography of AT and obits of the kings of the regnal-canon are shown in bold.

As can be seen while the chronology of most of FM's non-regnal entries is within two years of that of the Clonmacnoise chronicle there is no consistency in either the magnitude or sign of the differences Δ, and moreover occasional entries are asynchronous by up to ±13 years. The important implication of this result is that FM's chronology is untrustworthy in either absolute or relative terms over the entire extent of its regnal-canon.

The remarkably erratic character of FM's chronology naturally prompts the question as to how such profound disorder arose. To examine this I consider the matter of how Mícheál Ó Cléirigh and his co-compilers reduced his formidable array of sources to a single unified text. Ó Cléirigh in both his prefaces asserted that, 'The chroniclers and learned men who were engaged in extracting and transcribing this book from various books, were: [six names].'[81] Thus any hypothesis of the method used by Ó Cléirigh to compile all these sources must accommodate up to six compilers excerpting and writing simultaneously. The hypothesis must also account for the complex pattern of largely random chronological displacement of many entries in FM relative to the chronology of the sources used, cf. Figure 43 above. First we note that neither of the existing manuscript pairs, MSS C+H or A+P, can be the result of the 'writing' of these compilers, because neither exhibits a sufficiently large number of scribal hands, for in these four MSS protracted sequences of annals have been written by just one scribe.[82] It must therefore be the case that the text written by these compilers in the first phase of the compilation when excerpting their sources has been lost, and because this constituted the initial phase I shall refer to the resulting text as the 'Initial Draft'. Now for six compilers to be able simultaneously excerpt multiple sources into one file it is obvious that this Initial Draft must have been in a dismembered state. Examination of MS UCD OFM A16 shows that Conaire Ó Cléirigh took Mícheál Ó Cléirigh's SR and systematically computed and interpolated the regnal AM and AD series into it. I suggest that next, each regnal entry of SR together with its AM or AD datum was transcribed onto a separate sheet of paper. Finally from the arrival of the Fir Bolg in AM 3266 onwards year headings were inscribed, one per sheet of paper, so that every year between the regnal obits was fully represented with ample blank space available for entries. In this way FM's entire regnal-canon and AM/AD apparatus, in perfect synchronism with SR, was prepared in advance. This would then allow all compilers to excerpt and inscribe simultaneously from separate sources just so long as no two compilers required to simultaneously access the same year, which conflict could be easily avoided by their working on disparate intervals. For any given event this arrangement conferred upon the first compiler inscribing an entry for that event the authority to determine its chronology. In cases where the event was registered in multiple sources then subsequent

---

81 O'Donovan, *FM* i, p. lxiv, 'As iatt na Croinicidhe, & an taos ealadhna do bháttar acc sccriobhadh an leabhair sin, & aga theglamadh a leabhraibh éccsamhla. ...' O'Donovan's translation of 'acc sccriobhadh' as 'transcribing', is inaccurate; Walsh, *Gleanings*, 75 (short preface). Cf. Cunningham, *Making FM*, 107–54 ('Methodology of the Four Masters'). **82** Cunningham, *Making FM*, 155–90 (Compares the FM MSS).

compilers had either to accept the initial chronology, to relocate the initial entry, or to duplicate the event under another year. With the authority to determine the chronology of the compilation distributed amongst six compilers it is not difficult to understand that the chronology of many entries would be effectively randomized, particularly in the first millennium where there is sustained asynchronism between the regnal chronology of the Moville-Clonmacnoise chronicle and that assumed by Mícheál Ó Cléirigh. This indeed is just what is observed in FM. One can also see that a document produced by such a process would contain, apart from multiple hands and variant orthographies, many textual variations, particularly where translation from Latin to Irish was required. It would also contain, in cases where compilers had missed an earlier inscription, multiple entries of an event. However, as it is the case that duplicate entries are rare in FM it is apparent that in a second phase virtually all such instances were identified and resolved to a single entry, and an earnest endeavour made to normalize orthography and style. I suggest that the manuscript pair MSS C+H is the result of this process of normalization and hence will refer to it as the 'Normalized Draft'. This pair of MSS shows numerous interlinear and marginal additions, evidently the result of collation of the Normalized Draft with supplementary sources, as well as some further textual emendations, whereas in the pair of MSS A+P these additions and emendations are generally incorporated by the first hand. Thus it is clear, as Walsh also recognized in his proposal for a new edition of FM, that MSS A+P represent the final compilation achieved by Mícheál Ó Cléirigh and his co-compilers.[83] Hence I term it the 'Final Draft', and the process outlined above may be summarized as the sequence:

Multiple sources → Initial Draft [lost] → Normalized Draft [C+H] → Final Draft [A+P]

Given the administrative complexity of this compilation process and the grievous chronological errors it inherited from Gilla Cóemáin's regnal-canon it is not to be wondered at that FM, notwithstanding its wealth of chronicle sources and awesome number of entries, was deeply flawed as a chronicle by its profoundly erratic chronology.

Indeed this last comment applies equally to the entire corpus of regnal-canon chronicles, for it must be acknowledged that none of those scholars who developed the regnal-canon chronicle tradition from the eleventh to the seventeenth centuries ever achieved sufficient competence at historical

---

83 Walsh, *Four Masters*, 12–13 (final compilation); cf. Cunningham, *Making FM*, 188–9 'Walsh's observation is correct although the nature of the variation identified is rather less significant in respect of the post-1170 annals.'

chronology to overcome the grievous anachronisms introduced by the Cashel regnal-canon. For these scholars, and for Irish historical writing in general, the compilation and adoption of the Cashel regnal-canon as authoritative in the early eleventh century was a chronological disaster. Nor alas did the disruptive influence of the Cashel canon cease with Ó Cléirigh's compilation of FM, for its authority is readily observed in Seathrún Céitinn's widely disseminated *Foras Feasa ar Eirinn* (*c.*1634), O'Flaherty's *Ogygia* (1685), and Charles O'Conor's *Dissertations on a History of Ireland* (1753, 1766). In the nineteenth century John O'Donovan's decision to devote his exceptional talents and energy to the production of a printed edition of FM, rather than one of the texts of the Clonmacnoise or Cuana groups, re-vitalised the regnal-canon tradition. O'Donovan's prestigious publication has inspired generations of students of Irish history down to the present day, so that popularly FM is usually regarded as the archetype of the Irish Annals.[84] All of this has contrived to sustain the legacy of the Cashel regnal-canon and hence to obscure and distort the chronology of medieval Irish history.

Summary of the evolution of regnal-canon chronicles

Circa 908 – Cormac m. Cuileannáin compiled a series of tripartite canons listing Irish kings from the Fir Bolg to the Tara/Armagh/Cashel succession over *c.*1262 BC–AD 763. The Moville chronicle was his primary source for the regnal successions of the Christian era.

Circa 1014 – At Brian Borúma's instigation Cashel scholars extended Cormac's canons to show Brian as the ultimate king of both the Tara and Cashel regnal successions. These extended canons constituted part of the incomplete Psalter of Cashel.

Circa 1056 – Flann Mainistrech composed two poems celebrating the Tara regnal succession for the Christian era based upon the Cashel regnal-canon.

Circa 1072 – Gilla Cóemáin composed two poems celebrating the Tara regnal succession from the Fir Bolg to Brian Borúma in which he systematically cited regnal years, the majority of which were taken from the Cashel regnal-canon.

Circa 1072–1166 – Armagh scholars employed Gilla Cóemáin's poems as the chronological basis for the compilation of LG in which the post-Patrician era incorporated annals from the Clonmacnoise chronicle selectively emphasizing Armagh affairs.

Circa 1423 – Maoilín Ua Maoil Chonaire based the pre-Patrician section of his Uí Maoil Chonaire-II chronicle on LG, while for AD 432–1223 he conflated LG with the secularized version of the Clonmacnoise chronicle. This was followed

---

84 Mac Niocaill, *MIA*, 18 and F.X. Martin *idem*, 6 both make this point.

by his recompilation of the Connacht and Fermanagh chronicle over 1224–1423 as discussed in chapter 9.

Circa 1609 – Calloch O'More acquired either Uí Maoil Chonaire-II or a contemporaneous copy of it and annotated it.

1627 – Conell Mageoghagan translated Calloch's annotated edition of Uí Maoil Chonaire-II, leaving numerous lacunae and introducing many interpolations including his own marginal AD that are erratic up to the thirteenth century. While Mageoghagan's autograph is lost we possess a number of relatively early copies of it, and these constitute MB.

1630 – Micheál Ó Cléirigh compiled *Seanchas Riogh Eireann*, a comprehensive chronicle of the supposed 'kings of Ireland', basing it upon Gilla Cóemáin's aforementioned poems, except that Ó Cléirigh emended the regnal years to synchronize Flood and Incarnation with the Septuagint AM 2242 and 5200, and Dathí m. Fiachrach and Brian Borúma's obits at AD 428 and 1013.

1631 – Micheál Ó Cléirigh and others compiled an edition of LG reproducing exactly the Septuagint chronology and regnal succession of his *Seanchas Riogh*.

1632–6 – Micheál Ó Cléirigh and others compiled nine major Irish chronicles together, reproducing exactly the Septuagint chronology of his *Seanchas Riogh* and introducing a systematic AM/AD chronological apparatus. While the primary compilation is lost two subsequent copies survive and these constitute FM, and collation with the Clonmacnoise group shows FM's chronology to be seriously distorted at least up to the eleventh century.

Circa 1634 – Seathrún Céitinn alias Geoffrey Keating compiled his *Foras Feasa ar Eirinn* apparently drawing upon Ó Cléirigh's *Seanchas Riogh* for his regnal succession.[85]

Circa 1685 – Roderick O'Flaherty compiled his *Ogygia* employing the Armagh MS of MB as the primary source for his regnal succession, but making an independent attempt to impose his own interpretation of Vulgate chronology.

---

85 Mc Carthy, 'Irish regnal canon', *s.v.* 'Foras Feasa ar Eireann' (Keating's synchronisation of the Incarnation with the reign of Criomhthann Nia Nair, as in *Seanchas Riogh*).

CHAPTER ELEVEN

Final compilation stages

The preceding chapters have identified, as far as possible, the major compilation stages lying behind the groups of our chosen texts, and it now remains to identify the individual characteristics of each of these texts relative to those major compilations. It may be helpful here to recall that the concluding stages of the compilation process include both additive and subtractive mechanisms. The former arises because the later compilers usually embed their additions into an earlier compilation. It should not be assumed that these additions must appear at the end of the text for in several instances they occur near the beginning, and in general additions may be made anywhere, though it is usually the case that the additions at the end are the most numerous. For the purposes of discussion the only requirement is that we are able to reliably identify them as one of the later phases of compilation, and then we refer to them collectively as an end chronicle. The subtractive mechanism whereby the later compiler has regularly reduced or abandoned entries from an earlier compilation is likewise common, and we term the result an abridgment of the source chronicle.

Clonmacnoise group

Commencing with the Rawl. B. 502 text of AT we recall that both the date and codicological evidence of this MS imply that it was written at Clonmacnoise. Further we note that the last phase of identifiable compilation is represented by the glosses, and Best's identification of the glossator of ff. 9–12 as 'interpolator H' of *Lebor na hUidre* suggests that after its completion in *c.*1100 Rawl. B. 502 remained in use in Clonmacnoise. An unidentified scribe has glossed the earlier ff. 1–9 and some of these glosses have been subsequently incorporated into the main text of Rawl. B. 488, cf. plates 2 and 3. A critical examination of all these glosses against the main texts of both Rawl. B. 502 and 488 is a major desideratum, together with the completion of a critical edition of AT.

Turning next to Rawl. B. 488, we have in chapter 9 concluded that the major compilation behind this was a late thirteenth-century secular adaptation of the Clonmacnoise chronicle by the Uí Maoil Chonaire to the purview of their patrons, the Uí Chonchobair, and this has been designated Uí Maoil Chonaire-I. Indeed Dumville characterized the compiler of AT's archetype as, 'a rather hard-headedly secular-minded chronicler who rejected the natural marvels, most of the ecclesiastical obits, and further entries having a bearing on Church-affairs.'[1] As we have seen the most significant ecclesiastical obits that were omitted in this process were those of the *comharba* of Clonmacnoise.[2] Consequently, we must conclude that the singular obit of Tigernach Ua Braein, *comharba* over 1071–88, represents an addition made sometime between that Uí Maoil Chonaire-I compilation and the transcription by the scribe of Rawl. B. 488 in the later fourteenth century. This obit represents therefore a crucial witness to a later stage in the compilation of this MS and it requires further examination beyond that already given in chapter 6, p. 191 ff. There it was shown that a compiler identified as 'Tigernach-admirer' had restored Tigernach's obit to a position corresponding exactly with that of CS, so that it is helpful to compare the two obits, which with their contractions expanded read:

AT 1088.4:Huc usque Tigernach scribsit ocht.ar.ochtmogait quieuit.
CS 1088.4: Tigernach H. Braín, do Sil Muiredhaigh, comarba Ciarain Cluana muc Nois ocus Comain, quieuit.

Here we may first note that Tigernach-admirer's priorities were to emphasize Tigernach's contribution to writing the text and the year of his death, while he omitted all the details of his familial and tribal origins, and his ecclesiastical affiliation and status. His primary objective was not therefore simply to restore Tigernach's obit. Second we note the form in which he identified the year, 'ocht.ar.ochtmogait', for this is unmistakably the Uí Duibhgeannáin style of *Anno Domini*, expressed in Irish using the particle 'ar' and commencing from the least significant digit. Third since neither AT nor CS exhibit AD at this or adjacent years and this is indeed the year 1088, it appears that Tigernach-admirer himself accurately supplied 'ocht.ar.ochtmogait'. Fourth, we see that Tigernach-admirer wrote substantially in Latin making it most unlikely that he was responsible for the widespread degradation of the Latin in Rawl. B. 488, which is thus more likely to have arisen at the earlier Uí Maoil Chonaire com-pilation. Hence I conclude that Tigernach-admirer was of the Uí Duibhgeannáin and he was here primarily concerned to register his appreciation for Tigernach's earlier contribution to the compilation of his exemplar and the AD limit of that contribution. This being so it is appropriate to investigate any other evidence of an Uí Duibhgeannáin association with Rawl. B. 488. The most extensive evidence is the marginal AD system-B over AD 978–1045, 1064–1178 written systematically as 'ais in tigerna', most likely in the sixteenth century, cf. chapter 2, p. 23. As well we have the marginal inscription by Brian Mac Diarmada written

1 Grabowski & Dumville, *Chronicles*, 155–83 (AT vs CS), 182 (cit.), cf. Ó Muraíle, *Celebrated antiquary*, 103–4 (AT vs CS).   2 Grabowski & Dumville, *Chronicles*, 158–9 (Clonmacnoise obits unique to CS).

on f. 4^r with the date '1584', at which time Mac Diarmada with the support of the Uí Duibhgeannáin was compiling LC. We have therefore good evidence of an association between the Uí Duibhgeannáin and this MS extending from the compilation of its exemplar to the closing decades of the sixteenth century.

While the scribe of Rawl. B. 488 has not been identified Ó Cuív, following Best and Oskamp, has noted that he was the same scribe who wrote the passages from LG found in RIA MSS 537–9, and who also contributed to 'the composite manuscript commonly known as 'Leabhar Buidhe Leacáin' ('Yellow Book of Lecan') which originated in the Mac Fhir Bhisigh school in Sligo and which may have been written in the period 1350–70.'[3] This association with the Yellow Book of Lecan then places this scribe in the latter half of the fourteenth century in a secular context deep in the province of Connacht, and this led Ó Muraíle to hypothesize that Rawl. B. 488 'had lain at Lackan for so long that it had come to be thought of as a product of the family [sc. Mac Fhirbhisigh].'[4] However, a distinctive feature of this particular scribe's work is that he wrote a neat, compact hand in two columns without ruling, so that the lines of text in his left and right columns do not remain in absolute synchronism.[5] Another distinctive feature is his strong inclination to right justify the lines of related text so that as a consequence the right-hand ends of long sequences of his lines of text are in close alignment. These features may be observed in plate 3, and in the samples of his work reproduced by Oskamp.[6] Now there is also good evidence that these were characteristics of Uí Duibhgeannáin scribes in general for they are also found in the approximately contemporaneous contributions of Magnus Ua Duibhgeannáin to the Book of Ballymote, written in the last decades of the fourteenth century.[7] These same features are still evident about two centuries later in the work of the Uí Duibhgeannáin scribes who contributed to the compilation of CT, and also with less consistent right justification in Pilip Ua Duibhgeannáin's contribution to LC, cf. plates 10–11. Thus in consequence, on the basis of the AD date 'ocht.ar.ochtmogait', the sustained 'ais in tigerna' marginalia, Brian Mac Diarmada's marginal entry for 1584, and on the unruled, right justified features of the writing I conclude that Rawl. B. 488 was an Uí Duibhgeannáin compilation of the late fourteenth century based upon Uí Maoil Chonaire-I, and that it remained in the possession of the Uí Duibhgeannáin at least until the end of the sixteenth century. Collation of parallel passages of Rawl. B. 502 and 488 shows the latter to be both an abridgment and textual

---

3 Ó Cuív, *Catalogue*, 144 (cit.). Best, 'Yellow book', 190–2 and Oskamp, 'Yellow book', 102–3 (scribe of Rawl. B. 488). Both Best and Oskamp considered Rawl. B. 488 to be part of the 'Yellow Book', but their hypothesis has been disproven by O'Sullivan, 'Yellow book', 177–81. 4 Ó Muraíle, *Celebrated antiquary*, 102 (cit.). 5 Ó Cuív, *Catalogue*, 143 (neat hand with no ruling). 6 Oskamp, 'Yellow book', plates I–VII opp. p. 108 (MS samples). 7 Atkinson, *Ballymote*, 445 (written & signed by Magnus Ua Duibhgeannáin).

degradation of the former, from which it is clear that before Rawl. B. 502 was truncated at AD 140 it preserved a far more substantial and textually superior edition of the Clonmacnoise chronicle than has been transmitted by Rawl. B. 488.

Turning next to CS we find that its final compilation stage is associated directly with the Meic Fhirbhisigh in that its primary MS, TCD 1292, was written by Dubhaltach Mac Fhirbhisigh, who, as Hennessy and Ó Muraíle remarked, was concerned to reproduce carefully some aspects of his exemplar. However, Dubhaltach's concern did not extend to either his exemplar's orthography or grammar for he was inclined to modify these to contemporary norms, nor as we shall see did it extend to its content.[8] Regarding the character of Dubhaltach's reproduction of his exemplar most discussions have focussed upon two interjections in the pre-Patrician section of the text, the first of which has been already discussed as the 'preface' in chapter 3, p. 62. With one exception scholars have assumed Dubhaltach to be the author of these interjections, but no actual evidence for this has been offered.[9] However, Ó Muraíle, who dated Dubhaltach's completion of CS to c.1640, has pointed out a number of seventeenth-century orthographical features of these interjections. Namely the use of the Ó Cléirigh affectation of 'cc' for 'g', the late orthography of 'lécchtóir', and the use of the word 'athcumair' found otherwise almost solely in seventeenth-century texts. These late features together with Dubhaltach's parallel use of the word 'léghthóir' twice in the colophon to his translation of the rule of S. Clare in 1647, and four times in the preface to his Book of Genealogies written in 1650, lead me to conclude that he was indeed the author of these two interjections.[10] However, careful examination of the text of CS shows that these two are but part of a series of ten interjections, and in order to examine this matter further I cite translations of all ten in Figure 44.

Now since he has signed I.10 it is indisputably by Dubhaltach and it shows that his exemplar was old and had sustained a serious lacuna that must have been considerably greater than his estimate of 'two leaves' since all annals for the years 723–803 are missing. Of the nine remaining interjections scholars have studied only I.1 and I.5, considering them both to be interdependent and to reflect upon the character of Dubhaltach's compilation of CS. Of these studies, of which Ó

8 Hennessy, *CS*, ix–x (scribe of TCD 1292), xxxvi (orthography & grammar); Ó Muraíle, *Celebrated antiquary*, 97–8 (scribe), opp. 41, 104–6 (Dubhaltach's reproduction of a lacuna), 103 (updating orthography).   9 Dubhaltach's authorship of the two interjections: Hennessy, *CS*, xxviii–xxx; O'Donovan, *FM* i, p. lxv n. g; O'Curry, *MM*, 126–7; Grabowski & Dumville, *Chronicles*, 156. Ó Muraíle, *Celebrated antiquary*, 102 registers the following doubt: 'the abridging of the text – for which ... apologies are expressed twice near the beginning of the manuscript – might not have been done by Dubhaltach but may instead be the work of some earlier member of Clann Fhir Bhisigh.'   10 N. Ó Muraíle, personal communication, 30 August 2006 (orthographical details – the affectation of 'cc' for 'g' is found erratically throughout CS); idem, *Celebrated antiquary*, 102, 372 (CS date), opp. 104, 139 (S. Clare colophon facsimiles), 166, 201 n.10 (date of preface); idem, *Book of Genealogies* i, 182–6 L. Gen. 15.5, 16.1, 17.2, 18.2 ('léghthóir' instances).

Sigla	CS pg.	Interjection
I.1	3	Incipit Chronicum Scotorum, i.e. The Chronicle of the Scoti is begun here. Understand, Reader (*lécchtóir*), that for a certain reason, and plainly to avoid tediousness, what we desire is to make a short (*athcumair*) Abstract and Compendium of the History of the Scoti only in this copy, leaving out the lengthened details of the Books of History; wherefore it is we entreat of you not to reproach us therefor, as we know that it is an exceedingly great deficiency.
I.2	3	*In this year the daughter of one of the Greeks came to Hibernia ... Cesar ...* This the antiquaries of the Scoti do not relate.
I.3	9	*Nimhed, son of Adhnoman .uu. came ...* as it is related in the Invasions of Erinn.
I.4	9	*A.M. 2355. At this time the Fir Bolg occupied Erinn.* But this has not been proved.
I.5	9–11	You have heard from me, O Readers (*legnicch*), that I like not to have the labour of writing this section (*tslecda*) imposed on me, wherefore it is that I beseech of you, for the sake of true friendship, not to reproach me for it (if the reason thereof is understood by you), for it is certain that it is not the Clann Firbisigh who are in fault.
I.6	11	*Milidh, son of Bile, proceeded ... to Egypt, after the slaying of Reflor ...* (as it is found in the Invasions of Erinn); and understand not that it was soon after the death of Nel in Egypt, but many years indeed after it, that ...
I.7	11	*His great fleet consisted of 100 ships,* as the vellum relates from which this copy has been drawn;
I.8	15	*the sons of Milidh ... assumed the sovereignty of Erinn ...* and so forth.
I.9	15	I pass to another time, and He Who Is will bless it.
I.10	124 n.2	A front of two leaves of the old book out of which I write this is wanting, and I leave what is before me of this page for them. I am Dubhaltach Firbisigh.

Figure 44. The ten interjections found in CS are identified with sigla I.1–10, and with page numbers are cited from Hennessy's edition of CS with his translations of them in plain font. Relevant proximate text and Irish words are cited in italic.

Muraíle made an excellent summary, by far the most substantial was that of Dumville who made a detailed comparative study of AT/CS over 974–1150. In the beginning of this study Dumville, having first cited both I.1 and I.5, inferred that:[11]

It is clear, then, that what Mac Firbhisigh is saying is that he has savaged the *Leabhar Oiris* or *Leabhar Gabhála Érenn*, as being unnecessary for his present

11 Ó Muraíle, *Celebrated antiquary*, 103–4 (summary); Grabowski & Dumville, *Chronicles*, 153–83 (study), 156 (cit.).

purpose. There is no implication, I think, in what he says that the whole work is a sustained abbreviation of the entire text of his exemplar.

Thus Dumville concluded that *both* I.1 and I.5 identified Dubhaltach's intention to abridge only the Irish origin legend section of his exemplar. However, Dubhaltach's interjection I.5, 'You have heard from me', cannot logically be taken to refer to interjection I.1 in order to explain why he resented writing this section, since I.1 has already signalled his intention to omit unwanted material. Moreover, the material he is abridging in this section actually recounts the origin of the Scoti, which is just the material his interjection I.1 has stated that he intends to include in his copy. Rather I.1, both by its content and prefatory position applies to the *whole* subsequent text, as indeed is borne out by the virtual absence of world history material in CS relative to AT/AR. On the other hand interjection I.5 refers only to the earlier part of the text, cf. 'this section (*an tslecda so*)', and indeed the prior interjections I.2 and I.4 both raise objections against the material just transcribed. Furthermore I.3 abridges the account of Nemedh by pointing out that it is related in the 'Invasions of Erinn', i.e. *Lebor Gabála*. Consequently, it appears that the interjection I.5 which follows, 'You have heard from me O Readers, that I like not the labour ... ', refers to these three previous brief interjections I.2–4, and *not* to interjection I.1 as has been generally supposed. It appears in fact that Dubhaltach was having difficulty transcribing this Irish origin legend section of his exemplar because he found that it repeatedly conflicted with the version of the 'Invasions of Erinn' that he knew. At I.6 he went on to remark a chronological conflict concerning Milidh and Nel, and at I.7 he assigned responsibility to 'the vellum' for the stated size of Milidh's fleet. Finally at I.8 he truncated the account of the sons of Milidh with, 'and so forth', at which point he abandoned the origin legend of Ireland altogether and proceeded to the time of Patrick with I.9, 'I pass to another time ...'. And indeed collation of this section of CS with LG shows that its account of the 'Invasions' repeatedly diverges from all of the known later medieval recensions of LG. For example, they all make Cesar a grand-daughter of Noah and hence of Hebrew descent rather than Greek.[12] It should be recalled that this Annalistic account of the Irish origin legend originated with the Moville compiler in the middle of the eighth century, and versions cognate with that of CS are found in AR/AI/AB.[13] It is not to be wondered at, therefore, that the version with which Dubhaltach was familiar in the middle of the seventeenth century significantly differed from that written

---

12 Compare Hennessy, *CS*, 2–14 with Macalister *LG* ii, § 174–5, 187, 103–7, 199–200, 207; *LG* iii, § 208–10, 214–15, 219, 216, 219–20, 237; *LG* iv, §303, 306; *LG* ii, § 104, 126–32; *LG* v, 385–6, 395, 387. Scowcroft, '*LG* I', 104 (Cesar grand-daughter of Noah); Carey, 'Cesair legend', 38–9 (early versions of the Cesair legend).   13 Jaski, 'Irish origin legend', 36, 40 (Annals vs LG).

nine hundred years earlier. Thus it seems clear that these nine interjections by Dubhaltach constitute a unity and they identify two quite distinct abridgments. In the first of these Dubhaltach advised regretfully that his transcription of his exemplar, the 'old book', would include only the history of the Scoti, and indeed collation of CS with AT/AR shows that this is substantially the case for Dubhaltach abandoned virtually all of the world history entries. However, the very occasional cryptic papal and imperial entries, e.g. CS 524.2 'Ioannes papa quieuit', 602.8 'Mauricius moritur', show that Dubhaltach did not adhere absolutely rigidly to his 'Scoti' policy, and confirm that such world history entries indeed existed in his exemplar. In the second and textually earlier abridgment, Dubhaltach found while transcribing his exemplar's Irish origin legend that it repeatedly conflicted with the version of *Lebor Gabála* that he knew, so even though it referred specifically to the history of the Scoti he variously contradicted, abridged, or omitted it. In summary, these interjections show us that from the very outset it was Dubhaltach's intention to substantially abridge his exemplar, and in the event his abridgment of the Irish origin legend was particularly severe.

Next regarding the content of Dubhaltach's exemplar, Dumville's invaluable tabulation of AT and CS unique entries over 975–1150 has demonstrated comprehensively that CS transmits numerous ecclesiastical obits lost from AT, and in particular it substantially preserves the succession of Clonmacnoise *comharba*. It is evident therefore that Dubhaltach's exemplar was *not* derived from the secular edition of the Clonmacnoise chronicle compiled by the Uí Maoil Chonaire and from which AT derives, but rather from a more comprehensive edition preserving the Clonmacnoise ecclesiastical content of that chronicle. Thus Dubhaltach's 'Scoti' policy fortunately resulted in the transmission in CS of many Irish ecclesiastical entries recorded in Clonmacnoise that had been lost in the compilation sequence of AT. On the other hand Dumville's identification of AT-unique entries over 975–1150 shows us that CS has lost a considerable number of Clonmacnoise chronicle secular entries over that interval.[14] While it is not possible to be sure whether these secular losses were incurred by Dubhaltach in his abridgment, or earlier by the compiler of his exemplar, it is clear that this earlier compiler had comprehensively transmitted the Clonmacnoise ecclesiastical material.

Turning to consider the origin of Dubhaltach's exemplar it appears certain from the concluding assertion in his interjection I.5 that, 'it is not the Clann Firbisigh who are at fault', that his exemplar was compiled by a member of the Meic Fhirbisigh. Consequently, his identification here must be taken together with his commitment in I.1 to leave out 'the lengthened details of the Books of

14 Dumville & Grabowski, *Chronicles*, 184–9 (CS-unique entries), 190–205 (AT-unique entries).

History (*na leapar airisin*)' as a reference to a Leabhar Airisin Meic Fhirbhisigh, and his acknowledgement that this represented a formidable chronicle. Regarding our knowledge of Mac Fhirbhisigh possession of substantial chronicles, the earliest reference to such is by Micheál Ó Cléirigh in his longer preface to FM written in 1636 wherein he listed the sources he had used to compile the first volume of FM extending from the Flood to AD 1207. The last of these sources he described as follows:[15]

> Leabhar Oirisean Leacain Meic Firbisicch ... was procured for them after the greater part of the book had been written, and from it they transcribed every copious matter they found which they considered necessary which was not in the first books they had, for neither the book of Cluain nor the Book of the Island had anything beyond the year of the age of our Lord 1227.

It is explicit from this that by 1636 Ó Cléirigh had acquired Mac Fhirbhisigh annals that extended not only over Flood–AD 1207 but beyond AD 1227, and which contained material not in his other sources. Next regarding the relationship between CS and FM, Hennessy pointed out that many entries 'common to the Annals of the Four Masters and the present chronicle [CS], are not found in any other volume of Irish Annals now known to be in existence.'[16] It is certain therefore that over Flood–AD 1207 CS/FM share a common Mac Fhirbhisigh annalistic source which was known to both Micheál Ó Cléirigh and Dubhaltach as 'Leabhar Airisin [Lecain] Meic Fhirbhisigh'. The next reference to this work is by Dubhaltach in 1649 in his Book of Genealogies where, having first used 'Leabhar Airsion Fhearghail Uí Ghadhra', i.e. FM MS C, to compile his regnal succession over AM 2242–AD 1166, he continued with the reign of Ruaidhrí Ua Conchobhair 'according to the Book of History of Leacán Meic Fhir Bhisigh'.[17] Then sixteen years later in 1665 Dubhaltach disclosed further details of this Mac Fhirbhisigh 'Book of History' when he compiled a list of Irish bishops for James Ware which he prefaced and concluded as follows:[18]

> [§1] The ensueing bishops' names are collected out of severall Irish ancient and modern manuscripts, viz. of Gilla-Isa Mac Ferbisie's Annals written afore the yeare 1397 ... and out of others the Mac Ferbisies' Annals ...
> [§143] Huc usque [1530] the Mac Ferbisies Irish Annals furnished this collection.

---

15 Ó Muraíle, *Celebrated antiquary*, 20 (cit.), cf. O'Donovan, *FM* i, p. lxv.   16 Hennessy, CS, xxxviii (cit.). Ó Muraíle, *Celebrated antiquary*, 100 was mistaken when he attributed to Hennessy the assertion that the CS entry regarding the synod of Uisneach in 1111 is also found in FM. Hennessy, idem, xxxviii–ix cited the CS entry in support of his hypothesis that Dubhaltach's exemplar was compiled by Gillachrist Ua Maeileoin of Clonmacnoise.   17 Ó Muraíle, *Celebrated antiquary*, 178 (L. Gen regnal succession); idem, *Book of Genealogies* iii, 4 (date & Leabhar Uí Ghadhra), 41 (cit.), 4–42 (regnal succession).   18 Ó Muraíle, *Celebrated antiquary*, 250 (cits.), opp. 233 (facsimile of BL Add. 4799 f. 18ʳ). In 1666 Dubhaltach translated for Ware other Mac Fhirbhisigh annals, the 'Annals of Lecan' for the years 1443–68, cf. *idem* 271–2.

Here Dubhaltach indicated that he had in his possession annals that were originally compiled by Giolla Íosa before 1397, and subsequently extended by others of the Meic Fhirbhisigh at least as far as 1530.[19] Now given that the ecclesiastical entries that Dubhaltach transcribed into his Bishops' list are just the same sort of entries that Grabowski and Dumville showed were the distinctive feature of CS vis-à-vis AT, I submit that the only reasonable conclusion is that Dubhaltach used exactly the same Mac Fhirbhisigh Leabhar Airis as the source for his earlier compilation of CS.[20] That is, CS was simply Dubhaltach's abridgement of the Leabhar Airis of Giolla Íosa, and this explains why he felt obliged to make such a prominent apology in I.1. Thus when Dubhaltach compiled CS in c.1640 the section of Leabhar Airisin Meic Fhirbhisigh compiled by Giolla Íosa before 1397 would have been about 240 years old, and hence accord with Dubhaltach's description of his exemplar as an 'old book' exhibiting a serious lacuna. Collation of the 130 bishops' names listed by Dubhaltach over 678–1530 against those of FM provides further evidence supporting this identification since nearly every one of them also appears in FM, in most instances appearing either first, second, or last in the list of entries in accordance with their late addition to FM remarked by Mícheál Ó Cléirigh. On the other hand, in accordance with Dubhaltach's commitment to abridge his source, only a small number of these bishops appear in CS, notably the Clonmacnoise succession.[21]

Regarding Dubhaltach's motive for making this abridgment, in 1996 Ó Muraíle presented a convincing argument that it 'could well be that Dubhaltach copied the *Chronicum* for [John] Lynch at about the same time that he transcribed the Fragmentary Annals for that same scholar.' Dr John Lynch, 1599–c.1677, was a historian, friend and patron of Dubhaltach, who was educated in Galway and France, ordained in 1625, and made archdeacon of Tuam in c.1630. Subsequently he returned to France and there published a number of books, the first in 1662 entitled *Cambrensus Eversus* was his refutation of the criticisms of Ireland and Irish Christianity by the Welsh cleric Giraldus Cambrensis c.1146–1220.[22] If CS was compiled specifically for Lynch's polemical work then this would very satisfactorily explain Dubhaltach's inclusion of Irish ecclesiastical affairs, and especially Clonmacnoise affairs, and also its original truncation at 1135. It would also explain his rather mysterious remarks in I.1 that 'For a certain reason ... what we desire is to make a short Abstract and Compendium of the Scoti only

19 Ó Muraíle, *Celebrated antiquary*, 16–21 (Giolla Íosa).   20 Grabowski & Dumville, *Chronicles*, 153–83 (CS vs AT entries).   21 I wish to express my gratitude to Nollaig Ó Muraíle for his generosity in supplying me with a copy of his own annotated edition of this bishops' list, transcribed from BL Add. MS 4799 ff. 18ʳ–21ᵛ, from which these FM/CS collations have been made.   22 Ó Muraíle, *Celebrated antiquary*, 100, 394 (citation & *Cambrensus Eversus*), 65–6 (Lynch). 88–9 (Fragmentary annals copy); the full title of Lynch's book is *Cambrensus Eversus, seu potius Historica Fides in Rebus Hibernicis Giraldo Cambrensi Abrogata*.

in this copy', and that in I.5, 'I beseech of you, for the sake of true friendship, not to reproach me.' These remarks indeed suggest that Dubhaltach was compiling CS with a specifically Irish Christian purview for the use of a close friend, and they fit remarkably well with his known relationship with Lynch. In summary, CS comprises an extensive abridgment by Dubhaltach Mac Fhirbhisigh of earlier annals compiled by Giolla Íosa Mac Fhirbhisigh from the Clonmacnoise chronicle. In his abridgment Dubhaltach omitted much of the Moville compiler's Irish origin legend and nearly all world history entries, and he substantially revised the orthography of his source to seventeenth-century style.

Finally turning to AR I have already discussed in chapter 2 in some detail the compilation by Brendan O'Conor in 1641 of its only MS, Bruxelles Bibl. Royale 5301–20. There we found that O'Conor's interjection 'Adversaria rerum Hiberni[ae] quae excerpta ex mutila historia D. Cantwelij' written at the head of his transcription shows that he, like his close contemporary Dubhaltach Mac Fhirbhisgh, was initially intent on abstracting principally Irish entries but he subsequently relented and transcribed some world history entries. Examination of the microfilm also shows that O'Conor transcribed entries only intermittently, and did not continue his transcription to the end of his exemplar. Thus the conclusion that his compilation represents a substantial abridgment of his exemplar, of which we have only his cryptic description, 'mutila historia D. Cantwelij'. Collation of post-Patrician AR against AT/CS confirms this conclusion, and it also discloses that AR transmits both world history entries omitted from CS and ecclesiastical entries omitted from AT. This therefore implies that 'historia D. Cantwelij' had not descended directly from either of these but rather from the Clonmacnoise chronicle independently, and because of AR's mutually exclusive range relationship with Rawl. B. 502 I have suggested that the 'historia' was in fact a good copy of the now missing sections of this Rawlinson MS. In summary the final compilation stage of AR appears to have severely abridged an exemplar which represented a good but already lacunose copy of the Clonmacnoise chronicle. The stemma in Figure 45 summarizes the descent relationships for the four primary Clonmacnoise MSS from their parent Clonmacnoise chronicle.

Cuana group

Commencing with AU I first consider the compilation of its penultimate stage, i.e. the compilation of its primary MS TCD 1282 (MS H). The most readily identified contributor to this was Cathal Óg Mac Maghnusa of Seanad on Loch Erne, about six miles south-east of Enniskillen, whose obit at 1498 in AU describes him as follows:[23]

23 Mac Carthy, *AU* iii, 430–1 (cit. – the emphasis Mac Carthy gives as 'an leabhuꞃ sa/THIS

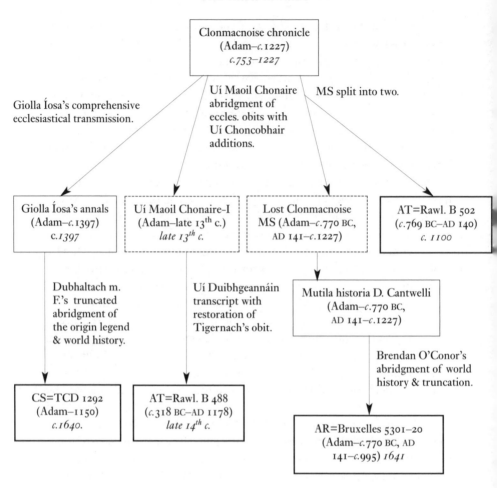

Figure 45. A stemma illustrating the descent of the four primary Clonmacnoise MSS from the Clonmacnoise chronicle, where the existing MSS are identified by thick rectangles, attested works by light rectangles, and hypothesized works by dotted rectangles. Ranges are given in parentheses and dates where known are shown in italic, and those dates shown as ranges identify the accumulation of annals over those years. The comments beside arrows identify the salient characteristics of the compilation stages.

> Mac Maghnusa Mag Uidhir, died this year: namely Cathal … one who was full of grace and of knowledge in every science, both law and divinity, physic and philosophy, and knowledge of Gaidhelic also to the time of this decease, and one that projected and collected and compiled this book from very many other books (*nech ro chumdaigh ⁊ ro theglaim ⁊ ro thinoil an leabhur sa a leabhraibh ilímdaibh ailibh*).

BOOK', does not exist in the MS, cf. Ó Muraíle, *AU* i, frontispiece reproducing Cathal Óg's obit on TCD 1282 f. 139ᵛ).

Now while this obit credits Mac Maghnusa with having 'projected and collected and compiled this book from very many other books' it makes no mention of writing, and it is important to note that the preceding rather fulsome praise for his learning omits all mention of history. It suggests therefore that Mac Maghnusa's role was principally that of patron providing the source books, fiscal support, and leadership, and this role accords well with his major ecclesiastical and political responsibilities as effectively acting bishop of the Clogher diocese from 1484, and head of the Mac Maghnusa clan from 1488.[24] However, Mac Carthy in his introduction to AU also identified him as 'the Compiler' and 'the canonist' and attributed a scribal role to him, asserting:[25]

> ... on the blanks left, in the usual way, between the years for additions and on the margins, a court hand, evidently of the Compiler (who else would have been at pains to record the birth-days of his children?) made entries, some in Irish, others in Latin.

Mac Carthy further attributed to Mac Maghnusa the intermittent ferial and epactal data inserted into the spaces left by the principal scribe, Ruaidhrí Ua Luinín, in the following glowing terms:[26]

> Mac Manus ... neither tampered with the text, vitiated the dating, nor omitted the solar and lunar notation, but, side by side with the chronological errors he was unable to correct, preserved the criteria whereby they can with certainty be rectified.

With these confident assertions, supported only by his rhetorical question concerning birth-day entries, Mac Carthy made Mac Maghnusa the singular compiler of the text and chronological apparatus of AU, and notwithstanding his weak evidence they proved very influential for they were effectively repeated subsequently by Gwynn, Mac Niocaill and Ó Muraíle. Indeed they tended to become more emphatic in time, cf. Ó Muraíle in 1998:[27]

> Cathal Óg was a man of many talents. First and foremost he deserves to be remembered as a scholar whose crowning achievement was the compilation of these Annals of Ulster ... [and] the second of the four 'successive hands of interpolators and glossators' ...

Even though Gwynn, Mac Niocaill, and Ó Muraíle also acknowledged the contributions of Ua Luinín and Ua Caiside to the compilation of AU, they saw Mac

---

24 Ó Muraíle, *AU* i, [14–15] (ecclesiastical and political roles). 25 Mac Carthy, *AU* iv, pp. ii (cit.), viii ('a canonist'). 26 Mac Carthy, *AU* iv, p. ix (cit.). 27 Ó Muraíle, *AU* i, p. [13] (cit.); Gwynn, 'Cathal Mac Magnusa' ii, 373 wrote of 'the fine sense of accurate scholarship which was a special gift of Cathal Mac Maghnusa. When he has an ancient text before him, he copies it (or has it copied) with the utmost fidelity'; Mac Niocaill, *MIA*, 36–7 'the person responsible for the compilation of U, [AU was] Cathal Mac Maghnusa ... some of the additions are family

Maghnusa as the 'scholar' principally responsible for the compilation of the text of AU up to his death in 1498.[28] One consequence of this was that in 1998 a stone monument was erected on Belleisle, formerly Seanadh, on Lough Erne, celebrating the quincentennial of Mac Maghnusa's death and bearing an inscription describing him as 'Compiler of the Annals of Ulster (*Teaglamaí Annála Uladh*)'.[29]

However, the picture regarding the compilation of AU began to alter radically in 2001 when Brian Ó Cuív identified Ruaidhrí Ua Caiside as the scribe of ff. 1–32[rag] Rawl. B. 489 (MS R), for Ó Cuív remarked Ua Caiside's preference for Arabic numerals. And indeed subsequent collation of the Arabic numerals in these folios with those appearing in chronological criteria and many of the interpolated entries in MS H, including the birth entries of Mac Maghnusa's children, showed Ua Caiside to have been the scribe of them all. In fact Ware had already identified Ua Caiside in 1639 as the scribe of the interpolations in the first part, and of the completion of the latter part of MS H.[30] With this identification Mac Carthy's slender basis for attributing a scribal role to Mac Maghnusa disappeared and the focus shifted instead to Ua Caiside. Regarding his background, the Uí Caiside entries in AU show the family to have been hereditary physicans to the Meig Uidhir, and located at Cuil, county Fermanagh. Ua Caiside's insertion of most of these Uí Caiside entries together with his strong interest in numerical and chronological matters, suggest therefore that his educational background lay in the tradition of medieval medicine. However, his actual career appears to have been ecclesiastical in that he was appointed vicar of Kilskeery in county Tyrone and by 1502 was archdeacon of Clogher. Some of the entries that he interpolated disclose a knowledge of canon law, e.g. AU 449.1, '… see the gloss on the *Clementinae*, i.e. *de magistris* at the word *Bononiensis*', the *Clementinae* being canon law decretals issued by Pope Clement V in 1314. His involvement with ecclesiastical legal and historical material evidently continued for in *c.*1525 he compiled the *Register of Clogher* for Patrick Ua Cuilinn, bishop of the diocese.[31]

A survey of the entries that Ua Caiside added to MS H shows that they commonly exhibit some very distinctive textual and chronological features, notably:

a) His preference for using Arabic numerals.

b) His desire either to furnish chronological precision, or to emend existing chronology.

memoranda by Cathal Mac Maghnusa himself'; Mac Airt & Mac Niocaill, *AU*, ix, 'One of the interpolating hands (H²) is that of Cathal Mac Maghnusa.' **28** Gwynn, 'Cathal Mac Magnusa' i, 233–5; Mac Niocaill, *MIA*, 37; Ó Muraíle, *AU* i, [6–7, 18–19] (acknowledgements of Ua Luinín & Ua Caiside). **29** Ó Muraíle, *Cathal Óg*, 68 (inscription). **30** Ó Cuív, *Catalogue*, 157 (Ua Caiside scribe of MS R ff. 1–32); Mc Carthy, 'AU compilation', 74 fig. 1 (Ua Caiside's Arabic numerals in MSS H & R), 76–7 (Ua Caiside's contribution to MS H); Ware, *De scriptoribus*, 83 (identified Ua Caiside as second scribe of MS H) **31** Ó Gallachair, 'Clogherici', 152–4 (Ruaidhrí Ua Caiside's biography); Mac Carthy, *AU* iv, p. viii (gloss mistakenly attributed to Mac

c) His frequent use of brief phrases emphasizing the year as 'in bliadhain-si' or 'hoc anno' or 'hic', that are all incongruent in an annalistic context and to which elements I shall refer as *temporal emphatics*.

Ua Caiside's entries recording the births of two of Mac Maghnusa's children illustrate these features, here highlighted in italic:[32]

> AU 1482.11: *Hoc anno in Estate* natus est Cormacus, filius Caroli iuuenis.
> AU 1485.27: *Hic* natus est Connactius, filius Caroli Iuuenis, *5 Kalendas Februarii, feria 6.*

Initially I inferred from Ua Caiside's emphasis on chronological matters that his role had been that of the chronologist for the compilation of MS H up to 1489.[33] Subsequently however I discovered entries that were written by Ua Luinín and that exhibited the very same characteristics as Ua Caiside's interpolations. For example:[34]

> AU 1395.1: Pilib Mag Uidhir do eg *in bliadhain-si* ... fa buaidh ongtha 7 aithrighi *17 Kl. Apr.*
> AU 1420.7: Maighistir Matha h-Ua Banain, persun 7 oirchinnech Daire Maelaín, d'h-eg *6 Idus Septimbris.*
> AU 1420.8: Goffraigh h-Ua Daimhin d'h-eg *13 Kalendas Iulii* ...

Here we find Arabic numerals, precise Julian dates and a temporal emphatic all written by Ua Luinín, and the clear implication of this is that it was Ua Caiside who had drafted the exemplar that Ua Luinín transcribed. Furthermore that Ua Caiside's compilation of Ua Luinín's exemplar was not restricted just to the later centuries is shown by the existence of seventy-seven occurrences of entries containing the temporal emphatics 'hoc anno' or 'hic' over 436–1179. Ua Luinín wrote sixty-one of these and Ua Caiside the remaining sixteen. Of these seventy-seven entries forty-two commence with 'uel', so that these all provide a duplicate entry with an alternative chronology showing their compiler to have been collating two disparate sources. In confirmation of this inference eighteen of the seventy-seven incorporate interjections identifying 'alios', 'alium librum', 'in aliis libris', 'alii dicunt', 'Dicunt Scoiti' or 'Librum Monachorum' as their sources.[35] Moreover, examination of a further five interjections attributing entries to Dub dá Leithe shows that these were written jointly by Ua Caiside and Ua Luinín, cf. Figure 28, p. 225. A distinctive textual feature of all these

---

Maghnusa); Nicholls, *'Register of Clogher'* 361, (compilation).   **32** Mac Carthy, *AU* iii, 256, 260, 262, 268, 280, 284, 300, 310, 366 (birth entries of Mac Maghnusa's children).   **33** Mc Carthy, 'AU compilation', 76 (Ua Caiside as chronologist).   **34** Mac Carthy, *AU* iii, 30 obscures the MS H Arabic '17' of AU 1395.1 as 'decimo septimo'.   **35** AU 436.3, 469.1, 483.2, 490.3, 535.5, 544.4,

interjections is that they commence '[uel] sic in Libro Duibh da Leithi …'. Furthermore examination of the thirteen interjections attributing entries to Cuana, cf. Figure 23, p. 198, shows that eight commence with essentially the same attribution as the Dub dá Leithe interjections, viz., 'sic in Libro Cuanach …'. Twelve of the Cuana entries duplicate existing entries and hence supply an alternative chronology for them. Finally three employ the temporal emphatics 'isto anno' or 'isto', and one of these explicitly remarks an alternative chronology, viz. AU 602.3: 'Omnia quae scripta sunt in anno subsequente, inueni in Libro Cuanach in isto esse perfecta.' While these use 'isto' rather than 'hoc', the other textual and chronological features of these Cuana interjections identify them all as the work of Ua Caiside.

In consequence I conclude that all of these interjections, even when written by Ua Luinín, are actually the work of Ua Caiside collating and inscribing in the exemplar subsequently copied by Ua Luinín. Thus the editorial compiler of the text and chronological apparatus of AU was Ua Caiside, not Mac Maghnusa. This is not of course to deny Mac Maghnusa's influence as patron upon the compilation for a survey of the fifteenth century shows numerous entries referring to his family and extending over his lifetime, cf. Figure 46, p. 321. Indeed the birth entries of Mac Maghnusa's children entered by Ua Caiside are a clear demonstration of his influence on the content of the compilation. All the decisions regarding the generous spacing of the layout cf. plate 7, the sources to be used, and the Fermanagh clans to be documented in the fifteenth-century section, were no doubt taken by Mac Maghnusa as patron. His influence surrounds the compilation for he organized and paid for the work and so his name was attached to it. Furthermore there is independent evidence of his support for scholarship in the copy of *Félire Óengusso* written for him by Ua Luinín.[36] On the other hand Ua Caiside's influence was at the inner level of the entries and chronological apparatus, and here it is both ubiquitous and conspicuous once his traits are distinguished. The importance in recognizing Ua Caiside as the editorial compiler of AU lies in the implications of his evident lack of training as an annalist, and his inadequate skills as both chronologist and copyist. For it was these inadequacies that resulted in the myriad duplicate entries in the earlier Christian centuries and the textual emendations distributed throughout the compilation. These were the features that prompted Mac Niocaill to describe it as having 'been carpentered together in, often, a fumbling fashion'.[37]

655.7 'alios'; AU 438.2, 498.4, 516.2, 663.7 'alium librum'; AU 789.7 'in aliis libris'; AU 452.1, 461.2, 607.1 'alii dicunt'; AU 491.1 'Dicunt Scoiti'; AU 511.4, 527.3 'Librum Monachorum' – the 'Librum Mochod' of Hennessy, *AU* i, 42 and Mac Airt & Mac Niocaill, *AU*, 68 is the result of a mistaken rewriting of Ua Caiside's 'Monachorum' in MS H.   **36** Ó Muraíle, *AU* ii, [14], and idem, *Cathal Óg*, 18 (*Félire Óengusso* in the Franciscan Library, Killiney, MS A7).   **37** Mac Niocaill, *MIA*, 21 (cit.); Ó Muraíle, 'Ó Cianáin', 423–30 (Ua Caiside's textual emendations); Mc

Regarding the sources employed by Ua Caiside in this compilation in chapter 9 I have proposed that the principal was a Fermanagh chronicle compiled by the Uí Chianáin commencing with Adam and extending up to *c.*1483. To this Ua Caiside made many additions from the Books of Cuana, Dub dá Leithe, the Monks (*Monachorum*), and other unidentified works. It was this interpolated edition of the Uí Chianáin Fermanagh chronicle that Ua Luinín transcribed up to *c.*1483, followed by a continuation compiled by Ua Caiside. Ua Luinín stopped his transcription at the bottom of f. 129^v in the middle of an entry, partway through 1489, and it seems likely that this abrupt cessation was a consequence of Mac Maghnusa's death in 1498. Ua Caiside subsequently took up the role of scribe and by 1505 had completed ff. 130–43 covering 1489–1504 in an improving facsimile of Ua Luinín's hand. In these circumstances it appears most likely that Ua Caiside was the author of the obit for Mac Maghnusa in AU.[38] The fulsome character of the obit is not altogether surprising when one reflects that it was Mac Maghnusa who afforded the untrained Ua Caiside the opportunity to work on some of the best chronicle material known to exist in Ireland in the fifteenth century. While we must be grateful to Mac Maghnusa for his initiative in undertaking the compilation of the Uí Chianáin chronicle with other early sources, we may wonder at his choice of editorial compiler. However, the warm praise accorded by some modern scholars to Mac Maghnusa for accurate transcription of antique sources is misplaced and belongs rather to Ua Luinín and the Uí Chianáin chroniclers who preceded him. For indeed the entries concerning the Uí Luinín in AU show that Ruaidhrí Ua Luinín was a member of a hereditary erenagh family from Ard in county Fermanagh. From the superior quality of his writing in both AU and *Félire Óengusso* it is obvious that he was a highly trained and professional scribe, and from the extent of his contribution it is clear that he was the principal scribe engaged by Mac Maghnusa for the compilation.

Turning next to the final stage in the compilation of AU, which was undertaken first by Ua Caiside and then by Ua Luinín writing MS R using MS H as their exemplar. The superior quality of both MS R's vellum and decoration show that it was intended to be a significantly more prestigious production than its exemplar. Their joint work extends over 431–1506 and so omits the entire pre-Palladian section of MS H, but adds an extension of two years. Ua Caiside's omission of the pre-Palladian section, which in MS H required about eighteen folios, helped to initiate the mistake insisted upon by modern scholarship that the 'Annals of Ulster start at 431'.[39] Ua Caiside wrote 431–952 on ff. 1–32ra in

Carthy, 'AU compilation', 76–7 (Ua Caiside's deficient chronological skills). **38** Mc Carthy, 'AU compilation', 75 (Ua Caiside scribe of ff. 130–43), cf. Ó Muraíle, *Cathal Óg*, vi (author of obit). **39** Hughes, *Early Christian Ireland*, 144 (cit.); Mc Carthy, 'AU compilation', 77–84 (scholarship

a very convincing facsimile of Ua Luinín's hand, except that he frequently but erratically substituted Arabic numerals for the Roman numerals of MS H.[40] He also made numerous minor textual and orthographic modifications to the entries, but these are not registered in either the Hennessy or Mac Airt and Mac Niocaill editions of this part of AU. Regarding Ua Caiside's own additions to MS H, some of these including all his ferial and epactal data appear incorporated into the main text, some appear interlinearly, some are enlarged, and some do not appear at all. Since it seems unlikely that Ua Caiside would repeatedly omit his own additions I infer from these instances that they do not represent omissions by him but rather they are the result of additions he made to MS H *after* he had completed his section of MS R. This implies thereby that MS H remained accessible to Ua Caiside, and probably in his possession.

Ua Luinín took over the compilation in the second line of 952 and at the very next kalend he fully restored the Roman numerals of the AD of MS H and maintained consistency with his exemplar in this regard thereafter. However, examination of Mac Carthy's apparatus in AU ii–iii shows fairly frequent textual and orthographic variations between MSS R and H over Ua Luinín's section. Some of these appear to be deliberate emendations by Ua Luinín to Ua Caiside's entries. For example in the obit for David Ua Duibgennain at AU 1398.1 Ua Luinín added the words 'in history (*re seanchas*)' to his title of 'professor (*ollam*)', and he omitted Ua Caiside's chronological refinement of 'in the beginning of the Spring'.[41] On the other hand it seems likely that some items Mac Carthy marked as omissions in MS R represent rather subsequent *additions* by Ua Caiside to MS H. Ua Luinín's termination at 1506 leaving blank vellum on f. 107vb suggests that he completed his scribal contribution in 1507. The continuation over 1507–28 was written incrementally on ff. 107vb–119rb by two further competent scribes working together.[42] At the end of their annals for 1528 a fifth scribe added a two-line entry at the bottom of f. 119rb followed by a six-line entry at the top of f. 119va which includes the obit of Ruaidhrí Mac Craith 'for whom was written this book', and that of Ruaidhrí Ua Luinín 'the one who wrote choice (*forgla*) part of this book.'[43] Immediately below these another much better scribe subsequently added duplicate obits in panegyric style for both men, but not mentioning the book. Following this up to ten scribes wrote the annals for 1529–41 and these conclude with the obit for Ruaidhrí Ua Caiside asserting that he 'wrote this book for the greater part (*pro*

asserting '431'), 87–8 (codicology of MS H), 91–2 (MS H's missing pre-Palladian folios).   **40** Ó Cuív, *Catalogue*, 158 'the two hands are similar in many respects, both being extremely neat'; Mc Carthy, 'AU compilation', 74 fig. 1 (Ua Caiside's Arabic numerals).   **41** Mac Carthy, *AU* iii, 38–9 (cits.).   **42** Ó Cuív, *Catalogue*, 159 (scribes 3 & 4); Mc Carthy, 'AU compilation', 93 (mistakenly asserted Ua Luinín's last entry was at 1507).   **43** Mac Carthy, *AU* iii, 573 (cits.).

maiori parte)', and appropriately concluding by citing Ua Caiside's own praise for Mac Maghnusa's 'knowledge of every science, both law and divinity, physic and philosophy, to the time of his death.'[44] Thereafter entries comprise just intermittent year headings and occasional obits. From this sequence of scribes, entries, and obits it appears that over 1507–28 MS R remained in the control of Ua Luinín for whom scribes three and four served as competent amanuenses maintaining the chronicle. Following Ua Luinín's death MS R appears to have transferred to Ua Caiside's control for whom about ten different scribes served as amanuenses until his death in 1541, after which it was no longer maintained regularly.[45] It seems to have been the resulting confusion of scribal hands over 1529–41 that prompted Ua Luinín's grandson Matha to complain in 1579 in an inscription on f. 125vb, 'I regret how badly the son of Ua Caiside wrote these five or six folios at the end of this book ...'[46] Since Matha could not possibly have considered the annals of 1529–41 all to be the work of a single scribe, his criticism was apparently directed at Ua Caiside's poor choice and supervision of his various amanuenses. The statement in Ua Caiside's obit that he 'wrote this book for the greater part' has been rejected as 'simply not true', and as an 'incorrect statement'.[47] However, when it is appreciated that Ua Caiside had

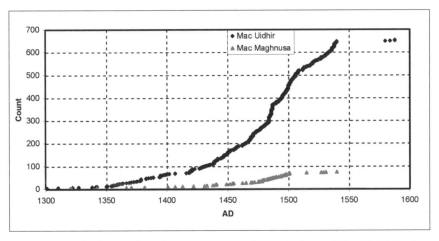

Figure 46. Plot of the cumulative count of AU entries referring to 'Mag Uidhir' and to 'Mac Maghnusa', as registered by Mac Carthy AU iv, 246–53 and 234–6.

---

44 Mac Carthy, *AU* iii, 428–30 (Mac Maghnusa's obit), 632 (Ua Caiside's obit). 45 Ó Cuív, *Catalogue*, 159–60 (scribes over 1529–41); Byrne, *Irish script*, 32 '[MS R] was continued after ... 1528 by Ruaidhrí Ó Casaide (O'Cassidy), archdeacon of Clogher, and the annalistic record ceases with O'Cassidy's death in 1541.' 46 Ó Cuív, *Catalogue*, 160 (cit.), cf. *AU* iii, 628 n. 6. 47 Gwynn, 'Cathal Mac Maghnusa' ii, 382 (cit.); Ó Cuív, *Catalogue*, 158 (cit.).

compiled much of the exemplar used for MS R it can be seen that the statement is appropriate to that particular sense.

Finally we may obtain some idea of the attitudes taken by Ua Caiside and Ua Luinín towards the Meig Uidhir, the pre-eminent clan in Fermanagh in their time, and the Meic Maghnusa, patron of AU, by plotting their entry counts over 1300–1600, cf. Figure 46. The majority of the Mac Maghnusa entries are confined to Cathal's own lifetime *c.*1438–98 and a lacuna follows 1501, but over the last decade or so of Ua Caiside's life there is a brief resurgence. It seems likely that this distribution reflects Ua Caiside's admiration for Cathal and his family and Ua Luinín's relative indifference. Regarding the Meig Uidhir it can be seen that their account in the Uí Chianáin chronicle commenced effectively at *c.*1350 and steadily intensified thereafter. By 1440 this rate exceeds five entries per annum and this rate is maintained or exceeded until Ua Caiside's death in 1541. It is particularly intense over the years 1484–9, which represents the continuation of the Uí Chianáin chronicle compiled by Ua Caiside while Mac Maghnusa was still alive, and so probably reflects something of Cathal's own admiration for the Meig Uidhir.

In the foregoing I have examined the final stages of the compilation of AU in considerable detail because it is undoubtedly the most important witness to the origin and evolution of the Cuana group. For its companions AB/AI a brief review must serve. Thus regarding AB, in chapter 7 it has been shown that this is substantially an abridgment of Liber Cuanach up to *c.*1178. Two distinct series of additions have been made to this, the first an end chronicle of Boyle abbey and Cistercian affairs over 1148–1228, cf. Figure 26, p. 219. The second and final series furnish an end chronicle of Holy Trinity affairs from 1229 to its conclusion at 1257.[48] Turning lastly to AI, in chapter 7 it has been shown that *c.*1065–81 an Emly compiler, Flann Cuileain, embedded a substantial Munster chronicle in a combination of Liber Cuanach and the Clonmacnoise chronicle, supplying an accurate kalend+ferial+epact apparatus at least over 779–1081. Then *c.*1093 a Lismore compiled severely abridged this Emly compilation and added to it a Lismore end chronicle. Subsequently, as Best and Mac Airt documented in great detail, a total of thirty-eight hands incrementally made separate additions to it, each in its turn providing an end chronicle to the preceding stage.[49] Of these Mac Airt concluded that only 'the annals of 1092 to 1214 and from 1258 to 1285 are to be taken as contemporary, or about contemporary' and so these additions represent contemporaneous Munster chronicles.[50] Mac Airt deduced that over 1093–1130 these additions were made at Lismore. There has been no analysis made of the sources used for the non-contemporaneous additions, but Mac Airt dated

---

48 Freeman, *AB* 42 (1925), 281–96 (Boyle Abbey), 296–305 (Holy Trinity).   49 Hands: Best & Mac Neill, *AI facsimile*, 9–24 and Mac Airt, *AI*, xxx–xlvi.   50 Mac Airt, *AI*, xxxi (cit.).

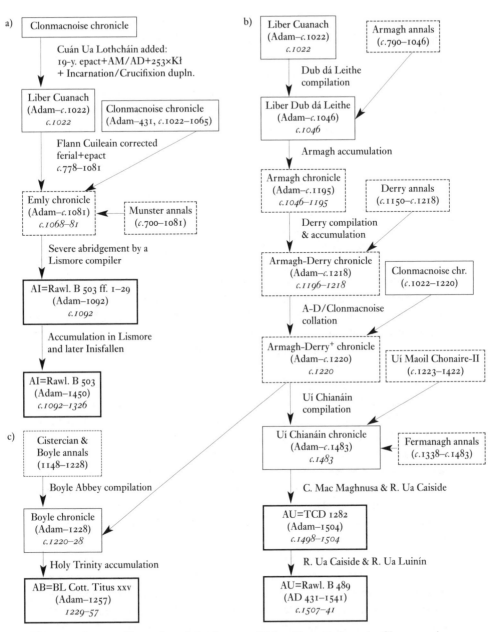

Figure 47. Stemma illustrating: a) the descent of Liber Cuanach from the Clonmacnoise chronicle and thence AI; b) the descent of AU from Liber Cuanach; c) the descent of AB from the Armagh-Derry⁺ chronicle. As in Figure 45, p. 314, existing MSS are identified by thick rectangles, attested works by light rectangles, and hypothesized works by dotted rectangles. Ranges are in parentheses and compilation dates where known are shown in italic and those shown as a range of years imply the accumulation of annals.

two of the six hands that completed the annals over 1286–1326 to approximately the mid-fourteenth century, and he identified the last two of these that wrote 1325–6 as 'evidently the work of Inisfallen scribes'.[51] Best and Mac Airt also identified a total of sixteen later hands that made occasional additions to the MS. These hands range in date from the thirteenth to the seventeenth century, and they register entries up to 1450.[52] In Figure 47 stemma illustrating the descent of AU/AI/AB from the Clonmacnoise chronicle via Liber Cuanach are given.

Connacht group

Since the later compilation of both CT and LC have been examined in some detail in chapters two and nine a brief résumé will serve here. First regarding CT, the discussion of chapter 2 has demonstrated that the third and last scribe C of the primary MS who wrote the years 1479–1544 was likely Seán Riabhach Ua Duibhgeannáin writing c.1578, and that he did not complete his transcription. This then was the final stage of the compilation of CT. The discussion in chapter 9 has shown that this section represents an incomplete transcript of an abridgment of the Uí Duibhgeannáin chronicle. On the other hand the material before 1479 represents a modest abridgment of Uí Maoil Chonaire-II as far back as 1224, but which then abandoned all entries before that year, cf. Figure 38, p. 262.

Turning next to LC the discussion of chapter 2 has shown that the years 1577–90 of L4 represent a record of contemporary events. On the other hand sections L1–3 represent a compilation made over 1588–9 by Uí Duibhgeannáin scribes collaborating with Brian Mac Diarmada. Thus the final stages of LC comprise the annals for 1588–90 of L4 together with L1–3 all written over the years 1588–90. The sections L1–3 provide a lacunose account of 1014–1577 which the Uí Duibhgeannáin scribes abridged first from the Armagh-Derry[+] chronicle for 1014–1220, followed by Uí Maoil Chonaire-II for 1223–1316, followed by the Fermanagh chronicle for 1413–78, followed by the Uí Duibhgeannáin chronicle for 1479–1577, cf. Figure 38, p. 262. It is most unfortunate that neither of these Connacht compilations has transmitted any of the content of Uí Maoil Chonaire-II prior to 1224, for this has left an apparent Connacht vacuum for the entire early medieval and pre-historical periods. The content of this lacuna can however be partly reconstructed by consultation of MB's English translation of Uí Maoil Chonaire II for Adam–1223, though allowance must be made for Mageoghagan's own additions for which see below. When this is done it can be seen that Maoilín

51 Mac Airt, AI, xxxix–xl, 'Hand 35 … is apparently of the mid-fourteenth century'; 'Hand 36 … written … before No 30, who flourished probably within fifty years after 1311'; 'Hand 37 is that of a contemporary'; 'Hands 38 and 39 … are evidently the work of Inisfallen scribes.'
52 Additional hands: Best & Mac Neill, AI facsimile, 24–5 and Mac Airt, AI, xl–xli.

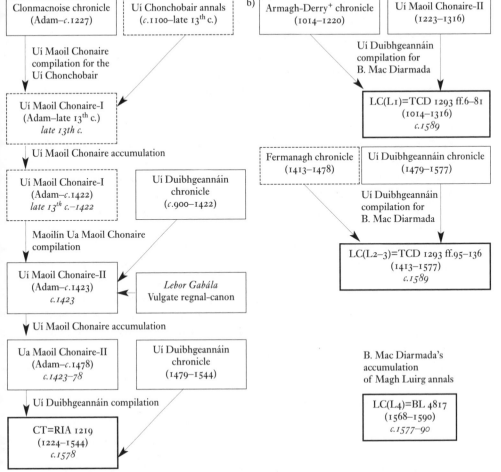

Figure 48. Stemma illustrating: a) the descent of CT, and b) the descent of LC. As in Figure 45, p. 314, existing MSS are identified by thick rectangles, attested works by light rectangles, and hypothesized works by dotted rectangles. Ranges are shown in parentheses and compilation dates where known are shown in italic, and compilation ranges imply accumulation of annals.

Ua Maoil Chonaire emended the regnal series of *Lebor Gabála* in order to reconcile the interval Flood–Incarnation, i.e. Cessair–Fachtna Fathach 16, to the Vulgate chronology of $3952-(1656-1) = 2297$ years. Also by adjusting a relatively small number of regnal years in the Christian era he brought the interval summation of regnal years into closer correlation with the major epochs of Patrick's *uenit* and Brian Boroimhe's obit.[53] In Figure 48 stemma illustrating the descent of CT/LC are given.

---

53 Mc Carthy, 'Irish regnal canon', *s.v.* 'MB – Mageoghagan's Book' (Vulgate chronology &

Regnal-canon group

I commence by considering the final compilation stage of MB that Conall Mageoghagan embarked upon in 1627. In chapter 10 it has been shown that his principal source was essentially Uí Maoil Chonaire-II extending at least over Adam–1408 which he undertook to translate for his relative Terence Coghlan. However, in his compilation Mageoghagan did a great deal more than mere translation of this principal source, mainly in the form of severe abridgment. I shall examine first his handling of the chronological apparatus and then of the entries. For the chronological apparatus he completely abandoned all the kalends and ancillary series of his source and replaced them with his own marginal AD. Mageoghagan also emphasized the regnal-canon by inscribing the name of the ruling king at the head of each page, cf. plate 12. By these means he effected a transformation of Uí Maoil Chonaire-II from the kalends to the regnal-canon tradition. When Mageoghagan's own marginal AD is collated against the chronology of the other annals it shows substantial and sustained anachronism over 432–1021. Specifically over 432–59 it is in arrears, over 481–627 it is nearly always in advance, over 633–1021 it is again in arrears, while over 1022–1408 it maintains close synchronism with respect to the other annals. Mageoghagan's marginal AD runs intermittently from 425 to 634, but from 637 onwards it is generally continuous with the exception of numerous discontinuities. While some of these are likely to be the result of transcription errors by either Denis Murphy or Tadhg O'Daly, the scribe of his exemplar, others synchronized to substantial lacunae in MB's entries are likely Mageoghagan's responsibility. For example over 432–1022 the following discontinuities associated with lacunae are found in Murphy's marginal years: 701→710, 795→798, 848→863, 888→897, 925→929, 958→970, 996→1008. Both the fact that corresponding discontinuities are found in the primary MS BL 4817 and that the marginal AD does register these lacunae support the attribution of these omissions and marginal AD to Mageoghagan. But because Mageoghagan asserted that there were 'leaves' and 'years' missing from the 'old booke' it has generally been assumed that these were the cause of lacunae in the text of MB.[54] However, the occasional appearance of single entries within some of these lacunae suggest rather that Mageoghagan himself was in these instances deliberately abridging his exemplar by skipping over consecutive series of years.[55] When we turn to consider MB's

Fachtna Fathach). **54** Murphy, *AC*, 215 'There are soe many leaves lost or stolen out of the ould Irish book', and 258, 'Here there are certaine years missing in mine ould Booke'; Sanderlin, *Conell Mageoghagan*, 3 'In AClon [MB] itself there are <u>lacunae</u> which may well be evidence for the poor condition of the original.' **55** Mc Carthy, 'Synchronization', *s.a.* 705–12 see MB's solitary regnal incipit for Feargall *s.a.* 710, and *s.a.* 849–61 see MB's solitary entry for 'fforannan and Dermott' *s.a.* 852, cf. Murphy, *AC*, 122, 140.

entries we find that this abridgment is consistent with the distribution of his entries from within each year. For indeed when MB's entries are collated against parallel entries in AT/CS/AU/CT/LC we repeatedly find a high incidence of either the very first or the very last entries, which strongly suggests that Mageoghagan was simply translating a small sample of entries from each year, regularly choosing that entry immediately preceding or succeeding the kalend. For example over the fifty years 650–99, while MB has far less entries than AT, in forty-six years MB has the first and/or the last AT entry. It is likely this feature of his *modus operandi* which is responsible for the characteristic that when unique entries do occur in MB they are often found as the very last entry under the year.[56] Mageoghagan's wholesale abridgment of his source together with the numerous inaccuracies and discontinuities in his marginal AD discloses a markedly *ad hoc* attitude on his part towards his compilation. Indeed this is apparent in his concluding interjection 'Here endeth this Booke', which is ambiguous as to whether it was his 'old booke' or his own translation that ended at this point.

On the other hand Mageoghagan made numerous additions of his own, often prefixed by addressing himself to 'Brother', 'Reader', 'you', or referencing 'mine author', or placing brief additions within parentheses. Most of these appear to be spontaneous additions recited from Mageoghagan's personal knowledge of the matter to hand, such as his impromptu listing of the contemporaneous families that he considered descended from the four sons of Milidh:[57]

> ... before I proceed any further **I will Laye Down unto you** the severall septs descended of Heremon *especially the cheefest of them*, and then after the septs of Heber, Ire, and Lauthus, **to the end the Reader may know them.** O'Neale ... *with Divers others* are the o'Neals of the West ... *and others are Descended of Heremon, but not of the o'Neals but of other collatterall kinsmen. Also ... and others are of the said Descent.* The scepts of Ire, son of Miletus, are Magenis Viscount of Ivhagh ... *&c.* The scepts of Heber the white ... *some say that Powers ... are of the said sept. o'Keruell too whoe should not be forgotten.* The scepts of Lauthus ... and *others &c.*

Here Mageoghagan's own address to his reader is emphasized in bold and his repeated informal elements in italic, indicating that his compilation here was spontaneous. Certainly, with the exceptions only of one brief allusion to O'Sullivan's *Historiae Catholicae* and two to Calloch O'More he cites no sources for his additions.[58] His most substantial formal additions are his genealogies of three contemporaries, Randolph earl of Antrim, Henry earl of Thomond, and Arthur Magennis viscount of Iveagh who is also mentioned in the citation given above.[59] Mageoghagan's anachronistic interpolation of these genealogies immediately after

---

56 Murphy, *AC*, s.a. 801, 809, 813, 818, 822, 824, 827, 836, 842, 863, 871 (MB-unique entries; I am grateful to Bart Jaski for bringing this phenomenon and these examples to my attention). 57 Murphy, *AC*, 29–30 (cit.). 58 Murphy, *AC*, 14, 25 (O'More), 25 (O'Sullivan). 59 Murphy,

the Norman invasion and addressing Terence Coghlan directly as 'For your better instruction Brother ...', seems intended to demonstrate to him that notwithstanding the Norman and English invasions of Ireland the pedigrees of the seventeenth-century nobility still derived from the Milesians. It is in effect a reaffirmation of his claim in the preface that the Psalter of Cashel contained 'all the inhabitations, events and Septs that lived in this Land from the first peoplinge, inhabitation, and Discoverie.'[60] In contrast to his emphasis on noble pedigrees collation of those MB entries referring to members of the Mageoghagan family with the parallel entries from CT/LC shows that Mageoghagan did not enlarge on these. In summary, in his compilation of MB Mageoghagan profoundly abridged the content of his Uí Maoil Chonaire-II exemplar, and he added numerous informal entries based on his own general knowledge. Chronologically, by abandoning all the kalends and ancillary series while leaving Maoilín Ua Maoil Chonaire's regnal series of Uí Maoil Chonaire-II intact, Mageoghagan produced the first known edition of annals in the regnal-canon tradition.[61] While we have no contemporary account of how MB was received it is surely significant that within five years the most formidable Irish annalistic compilation ever undertaken, Ó Cléirigh's FM, would likewise employ the regnal-canon as its primary chronological apparatus.

Examination of both the text of FM and its two prefaces show that it was intended by Mícheál Ó Cléirigh to comprehensively represent the chronicles of Ireland. Consequently, FM constitutes in effect a wide-ranging compilation of Irish chronicles and on this account a substantial examination of its sources is warranted here. As discussed in chapters two and ten the compilation of FM is witnessed by two manuscript pairs, viz. MSS C+H and A+P, which in both cases are accompanied by contemporaneous prefatory material. Prefixed to MS A, and also formerly to MS C when it was transcribed in 1735 into what is now TCD 1300, are the dedication to Fearghal Ó Gadhra followed by the short preface and six testimonials. On the other hand on two vellum folios inserted in MS P between the years 1207 and 1208 are found the dedication followed by the long preface. Collation of these two dedications strongly suggests that that of MS P is based upon that of MS A, and the same holds true of the long and short preface, as will be discussed below.[62]

Turning first to consider the sources we find that the short preface lists five, indicating approximately the range of the first two, while the long preface

AC, 209–13 (genealogies). 60 BL Add. 4817 f. 3ᵛ, cf. Murphy, AC, 7–8 (cit.). 61 O'Donovan, FM i, p. lxiv n.b simply stated that MB represented a translation of the 'original' Book of Cluain-mic-Nois. 62 O'Donovan, FM i, pp. lv–lxi (dedication), lxiii–lxvii (long preface), lxviii–lxxi (testimonials); Walsh, Gleanings, 71–4 (dedication), 74–6 (short preface), 77–80 (testimonials). MS P's dedication omits the two names 'm corbmac gaileng' and 'm luighdeach luaighne', and replaces the genealogy from 'm tantt ... m. Adam' with 'etcetera', cf. FM i, pp. lix–lxi. It also omits many length marks.

repeats these five and adds four more with further details of the ranges of six sources. Translations of Ó Cléirigh's descriptions of these sources are listed in Figure 49 in the order of their appearance, together with his details of their range.

FM sources	Range
1. Book of Cluain-mic-Nois. [S & L]	– Not beyond 1227
2. Book of the Island of Saints in Loch Ribh. [S & L]	– Not beyond 1227
3. Book of Seanadh Mic Maghnusa in L. Erne. [S & L]	–1532
4. Book of Clann Ua Maelchonaire of county Roscommon. [S & L]	–1505
5. Book of the O'Duigenans of Kilronan of county Sligo. [S & L]	900–1563
6. Book of Lecan Mic Firbisigh. [L]	– Beyond 1227
7. Book of Cucogry, son of Dermot, son of Tadhg Cam O'Clerigh. [L]	1281–1537
8. Book of Mac Bruaideadha (Maoilin Og). [L]	1588–1603
9. Book of Lughaidh O'Clerigh. [L]	1586–1602

Figure 49. The names of nine sources given by Michéal Ó Cléirigh in his short preface (S) and long preface (L) to FM, together with their range where given.[63]

Given its primary position in both prefaces it is apparent that the Book of Cluain-mic-Nois was regarded by Ó Cléirigh as a fundamental source, and hence its accurate identification is of paramount importance. Hennessy considered this question and he pointed out that the interjections referring to the Book of Clonmacnois at FM 964.7 and 1005.7 allude to entries which are found otherwise only in CS, and also that, 'Many other entries, also common to the Annals of the Four Masters and the present chronicle [sc. CS], are not found in any other volume of Irish Annals now known to be in existence.'[64] Hennessy's review and a further interjection referring to 'Sliocht liubhair Cluana mic Nóis' at FM 1022.2 led Ó Muraíle to conclude, 'That the *Chronicum* is to be identified with the collection of annals called *Leabhar Cluana mic Nois* which the Masters name as one of their sources ... is virtually proved.'[65] On the other hand Oskamp had earlier emphatically identified Ó Cléirigh's source with AT.[66] However, collation of the entry at FM 1022.2 attributed to 'Lebhar Cluana Mic Nóis' with the cognate entries found in both AT and CS does not support either of these identifications:

---

63 O'Donovan, *FM* i, pp. lxiv–lxvii (long preface sources); Walsh, *Gleanings*, 75 (short preface sources); Gwynn, 'Cathal Mac Maghnusa' ii, 370–1 (identifications of some of these sources). 64 Hennessy, *CS*, xxxvi–viii ('Book of Clonmacnois', however he did not make any conclusive statement regarding the relationship between it and CS). 65 Ó Muraíle, *Celebrated antiquary*, 100–1 (cit.). 66 Oskamp, 'Yellow book', 112–13 (AT identification).

AT 1022.4	FM 1022.2	CS 1022.3
Mael Sechlainn **Mor** mac Dondchadha, aird-rí Erenn uili, 7 **tuir** chongbala einigh 7 uáisle iarthair domain uile, do ég a Cro Ínis Locho Aindinn in .xl.iii. anno regní sui.	Maoileachlainn **Mór**, mac Domhnaill, mic Donnchadha, **tuir** ordain, 7 oireachais iarthair dhomhain, do écc h-í c-Cró Inis Lócha h-Ainind, iar m-beith trí bliadhna cethrachat i righe uas Erinn, *madh iar Lebhar Cluana Mic Nóis*	Maolseclainn mac Domnaill mac Donnchadha airdri Erenn uile, tuile ordain iartair domain, do éc i g-Croinis Locha Ainninne in .xliii. anno regni sui.

While FM shares 'mac Domhnaill' and 'ordain' with CS, it also shares 'Mór', 'tuir' and two separate qualities attributed to Maolsechlainn with AT. These relationships, which recur whenever we collate entries common to AT/CS/FM, suggest rather that Ó Cléirigh's source was the antecedent of *both* AT and CS. Apropos the four entries highlighted by Hennessy at FM 806.6, 842.13, 964.7, 1005.7 because he found them only in FM and CS, it must be observed that they all fall within a lacuna of AT, so we cannot infer uniqueness from them regarding the relationship between FM and CS. Rather it is clear that Ó Cléirigh's Book of Cluain-mic-Nois derived from the antecedent of AT and CS which in chapter 6 we have shown on independent grounds did indeed extend to *c.*1227, cf. Figure 20, p. 173. In these circumstances I conclude that Ó Cléirigh's Book of Cluain-mic-Nois, like that of Giolla Íosa's, derived directly from the Clonmacnoise chronicle, cf. Figure 45, p. 314. For reasons given below I consider it likely that Ó Cléirigh's copy of this work was seriously lacunose.

Regarding Ó Cléirigh's second source we first note that the abovementioned interjections at FM 964.7 and 1005.7 also attribute these entries to the Book of the Island, viz. 'S. liub an oilen, & Cl m. Nois', and 'Sliocht liubhair Cluana Mic Nóis, & liubhair an Oilén .i. Oilen na Naomh for Loch Ribh' respectively.[67] Similarly Ó Cléirigh grouped these two sources together in both prefaces when he asserted that neither extended beyond 1227. These correspondences, together with the proximity of Loch Ribh to Clonmacnoise suggest that these two sources were closely related and Ó Cléirigh considered them as a pair. Furthermore examination of the distribution of FM references to 'Loch Ribh' shows twenty-six between 742 and 1227 and only one thereafter. Moreover, all four entries between 1189 and 1227 are unique to FM. On the other hand there are absolutely no references in FM to any 'Island of Saints' in Loch Ribh or anywhere else. Rather the only substantial group of entries in FM referring to an ecclesiastical establishment in Loch Ribh before 1227 are sixteen references over 719–1193 to Inis Clothrann where the sixth-century foundation of

67 O'Donovan, *FM* ii, 686–7 n. v (FM 964.7), 755 (FM 1005.7).

S. Diarmuid was located. These are at their most frequent over 1136–93, and these include an obit at 1160 for Giolla na Naemh Ua Duinn, 'fer léighinn Insi Clothrann, saoi senchusa, & dána'.[68] I conclude therefore that Ó Cléirigh's Book of the Island refers to a mid-twelfth century Inis Clothrann transcript of the Clonmacnoise chronicle to which had been added an end chronicle of the monastery there. Since the evidence of the lacunae in AT/AR suggest that the MS of the Clonmacnoise chronicle was dismembered by the later fourteenth century, cf. Figure 45, p. 314 above, it seems virtually certain that in 1636 Ó Cléirigh's Book of Cluain-mic-Nois was likewise lacunose and he was using the Book of the Island to fill these lacunae. Earlier scholars have identified a number of different chronicle texts with this Book of the Island, but there has been no serious attempt made to establish any relationship between these proposed texts, FM and Loch Ribh. Amongst these proposals Gwynn's assertion that 'there can be little doubt that we owe to this lost Book [of the Island] a long series of entries concerning kings and abbots of Leinster', was made without any justification whatsoever.[69] While the Clonmacnoise chronicle is by far the most likely ultimate source of such Leinster entries, in FM they may have been transmitted wholly or partially via the Books of Cluain-mic-Nois, the Island, or Lecan Mic Firbisigh. Finally it should be noted from Figure 49, p. 329, that Ó Cléirigh gave no earlier termini for the Books of Cluain-mic-Nois, the Island, Seanadh Mic Maghnusa, Clann Ua Maelchonaire, or Lecan Mic Firbisigh. The implications of Ó Cléirigh's omissions are, based upon what we know independently concerning the ranges of these works, that they all commenced either at Adam if complete, or deep in Irish prehistory if they had lost their initial folios.

Ó Cléirigh's third source was identified by Gwynn as, 'beyond any doubt the A-text of the Annals of Ulster', i.e. TCD 1282, though again he did not explain the basis for his identification. However, collation of FM and AU indeed supports his conclusion, which also conforms to what is known of the history of both TCD 1282 and Rawl. B. 489. For example, the obits of Eoin Ua Cairbri and Paidin Ua Congaile added into TCD 1282 by Ruaidhrí Ua Caiside but *not* found in Rawl. B. 489, are both in FM.[70] However, since TCD 1282 has been shown to have terminated at 1504, and Ó Cléirigh stated his Book of Seanadh extended to 1532, it appears that when acquiring TCD 1282 from Ussher he had obtained copies of some of the later entries of Rawl B 489 which extends continuously to 1541.[71] For indeed collation over 1505–32 shows that FM reproduces the substance of many Rawl. B. 489 entries. Also, as noted above, Ó Cléirigh cited no starting year for this source, suggesting that at that time

---

68 Bhreathnach, 'Two contributors', 107–11 (Giolla na Naemh).   69 Identifications of the book of the island: Ware, *De scriptoribus*, 75; O'Donovan, *FM* ii, 754; Ó Cuív, *Catalogue*, 152; Gwynn, 'Cathal Mac Maghnusa' ii, 370.   70 Mac Carthy, *AU* ii 496 & 522, cf. FM 1353.1 & 1365.1 (obits). 71 Mc Carthy, 'AU compilation', 70–2, 92 (ownership of AU MSS).

TCD 1282 commenced deep in Irish pre-history and not, as repeatedly asserted in modern times, at 431. Indeed it may well be that it was the dismemberment of this MS by the compilers of FM that contributed to the loss of two complete gatherings from TCD 1282, one from the very start and the other from the centre of the volume.[72]

Ó Cléirigh identified his fourth source collectively with the Uí Maoil Chonaire of county Roscommon, and there are good grounds to identify this with Uí Maoil Chonaire-II compiled by Maoilín in c.1423 and continued by his successor ollamhs to 1478, cf. chapter 9. While Ó Cléirigh's terminus of 1505 falls shortly thereafter, the difference is reasonably explained by assuming that, as in the case of AU, their copy had acquired a short end chronicle. The fifth source listed by Ó Cléirigh he identified with the Uí Duibhgeannáin of Kilronan, hereditary ollamhs to the Síl Maolruanadh and Conmhaicne, which family took over and extended the compilation of Uí Maoil Chonaire-II. Ó Cléirigh's terminus of 1563 falls just two decades after the date of c.1542 that has been deduced for the first phase of the Ua Duibhgeannáin compilation, and as in the previous two cases the difference can be understood in terms of their source copy having acquired a short end chronicle. On the other hand Ó Cléirigh stated explicitly that this source commenced at 900, showing that he did not consider that the Uí Duibhgeannáin chronicle extended back to early Christian Ireland.

The remaining sources are only cited in the long preface of MS P, and the first of these is the Book of Lecan Mic Firbisgh. Ó Cléirigh wrote that they transcribed from this 'every copious matter they found which they considered necessary which was not in the first books they had, for neither the Book of Cluain nor the Book of the Island had anything beyond the year of the age of our Lord, 1227.'[73] This description effectively rules out CS as a possibility since it does not extend anywhere near as far as 1227. Rather the most credible identification of this source is the annalistic collection described by Dubhaltach Mac Fhirbhisigh in the preface to his 'Bishops list' compiled for James Ware in 1665 as, 'Gilla Isa Mac Ferbisie's Annals written afore the year 1397 ... Huc usque [1530] the Mac-Ferbisies' Irish Annals furnished this collection', as both Ó Muraíle and Ó Concheannain have concluded.[74] As already discussed Dubhaltach stated that he had employed these annals as a source for his 'Bishop's list', and indeed collation of his list with FM shows that they share a common source. Moreover, in FM virtually all these episcopal entries appear either in the first, second, or the last position, indeed suggesting that they were late additions to the compilation as Ó Cléirigh stated. Hence I conclude that

72 Mc Carthy, 'AU compilation', 79–84 (belief that AU started at 431), 90–3 (range of AU and lost gatherings). 73 Ó Muraíle, *Celebrated antiquary*, 20 (cit.), cf. O'Donovan, *FM* i, p. lxv. 74 Ó Muraíle, *Celebrated antiquary*, 250 (cit.), 20 (identification); Ó Concheannain, 'Giolla Íosa', 394 (identification).

Giolla Iosa's annals to c.1397, together with their continuation by his kinsmen to 1530 were the source employed by Ó Cléirigh, for the use of such a source would provide an important authority for his own compilation, and indeed this appears to be one of his intentions in emphasizing his use of it.

Paul Walsh identified the author of the seventh source, Cúchoighriche Ó Cléirigh, as the son of Diarmad †1522, son of Tadhg Cam †1492, but little else is known about him.[75] Likewise nothing else has survived concerning his book. However, since he belonged to a family who provided the hereditary ollamhs to the Uí Dhomhnaill of Tir Chonaill from the late fourteenth century, it seems likely that this work provided Ó Cléirigh with the many records of that family found distributed in FM from 1281 to 1537. Indeed FM 1281.2 furnishes an account of the battle of Disert-da-chrioch won by the Cineal Chonaill at which their leader Domhnall óg Ua Dhomhnaill was slain. This entry is a substantial and admiring account of Domhnall and his fallen allies and concludes, 'many other of the sons of lords and chieftains [are] not enumerated here.' It is clear then that this entry is taken from a longer source and given its subject and attitude it seems very likely to be taken from the start of Cúchoigriche Ó Cléirigh's book. Examination of O'Donovan's index shows that the Uí Dhomhnaill are closely documented in the interval 1281–1537; for example, of the total of seventy-seven references to the 'O'Donnells of Tirconnell', fifty-five fall within 1281–1537.[76]

Regarding the author of the eighth source, Maoilín Óg Mac Bruaideadha, a warm tribute to his scholarship accompanies his obit at FM 1602.18, and a citation from one of his historical poems is also given, presumably from his book. At FM 1582.36 the obit of his father Maoilín describes him as the ollamh in history to the Uí Briain, and at FM 1563.8 the obit of his uncle Diarmait describes him as ollam of the Uí Bracain and Uí Fermaic, who O'Donovan located in the baronies of Ilbrickan and Inchiquin in county Clare. At FM 1599.15 a detailed account is given of an attack by Aodh Ruadh Ó Domnaill on Thomond, including Clare, of whom Maoilín Óg requested the return of his cattle and Aodh Ruadh obliged, and a subtle quatrain by Maoilín Óg is cited. It seems very likely then that the accounts of this attack at least, and of course the quatrain cited with his obit, come from Maoilín Óg's book.[77] Subsequently it was Maoilín Óg's son, Conchobhar, with an address at Cill Chaoide, alias Kilkeedy, in county Clare, who provided the second secular testimonial for FM. Finally a note in the Psalter of Caimín shows that Mícheál Ó Cléirigh was 'acquainted with [Concobhair] Mac Bruaideadha, and with his sones Flann and Bernard'.[78] These and other connections between the Ó Cléirigh and Mac

75 Walsh, O'Cleirigh family, 11–12 (identification of Cúchoighriche)   76 O'Donovan, FM vii, 308 (O'Donnell index).   77 O'Donovan, FM v, 1790 (Maoilín's obit), 1596 (Diarmait's obit); idem, FM vi, 2320 (Maoilín Óg's obit & tribute), 2096–104 (attack).   78 O'Donovan, FM i, p. lxix

Bruaideadha families prompted Jennings to suggest 'that between the two bardic families of Tirconaill and Thomond there was more than a mere professional friendship', and given the Clare origin of the Ó Cléirigh family this hypothesis indeed seems likely.[79]

Finally the ninth source, the Book of Lughaidh O'Clerigh, which work was first tentatively identified by O'Curry and subsequently emphatically by Walsh with the Life of Aodh Ruadh Ó Domhnaill.[80] Lughaidh Ó Cléirigh's father, Maccon, died in 1595 while Lughaidh was still alive in 1616, and he also contributed at least four poems to the Contention of the Bards, and composed an elegy for Baothghalach Mac Aodhagáin.[81] Recently Pádraig Breatnach has detailed the textual relationship between Lughaidh's Life and FM 1587–1602, so that of Mícheál Ó Cléirigh's later sources Lughaidh's book is the best documented.[82] Thus it emerges that the last three sources cited by Ó Cléirigh are effectively chronicles of the affairs of the Uí Domhnaill of Tirconnell. Hence in summary, FM may be briefly described as a conflation of abridgments of the Clonmacnoise and Connacht chronicles, embedded in Ó Cléirigh's own Septuagint recension of Giolla Cóemáin's regnal chronicle, to which he added an Ua Domhnaill end chronicle. While Ó Cléirigh's list of sources certainly cannot be regarded as comprehensive since in both prefaces he asserted that more sources were used that 'would be tedious to name', it does seem clear that his list identified the sources that he regarded as authoritative and prestigious.[83]

It remains to fulfil the undertaking of chapter 2 to consider the question of the relationship of the surviving MSS of FM to what we know of the history of the Franciscans in Louvain, and of Fearghal Ó Gadhra †c.1660.[84] For, as Ó Muraíle demonstrated in his landmark paper of 1987, there has existed serious conflict in scholarly interpretations of the various MSS and the accounts concerning them.[85] Much of this confusion has in fact arisen from the indiscriminate use of the simple title 'Annals of the Four Masters', with no attempt to identify which of the copies or parts thereof is intended. All scholars have agreed that both the Louvain convent and Ó Gadhra were to receive a copy of the work, and relying on the long preface they have all assumed that both these copies were of the complete compilation, which was to be divided into two parts.[86] However,

(Conchobhar's testimonial); Walsh, 'Travels' (cit.), 132, cf. Ó Muraíle, *Irish leaders*, 361. 79 Jennings, *Michael O Cleirigh*, 155 (cit.).   80 Life of Aodh Ruadh: O'Curry, *MM*, 22; Walsh, *Ó Cléirigh family*, 15–16, Walsh, *Aodh Ruadh* ii, 1.   81 Walsh, *Ó Cléirigh family*, 16 (Lughaidh Ó Cléirigh).   82 Breatnach, ' Aodha Ruaidh', 129–46 (FM & Aodh Ruadh), cf. Ó Muraíle, 'Aodha Ruaidh', 112–13, 120 .   83 O'Donovan, *FM* i, p. lxvii '& leabair oirisen oile nach iatt ro badh eimhelt dainmniughadh'; Walsh, *Gleanings*, 75 'Do bhátor aroile do leabhraibh aca ro badh eimhilt dáireamh.'   84 Boyle, 'Fearghal Ó Gadhra', 25 (obit).   85 Ó Muraíle, 'Autograph MSS', 76–83 (conflicting accounts), 88–95 (excellent summary of the MSS).   86 For example Sullivan, 'Slane manuscript', 78 wrote of the 'set made for the patron of the undertaking, Fergal O'Gara, ... and the set taken to Louvain.'

there has been repeated conflict regarding at which year this division was to be made so that 1171–2, 1207–8 and 1332–4 have all been proposed. The responsibility for this confusion rests squarely with Micheál Ó Cléirigh who wrote in his long preface that the 'book is divided into two (*Atátt an leabhar randta ar dó*)', and that the second book 'begins with the year 1208 (*an dara leabhar darab tosach an bliadain si 1208*)'. Then in the very next sentence he wrote that he and the two other Ó Cléirighs had written the 'last book (*an leabhar deidhenach*)' from 1332 to 1608.[87] This irreconcilable conflict, together with the fact that MSS A and C conclude at 1169 and 1171 respectively, has wrought widespread confusion regarding the matter of the division.

However, it is the case that no scholar has included in their analysis of the situation the differences and conflicts presented by Micheál Ó Cléirigh's two prefaces. These differences relate to FM's range, parts, sources, compilers, and signatories. Regarding the range and parts the short preface makes no mention whatsoever of any division in the text, which it asserts concluded at 1333. On the other hand the long preface unequivocally states that it was in two parts that extended to 1608. While both of these prefaces were signed and dated 10 August 1636 by Ó Cléirigh, the long preface exhibits substantial textual dependence upon the short preface, virtually the whole of which is either repeated verbatim or paraphrased. Since the long preface has several instances of internal contradiction, one example of which has been given above, whereas the short preface has none, it is clear that even though both were given the same date, Ó Cléirigh did, in fact, write the short preface first. Accompanying both prefaces is the dedication to Fearghal Ó Gadhra written by Micheál Ó Cléirigh in formal but affectionate terms, and declaring that the compilation had finished on 10 August 1636, the very date of both prefaces. We are obliged to conclude therefore that on this date Ó Cléirigh envisaged the production of not two *identical* copies as has been assumed, but of two very different copies. Namely a single-part version extending to 1333, and a two-part version divided at 1207–8 and extending to 1608. Which of these versions did Ó Cléirigh intend for Ó Gadhra, and which for Louvain? Since the short preface was signed first by five of the six compilers and then by the four attendant Franciscan friars, whereas the long preface was signed *only* by the Franciscans, this suggests that the single-part version was intended for Ó Gadhra and the two-part version for Louvain. Furthermore since John Colgan did annotate MS A in Louvain I conclude that Ó Cléirigh's intention was indeed that Louvain should receive the polished Final Draft, and Ó Gadhra should receive the preliminary and lower grade Normalized Draft, cf. chapter 10 p. 300 for definitions of these drafts. Now since both the prefaces and the dedication acknowledge that it was

---

87 O'Donovan, *FM* i, p. lxiii, lxvi (cits.).

O Gadhra that 'gave the reward of their labour to the chroniclers', and this involved supporting up to six highly educated men over four years and providing at least three thousand sheets of paper, it is not hard to see that on 10 August 1636 Micheál Ó Cléirigh embarked upon a course fraught with peril. Whilst we have no evidence of an actual clash occurring, the disposition of the surviving MSS strongly suggests that Ó Cléirigh's plan to send the entire Final Draft to Louvain was never completed.[88]

To consider this matter more closely I pose the question – when Micheál Ó Cléirigh wrote in his dedication to Ó Gadhra that, 'this book ... was finished ... on the tenth day of August, 1636', to which draft was he referring, the Initial, Normalized, or Final Draft? Since in fact both MSS H and P extend to 1616 this implies that *neither* Normalized *nor* Final Drafts were complete on 10 August 1636. Rather it suggests that on that date the Initial Draft had reached 1608, the Normalized Draft reached 1333 and the Final Draft reached 1169, and that it was these latter that Micheál Ó Cléirigh despatched respectively to Ó Gadhra and to Louvain. The fact that the Louvain despatch ended precisely at the year of the Norman invasion of Ireland suggests that Colgan, whose interest lay in early Irish Christian history, had put pressure on Ó Cléirigh for this section. Furthermore, the continuation of both MSS H and P to 1616 shows that both these compilations were subsequently extended eight years past Ó Cléirigh's specification of '1608'. At the same time MS H's starting year of 1334 bears witness that the Normalized Draft to 1333 had indeed been despatched to Ó Gadhra, just as Micheál Ó Cléirigh proposed in his short preface. This is further confirmed by Dubhaltach Mac Fhirbhisigh's acknowledgement of 'Leabhar Airision Fhearghail Uí Ghadhra' as his principal source for the regnal-canon in his *Leabhar Genealach* compiled in Galway in 1649.[89] What then became of the remainder of the Final Draft from 1170 to 1616, preserved in MS P? Remarkably MS P is completely lacking in marginalia that might indicate its location or ownership, and we have no direct information concerning its whereabouts until *c.*1762 when it was certainly in the possession of Charles O'Conor of Belanagare as we shall see.[90] In great contrast to this we know when and from whom O'Conor received MS C for he himself inscribed consecutively onto a fly-leaf of the MS:

a) That Seán Mac Craith, a medical professor in Dublin, had had the volume bound at his own expense in 1735.

88 O'Donovan, *FM* i, pp. lvii, lxiii (rewards); Walsh, *Gleanings*, 75 (rewards); O'Sullivan, 'Slane manuscript', 82 (hypothesis of Louvain origin for MS P).   89 Ó Muraíle, *Book of Genealogies* iii, 4 (acknowledgement, date & place), cf. idem, *Celebrated antiquary*, 178.   90 Ó Muraíle, 'Autograph MSS', 95 (MS P summary), 82, 'it [MS P] is in fact quite devoid of extraneous matter of any kind.'

b) That in 1734 he, Charles O'Conor, had been given custody (*a urlamhas do thabhairt do*) of the volume by Brian Ó Gadhra, the archbishop of Tuam.
c) An obit recording Brian Ó Gadhra's death on 3 April 1740 which reiterated that it was he who had entrusted O'Conor with the volume (*ro thiodhlaic an leabhar so dhamh*).

On the authority of these statements it cannot be doubted that O'Conor had been given custody of MS C in 1734 by archbishop Brian Ó Gadhra, Fearghal's grandson, and as we shall see he reiterated this in 1756. Since in 1734 O'Conor was aged just twenty-four it appears that his uncle, bishop O'Rourke of Killala who had earlier acted as his tutor in Irish studies, prevailed upon Brian Ó Gadhra to entrust custody of MS C to the young O'Conor. Unfortunately when Charles O'Conor's own grandson, the Revd Charles O'Conor, came to document his grandfather's acquisition of MS C he introduced serious confusion. For in 1818 when he catalogued MS C as part of the Stowe collection, notwithstanding the inscription on its flyleaf, he wrote:[91]

> This volume was carried into Spain by *Colonel O'Gara*, who commanded the Irish regiment of Hibernia, in the Spanish service, in 1734. He sent it to his relative, the late Charles O'Conor, of Belanagare, as the person best qualified to make use of it …

The reference here to 'Colonel O'Gara' is to Oliver O'Gara †*c.*1761, Charles O'Conor's second cousin on his father's side. Now this account *cannot* refer to MS C, which we know was entrusted in 1734 to O'Conor by archbishop Brian Ó Gadhra. Rather since we know Charles O'Conor did indeed obtain two volumes of FM it is apparent that the Revd O'Conor conflated the accounts of how his grandfather acquired these two volumes. The actual relationship between Colonel O'Gara and MS volumes of FM emerges in a letter written by Charles O'Conor to his friend Dr Curry in 1756 when an un-named ecclesiastic had challenged his custody of MS C as follows:[92]

> I shall write to Colonel O'Gara in St. Sebastian, where he is quartered with his regiment, and reproach him with giving more of his confidence to a little, ignorant ecclesiastic than to me, his nearest relation in this kingdom; his father and mine being brother and sister's children. This expedient will, I hope, confirm the book to me. In 1734 I got that work, through the interest of Bishop O'Rorke, my uncle.

Now both this challenge and Charles O'Conor's proposed appeal to Colonel O'Gara on the grounds of their consanguinity shows unequivocally that Charles

---

91 O'Conor, *Bibliotheca* i, 113 (cit.) cf. O'Donovan, *FM* i, p. xvi.   92 Ward & Ward, *Letters* i, 17 (cit.), cf. O'Donovan, *FM* i, p. xvi; O'Conor, *Rerum Hib.* i, 51 cited it incompletely, and idem iii, p. ix cited it with an incorrect addressee.

O'Conor did not own MS C. Moreover, it shows that both the un-named ecclesiastic and Charles O'Conor considered in 1756 that authority regarding possession of MS C resided with Colonel O'Gara. This information, together with the Revd O'Conor's statement that Colonel O'Gara had carried a volume of FM with him to Spain, that cannot be MS C, and which he subsequently sent to Charles O'Conor for his use, show that Colonel O'Gara occupied a singularly powerful position with respect to FM MSS. Moreover, since we know MS C remained in Charles O'Conor's possession, it seems that his custody of it was indeed confirmed by Colonel O'Gara. Furthermore examination of Charles O'Conor's correspondence shows that he had in fact obtained MS P between 3 October 1760 and 12 June 1762. For on the former date he wrote to Dr Curry that 'there is a chasm of fifty-four years in my Irish Annals, that is from 1170 to 1224', and these are respectively within one year of the end of FM MS C and the start of CT, i.e. RIA 1219, in O'Conor's possession since 1744. Thus this statement effectively confirms his custody of MS C in 1760. Then on 12 June 1762 O'Conor wrote to Dr Curry that 'Of these literary and poetical compositions from the conquest to the year 1631, I have a quarto volume of 1,000 pages.' Thus by this date the 'chasm' no longer existed and he wrote in terms of a singular 'quarto volume', and since MSS C+P comprise about 1,100 quarto pages his description is indeed appropriate to them. On 25 July 1763 O'Conor wrote to Dr Frances Sullivan of TCD proposing that the 'Annals of the Four Masters ... ought to be printed accurately', and on 1 September 1767, referring to his own source material, he wrote that 'there are abundant materials in the *Annals of the Four Masters* from the tenth to the seventeenth century.'[93] These references show that by 12 June 1762 O'Conor had custody also of MS P and was subsequently endeavouring to publish it with MS C and to make them available to other scholars. This sequence of events and the Revd O'Conor's assertion that Colonel Ó Gadhra had 'sent' a volume of FM to Charles O'Conor imply then that in fact it was MS P that was entrusted by Colonel O'Gara to his custody in c.1762. In his correspondence while Charles O'Conor referred to 'my Connacht Annals' he never applied 'my' to these FM volumes and in the event he did lose custody of MS P towards the end of his life.[94]

Thus the evidence points to the conclusion that *both* MSS C and P had earlier been in the possession of the Ó Gadhra family, and so notwithstanding Mícheál Ó Cléirigh's intention to send the Final Draft, i.e. MSS A+P, to Louvain, it appears that MS P was in fact sent to Fearghal Ó Gadhra.[95] While

---

93 Ward & Ward, *Letters* i, 99 ('chasm'), 134 ('quarto volume'), 165 (publication), 222 ('abundant materials').   94 By 1781 MS P was in the possession of William Burton in Dublin, see Matthew Young's account of the lacunae of AU/AT/LC/FM suffixed to the copies of FM MSS C and P, now RIA MSS 988–92, cf. Mulchrone, *Catalogue RIA*, fasc. xxii, 2828, and also O'Sullivan, 'Irish manuscripts', 245 item H.2.   95 George Petrie also concluded that MS P had been in the

we have only circumstantial evidence concerning this, when one contemplates the scale of the compilation supported by Fearghal Ó Gadhra and the disparate treatment of him proposed by Micheál Ó Cléirigh's short preface, it is not difficult to believe that some passionate forces were unleashed. Furthermore, recognizing that MS P was sent to Fearghal Ó Gadhra provides a basis to explain both the lacuna in MS C from 1171–1333, and the reports of two volumes ('duo tomi') of 'Annalium Hiberniae Quatuor Magistrorum' in Louvain in c.1658 and c.1673. The first of these reports appears in an inventory made by Thomas O'Sheerin of the manuscripts and books in Colgan's study, and it is clear from the details he provided about their position and status that he compiled it very shortly after Colgan's death in c.1658.[96] The first entry under 'Index Librorum Hiberniae in Papiro' is 'Annalium Hiberniae – tomi duo', and since Bonaventure O'Docherty subsequently glossed this as 'Quatuor Magistrorum' it is virtually certain therefore that in c.1658 such text of FM as was in Louvain was in two volumes.[97] Subsequently, following O'Sheerin's death in 1673, O'Docherty in turn made a 'Catalogus Manuscriptorum tam Latinè quam Hibernicè, olim in Camera R.P. Colgani repertorum, quibus postea R.P. Sirinus usus fuit.' In this he repeated and enlarged the entry in O'Sheerin's inventory as, 'Annalium Hiberniae Quatuor Magistrorum Hibernicè (communiter *Annales Dungallenses* appellati quia in conventu Dungallensi scripti) duo tomi, in fol. cum indice eorumdem, in folio, et alio indice.'[98] These entries leave no room for doubt that by 1658, there were two volumes identified as 'Annalium Hiberniae Quatuor Magistrorum' in Louvain, and by 1673 also indices to them.

The Louvain Franciscan MSS were transferred to S. Isidore's in Rome around the time of the French revolution and in c.1854 Charles Mac Donnell reported that, 'the second volume of the autograph exemplar of the Four Masters, formerly at S. Isidore's, is now in the Barberini Library.' However, all subsequent searches have failed to locate this volume. One of these two volumes can be securely identified with MS A since that was annotated by Colgan, but

---

possession of the Ó Gadhra family, cf. O'Donovan, *FM* i, p. xviii, 'the Manuscript now bought for the Acadamy [*sc.* MS P] ... passed from the representative of the O'Gara family into the hands of Mr. Charles O'Conor.' **96** UCD Killiney MS A34 item 1 (inventory); Dillon et al., *Catalogue*, 74 and Fennessy, 'Printed books', 83 did not identify the hand or the date. The hand is established by comparing it with O'Sheerin's four signed letters to Francis Harold, MS Killiney D.5 pp. 9, 15–16, 177–8, 237. The date is established by O'Sheerin's description of Colgan's Saint's Lives for April to December as 'Vitae SS.rum nondum editae', of which 'plures ex praedictis vitis manent supra easdem in cesta', pp. 5, 11. O'Sheerin's precise location for the unedited Lives implies Colgan's death. **97** Bonaventure O'Docherty subsequently emended the entry by striking through the last two words and writing superlinearly, 'Quatuor Magistrorum Hib. Tomi duo cum Index eorumdem'. **98** UCD Killiney MS A34 item 2, pp.1, 3 (cits.). O'Docherty identified himself on p. 13, 'Ita attestor fro Bonra Docharty.' The manuscript inventory was published by Mac Donnell, 'Colgan MSS', 95–103 (inventory), 98 (FM entry).

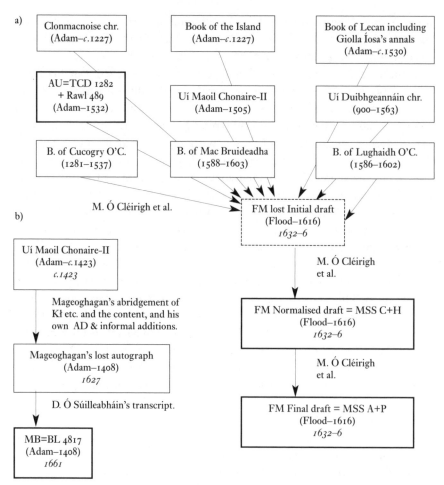

Figure 50. Stemma illustrating: a) the descent of FM, and b) the descent of MB. As in Figure 45, p. 314, existing MSS are identified by thick rectangles, attested works by light rectangles, and hypothesized works by dotted rectangles. Ranges are shown in parentheses and compilation dates where known are shown in italic, and compilation ranges imply accumulation of annals.

what of the second?[99] I suggest that when MS P was sent to Fearghal Ó Gadhra, because he then had duplicates of the years 1170–1333, it was resolved that Louvain should receive these duplicates. However, it was the latter section of the Normalized Draft that was sent thus creating the lacuna in MS C, and whether by oversight or deliberately the two years 1170–1 were retained, leaving Louvain with a second smaller volume extending from 1172 to 1333, and a

99 Ó Muraíle, 'Autograph MSS', 84 (searches). On p. 83 he observed that 'Mac Donnell does not say that he actually laid eyes on the volume', and concluded that 'his testimony is no better than

lacuna for the years 1170–1. This then was the second volume catalogued in Louvain, and asserted by Mac Donnell in 1854 to be in the Barberini Library but never subsequently found. In summary it emerges that hypotheses based simply upon the long preface of two 'Louvain' and two 'Ó Gadhra' volumes of FM cannot adequately explain the known sequence of events, the conflicts inherent in the two prefaces, or the disposition of the surviving MSS. Instead I have proposed three separate phases of MS transmission: in the first phase Louvain was sent MS A and Ó Gadhra was sent MS C then extending to 1333, in the second phase Ó Gadhra was sent MS P, and in the third phase Louvain was sent the years 1172–1333 of MS C by Ó Gadhra. This leaves unaccounted the remaining MS H for which there is no indication that it was ever in either Ó Gadhra hands or Louvain. It was so heavily annotated by O'Flaherty in the late seventeenth century it seems he must have owned it, after which nothing is known until it appeared in Dublin in 1724 where it has been ever since.[100] A stemma showing the descent of MB and FM is given in Figure 50.

hearsay'. But Mac Donnell was earnestly attempting to locate Colgan's lost works and his interest in the second FM volume in the Barberini was that it supplied a possible location for these lost works. Given this and the then incomplete Barberini catalogue it would be remarkable that he did not search for Colgan's works proximately to the now missing second Louvain volume. 100 Ó Muraíle, 'Autograph MSS', 92–4 (MS H).

CHAPTER TWELVE

Reliable Annalistic chronology

When a chronicle entry is used as a source for historical information the following two issues must be carefully considered: a) The semantic fidelity of the entry to the original record of the event; b) The reliability of the chronological apparatus in placing the event in time. Regarding semantic fidelity, while certainty is rarely attainable, a great deal of reassurance can be obtained by collating all surviving versions of the entry and identifying its earliest form. Then, wherever possible, this earliest form must be collated semantically with all available independent records of the event as a crosscheck upon its fidelity. Regarding chronological reliability, again identification of the earliest form of the chronological apparatus is the essential first step, and this similarly must be accompanied wherever possible by collation with all independent chronological data.[1] Guidance in the matter of identifying the earliest forms of both entries and chronological apparatus is available from the preceding chapters, which have identified the hierarchical relationships existing between the different groups. Of these in general the Clonmacnoise group preserves the earliest semantic form of the entries and chronological apparatus, the Cuana group represents a continuation of Cuán Ua Lothcháin's eleventh-century revision to the chronology of the Clonmacnoise chronicle up to c.664, while the Connacht group represents a continuation of the Clonmacnoise chronicle in Connacht from the later thirteenth century. On the other hand the regnal-canon group represents an entirely separate chronological tradition initiated in the early tenth century by Cormac mac Cuileannán that was introduced into the Connacht group by Maoilín Ua Maoil Chonaire in c.1423, and finally accorded primacy by Conall Mageoghagan in 1627. The matter of semantic fidelity will not be further considered here; rather the purpose of this chapter is to review our available sources over the entire range of the Annals and to identify as far as possible the chronologically reliable source or sources for each era.

Before proceeding there are a number of clarifications needed regarding the presentation of this review. First, the rectification of all scribal errors in the chronological apparatus will simply be assumed. Second, since the typical annalistic chronological apparatus comprises multiple parallel series, e.g. kalends, ferials, AD, it quite often happens that only some of these series can be

1 Mc Carthy, 'S. Brigit', 258–79 illustrates both techniques.

classified as reliable and it is just these that we wish to identify. Third, in order to simplify the specification of AD ranges all small lacunae and relatively short reliable series will be omitted from the discussion. Fourth, because our sources represent the accumulated work of many compilers working to different standards over hundreds of years it often happens that series of the resulting apparatus may be classified as reliable for only part of their total range. Finally, a series of the chronological apparatus will be classified as *reliable* over a specified AD range M to N if it:

a) Identifies a total of exactly N–M+1 Julian years.
b) Maintains precise synchronization with the Julian calendar for kalends and ferials, and with the ecclesiastical calendar for epacts and AD.
c) Locates all those events recorded in the source with independent chronology either precisely or closely to their independent chronology.

This definition ensures that those series classified as reliable maintain precise synchronism with the Julian and ecclesiastical calendars, and also conform closely to the independently available chronology, while allowing some small divergence between them. It also ensures that the concatenation of a sequence of such reliable series is similarly reliable. For discussion it is convenient to divide the full range of the Annals into the following three eras based upon the ranges of the surviving MSS of the Clonmacnoise and Connacht groups, namely the pre-Christian era, AD 1–1178, and AD 1014–1590.

Pre-Christian era

While the Clonmacnoise, Cuana and regnal-canon groups all provide a chrono-logical apparatus for parts of this era, only AT/AI/AB have preserved something of the form of the pre-Christian section of Rufinus' chronicle. Of these it is AT which best preserves both the kalend and Old World dynastic series. Examination of Rawl. B. 502, our best MS for AT, shows a total of 769 kalends and eighteen Old World dynastic series, some vestigial, before the year of the Incarnation.[2] Very little work has been undertaken on this material and until recently the only published evaluation of its chronology was that in 1913 by Mac Neill based upon his partial collation with Jerome's chronicle. This account is unfortunately adversely influenced by Mac Neill's *Irish world-chronicle* hypothesis, namely that it was the result of a relatively late and ill-contrived Irish compilation from

---

2 Stokes, *AT*, 9 omits a kalend before 'Dinastia Ægiptiorum', 31 omits a kalend before 'Húc usqus [sic] Siria'; Mc Carthy, 'Status', 117, 142–3 (dynastic series); idem, 'Bede's primary source', 5 (Table 1 – dynastic series).

assorted Western chronicles, in particular Bede's DT and DTR.[3] Because of this Mac Neill's conclusions are very misleading. However, in 1972 Morris and in 1998 Mc Carthy published preliminary collations that raised serious questions concerning Mac Neill's conclusions.[4] More recently Mc Carthy has published critical collations between AT/AI and DT/DTR which show unmistakeably that the Iona chronicle had inherited its kalends, Age structure, and Vulgate AM from Rufinus' chronicle, cf. chapter 4, p. 125 ff. It was a copy of the Iona chronicle sent in c.687 by Adomnán, abbot of Iona, to Aldfrith, king of Northumbria, that subsequently provided Bede with both his Age structure and Vulgate chronology for both DT and DTR.[5] However, to obtain a reliable Annalistic chronology for the pre-Christian era it will be necessary to first comprehensively collate the common entries of AT/AI/AB with those of DT/DTR, the surviving fragments of Eusebius' chronicle, together with the Jerome and Armenian recensions, and other sources of pre-Christian history accessible to Rufinus.

Regarding the status of the chronological apparatus of the pre-Christian section of the Cuana group, this is witnessed only by AB and its evidence shows that Cuán Ua Lothcháin extended both the ferial series of Rufinus' chronicle and his own annalistic epactal series back to Adam and effectively maintained the Vulgate AM chronology of the Clonmacnoise chronicle. This conclusion is also confirmed by AU's pre-Palladian AM synchronisms which are all based upon AM 3952, the Vulgate date for the Incarnation.[6] However, the very lacunose character of AB over the pre-Christian era severely hampers the detailed identification of Cuán's handling of its chronology. Finally regarding the pre-Christian era of the regnal-chronicle group, in chapter 10 it has been shown that its earlier chronology is the result of an eleventh-century compilation based upon otherwise unattested Irish regnal series exhibiting serious asynchronism with Biblical chronology. Accordingly the pre-Christian chronology of this group must be considered completely untrustworthy.

AD 1–1178

It is remarkable that even though our MSS of both AT and CS exhibit serious lacunae and the latter has suffered severe abridgment up to AD 335, nevertheless when taken together they provide a continuous kalend series extending from c.769 BC to 1178, with a lacuna of only thirty-seven years for 767–803. In the

3 Mac Neill, 'Authorship', 41–5 (compilation), 50–9 (structure), 53–9 (evaluation of chronology), 76–7 (Bede's DT & DTR).   4 Morris, 'Chronicle of Eusebius', 80–93, and Mc Carthy, 'Status', 142–8 (preliminary collations).   5 Mc Carthy, 'Bede's primary source', 12–15 (collations), 22–3 (Iona chronicle), 24–7 (Adomnán), 24–5 (Aldfrith).   6 Mc Carthy, 'AU apparatus 82–1019', 265, 272 (AU's synchronisms).

Christian era this kalend series is paralleled by a ferial series for AD 1–655, and by ferial, epactal and AD series for 1020–1178, and as well, scattered over the entire range are entries referring to European and astronomical events for which we have independent chronological data. As a consequence it has been possible to make a comprehensive and critical appraisal of the chronological apparatus of the Clonmacnoise group and this has been both published and made available on the Internet since 1998. This being so it is not proposed to present more than a summary account here.[7]

After the kalends the ferials represent the most extensive series of AT and CS, and because they extend over the first seven centuries where the chronological problems are the most severe, they are crucial for the detection and correction of scribal kalend omissions and interpolations. The method rests upon the Julian calendar systematically arranging three consecutive common years of 365 days followed by a bissextile year with 366 days, and as a result the ferial of the kalends of January must follow a twenty-eight year cycle called the solar cycle. Since $365=7\times52+1$ then following common years the ferial of the kalends of January must increment by one, and following bissextile years by two. As a consequence of this the solar cycle possesses a very regular numerical structure that may be best displayed by tabulating it as seven groups of four successive years as shown in Figure 51.

Years	1–4	5–8	9–12	13–16	17–20	21–24	25–28
Common	K.uii.	K.u.	K.iii.	K.i.	K.ui.	K.iiii.	K.ii.
Common	K.i.	K.ui.	K.iiii.	K.ii.	K.uii.	K.u.	K.iii.
Common	K.ii.	K.uii.	K.u.	K.iii.	K.i.	K.ui.	K.iiii.
Bissextile	**K.iii.**	**K.i.**	**K.ui.**	**K.iiii.**	**K.ii.**	**K.uii.**	**K.u.**

Figure 51. The twenty-eight year solar cycle displaying the ferial of the kalends of January for seven iterations of three common years followed by a bissextile year. The kalends of bissextile years are in bold to emphasize their distinction. To obtain the ferial of the kalends of January for any Julian year this table should be indexed by the remainder of its AD divided by twenty-eight. For example, $664=23\times28+20$ so that AD 664 is bissextile with K.ii; in the case that the remainder is zero the year 28 is indexed.

This table highlights a most valuable property of the solar cycle, namely that over any interval of four consecutive years the ferial must either increment by five or, if that result exceeds seven, then decrement by two. This may be confirmed by comparing the data across the rows of Figure 51. This property

7 Mc Carthy, 'Chronology'; idem, 'Synchronization', (Internet); Mc Carthy & Breen, 'Astronomical observations', *passim* (independent data).

confers a most powerful error-detection safeguard on ferial series since it does not require prior knowledge of the location of bissextile years, so that it allows systematic identification and correction of corrupt kalends and ferials. When this is combined with the parallel collation of the chronological apparatus and the entries of AT and CS then a valuable insight into the chronological apparatus of their common source is obtained.[8] What emerges is a kalend+ferial sequence which commenced at the Incarnation in synchronism with the Julian year and continued thus to AD 90. Thereafter a series of bissextile errors render the ferial sequence anachronistic up to 399 following which ferial synchronism with the Julian year is restored. However, at 425 a sudden hiatus occurs in the ferial series with the result that nearly all the subsequent ferials to the seventh century are asynchronous, and critical analysis shows that this hiatus and subsequent asynchronism were the result of deliberate corruption.[9] In chapter 4 I have concluded that these disruptions were the consequence of Ecgberht's revision of the Iona chronicle in $c.727$. When however the chronological accuracy of the kalend+ferial series is checked for those events with independently known chronology, it is immediately apparent that seven consecutive kalends have been lost at the point of the hiatus at 425. Following that a further six kalends were lost somewhere between 612 and 664.[10] Thus in all thirteen kalends were lost as a result of Ecgberht's revision and the matter of their restoration must be carefully considered. Regarding the first seven, since these

Event	Independent AD	Un-restored AD	Δ	Restored AD
Solar eclipse 2 Aug. 612	612	612	0	612
Isidore's *Chronica Maiora*	615	615	0	615
Volcanic eruption of AD 627	627	623	4	627
Baptism of Edwin	627	623	4	627
Lindisfarne founded	635	630	5	635
Heracleonas reigned	641	636	5	641
Death of Aidan	651	646	5	651
Death of Penda	655	650	5	655
Death of Cumine Fota	661	656	5	661
Solar eclipse 1 May 664	664	658	6	664

Figure 52. Tabulation of those events in AT/CS between 612 and 664 for which an independent AD is available. Beside this is tabulated the AD of these events in the un-restored kalend chronology of AT/CS, the difference Δ between these, and the restored AD.

8 Mc Carthy, 'Chronology', 212–20 (collation & correction demonstration).   9 Mc Carthy, 'Chronology', 227–9 (deliberate corruption).   10 Mc Carthy, 'Chronology', 223–7, esp. table 5

were consecutive then they must be restored at 425–31, but the remaining six are clearly not consecutive and the best we may do in these circumstances is to distribute them so as to ensure that those events for which we have an independent AD are restored to that year. Between 612 and 664 we have ten such events and these are tabulated in Figure 52 followed by their independent AD, the un-restored AD, and the difference Δ between these.

As can be seen no kalends have been lost in the intervals 612–15 or 635–61, but four are missing in the interval 615–27, one in the interval 627–35 and another in 661–4. Distributed uniformly the first four kalends may be placed at 617, 620, 623 and 626, the next at 631 and the last at 662. With these six kalend restorations all ten events for which we have an independent chronology will be restored precisely to their appropriate AD as is shown in the final column of Figure 52.[11] Whilst these restorations thus achieve precise synchronization for those events with independently attested chronology, and they also maintain the chronological ordering of all entries, it must be acknowledged that there is significant uncertainty in the absolute chronology of some unattested events. Namely in the interval 616–26 there is an uncertainty of ± 4 years in the restored AD for all unattested entries, and for 628–34 and 662–3 an uncertainty of ± 1 year. At the same time it should be emphasized that these kalend restorations do not perturb in any way the chronological ordering of the entries.

Finally we must consider the matter of the lacuna in AT/CS for the interval 767–803. I consider that we may reliably restore both the chronology and much of the content for the Clonmacnoise chronicle over this lacuna from AU for the following reasons:

a) Cuán Ua Lothcháin employed the Clonmacnoise chronicle as his principal source in compiling this section of the Liber Cuana, see chapter 7.
b) The kalend chronology of AU corresponds virtually identically to that of AT for their common events over 664–766, and to that of CS over 804–904, so that for at least a century on either side of the lacuna AU's kalends and common events maintain synchronism with those of AT and CS.[12]
c) There is no evidence of any chronological dislocation in AU over 763–803, and indeed accurate eclipse entries at 773 and 788 confirm its accuracy at these two years.[13]

(lost kalends).   11 Mc Carthy, 'Synchronization', 'Introduction' and s.a. 617, 620, 623, 626, 631, 662. Note that in editions 1–3 of these tables kalend restorations were made at 614, 619, 624, 629, 634, 659. The procedure given above correctly synchronizes all events with independent chronology, and so represents a significant improvement and has been implemented in edition 4. 12 Mc Carthy, 'Synchronization', s.a. 664–766, 804–904 (AT/AU & CS/AU synchronism). 13 Mc Carthy & Breen, 'Astronomical observations', 123–4 (eclipses).

Thus there are substantial grounds on which to conclude that AU accurately represents the kalend chronology and indeed the content of the Clonmacnoise chronicle for 767–803, and so AU may be used to restore its chronology over this interval. On the same grounds following 904 where CS lacks a kalend found in AU at 905, and likewise at 980 we restore kalends to CS at these years. Finally for 1018–1178 the kalend, ferial, epactal, and AD series of AT, either with CS or alone, provides a comprehensive apparatus precisely synchronized with the Julian and ecclesiastical calendars, and with many events for which an independent chronology is available. The two additional series introduced by Cuán and adopted in the Clonmacnoise chronicle from c.1022, the epact, and AD, both derive from the Paschal tract compiled in 525 by Dionysius Exiguus †c.550. In this Dionysius substituted AD 532 for the year Diocletian 248, and he based his Paschal table upon a nineteen-year cycle of epacts that represent the age of the moon (*luna*) computed on the eleventh kalends of April (22 March). Cuán adjusted these Dionysiac epacts to the Annalistic datum of the kalends of January to obtain the nineteen-year cycle of Annalistic epacts shown in Figure 53.[14]

Index	1	2	3	4	5	6	7	8	9	10	11	12	13	14	15	16	17	18	19
Epact	9	20	1	12	23	4	15	26	7	18	29	10	21	2	13	24	5	16	27

Figure 53. The cycle of Annalistic epacts derived by Cuán Ua Lothcháin from the Dionysiac Paschal tract. To compute the epact for any Julian year add one to its AD and index the cycle by the remainder on division by nineteen. For AD 438 for example, 438+1=439=23×19+2 so the index is two and AD 438 has epact 20; if the remainder is zero then the index is nineteen.

After 1022 when the epacts introduced by Cuán were correctly synchronized the resultant four-series apparatus was the most substantial reliable apparatus ever achieved in Irish chronicles, and it stands in conspicuous contrast to the preceding centuries of simple kalends, cf. Figure 55, p. 353. However, it was also an instance of substantial over-specification since any one of the ferial, epactal, or AD series alone would have been sufficient to securely sequence the kalends. And indeed in the ensuing centuries first the epacts and then ferials were to be abandoned. In summary then, between them AT and CS present a reliable and consistent chronology extending from AD 1 to 1178, with the exceptions of 425–31 and those parts of the interval 616–63 where uncertainties in absolute chronology arise from kalend loss, and their lacuna for 767–803, which must be supplied from AU. Regarding the third member of the Clonmacnoise group,

14 Mc Carthy, 'Emergence of AD', 36 (Diocletian 248), *passim* (AD); Krusch, *Studien*, 70–4 (Dionysius' tract), cf. Wallis, *Reckoning*, 64–8, 130–1 (Dionysiac epacts); Mc Carthy, 'Status', 263–4 (annalistic epacts).

AR, while its kalend and ferial series have suffered severe attrition at the hands of its scribe, Brendan O'Conor, enough remains to show that it synchronizes with AT/CS over 402–79 and 550–601.[15]

Regarding the Cuana group, examination of AU's pre-Palladian apparatus discloses that Cuán profoundly distorted the chronology of his Clonmacnoise source over *c.*82–*c.*387; for he introduced duplicate Incarnation and Crucifixion entries in the mid-third century that necessitated the subsequent interpolation of 253 kalends over 254–431. Then over 431–663 Cuán restored only five of the six missing kalends with the result that his AD series was one year in arrears from thence to 1013. From 664 on collation of AU's chronological apparatus and common events with those of the Clonmacnoise group shows that AU's kalend series is reliable for 664–1178, and its ferial, epactal, and AD series for 1014–1178. For AI there has not been an opportunity to collate its apparatus comprehensively but to judge from Mac Airt's account and from sample checking, its kalend, ferial, and epactal series appear reliable for 973–1178.[16] Of the Connacht group LC is reliable over 1014–1178 as may be expected since over these years LC transmits the Armagh-Derry[+] chronicle, cf. Figure 38, p. 262. On the other hand for the regnal-canon group both of its members are demonstrably profoundly unreliable over the interval AD 1–1021, cf. Figure 43, p. 299.[17] From 1022 on however the AD series of MB/FM follow closely but not precisely the AD chronology of the Connacht group.

AD 1014–1590

It is indeed fortunate that the range of the surviving MSS of the Clonmacnoise group substantially overlap those of the Connacht group, for when these are collated it shows that their kalend, ferial, epactal and AD series effectively agree for the entire overlap 1014–1178, cf. Figure 55, p. 353. Furthermore, when the kalend and AD series of LC and CT are collated it emerges that they both maintain synchronism with the Julian and ecclesiastical calendars over their entire range of 1014–1590. This is the case notwithstanding lacunae in LC/CT at 1139–69, 1394–8, 1572–6, and these synchronized series extending over 577 years, which also include synchronous ferials over 1014–1478, represent a most impressive achievement in itself.[18] When taken with the many events with synchronous independent chronology this provides compelling reasons to regard the chronology of the Connacht group as comprehensively reliable over this interval. This important fact has never been acknowledged in modern times. First Hennessy in his extensive introduction to his edition of LC,

15 Mc Carthy, 'Chronology', 249–50 (AR ferials).   16 Mac Airt, *AI*, xxiv–xxix, xliv (dating). 17 Mc Carthy, 'Synchronization', *s.v.* 'Tables 4–5' (FM unreliability).   18 AT and AU may be used to restore the 1139–69 lacuna, and AU that of 1394–8.

wherein he incorporated parts of CT to fill out LC's lacunae, neither remarked their synchronism nor provided any discussion whatsoever of their chronology. Then it was most unfortunate that Freeman in his account of the elaborate chronological apparatus of CT chose to place the emphasis of his discussion upon the exotic additional series and their problems, and to make repeated derisory comments regarding them that exposed his own shortcomings, while overlooking the fundamental kalend and AD series.[19] In this way the essential integrity of the key chronological series of the Connacht group has been over-looked, and instead chronological priority has been accorded to Mac Carthy's edition of AU. For example, Mac Niocaill when comparing the chronology of LC and AU over 1191–1223 wrote, 'in the relationship of L1 [LC] with U [AU] there is *evidence of disturbance in L1's text.*'[20] Here, because he found LC's chronology differed from that of Mac Carthy's edition of AU Mac Niocaill simply assumed the 'disturbance' to be in LC.

In fact in his two volumes of AU Mac Carthy relentlessly supplied ferials and epacts absolutely regardless of the MSS readings, and prompted by James Ware's marginal AD annotations in Rawl. B. 489 over the interval 1265–1378 he interpolated alternative values into the AD series. The truth of the relationship between LC/CT and AU can only be established by systematic collation of the MS chronological data of TCD 1282 in the *prima manu* of Ua Luinín against that of LC/CT, together with their common events. This has been done and made available on the Internet and it reveals that AU's kalend, ferial, epactal, and AD series are *all* asynchronous to the Julian and ecclesiastical calendars over the interval 1192–1378. It shows that in fact kalends were interpolated into AU at 1192 and 1314, and kalends were omitted at 1223, 1263, 1266, 1272, 1286, 1371, 1373. Since these two interpolations and seven omissions were all registered in the AD series, over 1192–1223 and 1263–1378 AU's AD chronology is asynchronous by between one and five years.

These kalend interpolations and omissions had significant consequences for both MSS of AU and for Mac Carthy's edition, and so it is worth considering them in some detail. The sequence of events was as follows. After the completion of TCD 1282 in *c.*1505 Ruaidhrí Ua Caiside collated it with a now lost member of the Connacht group that resembled LC, and he marginally interpolated numerous entries, locating them by synchronizing the AD that appeared in each text. He was clearly either unaware of or indifferent to the kalend interpolations and omissions because his interpolations over 1192–1223 are displaced by one year, and those for 1263–1378 by between one and five

---

19 Freeman, *CT*, xiv–xx, did not even identify the kalends as part of the chronological apparatus. His allusions to 'characteristic peculiarity', 'violent irregularities', 'the compiler's happy-go-lucky procedure', 'a piece of playful archaism' and 'scribal foolery' are all gratuitous and reflect Freeman's weak grasp of chronology. 20 Mac Niocaill, *MIA*, 31 italic emphasis added.

years. Then about a century later James Ware collated Rawl. B. 489, which does not incorporate these particular interpolations of Ua Caiside, with a member of the Connacht group, and where he found that the AD of common events differed he inscribed the Connacht AD in the margin of Rawl. B. 489. Since Ware annotated the years 1265–1378 in this way the MS he used may have been that which he described in his catalogue of 1648 as, 'Pars Annalium coenobij S. Trinitatis de Loghkea, videlicet ab anno Domini 1249. usque ad annum 1408. ex Hibernico idiomate in Anglicum versa, in 4.'[21] Use of this copy beginning only at 1249 would help explain why Ware did not identify and annotate the asynchronisms in AU over 1192–1223. Finally came Mac Carthy who, having systematically supplied ferial and epactal series for his edition regardless of the MSS readings, turned in his introduction to discuss what he termed 'misdating' over 1191–1378. Here Mac Carthy briefly acknowledged the existence in TCD 1282 of a, 'serious error, continued through more than a century (1265–1378) and accumulating by accretions of from two to five years.' But Mac Carthy blamed this 'serious error' on the 'ignorance of chronistic criteria on the part of the summarist', and he claimed that the text itself, 'preserved these [ferial and epactal] data to an extent quite sufficient to have obviated the deviation in question.'[22] Mac Carthy's claim that the chronological integrity of AU's text had been preserved by the ferial and epactal data was both untrue and deeply misleading. Over the 154 years of 1225–1378 the primary MS TCD 1282 has just thirty-six ferials of which fourteen are corrupt, and twenty epacts of which sixteen are corrupt. Moreover, there are no ferial or epactal data proximate to the years 1263, 1266, 1272, 1286, 1314, 1371, or 1373 that would allow anyone to detect the kalend interpolations and omissions there. The truth is that Mac Carthy, prompted by Ware's marginal AD annotations in Rawl. B. 489, followed Hennessy's LC over 1263–1378.[23] In this way Mac Carthy effectively denied AU's asynchronism over 1192–1223, and in his footnotes to these years he made collations with Hennessy's edition of LC in such a way as to create the impression that the latter verified the chronology of AU. Namely nearly all of Mac Carthy's collations in the interval 1192–1223 referring to 'the *Annals of Loch Ce* (*ad. an.*)' refer to those entries interpolated into TCD 1282 by Ruaidhrí Ua Caiside by synchronizing their AD, and hence are indeed synchronized with LC. But Mac Carthy systematically ignored all those entries written by Ua Luinín in *both* TCD 1282 and Rawl. B. 489, found also in LC, and whose AD chronology repeatedly conflicts with that of AU. For example the first three entries of LC 1193 appear at AU 1194 but Mac Carthy noted only that the last two entries of AU 1194, both interpolations by Ua Caiside, appear in LC 1194. On the few occasions that Mac Carthy did acknowledge the chronological

---

21 O'Sullivan, 'Finding list', 90.   22 Mac Carthy, *AU* iv, p. xcix.   23 Mac Carthy, *AU* ii, 332 n. 1.

conflict between AU and LC he did so to try to argue AU's supposed priority. For example, for the obit of Domnall Ua Brolchain which is placed by both LC 1202.12 and AU 1203.4 on the fifth kalends of May [27 April], Mac Carthy wrote, 'It fell on Sunday in the present year [1203]. This goes to prove that the *Annals of Loch Ce* (followed by the *F.M.*) err in assigning the obit to 1202; in which the 27th fell on Saturday, a day of no particular note.'[24] This purported 'proof' rests entirely upon Mac Carthy's unverifiable assumption that the day in question should be a Sunday. In these circumstances there are no possible grounds for according to AU over 1192–1378 the chronological priority conjured by Mac Carthy's edition and introduction. Rather it must be recognized that over these years AU clumsily combines copies of the Armagh-Derry[+] chronicle with Uí Maoil Chonaire-II, abandoning most of their ferial series from 1169 onwards, and seriously distorting their kalend chronology over 1192–1378. Consequently, it emerges that over 1192–1378 LC/CT represent the only reliable source for Annalistic chronology.

Regarding the Cuana group, the kalend and AD series of AU is reliable for 1014–1191 and 1379–1541. But with respect to AU's ferial and epactal series, Mac Carthy so comprehensively supplied ferial and epactal data that his edition creates the impression that AU invariably provided such data. However, in fact the MSS more often supply just blank space, and reliable ferial series occur in AU only for 1014–1168 and 1379–1500, while reliable epacts occur only for 1014–1191; the remainder was all Mac Carthy's invention.[25] Indeed regarding

Group	Source	Ranges of reliable chronological criteria
Clon.	AT	K: 1–358, 488–766*, 974–999; KFEA: 1020–1178.
Clon.	CS	K: 336–722*, 804–1021; KFEA: 1022–1150.
Cuana	AU	K: 664–1013; KFEA: 1014–1132, 1156–1191; KFA: 1379–1500; KA: 1501–41.
Conn.	LC	KFEA: 1014–1139, 1170–1223; KFA: 1224–1316; KA: 1413–1590.
Conn.	CT	KFA: 1224–1478; KA: 1479–1544.

Figure 54. A summary tabulation of the reliable Annalistic chronological series available over the range AD 1–1590. The prefixes to each range of AD years indicate the reliable series provided by the source, where K=kalends, F=ferials, E=epacts, A=AD. Minor lacunae and relatively short reliable series have been omitted in order to simplify the presentation of the ranges, and at '*' thirteen kalends are assumed restored to AT/CS over 425–31, 615–64.

24 Mac Carthy, *AU* ii, 240 n. 2.   25 Mac Carthy, *AU* ii, *passim*, generally identified these by placing his ferial and epactal additions in square brackets between [a...a] and then recording '[a-a] blank space, A,B' in his apparatus.

Annalistic epacts in general it is the case that since those of LC/CT are asynchronous to the ecclesiastical calendar from 1235 onwards, epacts were in fact continued accurately only for about two centuries after Cuán introduced them in *c.*1022. This is just the interval during which these annals remained in an ecclesiastical environment, viz., in the monasteries of Clonmacnoise, Armagh and Derry. Mac Carthy was quite mistaken therefore in his belief that the 'Paschal Cycle was the basis of the Irish Chronicle.'[26] Rather epacts were an ecclesiastical series that flourished only from *c.*1022 to 1235, and the attempts by later compilers to extend them in both the Cuana and Connacht groups were unsuccessful. As regards AI, until its apparatus has been fully collated no proper judgement can be made regarding its reliability after 1178. Finally, regarding the regnal-canon group, since Mageoghagan compiled MB from Uí Maoil Chonaire-II it is likely that he based his own marginal AD upon that of his source. In this case one would expect his AD to be accurate from 1022 onwards and this is indeed supported by sampling the AD and entries of Murphy's edition, but nevertheless it remains to be demonstrated comprehensively. Similarly for FM the indications are that its AD chronology post 1022 is substantially reliable but again this remains to be demonstrated.

We may summarize the foregoing discussion in tabular form by listing for the members of each group the ranges over which the criteria of its chronological apparatus has been established as reliable, and this is shown in Figure 54.

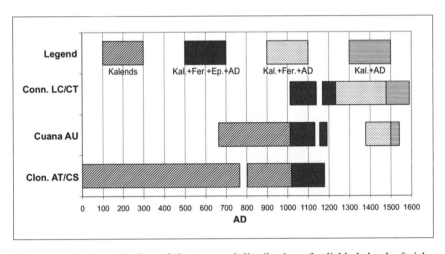

Figure 55. A schematic view of the temporal distribution of reliable kalends, ferials, epacts, and AD between the Clonmacnoise, Cuana and Connacht groups. Again small lacunae and short reliable series have been omitted in order to simplify the diagram.

26 Mac Carthy, 'Palatino-Vaticanus', 361 (cit.).

It is very helpful to view these results graphically over the entire range 1–1590 in terms of the separate contributions of each group to reliable chronological series, and this is shown in Figure 55. This shows graphically that over the first millennium it is the kalend series that provides the reliable basis for Annalistic chronology. Then for about two centuries following Cuán's introduction of epacts and AD these, together with ferials, represent the climax phase of the Annalistic chronological apparatus. With the move to Connacht and the Uí Maoil Chonaire in the thirteenth century the epacts lost synchronism by 1235, and by 1479 the ferials were abandoned by the Uí Duibhgeannáin leaving just kalends and AD. In Fermanagh the Uí Chianáin were a little more conservative, maintaining synchronized ferials for 1379–1483 and these were continued by Ruaidhrí Ua Caiside to 1500. Thus it can be seen that over much of the range 1–1590 we have two or more sources that provide reliable chronological series to serve as the basis for Annalistic chronology. The chronological collations that are summarized in Figure 54 and Figure 55 have been made available on the Internet, and these may be used to supply a reliable chronology for entries from other sources whose chronological apparatus is deficient.[27] For example, AR, AB, and AU over 81–663, 1192–1378, and also to correct the chronology of the many misplaced entries found in common with MB and FM.

27 At www.irish-annals.cs.tcd.ie

Epilogue

Before concluding I wish to briefly review the whole process of Irish chronicling from its inception to its conclusion, to justify my initial insistence upon including the chronological apparatus, codicology and palaeography in the analysis of chronicles, and to outline the chronicle material that has not been examined in this study.

Twelve centuries of Irish chronicling – from Bethlehem to Bundrowes

The practice of chronicling events on an annual basis flourished in Ireland for about twelve centuries and expanded to formidable proportions, and having reviewed the details of this expansion in the previous chapters it is worthwhile now to briefly consider the process as a whole. There are two key events that clearly mark the inception and conclusion of this process, namely S. Jerome's adoption of the Hebrew Bible as the primary Biblical authority in *c.*391 and Mícheál Ó Cléirigh's compilation of FM over 1632–6. The first of these arose from Jerome's endeavours to establish the Biblical text from the various existing editions of the Septuagint, the Greek Biblical translation used by the Christian diaspora from earliest times. However, when Jerome compared his own collected editions of the Greek Bible with the six parallel collations of Hebrew and Greek editions in Origen's *Hexapla*, he concluded that the Hebrew Bible provided the only authoritative source for the text. Thus from *c.*391 onwards he designated the Hebrew Bible as the 'Hebrew truth (*Hebraica ueritatis*)', and over *c.*391–404 he translated the Hebrew Bible into Latin. Subsequently Jerome's translation was accepted as the authoritative edition of the Bible by the western Church and hence was termed the 'universal edition (*editio vulgata*)' or Vulgate. However, with his adoption of the primacy of the Hebrew Bible Jerome also confronted all subsequent Latin Christian scholars with the irresolvable conflict between the Hebrew chronology and that of the Septuagint. In particular he effectively rendered obsolete the Biblical chronology of both Eusebius' chronicle of *c.*325 and his own Latin translation of this made in *c.*380.

Rufinus of Aquileia was a unique western witness to Jerome's conclusion that the Septuagint must be rejected and primacy accorded instead to the Hebrew Bible. Further, it is a principal conclusion of this study that it was Rufinus who, in the very productive years following his return to Italy in 397, undertook the compilation of a world chronicle reflecting Hebrew Biblical chronology. Rufinus embedded this distinctive Hebrew Biblical chronology in a chronicle employing the kalend+ferial apparatus that he knew from the Paschal tract of Anatolius of Laodicea. In his compilation Rufinus also inserted numerous interjections remarking conflicts between the chronology of the Hebrew Bible, the Septuagint and the chronicles of antiquity. In normal circumstances we would expect this compilation to have taken root amongst Rufinus' supporters in his native Italy. However, circumstances prevailed against this when in 409 the army of Goths led by Alaric blockaded Rome and then invaded the rest of the Italian isthmus, and Rufinus and his colleagues were driven thence into Sicily where he died. Thereafter the circumstantial evidence implies that Rufinus' chronicle travelled westward via Sulpicius Severus in southern Gaul and reached Ireland by c.425. Thus in less than two decades Rufinus' chronicle reflecting the chronological consequence of Jerome's adoption in Bethlehem of the primacy of the Hebrew Bible had reached the western extremity of Europe, and it was here that it took root.

The evolution of Rufinus' chronicle in Ireland and Britain over the succeeding twelve centuries is, I trust, adequately reviewed in the summaries at the conclusions of chapters four to ten, and the stemma of chapter eleven. But a cryptic recitation here of some of the places and persons who were involved with this evolution will help to underline the wide distribution and manifold contributions to this evolution process in the Insular context. For places we have: Leinster, Louth, Iona, Northumbria, Moville, Clonmacnoise, Armagh, Emly, Lismore, Derry, Boyle, Cluain Plocáin, Kilronan, Lisgoole, Lecan Mac Fhirbhisigh, Seanadh, Loch Cé, Lemanaghan and Bundrowes. For persons we have: Auxilius, Secundinus, Iserninus, Mochta, Finnian, Columba, Adomnán, Aldfrith, Bede, Cuán Ua Lothcháin, Dub da Leithe, Flann Cuilleain, Tigernach Ua Braein, Duinnin Ua Maoil Chonaire, Pilib Ua Duibhgeannáin, Maoilín Ua Maoil Chonaire, Giolla Íosa Mac Fhirbhisigh, Cathal Mac Maghnusa, Ruaidhrí Ua Caiside, Ruaidhrí Ua Luinín, Brian Mac Diarmada, Conall Mageoghagan and Mícheál Ó Cléirigh. This list of twenty-three names certainly represents only a small fraction of the total number of compilers who participated in the twelve centuries of Irish chronicling.

The event that in my view marked the conclusion of the evolution of Rufinus' chronicle was the compilation of FM over 1632–6 by Mícheál Ó Cléirigh in Bundrowes, for in this final flourish he rejected most of the distinctive features of Rufinus' chronicle. Namely Ó Cléirigh substituted the Septuagint chronology for the Vulgate, he discarded all the world history, he repudiated the use of Latin, and he abandoned the kalend+ferial apparatus replacing it with an Irish regnal succession and AM/AD written in Irish and Arabic numerals. Thus Ó Cléirigh's compilation in Bundrowes rejected nearly all of the key features of the tradition of Rufinus' chronicle, and so with FM we may fairly consider that the evolution ceased. This is not of course to represent that scholarly interest in Rufinus' tradition then ceased for copies of the earlier editions have been repeatedly made since, such as the abridgments by Dubhaltach Mac Fhirbhisigh and Brendan O'Conor in *c*.1640–1, all the way down to the published and electronic editions of the present day.

Necessity for a comprehensive analysis of chronicle features

In the introductory chapters to this book I emphasized the importance of including the chronological apparatus in the analysis of a chronicle, and also of comprehensively identifying the codicological and palaeographic features of its MS(S). I wish here to justify these requirements by briefly revisiting instances where these considerations have lead to valuable insights into the compilation of our Annals. For examples:

1. Examination of the chronological apparatus of pre-Palladian AU, together with codicological and palaeographic features of MS H shows that the original compilation of AU commenced deep in the Biblical period, undoubtedly at Adam. Hence these considerations are sufficient to show that the frequently repeated hypothesis that AU commenced at AD 431 is unsustainable.

2. Collation of the imperial regnal series of AI/AT/AU/DT/DTR shows that they *all* derive from a common source extending as far as *c*.685. This in turn implies that Bede's principal world history source for his DT/DTR compilations came from Iona during the abbacy of Adomnán. In consequence the hypothesis that the Annalistic world history derived from Bede's chronicles is unsupportable.

3. Collation of the kalend+ferial apparatus and the common entries of post-Incarnation AT/CS shows that thirteen kalends were deliberately deleted from the Iona chronicle, namely seven kalends over 425–31 and six more over 612–64. The synchronism between these kalend deletions and the Annalistic papal chronicle over 431–608 shows that both were work of an Iona proponent of Roman ecclesiastical traditions, suggesting thereby Ecgberht †729. This inference is supported by the synchronization of the Anglo-Saxon chronicle over 611–718 with the termination of the papal chronicle. Moreover, no examination of the Annalistic entries purporting that S. Patrick's Irish mission commenced at 432 has ever considered the

implication of the seven preceding years having been purposefully removed from the chronicle. In fact the proximity of these perturbations and the emphasis of the Patrician entries upon episcopacy lead to the conclusion that Ecgberht was responsible for them.

4. The observation that the first appearance of ferial+epact expressed in Irish in AT is synchronised to Tigernach Ua Braein's term as *comharba* at Clonmacnoise over 1071–88 leads to the conclusion that Tigernach instituted an enduring reform in the chronological apparatus of the Clonmacnoise chronicle. This alone provides sufficient grounds to reject Ware's oft repeated hypothesis of Tigernach's compilation of all of AT up to 1088.

5. Examination of the many diverse chronological criteria of the apparatus of CT over 1224–1590 shows that all series exhibit either a lacuna or a discontinuity or both over 1423–32, implying that the major Uí Maoil Chonaire compilation of the fifteenth century may be dated to *c.*1423 and hence associated with the ollamh, Maoilín Ua Maoil Chonaire †1441.

I trust that these examples attest to the value of including evaluations of the chronological apparatus, codicology, and palaeography in any analysis of chronicle material. There is indeed a great deal more that can be investigated in this way with the Irish Annals and this book represents only a beginning, but I hope that it has demonstrated these Annals to be a unique extension of the Latin Christian chronicling tradition initiated in Palestine by Jerome and Rufinus. As such the Irish Annals are compilations to be treasured.

Outstanding chronicle compilations

The following three published annalistic compilations were omitted from this study, namely *Mac Carthaigh's Book*, the *Miscellaneous Annals* and the *Fragmentary Annals*.[1] All three were omitted because in my judgement the additional complexity needed to incorporate them into the taxonomy and discussion would not be compensated by substantially increased insight into the evolution of the principal annals. Likewise, a considerable number of fragmentary annalistic MSS, mostly unpublished, have been passed over in this study. These omissions also arose from a need to keep the scale of the analysis within reasonable limits, and the omissions are definitely not intended to make a value judgement on the works themselves which rather all possess their own intrinsic interest and merit their own study. A case in point is the fragment MS

---

1 Ó hInnse, *Miscellaneous annals*, (editions of *Mac Carthaigh's Book* & *Miscellaneous Annals*); O'Donovan, *Three Fragments* and Radner, *Fragmentary annals*, (editions of the *Fragmentary Annals*).

Edinburgh, National Library of Scotland, Gaelic II ff. 79, 88 covering the years 1360–1402, which Mac Niocaill published in 1958 and in his 1975 monograph he included it anonymously in his stemma of AU/CT/LC for the late fourteenth century.[2] I believe the scribe may be Ruaidhrí Ua Luinín and that they relate to the problem of AU's lost kalends over 1263–1378, but a serious study of this fragment is required before these hypotheses may be accepted. The MSS of the aforementioned published and unpublished annals are listed in appendix 1 under 'Unclassified MSS'. Finally, another collection of Irish chronicles not considered here is that listed by Mac Niocaill under the heading 'Anglo-Irish Annals', pointing out that this described their 'stance', that is their purview, and not their language which is normally Latin.[3] While the content of these works is naturally of historical interest, they issue from a completely different chronicling tradition and consequently can throw no light upon the evolution of the Irish Annals.

2 Mac Niocaill, 'Cáipéisí', 33–42 (edition); Mac Niocaill, *MIA*, 35 identified them as 'some fragmentary annals for the years 1360 to 1402 (by their own dating) which are demonstrably brother to one of the sources of U', but his stemma in figure 6 on the same page simply refers to them as 'Fragment'. 3 Mac Niocaill, *MIA*, 37 (Anglo-Irish 'stance'), 41 (list).

Manuscript witnesses to the Annals

Where two shelf marks are cited in modern usage, the older has been given in parentheses.

CLONMACNOISE GROUP

AT – see O'Grady, *Catalogue*, 1–3 for nos. 4–5.
1. Rawl. B. 502 (*c.*1100).
2. Rawl. B. 488 (saec. xiv²).
3. TCD 1292 (H.1.18) (saec xvii) – Copied from no. 2.
4. BL Egerton 104 (saec xix) – Copy of *c.*320 BC–AD 1163 from no. 3.
5. BL Egerton 94 (saec. xix) – Copy of no. 4.
6. RIA 686 (23.P.5) (*c.*1765) – Copy of *c.*320 BC–AD 718, 1067–1159.
7. RIA 826 (D.vi.1) (saec. xix) – Collation by the Revd O'Conor of AT/FM/AI/AB.
8. RIA 1239 (D.vi.2) (saec. xix) – Copy by the Revd O'Conor.
9. RIA 1240 (E.i.2) (saec. xix) – Copy by the Revd O'Conor.

CS – see Ó Muraíle, *Background*, ii p. 326 ff. for these sigla and details.
1. H=TCD 1292 (H.1.18) (*c.*1640).
2. A=American Irish Hist. Soc. MS (1711?).
3. G=NLI G 431 (*c.*1760).
4. P=RIA 686 (23.P.5) (*c.*1765) – Range *Patritius natus* – AD 1135.
5. E=RIA 1240 (E.i.2) (*c.*1810).
6. L1=RIA 167 (23.O.8) (1830).
7. L2=RIA 168 (24.C.30) (1839).
8. L3=Sheffield 1 (1839).
9. L4=Torna xxxii (*c.*1839).
10. L5=Waterford, Coláiste Eoin 11 (1840).
11. L6=NLI G.75 (1840).
12. L7=Maynooth College M 104 (1841).
13. L8=Fermoy, Coláiste Cholmáin 10 (1841).
14. L9=RIA 169 (23.O.30) (1842).

AR
1. Bruxelles Bibl. Royale 5301–20 pp. 97–162 (1641).

CUANA GROUP

AU – see Mac Carthy, *AU* iv, pp. i–xiii for the sigla and details of nos. 1–6.
1. H=TCD 1282 (H.1.8) (*c.*1505).
2. R=Bodleian, Rawl. B. 489 (*c.*1508).
3. C1–2=BL Add. 4795 ff. 1–108 – Translation for Ware of 431–1307.
4. C3=BL Add. 4789 ff. 203–326 – Translation for Ware of 1156–1303, 1486–1504.
5. D=BL Add. 4784 ff. 21–32 – Latin translation of 1200–1300.
6. E+F=TCD 574 (E.3.20) (saec. xvii) – Copy of 431–665 with partial Latin translation.
7. RIA 822–3 (3.C.16–17) (1840) – O'Curry transcript of no. 1.
8. RIA 824–5 (E.iii.1, E.ii.3) (*c.*1800) – Copy by the Revd O'Conor of 431–765, 1156–1303.

AI – see Mac Airt, *AI* pp. xi–xiii for nos. 1–9.
1. Bodleian Rawl. B. 503 (*c.*1092–1326)
2. BL Add. 4787 (1624) – Extracts by Ware from 432.
3. BL Add. 4799 – Full translation by Mac Fhirbhisigh.
4. BL Add. 4791 – Excerpts for 1170–1308.
5. BL Add. 11215 (1789) – Excerpts referring to the Vikings.
6. TCD 804 (F.1.18) – A copy of nos. 2 and 3.
7. RIA 826 (D.vi.1) (saec. xix) – Excerpts by the Revd O'Conor.
8. RIA 593 (24.B.20) (saec. xix) – English translation of O'Conor's edition.
9. RIA 1110 (12.I.5) (1843) – Translation of 624–1196.
10. TCD 1324 (H.3.5) – Part of 1120–83 by Maurice Gorman.

AB
1. BL Cotton Titus A xxv (*c.*1257).
2. TCD 574 (E.3.20) – Virtually a full transcript of no. 1.
3. BL Add. 6917 ff. 205–57.
4. BL Add. 4791 ff. 162–74 (saec. xvi) – Extracts over *c.*347–1240.

CONNACHT GROUP

CT
1. RIA 1219 (C.iii.1) ff. 1–90 (saec. xvi)
2. TCD 1278 (H.1.1–2) (1764) – Copy of no. 1 by Maurice O'Gorman.
3. RIA 986–7 (23.F.7–8) (1783) – Copy of no. 1 by Maurice O'Gorman.
4. BL Add. 4822 – See O'Sullivan 'Finding list', 80, 90.

LC – see Mac Niocaill, *MIA*, 40 for the sigla L1–3.
1. L4=BL Add. 4792, ff. 19–32 (*c.*1575–90).
2. L1–3=TCD 1293 (H.1.19) ff. 1–136 (1589–90).

MB – see Sanderlin, *PRIA* 82 C (1982) 112 for the sigla of nos. 1–8, 10–11.

1. B=BL Add. 4817 (1661).
2. A=Armagh Robinson Library, ff. 1–104 (1660).
3. T=TCD 673 (F.3.19) (1685).
4. N9=NLI 919 (1685?).
5. N7=NLI 767 (*p.* 1735).
6. R9=RIA 1048 (24.E.19) (saec. xviiii).
7. R1=RIA 1047 (24.E.11) (1842).
8. M=S. Patrick's Coll., Maynooth, O'Renehan vol. 63 (saec. xviiii).
9. Leipzig, Universitätbibliothek Albertina, Whitley Stokes MS., 1919 D 639 (1894).
10. W1=BL Add. 4787 (*c.*1650) – Citations only.
11. W2=BL Add. 4791 (*c.*1650) – Citations only.

FM – see Ó Muraíle, 'Autograph MSS', 75–6 for the sigla of nos. 1–4.

1. A= UCD OFM, A 13.
2. P= RIA 687–8 (23 P 6–7).
3. C= RIA 1220 (C.iii.3).
4. H= TCD 1301 (H. 2. 11).
5. RIA 988–9 (23.F.2–3) – A copy of no. 3 by Brennan in *c.*1781.
6. RIA 990–2 (23.F.4–6) (saec. xviii) – Copy by M. O'Gorman of 1397–1611.
7. TCD 1300 (H.2.9–10) (*c.*1734) – Copy of no. 3 by H. O'Molloy.
8. BL Add. 4784 (saec. xvii¹) – Post-Patrician excerpts.
9. BL Egerton 103 (saec xix) – Copy of no. 4 for 1334–1580 by E. O'Reilly.
10. TCD 1279 (H.1.3–5) (saec. xviii) – Copy of AM 2242–AD 1172 by M. O'Gorman.
11. RIA 568 (23.O.38) (saec. xix) – Copy of AD 76–919.

1. NLI G5–6 (saec. xv) – *Mac Carthaigh's Book*, see Ó hInnse (1947) 2–115.
2. Rawl. B. 488 ff. 27–8 (saec xv) – *Miscellaneous Annals I*, see Ó hInnse (1947) 116–42.
3. Rawl. B. 488 ff. 29–34 (saec xv) – *Miscellaneous Annals II*, see Ó hInnse (1947) 142–85.
4. Bruxelles Bibl. Royale 5301–20 pp. 1–70 – See Radner *Fragmentary Annals*.
5. TCD 1337 (H.3.18) end leaves (saec. xiv) – See Gwynn 'Fragmentary annals'.
6. BL Add. 30512 ff. 39ʳ–40ʳ (saec. xv) – See Mac Niocaill 'Ánnála Gearra'.
7. TCD 1372 (H.4.31) pp. 99, 100, 106 – See Walsh 'Memoranda'.
8. TCD 1293 (H.1.19) f. 140 – See Walsh 'Tirconaill Annals'.
9. RIA 936 (C.vi.1) pp. 480–4 – See Walsh 'Fir Manach Annals'.
10. TCD 1372 (H.4.31) pp. 98, 103 & H.4.25 pp. 190–1 – See Walsh 'Leinster Annals'.
11. Edinburgh NLS Gaelic MS 2, ff. 79, 88 (saec. xv) – See Mac Niocaill 'Cáipéisí'.
12. TCD 1281 (H.1.7) (1765) – 'Dublin Annals of Inisfallen', see Mac Airt, *AI*, vii–viii.
13. BL Egerton 98–9 (1783) – Copy and English translation of no. 12 for *c.*250–1320.
14. BL Egerton 96 (1808) – Lacunose copy of no. 13 over *c.*250–1320.
15. BL Egerton 97 (1820) – Copy of no. 14.
16. RIA 821 (3.B.18) (1830) – For *c.*250–1435 & attributed to Inisfallen.

Survey of Annalistic verse up to AD 1000

NOTES

1. All verse in AU MS H, except that at AU 856.6, 920.10, 1207.2, 1365.7–8, has been added marginally, mostly by Ua Luinín over 622–809. Mac Airt & Mac Niocaill record that he mostly inserted it *in prima manu* (H), but thereafter in his emending hand (H¹). Subsequently further quatrains were added by Ua Caiside (H²). These have been identified below as H=plain font, H¹=italic font, H²=bold font.

2. Most verses are quatrains=q, but at AD 484 and 738 there are lines=l. Peter Smith informs me that these quatrains are typically composed in the metric called *deibide*.

3. Verse certainly does not cease at AD 1000. AU has verse, inscribed by Ua Luinín and Ua Caiside as follows: AD 1004(2xH¹), 1006(H¹), 1013(H¹), 1020(H), 1022(2xH¹), 1024(H¹), 1032(H¹), 1049(H¹), 1056(H¹), 1060(H²), 1065(H²), 1067(H²), 1080(H²), 1086(2xH²), 1088(H²), 1099(H²), 1207(H), 1343(H), 1357(H), and 1365(H). This is the last verse in TCD 1282 but Rawl. B. 489 has a quatrain at 1536.

4. CS has post-1000 verse just at 1016 and 1022, and AT has the same quatrain at 1022, and while this and AU 1022 refer to the same event, Mael Seachnaill's death, the AT/CS quatrain differs from that of AU, evidently reflecting the contrasting Clonmacnoise and Armagh purviews.

5. Post-1000 verse is also found in CT at 1233.3, 1249.11, 1270.18, 1274.2–4, 1278.2, 1288.3, 1293.2, 1316.5, 1350.4, 1365.7, 1368.2, 1384.1, 1405.15 and 1562.1. In LC corresponding verse is found at 1233.3, 1249.15, 1270.7, 1274.1–3, 1278.1, 1288.2, 1293.1, 1384.2, and 1405.14.

6. Many of the pre-1000 verses listed below are found in FM, although Cunningham has noted that some in O'Donovan's edition are subsequent interpolations by Henry Burc and she has stated that FM's 'use of verse is very selective as compared with' AT/CS. However, FM also has unique pre-1000 verse and its verse continues to 1602.[1]

7. The pre-Incarnation verse is dated by Vulgate AM, while the sychronised AD has been used for all verse of the Christian era, and 'lac.' identifies all MS lacunae.

AM	Event	AT	CS	AR	AB	AI	Attribution
1656	Age 1 =1656 y.	lac.	1xq	–	–	lac.	an Gaoideal
–	Age 2 = 292 y.	lac.	1xq	1xq	–	lac.	poeta
1948	Age 2 ends at AM 1948	lac.	–	1xq	–	lac.	poeta
–	Age 3 = 942 y.	lac.	1xq	1xq	1xq	1xq	poeta, AB marginal.
2890	Age 3 ends at AM 2890	lac.	–	1xq	1xq	1xq	-, AB marginal.
–	Age 4 = 473 y.	lac.	lac.	1xq	1xq	1xq	poeta, AB marginal.

→

1 Cunningham, *Making FM*, 95 n. 82 (Henry Burc), 92 (cit.), 91–5 (verse in FM).

AM	Event	AT	CS	AR	AB	AI	Attribution
3363	Age 4 ends at AM 3363	–	lac.	1xq	1xq	1xq	poeta, AB marginal.
–	Age 5 = 589 y.	1xq	lac.	lac.	–	1xq	poeta
–	Incipit reg. Persarum – AI§171	–	lac.	lac.	–	2xq	–
–	Reg. Artaxerxes – AI§186	–	lac.	lac.	–	5xq	poeta
–	Reg. Darius Arsami – AI§191	–	lac.	lac.	–	2xq	poeta
–	Reg. Alexander – AI§193	–	lac.	lac.	–	4xq	file
3952	Incarnation at AM 3952	1xq[2]	lac	lac	–	1xq	poeta

AD	Event	AT	CS	AR	AU	AI	Attribution
1	Age 6 starts at AM 3952	1xq	–	lac.	lac.	1xq	poeta
352	Eochaid Muigmedon reg.	1xq	–	–	–	–	–
462	Mors Laeghaire	lac.	1xq	–	–	–	Poeta
484	Oilill Molt tuitim	lac.	10xl	lac.	–	–	Bec Mac De
489	Cath Cella Asnada	2xq	1xq	lac.	–	–	–
491	Patricius q.	1xq	1xq	lac.	1xq[3]	–	–
501	Cath Seghsa	2xq	2xq	lac.	–	–	Cendfaelad
507	Cath Fern Midhi	1xq	1xq	lac.	–	–	–
513	Q. Earc	1xq	1xq	lac.	–	–	Patricius
514	Cath Droma	1xq	1xq	lac.	2xq[4]	–	Cendfaeladh
520	Colamcille natus	1xq	1xq	lac.	–	–	–
525	Cath Luachra	1xq	1xq	lac.	–	–	–
531	Cath Eiblinde	1xq	1xq	lac.	–	–	Cendfaeladh
532	Bádudh Muircertaig	7xq	6xq	lac.	–	–	S. Ceirnecho (CS)
533	Dormitatio Mochtai	2xq	–	lac.	–	–	–
542	Cath Sligighe	2xq	2xq	lac.	–	–	–
543	Obit Ciaran	1xq	1xq	lac.	–	–	Ciaran
558	Cluana ferta fund.	1xq	1xq	–	–	–	–
560	Cath Chuile Dremni	3xq	3xq	2xq	–	–	Coluimcille
562	Cath Mona Daire	4xq	4xq	–	5xq	–	Cendfaeladh
565	Cath Gabra Life	2xq	–	–	–	–	–
568	Bas Ainmereach	1xq	1xq	–	1xq	–	–
572	Cath Femin	1xq	–	–	–	1xq[5]	AT -, AI Patricius
572	Brenaind Birra q.	1xq	–	–	–	–	–
585	Cath Bhealaig	1xq	1xq[6]	–	–	–	–
592	Cath Eudhuind	1xq	–	–	–	–	–
593	Q. Coluimcille	1xq	1xq	1xq	–	–	–
595	Bass Cumascaigh	1xq	–	–	–	–	–
596	Cath Duin Bolc	2xq	2xq	–	–	–	coniungs [i.e. Aed's wife]
602	Iug. Colman Rimedha	1xq	1xq	–	1xq	–	→

2 In AT this quatrain is anachronistically located at the *start* of Age 5.   3 AU's quatrain is only in Rawl. B. 489 and while on the same theme it differs from that in AT and CS.   4 These two quatrains are by Ua Luinín at AU 515.1, the second of which is repeated by Ua Caiside at AU 516.3.   5 AI's quatrain differs from that of AT.   6 The quatrain appears to be misplaced in CS.

AD	Event	AT	CS	AR	AU	AI	Attribution
602	Iug. Aedh Slaine	1xq	1xq	–	*1xq*	1xq[7]	AT/CS/AU -; AI Aed Alláin.
602	Iug. Aedha Roin	–	1xq	lac.	**1xq**	–	–
603	Bas Brannduib	1xq	1xq	lac.	**1xq**	–	–
603	Saran Saebderg	2xq	2xq	lac.	**1xq**	–	Caillech Laigen
608	Bass Aeda m. Colgon	2xq	2xq	lac.	–	–	–
610	Cath Odhba	1xq	1xq	lac.	–	–	–
617	Bass Fergusa	2xq	–	lac.	**2xq**	–	–
618	Aedh Bennan q.	2xq	–	lac.	–	–	–
618	Fingen mac Aedha m.	1xq	–	lac.	–	–	Coniunx Fingen
622	Conaing dimersus	2xq	2xq	–	1xq	–	Nindine eices
623	Expugnacio Ratha Guala	1xq	–	–	1xq	–	Fiacha
625	Guin Dóir m. Aedha	1xq	–	–	–	–	Failbe Fland
625	Guin Dóir m. Aedha	1xq	1xq	–	–	–	Mathair Dóir
626	Mongan interit	3xq	3xq[8]	–	2xq	–	Bec Boirche
628	Bellum Cairn Feradhaigh	–	–	–	1xq	–	–
631	Cath Dúine Ceithirn	1xq	–	–	–	–	–
643	Domnall Brecc interfectus	–	–	–	2xq	–	Cuimméne
648	Mael coba iugulatus	1xq	–	–	–	–	–
649	Ragallach mac Uatach	3xq	–	–	–	–	–
649	Bellum Cairn Conaill	–	–	–	2xq[9]	–	Guaire
651	Guin da mac Blaithmeic	2xq	2xq	–	3xq	–	Maelodran (AU)
654	Fursu pausauit	1xq	–	1xq	–	–	–
657	Mors Ceallaig	–	–	–	**1xq**	–	–
662	Cummeni & Saran q.	–	–	–	**1xq**	–	–
669	Mors Maele Fothartaigh	–	–	–	1xq[10]	–	Cenn Faelad
671	Iugulatio Seachnusaigh	1xq	1xq	–	1xq	–	–
688	Bellum Imlecho Pich	–	–	–	4xq	–	Gabaircenn
695	Cath Grellaigh	2xq[11]	–	–	2xq	–	Moling
695	Cath Grellaigh	1xq	–	–	–	–	Adhomnan
722	Cath Almuine	3xq	3xq	–	–	–	Cú Bretan
722	Cath Almuine	3xq	3xq	–	–	–	Nuadha hua Lomthuile
738	Cath Senaig/Uchbad	1xq	lac.	–	–	–	Samthand
738	Cath Senaig/Uchbad	2xq	lac.	–	–	–	[Quidam]
738	Cath Senaig/Uchbad	1xl	lac.	–	–	–	Aedh Allain fein
742	Cathal m. Finguine mor.	–	lac.	–	–	1xq	Mór Muman
743	Bellum Serethmaighe	–	lac.	–	1xq	–	Aedha Aldan
747	Cú Cuimne obiit	–	lac.	–	2xq	–	Muine Chon Cuimne
759	Bellum Emnae Machae	–	lac.	–	4xq	–	–
764	Frosa i Crich Muiredaigh	–	lac.	–	3xq	–	–
778	Cath Forcalait	lac.	lac.	–	1xq	–	–
780	Fuga Ruadrach	lac.	lac.	–	1xq	–	–
781	Bellum Rige	lac.	lac.	–	1xq	–	–

→

7 AI's quatrain differs from that of AT/CS/AU. **8** CS splits its first quatrain from its second and third quatrains with obits relevant to the latter two. **9** AU hand not identified by Mac Airt & Mac Niocaill, *AU*. **10** Quatrain by Ua Luinín and attribution by Ua Caiside. **11** AT has Adomnán's quatrain between Moling's two quatrains.

AD	Event	AT	CS	AR	AU	AI	Attribution
784	Rigdal Donnchad & Fiachnae	lac.	lac.	–	1xq	–	–
797	Mors Innrechtaigh	lac.	lac.	–	1xq	–	–
797	Bellum Droma Rigin	lac.	lac.	–	1xq	–	–
809	Indredh nUlad	lac.	–	–	2xq	–	–
810	Uastatio Luighne	lac.	–	–	1xq	–	–
815	Mors Muirgusa	lac.	–	–	1xq	–	–
824	Orggain Benncair	lac.	–	–	1xq	–	–
834	Ceallach m. Brain mor.	lac.	–	–	1xq	–	–
840	Innriud Mide & Breg	lac.	–	–	1xq	–	–
841	Slogad la Neill	lac.	–	–	1xq	–	–
846	Niall m. Aedha mor.	lac.	–	–	1xq	–	–
851	Cinaedh m. Conaing demers.	lac.	–	–	1xq	–	–
857	[Synchronism on Nicaea]	lac.	–	–	1xq[12]	–	Cellach
868	Bellum Cill Oa nDaighri	lac.	–	–	2xq	–	–
878	Garfith decollatus	lac.	–	–	2xq	–	–
879	Aedh m. Neill dorm.	lac.	–	–	2xq	–	–
883	Braen m. Tigernaigh occ.	lac.	–	–	1xq	–	–
887	Mael Mura mor.	lac.	–	–	2xq	–	–
895	Cellach iug.	lac.	–	–	1xq	–	–
895	Ard Macha do orcain	lac.	–	–	1xq	–	–
903	Mael Finnia mor.	lac.	–	–	3xq	–	–
908	Bellum Bealaigh Mugnai	lac.	3xq	–	–	–	[Dallan mac Mór]
909	Cerball mor.	lac.	1xq	–	–	–	–
912	Muiredhach & Gairbith [m.]	lac.	–	–	2xq	–	–
914	Slogad la Niall	lac.	–	–	1xq	–	–
915	Oengus h Mael Sechnaill m.	lac.	–	–	1xq	–	–
916	Flann defunctus	lac.	1xq	–	–	–	–
919	Bellum re nGentibh	lac.	–	–	4xq	–	–
921	Flaithbertach mor.	lac.	–	–	1xq[13]	–	–
923	Ligach mor.	lac.	1xq	–	–	–	Gilla Mochuda
929	Ceile q. [synchronism on AD]	lac.	–	–	1xq	–	–
929	Slogadh la Donnchad	lac.	–	–	1xq	–	–
943	Muirchertach do m.	lac.	–	–	1xq	–	–
980	Domnall H. Neill obiit	–	–	–	3xq	–	Mac Coisse
980	Murgon fin.	–	–	–	1xq	–	–

12 This synchronism by Ua Luinín (H) is *not* marginal and it remarks 533 years from Nicaea, which took place in AD 325, and from 325 to 857 is indeed 533 years when reckoned inclusively, viz. (857-325)+1=533. 13 This quatrain by Ua Luinín (H) is *not* marginal.

The regnal-canon

The following tables represent a reduced version of the online collation at:

www.irish-annals.cs.tcd.ie

Specifically, the regnal years and remarks have been removed, so that it will fit across one page.

Sigla, editions and references

The following are the sigla used for the different editions included in this collation, and also the methods used to reference them:

LS   K. Meyer, 'The Laud synchronisms', referenced by page and line number.

AI   S. Mac Airt, *AI*, referenced using Mac Airt's paragraph numbers §345–86.

EE   The poem *Eremon is Eber ard* of which no published edition exists, so the facsimile in K. Mulchrone, *The Book of Lecan* facsimile ff. 33^{r-v} has been used. It has been referenced by its facsimile line number prefixed by a=33ra, b=33rb, c=33va, d=33vb. The earlier copy at ff. 14–15 is missing two verses.

FL   Flann Mainistreach – R. Best & M O'Brien, *The Book of Leinster* iii, 504–15 for the poems *Rig Themra dia tesband tnú* §§1–35 and *Rig Themra toebaige iar tain* §§1–52, which have been referenced by their quatrain number.

GC   Gilla Cóemáin's poems, *Hériu ard inis na rrig* §§1–151, and *At-tá sund forba fessa* §§1–37 which are numbered thus by Peter Smith in his critical edition, *Three historical poems ascribed to Gilla Cóemáin – A critical edition of the work of an eleventh-century Irish scholar*. See also the editions in Best & O'Brien *The Book of Leinster* iii, 471–503.

LL   The *Book of Leinster* i edition of *Lebor Gabála* by R. Best, O. Bergin, & M. O'Brien whose reigns have been referenced by their line number. This is the earliest edition of LG *a* and its regnal years are virtually identical with those tabulated under LG.

LG   R.A.S. Macalister's *Lebor Gabála Érenn* i–v, referenced by his paragraph numbers, and the reign references have been taken from LG *a* = LG R^1.

MB   Mageoghagan's Book, i.e. D. Murphy, *Annals of Clonmacnoise*, referenced by page and line number.

SR   Michéal Ó Clérigh's *Seanchas Riogh Fireann* of 1630 from P. Walsh *Genealogiae Regum et Sanctorum Hiberniae*, referenced by paragraph number.

FM   J. O'Donovan, *Annala Rioghachta Eireann – Annals of the Kingdom of Ireland* i–vi, has been referenced by the FM year and CELT entry number.

AD   In Table 3 the synchronized AD of the obits of the post-Patrician kings have been cited.

TABLE I. KINGS OF IRELAND FOR THE PRE-CHRISTIAN ERA — CEASAIR TO
EOCHAIDH FEIDHLEACH

Pre-Incarnation regnal references

Reign	LS	EE	GC	LG	LL	MB	SR	FM
1. Ceasair et al.	–	–	1–4	166	440	11.15	–	2242.1
2. Partholón et al.	–	–	5–6	199	475	13.3	–	2520.1
3. Neimidh et al.	–	–	7–13	237	608	14.21	–	2850.1
Fir Bolg	–	–	14–18	278	857	14.18	–	3266.1
4. Slainghe m. Deala	471.3	–	19	280	877	16.17	1	3267.1
5. Rudhruidhe	471.5	–	20	280	878	16.17	2	3269.1
6. Gann & Geanann	471.5	–	20	280	879	16.18	3	3273.1
7. Sengainn	471.6	–	21	280	880	16.19	4	3278.1
8. Fiacha	471.7	–	21	280	881	16.19	5	3283.1
9. Rionnál	471.8	–	22	280	883	16.20	6	3289.1
10. Foidhbhgen	471.9	–	22	280	884	16.21	7	3293.1
11. Eachdhach m. Erc	471.10	–	23	280	886	16.21	8	3303.1
Tuaithe de Danonn	–	–	–	306	1049	17.13	–	3303.1
12. Bres	471.14	–	25	310	1073	17.24	1	3310.1
13. Nuadhat Argatlaimh	471.13	–	24	310	1074	17.29	2	3330.1
14. Lugh Lamhfada	471.15	–	26	312	1097	18.1	3	3370.1
15. Eochaidh Ollathar	471.16	–	27	313	1106	18.3	4	3450.1
16. Dealbhaeith	471.17	–	28	315	1124	18.3	5	3460.1
17. Fiachaidh m. Dealbhaeith	471.19	–	28	315	1125	18.4	6	3470.1
18. Mac Cuill, Mac Cecht, & Mac Greine	471.20	–	29–30	315	1128	18.4	7	3500.1
Rioghaibh M. Mileadh	471.25	–	–	386, 469	1457	21.15	–	3500.1
19. Ereamhón & Éber	–	a.11	31	471	–	28.5	1	
20. Ereamhón	474.20	a.14	32	472	1822	28.13	1	3516.1
21. Muimhne et al.	474.23	a.16	33	499	1859	30.13	2	3519.1
22. Er et al.	–	–	34	500	1861	28.11	3	3519.2
23. Irial Fáidh	474.25	a.18	35	501	1864	31.1	4	3529.1
24. Ethrel m. Ireoil	474.26	a.20	36	502	1913	31.10	5	3549.1
25. Conmaol m. Emhir	474.27	a.22	37	504	1992	31.14	6	3579.1
26. Tighernmas	474.29	a.26	38	505	2020	31.19	7	3656.1
27. Ere gan rígh	–	–	–	–	–	–	8	3663.1
28. Eochaidh Eudgadhach	474.34	a.28	39	506	2034	–	9	3667.1
29. Sobairce & Cermna	475.1	b.8	40–1	507	2098	32.14	10	3707.1
30. Eochaidh Faobarghlas	475.3	–	42	508	2169	32.24	11	3727.1
31. Fiachach Labhrainne	475.4	a.30	43	509	2207	32.30	12	3751.1
32. Eochaidh Mumo	475.5	a.32	44	510	2213	33.8	13	3772.1
33. Aenghus Olmucadha	475.6	a.34	45	511	2231	33.10	14	3790.1
34. Enna Airgthech	475.8	a.36	46	512	2308	33.18	15	3817.1
35. Roitheachtaigh m. Maoin	475.9	a.38	47	513	2312	33.22	16	3842.1
36. Sédna m. Airtri	475.10	b.13	48	514	2315	33.24	17	3847.1
37. Fiachaidh Fionscothach	475.11	b.17–19	49	515	2317	33.26	18	3867.1
38. Muineamhón	475.12	a.40	50	516	2322	34.1	19	3872.1
39. Failderdóid	475.13	a.42	51	517	2325	34.5	20	3882.1

→

	Pre-Incarnation regnal references							
Reign	LS	EE	GC	LG	LL	MB	SR	FM
40. Ollamh Fothla	475.15	b.25	52	518	2331	34.9	21	3922.1
41. Fionnachta	475.21	b.29	53	519	2335	35.6	22	3942.1
42. Slanoll	475.22	b.31	54	520	2338	35.9	23	3959.1
43. Ghedhe	475.24	b.33	55	521	2341	35.15	24	3971.1
44. Fiachaidh Fionnailches	475.25	b.35	56	522	2344	35.23	25	3991.1
45. Bernghal	475.27	b.39	57	523	2346	35.27	26	4003.1
46. Oilioll m. Slanuill	475.28	b.37	58	524	2348	35.32	27	4019.1
47. Siorna	475.32	a.44	59–60	525	2400	36.1	28	4169.1
48. Rotheachtaigh m. Roain	475.42	a.46	61	526	2445	36.13	29	4176.1
49. Elim	476.1	a.48	62	527	2448	36.16	30	4177.1
50. Giallchaidh	476.2	b.1	63	528	2450	36.19	31	4186.1
51. Art Imleach	476.6	b.4	64	529	2453	36.23	32	4198.1
52. Nuadha Fionn	476.7	b.6	65	530	2455	36.26	33	4238.1
53. Breas	476.8	d.20	66	531	2457	36.29	34	4247.1
54. Eochaidh Apthach	476.9	–	67	532	2459	36.34	35	4248.1
55. Fionn m. Bratha	476.10	–	68	533	2461	37.6	36	4270.1
56. Sédhna Ionnarraidh	476.11	–	69	534	2466	37.8	37	4290.1
57. Siomón Brec	476.12	–	70	535	2467	37.12	38	4296.1
58. Duach Fionn	476.13	b.15	71	536	2469	37.15	39	4306.1
59. Muiredhach Bolgrach	476.14	–	72	537	2471	37.18	40	4307.1
60. Enna Derg	476.15	b.21	73	538	2473	37.20	41	4319.1
61. Lughaidh Iardonn	476.17	b.23	74	539	2475	37.22	42	4328.1
62. Siorlamh	476.18	b.47	75	540	2477	37.24	43	4344.1
63. Eochaidh Uairches	476.19	b.27	76	541	2479	–	44	4356.1
64. Eochaidh Fiadhmuine & Conaing Begeaglach	476.20	–	77	542	2487	37.28	45	4361.1
65. Lughaidh Laimhderg	476.22	–	78	543	2490	37.32	46	4368.1
66. Conaing Begeaglach	476.24	–	79	544	2491	37.33	47	4388.1
67. Art m. Luighdheach	476.26	b.41	80	545	2494	38.1	48	4394.1
68. Fiachaidh m. Muiredhaig	–	–	80A	–	–	–	49	4404.1
69. Oilioll Fionn	476.27	b.45	81	546	2497	38.3	50	4415.1
70. Eochaidh m. Oiliolla	476.28	b.49	82–3	547	2505	38.12	51	4422.1
71. Airgetmar	473.24	c.1	84	548	2508	38.18	52	4452.1
72. Duach Ladhgrach	473.25	b.43	85	549	2510	38.21	53	4462.1
73. Lughaidh Laghdhe	473.26	c.3	86	550	2512	38.23	54	4469.1
'réim riograidhe'	–	–	–	–	–	–	59	–
74. Aodh Ruadh	473.27	c.6	87	–	2514	38.25	60	4476.1
75. Diothorba	–	c.8	88	–	2514	38.25	61	4483.1
76. Ciombaoth	173.?8	c.10	89	551	2514	38.27	62	4490.1
77. Aodh Ruadh	473.27	c.6	87	–	2514	38.32	63	4497.1
78. Diothorba	–	c.8	88	–	2514	38.32	64	4504.1
79. Ciombaoth	473.28	c.10	89	551	2514	38.32	65	4511.1
80. Aodh Ruadh	473.27	c.6	87	–	2514	38.32	66	4518.1
81. Diothorba	–	c.8	88	–	2514	38.32	67	4525.1
82. Cimbaoth	473.28	c.10	89	551	2514	38.32	68	4532.1

→

					Pre-Incarnation regnal references			
Reign	LS	EE	GC	LG	LL	MB	SR	FM
83. Macha & Cimbaoth	–	–	89	551	2514	38.32	69	4539.1
84. Macha	473.29	c.9	90	552	2699	39.26	70	4546.1
85. Reachtaidh Righderg	473.32	c.12	91	553	2702	41.23	71	4566.1
86. Ughaine Mhór	473.33	c.15	92	554	2706	41.32	72	4606.1
87. Badbchadh m. Eathdhach	–	–	92A	–	–	–	73	4606.2
88. Laoghaire Lorc	473.37	–	93	555	2789	43.23	74	4608.1
89. Cobhthach Caol	473.38	c.17	94	556	2782	43.24	75	4658.1
90. Labhraidh Loingseach	474.1	c.19	95	557	2799	44.13	76	4677.1
91. Melghe Molbthach	474.2	c.22	96	558	2802	44.23	77	4694.1
92. Modh Corb	474.3	c.24	97	559	2805	44.25	78	4701.1
93. Aengus Ollamh	474.4	c.26	98	560	2807	44.28	79	4719.1
94. Irereo m. Melghe	474.5	c.28	99	561	2809	44.31	80	4726.1
95. Fior Corb	474.6	c.30	100	562	2810	45.1	81	4737.1
96. Conla Caomh	474.7	–	101	563	2812	45.3	82	4757.1
97. Oilill Caisfhiaclach	474.8	c.32	102	564	2813	45.5	83	4782.1
98. Adamar m. Fir Cuirb	474.9	c.34	103	565	2815	45.8	84	4787.1
99. Eochaidh Ailtlethan	474.10	c.36	104	566	2817	45.9	85	4804.1
100. Fearghus Fortamhail	474.11	c.38	105	567	2818	45.11	86	4815.1
101. Aenghus Tuirmeach	474.12	c.40	106	568	2819	45.13	87	4875.1
102. Conall Collamrach	472.20	–	107	569	2833	45.21	88	4880.1
103. Nia Sedhamain	472.21	c.42	108	570	2835	45.23	89	4887.1
104. Enna Aighnech	472.22	d.30	109	571	2836	45.24	90	4907.1
105. Criomhthann	472.23	–	110	572	2838	45.27	91	4911.1
106. Rudhruighe	472.24	c.44	111	573	2839	46.1	92	4981.1
107. Ionnat Mar	472.26	c.45	112	574	2870	46.14	93	4990.1
108. Breasal Bóidiobhadh	472.27	c.46	113	575	2872	46.17	94	5001.1
109. Lughaidh Luaighne	472.28	c.48	114	576	2875	46.27	95	5016.1
110. Congal Claroinech	472.29	c.50	115	577	2877	46.29	96	5031.1
111. Duach Dallta	472.30	d.2	116	578	2878	47.1	97	5041.1
112. Fachtna Fathach	472.31	d.3	117	579	2879	47.6	98	5057.1
113. Eochaidh Feidhleach	472.32	d.5	118	580	2880	47.15	99	5069.1

TABLE 2. KINGS OF IRELAND FOR THE PRE-PATRICIAN ERA
EOCHAIDH FEIDHLEACH TO DATHÍ M. FIACHRACH

Reign	Pre-Patrician regnal references							
	LS	FL	GC	LG	LL	MB	SR	FM
113. Eochaidh Feidhleach	472.32	2	118	580	2880	47.15	99	5069.1
114. Eochaidh Airemh	473.1	3	119	581	2881	48.1	100	5084.1
115. Ederscel m. Eoghain	473.2	4	120	582	2883	48.4	101	5089.1
116. Nuadha Necht	473.3	5	121	583	2889	48.6	102	5090.1
117. Conaire Mór	473.4	6	122	584	2891	48.9	103	5160.1
118. Erinn gan rígh iar c-Conaire	–	–	123	–	–	–	104	5165.1
119. Lughaidh Sriabh	476.31	7	124	585	2893	49.1	105	5191.1
120. Concubhar Abhradhruadh	476.35	8	124	586	2895	49.13	106	5192.1
121. Criomhthann Nia Nair	476.37	9	125	587	2897	49.16	107	9.1
122. Chairbre Caitcend	476.40	10	126	588	2903	49.25	108	14.1
123. Feradhach Fiond	477.1	11	127	589	2905	50.12	109	36.1
124. Fiatach Fionn	477.4	12	128	590	2907	50.14	110	39.1
125. Fiachaidh Fionnfolaidh	477.5	13	129	591	2909	50.17	111	56.1
126. Elim m. Conrach	477.8	14	130	592	2910	50.19	112	76.1
127. Tuathal Techtmar	477.15	15	131	593	2924	52.11	113	106.1
128. Mal m. Rochraidhe	477.22	16	132	594	2952	54.23	114	110.1
129. Feidlimidh Reachtmhar	477.23	17	132	595	2955	54.26	115	119.1
130. Cathaoir Mor	477.25	18	133	596	2959	57.5	116	122.1
131. Conn Cedcathach	477.27	19	134	597	2961	58.8	117	157.1
132. Chonaire m. Modha	477.35	20	135	598	2963	59.30	118	165.1
133. Art m. Cuinn	477.37	21	136	599	2964	59.32	119	195.1
134. Lughaidh m. Niadha	477.42	22	137	600	2967	60.1	120	225.1
135. Ferghus Duibhdhedach	478.1	23	138	601	2969	60.3	121	226.1
136. Corbmac m. Airt	478.3	24	139	602	2971	60.5	122	266.1
137. Eochaidh Gondat	478.7	25	140	603	2974	60.24	123	267.1
138. Cairbre Liffechair	478.10	26	141	604	2975	60.26	124	284.1
139. da Fothadh	478.13	27	142	605	2977	62.16	125	285.1
140. Fiachaidh Sraibhtine	478.15	28	143	606	2980	62.19	126	322.1
141. Colla Uais	478.16	29	144	607	2982	63.4	127	326.1
142. Muireadhach Tíreach	478.18	30	145	608	2983	63.17	128	356.1
143. Caolbhadh m. Cruinn	478.20	31	146	609	2985	63.21	129	357.1
144. Eochaidh Muighmhedhoin	478.21	32	146	610	2987	63.23	130	365.1
145. Criomhthann m. Fiodhaigh	478.22	33	147	611	2988	64.8	131	378.1
146. Niall Naoighiallach	478.23	34	148	612	2990	64.18	132	405.1
147. Dathí m. Fiachrach	478.24	35	149	613	2992	64.31	133	428.1

TABLE 3. KINGS OF CHRISTIAN IRELAND FOR THE PRE-NORMAN ERA LAOGHAIRE M. NÉILL TO RUAIDHRÍ UA CONCHOBHAIR

Post-Patrician regnal references

Reign	LS	FL	GC	AI	LG	LL	MB	SR	FM	AD
148. Laoghaire m. Néill	478.25	1–2	1	345	614	2999	65.3	1	458.1	462
149. Oilill Molt	478.30	3	2	346	615	3002	71.24	2	478.1	484
150. Lughaidh m. Laoghaire	478.32	4	3	347	616	3009	73.2	3	503.1	509
151. Muirchertach m. Muiredhoigh	478.35	5	3	348	617	3013	75.3	4	527.1	532
152. Tuathal Maolgarbh	479.1	6	4	349	618	3018	78.1	5	538.1	543
153. Diarmaitt m. Cerrbeoil	479.3	7	4	350	619	3024	80.27	6	558.1	563
154. Domhnall & Feargus mm. Muirchertaigh	479.8	8	5	351	620	3029	88.27	7	561.1	565
155. Eochaidh m. Domnaill & Baodan m. Muircheartaigh	479.10	9	5	353	621	3032	88.29	8	563.2	571
156. Ainmire m. Sedna	479.12	10	5	352	622	3036	90.10	9	566.1	568
157. Baodan m. Nindeadha	479.13	11	6	–	623	3037	88.28	10	567.1	584
158. Aodh m. Ainmirech	479.15	12	6	354	624	3039	90.13	11	594.1	596
159. Aodh Sláine & Colman Rimidh	479.16	13–14	7	355	625	3044	97.7	12	600.4	603
160. Aodh Uairiodhnach	479.19	15	7	356	626	3049	98.24	13	607.1	610
161. Maol Cobha m. Aodha	479.20	16	8	357	627	3052	98.25	14	610.3	613
162. Suibhne Meann	479.21	17	8	358	628	3055	99.19	15	623.2	630
163. Domhnall m. Aodha	479.23	18	8	359	629	3060	100.25	16	639.2	643
164. Chonall & Cheallach mm. Maol Cobo	479.27	19–20	9	360	630	3064	103.13	17	656.2	653
165. Diarmait & Blathmac mm. Aodha Sláine	479.29	21	9	361	631	3068	107.6	18	664.2	664
166. Seachnusach m. Blaithmic	479.30	22	10	362	632	3071	107.23	19	669.1	671
167. Cend Faoladh m. Blaithmic	479.31	23	10	363	633	3074	108.17	20	673.1	675
168. Fionachta Fleadhach m. Dunchadha	479.32	24	10	364	634	3076	108.31	21	693.3	695
169. Loingseach m. Aongusa	479.34	25	11	365	635	3080	110.30	22	701.2	703
170. Congal Cinn Maghair	479.35	26	11	367	636	3083	112.5	23	708.3	710
171. Ferghal m. Maoile Dúin	479.36	27	11	368	637	3085	112.7	24	718.1	722
172. Fogartach m. Néill	479.38	28	12	369, 366	638	3087	113.1	25	719.1	724
173. Cionaedh m. Iorgalaigh	479.39	29	12	370	639	3089	115.14	26	722.2	728
174. Flaitbertach m. Loingsigh	479.41	30	12	371	640	3092	115.15	27	729.1	734
175. Aodh Allan m. Ferghaile	479.42	31	12	372	641	3094	115.17	28	738.4	743
176. Domhnall m. Murchadha	479.43	32	13	373	642	3097	118.2	29	758.6	763
177. Niall Frosach m. Ferghaile	480.28	33	13	374	643	3099	121.5	30	765.17	770
178. Donnchadh m. Domhnaill	480.29	34	14	375	644	3102	122.17	31	792.1	797
179. Aodh Oirdnidhe m. Néill	480.30	35	14	376	645	3104	128.6	32	817.11	819

→

Post-Patrician regnal references

Reign	LS	FL	GC	AI	LG	LL	MB	SR	FM	AD
180. Conchobhar m. Donnchada	480.31	36	15	377	646	3108	130.30	33	831.1	833
181. Niall Caille m. Aedha Oirdnidhe	480.34	37	15	378	647	–	135.14	34	844.16	846
182. Mael Sechlainn m. Mael Ruanaidh	480.35	38	16	379	648	3112	140.24	35	860.10	862
183. Aodh Fhinnliath m. Néill Caille	480.36	39	16	380	649	3117	141.3	36	876.15	879
184. Flann Sionna m. Maoilechlainn	481.1	40	17	381	650	3120	144.1	37	914.10	916
185. Niall Glúndubh m. Aedha Finnleith	481.2	41	17	382	651	3126	145.18	38	917.7	919
186. Donnchadh m. Floinn	481.3	42	18	383	652	3128	146.24	39	942.13	944
187. Conghalach m. Maoil Mithigh	481.4	43	18	384	653	3131	154.13	40	954.7	956
188. Domhnall m. Muirchertaigh	481.5	44	19	–	654	3135	157.3	41	978.4	980
189. Maolsechlainn Mór m. Domhnaill	481.6	45–6	20	–	655	3139	158.32	42	1001.1	1004
190. Briain m. Cinnéittigh	481.7	47	20	385	656	3145	165.24	43	1013.1	1014
191. Maoileachlainn Mór m. Domhnaill	481.8	48–9	20A	386	657	3149	168.1	44	1022.2	1022
192. Diarmait m. Mael na mBó	–	–	–	–	658	3158	173.2, 176.25	–	1072.3	1072
193. Toirrdhealbhach Ua Briain	–	–	–	–	659	3167	180.23	1	1086.9	1086
194. Muirchertach Ua Briain	–	–	–	–	660	3170	184.27	2	1119.4	1119
195. Toirrdhealbhach Ua Conchobhair	–	–	–	–	661	3184	189.27	3	1156.9	1156
196. Muirchertach Ua Lachlainn	–	–	–	–	662	3198	201.5	4	1166.11	1166
197. Ruaidhri m. Toirrdelbaig Ua Conchobhair	–	–	–	–	663	3202	206.11	5	1198.2	1198

Bibliography

Abbot, T., & Gwynn, E.   *Catalogue of the Irish manuscripts in the Library of Trinity College Dublin* (Dublin 1921).

Anderson, A.O.   *Early sources of Scottish history, AD 500 to 1286* i–ii (Edinburgh and London 1922).

Anderson A.O., & Anderson M.O. (eds)   *Adomnan's Life of Columba* (Edinburgh 1961; Oxford 1991).

Anderson, M.O.   *Kings and kingship in early Scotland* (Edinburgh and London 1973).

Anscombe, A.   'Dr Mac Carthy's lunar computations', *ZCP* 4 (1903) 332–8.

Atkinson, R. (ed.)   *Book of Ballymote: a photographic facsimile with introduction* (Dublin 1887).

Baillie, M.G.L.   'Marking in marker dates – towards historical precision', *World Archaeology* 23:2 (1991) 233–43.

Baillie, M.G.L.   'Dendrochronology raises questions about the nature of the AD 536 dust-veil event', *The Holocene* 4:2 (1994) 212–17.

Baillie, M.G.L.   'Patrick, comets and Christianity', *Emania* 13 (1995) 69–78.

Bannerman, J.   'Notes on the Scottish entries in the early Irish annals', *Scottish Gaelic Studies* xi (1968) 149–70, repr. in his *Studies*, 9–26.

Bannerman, J.   *Studies in the history of Dalriada* (Edinburgh 1974).

Barnard, T., Ó Cróinín, D., & Simms, K. (eds)   *A miracle of learning* (Aldershot and Brookfield VT 1998).

Bernard, E.   *Catalogi Librorum Manuscriptorum Angliae et Hiberniae* (Oxford 1697).

Best, R.I. (ed.)   'The Leabhar Oiris', *Ériu* i (1904) 74–112.

Best, R.I.   'Palaeographical notes – the Rawlinson B 502 Tigernach', *Ériu* 7 (1914) 38–57.

Best, R.I.   'The Yellow Book of Lecan', *Jnl. of Celtic Studies* I (1949–50) 190–8.

Best, R.I., Bergin, O., & O'Brien, M.A. (eds)   *The Book of Leinster formerly Lebar na Núachongbála* i–v (Dublin 1954–67). See also A. O'Sullivan.

Best, R.I., & Mac Neill, E. (eds)   *The Annals of Inisfallen reproduced in facsimile …* (Dublin and London 1933).

Bhreathnach, E.   'Two contributors to the Book of Leinster – bishop Fin and Gilla na Náem Úa Duinn' in M. Richter & J.-M. Picard (eds), *Ogma: essays in Celtic studies in honour of Próinséas Ní Chatháin* (Dublin 2002) 105–14.

Bhreathnach, E.   *The kingship and landscape of Tara* (Dublin 2005).

Bhreathnach, E., &   *'Baile Chuinn Chétchathaig*: Edition' in Bhreathnach, *Kingship of*
Murray, K. (eds)   *Tara* (2005) 73–94.

Bieler, L.   *The life and legend of St Patrick* (Dublin 1949).

Bieler, L. (ed.)   'Adamnan *De locis sanctis*' in CCSL 175 (Turnhout 1965) 219–97.

Bieler, L. (ed.)   *The Patrician texts in the Book of Armagh* (Dublin 1979).

Bieler, L. (ed.)   *Clavis Patricii II: Libri Epistolarum Sancti Patricii Episcopi* (Dublin 1993).

Binchy, D.   'Lawyers and chroniclers', in B. Ó Cuív, *Seven centuries of Irish learning 1000–1700* (Cork 1961, repr. 1971) 50–61.

Binchy, D.   'Patrick and his biographers: ancient and modern', *Studia Hibernica* 2 (1962) 7–173.

Bindon, S.H.   'On the MSS. relating to Ireland in the Burgundian Library at Brussels', *PRIA* iii (1846–7) 477–502.

Boyle, A.   'Fearghal Ó Gadhra and the Four Masters', *IER* 100 (1963) 100–14.

Breatnach, P.   'Irish records of the Nine Years' War: a brief survey, with particular notice of the relationship between Beatha Aodha Ruaidh Uí Dhomhnaill and the Annals of the Four Masters' in P. Ó Riain (ed.), *Beatha Aodha Ruaidh* (London 2002) 124–47.

Burgess, R.W.   'Dates and editions of Eusebius' *Chronici canones* and *Historia ecclesiastica*', *Journal of Theological Studies* NS 48:2 (1997) 471–504.

Byrne, F.J.   'The Ireland of St Columba' in J.L. McCracken (ed.), *Historical Studies* 5 (1965) 37–58.

Byrne, F.J.   'Seventh-century documents', *IER* 108 (1967) 164–82.

Byrne, F.J.   *Irish kings and high kings* (London 1973, 1987; repr. Dublin 2001).

Byrne, F.J.   *1000 years of Irish script* (Oxford 1979).

Byrne, F.J.   *'Ut Beda boat:* Cuanu's signature?', in P. Ní Catháin and M. Richter (eds), *Ireland and Europe in the Early Middle Ages: texts and transmission* (Dublin 2002) 45–67.

Byrne, F.J.   'Ireland before the battle of Clontarf' in Ó Cróinín (ed.), *New history* i (2005) 852–61.

Byrne, F.J.   'Ireland and her neighbours, *c.*1014–*c.*1072' in Ó Cróinín (ed.), *New history* i (2005) 862–98.

Byrne, F.J., &   'Two Lives of Saint Patrick – *Vita Secunda* and *Vita Quarta*',
Francis, P. (eds)   *JRSAI* 124 (1994) 5–117.

Camden, W.   *Britannia* (London 1600).

Capelli, A.   *Dizionario di abbreviature Latine ed Italiane* (Milan 1985).

Carey, J.   'Origin and development of the Cesair legend', *Éigse* 22 (1987) 37–48.

Carey, J.   'The ancestry of Fénius Farsaid', *Celtica* 21 (1990) 104–12.

Carey, J.   *A new introduction to Lebor Gabála Érenn*, ITS monograph (London 1993).

Carey, J.   *The Irish national origin-legend: synthetic pseudo-history*, Quiggin pamphlets on the sources of mediaeval Gaelic history 1 (Cambridge 1994).

Carney, J.   *Studies in Irish literature and history* (Dublin 1955)

Carney, J.	*The problem of St Patrick* (Dublin 1961).
Carney, J.	'The Ó Cianáin miscellany', *Ériu* 21 (1969) 122–47.
CELT	*CELT: The online resource for Irish history, literature and politics* at the url: *www.ucc.ie/celt/*
Charles-Edwards, T.	*The Chronicle of Ireland* vol. 1 (Introduction, Edition), vol. 2 (Glossary, bibliography, indices, maps) (Liverpool 2006).
Clancy, T.O., &. Márkus, G	*Iona: the earliest poetry of a Celtic monastery* (Edinburgh 1995).
Colgan, J. (ed.)	*Acta Sanctorum Hiberniae* i–ii (Louvain 1645). The preface, which consists of nine pages, is unpaginated so I have used [1]–[9].
Colgrave, B. (ed.)	*Two Lives of Saint Cuthbert* (Cambridge 1940).
Colgrave, B., & Mynors, R.A.B. (eds)	*Bede: Ecclesiastical history of the English people* (Oxford 1991).
Comyn, D., & Dinneen, P. (eds)	*Foras Feasa ar Éirinn le Seathrún Céitinn: The history of Ireland* i–iv, ITS 4, 8, 9, 15 (London 1902, 1908, 1908, 1915).
Connellan, O. (ed.)	*The Annals of Ireland, translated from the original Irish of the Four Masters* (Dublin 1846).
Croke, B.	*Count Marcellinus and his Chronicle* (Oxford 2001).
Cross, F.L., & Livingstone, E.A.	*The Oxford dictionary of the Christian Church* (Oxford 1983). Cited as *ODCC*.
Cunningham, B.	'The making of the Annals of the Four Masters', Ph.D. thesis University College, Dublin (2005).
Cunningham, B., & Gillespie, R.	*Stories from Gaelic Ireland: microhistories from the sixteenth-century Irish Annals* (Dublin 2003).
Cunningham, B., & Gillespie, R.	'James Ussher and his Irish manuscripts', *Studia Hibernica* 33 (2004–5) 81–99.
Davis, R. (ed.)	*The Book of Pontiffs (Liber Pontificalis)* (Liverpool 1989).
de Paor, L.	'The aggrandisment of Armagh', *Historical Studies* 8 (1971) 95–110.
de Paor, L.	*Saint Patrick's world* (Dublin 1993).
Dillon, M.	'Laud Misc. 610', *Celtica* v (1960) 64–76 and vi (1963) 135–55.
Dillon, M., Mooney, C., & de Brún, P.	*Catalogue of Irish manuscripts in the Franciscan library, Killiney* (Dublin 1969).
Dobbs, M.E.	'The history of the descendants of Ir', *ZCP* 14 (1923) 44–144.
Droysen, H. (ed.)	*Breviarium ab urbe condita* MGH AA ii (Berlin 1879) 1–182.
Duffy, S.	'The first Ulster Plantation: John de Courcy and the men of Cumbria', in T.B. Barry, R. Frame & K. Simms (eds), *Colony and frontier in medieval Ireland* (London and Rio Grande, OH 1995) 1–27.
Dumville, D.N.	'Some aspects of the chronology of the *Historia Brittonum*', *Bulletin of the Board of Celtic Studies* 25 (1974) 439–45.
Dumville, D.N.	'Ulster heroes in the early Irish annals: a caveat', *Éigse* 17 (1977–9) 47–54.

Dumville, D.N.	'Latin and Irish in the *Annals of Ulster*, A.D. 431–1050' in D. Whitelock, R. McKitterick, D. Dumville (eds), *Ireland in early medieval Europe* (Cambridge 1982) 320–41.
Dumville, D.N.	'Gildas and Uinniau' in M. Lapidge & D. Dumville (eds), *Gildas: new approaches* (Woodbridge 1984) 207–14.
Dumville, D.N.	'Language, literature, and law in medieval Ireland: some questions of transmission', *CMCS* 9 (1985) 91–8.
Dumville, D.N.	'On editing and translating medieval Irish chronicles: the *Annals of Ulster*', *CMCS* 10 (1985) 67–86.
Dumville, D.N.	'A millennium of Gaelic chronicling' in E. Kooper, *The medieval chronicle* (Amsterdam and Atlanta, GA 1999) 103–15.
Duncan, L. (ed.)	*Catalogue of Irish manuscripts in the Royal Irish Academy* fasc. xvii (Dublin 1935).
Elrington, C.R. (ed.)	*The life of James Ussher D.D.* vol. i of Ussher, *Whole works* (Dublin 1847).
Elrington, C.R. (ed.)	*The whole works of the most Rev. James Ussher, D.D.* i–xvii (Dublin 1847–64). Cited as 'Ussher, *Whole works*'.
Etchingham, C.	*Viking raids on Irish church settlements in the ninth century*, Maynooth monographs, series minor 1 (Maynooth 1996).
Etchingham, C.	'Les Vikings dans les sources documentaires irlandaises: le cas des annales', in É. Ridel, *L'Héritage maritime des Vikings en Europe de l'Ouest* (Caen 2002).
Fennessy, I.	'Printed books in St Anthony's College, Louvain, 1673 (F.L.K., MS A 34)', *Collectanea Hibernica* 35 (1996) 82–117.
Fennessy, I.	'Patrick Pearse and the Four (or Five) Masters', *Donegal Annual* 53 (2001) 81–7.
Fitzpatrick, E.	*Irish manuscripts in the Royal Irish Academy* fasc. xxiv (Dublin 1940).
Flower, R.	'The origin and history of the Cottonian annals', *RC* 44 (1927) 339–44, cf. Freeman, *AB* (1927).
Flower, R.	'Manuscripts of Irish interest in the British Museum', *Analecta Hibernica* 2 (1931) 310–29.
Flower, R.	*Catalogue of Irish manuscripts in the British Museum* iii (London 1953).
Foley, W.T., & Holder, A.G. (eds)	*Bede: a biblical miscellany* (Liverpool 1999).
Fraipont, J. (ed.)	'Bede *De locis sanctis*' in CCSL 175 (Turnhout 1965) 249–80.
Freeman, A.M. (ed.)	'The annals in Cotton MS Titus A xxv', *RC* 41 (1924) 301–30; 42 (1925) 283–305; 43 (1926) 358–84; 44 (1927) 336–61. Cited as *AB*
Freeman, A.M. (ed.)	'The annals of Connacht', *RC* 50 (1933) 1–23, 117–42, 272–88, 339–56; 51 (1934) 46–111, 199–301.
Freeman, A.M. (ed.)	*Annála Connacht: The Annals of Connacht (A.D. 1224–1544)* (Dublin 1944, repr. 1970). Cited as *CT*.
Giblin, C.	'The Annals of the Four Masters' in Thomas Davis Lectures, *Great Books of Ireland* (Dublin 1967) 90–103.

Gleeson, D., & Mac Airt, S. (eds) 'The annals of Roscrea', *PRIA* 59C (1959) 137–80. Cited as *AR*.

Grabowski, K., & Dumville, D. *Chronicles and Annals of mediaeval Ireland and Wales* (Woodbridge, Suffolk 1984).

Grosjean, P. 'S. Patrice á Auxerre sous S. Germain. Le témoignage des noms Gaulois', *Analecta Bollandia* lxxv (1957) 158–80.

Gwynn, A. (ed.) 'Fragmentary annals from the west of Ireland', *PRIA* 37C (1926) 149–57.

Gwynn, A. 'John Lynch's *"De Praesulibus Hiberniae"'*, *Studies* xxxiv (1945) 37–52.

Gwynn, A. 'The Annals of Connacht and the Abbey of Cong', *Galway Archaeological Society Journal* 27 (1956–7) 1–9.

Gwynn, A. 'Archbishop Ussher and Father Brendan O Conor', in Franciscan Fathers, *Father Luke Wadding: commemorative volume* (Killiney 1957).

Gwynn, A. 'St Patrick and Rome', *IER* (April 1961) 217–22.

Gwynn, A. 'Cathal Mac Maghnusa and the Annals of Ulster', part i and ii, *Clogher Record* 2 (1958) 230–43, and 3 (1959) 370–84. Edited with introduction and notes by Nollaig Ó Muraíle *q.v.*

Gwynn, A. 'Brian in Armagh (1005)', *Seanchas Ardmhacha* ix (1978) 35–50.

Gwynn, E. (ed.) *The Metrical Dindsenchus*, in *Todd Lecture Series* vol. 8–11 (Dublin 1903–24).

Harrison, K. 'Epacts in Irish chronicles', *Studia Celtica* 12–13 (1977–8) 17–32.

Helm, R. (ed.) *Hippolytus Werke–Die Chronik* GCS 4 (Berlin 1955).

Helm, R. (ed.) *Eusebius Werke–Die Chronik des Hieronymus*, GCS 7 (Berlin 1956).

Hely, J. *Ogygia, or a chronological account of Irish events* (Dublin 1793). See O'Flaherty *Ogygia*.

Henderson, I. 'Applecross and the Pictish and Dalriadic entries unique to the Annals of Ulster, *c*.675–*c*.730 A.D.' in E. Meldrum, *The dark ages in the Highlands* (Inverness 1971) 43–9.

Hennessy, W.M. (ed.) *Chronicum Scotorum: a chronicle of Irish affairs from earliest times to A.D. 1135* (London 1866, repr. Wiesbaden 1964). Cited as *CS*.

Hennessy, W.M. (ed.) *Annals of Loch Cé: a chronicle of Irish affairs, 1014–1690* i–ii (London 1871, repr. Dublin 1939). Cited as *LC* and includes an edition of CT for AD 1316–1412.

Hennessy, W.M. (ed.) *Annála Uladh: The Annals of Ulster* i (Dublin 1887, 1999), reproducing AD 431–1056. Cited as *AU* i, see also B. Mac Carthy, *AU* and Ó Muraíle, *AU*.

Herbert, M. *Iona, Kells and Derry* (Dublin 1996).

Historical Manuscripts Commission *Report on the Franciscan manuscripts preserved at the Convent, Merchants' Quay, Dublin* (Dublin 1906).

Hogan, E. *Onomasticon Goedelicum* (Dublin and London 1910).

Hughes, K. *Early Christian Ireland: introduction to the sources* (London 1972).

Hull, V. 'The Middle Irish preterite passive plural in the Annals of Ulster', *Language* 28 (1952) 107–8.

Hull, V.	'The preterite passive plural in the Annals of Inishfallen', *ZCP* 24 (1953–4) 126–7.
Hull, V.	'The infixed and independent objective pronoun in the Annals of Inishfallen', *ZCP* 24 (1953–4) 136–8.
Hussey, J.M.	*The Byzantine Empire* in *The Cambridge medieval history* vol. 4 (Cambridge 1966).
Hyde, D.	*A literary history of Ireland* (London and New York 1899, 1967) 38–43 ('Ch. IV: How far can native sources be relied on?'), 573–82 ('Ch. XLI: The Irish Annals').
Ireland, C.	'Aldfrith of Northumbria and the learning of a *sapiens*' in A. Kathryn, E.E. Sweetser & C. Thomas (eds), *A Celtic florilegium* (Lawrence, MA 1996).
Jaski, B.	'Additional Notes to the Annals of Ulster', *Ériu* xlvii (1997) 103–52.
Jaski, B.	*Early Irish kingship and succession* (Dublin 2000).
Jaski, B.	'The invention of tradition', pers. correspondence to D. Mc Carthy, *c.* Dec. 2002.
Jaski, B.	'We are of the Greeks in our origin: new perspectives on the Irish origin legend', *CMCS* (2003) 1–53.
Jaski, B.	'The genealogical section of the Psalter of Cashel', *Peritia* 17–18 (2003–4) 295–337.
Jaski, B.	'Aeneas and Fénius: a classical case of mistaken identity' in *Texts and identitites in the early Middle Ages* by R. Corradini, R. Meens, C. Pössel & P. Shaw (eds), (Vienna 2006) 17–33.
Jennings, B.	*Michael O Cleirigh: chief of the Four Masters and his associates* (Dublin and Cork 1936).
Johnstone, H. (ed.)	*Annals of Ghent / Annales Gandalenses* (New York 1951).
Jones, C.W. (ed.)	*Bedae opera de temporibus* (Cambridge, MA. 1943).
Jones, C.W. (ed.)	'Chronica maiora' in *Bedae venerabilis opera*, CCSL cxxiii B (Turnhout 1977) 461–535.
Jones, C.W. (ed.)	'De temporum ratione' in *Bedae venerabilis opera*, CCSL cxxiii B (Turnhout 1977) 241–544.
Jones, C.W. (ed.)	'De temporibus liber' in *Bedae venerabilis opera*, CCSL cxxiii C (Turnhout 1980) 579–611.
Jones, C.W. (ed.)	'Epistola ad Pleguinam' in *Bedae venerabilis opera*, CCSL cxxiii C (Turnhout 1980) 613–26.
Jones, C.W. (ed.)	'Epistola ad Vvicthedum' in *Bedae venerabilis opera*, CCSL cxxiii C (Turnhout 1980) 631–42.
Karst, J. (ed.)	*Eusebius Werke: Die Chronik aus dem Armenischen Übersetz* GCS Band V (Leipzig 1911).
Keating, G.	*Foras Feasa ar Éirinn*, see D. Comyn.
Kehnel, A.	*Clonmacnois: the Church and Lands of St. Ciarán* (Münster 1997).
Kelleher, J.V.	'Early Irish history and pseudo-history', *Studia Hibernica* 3 (1963) 113–27.
Kelleher, J.V.	'The pre-Norman Irish genealogies', *Irish Historical Studies* 16 (1968) 138–53.

Kelleher, J.V. 'The Táin and the Annals', *Ériu* 22 (1971) 107–27.

Kelly, F. *A guide to early Irish law* (Dublin 1988).

Kelly, J.N.D. *Jerome: his life, writings, and controversies* (London 1975).

Kenney, J.F. *The sources for the early history of Ireland: an introduction and guide*, i *Ecclesiastical* (New York 1929).

Knaepen, A. 'L'histoire Greco-Romaine dans les "Chroniques" de Bede le Venerable (*De temporibus* ch. 17–22 et *De temporum ratione* ch. 66–71)' in Erik Kooper (ed.), *The Medieval Chronicle III: Proceedings of the 3rd international conference on the medieval chronicle* (2004) 76–92.

Knott, E. *An introduction to Irish syllabic poetry of the period 1200–1600* (Dublin 1934, repr. 1957, 1966).

Krusch, B. *Studien zur christlich-mittelalterlichen Chronologie: Die Enstehung unserer heutigen Zeitrechnung*, Abhandlungen der Preuss. Akad. (Berlin 1938).

Lawlor, H., & Oulton, J.E.L. (eds) *Eusebius, bishop of Caesarea – The Ecclesiastical history and the Martyrs of Palestine*, i–ii (London 1928).

Leech, R.H. '*Cogadh Gaedhel re Gallaibh* and the *Annals of Inisfallen*', *North Munster Antiquities Journal* 11 (1968) 13–21.

Lizeray, H. (ed.) *Le livre des quatre maîtres: Annales du royaume d'Irlande, depuis les origines jusqu'à l'arrivée de saint Patrice* (Leroux 1882).

Mac Airt, S. (ed.) *The Annals of Inisfallen (MS Rawlinson B 503)* (Dublin 1951). Cited as *AI*.

Mac Airt, S. (ed.) 'Middle-Irish poems on World-kingship', *Études Celtique* vi (1953–4) 255–81, vii (1955–6) 18–45.

Mac Airt, S. 'The chronology of St Patrick', *Seanchas Ardmhacha* vol. 2 no. 1 (1956) 4–9.

Mac Airt, S., & Mac Niocaill, G. (eds) *The Annals of Ulster (to A.D. 1131)* (Dublin 1983). Cited as *AU*.

Macalister, R.A.S., & Mac Neill, E. (eds) *Do Ghabhálaibh Érend* (Dublin n.d. [1918]). A partial edition of M. Ó Clérigh's recension of LG from RIA MS 617 (23 K 32).

Macalister, R.A.S. (ed.) *Lebor Gabála Érenn* i–v in ITS vols. xxxiv, xxxv, xxxix, xli, xliv (Dublin 1938–56).

Macalister, R.A.S. 'The sources of the Preface to the "Tigernach" Annals', *Irish Historical Studies* iv, 13 (1944–5) 38–57.

Mac Cana, P. 'The rise of the later schools of *filidheacht*', *Ériu* 25 (1974) 126–46.

Mac Cana, P. *The learned tales of medieval Ireland* (Dublin 1980).

Mac Carthy, B. 'The Codex Palatino-Vaticanus, No. 830', *Todd Lecture Series* vol. iii (Dublin 1892).

Mac Carthy, B. (ed.) *Annála Uladh: The Annals of Ulster* ii–iv (Dublin 1893, 1895, 1901, 1999). Vol. ii–iii reproduce AD 1057–1588 with some lacunae, and vol. iv contains the Introduction and Index. Cited as *AU* ii–iv, see also Hennessy, *AU* and Ó Muraíle, *AU*.

Mc Carthy, D.P. 'Chronological synchronisation of the Irish Annals' at: www.irish-annals.cs.tcd.ie

Mc Carthy, D.P.   'Collation of the Irish regnal canon' at: www.irish-annals.
                       cs.tcd.ie.
Mc Carthy, D.P.   'Easter principles and a fifth-century lunar cycle used in the British
                       Isles', *Journal for the History of Astronomy* xxiv (1993) 204–24.
Mc Carthy, D.P.   'The chronological apparatus of the annals of Ulster AD
                       431–1131', *Peritia* 8 (1994) 46–79.
Mc Carthy, D.P.   'The origin of the *latercus* Paschal cycle of the insular Celtic
                       churches', *CMCS* 28 (1994) 25–49.
Mc Carthy, D.P.   'The Lunar and Paschal tables of *De ratione paschali* attributed
                       to Anatolius of Laodicea', *Archive for History of Exact Sciences*
                       49:4 (1996) 285–320. Reprinted in McCarthy & Breen, *De
                       Ratione Paschali* (2003) 148–30.
Mc Carthy, D.P.   'The Biblical chronology of James Ussher', *Irish Astronomical
                       Journal* 24 (1997) 73–82.
Mc Carthy, D.P.   'The status of the pre-Patrician Irish Annals', *Peritia* 12 (1998)
                       98–152.
Mc Carthy, D.P.   'The chronology of the Irish annals', *PRIA* 98C:6 (1998) 203–55.
Mc Carthy, D.P.   'The chronology of St. Brigit of Kildare', *Peritia* 14 (2000) 255–81.
Mc Carthy, D.P.   'Topographical characteristics of the *Vita Prima* and *Vita
                       Cogitosi Sanctae Brigitae*', *Studia Celtica* xxxv (2001) 245–70.
Mc Carthy, D.P.   'The chronology and sources of the early Irish annals', *Early
                       medieval Europe* 10:3 (2001) 323–41.
Mc Carthy, D.P.   'The chronology of St. Colum Cille', *An Tionól* 24 Nov. 2001
                       DIAS www.celt.dias.ie/english/tionol/tionol01.html
Mc Carthy, D.P.   'The emergence of *Anno Domini*' in G. Moreno-Riaño &
                       G. Jaritz (eds), *Time and eternity* (Turnhout 2003) 31–53.
Mc Carthy, D.P.   'The chronological apparatus of the *Annals of Ulster* AD
                       82–1019', *Peritia* 16 (2003) 256–83.
Mc Carthy, D.P.   'The original compilation of the *Annals of Ulster*', *Studia Celtica*
                       38 (2004) 69–96.
Mc Carthy, D.P.   'Bede's primary source for the Vulgate chronology in his
                       chronicles in *De temporibus* and *De temporum ratione*' in I.
                       Warntjes & D. Ó Cróinín (eds), *Proceedings of the 1st international
                       conference on the science of computus in Ireland and Europe, AD
                       400–850* (Turnhout 2010) 159–89.
Mc Carthy, D.P., &   'An evaluation of astronomical observations in the Irish
  Breen, A.   annals', *Vistas in Astronomy* 41:1 (1997) 117–38.
Mc Carthy, D.P., &   'Astronomical observations in the Irish annals and their
  Breen, A.   motivation', *Peritia* 11 (1997) 1–43.
Mc Carthy, D.P., &   *The ante-Nicene Christian Pasch: De ratione paschali The
  Breen, A.   Paschal tract of Anatolius, bishop of Laodicea* (Dublin 2003).
Mc Carthy, D.P., &   'The "lost" Irish 84-year Easter table rediscovered', *Peritia*
  Ó Cróinín, D.   6–7 (1987–8) 227–42.
Mac Donald, A.D.S.   'Notes on the terminology in the Annals of Ulster 650–1050',
                       Peritia 1 (1982) 329–33.

Mac Donnell, C. 'MSS. of the celebrated John Colgan, preserved at St. Isidore's, Rome', *PRIA* vi (1854) 95–112.

Mac Eoin, G. 'The interpolator H in Lebor na hUidre' in J.P. Mallory & G. Stockman (eds), *Ulidia: Proceedings of the First International conference on the Ulster cycle of tales* (Belfast 1994) 39–46.

McClure, J., & Collins, R. (eds) *Bede: The ecclesiastical history of the English people, The Greater Chronicle, Bede's letter to Egbert* (Oxford 1999).

Mac Fhirbhisigh, D. See Ó Muraíle, N., *Book of Genealogies*.

Mac Neill, E. 'An Irish historical tract dated AD. 721', PRIA 28C (1910) 123–48.

Mac Neill, E. (ed.) 'Poems by Flann Mainistrech on the dynasties of Ailech, Mide and Brega', *Archivium Hibernicum* ii (1913) 37–99.

Mac Neill, E. 'The authorship and structure of the "Annals of Tigernach"', *Ériu* 7 (1913) 30–120.

Mac Neill, E. 'On the reconstruction and date of the Laud synchronisms', *ZCP* 10 (1915) 81–96.

Mac Neill, E. 'The Hymn of St Secundinus in honour of St Patrick', *Irish Historical Studies* 2:6 (1940–1) 129–53.

Mac Niocaill, G. (ed.) 'Annála Gearra as Proibhinse Ard Macha', *Seanchas Ardmhacha* 3:2 (1958–9) 337–40.

Mac Niocaill, G. 'Cáipéisí ón gCeathru Céad Déag', *Galvia* v (Galway 1958) 33–42.

Mac Niocaill, G. 'Annála Uladh agus Annála Locha Cé 1014–1220', *Galvia* vi (Galway 1959) 18–25.

Mac Niocaill, G. *The medieval Irish Annals* (Dublin 1975).

Mac Niocaill, G. 'The Irish-language manuscripts' in P. Fox (ed.), *Treasures of the Library: Trinity College, Dublin* (Dublin 1986).

Maund, K. 'Sources of the "world chronicle" in the Cottonian annals', *Peritia* 12 (1998) 153–76.

Meckler, M. 'The Annals of Ulster and the date of the meeting at Druim Cett', *Peritia* 11 (1997) 44–52.

Meyer, K. (ed.) 'Mitteilungen aus irischen Handschriften', *ZCP* 5 (1905) 21–25, 495–504.

Meyer, K. (ed.) 'The Laud synchronisms', *ZCP* 9 (1913) 471–85.

Migne, J.P. (ed.) *Patrologia Latina* i–ccxxi (Paris 1844–64).

Miller, M. 'The chronological structure of the Sixth Age in the Rawlinson Fragment of the "Irish World-Chronicle"', *Celtica* 22 (1991) 79–111.

Moisl, H. 'The Bernician royal dynasty and the Irish in the seventh century', *Peritia* 2 (1983) 103–26.

Mommsen, T. (ed.) 'Prosperi Tironis epitoma chronicon', MGH *Chronica Minora* i (Berlin 1892) 341–485.

Mommsen, T. (ed.) 'Isidori iunioris episcopi Hispalensis chronica maiora', MGH *Chronica Minora* ii (Berlin 1894) 391–488.

Mommsen, T. (ed.) 'Historia Brittonum cum addimentis Nenii', MGH *Chronica Minora* iii (Berlin 1898) 111–222.

Mommsen, T. (ed.)   *Gestorum pontificum Romanorum* i, MGH (Berlin 1898).

Mommsen, T. (ed.)   'Bedae chronica maiora ad A. DCCXXV. eiusdem Chronica Minora ad A. DCCIII.', MGH *Chronica minora* iii (Berlin 1898) 223–354.

Moody, T.W., Martin, F.X., & Byrne, F.J. (eds)   *A chronology of Irish history to 1976*, vol. viii of *A New history of Ireland* (Oxford 1982).

Morris, J.   'The Chronicle of Eusebius: Irish fragments', *Bulletin of the Institute of Classical Studies* 19 (1972) 80–93.

Morris, J. (ed.)   *Nennius: British history and the Welsh Annals* (London 1980).

Mosshammer, A.A.   *The Chronicle of Eusebius and Greek chronographic tradition* (Lewisburg and London 1979).

Muhlberger, S.   *The fifth-century chroniclers: Prosper, Hydatius and the Gallic chronicler of 452* (Leeds 1990).

Mulchrone, K.   *Catalogue of Irish manuscripts in the Royal Irish Academy* fasc. xx (Dublin, 1936) 2451–2578; fasc. xxvi (Dublin 1942) 3221–3356.

Mulchrone, K. (ed.)   *The Book of Lecan*, vol. ii in *Irish Manuscripts Commission facsimiles in collotype of Irish manuscripts* (Dublin 1937).

Mulchrone, K., & Fitzpatrick, E.   *Catalogue of Irish manuscripts in the Royal Irish Academy* fasc. xxvii (Dublin 1943).

Murphy, D. (ed.)   *The Annals of Clonmacnoise, being Annals of Ireland from the earliest period to A.D. 1408, translated into English A.D. 1627 by Conell Mageoghagan and now for the first time printed* (Dublin 1896, repr. Felinfach, Wales 1993). Cited as AC.

Murphy, F.X.   *Rufinus of Aquileia (345–411): his life and works* (Washington D.C. 1945).

Murphy, G.   'On the dates of two sources used in Thurneysen's Heldensage', *Ériu* xiv (1952) 145–56.

Nelson, J.L. (ed.)   *The annals of St.-Bertin: ninth-century histories.* vol. 1 (Manchester 1991).

Nicholls, K.W. (ed.)   'The Register of Clogher', *Clogher Record* 7:3 (1971) 361–431.

Nicolson, W.   *The Irish historical library* (Dublin 1724).

Ní Shéaghdha, N.   *Catalogue of Irish manuscripts in the National Library of Ireland* fasc. i (Dublin 1967).

O'Brien, M.A. (ed.)   *Corpus genealogiarum Hiberniae* (Dublin 1962).

Ó Buachalla, L.   'The construction of the Irish annals 429–466', *Journal of the Cork Historical and Archaeological Society* lxiii (1958) 103–16.

Ó Buachalla, L.   'Notes on the Early Irish Annals, 467–550', *Journal of the Cork Historical and Archaeological Society* lxiv (1959) 73–81.

Ó Catháin, D.   'John Fergus, MD, eighteenth-century doctor, book collector and Irish scholar', *JRSAI* 118 (1988) 139–62.

Ó Catháin, S.   'Some studies in the development from Middle to Modern Irish based on the Annals of Ulster', *ZCP* 19 (1933) 1–47.

Ó Concheannain, T.   '*Lebor Gabála* in the book of Lecan' in Barnard et al. (eds), *A miracle of learning* (1998) 68–90.

Ó Concheannain, T.   'A medieval Irish historiographer: Giolla Íosa Mac Fhir Bhisigh' in Smyth (ed.), *Seanchas* (2000) 387–95.

O'Connell, D.J.   'Easter cycles in the early Irish Church', *JRSAI* 66 (1936) 67–106.

O'Conor, C.   *Dissertations on the Antient history of Ireland* (Dublin 1753).

O'Conor, C.   *Dissertations on the history of Ireland* (Dublin 1766, 1812).

O'Conor, C.   *The Ogygia vindicated* (Dublin 1775). See O'Flaherty.

O'Conor, C. Revd   *Bibliotheca MS. Stowensis* i–ii (Buckingham 1818).

O'Conor, C. Revd   *Rerum Hibernicarum Scriptores Veteres* i–iii (Buckingham 1814, 1825, 1826).

Ó Corráin, D.   'A handlist of publications on early Irish history', *Historical Studies* 10 (1976) 172–203.

Ó Corráin, D.   'Creating the past: the early Irish genealogical tradition, Carroll lecture 1992', *Peritia* 12 (1998) 177–208.

Ó Cróinín, D.   'An Old-Irish gloss in the Munich computus', *Éigse* 18 (1981) 289–90.

Ó Cróinín, D.   'Mo Sinu maccu Mín and the computus at Bangor', *Peritia* 1 (1982) 281–95.

Ó Cróinín, D. (ed.)   *Sex Aetates Mundi* (Dublin 1983).

Ó Cróinín, D.   'Hiberno-Latin *Calcenterus*', *Peritia* 1 (1982) 296–7.

Ó Cróinín, D.   'Early Irish annals from Easter tables: a case restated', *Peritia* 2 (1983) 74–86.

Ó Cróinín, D.   'A seventh-century Irish computus from the circle of Cummianus', *PRIA* 82C: 11 (1982) 405–30.

Ó Cróinín, D.   'The Irish provenance of Bede's computus', *Peritia* 2 (1983) 229–47.

Ó Cróinín, D.   'Rath Melsigi, Willibrord, and the earlies Echternach manuscripts', *Peritia* 3 (1984) 17–49.

Ó Cróinín, D.   'New light on Palladius', *Peritia* 5 (1986) 276–83.

Ó Cróinín, D.   'The date, provenance and earliest use of the works of Virgilius Maro Grammaticus', in G. Bernt, F. Rädle & G. Silagi (eds), *Tradition und Wertung: Festschrift Franz Brunhölzl* (Sigmaringen 1989) 13–22.

Ó Cróinín, D.   'Early Echternach fragments with Old Irish glosses', in G. Kiesel & J. Schroeder (eds), *Willibrord, Apostel der Nederlande, Gründer der Abtei Echternach. Gedenkgabe zum 1250. Todestag des angelsächsischen Missionars* (Luxembourg 1989) 135–43.

Ó Cróinín, D.   *Early medieval Ireland 400–1200* (London 1995).

Ó Cróinín, D.   'The computistical works of Columbanus' in M. Lapidge (ed.), *Columbanus, studies on the Latin writings* (Woodbridge 1997) 264–70.

Ó Cróinín, D.   'Bede's Irish computus' in D. Ó Cróinín, *Early Irish history and chronology* (2003) 201–12.

Ó Cróinín, D.   *Early Irish history and chronology* (Dublin 2003). This volume reproduces all of Ó Cróinín's publications on *computistica* up to 2003.

Ó Cróinín, D. (ed.)   *A New history of Ireland* I (Dublin 2005).

Ó Cuilleanáin, C.   'The Dublin Annals of Inisfallen' in S. Pender (ed.), *Féilscríbhinn Torna* (Cork 1947) 183–202.

Ó Cuív, B. (ed.)   'A fragment of Irish annals', *Celtica* 14 (1981) 83–104.

Ó Cuív, B. (ed.)   'Elegy on Féilim Mac Maghnusa Méig Uidhir Ob. 1487', *Celtica* xxiii (1999) 261–8.

Ó Cuív, B.   *Catalogue of Irish language manuscripts in the Bodleian library at Oxford and Oxford College libraries* (Dublin 2001).

O'Curry, E.   *Lectures on the manuscript materials of ancient Irish history* (Dublin 1861, repr. 1995). Cited as *MM*.

O'Donovan, J. (ed.)   'Annals of Dublin', *Dublin Penny Journal* 1:22 (1832) 102–4; 1:38 (1833) 299; 1:40 (1833) 315.

O'Donovan, J. (ed.)   'The Annals of Ireland, from the year 1443 to 1468 translated from the Irish by Dudley Firbisse ...', *Miscellany of the Irish Archaeological Society* 7 (1846) 198–302.

O'Donovan, J. (ed.)   *Leabhar na g-Ceart* (Dublin 1847).

O'Donovan, J. (ed.)   *Annala Rioghachta Eireann: Annals of the Kingdom of Ireland* i–vii (Dublin 1848–51; repr. New York 1966). Cited as *FM* i–vii.

O'Donovan, J. (ed.)   *Annals of Ireland: three fragments copied from ancient sources by Dubhultach Mac Firbisigh* (Dublin 1860).

Ó Duinnín, P.   *Me Guidhir Fhearmanach, The Maguires of Fermanagh* (1917).

O'Dwyer, B.W.   *The conspiracy of Mellifont, 1216–1231* (Dublin 1970).

O'Dwyer, B.W.   'The annals of Connacht and Loch Cé and the monasteries of Boyle and Holy Trinity', *PRIA* 72C (1972) 83–101.

Ó Fiaich, T.   'The contents of Mac Carthaigh's Book', *IER* 5S 74 (1950) 30–9.

Ó Fiaich, T.   'The Church of Armagh under lay control', *Seanchas Ardmhacha* 5 (1969) 75–127.

O'Flaherty, R.   *Ogygia, seu, Rerum Hibernicarum Chronologia ...* (London 1685). See J. Hely, *Ogygia*.

O'Flaherty, R.   *The Ogygia vindicated against the objections of Sir George Mac Kenzie* edited by C. O'Conor (Dublin 1775).

Ó Gallachair, P.   'Clogherici – A dictionary of the diocese of Clogher (1535–1835)', *Clogher Record* 1:4 (1956) 137–60.

O'Grady, S.   *Catalogue of Irish manuscripts in the British Museum* I (London 1926).

Ó hInnse, S. (ed.)   *Miscellaneous Irish annals, A.D. 1114–1437* (Dublin 1947).

Ó hUiginn, R.   'Tomás Ó Máille', *Léachtaí Cholm Cille* 27 (1997) 83–122.

Olmsted, G.   *The Gaulish calendar* (Bonn 1992).

O'Kelleher, A , & Schoepperle, G. (eds)   *Betha Colaim Chille. Life of Columcille compiled by Maghnas Ó Domhnaill in 1532* (Urbana, IL 1918; repr. Dundalk 1994).

O'Lochlainn, C. (ed.)   *Irish men of learning: studies by Father Paul Walsh* (Dublin 1947).

O'Loughlin, T.   'The library of Iona in the late seventh century: The evidence from Adomnán's *De locis sanctis*', *Ériu* 45 (1994) 33–52.

O'Loughlin, T.   'Adomnán's *De locis sanctis*: A textual emendation and an additional source identification', *Ériu* 48 (1997) 37–40.

Ó Lúing, S.   'William Maunsell Hennessy, Celtic scholar, 1829–89', *Journal of the Kerry Archaeological and Historical Society* 19 (1989) 80–120.

Ó Máille, T.   *The language of the Annals of Ulster* (Manchester 1910).

Ó Mórdha, E.   'The place-names in the Book of Cuanu' in A.P. Smyth (ed.), *Seanchas* (2000) 189–91.

Ó Muraíle, N.   'The autograph manuscripts of the Annals of the Four Masters', *Celtica* 19 (1987) 75–95.

Ó Muraíle, N.   'Background, life and writings of Dubhaltach Mac Fhirbhisigh' i–ii, Ph.D. thesis University College, Maynooth (1991).

Ó Muraíle, N.   *The celebrated antiquary Dubhaltach Mac Fhirbhisigh (c.1600–71): his lineage, life and learning* (Maynooth 1996).

Ó Muraíle, N.   'Seán Ó Donnabháin: "An cúigiú máistir"', *Léachtaí Cholm Cille* 27 (1997) 11–82.

Ó Muraíle, N.   ʌnnʌLʌ uLʌdh: *Annals of Ulster from the earliest times to the year 1541* i–iv (Dublin 1998). A facsimile reprint of Hennessy & Mac Carthy *AU* i–iv, with Nollaig Ó Muraíle's 'Introduction to the 1998 reprint', on vol. i pp. [1]–[45]. Cited as Ó Muraíle, *AU* i–iv.

Ó Muraíle, N.   *Cathal Óg Mac Maghnusa and the Annals of Ulster* McManus Clan Association (Enniskillen 1998). See also Gwynn, A., 'Cathal Mac Maghnusa'.

Ó Muraíle, N.   'Paul Walsh as editor and explicator of *Beatha Aodha Ruaidh*' in P. Ó Riain (ed.), *Beatha Aodha Ruaidh* (London 2002) 98–123.

Ó Muraíle, N. (ed.)   *Irish leaders and learning through the ages: Paul Walsh essays collected, edited and introduced* (Dublin 2003).

Ó Muraíle, N. (ed.)   *Leabhar Genealach: The great book of Irish genealogies* i–v (Dublin 2005).

Ó Muraíle, N.   'The learned family of Ó Cianáin/Keenan', *Clogher Record* xviii:3 (2005) 387–436.

Ó Murchadha, D.   *The Annals of Tigernach: Index of names* (Dublin 1997).

O'Neill, T.   *The Irish hand* (Mountrath, Co. Laois 1984).

O'Rahilly, T.F.   *The two Patricks* (Dublin 1942).

O'Rahilly, T.F.   *Early Irish history and mythology* (Dublin 1946, repr. 1971).

Ó Riain, P.   'Finnian or Winniau?' in P. Ní Chatháin & M. Richter (eds), *Irland und Europa. Die Kirche im Frühmittelalter* (Stuttgart 1984) 52–7.

Ó Riain, P. (ed.)   *Corpus Genealogiarum Sanctorum Hiberniae* (Dublin 1985).

Ó Riain, P.   'The psalter of Cashel: a provisional list of contents', *Éigse* 23 (1989) 107–30.

Ó Riain, P.   'Anglo-Saxon Ireland: the evidence of the Martyology of Tallaght' *H.M. Chadwick memorial lecture 3* (Cambridge 1993).

Ó Riain, P. 'Finnio and Winniau: A question of priority' in R. Bielmeier & R. Stempel (eds), *Indogermanica et Caucasica* (Berlin and New York) 407–14.

Ó Riain, P. 'Finnio and Winniau: a return to the subject' in J. Carey, J.T. Koch & P.-Y. Lambert (eds), *Ildánach Ildírech: a festschrift for Proinsias Mac Cana* (Andover and Aberystwyth 1999) 187–202.

Ó Riain, P. (ed.) *Beatha Aodha Ruaidh: the life of Red Hugh O'Donnell. Historical and literary contexts*, ITS subsidiary series 12 (London 2002).

Ó Riain, P. *Feastdays of the saints: a history of Irish martyrologies* (Brussels 2006).

Orpen, G.H. *Ireland under the Normans, 1169–1333* i–iv (Oxford 1911–20).

Oskamp, H.P. '"The Yellow Book of Lecan proper"', *Ériu* 26 (1975) 102–19.

O Sullevenus, P. *Historiae Catholicae Iberniae Compendium* (Lisbon 1621).

O'Sullivan, A. (ed.) *The Book of Leinster formerly Lebar na Núachongbála* vol. vi (Dublin 1983). See also Best & Bergin, *Book of Leinster*.

O'Sullivan, A., & W. 'Three notes on Laud Misc. 610 (or the Book of Pottlerath)', *Celtica* ix (1971) 135–51.

O'Sullivan, H. 'Irish Annals of the eleventh and twelfth centuries', M.A. thesis University College, Dublin (1970).

O'Sullivan, W. 'The Irish manuscripts in case H in Trinity College Dublin catalogued by Matthew Young in 1781', *Celtica* xi (1976) 229–50.

O'Sullivan, W. 'Ciothruadh's Yellow Book of Lecan', *Éigse* 18 (1981) 177–81.

O'Sullivan, W. (ed.) 'Correspondence of David Rothe and James Ussher, 1619–23', *Collectanea Hibernica* 36–7 (1994–5) 7–49.

O'Sullivan, W. 'A finding list of Sir James Ware's manuscripts', *PRIA* 97C (1997) 69–99.

O'Sullivan, W. 'The Slane manuscript of the *Annals of the Four Masters*', *Riocht na Midhe* 10 (1999) 78–85.

Pertz, G.H. (ed.) 'Annales Fuldenses, 680–901' in MGH *Scriptores* i (1826) 337–415.

Petavius, D. *De doctrina temporum* (Paris 1627).

Petrie, G. 'On the history and antiquities of Tara Hill', *Transactions of the Royal Irish Academy* xviii (Dublin 1839) 143–9.

Pettiau, H. 'The officials of the church of Armagh in the early and central middle ages, to A.D. 1200' in A.J. Hughes & W. Nolan (eds), *Armagh: history & society: interdisciplinary essays on the history of an Irish county* (Dublin 2001) 121–86.

Phillimore, E. (ed.) 'The *Annales Cambriae* and Old Welsh Genealogies from *Harleian MS.* 3859', *Y Cymmrodor* 9 (1888) 141–83.

Radner, J.N. (ed.) *Fragmentary annals of Ireland* (Dublin 1978).

Reeves, W. (ed.) *The Life of St Columba* (Dublin 1857).

Reuter. T. (ed.) *The Annals of Fulda* (Manchester 1992).

Richardson, E. (ed.) *Hieronymus Liber de Viris inlustribus T.U.* Band 4 (Leipzig 1896).

Risk, M.H.   'Charles Lynegar, professor of the Irish language, 1712',
                          Hermathena 102 (1966) 16–25.

Routh, M.J. (ed.)   *Reliquae Sacrae* vol. ii (1844) 238–309.

Ryan, J.   'The two Patricks', *IER* (Oct. 1942) 241–52.

Sanderlin, S.   'Conell Mageoghagan and the Annals of Clonmacnois 433–1172',
                          Ph.D. thesis Cambridge University (1980).

Sanderlin, S.   'The manuscripts of the annals of Clonmacnois', *PRIA* 82C
                          (1982) 111–23.

Schmidt, J.   'Zu einer neuausgabe des annalen-fragments in der HS. Rawl.
                          B. 502' in H. Wagner & K.H. Schmidt (eds), *Akten des ersten
                          symposiums deutschsprachiger Keltologen* (Tübingen 1993)
                          267–86.

Schoene, A.   *Eusebi chronicorum libri duo* (Berlin 1866, repr. Dublin and
                          Zurich 1967).

Schwartz, E., &   'Die Kirchengeshichte' in *Eusebius Werke* GCS Band 2, Teil 1–3
  Mommsen, T. (eds)   (Leipzig 1903, 1908, 1909).

Scowcroft, R.M.   '*Leabhar Gabhála* Part I: The growth of the text', *Ériu* xxxviii
                          (1987) 79–140.

Scowcroft, R.M.   '*Leabhar Gabhála* Part II: The growth of the tradition', *Ériu*
                          xxxix (1988) 1–66.

Sharpe, R.   'Saint Mauchteus, *discipulus Patricii*' in A. Bammesberger &
                          A. Wollmann (eds), *Britain 400–600: Language and history*,
                          (Heidelberg 1990) 85–93.

Sharpe, R. (ed.)   *Adomnán of Iona: Life of St Columba* (London 1995).

Simms, K.   'The medieval kingdom of Lough Erne', *Clogher Record* 9:2
                          (1977) 126–41.

Simms, K.   'Charles Lynegar, the Ó Luinín family and the study of Seanchas'
                          in Barnard et al. (eds), *A miracle of learning* (1998) 266–83.

Smith, P.J.   'Early Irish historical verse: the evolution of a genre', in P. Ní
                          Chatháin & M. Richter (eds), *Ireland and Europe in the early
                          Middle Ages: texts and transmission* (Dublin 2002) 326–41.

Smith, P.J. (ed.)   *Three historical poems ascribed to Gilla Cóemáin: a critical edition
                          of the work of an eleventh-century Irish scholar* (Münster,
                          Germany 2007).

Smyth, A.P.   'The earliest Irish annals: their first contemporary entries, and
                          the earliest centres of recording', *PRIA* 72C (1972) 1–48.

Smyth, A.P.   *Warlords and holy men: Scotland AD 80–1000* (Edinburgh
                          1989).

Smyth, A.P. (ed.)   *Seanchas: studies in early and medieval Irish archaeology, history
                          and literature in honour of Francis J. Byrne* (Dublin 2000).

Stokes, W.   'Notes on the Annals of Ulster', *The Academy* 36:908–10 (1889)
                          207–8, 223–5, 240–1; *The Academy* 50:1271, 1273 (1896) 182–3,
                          223–4; *RC* 18 (1897) 74–86. Repr. in Ó Muraíle, *AU* i, [46–73.]

Stokes, W. (ed.)   *The Annals of Tigernach*, first published in *RC* 16 (1895)
                          374–419; 17 (1896) 6–33, 119–263, 337–420; 18 (1897) 9–59,

150–97, 267–303. The facsimile edition *The Annals of Tigernach* i–ii (Felinfach, Wales 1993) is paginated as 1–223, 224–466; this edition and pagination are cited in this book as *AT*.

Stokes, W. (ed.)   'The Dublin Fragment of Tigernach's Annals', *RC* 18 (1897) 374–90.

Stokes, W. (ed.)   'Annals from the Book of Leinster' in W. Stokes (ed.), *The Tripartite Life of Patrick* vol. ii (London 1897) 512–19.

Stokes, W. (ed.)   *Félire Óengusso Céli Dé: The Martyrology of Oengus the Culdée* (London 1905).

Thurneysen, R.   'Synchronismen der Irischen Könige', *ZCP* 19 (1933) 81–99.

Todd, J.H., & Reeves, W. (eds)   *The Martyrology of Donegal: a calendar of the saints of Ireland* (1864).

Todd, J.H. (ed.)   *Cogadh Gaedhel re Gallaibh* (London 1867).

Ussher, J.   'Corbes, Herenaches and Termon Lands' in Elrington, *Whole works* xi 419–73.

Ussher, J. (ed.)   *Veterum Epistolarum Hibernicarum Sylloge* (Dublin 1632) in Elrington, *Whole works* iv, 383–572.

Ussher, J.   *Britannicarum Ecclesiarum antiquitates* (Dublin 1639) in Elrington, *Whole works* v–vi.

Van den Gheyn, J.   *Catalogue des manuscrits de la Bibliothèque Royale de Belgique* vii (Bruxelles 1907).

Van der Brincken, A.D.   'Marianus Scottus – Unter besonderer Berücksichtigung der nicht veroffentlichen Teile seiner Chronik' *Deutches Archiv* (Köln 1961) 191–332.

Van der Brincken, A.D.   'Marianus Scottus als Universalhistoriker iuxta veritatem evangelii' in H. Löwe, *Die Iren und Europa im früheren Mittelalter* Teil 2 (Stuttgart 1982) 970–1009.

Van Hamel, A.G.   'The foreign notes in the Three Fragments of Irish annals', *RC* 36 (1915–16) 1–22.

Van Hamel, A.G.   'Über die vorpatrizianischen irischen Annalen', *ZCP* 17 (1928) 241–60.

Verbist, P.   'Reconstructing the past: the chronicle of Marianus Scottus', *Peritia* 16 (2002) 284–334.

Wainwright, F.T.   'Duald's three fragments', *Scriptorium* 2 (1948) 56–8.

Wainwright, F.T.   'Ingimund's invasion', *English Historical Record* 63 (1948) 145–69.

Waitz, G. (ed.)   'Mariani Scoti Chronici' in MGH *Scriptores* v (Hanover 1844) 481–568.

Walker, G. (ed.)   *Sancti Columbani opera* (Dublin 1970).

Wallis, F. (ed.)   *Bede: The Reckoning of Time* (Liverpool 1999).

Walsh, M., & Ó Cróinín, D. (eds)   *Cummian's Letter 'De Controuersia Paschali' together with a related Irish Computistical Tract 'De Ratione Conputandi'* (Toronto 1988).

Walsh, P.   *Gleanings from Irish manuscripts* (Dublin 1916, repr. 1933).

Walsh, P.   *Genealogiae Regum et Sanctorum Hiberniae* as appendices in *Archivium Hibernicum* 5–6 (1916–17) and separately (Dublin 1918).

Walsh, P. (ed.)   'Memoranda Gadelica', *Irish Book Lover* 19 (1931) 166–71.

Walsh, P. (ed.)   'Short Annals of Tirconaill', *Irish Book Lover* 22 (1934) 104–9, idem 24 (1936) 13.

Walsh, P. (ed.)   'Short Annals of Fir Manach', *Irish Book Lover* 23 (1935) 7–10.

Walsh, P. (ed.)   'Short Annals of Leinster', *Irish Book Lover* 24 (1936) 58–60, 87.

Walsh, P.   'Manuscripts of the Four Masters', *Irish Book Lover* 24 (1936) 81–3.

Walsh, P.   'Travels of an Irish scholar', *Catholic Bulletin* 27 (1937) 123–32.

Walsh, P.   *The O'Cleirigh family of Tír Conaill* (Dublin 1938).

Walsh, P.   'The dating of the Annals of Inisfallen', *Catholic Bulletin* 29 (1939) 677–82. Reprinted in Ó Muraíle, *Irish leaders* (2003) 477–83.

Walsh, P.   'The Annals of Loch Cé', *IER* 5S 56 (1940) 113–22.

Walsh, P.   'The Annals attributed to Tigernach', *Irish Historical Studies* 2:6 (1940–1) 154–9. Repr. in O'Lochlainn, *Irish men of learning* (1947) 219–25.

Walsh, P.   'The dating of the Irish annals', *Irish Historical Studies* 2:6 (1940–1) 355–75. See corrections by E.G. Quin *ibid.* 3 (1942–3) 107.

Walsh, P.   *The Four Masters and their work* (Dublin 1944).

Walsh, P.   'The learned family of O Duigenan' in O'Lochlainn (ed.), *Irish men of learning* (1947) 1–12.

Walsh, P.   'The learned family of O Maelconaire' in O'Lochlainn (ed.), *Irish men of learning* (1947) 34–48.

Walsh, P.   'The books of the O Duigenans' in O'Lochlainn (ed.), *Irish men of learning* (1947) 13–24.

Walsh, P. (ed.)   *The life of Aodh Ruadh O Domhnaill*, Part 1 – Text and Translation, Part 2 – Introduction and Glossary, ITS 42 (Dublin 1948, repr. 1957).

Ward, C.C & Ward, R.E. (eds)   *The letters of Charles O'Conor of Belanagare*, vol. 1 1731–71, vol.2 1772–90 (University Microfilm International, Ann Arbor, MI 1980).

Ward, R.E., Wrynn, J.F., & Ward, C.C. (eds)   *Letters of Charles O'Conor of Belanagare: a Catholic voice in eighteenth-century Ireland* (Washington D.C. 1988). Repr. only those letters considered relevant to its subtitle.

Ware, J.   *Archiepiscoporum Casseliensium et Tuamensium vitae ... Quibus adjicitur historia coenobriorum Cisterciensium Hiberniae* (Dublin 1626).

Ware, J.   *De praesulibus Lageniae sive provinciae Dublinensis* (Dublin 1628).

Ware, J.   *Edmund Spenser; a view of the state of Ireland ... The history of Ireland by Edmund Campion ... The chronicle of Ireland by Meredeth Hanmer ... Henry Marleburrought's chronicle* (Dublin 1633).

Ware, J.   *De scriptoribus Hiberniae. Libri duo* (Dublin 1639; repr. Farnborough 1966).

Ware, J.   *Librorum manuscriptorum Jacobi Waraei equities aur. catalogues* (Dublin 1648). Repr. in O'Sullivan, 'Finding list' (1997) 84–99.

Ware, J.   *Opusculo Sancto Patricio, qui Hibernos ad fidem Christi convertit* ... (London 1656).

Ware, J.   *Venerabilis Bedae epistolae duae* ... (Dublin 1664).

Ware, J.   *De Hibernia et antiquitatibus eius disquisitiones* (London 1654, 1658).

Ware, J.   *Rerum Hibernicarum, regnante Henrico VII* ... (London 1658). Suffixed to his *De Hibernia* (1658).

Ware, J.   *Rerum Hibernicarum Henrico octavo* ... (Dublin 1662).

Ware, J.   *Rerum Hibernicarum regnantibus Henrico VII, Henrico VIII, Edwardo VI, et Maria* ... (Dublin 1664).

Ware, J.   *De praesulibus Hiberniae commentaries* (Dublin 1665).

Warntjes, I.   'A newly discovered Irish computus: *Computus Einsidlensis*', *Peritia* 19 (2005) 61–4.

Warntjes, I.   'The Munich Computus and the 84 (14)-year Easter reckoning', *PRIA* 107C (2007) 31–85.

Zangmeister, C. (ed.)   *Paul Orosii historiarum adversum paganos Libri vii*, CSEL v (Vindobonae 1882).

Index